History of
Mary Washington College
1908–1972

Monroe Hall

History of Mary Washington College
1908–1972

Edward Alvey, Jr.

University Press of Virginia
Charlottesville

THE UNIVERSITY PRESS OF VIRGINIA
Copyright © 1974 by the Rector and Visitors
of the University of Virginia

First published 1974

The illustrations are reproductions of photographs
appearing in the college catalogues, annuals, and alumnae publications;
pictures taken for the college
by Judson Smith Studio and the Colony Studios;
and pictures appearing in
the Fredericksburg *Free Lance-Star* (used by permission).

ISBN: 0-8139-0528-1
Library of Congress Catalog Card Number: 73-92624
Printed in the United States of America

*This book is dedicated,
with admiration and affection, to*
GRELLET COLLINS SIMPSON
*whose love of learning
has inspired both faculty and students
in their quest for knowledge
and wisdom.*

Foreword

FOR many years—in fact, since the fiftieth anniversary of the founding of Mary Washington College—Dean Alvey and I have had numerous conversations regarding its history and evolution and the necessity at an appropriate time for someone to undertake the task of writing the life story of what has transpired on Marye's Heights since 1908. I must admit that in all of our conversations I had the advantage, because from the very beginning I felt completely convinced that the man I was talking with was the one person who could write the kind of history of the institution that I was interested in seeing brought into being.

I am sure that there have been—and still are—many persons either connected with the college or otherwise involved in its destiny who could have written a history of Mary Washington College. I am just as sure, however, that there has been only one person who would have written the history as we envisioned it in our many conversations.

As you will observe as you read this volume, Dean Alvey has allowed—encouraged, if you will—all facets of the college to intervene in the steady and controlled narrative which Time has created. He stops in his story to comment on persons, places, and things; he doesn't even try at times to disguise his identity as the storyteller. Neither does he try to conceal his own personal interests or points of view in the telling of the story. The pervasive sense of humor and comic spirit that have colored his genuine humanity and love of people come between the lines—and, oftentimes, even between the words.

The book that is now before you is Dean Alvey's history of Mary Washington College; it is also the official institutional history. The two histories coalesce into one. All of us are better for the fact that the time was ripe for the story to be written and that Dean Alvey, who had for so many years been one of the major personalities in the narrative, was ready in the wings to begin the story. For all of his talent as an author and all that he represents as a person and a long-time friend, it is a pleasure and a privilege for me to know that the history has been written and that the author is the man who should have written it. We who know him are deeply in his debt. Those persons who will become members of this academic community in the future will profit from the personal perspective that Dean Alvey has given to his history of the college—a college he has loved, served, and cherished over more than three decades of his life.

Actually, this project has been a work in progress ever since the author retired as dean of the college in 1967. There was no detail too minor for him to explore and no date too unimportant for him to verify. Above all, however, it appears to me that he has transmitted to us the essential spirit of the college and recorded the diverse contributions of the many persons who have made the institution what it is today. We are proud of his achievement in the present instance. Chiefly we are proud of him and his book.

GRELLET C. SIMPSON
President

June 29, 1973

Preface

THIS is the story of a college: its origin, its development, and its role as an institution of higher learning. It is more than an account of legislative enactments, board actions, and curriculum changes, although it does include these. It is essentially a record of people and their personalities—the students, the faculty, and the administrators who, over the years, made their impress upon the institution and helped to shape the ideas and ideals for which it stands today.

So, there are some twenty-five sketches of individuals who played a long and important role in the development of the college. There are descriptions of the students at various periods—how they lived, the subjects they studied, the recreations they enjoyed, and the contributions they made to the institution.

The growth of the college, both physically and academically, is traced in detail. An effort has been made to delineate the development of Mary Washington College from its establishment through an amendment to an appropriation bill by the General Assembly of Virginia in 1908 to its new status as an independent state college in July 1972.

In the preparation of the manuscript a variety of sources were consulted: minutes of the Normal School board, the teachers college board, the State Board of Education, and the Rector and Visitors of the University of Virginia; quarterly and annual reports of the chief administrative officer to these boards; minutes of faculty and committee meetings; reports of faculty and board committees; official publications of the college, such as annual catalogues and faculty handbooks; self-study reports; and miscellaneous documents relating to the purposes and progress of the institution.

Student publications have been a rich source of information on student life, especially the files of the college annual, newspapers, magazines, and student handbooks. Programs of plays, concerts, exhibitions, May Days, graduation exercises—all carefully preserved in the archives of the library—have furnished authentic information on the nature of these events. Articles by Dr. Carrol H. Quenzel, for twenty-five years, librarian of the college, have been a source of information on persons for whom college buildings were named.

Files of the Fredericksburg *Free Lance-Star* furnished contemporary accounts of persons and events. Interviews with dozens of persons who remember the "old days," letters and notes from former students and faculty members, and conferences with local citizens about the "school on the Hill" have been other sources of information. The list of such persons is, unfortunately, too long to enumerate here.

Special mention should be made of individuals who have aided in the preparation of the manuscript for publication. Dr. W. Wayne Griffith, now professor emeritus of English, and Dr. Eileen K. Dodd, professor emeritus of psychology, read the entire manuscript and made many suggestions. Carol Pridgen Gill, president of the Alumnae Association, and Levin J. Houston III, associate professor of music and book reviewer for the Fredericksburg *Free Lance-Star,* read the material and made comments. Mary J. Porter, reference librarian, E. Lee Trinkle Library, read the copy for editorial purposes. Mary Annette Klinesmith Kelly, associate professor of psychology and alumnae adviser, read the section on the Alumnae Association.

Barbara Alden, archivist of E. Lee Trinkle Library, has taken a keen interest in the project. She helped to locate needed material, to unearth specific facts, and to make available all the resources of the archives. She also read the manuscript carefully and made suggestions.

Finally, my wife, Frances, has been an unfailing source of encouragement, especially when difficult problems were encountered and the completion of the project seemed such a distant goal.

EDWARD ALVEY, JR.

Fredericksburg, Virginia
September 5, 1973

Contents

Foreword		vii
Preface		ix

History of the College, 1908–1972

I	Higher Education for Women	1
II	The Founding of the College	10
III	The College Opens	32
IV	College Life in the First Year	46
V	The Early Years, 1912–1914	58
VI	Significant Developments and Events, 1914–1919	69
VII	The 1920s	95
VIII	The College in 1928	132
IX	A Period of Change, 1929–1934	159
X	Development Accelerates: New Degrees, Faculty, and Facilities, 1934–1938	183
XI	Progress and Personalities, 1938–1941	231
XII	The War Years, 1941–1945	256
XIII	Coordination with the University of Virginia, 1944–1948	277
XIV	Postwar Developments, 1946–1949	293
XV	The Early 1950s	315
XVI	An Eventful Session, 1953–1954	333
XVII	The End of an Era, 1954–1955	342
XVIII	A New Era Begins, 1955–1956	359
XIX	The New Chancellor in Action, 1956–1957	372
XX	A Year of Change, 1957–1958	393
XXI	Continuing Growth, 1958–1960	410
XXII	Planning Ahead: The Early 1960s	434
XXIII	Academic Developments in the Mid-1960s	453
XXIV	New Majors, Degree Requirements, and College Calendar	465
XXV	New Buildings and Art Exhibitions	480
XXVI	Student Life in the 1960s	489
XXVII	Recent Developments, 1967–1972	499

Associations and Organizations

XXVIII	The Alumnae Association	517
XXIX	Student Organizations	546
XXX	The Honor System	556
XXXI	Clubs and Honor Societies	565
XXXII	Publications	597
XXXIII	Dramatics	606
XXXIV	The Library	621
XXXV	Gifts to the College	652
Index		657

History of
Mary Washington College
1908–1972

CHAPTER I

Higher Education for Women

NINETEENTH-CENTURY BEGINNINGS

HIGHER education for women was unheard of in the United States until Oberlin College admitted four women as regular, full-time students to the freshman class in 1837. This was some two hundred years after the founding of Harvard College in 1636. In the early days of our country, higher education was in a sense professional education, in that university graduates usually became lawyers, doctors, statesmen, or teachers in colleges or preparatory schools. Since these were regarded as men's occupations, there seemed little justification for the admission of women to the relatively small number of colleges then in existence.

In 1841 three of the young women who had been admitted to Oberlin became the first to receive bachelor's degrees that were really equivalent to those granted to men. In 1852 Antioch College, in Yellow Springs, Ohio, began a program of coeducation under the leadership of Horace Mann, its first president. The new state universities of the West were also pioneers in education for women. Iowa was coeducational from its beginning in 1856. Women began enrolling at the University of Wisconsin in 1860. The University of Michigan admitted its first women students in 1870.

Early arguments against the higher education of women seem strange today. One of the most commonly expressed concerns was what was believed to be a "difference between the male and female mind." Many leaders felt sincerely that women were inferior mentally to men and were unable to meet the standards set for men's higher education. A corollary to this argument was that standards would be lowered, the quality of instruction diluted, and that higher education itself would deteriorate under the distracting influence of women students.

Another argument mentioned frequently was the "diversity of pursuit and mission." Woman's place was in the home, as bearer and rearer of children, creator of an environment and atmosphere conducive to wholesome development, custodian of the family hearth, and helpmate of her husband, who was the wage earner and career person of the partnership.

The difference in physical strength between men and women was also advanced as an argument. It was asserted that women did not have "the stamina to endure a course of education as thorough and as extensive as that offered men." This objection seems to have caused apprehension among administrators, especially of women's colleges, who were careful to point out their concern for the health of the women students and the provisions for safeguarding their physical fitness.

In this connection it is interesting to note that, according to *Boston School Document No. 19* (Sept. 9, 1890), "At Wellesley College by its special attention to physical and hygienic culture, over 1,000 young women are required to enter a thorough course of physical training, and it is represented that these students pride themselves on their excellent physical condition which they first endeavor to attain before subjecting themselves to serious mental strain." Vassar required the study of physiology and hygiene in the freshman year at a time when no such requirement existed at Yale, Harvard, or Columbia. The University of Wisconsin provided medical care for women ten years before it was provided for men.

In time, proponents of higher education for women were able to point out that college did not undermine the health of women. In fact, female college graduates tended to be healthier than other women, not only because of the selective factors involved in college attendance but also because of the attention given to physical and health education, especially in the women's colleges.

Beginning about 1775, the female seminary idea spread rapidly, especially in the eastern and southern parts of the United States. These institutions made no pretensions to collegiate rank. They did offer a more liberal education for women. However, such leaders as Emma Willard, the founder of Troy Female Seminary, were ardent advocates of collegiate-level education for women, and public opinion for the establishment of women's colleges began to crystallize.

Wesleyan Female College, at Macon, Georgia, was chartered in 1836 with authority to grant academic degrees. In the same year Mary Lyon obtained a charter from the Massachusetts legislature for Mount Holyoke Seminary. Her administration of the institution and her concern for the education of women did much to further the cause. Between 1836 and 1860 seminaries for women multiplied rapidly, and they played an important part in establishing the need and feasibility of higher education for women. By 1861, when Vassar was chartered, the idea of a college education for women on a par with that for men was becoming well established. When Smith College opened in 1875, it had from the start a course of study almost identical with that of the leading men's colleges.

The Morrill Act of 1862, which established the land-grant colleges, gave an unexpected stimulus to the education of women. Most of the land-grant colleges of the West were coeducational from the start. In the 1890s even the eastern universities reacted to the demands for women's education. Tufts College opened all departments to women in 1892–93. Yale began admitting women to its graduate school in 1891–92. By the turn of the century, coeducation at the university level had achieved wide acceptance. In fact, newer institutions, such as Stanford and Chicago, were coeducational from the beginning.

In the South, however, the principle of separate education for women was still generally observed. Although some state universities admitted women, their actual number was kept down through the establishment of state colleges for women, such as those in Georgia and Florida. At the University of Virginia, a long struggle to admit women began in 1879, and by the 1890s it had taken the form of measures to establish a coordinate college for women.

EARLY WOMEN'S COLLEGES IN VIRGINIA

The first effort to provide more advanced education for women in Virginia was made about 1840 by a group of Methodists who obtained a charter for Buckingham Female College in Buckingham County. Buildings were erected, and the college opened with good prospects, but it closed after only a year or two.

In 1842 Mary Baldwin and Hollins were established, both originally by men from the North who were interested in education. The Reverend Joshua Bradley, a Baptist minister who had recently come to Virginia, conceived the idea of establishing a school of high quality for both sexes in the buildings and grounds of Botetourt Springs, formerly a popular summer watering place. A number of public-spirited citizens in the Roanoke Valley area joined in forming the Valley Union Educational Society of Virginia, which sponsored the new school. It opened in 1842 with nearly one hundred pupils but soon experienced financial difficulties that led to the resignation of Bradley, the principal, at the end of the first session.

The school struggled on until 1846, when Dr. Charles L. Cocke was asked to come from Richmond College to head what was then known as Valley Union Seminary. In 1852 the admission of boys was discontinued, and the renamed Female Seminary at Botetourt Springs became the first chartered institution for girls in the state.

In 1855, through the generosity of Mr. and Mrs. John Hollins of Lynchburg, the stock of the old corporation was bought and the institution placed under the control of a self-perpetuating board of trustees. The Hollins family gave varying amounts to the school over a period of time, while Dr. Cocke continued a presidency that lasted for fifty-five years. In 1855 the name was changed to Hollins Institute and subsequently, in 1911, to Hollins College.

With courses offered in the classics, mathematics, and philosophy, the institution set a high standard of scholarship, which attracted students from other states. However, like many colleges of the time it was forced to maintain a preparatory department to compensate for the general lack of a standard system of secondary education. The preparatory department existed at Hollins until 1912–13.

Mary Baldwin College at Staunton began as Augusta Female Seminary. Again a minister and a northerner was responsible for its establishment. The Reverend Rufus W. Bailey, from Maine, initiated a series of conferences with leading Presbyterians of Staunton and Augusta County with the idea of establishing a high-quality seminary for the education of girls.

A self-perpetuating board of trustees was set up, Bailey was elected principal with his wife as an assistant, and the school opened in temporary quarters with fifty students in the fall of 1842. It was so successful that the following year an agreement was made between the trustees of the seminary and the congregation of the First Presbyterian Church to erect a building on a lot adjoining and belonging to the church. Provision was made for three-fourths of the trustees to be ministers or members of the Old School Presbyterian Church.

Mary Baldwin, one of the first pupils, later became principal in 1863. Under her long administration (1863–97), the school achieved a national reputation for high standards of scholarship. In 1895 a new charter changed the name to Mary Baldwin Seminary and authorized the conferring of degrees. When Miss Baldwin died in 1897 she left a substantial sum to the school. In 1923 the name was changed to Mary Baldwin College. The preparatory department was discontinued entirely after 1928-29.

Sweet Briar College was established through the generosity of Indiana Fletcher Williams as a memorial to her only daughter, Daisy, who died at the age of sixteen. When Mrs. Williams died in 1900, she named four trustees to administer her principal bequest, a large estate of eight thousand acres, chiefly in Amherst County, and half a million dollars, a substantial sum in those days. The trustees were required to elect three others to join them in forming a board of directors.

The self-perpetuating board was instructed to establish and maintain on the estate a school or seminary to be known as the Sweet Briar Institute for educating white girls and young women "in sound learning and such physical, moral and religious training as shall in the judgment of the directors best fit them to be useful members of society." [1] The college was chartered in 1901 with the dual purpose of providing a sound education in the liberal arts and "practical training in certain artistic and industrial branches." [2] The new school opened formally in September 1906 with fifty-one students in attendance. Mary K. Benedict, a Yale Ph.D., was its first president.

Although Sweet Briar's curriculum was planned from the beginning to meet requirements for the bachelor of arts degree, not all applicants could meet the requirements as degree candidates. As a result, Sweet Briar admitted some subfreshmen students who offered as much as six units of high school work. The requirements soon became increasingly selective, and by 1919 the instructional program was limited to the liberal arts. The first A.B. degrees were granted in 1910 to five candidates. Sweet Briar grew in influence and prestige, especially during the administration of Dr. Meta Glass, who was president for twenty-one years, from 1925 to 1946. In 1949 Sweet Briar was awarded a chapter of Phi Beta Kappa.

Randolph-Macon Woman's College in Lynchburg was founded in March 1891 under the charter that had been granted by the General Assembly of Virginia to the original board of trustees of Randolph-Macon College, for men, in 1830, and that, in 1890, had been so amended as to authorize the establishment of other institutions of learning.

[1] Cornelius J. Heatwole, *A History of Education in Virginia* (New York: Macmillan, 1916), p. 297.
[2] *Ibid.*, p. 298.

At the time of its founding, Randolph-Macon Woman's College had as its stated purpose the provision for young women of educational advantages and opportunities equal to those offered in the best colleges for men. The project received strong financial support from the citizens of Lynchburg, who contributed substantial amounts in cash and land, and under the leadership of Dr. William Waugh Smith, raised an endowment fund of more than $100,000.

The new institution opened in 1893, with Dr. Smith as president. From its very beginning Randolph-Macon Woman's College established high standards of scholarship. Its carefully selected student body was drawn from a wide geographical area. In 1916 it became the first college for women to receive a charter of Phi Beta Kappa. Although related to the Methodist church, Randolph-Macon Woman's College is nonsectarian in its operation. Control is fully vested in a self-perpetuating board of trustees.

The present University of Richmond traces its beginnings to Dunlora Academy (1830) and the Virginia Baptist Seminary (1832). In 1840 a charter was granted to Richmond College to offer liberal arts courses, and this became the nucleus of the present university.

In 1914, when the college moved to its new campus in suburban Richmond, 22 former coeds in Richmond College formed the nucleus of a new division for women, known as Westhampton College, which began operation with an enrollment of 82. The same year the property of the Woman's College of Richmond, founded in 1854 as the Richmond Female Institute, was transferred to the trustees of Richmond College. The Woman's College ceased operation entirely in 1916, and 16 of its students enrolled in Westhampton. By 1920, when the college charter was amended and the name changed to the University of Richmond, there were 628 students and 46 faculty members.[3]

STATE-SUPPORTED HIGHER EDUCATION FOR WOMEN

When in 1869 Virginia adopted a new constitution, provision was made for a system of free public schools, with a state superintendent of public instruction and a state board of education. One of

---

[3] George M. Modlin, "University of Richmond, 1839–1955," *Addresses Commemorating the 125th Anniversary, University of Richmond*, pp. 9–11.

the requirements was that the "General Assembly shall establish, as soon as practicable, normal schools. . . ."

The first state superintendent, the Reverend William H. Ruffner, proceeded to put into effect the new constitutional provision for a system of public schools. His plan was passed by the legislature in 1870. In his first report Dr. Ruffner gave full statistics on the growth of normal schools in the eastern and central states and urged that provisions be made in Virginia for the training of teachers. Summer institutes were conducted in a few sections of the state, and in 1880 summer sessions for white teachers were held at the University of Virginia and for black teachers at Lynchburg.

In 1882 the first state conference of county and city public school officials was held in Richmond, with 89 of the 100 superintendents in attendance. Out of this meeting grew an added interest in public education in the state. Dr. Ruffner's struggle to establish normal schools was continued by R. R. Farr, who succeeded him as state superintendent of public instruction in 1882. The staffing of the newly established public schools presented a serious problem, for relatively few of the teachers had received adequate preparation for their work.

Other educational leaders joined Superintendent Farr in his plea for the establishment of normal schools. Dr. J. L. M. Curry, agent of the Peabody Fund, lent his aid and influence to the movement. As a result of their combined efforts, the state legislature in 1884 passed an act providing that a school should be located at Farmville for the express purpose of the "training of female teachers for the public schools."

This act, passed on March 7, 1884, established the first state institution of higher learning for women in Virginia. One month later the property of the Farmville Female College was deeded to the state, and its main building, part of the present Ruffner Hall, became the nucleus of the new institution. The legislature appropriated $5,000 for equipment and $10,000 for running expenses. Dr. Curry donated $5,000 from the Peabody Fund.

The act provided that the State Female Normal School for white teachers was to be managed by a board of thirteen trustees. The first board included Dr. Ruffner; Dr. Curry; Professor J. B. Minor of the University of Virginia; General S. C. Armstrong of Hampton Institute, an endowed institution founded in 1869 for the education of black teachers; and the state superintendent of public instruction, who served as an ex officio member. The new board immediately elected Dr. Ruffner as principal of the school.

In October 1884 the Normal School opened with 110 students.

From its founding the college at Farmville, known later as the State Teachers College and, since 1949, as Longwood College, has had a long and distinguished record of preparing teachers for the public schools of Virginia. Its thousands of graduates have rendered significant service to education in this and other states.

TWENTIETH-CENTURY DEVELOPMENTS

In the opening years of the twentieth century a new interest in education awakened throughout the South, but especially in Virginia. A new generation was coming into power, one that saw public education as a means of insuring the progress and future development of the state.

In 1901 the Southern Education Board was organized in a conference at Winston-Salem, North Carolina. A program of enlisting popular support for free schools was set up, with distinguished speakers such as Dr. Edwin A. Alderman, then president of Tulane University, as leaders. The new Virginia constitution of 1902 with its numerous and important educational provisions reflected this surge of interest in public education.

Successive legislative acts stimulated education through state aid for teachers' salaries, loans from the Literary Fund for constructing school buildings, and an act to insure the establishment of an agricultural high school in every congressional district. Actually these were not strictly agricultural schools, for they also offered college-preparatory programs.

With the aid of incentive funds and the work of the state examiners, the number of high schools increased rapidly. Cornelius Heatwole states that in 1906 there were about 75 so-called high schools in the state, only 10 of which were free and gave a four-year course.[4] However, the number increased rapidly. In the five-year period from 1905 to 1910, the number of high schools grew from 50 to 360. In an effort to standardize and improve quality, they were ranked as first-, second-, and third-grade high schools. Of the "standard" institutions operating in 1910, there were, according to Heatwole, 143 high schools giving a two-year course; 81 giving a three-year course; and 83 giving a four-year course.

By the time the new teacher-education institution at Fredericks-

---

[4] Heatwole, p. 329.

burg began operation there were about thirty schools and colleges in Virginia offering instruction for girls at varying levels of secondary school or college work. Some of these were under church control, while others were private or corporate undertakings.

In addition to the colleges already mentioned, some of the more important institutions for women then operating were Sullins College (Methodist), Bristol; Martha Washington College (Methodist), Abingdon; Blackstone College for Girls (Methodist), Blackstone; Southern Seminary (private), Buena Vista; Southern College (Methodist), Petersburg; Woman's College (Baptist), Richmond; and Virginia Intermont College (Baptist), Bristol.

Bridgewater College (Church of the Brethren) at Bridgewater; Virginia Christian College, later renamed Lynchburg College (Christian); and Shenandoah Collegiate Institute, later Eastern Mennonite College (United Brethren), at Dayton were coeducational.[5]

[5] *Ibid.*, p. 302.

CHAPTER II

The Founding of the College

THE LEGISLATIVE STRUGGLE

WHEN members of the General Assembly gathered in Richmond in January 1908, there was already a general recognition of the need for additional facilities for the preparation of teachers. As soon as it became evident that a new normal school, in addition to the one at Farmville, would be authorized, a number of cities and towns sought to have the institution located in their area. Finally the field of contenders narrowed down to Fredericksburg and Harrisonburg.

There ensued a vigorous legislative struggle between advocates of the two locations. The Senate selected Harrisonburg, while the House chose Fredericksburg. The resulting deadlock threatened for a time to block all efforts to establish a new school. C. O'Conor Goolrick, a young freshman member of the House of Delegates representing Fredericksburg, was pitted against the veteran Senator G. B. Keezell, of Harrisonburg, chairman of the powerful Senate Appropriations Committee.

The situation, however, was resolved by last-minute legislative strategy. With the assistance of Governor Claude A. Swanson, a coalition of forces representing the two contending cities was able to attach their respective bills as amendments to the general appropriations act of the session. The House had sought to have $25,000 included for a college at Fredericksburg, but in the form it came from the Senate the amended bill carried a $50,000 appropriation for a college at Harrisonburg. According to legislative procedure, the House had to give the bill final approval. It could strike out the appropriation for Harrisonburg, but it could not add the appropriation for Fredericksburg.

Faced with this dilemma, Goolrick and Senator Keezell held a hotel-room conference and agreed upon a compromise whereby both schools would be authorized. Former backers of the bill shook their heads in despair. The state could not afford two schools, they said, and the cause for a new teacher-training institution appeared lost.

On March 10, 1908, the crucial test came when the committee report recommending the compromise was voted on by the House.

The Founding of the College

It was accepted by the barest constitutional majority, without a vote to spare. The *Free Lance* of Fredericksburg reported that with the announcement of the results of the voting, "there was a scene of wild confusion, congratulations, and cheers." Approval by the closest of constitutional margins in both the House and the Senate meant that two new teacher-training institutions were authorized. Four days later, on March 14, 1908, the bill was signed into law.

The text of the act establishing the institution at Fredericksburg is of interest. As already indicated, it appears as a part of the appropriations bill, in which it was inserted after the last-minute action. Hence, as enacted, the provisions of the legislation appear under the title, "An Act appropriating the public revenue for the two fiscal years ending respectively the 28th day of February, 1909, and the 28th day of February, 1910. Approved March 14, 1908."[1] The pertinent sections of the act relating to the establishment of the colleges at Fredericksburg and at Harrisonburg read:

For the establishment of State normal and industrial schools for women, at Harrisonburg and Fredericksburg, the sum of seventy-five thousand dollars, of which the sum of twenty-five thousand dollars shall be for the school at Fredericksburg and shall be available on and after February twenty-eighth, nineteen hundred and nine, but not before.

The said schools shall be under the supervision, management and government of the boards of trustees, which shall consist of ten members each, to be appointed by the governor, by and with the advice and consent of the senate, to hold office for the term of four years; provided, that at the first appointment five of the members of each board shall be appointed for a term of two years, and five for a term of four years. The superintendent of public instruction shall be ex-officio member of the said boards of trustees, and any vacancy in said boards that shall be caused by death, resignation or otherwise shall be filled by the governor with the approval of the senate.

Second. The said trustees shall be bodies corporate under the name and style of State normal and industrial school for women at Harrisonburg and State normal and industrial school for women at Fredericksburg, respectively, with the right as such to plead and be impleaded in the courts, to receive all subscriptions, gifts and donations, real or personal, from any source whatever, the same by them to be held, invested, distributed, or expended for the best use and benefit of the said schools, and to exercise such other powers, and do such other acts

[1] *Acts and Joint Resolutions Passed by the General Assembly of the State of Virginia during the Session of 1908* (Richmond, 1908), p. 420.

which are necessary and proper to accomplish the end for which said schools are created. Said trustees shall from time to time make all needful rules and regulations for the government and management for said schools, fix the number and compensation of teachers and employees of said schools, and of said boards, and prescribe the preliminary examinations and conditions upon which students shall be received therein. Each of the said boards of trustees may appoint an executive committee, of which the superintendent of public instruction shall be a member, for the care, management and government of each of said schools, under the rules and regulations prescribed as aforesaid.

Third. The said trustees shall annually make and file with the said board of education a full report of their proceedings under this act, together with the report of the progress and condition of said schools. The trustees shall establish one of said schools within or near the corporate limits of Harrisonburg, in the county of Rockingham, Virginia, on a suitable site to be selected by said trustees, and one of said schools within or near the corporate limits of the city of Fredericksburg, in the county of Spottsylvania or Stafford on a suitable site to be selected by said trustees.

Fourth. Each county and city in the State shall be entitled to one pupil in each of said schools, who shall be nominated by the division superintendent of schools, and if any vacancy occur shall be filled by a like nomination, and each county and city in the State shall be entitled to one additional pupil in each school for each additional representative in the house of delegates above one, to be nominated in a similar manner, provided that the boards of trustees may increase the number of pupils, if they deem it expedient, said pupils to be selected as above. The said pupils so appointed shall be exempt from the charge of tuition. The boards of trustees shall prescribe rules for the selection of said pupils, their examination, and shall require of each pupil selected satisfactory evidence of an intention to teach in the public schools of this State for at least four years after leaving the said normal schools.

Fifth. For the purpose of the said schools there shall be paid out of the public treasury, from time to time, such sums as shall be appropriated to pay incidental expenses, the salaries of officers and teachers and to maintain the efficiency of the said schools; provided, that the Commonwealth shall not in any instance be responsible for any debt contracted or expenditure made by said institutions in excess of the appropriation made.

Sixth. The establishment of said school near or within the corporate limits of the town of Harrisonburg, in the county of Rockingham, is conditioned upon an appropriation of not less than fifteen thousand dollars cash to be paid by the town of Harrisonburg and the county of Rockingham, upon the establishment of said school; and the guaranteeing of a suitable site connected with the water, light and sewer

The Founding of the College

systems of said town, of not less than thirty acres of land for said institution at a cost not to exceed ten thousand dollars, said site and plans for said buildings to be submitted to and approved by the board of education, and the establishment of said school near or within the corporate limits of the city of Fredericksburg in the county of Spottsylvania, or Stafford, is conditional upon an appropriation of not less than twenty thousand dollars cash to be paid by the city of Fredericksburg and the county of Spottsylvania or Stafford upon the establishment of said school, and the site for said school and plans for buildings shall be submitted to, inspected and approved by the board of education.

Seventh. The superintendent of public instruction shall render to the second auditor an annual account of the expenditures for said institutions.

Governor Swanson, as authorized by this act, immediately appointed boards of trustees for the new schools. The Board of Trustees of the Fredericksburg State Normal and Industrial School for Women, the first governing body of this institution, met in Fredericksburg on April 27, 1908, and completed its organization.[2]

The original board consisted of the following members:

> Rev. J. Sidney Peters, Richmond, president
> Alden Bell, Culpeper, secretary
> E. J. Smith, Fredericksburg
> Judge R. H. L. Chichester, Stafford
> Dr. J. A. C. Chandler, Richmond
> George C. Round, Manassas
> Peter J. White, Richmond
> John T. Daniel, Cape Charles
> John A. Lesner, Norfolk
> J. W. Edmonds, Accomac
> J. D. Eggleston, Jr., state superintendent of
>   public instruction, Richmond, ex-officio

The board was a corporate body, with all the rights and duties enumerated in that act. The board held its second meeting in Fredericksburg on Tuesday evening, May 19, and Wednesday morning, May 20, 1908. One of its first actions was to select a president for the new institution. This was done in short order,

---

[2] An editorial welcoming members of the new board appeared in the *Daily Star* on April 28, 1908. Two days later another editorial urged the selection of the "Alms House property" as a site for the school.

when Edward Hutson Russell, one of the leaders in establishing the school in Fredericksburg, was unanimously elected.

At this two-day meeting the board adopted bylaws, appointed committees, elected Judge Chichester as treasurer, and, later on Wednesday afternoon, visited, "in carriages," several proposed sites for the school, accompanied by Professor Russell, former Mayor M. G. Willis, Colonel E. D. Cole, Henry Warden, and the Honorable C. O'Conor Goolrick. Thus, within two months after the passage of the act establishing the college, the governing board had been appointed, had held two meetings, and had selected a president for the new institution.

THE FOUNDER

Had it not been for the vigorous and influential work of C. O'Conor Goolrick, the legislative conflict over the establishment of the school might never have been resolved. Certainly the solution would not have been the location of a teacher-training institution at Fredericksburg.

Mr. Goolrick was born in Fredericksburg on November 25, 1876, the son of Judge John T. Goolrick and Frances Bernard Goolrick. He attended local schools and from 1894 to 1896 was a student at the Virginia Military Institute. He returned to Fredericksburg to engage in newspaper work for several years. Then in 1903 he entered the University of Virginia Law School, where he made an outstanding record; he wore proudly the Phi Beta Kappa key awarded him. Later he was to serve with distinction as a member of the board of visitors of the University from 1934 to 1946.

When Goolrick was elected to the House of Delegates in 1908 he was already known as a brilliant and capable lawyer. He was at his best in debate with opposing counsel or legislators, his keen intellect and quick wit demolishing many an adversary. However, he was never sarcastic or unkind. Always a gentleman, he was held in high regard by all who knew him, even his most implacable opponents in the courtroom, the legislative chambers, or the hustings.

Goolrick moved on to the state Senate in 1915 where he served for the next eight years. During this period he sponsored much important legislation. He was author of the workman's compensation bill of Virginia, copatron of the state's first compulsory education law, and a member of the 1918–19 commission that laid

The Founding of the College

the foundation for the county-unit system of public school administration.

Senator Goolrick is regarded by many as the father of the state highway system. He headed a legislative committee which, during 1916, 1917, and 1918, mapped out a system of state-maintained roads. In 1923 he found himself confronting a fellow senator, Harry F. Byrd, in an issue over the financing of the new state highway system. Goolrick favored a large bond issue, while Byrd championed a pay-as-you-go plan. The issue was debated vigorously. Byrd's program won. He went on to become governor and later United States senator.

Defeated in his campaign for reelection to the state Senate in 1923, Goolrick continued to serve his state as a private citizen with vigor and distinction. In fact, Byrd himself said, in a program in Fredericksburg organized to honor Goolrick, "He'll go down in history as one of the men who built up this state."

Goolrick was mentioned as a possible successor to Carter Glass in the United States Senate, but he refused to be considered. He served as city attorney of Fredericksburg for twenty-eight years and was, for a time, mayor of the city. He was a former president of the Virginia Bar Association and served as director of several corporations. For many years he was president of the Free Lance-Star Publishing Company. In 1950 he received the first B'nai B'rith award for distinguished service to his community. He was often referred to as Fredericksburg's most distinguished citizen.

Goolrick was especially proud of being called the "Father of Mary Washington College." For the 1944 *Battlefield* he wrote an account of the founding of the College. Simply and modestly, he described the legislative struggle he led to have the institution established at Fredericksburg. "It was a fight that will long be remembered in Virginia legislative history," he recalled.[3]

During the years that followed, Goolrick never lost his interest in the college, as the following pages indicate. He was a member of the board of visitors of the University of Virginia when Mary Washington College was affiliated with the university as its liberal arts college for women, and he lent his influence and persuasive skill to the accomplishment of this goal.

Goolrick died unexpectedly of a heart attack on June 4, 1960. He was eighty-three at the time but still active and vigorous. His wife, Nannie Osborne Ficklin Goolrick, and a daughter, Frances

---

[3] C. O'Conor, Goolrick, "A History of Mary Washington College," *Battlefield*, 1944, p. 9.

Goolrick Ashby, survived him. Governor J. Lindsay Almond ordered the flag in the State Capitol to be flown at half-mast, and Virginia leaders paid tribute to his accomplishments.[4] In 1967 the new million-dollar physical education building at the college was named in honor of Mr. Goolrick.

THE FIRST PRESIDENT

Edward Hutson Russell, selected by the board of trustees on May 19, 1908, to head the new school, was an experienced educator. Born in Petersburg on November 26, 1869, he attended the Henrico County public schools and the Richmond City High School. After graduating from the Virginia Military Institute in 1891, he studied law for a time at Richmond College. The teaching profession attracted him, however, and he began an educational career that extended over the next thirty years.

For two years he was school principal at Pulaski. Then he served for two years as commandant at Fishburne Military Academy. For the next eight years he was superintendent of schools in Bristol. During this time he founded and conducted a summer school for teachers at Emory and Henry College. In 1905 he became a member of the State Board of Public School Examiners for the First Circuit, which included Fredericksburg. During this period he founded and conducted the Summer School for Teachers at Fredericksburg.

Russell's experience as teacher, principal, superintendent, and school examiner gave him an intimate acquaintance with the public schools of his native state. He was closely identified with the preparation of teachers through the highly successful summer institutes he had conducted. His choice to head the new State Normal and Industrial School at Fredericksburg was acclaimed enthusiastically.

The new president brought to the position a dynamic energy and enthusiasm. He was a tall and powerful man, with a rich, resonant voice. His presence commanded attention and respect. Russell's enthusiasm for the new school led him at times to make somewhat extravagant statements about the resources and facilities of the institution, as is evidenced in passages found in the first catalogue and in others which appeared in some newspapers. However, his faith in the new school and his belief in its future were well justified, as the days to come were to prove.

[4] *Free Lance-Star,* June 6, 1960.

SELECTING THE SITE

Once it had been decided that the new normal school was to be located in Fredericksburg, a considerable controversy over the selection of the site developed. Members of the board of trustees were sharply divided. Some favored a tract of land then known as C. W. Jones's dairy farm, on Fall Hill Avenue, in the general area in which Mary Washington Hospital is now located. Others favored the heights west of the city where the college now stands. The area where the first buildings were constructed was known as Rowe's Wood, since most of the land belonged to Captain M. B. Rowe, who, at the time, owned and lived at Brompton. Captain Rowe also owned Altoona and quite a bit of other property in Spotsylvania County.

Advocates of the Jones's dairy farm tract insisted that the site was ideal, since it was level and would require little clearing or grading; that access to the city would be relatively easy; and that there was ample space for what expansion was then envisioned. Those in favor of the location west of the city admitted the validity of these arguments but pointed out that the heights overlooking the city would offer an attractive site for the new buildings, that the grove of trees would add beauty to the surroundings, and that the historic ground was an appropriate place to erect an institution dedicated to the acquisition and dissemination of knowledge.

In fairness to the advocates of the dairy farm site, it should be noted that between Washington Avenue and the proposed location on the heights, there was only one house standing, the Hopkins house off Littlepage Street. Direct access to the city was difficult. There was no road or sidewalk. Furthermore, a canal ran through the area, which was generally swampy. Older residents recall ice skating there in winter. The town limits extended only to Sunken Road, and the property proposed for the college was in Spotsylvania County.

For a time it looked as if the contention within the board would delay the beginning of work on the institution. At this point, as Goolrick put it, "Certain citizens of Fredericksburg interested themselves in the selection and successfully urged upon the Board choice of the present site." [5]

It was Goolrick himself who led the fight to build the school

---

[5] Goolrick, "Mary Washington College," p. 9.

in its present location. In a final stormy meeting of the board held in the old Exchange Hotel in Fredericksburg, the issue was settled by a vote taken in executive session. On March 2, 1909, the *Free Lance* was able to report:

The site offered by Captain M. B. Rowe won, with this understanding that suitable arrangements can be made in opening the street which runs through the Bradley property from a point on Washington Avenue between Col. E. D. Cole's home and the Mary Washington Monument lodge to the road at the foot of Rowe's woods.

The site embraces Rowe's woods and the heights to Guest's line [Snowden Farm] and a level plateau on the hill above. It contains 35 acres and the price paid is $187.50 per acre, or $6,662.50

The *Free Lance-Star,* in a fiftieth anniversary feature story by William Lakeman on March 13, 1958, reported that in August 1909 a deed for the sale was filed in Spotsylvania Courthouse, giving a purchase price of $8,516.70 for 45.4 acres. It was accompanied by a plat of "Rowe's Hill," as surveyed by Cecil Reid.

The site selected was admirably suited to "lend beauty and dignity to the new institution," even though it did involve greater initial expenditures for grading and access roads. What came to be known as "Normal Hill" and later College Heights provided a commanding view of the city to the east. Furthermore, it was historic ground.

In 1608 Captain John Smith sailed up the Rappahannock River on one of his earliest exploratory trips, discovering the village of the Seacobeck Indians and bartering with the natives there. Seacobeck Hall, the dining complex of the college, takes its name from this Indian village, located on or near the spot and visited by Captain John Smith and his party in 1608.

During the excavations for this building a considerable number of carefully carved arrowheads and even tomahawks were uncovered. Frederick M. Aldridge, an avid collector of Indian relics, gathered many of his specimens while Seacobeck Hall was under construction.[6]

The heights above the city became hotly contested ground during the Battle of Fredericksburg, December 12–13, 1862. Time and again the Federal troops sought to storm Marye's Heights but were repulsed, sustaining heavy losses. Gun emplacements have

---

[6] An account of Aldridge's collection is in David I. Bushnell, Jr., *The Manahoac Tribes in Virginia, 1608,* Smithsonian Miscellaneous Collections, XCIV, no. 8 (Washington, D.C.: Smithsonian Institution, 1935), p. 48.

The Founding of the College

been preserved in the area of the campus adjoining Framar, acquired by the college in 1946.

Mr. Goolrick re-created the scene in his inimitable way: "At break of day on December 13, 1862, might have been found here, as General Lee extended his lines north from historic Marye's Heights, Confederate infantry and artillerymen, calmly awaiting the gallant attack of General Burnside's Union brigades. When evening came at long last, the battle of Fredericksburg was ended; the guns were silent and only the challenge of the sentries and the cries of the wounded disturbed the stillness of the night. The stars looked down upon a battlefield where the tragedy of warfare was made glorious by the sublime valor of the American soldier." [7]

Even as late as 1937 evidences of the grim struggle were being uncovered. When grading was under way for the group of dormitories known as the Tri-Unit, cannon balls were found in the loads of dirt that were carted away, reminders of the heavy artillery bombardment that preceded the Federal attack on the very hill where the central buildings of the college now stand.

GROUND-BREAKING CEREMONIES

Ground-breaking ceremonies for the first building of the new normal school took place on the heights overlooking the city at eleven o'clock on Tuesday, December 14, 1909.

Dr. J. A. C. Chandler, superintendent of the Richmond public schools and president of the board of trustees, presided over an assembly of distinguished citizens, including the board of visitors of the new school, the mayor and other city officials, and members of the legislature. After an opening prayer by the Reverend John R. Rosebro, Dr. Chandler spoke briefly and then introduced Peter J. White, chairman of grounds and buildings. White outlined the work already done and pointed out that forty-seven years before, on this spot, "guns belched forth fire, and thousands of men were engaged in deadly conflict." [8]

Then Mayor H. Lewis Wallace threw the first shovelful of earth. E. H. Russell, president-elect, removed the second. Then Dr. Chandler invited the Honorable C. O'Conor Goolrick and the Honorable R. C. L. Moncure, as the members of the General Assembly responsible for establishing the school in Fredericksburg, to take the spade and join in the ground breaking. After

---

[7] *Ibid.*, p. 7.   [8] *Daily Star*, Dec. 16, 1909.

the Reverend R. A. Williams offered a prayer at the site, the ceremonies were continued at the courthouse.

A sizable crowd assembled there to hear the speeches and acknowledge their appreciation of the work done in behalf of the school. Again Dr. Chandler presided. He discussed briefly what the new school would mean to education in Virginia and expressed great hope for its success. He concluded by introducing C. O'Conor Goolrick as the "founder of the Normal School" in Fredericksburg.

Goolrick responded by acknowledging the help of Moncure and also of the Honorable Alden Bell, of Culpeper, who, as members of the legislature, had worked so hard to get the school located here. He concluded by urging a united effort to make the Normal School a success. Russell then made a short address, emphasizing that the new school would offer "industrial" as well as "classical" courses.

There followed speeches by A. B. Bowering, president of the city school board; the Honorable Alden Bell; and George C. Round, of Manassas, who introduced the first normal school bill in the legislature on March 14, 1874, and was at the time the oldest school trustee in the state. Then the Reverend J. H. Henderson spoke, emphasizing what the new school would mean to the religious life of the city with the added memberships and influence of the faculty and students in the churches.

At this point Russell made what the *Daily Star* described as "a very beautiful and happy address" in presenting a magnificent loving cup to Goolrick as the founder of the Normal School. A massive vessel of sterling silver, mounted on an ebony base, the cup was engraved on one side with the words, "Well done, good and faithful servant." The other side bears this inscription: "Presented to C. O'Conor Goolrick by his many friends on December 14, 1909, in appreciation of and gratitude for his work and service in the Legislature of 1908–09 for the location of the Normal School at Fredericksburg."

Russell paid an impressive tribute to Goolrick, speaking of his great service in behalf of the school. "But for Mr. Goolrick's tact, fearless pluck, and good diplomacy, we would not have the Normal here." Goolrick replied briefly but very feelingly. The *Daily Star* described him as "the hero of the hour" as various speakers paid tribute to his successful efforts. The exercises were concluded with a benediction by the Reverend Dr. R. J. McBryde.

The full text of Russell's speech in presenting the loving cup to Goolrick was printed in the *Daily Star* on December 16. He

The Founding of the College

chorus, directed by W. J. Phillips with the assistance of H. K. Sweetser, sang "in the most inspiring and impressive manner."

Placed in the cornerstone were a number of old coins, copies of the bylaws of the new school and the prospectus for 1911–12, newspapers of the day, and a souvenir program of the cornerstone laying.

The audience gathered on the grounds between the two new buildings, occupying seats in front of the speakers' stand or seeking relief from the sun by standing in the shade of the trees nearby. Only one critical comment appeared in the *Daily Star*'s exuberant account of the occasion. In this day before electric amplifiers, "The only drawback was that the [speakers'] stand was so far above the audience that the speakers could not be heard distinctly."

The principal address was given by Charles G. Maphis, secretary of the Virginia Education Commission, who for many years was dean of the University of Virginia summer session and founded the Institute of Public Affairs there. He spoke at length on the role of teachers in society, the recognition that should be given their work, and the importance of providing proper training for them.

"To the teacher," Mr. Maphis said, "is entrusted the noble work of shaping and fashioning human temples out of our boys and our girls, making them fit dwelling places for the immortal spirit of man." He spoke of the influence of teachers, citing examples from ancient and modern times. He concluded by emphasizing what this new teacher-training facility would mean to the Commonwealth of Virginia in improving the quality of teaching in its public schools. His address was printed in full on the first page of the *Daily Star* on July 5.

President Russell and State Senator John R. Saunders also spoke, and Professor A. B. Bowering brought greetings from the city of Fredericksburg. It was Governor William Hodges Mann, however, who really reached the heights of oratory and aroused the enthusiasm of the crowd.

The chief executive of the Commonwealth was an impressive figure in full dress uniform with his white beard and mustache. Always an eloquent speaker, he grew ecstatic as he dwelt upon "the fruit which this school will yield to our mother state in the years which are to come." The governor continued:

Tell me of the teachers, who, strong in body, pure in heart, and vigorous in intellect, will go out with abounding youth and enthusiasm to carry abroad the teachings, standards, and ideals of this institution and impress them with the best part of their character and life upon the youth of Virginia; teachers who will go throughout the length and breadth of the State sowing good seed, to blossom into an abundant harvest of beautiful lives, lives which will raise higher still the standards and ideals of this institution.

And then those who have been taught will teach others with constantly increasing force and power, and so the good work will go upward and onward from generation to generation, growing stronger and broader and deeper with advancing years, until at last heaven shall gather the immortal fruit and the men and women who have been educated in Fredericksburg, or by teachers educated there, shall go into the College of Angels above whose portals is written the motto, 'Eternal Progress'.[10]

At the close of the exercises President Russell announced greetings from Dr. J. L. Jarman, president of the State Normal School at Farmville, and Professor Julian A. Burruss, president of the State Normal School at Harrisonburg (later president of the Virginia Polytechnic Institute). The Honorable J. D. Eggleston, Jr., state superintendent of public instruction, sent a special message regretting that illness prevented his attending the exercises.

A number of school superintendents from nearby counties were present. Among them were John Washington, of Caroline; James Ashby, of Stafford and Spotsylvania; A. L. Terrell, of King and Queen; and W. G. Rennolds, of Essex and Richmond counties. Rennolds "brought with him applications for some young women from his division to enter the school." President Russell stated that enrollments from Rennolds's territory were leading all other school divisions at that time.

And so, on the day celebrated as the birthday of our independence, the cornerstone of a new college at Fredericksburg was laid with ceremony, music, oratory, and, most important, a deep sense of dedication.

BOARD ACTIVITIES AND STATE APPROPRIATIONS

The board of trustees met regularly throughout this early period under the capable leadership of Dr. J. A. C. Chandler. At a meeting in Fredericksburg on Monday evening, December 13, 1909, the board approved the contract for the dormitory building and authorized the executive committee to see that work was pushed

---

[10] *Daily Star,* July 5, 1911.

The Founding of the College

forward. It also prepared an estimate for appropriations to be asked from the next session of the legislature.

A few days later, on Wednesday, December 15, Russell, Alden Bell, and R. C. L. Moncure appeared before the Senate Finance Committee in Richmond to request appropriations for the school. They presented detailed schedules of the coast of completing and equipping the new school and also an analysis of the cost and current expenses for operation.

A total of $105,000 was requested. Of this amount $75,000 was for building, to be available in 1910, and $50,000 for the same purpose in 1911. The remaining $30,000 was for running expenses. Up to that time the school had received a total of $45,000, of which $25,000 was appropriated by the legislature when it established the school in 1908 and $20,000 was contributed by the city of Fredericksburg.

Records of the legislation enacted by the General Assembly of 1910 show that $50,000 was appropriated to the State Normal and Industrial School at Fredericksburg for the "building fund" for the fiscal year ending February 28, 1911, and $70,000 for buildings and equipment and $15,000 for support for the fiscal year ending February 29, 1912.[11] This represented a total of $120,000 available for buildings and equipment during the biennium covering roughly the years 1910 and 1911.

On March 7, 1910, Governor Mann announced the appointment of five members of the board of trustees for terms of four years commencing March 14, 1910:

>Alden Bell, Culpeper
>George C. Round, Manassas
>John A. Lesner, Norfolk
>Peter J. White, Richmond
>Saxon W. Holt, Newport News [12]

All except Holt had been members of the original board with two-year appointments, a plan designed for the interim period until a procedure could be begun of having half of the board up for appointment for four-year terms every other year.

By the time the college opened in 1911, C. O'Conor Goolrick had been appointed to the board and was chairman of the executive committee and also treasurer, Dr. Chandler continued to

---

[11] *Acts of Assembly*, 1910, pp. 404, 417.
[12] Executive Journal, Secretary of the Commonwealth, Feb. 1, 1910, to Feb. 1, 1914, p. 3, Archives, Virginia State Library, Richmond.

serve as president. The complete board, as listed in the first bulletin of the college, was as follows:

>Dr. J. A. C. Chandler, Richmond
>John T. Daniel, Cape Charles
>Hon. Alden Bell, Culpeper
>E. J. Smith, Fredericksburg
>Dr. A. S. Kemper, Lynnwood
>Rev. J. Sidney Peters, Richmond
>George C. Round, Manassas
>Peter J. White, Richmond
>Hon. S. W. Holt, Newport News
>Hon. C. O'Conor Goolrick, Fredericksburg
>Hon. J. D. Eggleston, Jr., superintendent of public instruction, ex officio, Richmond [13]

A typical meeting of the board of trustees was that held at the school on Tuesday, October 10, 1911, at noon.[14] The members of the board inspected the buildings and expressed their pleasure at the successful opening of the school. The possibility of an additional dormitory was discussed, since the present hall was already filled to capacity. Gunyon Harrison was appointed as superintendent of machinery, and C. L. Hudson as engineer for the session 1911–12. The board decided to devote its November meeting to the matter of preparing a budget for the next meeting of the state legislature.

Appointments to the board of trustees for four-year terms commencing March 14, 1912, were announced by the governor as follows:

>Charles G. Maphis, Charlottesville
>Charles O'Conor Goolrick, Fredericksburg
>J. A. C. Chandler, Richmond
>John T. Daniel, Cape Charles
>J. Sidney Peters, Richmond [15]

Maphis, a new appointee, was then secretary of the Virginia Education Commission and had been a principal speaker at the laying of the cornerstone of the new school. Dr. Chandler continued to serve as chairman of the board, Alden Bell as secretary, and C. O'Conor Goolrick as treasurer and chairman of the executive committee.

---

[13] *Bulletin*, 1911–12, p. 3.   [14] *Daily Star*, Oct. 11, 1911.
[15] Executive Journal, Secretary of the Commonwealth, 1910–14, p. 254.

The Founding of the College

State appropriations, as reported in the *Acts of Assembly*, reflect the efforts of the board to provide adequately for the support and development of the new institution. In 1912 the General Assembly appropriated the sum of $35,000 for support, $11,000 for furniture "and so forth," and $18,000 "to pay on note" for the fiscal year ending February 28, 1913.[16] It also appropriated $35,000 for support and $29,000 for "balance on debt" for the fiscal year ending February 28, 1914.

The General Assembly of 1914 appropriated $35,000 for support and $37,500 for a new dormitory building (first unit of Virginia Hall) for the fiscal year ending February 28, 1915. For the fiscal year ending February 29, 1916, it appropriated $40,000 for support and $5,000 for equipment. The 1916 General Assembly continued the $40,000 appropriation for support for each of the two fiscal years that followed and also $5,000 each year toward "heating plant, laundry, and equipment for same."[17] Incidentally, this laundry has continued to serve the college ever since. However, the heating plant became outmoded and was moved to a new location on College Avenue across from the campus in 1955. The repair and maintenance shops were located in the space occupied by the old heating plant; they were moved later to a site near the present golf course.

In 1918 the General Assembly raised its allocation for support to $50,000 for each fiscal year and $10,000 annually for "repairs, improvements, and additional equipment."[18] Thus, by the end of the first decade of operation, through the fiscal year ending February 29, 1920, the General Assembly had appropriated to the institution approximately $615,500, distributed as follows: for buildings and equipment (including original grant in act establishing the college), $275,500; for support, $340,000.

PREPARATIONS FOR OPENING

Plans for the opening of the new school proceeded throughout the year 1911. At a meeting of the board of trustees held on February 20, in the Corporation Commission Courtroom in the State Capitol at Richmond, dates for the first session were set. The opening was scheduled for September 11, 1911, and the session

---

[16] *Acts of Assembly*, 1912, pp. 252, 268.
[17] *Ibid.*, 1914, pp. 332-33, 357; *ibid.*, 1916, pp. 909, 930.
[18] *Ibid.*, 1918, pp. 709, 731.

would end on June 14, 1912. The president and the executive committee of the board were empowered to set the fees for room, board, and tuition. It was announced that a catalogue would be published as soon as possible.

The board decided to "postpone for the present the erection of the president's house on what was formerly the almshouse grounds, but this will be done as soon as possible."[19] Bids for construction were opened, and E. G. Heflin of Fredericksburg was the lowest bidder.

During what the *Daily Star* (February 21) described as the "lengthiest and most important meeting" of the board of trustees yet held, it was announced that the new dormitory building would provide accommodations for 140 students. Completion was expected by May 1. The administration building, "which will supply classrooms, offices, assembly hall, gymnasium, swimming pool, etc." was expected to be ready by the time the college opened.

"The total amount which will have been expended when the school opens its doors on September 26th next will approximate $200,000," according to the *Daily Star,* "so that some idea can be gathered from this as to the character of the buildings, etc."

At this meeting the board elected several faculty members for the new school. Professor Hugh S. Bird, superintendent of schools in Fredericksburg, was chosen to head the department of education. Others elected were W. N. Hamlet of Richmond, Virginia Stone of Montgomery, Virginia May Goolrick of Fredericksburg, and Annie I. Anthony of Campbell County. Marion C. Forbes of Richmond was selected as "head of the home," and Mrs. M. A. Horner, previously housekeeper for the Summer Normal at Fredericksburg, as housekeeper.

Some concern was expressed about the condition of roads leading to the school. The Board decided to ask the city of Fredericksburg to "secure proper approaches" and expressed the hope that "the county of Spotsylvania will contribute some work towards putting the roads in shape, as the county was not asked for any help in the construction of the school."

The board also voted to pay the city of Fredericksburg the sum of eight hundred dollars in consideration of the use of the city public schools as a training and observation school "on condition that money be used to increase the salary of the teachers in the public schools or to increase the number of said teachers." The

[19] *Daily Star,* Feb. 21, 1911.

board expressed the feeling that such an arrangement would be of mutual advantage to the city and to the Normal School.

Dr. Chandler, president of the board, presided. C. O'Conor Goolrick was elected treasurer of the board to succeed Judge R. H. L. Chichester, who had resigned. E. H. Russell, president of the school, and C. M. Robinson, its architect, also attended. John T. Daniel, board member from Cape Charles, was prevented from attending by bad weather.

During August and September 1911, the *Daily Star,* of Fredericksburg, carried a four-by-five-inch advertisement, at times on the first page, announcing the opening of the new college. The actual wording is of interest:

> State Normal School
> Session Opens
> September 26, 1911
> Free to Day Students Who Expect to Teach
> Tuition for Others $30.
> For full information as to Scholarships,
> Course of Study, Entrance Requirements, Etc.,
> see President E. H. Russell at his office in
> the Law Building.

It is interesting to note that several of the same issues carried an advertisement for the local private college still operating at that time. The display advertisement read:

> Fredericksburg College
> Session opens September 13th. Primary
> and Preparatory Departments in connection with
> the College. Every department thoroughly
> equipped. High standard maintained. Terms
> reasonable. For particulars address
> S. W. Somerville, President
> Fredericksburg, Va.

Some extravagance is evident in the statements made about the facilities and staff of the new institution. One affirmed that "a large and expert faculty has been secured from the graduate list of leading colleges and universities of the country."

Although no one can question the enthusiasm and dedication of the first faculty, the academic training of this small group left much to be desired. Not one of them held a degree higher than a master's. In fact, only two had master's degrees, two had bachelor's degrees, two had engineering degrees, two had M.D. degrees, and ten had no degrees at all.

According to the *Daily Star* of September 14, 1911, the new institution was equipped with "everything modern." The dormitory and the administration building being rushed to completion represented a total expenditure of $200,000, said the newspaper, which gave a detailed description of the two buildings.

The Dormitory (as it was called at the time) was described as modern in all of its appointments, with a "handsome" dining room accommodating three hundred people, a "commodious" kitchen, parlors "handsomely furnished" with mission furniture, "up-to-date" steam laundry, storage rooms, linen closets, offices, reading room, infirmary, rooms for the faculty, and fifty-one rooms for students, which "will accommodate 102 boarding students," and six "large and modernly appointed bathrooms."

It is difficult today to visualize the incorporation of all these facilities in one three-story building.

The building was heated with steam, and electricity for lighting was supplied by the school's own generating equipment. The six "gang baths" were designed to serve the student residents of the building. There were private baths for the "head of the home" and also for the "infirmary rooms." Each student room had a stationary stand with hot and cold running water. There were large closets on either side of the door. Furnishings included two single beds, two dressers, a student table, and chairs.

As of September 14, the Administration Building was still under construction. The newspaper stated that every effort was to be made to "have the work so carried on as not to interfere with the progress of the school."

President Russell announced that he and W. N. Hamlet had ordered equipment for "the Science Department, namely Chemistry and Physics, that will give the school an equipment equal to any in the state." He also said that equipment for the manual arts department, domestic science, and rural arts would be purchased "as soon as the heads of these departments arrive and Mr. Russell can confer with them."

These statements made two weeks before the opening of the school indicate an optimism which was to characterize the development of the new state college for women. For this entirely new institution, equipment and supplies all had to be ordered "from scratch." For example, the library was simply a small room with shelves and tables in the new administration building. Seats for twenty-four students were provided. Russell announced that

The Founding of the College

a faculty committee headed by Professor A. B. Chandler, Jr., who would teach Latin and social sciences, was preparing a list of books to be purchased for the library. Russell remarked later that the library collection began modestly with a Hagerstown almanac.[20]

This was only one of the many aspects of opening an entirely new institution. President Russell and his cohorts on the spot worked feverishly to get everything in readiness by the opening date. Some local cynics asserted that it could not be done, but the work progressed rapidly and with a will. By September 26, when faculty and students began to arrive, there were furnished rooms for them to occupy, food for them to eat and persons to prepare and serve it, classrooms in which they could teach and study, and a spirit of contagious enthusiasm that made it all seem a great adventure.

[20] Founder's Day address, March 14, 1949.

CHAPTER III

The College Opens

A NEW SCHOOL BEGINS

THE opening days of any college session are filled with excitement, activity, and at times confusion. There are new challenges to be met, new conditions to which to adapt, new friends to make, and new experiences to enjoy. A sense of anticipation and expectation permeates the atmosphere as students assemble and talk excitedly with each other. If this is true of established institutions, it is even more evident in the case of an entirely new school. A graphic account of the opening of the college appeared in Fredericksburg's daily newspaper.

The *Daily Star* for Tuesday, September 26, 1911, carried a feature story on the opening of the new normal school. Below a picture of President Russell, quaintly titled "Prof. E. H. Russell," and reproductions of architect's drawings of the Dormitory (Willard Hall) and the administration building (later to be named after President Russell), the following account appears:

Normal School Opens
———
A Full Attendance—No Delays
in the Work.
———
The Faculty—Public Opening Day
Will Be Held Soon, Etc.

The State Normal and Industrial School for Women opened in a blaze of glory Tuesday. A few pessimists did not think it possible for the buildings to be ready in time, but upon the Normal Hill was enacted Sept. 26th, the day for the scheduled opening, the most interesting educational scene this section of the State has ever witnessed.

The school is filled to its utmost capacity. Every room in the dormitory is taken. Some applicants could not be accommodated.

Nine lecture rooms are ready for use. These will suffice till the other rooms in the Administration building are completed.

Many visitors and friends of the school have inspected the buildings during the past week. All expressed themselves as delighted with the splendid equipment for the important work inaugurated Tuesday.

The school faculty have had their quarters in the building for several days and have been busy with committee work incident to the opening.

The College Opens

The student body consists of as bright, attractive and earnest an aggregation of young women as can be found in the State. The initial impression of the students was most favorable. While everything has an air of newness and strangeness to them, their living quarters are comfortable and convenient beyond their anticipations, and with the completeness of the equipment for their work they are jubilant over the prospect for a happy and successful session. They are contented and satisfied.

Arrangements have been made for twice a day mail service. In a few weeks the boardwalk will be constructed along the new road route, thus giving easy access to the city.

Tuesday was spent in the classification of students and in assisting them to become settled in their new home. There is no reason for delay in starting the class room work. A temporary schedule has been worked out, and it is probable that the instructors will meet their classes for a preliminary outline of work Wednesday or Thursday.

No elaborate exercises will be attempted for the opening, as the Assembly Hall is not yet ready and the head of the school and his assistants have been too busy with other more urgent matters incident to the work to permit it. It is probable, however, that a great opening day will be arranged for the near future, at which time people prominent in educational work throughout the State, the parents of the students and friends of the school will have an opportunity to visit the school and see it in action.

It is rather remarkable, but none the less gratifying, that in starting the electric machinery, the boilers, the kitchen ranges and all the plumbing there was no accident of any sort. This reflects great credit upon the contractors for the acceptable manner in which this work was installed.

A list of the officers and faculty follows this glowing account.

THE FIRST FACULTY

By the time the college opened, the entire faculty had been appointed and was on hand to begin work. President Russell had begun early to assemble his teaching staff. He had opened an office in the Law Building in Fredericksburg where he could interview candidates and discuss plans for the program to be offered at the institution then under construction. Early in the spring of 1911 appointments began to be announced as the board of trustees held its periodic meetings. By the time the first bulletin announcing the staff and curriculum changes appeared in June 1911, it was possible to give the names, teaching field, and academic training and experience of most of the faculty.

Perhaps the best idea of the kind of men and women who staffed the new college can be gathered from a special feature story that appeared in the local newspaper in the early fall. The *Daily Star* of November 17, 1911, published on the first page a group picture of the normal school faculty together with a brief educational biography of each. According to the enthusiastic reporter, "we present to our readers a good group picture of the faculty . . . [who] were chosen for their experience and special fitness for the work assigned them."

The photograph shows President Russell standing tall in the center of the front row, flanked by W. N. Hamlet and A. B. Chandler, Jr. Immediately behind this trio are the other three men on the staff: Gunyon M. Harrison, Professor Hugh S. Bird, and Dr. C. Mason Smith. On either side of this stalwart group are the twelve women members of the faculty, most of them arrayed in flaring, long white dresses with white shirtwaists and a bow of black ribbon tied tastefully at the throat. Hairstyles are predominantly side- or middle-parts to produce fairly impressive pompadours. Only two of the women dared to venture a slight smile for the cameraman, the young Dr. Anne Humphreys and Frances Withers, head of the household arts department. The men look stern and austere, except for the college physician, Dr. Smith, who radiates a confident glow.

It is a tribute to President Russell that he was able to assemble such a capable and well-trained group of people for the opening session of a new institution. Although the descriptions of their qualifications in published announcements appear extravagant and flamboyant, the dedicated individuals who began their work that fall presented an impressive background of training and experience in comparison to the typical normal school faculty of the period.

President Russell, as already noted, had attended Richmond College and V.M.I. and had had experience as a superintendent of schools, state school examiner, and conductor of summer courses for teachers.

A. B. Chandler, Jr., professor of Latin, who was later to become dean and then president, was a scholar of stature. He held B.A. and M.A. degrees from the University of Virginia and had significant publications and teaching experience to his credit before accepting the position at the new school.

W. N. Hamlet, professor of mathematics and science, was educated in the public schools of Lynchburg. He graduated from V.M.I. with a degree in chemical engineering and had also taken

The College Opens

courses at the University of Virginia and at Cornell University. After serving as high school principal at Ashland, Virginia, and Lonoke, Arkansas, he had gone to Richmond where for ten years he was assistant principal and head of the science department at John Marshall High School. For eight years he was professor of analytical chemistry in the department of pharmacy at the Medical College of Virginia. Subsequently, he served for three years as director of analytical chemistry in the medical department of the Medical College, a position he held at the time of his appointment to the faculty of the Normal School.

Hugh S. Bird, the head of the department of education, had been educated in the public schools of Petersburg and at what was then called Peabody Normal College, in Nashville, Tennessee. From 1888 to 1904 he had been professor of pedagogy at the College of William and Mary and director of the model and practice school there. He had also served as superintendent of public schools in James City County and the city of Williamsburg. Like Russell and Chandler, Bird had taught in the Virginia state summer schools for teachers, including that at the University of Virginia. He had had twelve years of experience in this work at the time of his appointment to the Normal School faculty. He was also superintendent of schools in Fredericksburg, a position he continued to hold.

Primary methods was taught by Virginia E. Stone, a graduate of Farmville State Normal School with twelve years of teaching experience. She had taught in several summer institutes for teachers, had taken special work at Teachers College, Columbia University, and had served as primary supervisor at the State Normal School at Farmville.

Instruction in household arts was the responsibility of Frances L. Withers, an experienced teacher who had studied at Martha Washington Seminary and Teachers College, Columbia University. She had also taken summer courses at Winthrop College and at the University of Virginia. Before joining the faculty in Fredericksburg she had taught household arts in a model manual training school in New Orleans.

Another teacher with wide experience, M. Catherine Straith, headed the work in rural arts. A native of Canada, she had studied and taught in Ontario. Later she had directed and written articles on school gardens in New York, New Jersey, and Pennsylvania. At the time of her appointment she was a member of the N.E.A. National Committee on School Gardens.

Olive M. Hinman was in charge of manual training and

drawing. She had studied at Farmville State Normal and at Teachers College, Columbia University. She had served as a special demonstrator in drawing for the Prang Company, manufacturers of drawing and painting supplies, and had taught and supervised drawing both in public schools and in summer institutes for teachers.

Virginia M. Goolrick was a native of Fredericksburg who had taught in the local schools for several years before taking charge of instruction in history at the new Normal School. She had held a scholarship in history at Teachers College, Columbia University, during the 1910–11 session and had also taught in summer schools for teachers.

Dora J. Dadmun was professor of English. A New Englander, she held an A.B. degree from Boston University and had taken summer courses at Harvard and Chautauqua. She had held school principalships in Wilmington and Hadley, Massachusetts.

Annie I. Anthony, in charge of modern languages, had attended the Danville College for Young Ladies and subsequently received both A.B. and A.M. degrees from Randolph-Macon Woman's College. She had had both school and college teaching experience, having been an instructor at the Valley Female College at Winchester and at the Clintwood Normal College.

Bernice M. White, director of music, had graduated from the New York Normal School at Courtland, taught music and directed choruses in Ithaca, and participated in music festivals there. She had taken summer work at Cornell and at New York University.

Cary Graves, director of physical education, held the A.B. degree from Presbyterian College for Women at Charlotte, North Carolina. She had also taken summer courses at the University of Virginia and Chautauqua School of Physical Education. She had previously been director of girls' gymnastics at Fredericksburg College.

Perhaps the most interesting person, academically and professionally, was Dr. Anne Humphreys, resident physician and instructor in biology. She was the daughter of Professor Milton W. Humphreys, long professor of Latin and Greek at the University of Virginia. After attending the Piedmont Female Institute in Charlottesville and Randolph-Macon Woman's College, Dr. Humphreys attended the University of Michigan as a student in medicine and surgery, graduating with honor in 1907. After interning in Minneapolis, she practiced medicine in Norfolk from 1909 to 1911. She was a member of local, state, and national medical asso-

The College Opens

ciations. She was still in her twenties when she joined the faculty at Fredericksburg.

A member of the first faculty who continued to teach until 1943 was Nora C. Willis, instructor in instrumental music. Miss Willis was a member of an old Fredericksburg family, had graduated in piano and theory of music from Fredericksburg College, and had taught piano for a time at the Woman's College in Richmond (later absorbed into Westhampton College). For the many years she taught at the college, Miss Willis entertained at frequent recitals and was always in demand as an accompanist. She was the principal teacher of piano until the 1940s. Miss Willis retired in 1943 and, shortly thereafter, married Charles M. Wattleworth. She died in 1969 at the age of 86.

Marion C. Forbes, head of the home, had graduated from Farmville and taught for several years. For the ten years immediately preceding her coming to Fredericksburg, she had been head of the home at Woman's College, Richmond.

Two other members of the original faculty were Gunyon M. Harrison, described as "Superintendent of Electrical Department and Assistant in Mathematics," and Dr. C. Mason Smith. Captain Harrison, as he was known after his World War I service, was a graduate in electrical engineering from V.M.I. He was also engaged in electrical contract work in Fredericksburg. Later he was to organize the Rifle Club at the college. Dr. Smith, consulting physician, received his M.D. from the University of Virginia. A member of numerous medical societies, he served as college physician for many years. His daughter, Jacquelin Randolph Smith, graduated from the college in 1937, the year in which she was May queen.

THE STUDENTS ARRIVE

The first session began with a student body of 110, which filled every available dormitory space. A complete list of the original registrants appeared in the *Daily Star*, October 4, 1911. This tabulation shows that thirty-two Virginia counties were represented. The largest groups came from Caroline (nine), Essex (twelve), and Spotsylvania (nine). Among the city residents, there were two students from Bristol, three from Richmond, one from Newport News, and fifteen from Fredericksburg.

The new school soon made its impact upon the community. On the first weekend after the college opened, the *Daily Star*

(September 30) noted: "There were a large number of students of the Normal School in town Saturday. A number of them patronized the merchants. The businessmen are beginning to realize that the school will be a great benefit to the trade interests of the city."

PURPOSE OF THE INSTITUTION

The first bulletin announcing the courses, fees, and other information concerning the new school, which appeared in June 1911, emphasized the role of the normal school. The language of the opening paragraphs (p. 8) is of interest:

The Normal School.

The idea has prevailed that anyone with an ordinary classical education was necessarily a teacher. To this fact is due the tardy recognition of the professional teacher. The knowledge of the subject matter is an essential, but it is not the only essential for the successful teacher. The knowledge of how to properly present that subject matter to others is of equal importance. Many of our best teachers, it is true, were not educated in Normal schools, but they have been successful in spite of that fact and not because of it.

It is impossible to secure the best results in our public schools without teachers who have been specially prepared for the profession. While the mission of the normal school, as the mission of all schools, is to prepare men and women for life service, the primary aim of the normal school is to offer an education that will peculiarly prepare persons for the teaching profession.

In further elaboration of the "purpose of the normal school at Fredericksburg," the catalogue continued (p. 9):

The purpose . . . is primarily to meet the needs of the public school system by offering an opportunity to the young women of the State to properly equip themselves to teach in the public schools. This school will aim to give the young women such an education as will not only make them superior teachers in the schoolroom, but leaders of thought in communities in which they make their homes.

Academic instruction will be given in such a manner as to cultivate the professional idea. The controlling thought will be to present the subject matter in such a way as to teach the student how to teach others. While it is primarily the object of this school to prepare teachers for the public schools, it must be recognized that the greater part of the life of the graduates of our normal schools is spent in the home circle rather than in the schoolroom. In order then to make the institution of the greatest possible value to the Commonwealth,

The College Opens 39

the energies of the school will be focussed upon those influences that contribute to the development and elevation of home life.

ADVANTAGES OF THE LOCATION

As was to be the case in all subsequent catalogue issues, the first bulletin emphasized the historical backgrounds of the city of Fredericksburg, its close association with the Washington family, and its strategic role in Civil War history.

Accessibility was also stressed: Fredericksburg was served by three "magnificent river boats" a week to and from Baltimore and also a line to Norfolk; twenty-four passenger trains a day on the main line north and south via the Richmond, Fredericksburg and Potomac Railroad; and daily passenger trains between Fredericksburg and Orange operated by the Potomac, Fredericksburg and Piedmont Railroad. There was no mention of highways. The city that was later to become a midpoint between Richmond and Washington on the heavily traveled U.S. Route 1 was at the time almost inaccessible by road.

Students traveled the fifty miles from Warsaw or Tappahannock by steamboat. College openings, holidays, and closing were set in terms of the steamship schedules of the Rappahannock River Line, for a large proportion of the students came from the towns bordering or adjacent to the reaches of the Rappahannock River below Fredericksburg.

THE BUILDINGS

As the 1912–13 catalogue (p. 20) stated proudly, the new buildings were "large, convenient, and handsome, and equipped with all modern conveniences." The Dormitory, later named Frances Willard Hall in honor of the famous temperance leader, was built in the shape of the letter H, with Ionic columns on the porches. It is interesting to note that apparently from the very first it became necessary to house three students in rooms planned originally for two girls. The same catalogue (p. 21) carried this sentence: "Each room can comfortably accommodate three persons, and is furnished with single iron beds, high-grade mattresses, and ample bedding."

The dormitory rooms were unusually large even for that day of spacious bedrooms. It is easy to understand the decision to house three girls in each room, especially when space was in such demand. From the very beginning, students not living in their own homes were expected to occupy college housing. Consequently, increases in enrollment necessitated expansion of dormitory accommodations. Dormitory No. 2 (Virginia Hall) was already under construction by the time the catalogue for 1913-14 went to press.

The Administration Building, later named Russell Hall in honor of the first president, was a spacious and handsome edifice. It was built in the shape of a cross, with Corinthian columns on the north and south porticoes. In the southeast corner of the basement was a small swimming pool, less than the size of an average classroom, with an adjoining dressing room. Across the hall were a manual training laboratory, a locker room for the gymnasium, and women's toilet facilities.

The east end of the basement also provided access to the gymnasium, a two-story affair extending down into a subbasement area. A short stairway from the outside entrance led down to the upper level where a corridor past the locker room extended to the balcony and "track" surrounding the gymnasium. A narrow concrete, tunnellike stairway led down to the main floor, which was the size of a standard basketball court.

For over fifty years, until the magnificent physical education facilities in Goolrick Hall were completed in 1967, the gymnasium was used for games, dances, and entertainments of various kinds. In the early sixties, the balcony was removed as unsafe, and fire escapes were built to the high windows recessed in deep wells, which afforded some light and ventilation to the area below. On the north side of the basement were the shops, heating plant, men's toilet, and a woodworking laboratory.

The first floor contained the "temporary library," offices of the president and the business manager, post office, and lecture rooms for "the departments" of history, modern languages, English, education, geography, sewing, and biology, along with a small lounge and a room used by the YMCA. The second floor housed the departments of household arts, chemistry, physics, rural arts, and manual arts. These were actually classrooms equipped with laboratory facilities. In addition, there was an auditorium seating nine hundred people.

The 1913-14 catalogue (p. 21) stated unequivocally, "This building is heated and ventilated by the most perfect heating and ventilating system known." There was a huge fan in the basement

The College Opens

to circulate heated air through the system of ducts leading into and out of each classroom. Unfortunately, this "most perfect" system was destined to be a continual problem, with rooms too cold in some parts of the building and too hot in others. The ventilation of the auditorium was hopelessly inadequate. There were windows only at the rear and behind the stage at the front. Nevertheless, the facilities were all new and up-to-date and were greeted with enthusiasm by students and faculty.

As originally planned, the new college was equipped for teaching industrial arts. The manual arts department occupied three of the large rooms in Monroe, with adjustable drawing tables, benches for woodworking, and tables for clay modeling, bookbinding, and other types of handwork. The department had its own clay kiln.

The rural arts department occupied two rooms. There were materials for studying school gardening, home gardening, plants, trees, and insects and apparatus for testing milk, seeds, and soils.

The new school boasted five pianos, an "electric lantern" for art appreciation and other illustrated lectures, and "a complete motion picture outfit."

The enthusiastic 1913–14 catalogue account (p. 23) of the college site, facilities, and equipment extended even to the physical environment: "The climate is ideal, and cannot be surpassed anywhere . . . magnificent view of the Rappahannock valley . . . location in a beautiful grove [containing] many varieties of our most attractive native trees. . . . In the center of the grounds is a spring of pure water."

Such were lavish descriptions of the locale that awaited the prospective student. With the faculty, the facilities, and the program of studies available, it is not surprising that the opening day found every dormitory space occupied with eager students.

REQUIREMENTS FOR ADMISSION

Requirements for admission were somewhat flexible. The 1911–12 bulletin (p. 21) specified that students must be at least "fifteen years old, of good moral character, and must have a thorough knowledge of the subjects taught in the grammar grades of the public schools." Students living close to a "good high school" were advised to complete the course offered there before applying to the Normal School. At a time when a high school education was not generally available in rural communities, some students enrolled for the basic work of the first two years of secondary schooling. A substantial number entered after completing only two years of high school work.

The bulletin stated further that "students will be classified according to their preparation. . . . Great care will be taken to place students where they can do the most effective work." The declaration was faithfully observed. In the early years of the college, the entire faculty joined with academic officials in interviewing students individually, assessing the extent and quality of their preparation, and assigning them to classes in which they could work most successfully. The "classification" of students occupied several days at the opening of each session.

COURSES OF INSTRUCTION

For the session of 1911–12 the bulletin (p. 19) listed seven courses, as the various curricula were then called, and a large number of subjects of study. There were two important courses.

1. The Regular Course. This was actually instruction on the high school level. As the catalogue stated: "As soon as the State high schools become sufficiently numerous and are developed so that conditions permit, it is the aim of the school to require for entrance to the regular course the equivalent of two full years of high school work, as outlined in the course required by the State for accredited high schools."

The bulletin continued: "Until these conditions prevail, the entrance requirements will be a thorough knowledge of Arithmetic, Geography, English, Grammar, United States History, Virginia History, Physiology and Hygiene, and other branches taught in the Grammar Grades of Virginia public schools."

2. The Professional Course. As the title implies, this was the standard two-year normal school course entitling the graduate to the professional diploma and the normal professional certificate issued by the State Board of School Examiners for a period of ten years and renewable thereafter.

The completion of four years of high school "academic work" (interpreted liberally) and a diploma from an accredited high school were prerequisites for admission to the two-year normal program. Students were permitted also to take this program if they had completed three years of high school work or the equivalent. In this case, they received the Virginia professional teachers certificate issued by the State Board of School Examiners for a seven-year period and renewable.

The professional elementary course was divided into specialization for primary grades or grammar grades. The required studies in the first year of the professional course consisted largely of methodology. There were methods in arithmetic, in reading, in geography, and in drawing, plus "General Method of Education," later called "General Theory of Education." There were also courses in general and child psychology, school management, "Observation of School Work," school music, nature study, and physical education.

The second year included studies in the history of education, the philosophy of education, music, physical education, "Virginia School History and School Law," and, most important of all, practice teaching in the training school.

Training school facilities were provided through the cooperation of the city of Fredericksburg, which offered "the full use of its public schools." Practice teaching under the direction of selected critic-teachers was available in classes ranging from the first grade through the fourth year of high school. Pupil enrollment totaled seven hundred. The head of the department of education, Hugh S. Bird, was also superintendent of schools of the city of Fredericksburg.

In addition to the courses designed to prepare students for teaching in the elementary grades, the offering included a variety of industrial arts courses. Completion of programs with such specialization led to the manual arts diploma, the household arts diploma, or the rural arts diploma.

An examination of the lists of graduates of the first five years reveals that the standard normal professional diploma, based on the two-year course beyond high school graduation, was the most popular. Only a few manual arts diplomas were awarded each year. The other special diplomas were rarely mentioned.

The number of subjects taught was quite large, especially when the size of the faculty is considered. As time went on, there was a trend toward the consolidation and integration of individual subjects of study, but an emphasis on methodology and practice teaching characterized these early years of the Normal School.

The rural arts diploma included courses in soils, botany, zoology, horticulture, entomology, dairying, poultry, nature study, and school gardening. By the 1915–16 session this had been reduced to courses in nature study, elementary agriculture, and school gardening.

EXPENSES

Since the new school was created primarily to prepare teachers for public schools, charges were extremely modest. In fact, tuition was free to all Virginia students who intended to teach at least four sessions in the public schools of the state. Enrollees with previous public school teaching experience were given full credit for the number of years they had taught.

In order to obtain free tuition, it was merely necessary to have an application form approved by the superintendent of the school division in which the applicant lived. No tuition was charged persons currently teaching in Virginia. Students from other states and Virginia students not teaching or preparing to teach were charged a tuition fee of $15.00 a term, or $30.00 for the session.

The charge for room and board, which included "all regular living expenses and laundry," was $67.50 a term, or $135.00 for the session. The medical attention fee was $3.00 for the session. A gymnasium uniform costing from $3.00 to $5.00 was required. The total cost of textbooks was from $3.00 to $8.00, depending on the courses taken. There were no extra fees for registration, diplomas, or laboratories.

For approximately $144.00 for the session, or less than $16.00 a month, a resident of Virginia expecting to teach could meet all expenses of the school. Only $30.00 additional was necessary for out-of-state students or nonteachers, of whom there were very few.

For students needing financial aid there was the State Loan Fund, from which small amounts could be borrowed at 4 percent interest. There was also a very limited number of student employment opportunities, which, if the total expense of attendance is a criterion, paid a very modest compensation indeed.

DISCIPLINE

Discipline was regarded as largely the "cultivation of the practice of self-control." Students were expected to do the right thing. There were "few iron-clad rules," said the 1911–12 bulletin (p. 15), but a constant effort to create "such an atmosphere and spirit as will cultivate an easy and natural desire for the best ideals in life."

The 1911–12 catalogue (p. 21) stated that "the Honor System will be maintained as fully as is practicable." It reported further:

The College Opens

As a supplement to official government and control, the students themselves have organized a Student Government League, which encourages and enforces honorable conduct in all matters pertaining to school life, and acts as a healthy deterrent to any over enthusiastic or thoughtless students who from such considerations might otherwise be guilty of infractions of the rules.

Every student is expected to exhibit the demeanor of a gentlewoman and to show considerate regard for others. Such a disposition should be the desire and life habit of a well-poised and refined woman.

However, the management will not hesitate, in deserved cases, to administer admonition and reproof. Should the conduct of any of the students justify it or the general good of the school require it, the President will confer with parents or guardians with reference thereto; and in proper cases students will be dismissed from the school.

CHAPTER IV

College Life in the First Year

SCHOOL COLORS AND ORGANIZATIONS

THE first year of the new school was an exciting experience for the newly gathered students. There were so many things to be done. Early in the fall a selection of school colors had to be made. Some students suggested the "rich orange and brown of the autumn leaves" on the trees surrounding the college. Others favored "the blue of the sky and the green of the cedars" on the hill. Still other color combinations were suggested, and rooms were trimmed with the various colors so that students might determine their reactions to them. Finally, an assembly was held to vote on the final choice. After much excitement and several ballots, the combination of blue and green was declared the winner.

The school colors were subsequently changed to brown and gold, which were used throughout the 1920s and most of the 1930s. When the name of the college was changed to Mary Washington in 1938, blue and white became the official colors. Since then, academic regalia, school publications, seals and pennants, and other insignia have used the familiar blue and white colors.

One of the first organizations to be established was the YWCA. A mass meeting of students held on Tuesday afternoon, October 24, 1911, was addressed by Claris Crane, field secretary of the National Young Women's Christian Association. A local association was organized and temporary officers were elected. Plans were made for affiliation with the National YWCA.[1] At a later meeting on November 28, the newly organized group adopted a constitution and elected permanent officers. Gay Wilson, who had been serving in an acting capacity, became the first president of the college YWCA.

The Y immediately began a program of service that made the organization a leading influence in the college. It led the observance of the National Week of Prayer; raised money for its projects through a Christmas bazaar; sponsored a public reception in January; gave a series of small entertainments and birthday parties throughout the year; and through Morning Watch meetings,

---

[1] *Daily Star*, Oct. 25, 1911.

Mission Study classes, and Bible classes ministered to the spiritual needs of the students.

Athletics played an important part in the life of the new institution. A varsity basketball team played a series of games with Fredericksburg High School. There were forty-seven members of the basketball subs. There was a tennis club with nineteen members, photographed for the 1913 *Battlefield* in middie blouses with ties and long white skirts reaching almost to the tops of their tennis shoes. The clay tennis courts were in the area immediately in front of Russell and Willard halls. From the way the rackets were being held in the photograph, the tennis of the day was a game of grace and delicacy rather than of aggressive serves and breathtaking returns.

There was a glee club of forty-seven members, with Ethel Taylor as president. Margaret Fraser, director of music at the college, conducted the group and Katherine Bartenstein was accompanist. Nora C. Willis, a member of the faculty for thirty-two years, taught piano. The enrollment of thirty-one students indicates the interest of young women of that day in piano lessons.

There were also literary societies, of course. Alice Chilton was the first president of the Russell Literary Society. Helen Lane Daniel headed the Woodrow Wilson Literary Society. There was even the Krokay Klub, posed in the annual dressed in long dark sweaters and white skirts, behind crossed croquet mallets. As might be imagined, there were several walking clubs, known as The Globe Trotters, The Sports, The Post Walking Club, each with its faculty sponsor and its roster of members.

Literally dozens of other clubs were formed. There were the regional clubs such as the Richmond Club; the Down the River Club, which had by far the largest number of members; the Caroline Club; the Hanover Club; the House of Lancaster Club; and the King and Queen Court. It is difficult to determine the purpose of many of the clubs. Apparently they were simply groups of congenial souls who got together from time to time, elected members, and posed for a page in the annual. Such were the Mother Goose Club, the Red Head Club, the Happy Dozen Club, and the Cynics' Club. The Better-to-Sew, My Dear Club announced that it met once a week on Saturday afternoon and that fudge or chocolate with marshmallows was usually served. Each member was supposed to entertain the club at least once during the session. There were a cotillion club (motto: "On with the dance, let joy be unconfined"), a dramatic club ("All the World's a Stage"), and even a rifle club.

RIFLE CLUB

The Rifle Club was organized by Gunyon M. Harrison, a graduate of Virginia Military Institute and a member of the first faculty of the college. Later Harrison was to serve with distinction in World War I, attaining the rank of captain. He was one of the organizers of the American Legion Post in Fredericksburg.

The *Battlefield* for 1914 (p. 65) listed fifty-seven members of the Rifle Club, a substantial portion of the entire student body. Sex Smith is listed as captain of the Rifle Club, Helen Phillips as manager, and Gunyon Harrison as organizer. The text that accompanied the list of members is of interest. It reads:

President Roosevelt, in his last message to Congress, said: "It is unfortunately true that the great body of our citizens shoot less and less as time goes on. To meet this, we should encourage rifle practice among schoolboys"—and we think among schoolgirls also.

There is no reason why a girl should not shoot as well as a boy. We think they need to know and understand the art of shooting and the use of firearms, and as a means to this end we have organized our Rifle Club. While at present our crack shots are few, there is no doubt but that the number is growing. Perfection comes slowly in all things worth while. Practice and rehearsals are needful for any act of life which we wish to perform well. Therefore we do not despair of being able shortly to produce a team of expert riflemen, able to compete with any.

At the writing of this article, we understand that it is the intention of the present Secretary of War to distribute among the schools and other rifle clubs some twenty thousand Krag rifles that are not in use by the standing army, for the object of encouraging rifle shooting among the young people throughout the country. If his idea is carried out, we will be a little in advance of the other schools and may call ourselves "The Pioneer Rifle Club of Virginia."

Apparently, the rifles were never actually delivered. The picture in the annual facing the club roster shows only two long-barreled rifles of ancient vintage and two of what used to be called BB guns. The photograph shows these weapons raised and aimed, fortunately not at the photographer, by the four students selected to display them.

The Rifle Club continued to function for several years. However, the number of members diminished the very next year, dropping to eighteen, with Grace K. Tanner, later a teacher of home economics at the college, as captain. The group photograph shows only four weapons, three BB guns and what appears to be

College Life in the First Year

a small pistol. The rest of the club members are pointing their index fingers, as if they were barrels of a pistol. Once again, aim seems to be at some object or person to the right of the photographer. However, smiling faces indicate no intention of doing bodily harm.

The following year, 1915–16, the Rifle Club was again flourishing with a membership of sixty-eight. Mary Rebecca Harrison was listed as president rather than captain. The threat of war was already apparent in the opening statement of the text: "Every good citizen of the United States should agree with President Wilson's policy of 'Preparedness' and since we all expect to be future citizens, why not prepare us?" No guns are in evidence in this year's picture. The writer of the text admitted that "at present our crack shots are few . . . but the number is growing."

When the 1917 *Battlefield* appeared, this country was at war. Gunyon M. Harrison had entered the service. To quote: "The club feels heavily the loss of its commander, Captain Gunyon M. Harrison; but while he is training riflemen, we are doing our best to become efficient riflewomen." Facing the club's group picture is a photograph of Captain Harrison in his uniform with boots and peaked felt hat, standing before a small tent. It is entitled "Our National Guard."

Apparently the Rifle Club did not survive the loss of its enthusiastic organizer. Captain Harrison did not rejoin the college staff upon his return from service. Incidentally, his wife, Cleora Segar Harrison, served as head of the home during the session 1918–19. She had previously held this position in the summer sessions from 1913 through 1918. The title of the position was changed when Mrs. C. L. Bushnell joined the staff as dean of women and professor of Bible in 1921.

The existence of a Rifle Club in the first year of the institution is of interest in view of the controversy over a proposed rifle range in the basement of the new physical education building during the late 1960s. Editorials in the college newspaper opposed the activity as "having no place in a woman's college" and as "encouraging an interest in firearms in a day when they are a menace." Plans for the proposed rifle range were abandoned.

PARTIES AND SOCIALS

The first party in the new school was held on Saturday evening, October 7, 1911. President and Mrs. Russell and the members of the faculty received the girls in the dining room, which had been cleared of tables and decorated with palms and ferns.

The grand march was led by Mr. and Mrs. Russell. "Many were the figure and steps which were introduced, and everyone gayly played 'follow the leader.' " For further entertainment piano and vocal selections were presented and a Virginia reel was danced by twenty girls in colonial costume. Refreshments were served at ten o'clock. Time for one more dance was allowed before the lights "dipped" to signal the end of the party. "The girls were all heard declaring as they left the hall that it was the 'best' party."[2]

Friendly relations existed between the new Normal School and Fredericksburg College. When the latter played Maryland Agricultural College in football on October 16, 1911, over seventy-five students from the Normal School attended and "rooted loyally for the local team." The *Daily Star* observed on October 18 that there was "only a small crowd to see the game other than the College and Normal School students."

College publications emphasized that all religious activities and associations sponsored by the school were "strictly non-sectarian." However, according to the first catalogue (p. 15), "Students will be expected to attend some church, preferably the choice of their parents." Local churches strove to outdo each other in welcoming the new students at the Normal School and providing "socials" for them. The Ladies' Aid Society of the Presbyterian Church was among the first to entertain the faculty at what was described as a "bountiful and elegant supper." The published menu indicates the lavishness of the repast. According to the newspaper (October 14), "the gathering broke up at a late hour, the guests from the Normal School being carried home in Mrs. Rodger's auto."

St. George's Episcopal Church simply reported that the young ladies of the Normal School were entertained in the parish house by the Sunday School teachers. An address of welcome, several musical numbers, and refreshments constituted the evening's entertainment.

The Methodist Church followed with an elaborate program of musical selections, recitations, humorous and serious addresses, and bountiful refreshments. The account of the festivities in the *Daily Star* on October 21, concludes with this sentence: "The ladies of the Normal School present were conveyed to and from the church in carriages provided by the committee in charge."

---

[2] *Ibid.*, Oct. 9, 1911.

College Life in the First Year 51

The Baptists were not to be outdone. Nearly an entire column in the *Daily Star* (October 28) was required to describe the "reception and social," which included an address of welcome; violin, vocal, and piano numbers; reading and recitations; and elaborate refreshments. An interesting feature of the account is a list of persons who "graciously tendered" their automobiles to transport "the student body and faculty, numbering more than 100 ladies and several gentlemen," from the school to the church. Apparently, automobiles were not such a rarity in Fredericksburg as early as 1911. Among the families furnishing cars are such familiar names as Warden, Embrey, Wheeler, Graves, Biscoe, Tompkins, Heflin, Kishpaugh, Jones, and Eastburn.

The round of entertainments continued with another reception and social "tendered by the ladies' societies" of the Presbyterian Church. There were the usual addresses of welcome, musical numbers, and recitations and refreshments. At this party the visitors from the Normal School and Fredericksburg College "were conveyed to and from the Church in automobiles, furnished and driven by Messrs. Henry Warden, W. S. Embrey, J. E. Rodgers, H. Curtis Biscoe, and Lynn Jones," as the *Daily Star* reported on November 11.

WALKWAYS AND WATER

Access to the city was a problem for students and faculty at the new school. In bad weather the new road (now Cornell Street) through the area from just below "Normal Heights" to Washington Avenue was almost impassable.

An editorial in the *Daily Star* (October 25, 1911) urged both Fredericksburg and Spotsylvania County to take action, "for the benefit of the merchants of this city," to construct a wooden or concrete sidewalk from the school grounds into the city. This would enable residents at the school to shop, attend church services, and visit socially during the winter months. Such a boardwalk was constructed later and served for many years as the chief way of access to the city for those at the school.

The same editorial called upon Spotsylvania County to build a permanent road way from the Plank Road (now William Street) into the school grounds, "a comparatively short distance." The writer pointed out that "citizens of the county are daily selling large quantities of meats and other supplies to the school and profiting thereby." The increase in land values because of the location of the school was also mentioned as a reason for the county supervisors to order that the work be done.

In his Founder's Day address at the college in 1949 (p. 12), Russell described some of the problems of the first year: "We started with approximately forty-seven acres of woodlands and fields, no roads or driveways. We built a dirt road to the city. The area between Washington Avenue and the school, all built up now, was a large area without a house. We built a long and beautiful boardwalk from Washington Avenue to the Administration Building. We had boardwalks in every direction—enough to make Atlantic City green with envy." Water was also a problem. Artesian wells were dug repeatedly without success. For many years one old hole remained behind Willard Hall. Finally, the college arranged to obtain water from the city.

ASSEMBLIES—AND DR. HUMPHREYS

From the beginning, chapel exercises were a regular part of the life of the school, with members of the faculty, ministers of the city, and others as inspirational speakers and leaders of devotions. In the early years of the college, these assemblies were held three mornings each week with attendance required.

During the fall these meetings provided opportunities to counsel students on various aspects of adjustment to their new environment. For example, at one of the October meetings the first year Dr. Anne Humphreys, resident physician and teacher of biology, spoke on how to dress for steam-heated rooms and discussed the ill effects of eating hurriedly.

To Dr. Humphreys were entrusted the physical examinations, which, from the beginning of the college, have been required, either prior to admission or during the first week or two of the session. On October 6, 1911, the *Daily Star* reported: "Dr. Humphreys has completed the physical examination of the students. She finds them in excellent physical health. This promises good for tennis and the basketball teams, which will be organized under Miss Graves. At present the students are taking their exercise on the tennis court and in the field under the direction of Miss Graves."

The college is indebted to Dr. Humphreys for the preservation of the evidences of the furious battle that took place on the present site of the school. While grading and landscaping were in progress on the grounds in November 1911, she noticed workmen about to level the war trenches and battery emplacements that still remained from the defense of Marye's Heights during the Battle of Fredericksburg. In spite of protests from the workmen that they had orders to level the ground, she was able to delay action until she could get in touch with school authorities. They ordered at once that the trenches and batteries should not be disturbed but should be kept in good order as objects of interest to visitors to the school.

DORMITORY LIFE

Dormitory life was strictly regulated by the sound of the bell, from the call to rise early in the morning until the signal for lights out at night. The bell rang to call to meals, to indicate beginning and ending of class periods, and to set the hours for study and quiet.[3]

A student during those early years recalls the tiptoed footsteps of Miss Forbes, the head of the home, as she made the nightly check of rooms after lights out had been sounded. A student who had failed to retire was severely reprimanded. Repeated violations of the rule could lead to campusing, which involved not only restriction to the college grounds but also suspension of the privilege of receiving visitors.

Even from the earliest days there was an approved calling list. Only men who had been vouched for by written recommendations were allowed to visit the students on the hill. The days and hours of calling were carefully specified, and only entertainment in the parlor or on the walkways surrounding the buildings was permitted. Young men who transgressed the regulations were put on the black list and deprived of the privilege of calling upon students.

For excitement at night during the hours of study there was always the possibility of a surreptitious visit to the kitchen for food. There was no "college shoppe," tearoom or snack bar in the early days. Hungry students stole down the steps from their rooms on the second and third floors to raid the kitchen, located at the rear of the first floor. One student recalls the breathless escape as the house mother sought to catch them in the pantry. However, it was after all a rather harmless thing, and only a reprimand resulted when it was detected.

[3] "The Crazy Old Bell," *Battlefield*, 1913, p. 16.

There was close contact between faculty and students. The college was small, and as one member of the first graduating class recalls, "Everybody knew everybody else." Students visited frequently in the homes of faculty members living on or near the campus. Picnics involving faculty and students were a favorite form of recreation. Clubs had socials during the winter months. There were trips to town for shopping, walks into the surrounding countryside, and informal get-togethers of friends in dormitory rooms.

WEEKEND VISITS

Weekend visits away from Fredericksburg, even to nearby towns, were a rarity, for transportation was mainly by train or steamship. In fact, it is hard to imagine the difficulties of travel by road in 1911. A party of motorists, led by an official of the roads department of the United States Department of Agriculture, left Fredericksburg at 3:00 P.M. for Washington. They traveled until midnight, when camp was pitched on the roadside. The journey was resumed at 8:00 A.M. Sunday, and the party reached Washington at 4:00 P.M.

The federal official characterized the road for the first twenty miles north of Fredericksburg as "the worst piece of roadway I ever saw." In the winter months farmers kept teams of horses or mules handy to drag cars through the morass of mud. It is interesting to note that this official advocated federal aid to supplement state funds to build a good road from Richmond to Washington, which, he said, would cost one million dollars, a fantastic sum to spend in those days.

Russell later related that on one occasion James Ashby, superintendent of schools in Stafford County, took him in his buggy to speak at Stafford Court House.[4] "It was a very narrow buggy," according to Russell; "mud was up to the horse's knees—rough road with rocks and mud. It took us two hours and a half to go ten miles. As we jolted and jostled along, I thought the Superintendent would mash the life out of me. When I reached Stafford Court House, I concluded that Mr. Ashby was the broadest educator I had ever ridden with."

[4] Founder's Day address, March 14, 1949, p. 8.

COLLEGE EXPENSES

Records of the "F.S.N.S. Supply Room" for the session of 1911–12 give a graphic picture of the cost of textbooks and supplies in those days. A typical account of one of the new students, Mary G – –, shows a total investment of about $8.00 for texts and other instructional materials for the first three months of the session.

Textbook prices were amazingly low. Lee's *History of the United States* cost $.65; Bennett's *Latin Grammar* was $.82; François's *Beginner's French* was only $.60; and Cheyney's *Short History of England,* one of the most expensive items listed, cost $1.32.

The markup in prices was ridiculously low. For example, Gildersleeve and Lodge's *Latin Grammar* cost $1.00 from the publishers. It was sold to students for $1.10. This 10 percent amounted to only a few pennies on most of the items sold. Classics, such as *The Merchant of Venice* and *As You Like It,* were sold for $.20 each. It is interesting to note the large number of pen holders and pen points that were sold – and pencils too – in the days before the ballpoint pen, or even the fountain pen, was a matter of general use.

A ledger in which expenditures were recorded from the chartering of the college in 1908 through the session of 1911–12 is among the archives in E. Lee Trinkle Library. It begins, appropriately enough, with the expense accounts of each member of the board of trustees for meetings held from May 1908 through 1912. With a few exceptions, the board met monthly. Expenses of attending a board meeting averaged $6.00 or $7.00. Expense accounts for as little as $.50 were paid by the state.

In 1911–12 the charge for a gymnasium suit and shoes totaled $4.00. The amount of cloth needed to produce the suits pictured in annuals and catalogues of that period must have been enormous. The voluminous garments seemed to have been used mainly for exercises with Indian clubs.

The ledger accounts also give an indication of the gradual development of the college. In 1909 there were bills for advertising for bids in the *Free Lance* and the *Washington Post.* In 1910 advertisements for bids on the administration building appeared in the Richmond *News Leader,* the Richmond *Journal,* the Richmond *Virginian,* the Richmond *Times-Dispatch,* and the Fredericksburg *Free Lance.*

SALARIES

Salaries in 1911–12 were modest indeed. Records indicate that the president of the college received $250 a month. Hugh S. Bird received $150 a month for the nine-month term. Two faculty members received $133.33 a month (a total of $1,200 for the session), and others received monthly salaries of $52.00, $62.50, $70.83, $75.00, $83.33, and, one person, $99.33. The college physician was paid $25.00 a month.

Each faculty member was charged $15.00 a month for board. It was a part of the teacher's contract that he take his meals in the dining hall. The $15.00 monthly charge also appeared as a credit to his account, but no refund was made if meals were not taken as stipulated. In other words, board was actually provided as a sort of fringe benefit, but it appeared as a charge that was then marked "paid."

MR. HAMLET

It is appropriate, perhaps, to close this section on the first session of the college with a sketch of W. N. Hamlet, one of the first professors selected by President Russell.

Mr. Hamlet taught at the college for thirty-one years (1911–1942). He and Nora C. Willis, instructor in piano (1911–1943), were the last two surviving members of the original faculty. During the first years of his professorship Mr. Hamlet taught both mathematics and science. Later, after Dr. Roy S. Cook joined the faculty, he concentrated on mathematics.

Mr. Hamlet was a conscientious and beloved teacher. He always seemed troubled when his efforts to teach a student were unsuccessful. He was unsparing of his time in helping slow students with their assignments.

During the Normal School days of the institution the mathematics taught consisted of a review of arithmetic designed for prospective elementary school teachers, a review of high school mathematics, and a course in business arithmetic. Later, when the college became a four-year institution, the mathematics curriculum was expanded to include advanced high school mathematics (geometry and trigonometry), geometry and the teaching of high school mathematics, and calculus.

For many years Mr. Hamlet continued to teach the course in

arithmetic for elementary grades. It was a requirement for certification as an elementary school teacher, and it frequently proved a stumbling block for otherwise well-qualified young women. Mr. Hamlet did his best to overcome the poor preparation of some of his students and their lack of aptitude for mathematical study. Occasionally he simply gave up.

He was a quiet man. Even with his long years of service to the college, he rarely ventured an opinion in faculty meetings. He habitually walked about the campus with his head down. A student here at that time remarked, with affectionate exaggeration, that the only way Mr. Hamlet knew his students was by their shoes.

He lived in his own house on College Avenue next to the house of Dr. Chandler. Both buildings are now owned by the college and are a part of the main campus. Mr. and Mrs. Hamlet loved growing things. Their house was surrounded by flower beds and almost hidden by thick shrubbery. There was even a fish pond with water lilies. The Hamlets also raised dogs, which they treated with great affection. Students of those days recall the dog houses and exercise yards that occupied the space just behind the house where part of the Tri-Unit now stands.

When Mr. Hamlet died in 1942, he left a farm in Spotsylvania County to the college as a "recreational area and bird sanctuary." For several years the Y retreat was held there each fall, and there were student government picnics in the spring. Mr. Hamlet's home in the city was sold to the college. After landscaping and remodeling it became a residence hall for students and was known as Hamlet House. Subsequently it was converted into a psychology clinic with specially equipped rooms for observing, testing, and counseling sessions. It now houses the testing and counseling services and contains the offices and records of the director of the counseling center.

CHAPTER V

The Early Years, 1912–1914

A SECOND SESSION STARTS

AFTER the usual summer institute for teachers, the second session of the Normal School opened on September 12, 1912. The catalogue for the session of 1912–13 listed a total registration of 131 students, all from Virginia. Most of them, in fact, were from the counties of eastern Virginia bordering the Rappahannock and Potomac rivers and from the city of Fredericksburg and nearby areas.

This catalogue, like all of those that followed, was illustrated with numerous pictures of buildings, facilities, and student life. The Dormitory and the Administration Building stand out starkly on the beginnings of a quadrangle, with tennis courts in the foreground. A few scattered young trees give little intimation of the lofty oaks and maples that now shade that part of the campus.

There were pictures of a "corner" in the dining room, a "section" of the swimming pool, and a "view in" the library, all of which show a major portion of each facility. The most impressive student picture is that of the Glee Club of 1911–12, all members in long white dresses, white shoes, and, where hemlines permit a glimpse, white stockings, with most of the girls wearing white hair ribbons, some with large bows.

Students frolic in front of the two buildings where "a tennis game" or "throwing a goal" is in progress. In the gymnasium students manage to perform calisthenic drills despite the voluminous bloomers and blouses they are wearing. All was not play, however, for interior views show girls "at work in chemical laboratory," "making book covers for use in library" (manual arts), "sewing" in the household arts department, and apparently examining seed sproutings in the rural arts laboratory.

COLLEGE DAYS

At the opening of the second session, on September 19, 1912, the YWCA gave a reception to the student body and faculty in honor of the new girls. After the receiving line a program of tableaux,

The Early Years 59

songs, and recitations was presented, followed by refreshments. In its second year the Y enlarged its membership and increased its activities. In addition to sponsoring the Bible and Mission classes at the school, it helped support a missionary in India and also established a scholarship to aid some needy student at the Normal School. A room in Russell Hall was set aside as a YWCA room, which the organization furnished with table, chairs, a rug, and window curtains. Weekly meetings, cabinet meetings, and small entertainments were held there.

Highlights of the 1912–13 session were a trip to Washington to see *Peter Pan;* the celebration of the fiftieth anniversary of the Battle of Fredericksburg on December 13; a concert by the Richmond College Glee Club; and on March 4, 1913, a trip to Washington by faculty and students to attend the inauguration of President Woodrow Wilson.

The trip to the inauguration afforded students an excellent opportunity to witness the pageantry of the occasion. Special trains were run to Washington from all directions. Contemporary accounts estimated the number of visitors at 300,000. Students from the Normal School must have been thrilled by the display of military power, the marching of the cadets from the United States Military Academy and the Virginia Military Institute. "A number of other military schools in Virginia were also in line," remarked the *Daily Star* reporter (March 4). The Washington Guards of Fredericksburg, under the command of Captain A. R. Bauman, made a fine showing. Over a thousand Princeton students accompanied the former president of their university on his journey to Washington to become the chief executive of the nation.

On the day before the inauguration, some five thousand women suffragettes paraded in a huge demonstration of "Votes for Women." That evening they staged an elaborate pageant on the steps of the Treasury building. The *Daily Star* (March 5) stated that dozens of participants were "dressed in the very lightest of gowns" and that several were later threatened with pneumonia. It must have been an inspiration to the young women of the period to see the fortitude and endurance of these pioneers in the struggle to win votes for women. It was an exciting time to be alive.

Lectures played an important part in the intellectual life of the college. During the session of 1912–13, the speakers included Dr. C. Alphonso Smith, on "The Ministry of Poetry"; Dr. W. B. Forrest, "The Influence of the Bible on English Literature"; Professor Charles G. Maphis, "Jefferson as Revealed in His Letters"; Vivian Conway, "Constantinople"; the Honorable A. J. Montague, "Lives of Lee and Jackson"; Governor William Hodges Mann, "Battle of Fredericksburg"; A. B. Bowering, "Personal Reminiscences of the Battle of Fredericksburg"; Dr. W. A. Kepner, "Animal Activities"; Professor T. S. Settle, "Rural School Improvement"; Dr. W. H. Heck, "School Sanitation."

In addition to such special lectures, the students presented a number of entertainments. Among those offered were "A College Minstrel," concerts by the Glee Club, a county fair, and a cantata, *The Garden of Flowers.* A high point in student entertainment in the second year of the school was the presentation on December 16, 1912, of *Alice in Wonderland,* a three-act play, with animal costumes designed by Olive Hinman of the faculty and made by students of the manual arts department. There were ladies and "gentlemen" of the court, pages, guards, dancers, and, of course, the Mock Turtle, the White Rabbit, and other characters. A photograph of the cast of principals and a tipped-in program of the production are featured in the 1913 *Battlefield.*

The first issue of the *Battlefield* was produced in the spring of 1913, when the first two-year graduating class received their diplomas. It was dedicated to President Russell. The editor in chief was Martha Belle Pearce, who later continued to take an active interest in the college.

Pictures, a list of activities, and a tribute in limerick style appear for each of the graduates. All were from Virginia, most of them from the Northern Neck or Piedmont sections of the state.

An idea of the verse may be gleaned from these two samples (p. 32):

> A student from Lancaster came;
> Sweet Alice may well be her name;
>   A vision we hold—
>   She'll not teach till she's old;
> Some knight will come urging his claim.

> There is a young lady named Mary;
> Not the one who was very contrary;
>   For this Mary is dear;
>   She is full of good cheer;
> And she *warbles just like a canary.*

The motto of the class was, appropriately, "Live on the Heights."

A new song was composed to the tune of "The Orange and the Black." The words were quite ethereal.

> When the stealthy darkness gathers
> And all the ways are dim,

The Early Years

> Across the misty valley
> There cometh unto him
> Who in the shadows walketh,
> A radiance, clear and bright,
> Whence, cheer and comfort giving,
> Shineth forth our Normal light.
>
> The mighty lamp of knowledge
> Can turn error's night to day;
> The lamps of faith and courage
> Drive fear's dark clouds away;
> Purity and truth and goodness
> Shine amid sin's blackest night.
> May each girl who leaves us carry,
> As she goes, such blessed light.

THE FIRST GRADUATES

The class of 1913 numbered thirty-two graduates, all from Virginia, who had completed the two-year normal school program:

> Katherine Bartenstein, Warrenton
> Elizabeth Lindsay Billingsley, Lignum
> Lottie Lee Broaddus, Smoots
> Mattie Hogge Bunkley, Tampico
> Mary Elizabeth Chesley, Fredericksburg
> Alice Chilton, Lancaster
> Elsie Coleman, Chase City
> Helen Lane Daniel, University
> Anna Elizabeth Diedrich, Waverly
> Ora Constance Green, Atlee
> Anne Ravenel Henry, Woodville
> Julia Westwood Keaton, Hampton
> Fannie Tyree Kennedy, Mineral
> Lucy Kennedy, Mineral
> Ruth Helen Lord, Richmond
> Buford Kirtley Lyne, Newport News
> Nettie Corbin Marye, Fredericksburg
> Annie Fontaine Nicholas, Scottsville
> Margaret Micou Nicholas, Scottsville
> Sally Henriette Norris, Fredericksburg
> Martha Belle Pearce, Richmond
> Ellen Pauline Perry, Fredericksburg
> Julia Anna Raiford, Ivor
> Verna Laurie Rooks, Cheriton
> Bertha Lumbard Scrimger, Sharps

Ethel Louise Taylor, Newport News
Elizabeth Dorothy Trible, Dunnsville
Winnie Davis Walker, Urbanna
Anne Latane Ware, Ware's Wharf
Virginia Isabel Willis, Lignum
Gay Vaughan Wilson, Richmond
Mary Isabella Wortham, Chase City

In addition to the class of 1913, the *Battlefield* also carried pictures of the classes of 1914 (fifty); 1915 (eleven); 1916 (thirty-one); 1917, (thirty-six); and 1918 (twelve). Of course, a fair number of students were enrolled who needed to complete two or three years of high school work at the institution before taking the two-year normal course that led to graduation and a diploma.

STUDENT LIFE, 1913-14

The class of 1914 was the first to use an officially adopted pin and ring, bearing the monogram *SNS* and the year. There were thirty-one graduates, all from Virginia. Susan Dabney Walker of Lynchburg was class president. Among the graduates that year was Ethel Hester Nash of Fredericksburg, who for many years was principal of Lafayette Elementary School. Miss Nash's eminence in her field was recognized by her election as president of the Department of Elementary School Principals of the National Education Association.

The annual that year was dedicated to Olive Hinman, teacher of manual training and drawing. Among the aspirations of the senior class mentioned in its last will and testament were a macadamized road to Washington, a soda fountain for refreshing drinks between classes, and a new dormitory.

There were fifty-four juniors and twenty-four "abridged juniors" in the class of 1915. In addition, there were classes of 1916, 1917, and 1918, who were actually taking high school work. Those in the class of 1918, who were taking second-year courses at the high school level, were known as preparatory students.

The YWCA and the Athletic Association continued to be leading organizations on the campus. In the fall the Y organized four Mission Study classes, with faculty members as leaders. The eight-week courses were concluded with a Foreign Mission pageant. In the spring there were four Bible classes, led by both teachers and students. Through its social service committee the Y aided poor families in Fredericksburg and sent flowers to the sick. It continued to support foreign mission work in India and to maintain a scholarship at the college. It also sponsored many social affairs, beginning with the reception for new students in the fall.

The Athletic Association sponsored class contests throughout the year for a trophy cup, which culminated in a Field Day held in the late spring. To mark this occasion there were field events, such as high and broad jumps, dashes, relays, and sack races. The popular yell was:

> Rah! Rah! Rah!
> That is true!
> All hurrah for Green and Blue!
> Hey! Hey! Hey!
> Do Your Best!
> Never meddle with S. N. S.!

Walking was encouraged by several clubs, with excursions to Falmouth, Gunnery Springs, Coal Springs, and other points of interest in the vicinity of Fredericksburg. Members of the faculty chaperoned the hikers. The Rifle Club continued to be one of the most active organizations on the campus. There were also two softball teams, the Tigers and the Giants.

An instrumental accompaniment with guitars and mandolins enhanced the singing of a student group called The Nightingales, whose aim was to outsing the Glee Club. The Eastern Shore Club composed of ten members, was organized with Emma Lankford as president.

Subject clubs made their appearance that year with the organization of Un Club à la Français. Members are pictured seated in a circle on the grass under a tree, each with a book, presumably in French, in her hands. The club motto was "En avant."

School songs continued to be composed. Josephine Marchant and Ruth Wickham composed the following words, sung to the tune of "A Merry Heart":

> There is a town that we all love so dearly—
>   You know it well; you know it well;
> By which the Rappahannock flows so clearly;
>   I need not tell—I need not tell.
> Here fought and bled the heroes of the Nation,
>   For freedom's right—for freedom's right;
> Each with a will and with determination
>   To show his might—to show his might.
>
> *CHORUS*
>
> Hearken! Hearken! Fredericksburg, once more!
> Hearken! Hearken! Fredericksburg, once more!

Tra-la-la-la! tra-la-la-la! tra-la-la-la! tra-la-la-la!
Hail, our Normal School! Tra-la-la-la! tra-la-la-la!

Upon the heights are halls so stately standing
    The grove above—the grove above;
There may be other structures more commanding,
    But these we love—but these we love.
Here flock the girls so early in September,
    With purpose high—with purpose high.
The faculty, we ever shall remember,
    To help them try—to help them try.[1]

News of the graduates of 1913 was a feature of the 1914 *Battlefield*. Most of them were teaching—at Sparta, Chancellor, Guinea, Beaver Dam, Lahore, Irvington, Frederick Hall, Bowling Green, Colonial Beach, Louisa—or in schools in Newport News, Richmond, and Ashland. Several had "schools to themselves," as one-room schoolhouses were euphemistically described.

Perhaps the one who went farthest from base was Jeanette Hess, who accepted a position in a large graded school at Dante, in the far southwestern part of the state. Teachers lived together in a bungalow on the mountainside near the school, where children of miners representing many nationalities attended. A severe case of typhoid fever caused her to return to Fredericksburg for hospitalization. She then taught for some fifty years in Spotsylvania County. At the time of her death in May 1972, she was still active in the Fredericksburg chapter of the Alumnae Association.

One graduate, Janetta Fitzhugh, was reported as continuing her education at Sweet Briar College. Another, Rachel Pearce, was enrolled at Richmond College.

The new teachers were confronted with large classes as they began their work. Classrooms of thirty-seven, thirty-eight, forty-two, and fifty-five students in the elementary grades were reported. Martha Belle Pearce, teaching in the Glen Echo School in Henrico County, had 42 "wide-awake, wriggling, willing workers."

The churches of Fredericksburg assisted eagerly in entertaining students at the Normal. A description of a Halloween party in the first years of the school gives an idea of what these events meant in the life of these girls away from home:

Reader, can you imagine for a moment or two, this scene: The old Plank Road winding in and out through the lane, bordered with trees on either hand, coming out into the open about a quarter of a mile from the dormitory, and leading up to the buildings themselves?

---

[1] *Battlefield*, 1914, p. 121.

The Early Years

And can you see from the windows of the dormitory, scores of automobiles coming through this lane, the lights glimmering between the trees here and there, and dashing through the big gate, sweeping down on the buildings with their bright lamps? And there, on the dormitory steps, stands a crowd of pretty and happy girls, talking and laughing with each other—and all so sweetly dressed! As each car stops, the girls jump in, and away it speeds around the corner, making room for another. Can you imagine this on Hallowe'en night, when the air is full of mystery—and can you explain it?

This is the explanation: About a week before Hallowe'en, the various churches sent invitations to the girls at the Normal, inviting those who attended their church to a reception on Hallowe'en night. So it was. . . .[2]

And there follows a breathless and enthusiastic account of the entertainment, the tables laden with sandwiches, cakes, ice cream, coffee, and fruits, and the return to the "stern and hard world of reality" on the hill.

Yearbook poems indicate a warm relationship between faculty and students. Popular teachers were the subjects of several pages of verse in the 1914 *Battlefield*. The tribute to President Russell (p. 124) is of interest:

> Mr. Russell is a great man;
> Mr. Russell is a pearl;
> Mr. Russell rules our school,
> And is loved by every girl.
>
> We go to Mr. Russell
> When home we want to go;
> He tells us all to hustle,
> And you bet that we're not slow.
>
> We even ask Mr. Russell
> If we may have a beau,
> For everything is all right
> If Mr. Russell says so.

Even in those days educational methodology and actual practice did not always agree. As an anonymous poet lamented (p. 124):

> Mr. Chandler, who teaches the subject, "Our Schools,"
> Uses no lesson plans nor definite rules.
> Then why should, in "Primary Methods," Miss Strong
> Make "Lesson Plans, Lesson Plans" her one great song?

[2] *Ibid.*, p. 128.

Mr. Tyner, in "Theory," is always remarking:
"In teaching, let the children do all the talking."
Says Mr. Hamlet, "If this be true,
Pray tell me what is the teacher to do?"

Miss Hinman says for "Spelling" there is not so much need;
"Get the thought, and thought only"—that is her creed.
But Miss Dadmun proclaims "Spelling" the high road to fame,
Demands, notes and marks each poor speller's name.

Now students tell me truly each one of you,
In just such a mix what are we to do?

In a less complex era, the simpler pleasures provided welcome respite from the routine of class attendance and study. A walk in the woods, game of tennis, birthday party for a roommate, box of food from home, Sunday night chafing-dish party, church social— these pleasures brought relaxation, fostered friendships, and made the long months between holiday visits at home pass more quickly and more enjoyably. And they built up a store of memories of college days that, for alumnae of the period, are still vivid and heartwarming after the passage of many years.

The home department, as it was then called, really sought to provide just that for teenage girls, many of whom were away from their homes for the first time. There was no dean of women in those days. The head of the home, who also served as registrar of the college, was Marion C. Forbes, who made the Dormitory a warm and friendly place in which to live, watched over the girls when they were sick, supervised their comings and goings, and listened to their problems. She also saw that the dining hall was operated properly, that special occasions and holidays were observed with appropriate decorations and menus, and that birthdays were recognized with cakes and candles, a custom that was carried on long after SNS became a more sophisticated institution. One of the early *Battlefields* featured an elaborate Thanksgiving Day menu that began with oysters on the half shell. One can imagine the treat this was for girls who were used to eating at home freshly tonged Rappahannock River oysters "shucked in their own liquor."

On May 16, 1914, the first May Day was held. With it was combined the Field Day and games that in previous years had been held each spring. The Field Day events began at nine o'clock, with the 50-yard dash, followed by the running high jump, "throwing the ball," 220-yard relay, standing broad jump, and other contests for a total of twelve events. Competition was among representatives of the four classes, with the prize "a $50 silver cup purchased by the Athletic Association of the State Normal School." The seniors, winners of the two previous field days, lost to the juniors by a score of 137 to 132½. By this narrow margin, they failed to win permanent possession of the trophy.

The *Daily Star* on May 18 reported that "a large gathering of people from Fredericksburg and neighboring country attested by their presence the great interest in these exercises which received frequent encores of applause." The exercises took place on the "lawn of the Normal School," immediately in front of Russell Hall. Prizes to the winners in the various athletic contests were donated by local merchants. A picture of the exercises, entitled "Crowning the Victors," appeared in the 1913–14 catalogue, along with a large number of other photographs depicting life at the college. There is even a full-page picture of the trophy cup presented that afternoon as a part of the May Day festival. The Honorable C. O'Conor Goolrick made the presentation to Eliza Peirce, president of the junior class.

The May Day program began with a processional led by the queen and her attendants, the senior Maypole dancers and then the classes, in order, with their colors. A May song was sung by the entire school. The May queen was crowned, and the Maypole dance, by the seniors, followed. There were then Spanish and Swedish folk dances and music by the Glee Club. At this point Goolrick presented the cup. The victors were crowned by the May queen, and the Reverend J. C. Hawk, after "an interesting address," delivered the prizes to the individual winners, who, presumably, were wearing the crowns presented by the May queen. A shepherd's dance and a garland dance and music by the Glee Club concluded the program, which ended with the school song.

The queen of the May was Janet LaCrosse, with Junia Graves as maid of honor. Queen's maids, heralds, a crown bearer, and a train bearer made up the rest of the court.

Class Day exercises were held in the auditorium of Russell Hall on Saturday morning, May 30. At eleven o'clock the seniors marched in singing their class song. After the welcoming address and "Remembrances of 1912–13–14," the seniors filed out of the auditorium followed by the audience, and all assembled on the steps of Russell Hall for the senior class prophecy and the placing of the 1914 class stone. The next scene of action was at the edge of the woods where the girls joined hands around a bonfire, singing and dancing as they cast into the fire their "hardest burdens." They returned again to the steps of Russell Hall for the last will and testament, which included expression of such hopes as a macadamized road from Washington Avenue to the Dormitory and a cement sidewalk for pedestrians only.

The baccalaureate sermon was delivered in Russell Hall on Sunday evening, May 31, by Dr. Collins Denny, bishop of the Methodist Episcopal Church of the South. Commencement exercises were held on June 1 at 8:00 P.M. in Russell Hall. The speaker was Professor John Calvin Metcalf of Richmond College, who was later dean of the Graduate School at the University of Virginia. His subject was "Idealism in Southern Literature." There were thirty-one graduates, all Virginians.

CHAPTER VI

Significant Developments and Events, 1914–1919

A NEW BOARD

THE original board of trustees for the State Normal and Industrial School for Women at Fredericksburg continued to function as the governing body of the school until July 1, 1914, when by action of the General Assembly, approved March 27, 1914, the control and supervision of the school was placed under a central "board of visitors for the State Normal schools for white women of Virginia," a corporation to be known as the Virginia Normal School Board.[1]

The act provided for a board of twelve members, one from each of the ten congressional districts plus two from the state at large. Appointments were to be made by the governor, subject to confirmation by the state Senate, for four-year terms. The state superintendent of public instruction was an ex officio member, as was the governor. The new board succeeded to "all the property, property rights, duties, contracts, and agreements now controlled by and vested in" the boards of trustees of the state normal and industrial schools for women at Fredericksburg, Harrisonburg, and Radford and the state female normal school at Farmville.

The act changed the names of the four institutions, dropping the "and industrial" part of the title for the schools at Fredericksburg, Harrisonburg, and Radford and providing that each be known simply as The State Normal School for Women at (name of location). The board was given the authority to manage the affairs of all four institutions, appointing officers, teachers, and employees "subject to the limitations of its funds and appropriations."

The act stipulated further that "it shall be the duty of the said board to prevent, as far as possible, unnecessary duplication of work in said schools, to provide for the correlation of the work of said schools with each other and with the primary and grammar grades and high schools of the state." The board was em-

[1] *Acts of Assembly*, 1914, chap. 322, pp. 567–68.

powered to grant certificates and, later, degrees; to confer with the presidents of the four institutions; and to "prepare all budgets to be presented to the General Assembly, and to make recommendations for maintenance and enlargement as the needs of the schools demand."

Members of the Virginia Normal School Board appointed in 1914 included:

>Honorable Richard B. Davis, president, Petersburg
>Judge John W. Price, vice-president, Bristol
>Brock T. White, Keezletown
>George B. Russell, Drake's Branch
>Alfred G. Preston, Amsterdam
>W. W. King, Staunton
>V. R. Shackelford, Orange
>Otho F. Mears, Eastville
>Oscar L. Shewmake, Surry
>D. D. Hull, Jr., Roanoke
>Merritt T. Cooke, Norfolk
>W. C. Locker, Richmond
>Governor H. C. Stuart, ex officio
>R. C. Stearnes, superintendent public instruction, ex officio, Richmond
>A. Stuart Robertson, secretary-auditor, Staunton [2]

The first meeting of the board was held in Richmond on July 10, 1914, at the request of Governor Henry C. Stuart, who, as presiding officer, called the group to order and stated the object of the meeting. Judge John W. Price was elected temporary chairman and V. R. Shackelford, temporary secretary.

At a second meeting on September 3, 1914, bylaws were adopted and the board organized with the Honorable Richard B. Davis as president, Judge Price, vice-president, and Shackelford, secretary. The board then elected the presidents of the Virginia normal schools: Dr. J. L. Jarman, Farmville; Dr. John Preston McConnell, Radford; Dr. Julian A. Burruss, Harrisonburg (later president of Virginia Polytechnic Institute); and E. H. Russell, Fredericksburg. (The latter's salary was $3,000 per annum, plus a house.) W. S. Chesley was elected treasurer and business manager of the institution at Fredericksburg at a salary of $1,500 per annum. Attorney General John Garland Pollard, later governor

---

[2] Minutes of the Virginia Normal School Board, inside cover, Archives, Virginia State Library, Richmond.

of Virginia, ruled that the new board might charge its expenses against the appropriations of the several institutions.[3]

Arrangements were made for the board to hold one meeting each quarter at the various schools in rotation. The group met at Radford in October, at Harrisonburg in December, and at Fredericksburg in March. At the third meeting a committee of three, consisting of Shackelford, W. C. Locker, and Oscar L. Shewmake, was appointed to act with the presidents in preparing courses of study, coordinating entrance requirements, and correlating the work of the several schools.[4]

EVENTFUL DAYS

The *Battlefield* for 1914–15 indicates the growth and development of the new institution. Dedicated to Bunyan Yates Tyner, professor of education, the publication reflects the active assistance of a faculty committee in producing a rather impressive and dignified publication.

The session of 1914–15 marked the first basketball game outside of the school's gymnasium. The team won a 14 to 9 victory over the YWCA team in Richmond, regarded as one of the best girls' basketball teams in the state. A gymnastic tournament was held in March, with a loving cup as the prize for the "best all-around gymnast."

On May 15, 1915, the May Day celebration was held. There were the crowning of the May queen, a Maypole dance, and other festivities. The usual spring Field Day followed the next day, with the victors in various events being crowned by the queen of the May.

It was not until the third session of the new college that the Student Government Association was organized (December 1, 1914). Its first officers were Theresa Inez Lynch, president; Elizabeth Cardwell Chenery, first vice-president; Lucy Lipscomb Duval, second vice-president; and Leam Snow Flippin, secretary.[5]

Interestingly enough, there were local sororities in the early years of the college. The *Battlefield* for 1915 (pp. 97–104) carried pictures of the members of two such organizations, along with seal, motto, and membership roster of seven or eight students each. Pi Sigma was described as founded in December 1911, while

[3] *Ibid.*, p. 31.   [4] *Ibid.*, p. 36.   [5] *Battlefield*, 1915, p. 64.

Phi made its appearance in November 1912. Both organizations seem to have been relatively short-lived, for there is no further mention of them in the annual or other college publications after 1915. However, it is possible that such clubs as the Sphinx, which appeared the following year, may have had some of the attributes of a secret society.

On October 23, 1914, a memorable visit to Annapolis was made. The girls left on an early train for Washington, where they boarded trolley cars to Annapolis (the W. B. and A. buses have long since superseded the trolley cars that ran between Washington, Baltimore, and Annapolis). Lieutenant Taylor Smith, U.S.N., the brother of the college physician, Dr. C. Mason Smith, made his home the headquarters of the group and conducted the students on a tour of the grounds and buildings. As one student recalls, "We were particularly interested in the tomb in the chapel where the body of John Paul Jones now rests, because of his associations with Fredericksburg, his 'only home in America.'"

The students were thrilled at the morning drills of the midshipmen, the dinner formation in response to the bugle call, and the martial music of the band. A football game followed that afternoon. Seated in a grandstand with the midshipmen, the girls helped cheer the team on to a victory over Western Reserve. As one student remarked on the way home, "If Annapolis was in Falmouth, life would be worth living." [6]

A field trip to Washington was also made that session. On January 22 a group of students visited a special exhibition of arts and crafts held in the Octagon House, once the home of Dolly Madison. Silverware, tapestries, prints, bookbindings, and jewelry, as well as laces and furniture, were featured in the exhibit, which had particular interest for students specializing in manual arts. After lunch the group managed to visit the National Museum, the Corcoran Gallery, the Congressional Library, and finally the White House. There the President himself met them. His "kindly and courteous greeting and cordial handshake went straight to our hearts" recalled one member of the group.[7]

Other, less exciting, events of the year were the YWCA opening reception in honor of the new students, a Halloween marshmallow roast given by the faculty for the students, the YWCA Christmas bazaar, the faculty Christmas tree celebration (with cornucopias filled with candy for all the students), and a YWCA book party.

[6] *Ibid.*, p. 118. [7] *Ibid.*, p. 121.

Among the visiting lecturers that year were Dr. W. H. Heck and Dr. Alfred Hall-Quest, both professors of education at the University of Virginia; Dr. Charles W. Kent, professor of English there; Dr. Henry Southwick, of Boston; and Rosewell Page, second auditor of Virginia.[8]

The Ben Greet Players presented *A Midsummer Night's Dream* and *She Stoops to Conquer*. Student productions were many and varied. They included a Lee-Jackson celebration; *An Afternoon with Mother Goose;* a minstrel show by the junior class; and an open-air concert by the Glee Club. It was indeed an eventful year.

GRADUATES AND CLASS ENROLLMENTS

The class of 1915 numbered forty-nine two-year diploma graduates. This year there was a graduate from Atlanta, Georgia; the rest were Virginians. There were fourteen seniors from Fredericksburg, indicating the community acceptance of educational opportunities offered by the new institution.

In addition to the class of 1915, the *Battlefield* for that year also listed memberships for the classes of 1916, 1917, 1918, 1919, and 1920. In the class of 1916, or students who were classified as having completed one year of the two-year normal course, there were forty-two members; the class of 1917, or students who had completed the equivalent of a four-year high school course, had thirty-nine members; the class of 1918, completing the third year of the high school course, numbered thirty-one. The classes of 1919 and 1920, completing the first or second year of high school work, numbered eight and nine, respectively.

THE FIFTH SESSION

The enrollment in 1915–16 was 249. The catalogue for that year contained a six-page folded insert picturing the entire faculty and student body as of April 27, 1916. Men and women faculty members all dressed in black or dark clothes are seated against a three-tiered background of young women dressed in white middy blouses and white skirts. Several students have pennants reading F. S. N. S. STATE NORMAL or S. N. S. FREDERICKSBURG. In the back ground of the panoramic view stand Willard Hall, Russell Hall, and Virginia Hall. The absence of trees gives a rather stark ap-

---

[8] *Catalogue,* 1914–15, p. 33.

pearance to the central quadrangle. However, there is a magnificent grove pictured from the east portico of Russell Hall.

Announcements of the college continued to emphasize the role of the normal school until its conversion to a teachers' college in the 1920s. Practice teaching was a prerequisite for graduation for many years. The following statement of the requirement is typical:

> As a prerequisite for graduation all candidates for diplomas must show evidence of ability to teach. Applicants for practice teaching must furnish satisfactory proof that they have the necessary academic requirements, and must have had classes in educational principles and methods of teaching school subjects. Our final estimate of a student teacher represents her ability as a woman and as a teacher to train children. She must show evidence of good scholarship, ability to present school work and to discipline a schoolroom, and a right attitude toward the serious work of training children.[9]

STUDENT TEACHING

Of interest in the early years was the close cooperation between the city of Fredericksburg and the Normal School in providing student teaching. Through an arrangement with the city school board the Fredericksburg public school served as the practice school for the Normal School. The first printed bulletin of the college, which announced the courses to be offered beginning September 26, 1911, carried (p. 24) a full-page picture of the "City Public School Building: The Training and Observation School for the State Normal."

The building designated to serve as the training school was known then as the Fredericksburg Public School. It was located at the corner of Caroline and Lewis streets. Both elementary and high school instruction were offered in this building, but student teaching there was limited to the primary and grammar grades.

The use of the building for high school instruction was discontinued in 1919 when the new Fredericksburg High School (now Maury Elementary School) was completed. The school then became Lafayette Elementary School. When the new Hugh Mercer School opened in the fall of 1969, the building was released from school use and the city made the space available to the Rappahannock Regional Public Library to house not only the collection

[9] *Catalogue*, 1915–16, p. 32.

moved from the Wallace Library Building but also many additional books and services.

The catalogue for 1912–13 (p. 28) described the new city school as "a large and handsome three-story brick building constructed, with its equipment, at a cost of about $45,000." All grades were represented in the school. The total enrollment in 1911–12 was 708. The same catalogue refered to efforts "being made through the cooperation of the Normal School and the City School Board to raise the standard of excellence of the training school so that it will become one of the model schools of the state in all of its departments." It also mentioned a course of study "now being worked out for the training school."

The "Training School Course of Study" published in October 1916 as an issue of the *Bulletin* of the State Normal School, was prepared under the general chairmanship of B. Y. Tyner, head of the department of education at the Normal School. The course of study committee consisted of Tyner; E. F. Birckhead, superintendent of the Fredericksburg city schools; Virginia E. Stone, primary supervisor, training school; and Charlotte L. Peoples, grammar grade supervisor, training school.

The bulletin is an impressive one, even after fifty years. Although it relied heavily upon detailed outlines of content by grades (1–4) and by subjects, it incorporated many suggestions for teaching procedures and classroom activities. The material was arranged and organized so as to be of maximum usefulness to the primary teacher. It was a source book of materials and procedures, arranged in most cases by months for the session's work in each grade.

Perhaps the most striking feature of the publication is that it represented the "combined effort of the heads of departments of the Normal School and the supervisors and teachers in the city elementary school." It is indicative of a high degree of cooperation between the college and the city school staff. Dean A. B. Chandler, Jr., was chairman of the subcommittee that prepared the geography sections of the course of study. Professor W. N. Hamlet led the group that prepared the arithmetic sections.

E. F. Birckhead, a graduate of William and Mary with a master's degree from Columbia University, was superintendent of schools and principal of the training school. Critic-teachers at that time were May Perrin, Myrtle Townes, Rebekah Peck, Helen Winston, Eliabeth Rice, and Carlotta Lewis. All except Miss Perrin were graduates of the State Normal School in Farmville.

Other teachers of the elementary grades that year were Anna Keim, Margaret Sacrey, Sally H. Norris, Theresa Dannehl, Selma Ulman, Maggie Honey, Mrs. Emma Euliss, Mrs. A. M. King, and Mrs. Elizabeth Courtney.

In those days, students who wished to prepare for high school teaching did their observation in the junior year in high school classes offered at the Normal School and in the senior year did their practice teaching in these classes at the Normal "under expert direction, supervision, and criticism." [10]

When it was proposed to discontinue offering preparatory work at the first- and second-year high school level at the Normal School, the objection was raised that this would deprive students of practice teaching in high school subjects. It was agreed to permit a more limited number of "preparatory students" in order that practice teaching at this level could continue.[11] Even as late as 1919–20 the catalogue outlined a four-year high school program. In the same catalogue (p. 48) appeared this interesting statement: "No student may enter the High-School Department of this school unless she has exhausted the high-school facilities of her home school, except under special circumstances. Any applicants falling under this head should consult the President of the school."

INSTRUCTION IN AGRICULTURE

School gardening was an important part of the curriculum in the early years. An area roughly between the present location of Seacobeck and Chandler halls was set aside for cultivation, and vegetables were raised for the school table. There were also "suitable yards for the scientific study of poultry." One student recalls the pen for pigs down the hill behind Willard Hall where leftovers from the dining hall could be readily fed them. Instruction in agriculture, one aspect of the industrial arts curriculum, was practical as well as theoretical. Students were expected to aid in the cultivation of the garden as well as to observe the germination of seeds and the ripening of vegetables.

One of the most fascinating pictures in the 1916–17 catalogue is captioned "Working in the School Garden." It shows forty or fifty girls, dressed immaculately in long white skirts, high-button

---

[10] *Catalogue*, 1919–20, p. 32.
[11] Minutes of the Board, March 18 and July 20, 1921.

shoes, white middy blouses with large black ties, and white sailor hats, all with hoes or rakes, working almost shoulder to shoulder in a mass attack upon what appears to be bare, dry soil. Two students in the foreground are even using small hand trowels in an effort to break the stubborn surface.

VIRGINIA HALL

The new dormitory was opened to students for the 1915–16 session. It was named Virginia Hall. Meanwhile, the first dormitory was named Frances Willard Hall. To the first floor of Virginia Hall were moved the offices of the president and his secretary, the dean, and the business manager; the library; the YWCA room; and the literary society halls. The infirmary was moved to the second floor of the new building. These moves made possible additional classroom space in Russell Hall and additional dormitory space in Frances Willard Hall.

PRESIDENT'S HOME

The president's home had been completed and occupied its place on the eminence overlooking the city, where it stood for many years. Known first as Ridge Crest, the building was a handsome structure, painted white, with a broad pillared porch extending across the front. A wide central hallway gave access to reception and dining rooms on either side. Above were two floors of spacious bedrooms. There was even an enclosed sun parlor.

After President Russell's resignation the residence was used to house faculty members, for President Chandler continued to occupy the house he owned on College Avenue next door to Mr. Hamlet. The residence was again a president's home when Dr. Combs assumed office. The Combs family lived temporarily in rooms in Willard Hall until the house was renovated for their use.

When Framar was purchased by the college, the president moved there, and the former residence was converted into dormitory space for students. Later, the large structure was moved slightly down the hill to provide space for the construction of Randolph and Mason dormitories. It then became the Spanish house, a residence for advanced students majoring in Spanish. A little card on the screen door now reads: "Gentlemen, please knock, *por favor.*"

A VICTORIOUS TRIP

Athletics continued to have an important role in the life of the college. Basketball attracted sixty girls who reported for practice and played in match games. The account of a trip to Washington to play the YWCA there affords a vivid picture of the thrills and enthusiasm such an opportunity produced:

We were all so happy—yes, we were going on an early train and that meant more time in Washington to have a good time we hoped, to become tired out our chaperones feared; but we were gay, and when all of the girls came out with us, to bid us a pleasant trip and make us know that their good wishes for success attended us, we entered the jitney with hearts that were confident of a successful day.

The trip to our Capital City was very interesting and, because the first time that many of us had been to Washington we were all eager for the first view. The Union Station proved a wondrous sight. But we were looking for other things, and soon were being ushered through the Capitol and the Congressional Library, both of which were exceedingly instructive.

How glad we were to arrive at the Ebbit, for we realized that it was quite a long time since we had had our breakfast at the Normal Dining Hall. The dinner was in harmony with our appetites, and we appreciated Mr. Harrison's jokes even when they were on some of us; we had to be good sports.

The rest of the day must be divided so that we could continue our sight-seeing, rest, and play the game which we had almost forgotten. We went through the White House, and saw many buildings which we remember as wonderful structures. Then we rested for the game. We tried to relax and forget, but there was much to think about.

The game—I've almost forgotten to mention it—and that's what we came for! Oh, yes, it was quite a hard game, between the Washington Y. W. C. A. and our team, but because we always held the score at least two points ahead our hopes were never dimmed. And we had such an encouraging audience in the gallery, who spurred us on with their cheers. When the game was won with the score of 16 to 7, and we knew that the 'phone message to our school-mates would be the one that they expected, we were truly happy.

Our good time was continued at the Y. W. C. A., where we dined with the same girls, with whom we had played. Then we returned to the gymnasium to see the game played between the George Washington University and the Ingram teams. This we watched with interest, but we had to leave before the end of the game to catch the train back to Fredericksburg.

. . . When we returned to our dear old Normal we were given a hearty welcome, and then we knew how much our victory meant to those at home as well as to our team and coach.[12]

VISIT TO RICHMOND

An idea of life in those unsophisticated days may be gathered from an account in the *Battlefield* for 1916 (pp. 102–3) of a trip to Richmond to attend a concert given by Geraldine Farrar.

"Eleven of our girls, chaperoned by Misses Fraser and Atkinson, left Fredericksburg on the one-seventeen train." Mr. Russell met them at the station and convoyed them to the Jefferson Hotel where rooms had been engaged. Afternoon activities included a shopping tour and a "delightful automobile drive" to the country club and to the "College at Westhampton." The "culinary art" was enjoyed to its perfection at the YWCA cafeteria. *"Such* fried chicken, *such* salad, *such* everything, all for thirty-five cents."

The students hurried back to the Jefferson to dress for the concert. On arrival at the City Auditorium they were ushered down to front-row seats "past hundreds of Richmonders, resplendent in dress suits, beautiful evening gowns and many sparkling jewels. "For the next two hours we sat enthralled at the seat of sweet music. The peerless Farrar proceeded to weave about us the spell of her charming personality and exquisite vocal art." Afterwards Russell gave an impromptu ice cream party.

The next morning, unfortunately, the group was late in rising and "our beloved Cafeteria" was closed. However, Russell arranged for the party to have breakfast at Murphy's Hotel. There followed a tour of the Capitol and an appointment to meet Governor Stuart. "We enjoyed his hearty handshake, cordial manner, and good jokes." The group took jitneys to Elba station where they boarded the twelve-one for Fredericksburg, after "one of the pleasantest experiences of our school days."

OTHER EVENTS

YWCA presented *The Girls of Yesterday and Today,* a historical pageant marking the fiftieth anniversary of the national organization. It was given in the auditorium of Russell Hall. The YWCA also gave several receptions and held a county fair. Visiting speakers included John Stuart Bryan, Fairfax Harrison, and Henry W.

---

[12] *Battlefield,* 1916, p. 61.

Anderson. Kate Langley Bosher gave readings, and the Ben Greet Players presented *As You Like It* and *Twelfth Night*.

There were the usual Glee Club concerts, Dramatic Club plays, the annual Field Day, and the annual Gymnasium Tournament, as well as other student entertainments. Intramural competition in basketball was part of the athletic program, with cups awarded to first-, second-, and third-place winners (the junior class, the senior class, and the sophomore class). In view of the number and variety of events it sponsored, the YWCA seems to have been the most prominent organization on the campus. However, the Athletic Association was a close second, with the basketball team, track team, sports day with trophies, and its intramural competitions.

Literary societies provided extracurricular intellectual stimulus in most colleges and preparatory schools in those days. There were two at the Normal School, both started the second year of its operation. An idea of their nature can best be gained from some of the activities reported for 1915–16.[13]

The Woodrow Wilson Literary Society studied the lives and works of Robert Louis Stevenson and Eugene Field. It debated such topics as compulsory education laws and equal suffrage for women in Virginia. It also studied "Women of Achievement," such as Mabel Boardman and Frances Willard.

The Russell Literary Society, with fifty-five members, also met weekly. It reported a study of famous and successful women, a long list of them ranging from Queen Elizabeth to Gene Stratton-Porter and Geraldine Farrar. The society also studied Southern statesmen and the customs of their times although there is no indication of the identity of the statesmen studied. Kate Langley Bosher, "celebrated Virginia novelist and short story writer," spoke at an open meeting of the society in March 1916 and read two of her short stories, "Horatius" and "Household Management."

The Glee Club was organized in 1911 under direction of Bernice White, head of the department of music. It gave its first public entertainment, "An Evening with the Masters of Music and Painting," produced "in connection with the Manual Arts Department." The next session (1912–13), under the direction of Margaret Elizabeth Fraser, then head of the department of music, the club gave three public entertainments "in connection with the Piano Class."

[13] *Ibid.*, pp. 72–73, 76–78.

In the spring of 1913 the Glee Club gave a cantata, *The Garden of Flowers*. The following spring it put on an operetta, *The American Girl*. By the spring of 1915 the Glee Club was entertaining the District Teachers Meeting, giving an open-air concert, and singing at the May Day festival and at the baccalaureate service. It also entertained the Richmond College Glee Club.

No description of college life in those days is complete without mention of the college "jitney," an open-air affair on a Ford chassis with benches on both sides, which normally seated about ten or twelve students, depending upon how close together they sat and whether they tried to turn sideways and lean on the backrest to view the scenery and wave to friends. Pictures of the jitney bus appear in several publications. It was even celebrated in verse by a contributor to the 1916 *Battlefield* (p. 98):

> The jitney bus from morn till night
> Does travel up and down
> The hills of our dear Normal School
> To take us all to town.

THE GRADUATES

The *Battlefield* for 1916 published individual and class pictures for a total of 229 students, arranged by classes:

Class of 1916 (Senior)	35
Class of 1917 (Junior)	74
Class of 1918 (Sophomore)	49
Class of 1919 (Freshman)	21
Class of 1920 (Preparatory)	20
Class of 1921 (Sub preparatory)	21
Mature Students (Special)	9

The catalogue for that session (p. 85) shows that thirty-one of the graduates received the regular diploma (preparation for teaching in the elementary grades); three the household arts diploma; and one the industrial arts diploma. Even at that time the industrial part of the program was not attracting significant enrollment.

The Reverend William E. Thompson of Norfolk gave the commencement address, and the Reverend E. T. Wellford of Newport News delivered the baccalaurate sermon. The *Battlefield* for 1916 was dedicated to Mr. Chandler, "whose wise instruction, cheerful assistance, and sound leadership it has been our good fortune to enjoy." The copy of the annual in the Archives is inscribed: "Presented to the Mary Washington College Alumnae Association, February 9, 1940, by Mrs. A. B. Chandler."

ROY S. COOK

In his report to the Normal School board in September 1916, President Russell announced the appointment of Roy Selden Cook as assistant in science and mathematics. Thus began an association with the college that was to continue, with some interruptions, for the next thirty-three years.

Dr. Cook was born in Batesville, Albemarle County, on September 1, 1890. He attended nearby Miller School. Upon his graduation there he was awarded a scholarship to the University of Virginia where he majored in chemistry. While he studied at the university, he also taught chemistry at Charlottesville High School. It was there that he met his future wife, Virgie Via, whom he taught in her senior year. Upon graduation from the University of Virginia in 1915, he spent a year as principal of Accomac High School. He joined the faculty of the Normal School the following year.

Dr. Cook first served as assistant to W. N. Hamlet, teaching courses in both science and mathematics. For a time, he lived in Hamlet's house. In 1918 the call to military service terminated his teaching temporarily. He went overseas and served on the western front during the fall of 1918. He returned to the college in 1919 but left after a year to continue his studies at the University of Virginia.

Dr. Cook taught part time at the Miller School while getting his master's and doctorate in chemistry at the university. His record was distinguished, and upon receiving his Ph.D. in June 1925 he was honored by election to Sigma Xi. He was married the following September and brought his bride to Fredericksburg as he resumed his teaching at the college. During her first years here, Mrs. Cook was both student and faculty wife. She received her B.S. in 1931.

Dr. and Mrs. Cook were truly inseparable companions. They never spent a night away from each other during their entire married life except when Dr. Cook was in the hospital for periodic eye examinations. An accidental collision in a dark hallway with the protruding knob of a chest of drawers while visiting in a friend's home caused what later proved to be a serious eye injury. In time cancer developed, and finally the eye was removed at Johns Hopkins University Hospital. However, Dr. Cook's spirits were never dimmed. He was always bright and cheerful.

Dr. Cook's contributions to the college were many and extended over a long period of time. For over twenty years he served as a chairman of Joint Council, the faculty-student governing body in charge of discipline. He also helped edit the *Bayonet*, the student handbook. Rock collecting was one of his hobbies. For many years, cases containing his carefully labeled collection of hundreds of specimens stood in the hall of Monroe outside the chemistry laboratory.

Dr. Cook taught both chemistry and physics. He built up the college's stock of chemicals and made additions to the laboratory equipment. When the science department moved from Monroe to the second floor of Chandler Hall, the former training school building, Dr. Cook supervised the arrangement of the rooms. There was one laboratory for chemistry and another for physics, with a stock room in between opening into both laboratories. Facilities were limited and there were few advanced courses in chemistry, but the quality of instruction was high.

Shelves of chemical supplies extended all the way to the ceiling of the lofty room. Dr. Cook was not tall, but he went up and down the ladders on each side of the stock room with an agility and a cheerfulness that was a pleasure to behold. He knew where each jar and bottle was located, and how much of each of the hundreds of chemicals was on hand.

The chemistry lecture room, with demonstration table, was just across the hall. It seated sixty or seventy students. Usually there were two laboratory sections for each lecture class. Because of the limited facilities, laboratory sections began at 8:00 A.M. and ran continually until 5:00 or even 6:00 P.M. Demonstrations were set up early in the morning or during the lunch hour.

Dr. Cook was sponsor of the Science Club for years. When a chapter of Chi Beta Phi national honorary scientific fraternity was installed in 1945, he became a charter member. After his death the chapter established a loan fund, later converted into a scholarship fund, in his memory. Each year Chi Beta Phi holds an auction, when donations and volunteer services of students and faculty are sold to the highest bidder. Students bid for having breakfast served in their room by a fellow student, for cakes and candies, or for dinner for two in a faculty home. Proceeds have made possible at least two $350.00 grants in aid annually to outstanding students in science. Dr. Cook would have relished this recognition of achievement.

Dr. and Mrs. Cook took their meals in the college dining hall for many years. Mrs. Cook was always there with the car to meet him when his classes were over. She blew the horn once to indicate that she had arrived, and Dr. Cook always went to the window and adjusted the shade as a signal that he had heard.

Dr. and Mrs. Cook first sat at a table with Mrs. Bushnell. Later Mrs. Cook presided over their own faculty table. Their gracious attentions always put their guests at ease. Dr. Cook was a gentle man. He never said an unkind word about anyone. For twenty-one years he headed the science department. He was proud of his students and their accomplishments, and they sensed his concern with their progress. The *Battlefield* for 1949 was dedicated to him.

Dr. Cook taught continuously in both the regular and summer sessions. He had just begun his class on the morning of June 18, 1949, when he was stricken with a fatal heart attack. He was buried in Oak Hill Cemetery. Mrs. Cook still drives the 1940 Chevrolet they purchased together and which made so many trips back and forth to the campus. Dr. Cook never drove on account of his eyesight. The car is now thirty-three years old and has over 166,-000 miles on the speedometer. Mrs. Cook has steadily refused all offers from antique car fanciers.

WORLD WAR I

In 1916–17 the prospect of war was very real. Woodrow Wilson was doing his best to avoid entering the conflict, but he refused to accept "peace at any price." The moving picture *The Battle Cry of Peace* was shown to the student body, and *The Birth of a Nation* was shown later in the year. Gunyon M. Harrison, assistant in mathematics, was granted leave of absence and left as commanding officer of Company K, Second Virginia Regiment.

Plans were under way to equip a commercial department to offer instruction in typewriting, stenography, and bookkeeping and a "regular business course." The library, now housed in more commodious quarters on the first floor of Virginia Hall, had over three thousand well-selected volumes. Mary S. Yates, a graduate of the school who had taken special library training, was serving as a full-time librarian. The roster for 1916–17 lists 280 students, all except thirteen from Virginia. There were forty-two graduates that year, thirty-four receiving the regular diploma and eight the household arts diploma.

CURRICULUM

The catalogue for 1916–17 indicated few changes in curriculum. There were the usual preparatory courses covering the first and second years of high school work, the freshman and sophomore courses covering the third and fourth years of high school work, and the professional courses, or the two-year normal school program.

The latter were stabilized into five courses, indicated by Roman numerals:

    I. Preparation for teaching the primary grades
   II. Preparation for teaching the intermediate and grammar grades
  III. Preparation for teaching the first- and second-year high school grades
  IV. A course in household arts
   V. A course in industrial arts

Completion of any of the five entitled the student to a full diploma and the state normal school certificate, good for ten years and renewable thereafter. Methodology predominated in the first three programs. Practical courses such as cooking and table service, dressmaking, and home management were emphasized in the household arts curriculum. The industrial arts course included drawing, handwork, agriculture, and gardening as well as industrial arts.

EXPENSES AND SCHOLARSHIPS

After five years of operation, the college still kept the cost of attendance at a minimum. Prospective teachers were exempt from the tuition fee of $30.00 a session. "Board, including room rent, lights, fuel, laundry, bed linen, servant attention, and other necessary living expenses [was] $135.00 per session, or $15.00 per school month." [14]

Two new scholarships were announced by the United Daugh-

[14] *Catalogue*, 1915–16, p. 40.

ters of the Confederacy, one, valued at $150.00, named in honor of Matthew Fontaine Maury, "born in Spotsylvania County near Fredericksburg," and the other, valued at $135.00, to a graduate of a "first grade Virginia high school." Applicants for either scholarship were required to be lineal descendants of Confederate veterans.[15]

The bulletin for 1916–17 was the last of the profusely illustrated catalogues for a decade or more. Subsequent issues had only a frontispiece. One suspects that a limitation was placed on the number of pictures in such publications printed at state expense, as was the case in the 1920s. There were forty-two pages of pictures, plus a six-page folded insert showing a panoramic view of the entire faculty and student body.

Several of the pictures are of particular interest, affording as they do an idea of college life in those days. Included are a "wand drill" in the gymnasium; a class in industrial arts studying plants; the Stitch Club, each member holding a piece of embroidery; a view of the Field Day crowd entitled "Crowning the Victors"; and, most typical of the day, a view of the Old Plank Road, the narrow road that led from Fredericksburg past the Normal School to the west; and a picture of a small steamship, its lone funnel rising bravely in the midst of an open-air deck packed with people, with the caption, "Commodore Maury leaving with delegates from First District Teachers Conference." It was bound for points on the lower Rappahannock, including Tappahannock, where, with Fredericksburg, First District Teachers Meetings were held alternately. It was a great day for Fredericksburg when the meeting was held there.

On one occasion an elderly resident of the Northern Neck was accused of flirting with some of the young teachers on their way to Fredericksburg.

"You should be ashamed," said an indignant fellow passenger, also of mature years. "You with your white hair carrying on with these young girls."

"There may be snow on the mountain top, ma'am," was his reply, "but there is still fire in the valley." This rejoinder has survived for fifty years, a relic of that period of straw-hatted Gibson girls, with stiffly starched shirtwaists, and of gentlemen with high, stiff collars and white flannel trousers.

The following is a quaint section in the 1916–17 catalogue (p. 39):

[15] *Catalogue*, 1916–17, p. 36.

Students' Dresses

There is no necessity for, and this school distinctly discourages, the wearing either of costly or gaudy clothing. Neat, simple, inexpensive dresses fully meet all requirements. Especially to be avoided is the appearance by students in public wearing extreme styles in dress. Simplicity and modesty should characterize the dress of all students.

The entire student body is required to wear simple, white dresses whenever appearing as a body during Commencement Week.

Members of the graduating class are strongly advised to have Commencement dresses simple in design, made of cotton material, such as organdy, batiste, etc., and whose material costs not exceeding $10.00 in any case.

Lectures and entertainments in 1917–18 reflected the impact of the war. Dr. Douglas Freeman, of Richmond, gave an address on the war. Congressman C. C. Dill spoke on his experiences in France. Judge John T. Goolrick described the life of the private soldier.

Enrollment does not seem to have been affected by the war, as there were over 280 students registered. There were forty-nine graduates, twenty-seven in Courses I and II for elementary teaching, eleven in Course III for high school teaching (eighth and ninth grades), nine in Course IV (household arts), and two in Course V (industrial arts). These were the last graduates in industrial arts, a program which was discontinued that year.

Thus disappeared from the catalogue such courses as Home Mechanics 51–52–53, which included use of simple woodworking tools, simple soldering, textile printing, and treatment of floors, as well as Advanced Wood and Cement Work 71–72, including "important joints in wood construction" and concrete work such as "posts, blocks, sidewalks, troughs for feeding, flower pedestals." [16]

Throughout this period the Virginia Normal School Board concerned itself very closely with the operation of the institutions under its control. The four presidents submitted lengthy and detailed reports on both financial transactions and academic matters each quarter, and there were also annual reports summarizing developments during the session.

An examination of the minutes of the board indicates the careful supervision that its members gave to the normal schools. For example, at the same meeting at which the faculty and staff members for 1917–18 were elected, the board approved a number of

---

[16] *Catalogue*, 1918–19, pp. 107–9.

other recommendations by President Russell, including the following:

(7) That President Russell be authorized to pay Mr. A. B. Chandler for the Oliver typewriter belonging to him which the school has been using for several years.
(8) That the President of the school be authorized to sell one horse and purchase a Ford truck, at a cost not to exceed $400.00.[17]

Later, at a meeting in Harrisonburg on October 20, 1917, "Dr. Russell reported that he had been unable to get a suitable autotruck for $400.00, the amount he was authorized to spend at the last meeting of the Board, but could get a satisfactory truck for $435.00. On motion duly seconded, he was authorized to purchase the truck at $435.00." [18]

INFLUENZA EPIDEMIC

When the college opened in September 1918, the progress of the war was uppermost in the minds of everyone. Americans were advancing in their attack on the St. Mihiel salient, and General Pershing reported "ten thousand prisoners and sixty guns already taken and more to follow." [19] Two days later the St. Mihiel salient was eliminated, the number of prisoners rose to twenty thousand, and the Americans still pressed on.

William S. Hart, Alice Brady, Mae Marsh, and Douglas Fairbanks were featured in films on successive days at Pitts's Leader Theatre. The Fredericksburg Fair opened for its thirty-second Annual Agricultural Exhibition on September 17, and students converged on the State Normal School.

There was already an ominous note in the news, however. Spanish influenza was continuing its rapid spread over the country. Army camps reported 5,234 new cases of influenza and 644 new cases of pneumonia, with 155 deaths for the twenty-four hours preceding September 26.[20] On September 27, the *Daily Star* reported that "there are many cases of influenza in this city and community. At the Normal School there are a number of cases and in many families in the city there are one or more cases. In some instances, the entire families are ill."

On the same day, the city schools were closed for an indefinite period. Mayor Rowe issued a proclamation ordering "all places of

[17] Minutes of the Board, July 13, 1917, p. 89.   [18] *Ibid.,* Oct. 20, 1917, p. 91.
[19] *Daily Star,* Sept. 13, 1918.   [20] *Ibid.,* Sept. 26, 1918.

public assembly, including churches, Sunday schools, public schools, and all places of amusement, such as motion pictures and dance halls, to be closed until further notice."

Three days later the United States Surgeon-General reported 51,217 cases of influenza in army camps, with the number still growing. The marine barracks at Quantico was given permission to use as a hospital a large building there owned by Fredericksburg men, since all hospitals and other suitable buildings were filled to capacity with victims of influenza.

The epidemic continued to spread, with many more fatalities. In Washington even public funerals were banned. A single day brought 1,500 new cases and 40 deaths. Richmond reported 10,000 cases. All schools and churches were closed, and John Marshall High School was converted into an emergency hospital. Soon the entire nation was in the throes of the flu, as schools on the west coast closed.

The commander at Quantico requested the corporation court to turn over 224 pints of whisky seized in Fredericksburg to be used for medical purposes as the influenza epidemic struck down 1,500 marines. The request was granted.[21]

At the Normal School the influenza epidemic began to abate in early October. The *Daily Star* of October 2 reported: "The influenza at the normal school is largely decreased. There are only 50 cases now under treatment. There has not been a single death. The cases are very mild."

However, the next day, Virginia May Goolrick, a native of Fredericksburg who had been a member of the faculty from the opening of the college, died at the Normal School of pneumonia following an attack of influenza. She was sick only a few days. At the time of her death she was in charge of the department of history. The funeral was held on October 5. Pallbearers were C. O'Conor Goolrick, Chester B. Goolrick, A. B. Chandler, Jr., E. H. Russell, P. J. Daniel, and John Scott.

By then, the epidemic was on the wane in the area. On October 7 the *Daily Star* was able to report: "The greater number of students who have been sick with the Influenza at the Normal School have completely recovered and are ready to return to classes. There have been no new cases lately, and only a very few are still confined to their rooms. Every one is either better or convalescent, and it is hoped that work will soon be running smoothly again."

[21] *Ibid.*, Sept. 27, 1918.

In accordance with instructions from the Normal School board, students who had contracted influenza during the epidemic were charged a fee of $5.00 for the extra service rendered them. Russell reported that "there was not an objection or criticism raised by any patron of the school." [22]

During the epidemic Dr. H. M. DeJarnette, a Fredericksburg physician who was also a member of the Normal School board, rendered untiring and devoted assistance to the students and faculty on the Hill. He presented no bill for his services. In a letter recommending that he be compensated, President Russell wrote the board: "For the period of three weeks he attended daily and frequently at night normal school patients, gave much of his time and attention to looking after their welfare." [23] The board voted to pay Dr. DeJarnette fifty dollars. At the next meeting, in May, he declined to accept any compensation since he felt it would "establish a bad policy." [24]

It was not until early November that Fredericksburg schools were reopened after seven weeks of being closed. On November 8 Mayor J. P. Rowe revoked his proclamation of September 28, which had ordered all schools, churches, and places of amusement closed. The following Monday, November 11, 1918, the Armistice was signed and World War I ended.

OCCUPATIONS OF THE GRADUATES

The catalogue for 1918–19 (pp. 112–16) lists the occupations of the graduates of the classes of 1913, 1914, 1915, 1916, 1917, and 1918. Of the 215 diploma recipients over this six-year period, the first years of the college, 177 were teaching, 25 were married; 3 had clerical positions; 4 were listed "Home"; 1 was taking a nursing course; 2 were deceased; and, in the class of 1918, 1 was listed as doing Red Cross work, 1 war work, and 1 simply "Navy." There is no indication whether any of the married graduates were also teaching.

PRESIDENT RUSSELL RESIGNS

Early in 1919 there occurred a series of incidents, minor in themselves but the cumulative effect of which was to cause concern

[22] President Russell's report, April 10, 1919.
[23] Minutes of the Board, April 12, 1919, p. 114.
[24] *Ibid.*, May 9, 1919, p. 119.

about the administration of the school. In February a number of members of the faculty resigned, and as one observer reported, "all kinds of rumors were being circulated in the school and I fear, throughout the territory represented by our patronage." [25]

The board appointed a special committee to investigate conditions. The faculty was reported to be in a state of nervous tension, uncertain as to their status. Students were also excited, and morale was low. Rumors continued to plague the institution.

Matters reached a head at the board meeting held in Richmond on May 9, 1919. Judge John W. Price, president of the board, read the following letter of resignation from E. H. Russell:

May 9, 1919

The Virginia Normal School Board
Gentlemen:

For several years my health has been impaired and I feel impelled in justice to myself and the best interest of the school to herewith tender my resignation as President of the State Normal School for Women at Fredericksburg.

Very respectfully,
E. H. Russell [26]

The resignation was accepted and went into effect as of that day. The "duties and authority of the President were assigned to the dean until a new president is elected." Judge Price himself visited the school that evening and made the announcement of President Russell's resignation to a special meeting of the faculty. A. B. Chandler, Jr., took charge as acting president the next day. A student assembly was held that morning, at which Judge Price spoke briefly regarding the change in administration. A full account of the new developments appeared in the *Daily Star* that afternoon, May 10, under the headlines, "Mr. Russell Resigns; Ill Health Causes Retirement from Normal School; Mr. Chandler Acting President." The news story reported that Russell had presented his resignation the evening before to the Normal School board in session in Richmond, and that it had been accepted. The board designated Dean A. B. Chandler, Jr., as acting president for the remainder of the session and also selected him to take charge of the summer session to be held in June and July. Before adjourning, the board appointed a committee consisting of Judge Price, president of the board; Harris Hart, state superintendent of public instruction; and Dr. H. M. DeJarnette of Fredericks-

[25] Report to the Normal School Board, May 30, 1919.
[26] Minutes of the Board, May 9, 1919, p. 119.

burg to make a recommendation concerning the election of a permanent president.

The *Daily Star* article continued: "Mr. Russell's resignation ends a connection with the local school which has existed since the institution was established here in 1909, following the big legislative fight of the year previous. During the early years of the school, the president was called upon to perform an enormous amount of work, and largely as a result of this work Mr. Russell's health broke down, resulting in a long spell of sickness about two years ago. Since that time he has suffered from the effects of this attack and is still in bad condition. He will continue for the present to occupy the president's home at the school and will after taking a rest enter private business."

The article concluded with the statement that "President Russell leaves the institution with the personal good wishes of the faculty and students of the institution to which he has devoted his energies for the past eight years."

Thus Russell's connection with the institution he had helped to establish terminated rather abruptly. He and his family moved to Washington, where he entered the real estate business. The president's home became a faculty house, for Chandler had his own home on College Avenue next door to W. N. Hamlet's house.

The catalogue for 1919-20 referred to Russell Hall simply as the Administration Building. Later it was renamed Monroe Hall in honor of President James Monroe, who had lived in Fredericksburg. Russell Hall, the magnificent new dormitory erected in 1965 on the campus near Sunken Road, was named in honor of the first president of the school. Russell had died in 1956.

A NEW PRESIDENT

At a special meeting called by "telegraphic notice" for June 7, 1919, at the office of the state superintendent of public instruction in Richmond, the election of the new president was held, Judge Price, president of the board, presiding. After balloting, A. B. Chandler, Jr., was declared elected. In the words of the minutes, "Mr. Chandler was introduced, and in a happy speech, expressed his appreciation of the confidence of the Board in electing him as head of the Fredericksburg Normal School." [27]

[27] *Ibid.,* June 7, 1919, p. 123.

Algernon Bertrand Chandler, Jr., was an experienced educator. Born at Bowling Green on May 12, 1870, he received his preparatory school education in Midland and Bowling Green academies. His academic training included the B.A. and M.A. degrees from the University of Virginia, where he received a medal in oratory from the Washington Literary Society. He had also taken a special course in law at Washington and Lee University. Licensed to practice in 1895, Chandler formed a partnership with his brother, John W. Chandler, also a graduate of the University of Virginia, and they practiced law together in Atlanta for a few years. It was at this time that Chandler delivered the annual oration (on the life and character of Robert E. Lee) before the Virginia Society of Atlanta, an unusual honor for a young man of twenty-six. During the same year he gave the commencement address at the Georgia State Normal School at Milledgeville.

Chandler's keen interest in education led him to leave the legal profession and turn to teaching. Before entering public school work he had taught at Locust Dale Academy; at Nolley's School for Boys, in Richmond; and at Miss Ellett's School for Girls (now St. Catherine's School), also in Richmond.

After a period of service as principal of the Clifton Forge grade school and high school, Chandler returned to Richmond where he was principal of Leigh Public School for six years. He also taught English at Virginia Mechanics' Institute, a popular evening school for adults. He had been active in the state summer school for teachers at Fredericksburg, having conducted the program in 1910 and 1911. In the year preceding his appointment to the faculty of the Normal School he served as a state school examiner for the first circuit and secretary of the board.

Mr. Chandler was both a teacher and a scholar, as well as a capable administrator. He had written the Virginia supplement to Frye's *Grammar School Geography* and numerous professional articles for the magazine of the Virginia Teachers' Association, which he had served as vice-president. For three years he had edited the school page of the Richmond *News-Leader*.

Chandler was energetic and capable. He brought to his new position at Fredericksburg the dedication and enthusiasm characteristic of him. Serving first as professor of Latin, his contribution to the growth and development of the school was such that after three years he was made dean of the institution, the office he held at the time of his appointment to the presidency.

THE SESSION ENDS

The eighth annual commencement was held in the school auditorium on Monday evening, June 9, 1919, with fifty-one graduates. Each of them was given a bouquet of pink roses, as well as a diploma.

The speaker on this occasion was the Honorable Thomas J. Downing, whom President Chandler introduced as "the silver tongued orator of the Northern Neck of Virginia." The *Daily Star* (June 10) reported that "in most eloquent language he told the class that they had written finis to this page of their lives, but that the hand of hope was beckoning them on to new endeavors. . . . They were now going into the university of the world, where all nature is the faculty and all human beings the pupils."

In his address to the graduates President Chandler listed four aims that he hoped their alma mater would achieve:

1. With the differentiation of the work of the four state normal schools, Fredericksburg Normal would develop especially the music, industrial arts, and commercial courses.

2. The development of a school farm as a laboratory and source of food supply for the school.

3. The articulation of the institutional cookery and the service of the food with the instructional work in domestic science.

4. Training school facilities to be extended to include rural school observation and practice teaching.

CHAPTER VII

The 1920s

NEW PLANS AND PROJECTS

WHEN Chandler assumed the presidency of the Normal School he was thoroughly familiar with the institution, having served as professor and dean since its founding. One of his first problems was to find well-qualified replacements for the faculty members who had resigned the previous February. To do this it was essential to offer attractive salaries. President Chandler proposed for 1919–20 a salary scale that represented an increase of about 7 percent over the 1918–19 salaries. He also requested the authorization of two new positions. These requests were approved.[1]

Some ten new appointments, most of them replacements, were made at this time. They included Carrie Bell Vaughan, as head of the history department; M. Louise Ninde, as director of physical education; Elizabeth N. Williams, as director of music; Miriam H. Perrin, as assistant in English; Walter J. Young, as professor of biology, geography, and education; Anna P. Starke, as social director; and Dalia Lam Ruff, as assistant to the social director and to the registrar. Several new critic-teachers were appointed. Dr. Cook was back on the faculty after his war service with the A.E.F. in Europe.

Dr. Young was destined to play an important role in the college in the days to come. He was the only Ph.D. on the faculty at the time of his appointment. A graduate of Richmond College, he had earned his master's and doctor's degrees at the University of Pennsylvania. He taught biology, psychology, and philosophy at Hampden-Sydney College from 1911 to 1913 and philosophy and education at Richmond College from 1913 to 1918, serving as head of the department in each instance. Shortly thereafter he was a supervisor and summer school principal in Suffolk and a visiting professor at the Harrisonburg State Normal School summer session.

From 1919 to 1926 Dr. Young taught courses in the elementary education program at the college and worked with the student teachers in that field in city schools. During this time he also

---

[1] Minutes of the Board, June 7, 1919, p. 123.

served as pastor of the Massaponax and Zoan Baptist churches in Spotsylvania County.[2] He was an ordained minister, holding the B.D. and Th.M. degrees from Crozier Theological Seminary.

Dr. Young left the college in 1926 for a three-year period as head of the department of education at Winthrop College and another year at Henderson State Teachers College in Arkansas. He returned to Fredericksburg in September 1930 and served as professor of elementary education (1930–34), later professor of education and psychology (1934–38), and, finally, professor and chairman of the department of philosophy and psychology (1938–40). For many years he taught Education 165, Principles of Teaching-Elementary Grades, a course required of all candidates for the two-year diploma in elementary education and later for the degree course with a major in elementary education.

Dr. Young was an exacting and, at times, temperamental teacher. He always insisted upon and received the respectful attention of his students. He had a brilliant mind, and he was quick to dispose of educational philosophies not to his liking. He was somewhat traditional in his approach to teaching procedures, with command of subject matter as a fundamental objective.

Dr. Young founded and served as sponsor of two important organizations on the campus. In 1934 he organized Alpha Tau Pi as an honorary society for majors in elementary education. In the next few years several other colleges established chapters. The Alpha chapter continued to function until 1948, at which time the major in elementary education was discontinued. Dr. Young also sponsored the reestablishment of the Cotillion Club as an alternate dance organization to the German Club after which it was modeled.

Dr. Young lived across from the college in a small stone house. In his later years he was engaged in collaborating with Dr. Graves on a book on corelativity theory, which merged recent data from the fields of physics, psychology, and biology. Earlier, Dr. Young had published a number of articles and monographs. He was a member of the Royal Society of Arts in London and of several academies of science and learned societies in the United States.

He was still actively teaching at the time of his death on November 23, 1940. He had been ill for only a short time when he died at the age of fifty-seven. After Dr. Young's death his

---

[2] *Free Lance-Star*, Nov. 23, 1940.

widow was employed by the college for several years as a head resident in one of the dormitories.

The new social director, Anna P. Starke, had held various types of secondary school and college positions. She was the only Litt.D. on the faculty. The degree had been conferred by the Woman's College, Richmond. Miss Starke remained with the school for only two years, but her assistant, Dalia L. Ruff, continued her association with the institution for a total of thirty years.

Mrs. Ruff's first position was assistant to the social director and assistant registrar. In 1921, when Mrs. Bushnell came, Mrs. Ruff was made dietitian and assistant dean of women. For the next nine years, she held both positions and was also house mother in Willard Hall.

From 1930 to her retirement in 1949, Mrs. Ruff held the title of dietitian and director of dining halls. She continued to have complete charge of food services: purchases, meal planning, preparation, service (including supervision of student waitresses), and supervision of all dining hall employees. Even with her many responsibilities, Mrs. Ruff always had time to share a cup of coffee with a faculty colleague, a student, or a friend who dropped by casually.

During her entire association with the college, Mrs. Ruff lived on the campus, first in Willard Hall and then, when Seacobeck was completed, she occupied an apartment there. Her daughter, John (now Mrs. D. H. Strohecker), lived with her until graduating from the college in 1926. Mrs. Ruff's husband was killed tragically just ten days after her daughter was born. The widow decided to name the baby John, after her late husband. Mrs. Ruff never remarried.

When she died in 1951, the *Free Lance-Star* (March 14) referred to her as "friend of hundreds of college girls." Mrs. Ruff always seemed to sense when a lonesome freshman needed a motherly touch, and she was always ready to offer cheer with a warm smile and a friendly word. She was buried in the family cemetery in Lexington.

BUNYAN YATES TYNER

To succeed him as dean, President Chandler appointed Bunyan Y. Tyner, then head of the department of education and director of teacher training.

A native of North Carolina, Mr. Tyner had received his preparatory education at Buies Creek Academy, where he later went back to teach for a time. He received his bachelor's degree from Wake Forest College and his master's from Columbia University, with a special diploma in education from Teachers College.

After a period as teacher and principal in North Carolina schools, Tyner came to Fredericksburg in 1912 as professor of education and, later, head of the department. In addition to his teaching he also served as registrar both before and after his appointment as dean.

From 1919 to 1929 Tyner was second in command at Fredericksburg, as dean and dean of instruction. Both of these titles were used in the catalogues. He was closely associated with President Chandler in the developing program of the college.

Molly Coates, who was secretary to the dean and assistant registrar in the late 1920s, has described the fine working relationship between the president and the dean:

The administrative "set-up" at the College during my years there was especially impressive to me. I learned more about it first-hand, of course, when I worked in the office following my graduation, though both the President and the Dean were well-loved and highly respected during my student years also.

President Chandler, a rather plump, smallish man, was almost always the picture of cheerfulness, despite the many problems always facing him. He was enthusiastic, out-going, and friendly to all, informal in his contacts with others, but always understanding and helpful. He had a far-vision of what the college could and should be and worked unremittingly to achieve this goal. He was, however, inclined to be impetuous, and at times his eagerness and enthusiasm carried him beyond the practical or "realizable" in making his plans. On the other hand, Dean Tyner was quieter, with a quiet sense of humor, and more practical and "down-to-earth" in his proposals. Together they bore the main responsibility for the on-going of the College; with adjoining offices, they were frequently back and forth. In good humor and deep friendship, Dean Tyner was forever trying to "hold President Chandler down to "realities"; and President Chandler was forever trying to "spur" Dean Tyner on to enthusiasm for some of his idealistic aspirations. Between them (and they almost always arrived at a "middle ground of agreement") and together, they made a wonderful pair. They were both dedicatedly committed to their tasks and worked together as a team. There were of course, by the very nature of their positions, certain areas where the President made his unilateral decisions and the Dean made his—but there was a remarkable accord between them—and for the most part, with the faculty also. Faculty members were frequently brought into discussions pertaining to the academic aspects of the College and their advice both sought and heeded, insofar as the means were available. They both deserve an enormous amount of credit for having steered the College as successfully as they did through this crucial early period of its development and growth.³

Mrs. Tyner also taught at the College. From 1920 to 1928 she was professor of languages. Tyner was a likable man, tall, handsome, and rather stately. He was regarded with affection by students and colleagues. The *Battlefield* for 1915 was dedicated to him, with a fitting tribute: "To Bunyan Yates Tyner to whose wise counsel and guidance we are so deeply indebted and whose untiring energy has been expended without reserve in our behalf the 1915 *Battlefield* is affectionately dedicated by the Senior Class."

Ten years later, the annual was again dedicated to Dean Tyner. The *Battlefield* staff for 1925 wrote: "To Bunyan Yates Tyner Academic Dean whose lovable personality permeates the whole life of the college and upon whose wholesome counsel individuals and groups have leaned most profitably, this issue of the *Battlefield* is affectionately dedicated."

When President Chandler died in 1928, Dean Tyner was appointed acting president. After Dr. Combs became president, Tyner obtained a leave of absence to accept a teaching fellowship at Peabody College and to do graduate work there. From 1930 to 1932 he was dean of the college and head of the department of education at Winthrop College. From there he went to Meredith College where, from 1932 to 1954, he was head of the department of education and director of teacher training. He retired as professor emeritus of education in 1954.

Tyner was active in many professional and civic organizations. He was a member of the board of trustees of Campbell College from 1962 to 1965 and 1967 to 1970. In 1970 that college recognized his services by awarding him the honorary degree of doctor of humane letters. He was eighty-eight years of age at the time.⁴ For many years Dean Tyner resided in Raleigh, North Carolina, where he and his wife attended the annual meetings of the local chapter of the Mary Washington Alumnae Association. He died in 1973.

ASSIGNMENT OF SUBJECT FIELDS

On April 12, 1919, the Virginia Normal School Board adopted resolutions which it described as of very great importance to the

---
³ Letter to the author, Sept. 30, 1970, p. 10.
⁴ Letter to the author, Sept. 1, 1971.

future development of normal schools.[5] These resolutions put into effect the recommendations of its course of study committee, which had been charged with the responsibility of eliminating unnecessary duplication of effort in offering preparation for teaching. In brief, a function of the committee was to assign certain areas of specialization to each of the four normal schools.

The resolutions emphasized that the "most important function" of these schools was to train teachers for elementary schools. Hence, all four institutions would continue to offer two-year courses for the training of elementary teachers. Noting the increased demand for high school teachers, the board authorized all schools to continue to offer the first two years of preparation for specialization in the various subject fields, but, after July 1, 1921, only certain schools would be permitted to offer the third and fourth years of study. Under this plan, Farmville was assigned the four-year course for the training of high school teachers; Harrisonburg, for teachers of home economics; Radford, for training of supervisors of elementary schools and specialists in rural education; and Fredericksburg, for music, industrial arts, and commercial subjects. The only exception to this arrangement was that Fredericksburg was to offer the four-year commercial course in its entirety.

NEW COMMERCIAL DEPARTMENT

In accordance with this resolution, the Fredericksburg Normal School began at once to develop a commercial program. The catalogue for 1918–19 (p. 45) listed "Course V, A Commercial or Business Course," which was to be offered in the 1920–21 session.

The catalogue continued: "This course is primarily designed to prepare teachers of the commercial subjects, for which there is a rapidly growing demand in Virginia. Graduates of accredited high schools are eligible to this course. Upon completion of the two years the student is given the Diploma of the school and a State Certificate of equal dignity to that granted graduates in our other courses. This course is also open to Normal School and College graduates. See elsewhere in this catalogue a detailed outline of this course."

Although announcements of the new commercial program

---

[5] Minutes of the Board, April 12, 1919, pp. 114–15.

were enthusiastic, few persons believed that such courses would have broad appeal at the college level, especially since they were also available in high schools and business colleges. In fact, when the allocations by the course of study committee were first discussed with the heads of the normal schools, President Russell wrote a strong letter of protest to the committee members asserting that there was little likelihood that four-year programs in the field would attract students.

There was litle indication at that time that by the late thirties and early forties the commercial department at Fredericksburg would have a faculty of fourteen and a registration of over seven hundred students, or about half the entire college enrollment. The further development of this department is discussed later.

Plans went forward for developing the new department at Fredericksburg. In April 1920, the board authorized President Chandler to put in equipment for a "Commercial Teacher Training Course." [6] Accordingly, a small room in Monroe was equipped with a score of typewriters, and instruction began.

The catalogue for 1919–20 (pp. 59, 64) outlined the junior and senior years of the new program. Both consisted almost entirely of business subjects. In addition to typewriting, shorthand, and bookkeeping, there were business English, business arithmetic, and business writing, plus educational psychology, principles of study and teaching, and physical education. The senior year ("not offered until session of 1921–22") continued all of these business subjects and added commercial law, commercial geography, elementary economics, advanced bookkeeping, office practice, commercial education, and practice teaching.

By June 1921 Mr. Chandler had completed two years as president. The *Battlefield* for that year (pp. 11–12) carried an interesting report, written "at the invitation of the editorial staff" and entitled "Two Years of Progress." In his concise and matter-of-fact style, Chandler cited both small and great accomplishments:

On the material side we have recently laid concrete walks to the President's home and the Faculty home, rebuilt the driveway through the grove, secured a new Reo Speed-wagon for use by the practice-teaching Seniors, made improvements to the dining hall, added equipment to the kitchen, put in a new gymnasium floor, supplied fifty per cent additional equipment to the home economics department, laid a new gas main to the school, set out an orchard and erected a new fifty thousand gallon steel water tank.

[6] Minutes of the Board, April 16, 1920, p. 10.

On the academic, professional and recreational sides the school has introduced a new commercial teacher training course, added a critic teacher to Lee Hill School, established a practice and observation junior high school at Ruther Glen, adopted the group elective system in the course of study, further perfected the student government plan, revived and renamed the two literary societies, done a notable religious work through the Y. W. C. A., strengthened the physical education department, developing one of the strongest, if not the very strongest, basket-ball sextettes in the State, introduced a Lyceum series of entertainments with a large season membership, and provided moving pictures weekly for the students.

Looking ahead to the future, President Chandler continued:

For the session 1921–22 the institution will eliminate the high school or undergraduate department, placing the school upon a wholly professional basis; will add the senior year of the commercial teacher-training course, with an added member of the faculty in this department; will establish an additional practice school at Spotslyvania Court House for use by the high school seniors, with two critic teachers: will double the supervisory force; will expand the work of the Extension Bureau; will complete the new grammar grade course of study for the training school; will provide a full summer quarter for the summer of 1922; will refurnish the parlor of Frances Willard Hall; will add improvements to the kitchen, dining hall and service of meals, and will place only two girls in a dormitory room, with the possible exception of some corner rooms, in which three may be placed.

Subject to legislative appropriations, the Fredericksburg Normal also hopes, during the next two years, to add the second unit to Virginia Hall so as to provide cabinet rooms for the Y. W. C. A. and student government councils, literary society halls, Y. W. C. A. hall, guest rooms, enlarged library, kitchenette and the like. We hope to join the Administration Building with the central heating plant, to erect on our grounds an elementary training school, to build a concrete road through the grove, to extend our system of concrete walks, to erect a cold-storage plant, and establish at the school a health education center as the basis for an extension course for teachers in the health education of school children.

In concluding this recital of projects completed and future plans, Chandler generously expressed his debt to the cooperation of an able and loyal faculty and an enthusiastic and devoted student body. It was typical of the president that he renewed his pledge that "all the energies of my heart and brain shall be expended unstintingly in the promotion of the best interest" of the school and its development as a teacher training institution.

It is a tribute to President Chandler's care and good judgment in selecting new faculty and staff members that during his incumbency there came to the college men and women of high caliber who, as administrative officers and as faculty members, helped to shape the future of the school for the next quarter of a century. Outstanding among these new appointments was that of Mrs. Charles Lake Bushnell, who, in the fall of 1921, came to Fredericksburg as dean of women and professor of Bible.

NINA GOOKIN BUSHNELL

Nina Gookin Bushnell served as dean of women at the college from 1921 until her retirement in June 1950. During this long period of service she endeared herself to the hearts of thousands of students, who admired, respected, and loved her.

A native of Bristol, Mrs. Bushnell had attended the University of Tennessee and received the bachelor of arts degree there. Before coming to the college, she had taught Latin at Reidsville High School in North Carolina and English at Winthrop College. For a time she was a school principal in Spartanburg, and then she went to the Synodical College at Fulton, Missouri, as dean of women. During World War I Mrs. Bushnell worked in France with a Virginia unit of the YWCA. Her husband, Charles Lake Bushnell, had died of typhoid fever in 1911.

Mrs. Bushnell's duties at the college were many and varied. A person of seemingly unlimited energy, she devoted herself unsparingly and unselfishly to the service of the institution. Her office in Virginia Hall was always open, day and night, seven days a week. She was always ready to confer with students, hostesses, or faculty members as well as with parents or guardians about student personnel problems. Much of her time during the day was devoted to this important role. She also served as hostess of Virginia Hall, the dormitory in which she resided.

As dean of women Mrs. Bushnell made the room assignments for all students. She also handled the permission cards on which parents indicated the privileges they wished their daughters to have, always, of course, within the framework of the regulations in the college handbook. Mrs. Bushnell's office saw to the preparation and distribution of the handbook.

As social director of the college, Mrs. Bushnell supervised all programs for recreation and entertainment. She always attended the final rehearsal of all programs given publicly by student organizations. She did not hesitate to eliminate any skit or dialogue that she felt to be offensive or in bad taste.

Mrs. Bushnell kept the social calling list, which men of the local community recall with a slightly grim smile in afteryears. In her own words, she "investigated the status of all men callers for the social calling list." Guest cards were issued from her office. No male caller could appear at a dormitory without first making sure that he had his guest card, which had to be presented each time to the dormitory hostess. Mrs. Bushnell issued all weekend permissions. Her office also supervised all "checking in and checking out" by students for local social privileges, such as dinners with dates, movies in town, visits in private homes, and attendance at parties sponsored by local groups.

In a report prepared for the State Personnel Office, Mrs. Bushnell described her office in Virginia Hall as the "Home Office" of the college. It served as the headquarters for general information. Taxi drivers invariably directed visitors to Mrs. Bushnell's office when they were uncertain where to go. The telephone in her office served as a sort of exchange for the college. There was no central switchboard. All long distance calls went first to 684, a familiar telephone number to everyone at the college.

Mrs. Bushnell kept the college clearance calendar, which was used to avoid conflicts in scheduling events or entertainments. For many years she directed the May Court, making a trip to Washington herself to choose the costumes at Garfinckel's or Woodward and Lothrop's. She also selected carefully the flowers that were to be carried. As social director, Mrs. Bushnell worked with the formal dances at the college serving as sponsor of the German Club for many years. As adviser to the *Battlefield,* the student annual, she supervised the layout and wrote much of the copy herself.

Mrs. Bushnell was a person of strong character and colorful personality. Everyone who knew her well respected her and recognized her genuine interest in the students. Her memory for their names and faces was legendary. Even after a period of years she could recall a former student's dormitory room number.

There were those who felt that Mrs. Bushnell kept too firm and active control of student affairs and that she tended to manage and direct what might have been more nearly student activities than "Mrs. Bushnell's touch." This was especially true of the May Court, the formal dances, and the *Battlefield.* A few timid students were awed by her presence, finding her a little too formidable. A few felt her rigorous standards of student dress—both at the college and for male callers—somewhat Victorian.

On the other hand, Mrs. Bushnell was a tremendous influence in the lives of students who attended the college during her years of service. She was always ready to assist, even lending students money from her own funds to go home quickly when an emergency arose. Students felt that in the office in Virginia Hall there was always someone to whom they could turn if help were needed.

Students of that day will remember the little "At Your Service" sign that hung above the push button of the buzzer used to summon her if she were "back in her room." The sign was always out except during the hour from 5:00 to 6:00 P.M. when she dressed for dinner.

Mrs. Bushnell always dressed for dinner. She felt that the evening meal should be a social as well as a gustatory experience, a time for relaxation but also for stimulating conversation. Appropriate dress and grooming were expected of all students, for the atmosphere of the evening meal was created not only by a physical setting of candlelight and modulated voices but by an ambience of gracious dining, which seemed to encompass both students and visitors.

Habitually, Mrs. Bushnell said grace for the evening meal. Promptly at six, entrance doors were closed, and a hushed silence fell as Mrs. Bushnell walked a few steps from her table toward the center of the room. There was never a signal for quiet. Silence was expected, and invariably, it was immediate as she came forward to speak.

Mrs. Bushnell's blessing was never formalized or stereotyped. Each evening she expressed in a few well-chosen words the thanks of the group for the blessings of the day and a plea for God's fellowship. These prayers were varied and particularized. They seemed to have a highly personal flavor, as if one were talking with a friend. As one visitor said with awe—and respect, too— "Mrs. Bushnell doesn't exactly pray to God; she talks with God." A brief hush always followed these blessings, and then conversation at scores of tables throughout the room suddenly seemed to sparkle as Mrs. Bushnell took a seat.

Often Mrs. Bushnell used the dining hall period for a lesson in good manners or "good breeding." She insisted that a lady's arms or elbows should not rest on the table when eating. "If you don't know what to do with your other hand, put it in your lap," she would say. Loud, boisterous laughter always produced a frown in that direction from Mrs. Bushnell's table. A knife or fork dropped on the floor was never entirely ignored, even if it were at some distance across the room. To Mrs. Bushnell, the social graces were part of one's education, especially that of young women. She knew the proper thing to do, and she shared her knowledge in a positive but kind manner. "A lady doesn't . . ." was the beginning of many little expressions of advice that she gave from time to time.

One of Mrs. Bushnell's memorable talks was on how to eat cherries with seeds in them—and many gallons were served as dessert in those days. "A lady never spits anything out of her mouth," Mrs. Bushnell would say. Mrs. Bushnell could say the word *spits* with such emphasis and intonation that one shared the revulsion she felt at the very mention of the word. "A lady never spits something, she *removes* it from her mouth." There followed a ladylike demonstration of a cherry seed's being removed delicately with the tip of the spoon and deposited carefully at the side of the plate. As one student put it in later years, "I believe they served those cherries so often because of the opportunity it gave to instill good table manners."

Mrs. Bushnell's instructions on eating soup were simple and to the point: "Always use the soup spoon in a motion away from the body. Always use the ice cream spoon toward the body." Thirty years later, one graduate still remembers the gravity with which these social graces were pronounced.

Sincerity and interest characterized these dining hall instructions. Former students of the college recall with appreciation the concern Mrs. Bushnell felt for their development of social graces as well as academic attainments. As one long-time faculty member expressed it, "Appreciation of Mrs. Bushnell came with maturity."

For visiting speakers and other guests of the college, dinner at "Mrs. Bushnell's table" was an event in itself. Ordinarily Mrs. Bushnell ate alone at a small table directly inside of the entrance doors of the south unit of the dining hall. Year after year, the figure in the dinner dress sat erect and poised, a living example of how a lady should sit at a table. No student left the dining hall until Mrs. Bushnell had given an almost imperceptible nod of dismissal to the table nearest her.

When visiting speakers were being entertained at dinner, conversation continued to sparkle at Mrs. Bushnell's table. The silver candlesticks had been polished to a gleaming radiance, and the light of the candles seemed to cast a spell as mints were passed and confidences exchanged. Mrs. Bushnell had a way of stimulating her guests by leading questions. Her own interest in current affairs was genuine and profound. She used to have a weekly current events session on Sunday evenings in the parlor of Virginia. Guests at her table found themselves caught up in serious discussions of current issues. There was always a rush to get to the auditorium in time for the formal address that evening.

Almost every student who attended the college during Mrs. Bushnell's era has some anecdote or vivid recollection of her. As one admirer put it recently, Mrs. Bushnell had charisma. She was liked—nay, loved—by the hundreds of students who experienced and cherished her influence. As one graduate remarked earnestly, "Next to my mother, I believe Mrs. Bushnell influenced my life most during the four years I was at the College."

Not everyone liked Mrs. Bushnell. However, there was no one who did not respect her. She did not try to relate to people in the modern sense of the word nor did she try to make people feel comfortable. She was the epitome of the social graces both in her office and on the campus, but she was always businesslike and efficient. One faculty member says he thought of her as being almost like royalty. He recalls seeing her in Miller and Rhoads once during a college vacation, and, "believe me, it was like seeing a queen off the throne."

On one occasion Mrs. Bushnell became quite concerned over rumors about a certain student that were being spread on the campus. That night she did not open the evening meal with the customary saying of grace. Instead, she gave a brief lecture on the pernicious results of repeating rumors. Then, in a very positive manner, she said, "Tonight I am isolated from you." She put out the candle on her table and left the dining room without eating.

On another occasion, students at Betty Lewis were alarmed when an intruder sought to enter through the open window of a first floor room. As usual, someone called Mrs. Bushnell. It was shortly after midnight, and the entire dormitory was agitated and disturbed. Characteristically, Mrs. Bushnell telephoned Hilldrup's taxi to have a car on the driveway near her office at Virginia Hall immediately. Dressing hurriedly, she rode one block down the hill to Betty Lewis and quieted the milling students. Later, in describing the incident a student said, "Mrs. Bushnell motored down, and all was well."

Mrs. Bushnell felt that the students were her personal responsibility. Once when an overwrought and despondent student threatened to take her own life, her roommate ran to Mrs. Bushnell, who always seemed to be there when an emergency arose. Mrs. Bushnell quieted the distraught girl. Then, with a keen sense of the kind of assurance that was needed, she called a house meeting in the parlor. As the girl sat in Mrs. Bushnell's office she was able to overhear her prayer for her, and the voices of the students as they joined in the Lord's Prayer at the end. Mrs. Bushnell stayed by the girl as she fell into a deep and relaxing sleep. Later she said, "Mrs. Bushnell saved my life that night."

Few students of later years knew of Mrs. Bushnell's active interest in sports in her earlier years at the college. She loved to dance, to swim, and to ride. An elderly resident of Fredericksburg recalls the first time he saw Mrs. Bushnell. It was in 1921, and she had just come to the college. A group of local citizens and some people from the Hill were taking a boat trip down the Rappahannock to participate in the opening of a new country club near Montross. When the boat anchored there, Mrs. Bushnell and President Chandler went below and donned bathing suits. Then they went swimming over the side of the boat. "I'll never forget it," says the resident.

On snowy days in winter Mrs. Bushnell used to set up a coffee urn and huge plates of doughnuts in the foyer of Virginia Hall. When classes changed at ten-thirty, word was passed around that Mrs. Bushnell had coffee and doughnuts ready in Virginia. It was just the thing for a midmorning snack on a brisk snowy day —long before *coffee breaks* or even the word *snack* had become part of our vocabulary.

Mrs. Bushnell retired from the college in 1950 at the age of seventy. She was still young in heart and spirit and seemed to possess tireless energy. For the next seven years she served as dean of women at Moravian College, Bethlehem, Pennsylvania. As a visitor there once remarked, "I felt Mrs. Bushnell's presence when I walked into the dining hall and saw the students having their evening meal by candlelight!"

In the summer of 1957 Mrs. Bushnell retired to Saint Petersburg, Florida. There she was active in the League of Women Voters and also worked as a Red Cross Gray Lady. Finally, advancing years necessitated her withdrawal from an active life. She moved into Bradenton Manor, a residence for retired persons at Bradenton, Florida, where she died on March 18, 1970.

Mrs. Bushnell always had a flair for the use of language. She loved words and used them affectionately and at times extravagantly. Perhaps the best summation of her ideals and character is to be found in the telegram that she sent to Chancellor Simpson in response to his request to name a new residence hall in her honor:

> With profound humility I have read your telegram and it is not understandable that so great honor has been accorded me. I beg of the board of visitors they will try to sense my profound gratitude but also to try to understand that I do not wish the publicity attendant on giving my name to the new dormitory though an honor anyone would covet. If I can but have a place in the hearts of the girls who knew me and shared in work and service and in rich comradeship I shall be content. Gratefully
>
> NINA BUSHNELL

WALLACE ALSOP AND IDA

In September 1922 William Wallace Alsop was employed by the college as chauffeur and general utility man. Known as Wallace to hundreds of students and faculty members during his long period of service, Wallace remained on the staff for the next thirty-four years, retiring in July 1956, at the age of seventy-five.

Wallace was born in Fredericksburg in 1881. He had worked locally and also in Washington before becoming a driver for R. G. Hilldrup, a local moving and storage firm. He had been employed by Hilldrup's for ten years at the time he left to work for the college in 1922.

For many years Wallace performed a wide variety of tasks. He was in general charge of the cleaning and maintenance of the trio of buildings on the hill. He drove student teachers back and forth to their duties at Falmouth and other nearby schools. He carried deposits to the bank. He saw that buildings were locked and unlocked, that lights were turned off when they should be, and that things were done that needed to be done.

Wallace made himself invaluable to the college. He was always on hand when needed and could always be counted on to do well what he was asked to do. In 1942 his title was changed to senior mechanic and according to his personnel record he was "placed in charge of all buildings on the campus except the dormitories." His title was changed in 1946 when he was classified as janitor foreman. Each change permitted a slight increase in salary.

When George Washington Hall was completed in 1941 Wallace really came into his glory. He was placed in charge of the new building, the pride of the college, and he literally carried the keys to all facilities there. He saw that the auditorium was unlocked and lighted for convocations, rehearsals, plays, and movies; that the roof garden was set up for dances with the portable lights in place; and that the Hall of Mirrors was shined and polished for the formal dances held there. Wallace was always the last to leave, turning out the lights and locking doors. On formal occasions he would put on a blue-gray uniform trimmed in red with gold braid and stand in the foyer as a sort of official doorman. He was proud of the uniform and he wore it with an air of authority.

Wallace was a man of inherent dignity. He was extremely polite but never servile. He was adamant in enforcing administrative regulations about the use of facilities in the auditorium. His tone was always respectful and at the same time it carried the calm assurance of authority. One of Wallace's interesting habits was the way he would say "Thank you, sir," or "Thank you, ma'am" whenever one greeted him with "Good morning, Wallace." In later years his hair turned gray, but he never lost his energy or his devotion to duty.

On the mural in the entrance foyer of George Washington Hall, Wallace is portrayed in a small panel between the information window and the corridor. Resplendent in his colorful uniform, he stands there alert and ready to help, one of the "old school" of people to whom duty and responsibility were a creed of life. Wallace died on July 7, 1968, at the age of eighty-seven. He was survived by his son, H. Wallace Alsop; two sisters, Ida Alsop Thornton and Clara Alsop Lee; three grandchildren; and six great-grandchildren.[7]

Wallace's sister Ida Alsop Thornton was also a long-time employee of the college. For many years she worked directly under Mrs. Bushnell, seeing that the parlors and other facilities of Virginia Hall were kept in spotless condition.

Ida came to work at the college in 1923 as a maid at a weekly salary of eight dollars. For the next thirty years, she served the institution faithfully and capably. Like Wallace, she was one of the old school, giving to her role at the college a dignity and sense of dedication that ennobled the work in which she was engaged. She stopped working at the end of the summer session in August 1953. Two months before this she had celebrated her

---

[7] *Free Lance-Star,* July 9, 1968.

seventy-sixth birthday. She was nearly ninety at the time of her death.

DEDICATION OF OPEN-AIR THEATRE

In 1923 an open-air theatre was constructed in the grove of trees just below the main campus. It was attractively situated on a natural slope that afforded an excellent view of the stage from the tiers of seats that extended up the hill. Its original seating capacity was approximately eight hundred.

The open-air theatre was dedicated under "ideal weather conditions" on Friday afternoon and evening, May 11, 1923. The next day the *Daily Star* gave a graphic and enthusiastic account of the proceedings in a front-page story headed "Big Day at Normal!"

In the afternoon part of the program the Glee Club sang and the Reverend Dudley Boogher gave an invocation, followed by addresses by President A. B. Chandler, Jr., Senator C. O'Conor Goolrick, State Superintendent of Public Instruction Harris Hart, and Governor E. Lee Trinkle. "In a sterling address" Hart "compared life to a stage," according to the *Daily Star,* and "traced the different kinds of actors."

Governor Trinkle first congratulated the young ladies and the school "upon the beautiful sylvan scenes that surround them." He called upon the future teachers to "banish ignorance from the grand old Commonwealth." The *Star* continued: "Professing himself to be a man of sentiment, the Governor simply swept the audience off their feet as he traced the ancient glories of the Old Dominion and of the long line of heroes who made Virginia their stamping ground."

An audience of over a thousand saw an evening production of Humperdinck's opera *Hansel and Gretel.* Lighting effects of blue and crimson suggested twilight scenes. Dancers performed under the direction of Pearl M. Hicks, and the Glee Club sang under the direction of Eva Taylor Eppes. "Visitors from a distance remarked upon the remarkable fullness and timbre as well as the sweetness and purity of tonal coloration in these young voices," who could be heard distinctly by the remotest members of the audience.

Thus the open-air theatre was dedicated with "eloquent addresses and a beautiful operetta." A congratulatory editorial in the same issue of the *Daily Star* characterized the new theatre as marking "another step in the remarkable development of this splendid Virginia educational institution. . . . The people of this section are very proud of this school and the work it is doing."

The senior class play, *A Midsummer Night's Dream,* was presented in the new outdoor setting. Commencement exercises were also held in the open-air theatre, with G. L. H. Johnson, superintendent of schools in Danville, as the main speaker.

In subsequent years the open-air theatre has been used extensively for May Day programs, commencement exercises, and student and professional performances. Later it was enlarged to seat sixteen hundred people, the stage rebuilt with Greek columns at the sides and rear, and the area extended to accommodate a large company of performers. New lighting was installed to facilitate evening performances during the spring, summer, and early fall.

BETTY LEWIS HALL

The need of additional dormitory facilities resulted in the construction of a new building at the foot of the hill just below the entrance to the college. In 1923 a group of Fredericksburg businessmen formed the Betty Lewis Building Corporation, which planned and financed the new facility and leased it to the college for use as a dormitory.

At a meeting of the executive committee of the Virginia Normal School Board on February 28, 1923, a contract between the college and the corporation was approved.[8] This agreement provided for a ten-year lease to the college at a yearly rental of 10 per cent of the actual cost of the structure when completed, estimated at between $36,000 and $40,000. The college was also to provide ordinary repairs and maintenance. The lease began as of September 15, 1923.

The new building was ready for occupancy in September 1923, and all space was immediately filled. In two years the board authorized a contract with the Betty Lewis Building Corporation for an addition to be erected at a cost of $28,500 and to be leased to the college at an annual rental of 10 percent of this cost.[9] The new addition was completed during the summer of 1925 and brought the total capacity of the building to 110 students.

[8] Minutes of Executive Committee of the Board, Feb. 28, 1923, p. 49.
[9] Minutes of the Board, Feb. 12, 1925, p. 3.

The college continued to use Betty Lewis as a residence hall for students until June 1930, when the availability of new dormitory space on the campus met the demand for rooming space. For the next seven years it was operated by the college as an apartment building. The building had been planned so that it could be readily converted into apartments when the college no longer had need of it. Rooms were arranged in suites, with a bath and kitchenette serving two or more connecting rooms, all of which were occupied as bedrooms when students were housed there.

In September 1937 the need for more dormitory space resulted in a reconversion of the building for student use. It was occupied for this purpose until the construction of additional residence halls made its use unnecessary, and it was sold at auction in 1972.

Betty Lewis Hall was named after the sister of George Washington who married the Revolutionary patriot Fielding Lewis. Born at Wakefield, she came to Fredericksburg at the age of five when the family moved to Ferry Farm across the Rappahannock from Fredericksburg. Betty was only seventeen when she married the widowed Lewis, then twenty-five. In 1752 he built Kenmore for his bride. For the next forty-four years it was her home. Eleven children were born there, only six of whom lived to adulthood.

Colonel Lewis had spent most of his fortune aiding the factory at Fredericksburg that manufactured arms for the Continental army. After his death in 1782, Betty continued to live at Kenmore for the next fourteen years. Until Mary Washington's death Betty enjoyed frequent visits with her mother, who lived just a short walk away in the house still standing at what is now the corner of Lewis and Charles streets. Betty Lewis died while visiting her daughter, Betty Lewis Carter, and her husband, Charles, at Western View, in Culpepper County. She is buried in the Carter family cemetery on the estate.

PHYSICAL EDUCATION MAJOR

The catalogue for 1922–23 announced a four-year course in physical education and supervision, leading to the degree of B.S. in education.

The new major was discussed at the board meeting on July 21, 1922, and it was agreed that the new program, if approved, would be offered only at the Normal School at Fredericksburg. The program as outlined was officially approved by the board at its meeting on January 27, 1923.[10] A listing of the required and elective courses appears in the catalogue announcing courses to be offered in 1923-24 (pp. 60-62).

The third-year major courses offered were playgrounds and pageantry; anatomy and kinesiology; physiology; history and principles of physical education; practical work (gymnastics, games, track events, apparatus work, and folk dances); and systems and organization (management of athletic programs, record keeping, and rules).

In the fourth year the major provided an advanced course in health education; educational and corrective gymnastics; physical diagnosis and anthropometry; practical work (Swedish gymnastics, dance, coaching, and officiating); and practice teaching.

The first two years of the program were devoted to basic courses in English, education, psychology, music, physical and health education, educational sociology, and principles of teaching. Physical education occupied three periods a week each quarter. As students began the major program, emphasis was placed on "standard fundamental training, developing physical soundness and proficiency, establishing the habit of successful study and work, and laying a professional foundation. . . . The first year is the year of personal development." [11]

Pearl M. Hicks, who had been director of physical education since 1920, headed the new major program. In 1924, Isabel M. Chappel, A.B., who had attended Winthrop College and the New Haven Normal School of Gymnastics, joined the faculty. Both Miss Hicks and Miss Chappel were experienced teachers of physical education.

NOW A TEACHERS COLLEGE

As early as 1922 it was proposed that the designation Normal School be changed to Teachers College. At a board meeting on January 12, 1922, President Duke, of Harrisonburg, made "an extensive and exhaustive report" on a questionnaire survey of a great number of institutions, which indicated "a steady and progressive tendency" to incorporate the word *college* in the name of such schools, with many becoming state colleges for women or state teachers colleges. After considerable discussion the board

---

[10] *Ibid.*, July 21, 1922, p. 43; Jan. 27, 1923, p. 46.
[11] *Catalogue*, 1922-23, p. 101.

passed a resolution "that it is the sense of this Board that it is not expedient at this time to change the name of the Normal Schools to Teachers' Colleges." [12]

Just two years later, however, the General Assembly, in an act approved February 13, 1924, changed its normal schools to teachers colleges. In the language of the act, "the State normal and industrial school for women at Fredericksburg shall hereafter be called 'the State teachers college at Fredericksburg.' " [13]

The change was not unexpected. In fact, the 1922–23 catalogue of the State Normal School for Women at Fredericksburg (p. 21) opened with the following statement:

This institution is doing the work of a teachers' college. It is on a four year basis, granting the degree of B.S. in Education for four years of college work based upon graduation from an accredited high school. The Fredericksburg Normal School is a member of the American Association of Teachers' Colleges. It is expected that the name of this institution will, within the next year, be changed to Teachers' College, in order that the name may be indicative of the actual work being done.

A diploma and the Normal Professional Certificate are granted upon the completion of the two years of our four year curriculum, the B.S. Degree and the Collegiate Professional Certificate being granted for the completion of the four years.

The same act also changed the name of the governing board of the institution from the Virginia Normal School Board to the Board of Virginia Teachers Colleges. The duties and rights of the new board, as enumerated in the legislation, were almost identical with those of the former board. The composition remained substantially the same, with Governor E. Lee Trinkle and State Superintendent of Public Instruction Harris Hart as ex officio members. W. C. Locker of Richmond became president of the board, replacing Virginius R. Shackelford of Orange.

The act was passed with the proviso that it was to become effective immediately. No time was lost in changing all publications, stationery, reports, and documents of the institution to reflect the status it now enjoyed. The catalogue of 1924–25 carried the title *State Teachers College, Fredericksburg, Virginia*. The first sentence proudly stated: "This institution is a State Teachers College."

The opening paragraph (p. 20) continued: "Originally or-

---

[12] Minutes of the Board, Jan. 12, 1922, pp. 34, 35.
[13] *Acts of Assembly*, 1924, pp. 14–15.

ganized in 1911 as a Normal School its work has grown and expanded to such an extent that the Legislature in 1924 changed its name to State Teachers College in order that its name may conform to the character of work done, that its students may enjoy the prestige due to the college name, and that the public school system of the State may reap the benefit of the services of teachers who are graduates of a Standard Teachers College."

NEW DEGREE PROGRAM

Even more exciting was the announcement that appeared in capital letters on the following page: "Important Addition: four year B.S. degree course for teaching academic subjects in the regular accredited four year high school has been added for the 1924-25 session. This is the outstanding development for next year. See page 45 for statement of this course."

Preparations for offering degree programs had been under way for some time. In fact, courses at the third- and fourth-year college level were already being offered in public school music, fine and industrial arts, commercial education, and physical education, "leading to the degree of Bachelor of Science in Education." [14]

The catalogue for 1922-23 (pp. 48-49) stated:

The Fredericksburg Normal School is a standard Teachers' College offering the degree of Bachelor of Science in Education. This degree is granted upon the completion of four years of work based upon graduation from an accredited high school. A student is privileged to major in any one of the following four special fields: (a) Public School Music and Music Supervision, (b) Fine and Industrial Arts and Art Supervision, (c) Physical Education and Playground Activities, (d) Commercial Subjects. This is the only Normal School in Virginia, and so far as we know, the only institution in Virginia of any type offering a four year course and a degree in any one of these four special fields.

We are emphasizing our degree courses in each of the four special fields, enumerated above, and invite outstanding high school graduates of the State to enter this institution, having in view the completion of a four year course and the acquisition of the degree. The administration of the school is especially interested in young women of this type and will be glad to correspond with them. The school is in a position to render financial aid to students through student aid positions, or loans, or both, and degree students are especially favored in these respects.

[14] *Catalogue,* 1921-22, p. 43.

The 1923–24 catalogue (p. 45) explained: "These courses are designed to prepare students for teaching any subjects in the Elementary, Junior and Senior accredited high schools, and are so arranged that the student may take majors and minors in those particular subjects which suit her tastes and for which she has had adequate basic preparation in her high school course."

Majors were available in the following areas:

A – Ancient Language (Latin), Modern Language (French), English, History, Mathematics, Science.
B – Public School Music and Music Supervision.
C – Fine and Industrial Arts and Art Supervision.
D – Physical Education and Play-ground Work.
E – Commercial Subjects.

A system of majors and minors provided flexibility and opportunity for electives. Upon completing the degree courses, students were awarded the collegiate professional certificate, the highest granted by the State Board of Education.

This certificate entitled the holder of a degree from a standard college or university who had completed at least eighteen semester hours in professional education courses, including student teaching, to teach all subjects in the elementary school and, in the high school, those subjects in which he had credit for twelve hours of college work in addition to two high school units in that field. Credit for six semester hours of college work was accepted for two high school units in any subject.

Three years of successful teaching experience, as attested by the presentation of statements from the division superintendents under whom the individual had taught, could be substituted for practice teaching provided at least eighteen semester hours' credit in education was offered in addition to practical experience. Actually, this exception was rarely utilized, for most of the students were not experienced teachers. Even the latter usually preferred to take practice teaching as a part of their degree program for the value of the experience and contact with the latest teaching procedures.

The collegiate professional certificate was valid for ten years and was renewable for periods of ten years upon completion of six semester hours of credit usually taken in summer school or by extension. This became the teaching certificate customarily granted to degree graduates of the state teachers colleges.

The normal professional certificate continued to be offered upon completion of the two-year course of study leading to teaching in the elementary grades. This two-year program was discontinued in June 1942.

DIFFERENTIATION POLICY ABANDONED

At a meeting on May 2, 1924, the course of study committee recommended to the governing board—now the Board of Virginia Teachers Colleges—that it adopt the following resolution: "No further effort will be made to continue differentiated courses at the various teachers' colleges. All institutions will be operated on the same basis."

Each institution was to offer a four-year course for high school teaching and a four-year program for elementary teachers. The two-year program for elementary teachers leading to the normal professional certificate was to be continued by all of the schools and organized so that transition to the third and fourth years and a college degree could be accomplished readily as the student was financially or otherwise able to do so.

The board set up minimum academic "constants," or requirements, for all degrees. It also directed that the two-year course for high school teachers and the two-year course in home economics be discontinued. The allocation of certain special subject fields continued. Harrisonburg proceeded to develop a strong program in home economics, while Fredericksburg strengthened its majors in commercial education, physical education, and school music.

At a meeting on May 24, 1924, the board adopted academic requirements for all degrees. It also set up credit-hour specifications for majors and minors. It specified six semester hours of student teaching, as well as four in physical education and two in hygiene, including the physical inspection of school children.[15]

As implemented at Fredericksburg, the new degree program required of all students three years of English, three years of physical education, and courses in hygiene, educational psychology, educational sociology, art appreciation, and applied sociology, as well as professional courses as principles of education, history of education, philosophy of education, school administration, and practice teaching. There was a complicated system of groups of electives to be chosen in accordance with the student's major subject. For example, a student majoring in commerce

---

[15] Minutes of the Board, May 24, 1924.

would take the "Group E: Commercial" electives each year, which really amounted to requirements in that particular curriculum.[16]

While these new developments were taking place, the college became a member of the American Association of Teachers Colleges, a recognition that added greatly to the prestige of the institution.

THE FIRST DEGREE GRADUATES

Curiously enough, the first degree was conferred in 1923 upon Frances Cornick Eckenrode, a native of Fredericksburg, who had taken the major portion of her work at another college. She was unable to return there for the final work for her degree because her presence was required at home. She was accepted as a special student at Fredericksburg in order to permit her to complete the degree requirements. State officials granted special permission for this to be done, and in June 1923 the first degree was conferred upon Miss Eckenrode before the program had actually been in operation long enough for other students then in the college to complete the requirements.[17]

In June 1924 three students completed the fourth year of college-level study in the newly inaugurated program and received their degrees. Molly Coates was granted the B.S. degree in commercial education; Sally H. Norris, the B.S. degree in education, majoring in public school music; and Leah Arden Lewis, the B.S. degree in education, with specialization in art education.

Molly Coates's association with the college was a long and varied one. She entered in the fall of 1919 to complete her high school course and prepare for college entrance a year later. When she finished the two-year diploma course, she discovered to her dismay that she was still too young to receive a teaching certificate. Happily, President Chandler and Dean Tyner arranged for her to work part-time in the dean's office and take the third and fourth years of the new degree course in commercial education just being instituted. Thus in 1924 she became one of the first three students to complete the degree course. She still recalls vividly the beaming face of President Chandler as he presented with pride the realization of a long-cherished dream. He also

---

[16] *Catalogue*, 1924–25, pp. 68–70.
[17] Letter from Molly Coates to author, Sept. 30, 1970, p. 5.

announced that all three recipients would join the college staff in the fall.

In the fall of 1924 Miss Coates joined the faculty as assistant registrar, assistant in the commercial department, and secretary to the dean. Although Dean Tyner was also officially the registrar, his many other duties meant that she really handled the work of that office, maintaining academic records, issuing transcripts, and preparing the periodic reports of student grades. In addition, she taught classes in typewriting and shorthand.

One of her greatest problems was preparing the individual student's schedule during registration so that conflicts could be resolved, subjects required for graduation completed, and any deficiencies made up. She found it difficult but challenging and rather rewarding when a satisfactory program was worked out.

During this period the college began offering evening courses in commercial subjects for interested townspeople. By virtue of having earned a teaching certificate in the Locker method of penmanship, Molly Coates was assigned that course in the evening school. She vividly describes the difficulty of spending a full hour making scrolls and push-pulls with the prescribed pen according to the official method, but her students cooperated wonderfully.

When funds made possible additional secretarial help in the administrative offices, she was given her choice of teaching or the latter. She chose to devote full time to the dean-registrar's office, where, for the next four years, she worked closely with Dean Tyner.

Miss Coates left the college in 1929 when Dean Tyner resigned. For some years she was executive secretary to an organization of doctors in Danville. In September 1956 she once again returned to the administrative offices of the college, this time as secretary to the new chancellor, Dr. Simpson. For the next twelve years she filled that important role in the college. She retired in June 1968 to Locust Toft, near Oak Grove, in her native Westmoreland County. Her hand-drawn Christmas cards with original verse to suit the occasion continue to delight her many friends on the faculty and staff and in the community.

THE MID-TWENTIES

In October 1924 the college published a small leaflet announcing the new degree program. After pointing out the superior opportunities for young women who had completed a four-year course, the announcement went on to this rather curious section, which is of interest especially in view of later efforts, finally successful in 1934, to obtain permission to offer the B.A. degree:

The B.S. vs. The B.A. Degree

The better type of Division Superintendents and High and Elementary School Principals in Virginia have already learned, and the public generally is now fast learning, the superiority of the B.S. Degree over the B.A. Degree for teachers in the various branches of the public school service. This superiority is readily understood when the content of the two Degrees is compared. In a word, it may be said that the B.S. Degree is based upon four years of college work after completing the course of an accredited high school, this college work being a proper combination and coordination of academic and education subjects including supervised student teaching in the particular branches in which the student is majoring and minoring; whereas, the B.A. Degree is usually based upon academic college subjects alone, these subjects being taken with no reference to the student's teaching them. The Teachers Colleges in Virginia are therefore naturally basing their four year courses upon curricula intended specifically to fit young women for the profession of teaching and are conferring the Degree of Bachelor of Science in Education on the completion of the four-year course.[18]

By the session of 1924–25 the faculty of the college had increased from the original fifteen to a total of some thirty-eight. President Chandler and Dean Tyner continued to head the administrative staff; Mrs. Bushnell was dean of women and also taught Bible; Dalia L. Ruff was dietitian and assistant dean of women; Molly L. Coates was assistant registrar and secretary to the dean; and Mrs. John C. Ferneyhough was treasurer and bookkeeper.

Other long-time faculty members who were then teaching included W. N. Hamlet, mathematics and science; Dr. Walter J. Young, social sciences; Eva Taylor Eppes, public school music and voice; and Nora C. Willis, piano. Supervisors in the training school department included Elinor Hayes, M. Josephine Jerrell, Beryl Barber Willis, and Helen W. Carmichael.

The degrees held by the faculty for 1924–25, as listed in the catalogue, included one doctorate (Dr. W. J. Young); ten master's degrees (including President Chandler and Dean Tyner); and thirteen various undergraduate degrees. Fourteen of the teaching and supervisory staff held no degrees, but were graduates of normal schools.

[18] "Degree for Teachers," *Bulletin* 10, no. 3 (1924).

There were only four men on the faculty: President Chandler, Dean Tyner, Dr. Young, and Mr. Hamlet. Dr. Cook was on leave of absence then, studying for a Ph.D. degree in chemistry at the University of Virginia.

By 1924 enrollment had increased markedly. There were 342 college students during the first two quarters of the 1923-24 session and 45 high school students. The following year marked an increase, possibly because of the new degree program, to 412 college students and 34 high school students. There were 52 evening commercial students. The summer school enrollment in 1924 was 452.

COLLEGE ACTIVITIES

College life in 1924-25 was enlivened with a variety of extra-curricular activities. The catalogue list (p. 32) gives a good idea of the important events during the year. The principal extra-curricula activities were:

Y. W. C. A. party to new students; Student Government party to new students; Convocation; party and dance given by second-year girls to first-year girls. Six numbers in the Artists Course as follows:
- Suzanne Keener and Assisting Artists
- Katherine Tift Jones and Georgia Price
- Scottish Musical Company in "The Bonnie Briar Bush"
- The International Artists
- Della Baker and the Balalaika Orchestra
- Maud Huntington Benjamin.

Annual reception of churches of the city to students; Hallowe'en demonstrations; inter-class basketball games; Thanksgiving holiday; Alumnae and Y. W. C. A. bazaar; Faculty Music Recital; Christmas Carols and stocking service; Y. W. C. A. New Year party; Address on "Authorship," by George Allen England; Virginia Reel Club Dance; Illustrated Lectures on Hygiene; Moving Pictures; Varsity Basketball Games vs. Marjorie Webster School of Physical Education, University of South Carolina, Richmond City Normal School, College of William and Mary; Annual Circus, benefit Athletic Association; Exhibit Physical Education Department; Plays by Students; Junior-Senior Reception; Glee Club Recital; Piano Recital by Music Department; Field Day by Physical Education Department and Athletic Club; Annual Trip to Washington and Luray; Senior Class Play; Senior Class Banquet; Alumnae Banquet and Reception; Baccalaureate Sermon; Commencement Address and Delivery of Diplomas and Degrees.

The 1920s

The Field Day program was a high point of the year. There were class contests in a wide variety of sports and events, including basketball, baseball, tennis, swimming, dashes, relay races, high and broad jumps, and the like. Points toward the silver trophy cup were accumulated throughout the session, but the winner was not determined until the culminating activities on Field Day. A small silver cup was also presented to the girl winning the greatest number of points in athletics during the year.

The May queen was crowned in connection with the Field Day program. She in turn awarded monograms and numerals to the members of the different class teams, the varsity basketball team, and winners of different athletic events. Students who won a thousand points in athletics in one year were awarded a school monogram.

KENMORE DEDICATED

On May 9, 1925, Kenmore was dedicated. Distinguished persons who had aided in the restoration of the historic home of Colonel Fielding and Betty Washington Lewis converged upon Fredericksburg for a celebration that drew between ten and fifteen thousand visitors. Governor E. Lee Trinkle was the speaker for the occasion. Students at the college took an active part in the proceedings. Dressed in colonial costumes, they served as hostesses, rode on floats, and performed a May dance on the afternoon program.

The *Battlefield* for 1925 (pp. 177–79) carried a picture of the restored residence, together with a two-page appraisal of what this newly dedicated shrine might mean to the nation in the days to come. It was entitled "Before a National Shrine–Kenmore."

MORE DEGREE GRADUATES

In June 1925 there were seven degree graduates: B.S. degrees in physical education were awarded to Frances Emily Abbitt, Page Harrison, Mary Lightner, Anne Murray, and Indie Lowry Sinclair; a B.S. degree in music to Willie Bivens; and a B.S. degree in science and mathematics to Helen Mills.

Miss Mills subsequently obtained the M.A. degree at Teachers College, Columbia University, and served as supervisor of mathematics and science in the campus training school from 1926 until the school was discontinued in 1938. She then became dean of women at Coker College in Hartsville, South Carolina.

NEW UNIT OF VIRGINIA HALL

On May 19, 1926, construction on the new unit of Virginia Hall was begun with $60,000 borrowed from state funds under the Noel Act as a self-liquidating dormitory project.

When completed, the new addition made possible dormitory accommodations for a total of 110 students on the second and third floors. On the first floor were the offices of the president, the dean of instruction, the registrar, and the treasurer, as well as the library, a faculty and board room, a book and supply room, a student activities room, and the campus post office. The office of the dean of women was on the second floor at the head of the stairs.

NEW FACULTY MEMBERS

The growing enrollment of the institution resulted in a number of new appointments to the faculty in 1925 and 1926. Of the group who began teaching at the college in September 1926 there were three persons whose aggregate years of service to the institution at their time of retirement totaled 127 years: Eileen Kramer Dodd, Oscar H. Darter, and Dorothy Duggan Van Winckel.

EILEEN KRAMER DODD

It was in the fall of 1926 that Dr. Eileen Kramer left her native Pennsylvania to come to Fredericksburg to teach at what was then the State Teachers College. At the time she was one of the few Ph.D.'s—and a woman Ph.D. at that—on the faculty at S.T.C.

Dr. Dodd (her married name) graduated from Muhlenberg College at Allentown in 1922. Subsequently, she attended New York University where she received the M.A. degree in 1924. Her thesis dealt with the psychological and educational ideas of G. Stanley Hall. She continued her graduate study at New York

University, receiving the Ph.D. degree in 1927. Her dissertation topic was "A Study of One Thousand Liberal Arts Students: The Relation between Their Intelligence Test Scores, Grade Averages, and Vocational Ambitions."

Before coming to Mary Washington Mrs. Dodd had taught in the public schools of Northampton and then served as dean of the Anewalt School at Cedar Crest College. She was also head of the department of education at Cedar Crest.

In her inimitable, effervescent way, Mrs. Dodd tells of her arrival on the campus in the fall of 1926:

I had never visited the College prior to my arrival there to teach. Mr. Chandler had met with me in Philadelphia while he was attending a National Education Association Convention there. Although I was considering two other positions at the time, Mr. Chandler talked so enthusiastically about the college and its future prospects that I decided to accept his offer. From then on, my life was cast in Fredericksburg.

I arrived in the late afternoon Sunday after a long, tiresome train trip that had begun at eight that morning. It was one of those unseasonably hot days in early September, and I was thoroughly wilted as I stepped from the train into the summery heat of what was to me a Southern town.

While I did not know it at the time, the R.F. and P. railroad station was being remodeled and not then in use. The train stopped at a temporary wooden shed some distance down the tracks. As I alighted, I wondered what kind of place have I come to?

There was only one taxi on hand, with a Negro driver at the wheel, and, as I shared the cab with other passengers, I asked him to take me to the college. He was uncertain where to deposit me—and I didn't know myself—so he took me and my two large suitcases to Mrs. Bushnell's office on the second floor of Virginia Hall.

I can imagine the appearance I made after that long day on the train. Mrs. Bushnell greeted me pleasantly and decided to call the Chandler residence to see where I was to stay. From hearing one end of the conversation, I gathered that Mrs. Chandler had asked if she should come in her car and take me to my quarters in the faculty annex. Mrs. Bushnell glanced at me for a moment and then replied, "I think she can manage."

And so I arrived at the faculty annex lugging my two suitcases. My first impressions were depressing. My room was on the first floor, next to the bath. There was a tired carpet on the floor, with a hole in it. The furniture consisted of an iron bed, a golden oak bureau—much the worse for wear—a desk, and a single straight-back chair. There were no curtains or draperies at the window. The entire room looked so bare and shabby.

However, when I looked out the window I saw a mimosa tree in full bloom. It was a glorious sight—and I decided to stay.

This was Sunday. My first meal at the College was that evening. It was a light supper consisting of rolls, lettuce and tomatoes, and jelly. At that time, I didn't care for tomatoes, but I ate them anyway, and then spread some jelly on the bread. I was hungry after the long day, and there really wasn't any way to get any other food.

After dinner I met Mary Phoebe Enders, and she was so kind and friendly. In fact, all of the girls in the house were wonderful to me. I began to feel that it might be a good place to stay—and so I stayed.

Students in those days were wonderful. They would come to see you and talk excitedly about their interests and adventures. And the group of teachers in the faculty house—Kate Trent, Elinor Hayes, Louise Elliott, Dorothy Duggan, Molly Coates, Ruth Palmer—were all young people. We had lots of fun together. On Sunday evenings we would share boxes of food from home that various ones would bring, or prepare a supper of waffles. And then we would all go to Sunday night vespers conducted by the Y.W. Everyone went. It was expected. And we all turned out for the various class and other benefits.

I was sponsor of the Junior Class my first year. We decided to have a goat as our symbol. One morning at breakfast we all appeared in the dining hall wearing white skirts and white sweat shirts decorated with a felt green goat. Then the seniors decided to have a distinctive symbol and they adopted a red devil as an emblem. So began the Devil-Goat rivalry that was to last for so many years. There was even a goat song, "Billy Goat," which Molly Coates and I wrote one night during convocation. During *convocation!* Can you imagine it?

Mrs. Dodd came to the college as professor of education, for, at the time, all courses in psychology were given in the department of education. Her specialty was tests and measurements ("I was a committee of one to administer and score all tests given at the college.") ; but she also taught courses in educational psychology and educational sociology. "In those days people taught what was needed to be taught," said Mrs. Dodd. "I taught United States history one session and even arithmetic for elementary grades. I remember now the difficulty one girl had in understanding latitude and longitude."

During the summer of 1930 she and Dr. James H. Dodd, the tall young professor from Mississippi, were married in the president's home at Cedar Crest College by the president of the college, Dr. William Curtis, who was a minister in the Reformed Church. After a honeymoon in Canada, they returned to Fredericksburg for the opening of college. For the next seven years they resided in an apartment at 404 Hanover Street in the home of Agnes Chewning. In 1937 the Dodds moved to their new home, Dodswood, located on a hill above William Street Extended, about a mile west of the college.

Mrs. Dodd always loved to "go to school." During the summers she took graduate courses at Lehigh University, the University of Pennsylvania, New York University, and the University of California. In the early 1950s, when there was much discussion of the Rorschach test, Mrs. Dodd took courses in its administration and interpretation at Duke University, "just to know more about the test."

She was one of the first of the faculty to offer an extension course in cooperation with the University of Virginia. For several years she conducted classes at Orange driving back and forth over the uncertain roads of that time.

For many years she served as faculty sponsor for Alpha Phi Sigma, the national honorary scholastic fraternity at the college. Under her leadership the organization brought many speakers and programs to the institution. It also sponsored teas, musicals, and even Sunday afternoon movies. Through award ceremonies and recognition exercises for students on the dean's list, Alpha Phi Sigma encouraged students to academic achievement. For many years, the organization awarded a cup to the senior having the highest average in the college. When the Darden Award was established in 1960, the Alpha Phi Sigma award became a recognition of the student attaining the highest average in her first two years at the college.

The thousands of students who have been in Mrs. Dodd's classes over the years remember her as a warm, enthusiastic, and capable teacher. Regardless of how many students were enrolled in each class—and her sections in general psychology and child psychology were always large—Mrs. Dodd knew each one of them.

She was always a patient listener to a student's problems, and her counsel was kind, sympathetic, and, most of all, constructive. Her keen perception of a young person's point of view made her an eagerly sought counselor, unofficially but most effectively.

Mrs. Dodd's home was a happy one. Dr. Dodd had courted her when they were both relatively new members of the faculty, and they had planned Dodswood together. Even though Dr. Dodd's visiting professorships took him to the Philippines for a year and to Hong Kong for another year, they never ceased to think of Fredericksburg, and they maintained an active correspondence with their friends back home. The "Dr. Dodd" of the couple was James Harvey. Mrs. Dodd always said she exchanged her doctorate for the Mrs. title when they were married.

During the many years that Mrs. Dodd served as head of the psychology department it was the most popular major on the campus. A number of her students went on to graduate study in psychology, qualifying for positions of responsibility as teachers and practitioners in the field. Mrs. Dodd kept up with large numbers of her former students.

Mrs. Dodd retired in 1970, after forty-four years of service to the college—and to her fellow man. Students admired her not only for what she knew and taught about psychology but for the life she lived and shared so generously with the students and her colleagues at Mary Washington. When a chapter of Phi Beta Kappa was installed at the college on February 22, 1971, she was elected to honorary membership.

OSCAR H. DARTER

Oscar Darter was a native of Tennessee. He had attended Carson-Newman College, at Jefferson City, Tennessee, before completing the diploma course at the State Normal School, in Ada, Oklahoma, in 1916. In the meantime he taught or served as principal of various schools. In 1917 he volunteered for the armed services in World War I. He served with distinction overseas, later becoming an instructor in the American Expeditionary Force in France after the armistice. He also attended the Sorbonne for a time.

Upon his return to the United States in 1919, Dr. Darter began a career of teaching that lasted for the next forty-one years. He served as superintendent of schools in several Oklahoma communities between 1919 and 1925. In the meantime he received his A.B. degree from the State Teachers College at Ada, Oklahoma, in 1922 and served as an instructor in the summer sessions there from 1922 to 1925. He then enrolled as a graduate student at Teachers College, Columbia University, and was awarded the A.M. degree there in 1926. He joined the faculty at Fredericksburg that fall as professor of history and head of the history and social science department, a position he continued to hold for thirty-four years until his retirement in 1960.

Dr. Darter was an energetic and enthusiastic teacher, with a genuine love for his work. In addition to carrying a full load of classes at the college—his specialty was the history of civilization —he organized the International Relations Club and was its sponsor and faculty director for many years. Along with Dr. Cook and Mrs. Ramey, he served as a member of the Joint Council, the disciplinary body of the college. He also was chairman of the chapel committee, scheduling semiweekly programs and presiding at many of them. He initiated a faculty forum.

In addition to his duties at the college, Dr. Darter enrolled for graduate study in history at George Washington University, commuting from Fredericksburg for courses there until, in 1948, he was awarded the degree of doctor of education (Ed. D.). His dissertation was entitled "Fredericksburg and Vicinity in Perspective: A Study of a Rural-Urban Colonial Neighborhood." An abstract appeared in *Summaries of Doctoral Dissertations,* 1947 and 1948, published by George Washington University in 1949.

Dr. Darter was a practicing as well as a teaching historian. In 1957 he published an expanded version of his doctoral dissertation under the title *Colonial Fredericksburg and Neighborhood in Perspective* (New York: Twayne Publishers, 1957). The same year the Bookman Associates published an illustrated pamphlet entitled *Historic Fredericksburg,* currently on sale at historic shrines in the city as a popular condensed account of the community. He has also written *The Darter-Tarter Family* (Richmond: Garrett & Massie, 1965) and *History of the Fredericksburg Baptist Church* (Richmond: Garrett & Massie, 1959).

Dr. Darter's interest in history led to his exploration of the colonial townsite of Marlborough, the early eighteenth-century seat of Stafford County and a flourishing Potomac port in the 1700s. Digging at the site of the town unearthed an elaborate system of boundary walls and foundations, along with hundreds of artifacts now at the Smithsonian Institution in Washington.

Upon his retirement Dr. Darter was appointed professor emeritus of history. He has continued to reside in his home just outside the Sunken Road entrance to the college.

DOROTHY DUGGAN VAN WINCKEL

Also appointed to the faculty in 1926 was Dorothy Duggan, a native of Tennessee. Her father was a professor at the University of Tennessee and served as superintendent of public instruction for the state of Tennessee. Miss Duggan, or Mrs. Edgar T. Van Winckel as she became after her marriage in 1952, graduated with the B.S. degree at the University of Tennessee. After a short period of teaching art both at the high school and college level, including the demonstration school at Peabody College, she received her M.A. degree in art from Peabody in 1926 and came to the College that fall. Thus began an association that was to last for many years.

At first, Dorothy Van Winckel taught all of the courses in art. She sponsored the Art Club, arranged student exhibitions, and was sponsor and then art adviser of the annual. Meanwhile, she continued her own creative activities and her special studies in the summer months.

From 1926 to July 1965 she served as chairman of the art department. As the staff grew larger and the number of courses increased, she concentrated on courses in figure sketching, block printing, and watercolor painting. The major in art continued to develop under her leadership and attracted more and more students.

Mrs. Van Winckel studied art at the Pennsylvania Academy of Fine Arts, the Art Students League in New York, and the Saugatuck Michigan School of Painting. She also held a Carnegie Scholarship for art study at Harvard University. Prints and watercolors have been her specialty, with exhibitions and awards from such groups as the Print Club of Philadelphia, the Washington Watercolor Club, the Norfolk Museum of Arts and Sciences, and the National Association of Women Artists. She has been represented in exhibitions sponsored by the Library of Congress (Parnell Exhibition of Prints) and the Society of American Graphic Artists.

Mrs. Van Winckel retired from the art department in July 1968. Her most recent showing was an exhibition of thirty-seven drawings, wood engravings, lithographs, oil paintings, and pastels, sponsored by the Fredericksburg Savings and Loan Association from May 21 to June 4, 1971. During this period, all but a few of these works of art were purchased by admiring visitors to the exhibition.

MARY PHOEBE ENDERS WILLIS

Also appointed in 1926 was Mary Phoebe Enders as instructor in physical education. A native of Maryland, she graduated at the Sargeant School for Physical Education, in Cambridge, Massachusetts. Upon coming to the college here, she continued her studies and received the bachelor of science degree in August 1929. She continued to teach until her marriage to Jere M. H. Willis, an attorney and former mayor of Fredericksburg.

In June 1944, when Mary Washington College became affiliated with the University of Virginia as the coordinate liberal arts college for women, she was appointed to the board of visitors. She served for two terms, or a total of eight years, until 1952. During most of this time, she was on the Mary Washington College committee of the board.

Mary Phoebe Willis describes her work on the board as an inspiring experience. It was a period of expansion and development. The fine arts center was erected, and both Brent Hall and later the Brompton estate were acquired by the college. Mrs. Willis has continued her service to the college by active participation in alumnae affairs.

CHAPTER VIII

The College in 1928

STUDENT ACTIVITIES BUILDING

As EARLY as 1922 a campaign was in progress among students, faculty, alumnae, and friends of the college to raise funds for a student-alumnae building. It was to be a rather elaborate structure containing not only a swimming pool but recreation rooms, alumnae offices, and other facilities now associated with student union buildings. It was to cost a minimum of fifty thousand dollars. Various ways of raising money were employed. In January 1923 a tearoom was opened in the rear basement of Willard Hall and operated by the local chapter of the Alumnae Association for the benefit of the proposed building.[1]

With a new major in physical education approved and in operation, the need for provision for instruction in swimming became urgent. The miniscule pool in the basement room of Monroe Hall was hopelessly inadequate. Early in 1926 further steps were taken to obtain the needed facility. President Chandler pleaded the case before a board meeting on January 18, 1926. At that time he had a very modest building in mind. He proposed that the college charge each student a special fee of five dollars for swimming facilities. In two years the revenue "would amount to $4,000.00 which," according to President Chandler, "would provide sufficient funds to build such a structure."[2] The proposal failed to receive approval.

An intensive campaign to raise money for the Student-Alumnae Building was made during the session of 1926–27. A leaflet describing the project stated that "the college has been endeavoring for four years to secure funds from students, alumnae, faculty, friends of education and of the college for this much needed building." Assured of a legislative appropriation of $25,000 if the college was able to raise the balance of the estimated $71,000 cost, campaign leaders sought to raise the sum needed before March 1, 1927, in order that construction might begin.

By the fall of 1926, the college had on hand a total of $7,000 cash in bank and $12,000 in unpaid pledges. Each alumna was

[1] *Catalogue*, 1923–24, p. 25.   [2] Minutes of the Board, Jan. 18, 1926.

now asked to give or raise $30.00 for the new building. Members of the faculty and student body were asked to make sacrifices and, through cooperative effort, raise a significant sum during the 1926–27 session.

Unfortunately, in spite of all efforts, the goal set was not attained. It became evident that other means of fund-raising were needed. President Chandler appeared before the board on April 29, 1927, and received approval for the construction of a Student Service Alumnae Building during the summer of 1927. He reported that he now had about $10,000 on hand from the previous drives and asked permission to have a "professionally conducted" campaign during August 1927 to raise "the remaining $10,000 needed." The board approved with the understanding that it was not obligated financially.[3]

The services of a fund-raising agency were obtained. Each solicitor was furnished with a "Workers' Sales Manual—Greater Fredericksburg Teachers College Service Building." This brochure explained how to approach contributors and how to answer their objections. The campaign bulletin gave answers to such objections as "I don't like the way the College runs things," "I won't get any benefit from the Service Building," and "Fredericksburg High School hasn't even a gymnasium."

Appeals were made to civic pride, to commercial benefits of having the college in Fredericksburg ("If you own a nickel's worth of real estate in this town, it is of greater value today because of the worth of this College"), and to the advantage of having such an institution in attracting new residents. President Chandler's five years of effort to raise the money were also referred to.

A printed list of pertinent questions and answers got to the heart of why one should contribute to a state institution, what businesses profited from the college, and whether local citizens were encouraged to visit the college. President Chandler was quoted as having offered the use of the swimming pool to high school girls in Fredericksburg. The local high school was already using the gymnasium in Monroe Hall for its practice sessions and its interscholastic games.

The campaign was launched on Tuesday afternoon, August 2, 1927, with a mobilization meeting at the campaign headquarters. That evening the four hundred students of the college staged a

[3] *Ibid.*, April 29, 1927.

twilight parade, led by the Elks Band, through the business section of the city to arouse interest in the project.

The *Free Lance-Star* the next day described the parade as "an attractive and inspiring sight," as students marched with locked arms in files of six abreast, dressed in white with brown and gold caps and carrying banners reading "Speak a Good Word for the College." Streets were filled with spectators.

The next morning there was an Early Bird Breakfast to organize the solicitors, after which they fanned out through the city in a whirlwind effort to obtain contributions. The "Sales Army" was headed by "Colonel" Claude Parcell, who was assisted by Mrs. Duff Green, "Major of the Women's Division." There were various team captains and lieutenants, with each team calling on about twenty-five persons. W. J. Ford was "Commanding General" of the drive.

The campaign was given front-page coverage by the *Free Lance-Star* except on Tuesday, when President Coolidge's "I do not choose to run for President in 1928" produced banner headlines. Fifty representative citizens worked as solicitors. There were daily report luncheons or dinners on Wednesday, Thursday, and Friday. These workers gave practically their full time to the intensive campaign. By the end of the week, when the drive was scheduled to end, a total of $23,500 had been pledged. It was decided to continue the campaign another week, which "the workers promised enthusiastically to do." On August 9 the newspaper described the response as "somewhat general," although many people in the city had not made contributions.

The final drive was successful, for at a campaign luncheon at one o'clock on Wednesday, August 10, it was announced that the goal of $35,000 had been reached, counting a few promised subscriptions from firms still awaiting final action by their boards or executives. The announcement was greeted with great enthusiasm, and it was stated that construction would begin immediately.

President Chandler was eloquent in thanking all workers and subscribers and the *Free Lance-Star,* as the paper reported on August 10. He declared, "It makes us extremely happy out at the college to know that through the untiring efforts of the Greater Teachers College Committee the funds have now been secured for the first unit of the building. . . . The College feels deeply indebted to its many friends who have rallied in this crisis." Some difficulty was experienced in collecting all of the amounts pledged. However, with the help of a state appropriation of $11,-

000, the amount needed was at hand, and construction was begun.

Work on the new swimming pool structure progressed rapidly. It was dedicated as the "first unit of the Student Service Building" on February 18, 1928, in the presence of faculty, students, notables from the city, and a considerable number of alumnae. Attorney General John R. Saunders came from Richmond to give the main address, and President Chandler outlined the history of the project. A program of "water stunts" followed, and the facility was then open for inspection. An interior picture of the pool dedication, with students in white lined up around the edges, appeared on the last page of the 1927–28 catalogue, which gave (p. 31) the following description of the new facility: "A commodious and modern swimming pool, costing $36,000.00, unsurpassed in its appointments by any pool in the State, has recently been completed and is open to all Students. The pool has the following features: 25 × 60 ft.; tile lined; splash trough; gallery for spectators; dressing rooms; showers; electric dryers; equipment room; chlorination, filtration and heat distributing machinery. It is used both on instructional and recreation basis."

Meanwhile, President Chandler had continued his efforts to obtain an appropriation to complete the Student-Alumnae Building as planned. On July 22, 1927, he appeared before the board to seek $35,000 "to match local funds" and complete the building, but no state funds were actually budgeted. At the time he also sought, without success, to obtain $18,000 for building and equipping a faculty apartment house.[4]

The new swimming pool, temporarily roofed over, for a time awaited the completion of the rest of the building above it. Later President Combs had the roof remodeled and replaced with terrazzo flooring and raised side walls, converting the area into an open-air roof garden.

For many years, the dances on the roof garden were a feature of college social life. At night, ornamental electrified lanterns were placed at intervals along the surrounding balustrade. From the dance floor the strains of soft music wafted across the campus on Friday or Saturday evenings during the summer session and in the early fall and late spring of the regular session.

A buffet for refrshements was set up at one end, where the dancers could refresh themselves with cups of brightly colored cold punch and small cakes made by the home economics department. Occasionally, on warm summer evenings, the lights were

---

[4] *Ibid.*, July 22, 1927.

dimmed so that dancers could enjoy the light of the moon and stars shining brightly above.

STUDENT TEACHING

Until 1934 every student who received a degree or diploma from the college was required to take courses that would qualify her for a teaching certificate in Virginia. This requirement included student teaching, or supervised teaching, which received much emphasis. The requirement was waived only in the most unusual circumstances.

The training school was regarded as the "practical workshop and educational laboratory" of the Normal School. As the catalogue of 1918–19 (pp. 32–33) stated, "it is necessary in the Training School to teach children and to train student teachers, and through the real development of the child the student gains most help in her own development as a teacher."

In his first report to the board as president, President Chandler devoted considerable space to the possible ways of improving the facilities for student teaching.[5] He proposed higher standards and higher salaries for the critic-teachers and their nomination jointly by the city superintendent of schools and the head of the department of education at the Normal School. He also proposed a cooperative agreement with Spotsylvania County so that seniors might get practice teaching in rural schools. This proposal resulted in the use of Lee Hill School, a two-room school near Fredericksburg, for training purposes.

Most of all, President Chandler desired to have a training school on the campus, operated and controlled by the Normal School. One of his first steps was to recommend such a project to the board. He indicated how such a school might be supported by payments made by the county and the city as tuition for the pupils from these political divisions whose schooling was provided for in this manner.

The construction of a campus training school was not to come for several years. The contract with the city for practice teaching in the elementary grades was renewed in 1919. The Normal School agreed to pay half the salaries of the critic-teachers and half the cost of the supplies, including heat, for the rooms used for student teaching.

[5] *Ibid.*, May 30, 1919, p. 2.

The arrangement with the city schools for elementary student teaching continued until June 1925, "maintained by a happy cooperation between the College and the City School Board."[6] During this period the Normal School published a 174-page course of study for history and geography, grades one through seven, developed in the "training schools" and organized and edited by Dr. Walter J. Young.[7]

However, occasional misunderstandings between city teaching staff and college supervisory personnel put an increasing strain on the cooperative agreement. Education instructors up on the Hill were said to have used their observation of teachers in the city schools in a highly critical fashion and to have "picked to pieces" the lessons they brought students to observe. In any case, the contractual agreement was discontinued after June 1925.

For several years preceding this severing of relations, the college had also been using the Lee Hill School for rural practice teaching in grades one through seven, the high school classes at the Normal School for student teaching at that level, and the Evening Business Extension School for practice teaching in commercial subjects, mainly typing and shorthand.

Now the college arranged to rent the adjacent property of Mrs. J. B. Mitchell as a training school. The board approved a five-year contract and authorized funds to put the building in shape.[8]

This was, at best, a makeshift arrangement. However, together with facilities and classes in Monroe Hall, the college was able to provide student teaching in grades one through eleven. Lee Hill School continued to be used for grades one through six, and now a new contract with Stafford County permitted the use of the Falmouth Elementary School for student teaching in those grades. A small bus was used to transport student teachers to the training centers off campus.

In August 1927 the college completed a five-year contract with the Spotsylvania County School board whereby the county would pay $900 a year toward the operation of the Lee Hill School; $2,500 a year toward the operation of the College Heights Elementary School (the rented structure described previously); and $20 per high school student per session in the College Heights High School (mainly classes in Monroe Hall). The college for its part agreed to bear all expenses of instruction and maintenance in these facilities. An interesting feature of the contract was the pro-

[6] *Catalogue*, 1923–24, p. 49.
[7] "History-Geography Syllabus for Elementary Grades," *Bulletin* 7, no. 4 (1922).
[8] Minutes of the Board, May 24, 1924, p. 66.

vision that the county school board agreed to "cooperate with the College in securing a legislative appropriation for an adequate training school building on the College campus."

President Chandler continued to urge the appropriation of funds for the training school building. At its meeting on January 18, 1928, the board authorized the inclusion of $70,000 in the budget for this purpose, and the General Assembly authorized the appropriation.[9] A site had already been selected and approved, and contracts for construction were immediately negotiated. It was hoped that the building could be ready for the opening of the 1928–29 session. College staff and faculty members were elated. At last, excellent provisions for observation and student teaching, elementary and high school, were to be had right on the campus itself.

THE NEW TRAINING SCHOOL

The erection of the new structure on the campus was announced with pride and enthusiasm. The 1927–28 catalogue (p. 31) carried the following notice: "A new training school building is now under construction on the campus of the College, at a cost of $70,-000.00. This building is to be modern in all its appointments. When completed no institution in the State will have superior practice teaching facilities to the Fredericksburg Teachers College, either for Elementary or High School work. This building will be ready for the regular session, 1928–29."

The frontispiece of the catalogue is a reproduction of the architect's drawing, by Charles M. Robinson, of the Campus Training School. It shows a series of classrooms facing the central campus which were not actually built, probably because of the cost. It was not until many years later that this part was added, when the building was no longer being used as a training school.

Very appropriately, the new school building was named Chandler Hall, in memory of the president who had worked so hard to get it established.

The school itself was known variously as the Campus Training School, College Heights High School, or simply the training school. With its equipment, it represented an expenditure of seventy-two thousand dollars. E. G. Heflin of Fredericksburg was the builder. The *Free Lance-Star* on September 4, 1928, described the

---

[9] *Ibid.*, Jan. 18, 1928.

The College in 1928

new building as "the handsomest and most complete of all the college group," containing classrooms, lavatories, offices, library, teachers' rest room, drinking fountains, and "every other needed modern facility both for the comfort and convenience of the teachers and students and for the program of education."

The building was a three-story structure. On the ground floor were classrooms for the primary grades, a home economics laboratory, storage rooms, and toilet facilities. The second floor contained classrooms for grades four, five, six, and seven, and some office space for staff members. The third floor housed the high school department. It included laboratories for biology and chemistry, the principal's office, and other office space.

In order to facilitate the teacher education program, observation rooms were provided on two of the floors, located between the two largest classrooms equipped with sliding doors that would permit closing off the spaces on either or both sides. Built on a slightly higher floor elevation, they provided space where a dozen or more college students could be seated as observers of the classes in progress on either side of them.

It was planned originally that auditorium and gymnasium facilities would be added later, but this idea was never carried out. In the early days of the new school, pupils used the gymnasium and auditorium in Monroe Hall. They also were permitted to use the college library. To the rear of the building an athletic field for the high school group was laid out, while smaller play spaces for the elementary children were provided on the sides of the school.

Great care was taken in planning and equipping the new school. It was staffed with a capable and experienced group of supervisors.

Selected as principal was C. Allmand Edwards, a graduate of Randolph-Macon College with a master's degree from Teachers College, Columbia University. Edwards had had considerable experience as a high school principal, having served in this capacity at Ashland, Burkeville, Toano, and Waverly in the eighteen years preceding his appointment. He also was supervisor of social studies.

Mr. Edwards and three of his supervisory staff worked at the Campus Training School until it was discontinued in 1938. They were Elinor L. Hayes, supervisor of the primary grades; Muriel I. Sanders, supervisor of languages; and Helen Mills, supervisor of mathematics and science.

Miss Hayes and Miss Mills were graduates of the college. Miss

Sanders had received her bachelor's degree from Westhampton College of the University of Richmond. All were working on master's degree programs at Teachers College, Columbia University; by 1932 all had been awarded their graduate degrees.

Other members of the first staff included Kate G. Trent, a graduate of Farmville, who served as supervisor of primary grades, and later grades four and five, until 1936; M. Josephine Jerrell White, a graduate of the Fredericksburg Normal School, who had held supervisory positions at the school since 1922; and Beryl B. Willis, also a diploma graduate, who had supervised student teachers since 1924.

The full-time staff in the training school had the assistance of a number of members of the regular college faculty in the supervision of student teachers. All of the special fields, such as physical education, art, music, and commercial subjects, were handled by instructors who were teaching these subjects in the college. This work was done as an extra service and was not usually considered a part of the teaching load, although classroom visits, conferences with student teachers, and the preparation of final rating sheets and grades were involved. Through such an arrangement the training school was able to offer an enriched program of studies at a time when many other schools were concentrating on the basic elementary school subjects and the high school units ordinarily required for graduation.

Student teaching was a serious business. In the elementary grades, students taught full time from nine to three daily for a quarter (three months). There was also a companion course in the afternoons on problems of teaching, as well as the daily conferences with the supervisor. The normal professional course students took only this work during the quarter in which they taught.

Since each supervisor usually had two elementary grades under her care, the student teachers really taught the classes. They were required to report to college earlier in September, for the train-training school followed the calendar of the Spotsylvania County schools. Ordinarily, two student teachers were assigned to an elementary classroom each quarter, so there was opportunity to alternate or to share teaching responsibilities. However, with preparation of lesson plans, organization of reading groups, and the creative job of teaching expected of them, there was little time for relaxation. Elementary majors who took the two-year diploma program first and then came back for their degrees did student teaching again in their senior year, but it was only on a part-time basis for one quarter, for there were other senior subjects to be taken.

Student teachers in high school subjects also had full responsibility for their classes. Miss Sanders supervised both English and Latin; Miss Mills had both science and mathematics. Again, there were frequently two student teachers to a classroom, who shared the responsibility. Students were expected to complete ninety hours of classroom teaching. In addition each had responsibility for sponsoring some type of extracurricular activity. Social science student teachers served as advisers for the Student Government Association in the training school and sponsored the International Relations Club there. English student teachers helped with the mimeographed newspaper and the annual and sponsored activities such as Book Week and special holiday observances. There were a choral club, a commercial club, basketball teams, a dramatic club, and various other organizations, all assisted by student teachers, most of whom were members of groups of a similar nature in the college itself.

Arrangements to transport pupils to the new school involved the cooperation of several agencies. The college purchased a "new Reo school bus" for the transportation of the upper grades of Falmouth School. The Spotsylvania County school board made contracts for the transportation of the Lee Hill children. The Stafford County school board contracted with the college to accommodate a number of high school pupils from that county.

The majority of the students came from Spotsylvania County. For a fixed sum paid annually by the county, the college agreed to provide instruction from the first grade through the high school and all costs of operating the school for children living in the Livingston school district. The county in turn agreed to provide bus transportation to the new school.

The new building was not completely ready for use on Monday, September 17, the date scheduled for its opening. Arrangements were made to hold classes temporarily in the old training school building and in classrooms in Monroe Hall for the ten days necessary to get furniture and equipment installed and the school building ready for occupancy. By early October the training school was in full operation with a total enrollment of some four hundred pupils. Of these, approximately one hundred were in the high school and three hundred in the elementary grades.

Elementary and high school pupils on the campus were to be a familiar sight until June 1938, when the training school was discontinued. A contract was signed with the city school board for student teaching in high school subjects and special fields such as art, music, and physical education in the elementary grades. A new off-campus program for apprentice teaching in the elementary grades was also initiated.

STUDENT REGULATIONS

Rules and regulations governing student life in the late 1920s seem archaic indeed in this day of permissiveness. Not only were hours of study, rest, and recreation specified, but walks about the campus, trips to town, and, above all, conduct with dates were carefully regulated.[10]

Study hour was from 7:15 to 10:00 every night except Saturday and Sunday. Students were required to be in their rooms, in Monroe Hall, or in the library. No visiting was allowed. If there should be any form of entertainment put on by the college in the evening, such as lyceums and/or special lectures—and all were "expected to come" to such programs—the study hour was observed from 3:30 to 5:30 in the afternoon.

A "recreation period" from 10:00 to 10:30 followed the study hour, when students were allowed to visit each other in their rooms. At 10:30 the quiet hour began with each student in her own room and "no unnecessary noise." At 10:30 the lights-out bell rang. From then until the rising bell, each room "should be quiet." Students were not allowed to use lights again before 5:00 A.M.

Students of those days tell of using lights in bathrooms or closets, with towels covering all cracks, to study late for a test, with risk of a call before Student Council if discovered. A more common practice when tests were in progress was to set the alarm at 5:00 A.M. and get in two good hours of study before the rising bell sounded at 7:00.

Rules were relaxed somewhat on Saturday and Sunday nights. Although dates were required to leave at 10:00 P.M., students could visit each other in their rooms until 10:30. Then began the fifteen-minute quiet hour, with lights to be out at 10:45. Vespers were held each weekday evening at 6:30 after supper in the parlor, conducted by the YWCA. On Sundays there was a morning watch, "to start the day right," and an evening Y service, varied and rather elaborate in nature, with songs, musical programs, and inspirational messages.

[10] *Student Handbook,* 1928–29, pp. 36–48.

The College in 1928

Students were allowed to take rural walks on Sunday "in groups of four or more." A maximum of three trips to town per week was allowed. Two of these could not be taken on the same day. The route to town was carefully specified. Students were to use Cornell and Lewis streets until reaching the center of town. Residents of these streets recall the steady click of heels on Sunday morning as students walked to and from church. On other days, the passersby moved in groups of two, three, or four, depending upon their class privileges.

Riding in automobiles was regarded as an especially pernicious pastime, fraught with danger for the unsuspecting students. Students were allowed to ride in cars only when accompanied by a member of the faculty or the immediate family; in a for-hire vehicle; or "directly to or from town with approved boys or men." Night riding was strictly forbidden. Violations of this rule resulted in campusing for months or, in the case of a repeated offense, suspension for an indefinite period.

The number of evening trips to town was quite limited. Sophomores were allowed to go one night a month, in groups of four, to movies or other approved entertainment. Juniors were allowed two night trips to town, still in groups of four, and seniors could go once a week, in groups of three or more.

Meals in town, at approved eating places, were also strictly limited, with the specifications varying according to class. Special permission to be absent from the dining hall had to be obtained from the dean of women. Dining room rules were carefully outlined. Students were required to attend all meals except Saturday and Sunday breakfast, when cuts were allowed. A record of attendance was kept and reported to the Student Government Association.

There was no cafeteria service, of course. Students were seated at tables of eight. Each table included some members of each of the four classes, with a junior or senior presiding. All meals were served family style, with student waitresses carrying the heavy trays to and from the kitchen. Students were expected to dress neatly for meals. Anything like slacks or hair curlers would be unheard of. At breakfast and lunch each table was dismissed as a unit by the hostess at that table. At dinner the dining room was dismissed as a whole by the dean of women. No one thought of rising from her chair until the signal for dismissal had been given, usually by a slight nod of the head from Mrs. Bushnell.

Some of the miscellaneous regulations seem amusing today. For example, the student handbook for 1928–29 (pp. 40–41) included the following rules:

1. Students shall neither stand nor walk on the streets with young men; nor are they to sit with them in automobiles or public places.

2. Students are not allowed to go to town on Sunday except to Sunday school and to church in the morning.

3. Students shall not enter drug stores or any other stores on Sunday.

4. Students are not permitted to walk through the grove with men at night. They may, however, walk up to the Tea Room with them on Saturday night.

5. Students shall be allowed to stroll on the campus with dates Sunday afternoon and to stroll through the Open-Air Theatre Grove. In addition, they shall be allowed to entertain on the campus in the afternoon anywhere within the area between Frances Willard, Virginia, and Monroe Halls.

6. Students are not to stroll beyond Betty Lewis at any time.

7. Students may go—without hats—to points as far as Hanover Street, beginning at the G. & H. Clothing Company, east, and extending west as far as corporate limits. No riding to or from this area. (Should students go beyond limits stipulated above, it becomes a rural walk, necessitating four in the group.)

The handbook for 1928–29 also contained the full text of all five verses of the Alma Mater song, with music by Mildred Stewart, class of '28. Usually, only the first and last verses were sung during the years that followed, when Alma Mater was sung to conclude every convocation and also at many other formal and informal gatherings of students.

JUNE 1928

Commencement activities on the weekend of June 2–4 followed the usual pattern. On Saturday evening there was the annual Alumnae Association banquet. Mrs. Bushnell welcomed the group, and Dean Tyner spoke. The alumnae dance followed. On Sunday morning the baccalaureate sermon was preached by the Reverend William A. Ryan, assistant pastor of the Seventh Street Christian Church in Richmond.

Graduation exercises were held the next morning at eleven o'clock before what was described as a record-breaking crowd. Rain forced the removal of the program from the open-air theatre to the auditorium of Monroe Hall. There were eighty-eight graduates, twenty-nine of whom were awarded the B.S. degree and fifty-nine received the two-year diploma. The principal address was delivered by Dr. Joy Elmer Morgan, editor of the *Journal* of

The College in 1928 145

the National Education Association. President Chandler gave a final message to the graduates.

SUMMER SESSION, 1928

The summer quarter for 1928, "for men and women" according to the catalogue, opened on June 11. It was now a full quarter of the college year, with first and second terms of six and five weeks, respectively. The opening enrollment of 250 was expected to increase to 300 by the end of the week.

Among the visiting professors that summer were Fred M. Alexander, president of the Virginia Education Association, who was working on his doctorate at Teachers College, Columbia University, at the time. Dr. Alexander later became director of secondary education at the State Department of Education and was the guiding spirit behind the new curriculum program launched throughout Virginia in 1933.

The summer session for 1928 closed with commencement exercises held in the open-air theatre on Friday evening, August 24. The speaker was Dabney S. Lancaster, secretary of the State Board of Education. Seniors marched in cap and gown. They were hooded by Dean Tyner and awarded their degrees and diplomas by President Chandler. The college Glee Club entertained with selections.

Two-year diplomas were awarded to twenty-nine students completing their work at that time. In addition, eight students finished their degree programs and received the degree of bachelor of science in education. The exercises closed with a "brief but impressive" message to the graduates by President Chandler.

A NEW SESSION BEGINS

The eighteenth session of the college opened on Tuesday, September 18, 1928, with an enrollment about fifty above the attendance of the previous session. The orientation program for freshmen began with a lecture at 1:45 P.M. by Dean Tyner, "Choosing Your Course, Explanations of Credits, Academic Standards, Records and Reports, Certification of Teachers, Diplomas and Degrees." The rest of the afternoon and the entire evening were devoted to registration (by alphabetical groups), physical examinations, and photographs, with time out for supper and a get-acquainted social hour of songs and yells.

Conferences with students, registration, and physical examinations continued throughout the next day and on into the evening, with a 45-minute break for a lecture by Mrs. Bushnell, "First Aid to the New Student, Social and Practical."

Thursday's activities for freshmen—hopefully they had managed to complete registration and "classification" by then!—included an open forum sponsored by the student government in the morning, tours of "Historical Fredericksburg, with guides," in the afternoon, and "complimentary moving pictures" that evening. Upperclassmen registered on Thursday, with no special orientation. Regular class work for all students began the next Thursday at 8:30, with the announced slogan, "A schedule for everybody and everybody following the schedule." Wisely, day students had been advised to register in advance, before September 15, "to avoid the rush at the opening."

NEW FACULTY MEMBERS

In the fall of 1928 there were quite a number of additions to the faculty. Among them were two persons who were to render long and distinguished service to the college: Dr. James Harvey Dodd and Mildred McMurtry Bolling.

JAMES HARVEY DODD

Dr. James Harvey Dodd was a native of Mississippi, born near the town of Chester on January 30, 1892. He received his A.B. degree from Western Kentucky College (now Western Kentucky University) in 1924, with a major in accounting and business administration.

Dr. Dodd continued his studies at Peabody College at Nashville, where he did advanced work in economics. He received his A.M. degree in 1925 and the Ph.D. degree in 1928. Dr. Dodd taught at Ward-Belmont School in Nashville from 1925 to 1927. During the session of 1927–28 he served as associate professor of economics and business administration at Franklin College, Franklin, Indiana, the position he held when called to Fredericksburg as professor of commercial education and head of the commercial department. When he joined the faculty in 1928 the commercial department was a relatively inconspicuous part of the college program, offering courses primarily in shorthand, type-

The College in 1928

writing, and accounting, with two other instructors on the staff.

In 1919 the Virginia Normal School Board had allotted certain fields to each of the then four state teachers colleges, "in order to avoid overlapping and duplication." The college at Fredericksburg was assigned the role of developing majors in commercial education and physical education in order to prepare teachers of these subjects for the public schools of Virginia.

Under Dr. Dodd's leadership the commercial major at Fredericksburg developed into a nationally known program. Curriculum V became the most popular major at the college. The enrollment in this field reached its peak about 1944, when there were over seven hundred students following the business education program (about one-half of the student body at the time), and the faculty in the department numbered fourteen.

Although many of these students were taking the two-year secretarial program then offered, the number of degree graduates was large; their services were sought widely as teachers of business subjects. This college was the first to arrange and require business experience for all of its degree majors in the department.

Dr. Dodd was a productive and nationally known scholar in the field of economics. In 1936 he published the first of his books, *Introductory Economics,* a widely used high school text that went through many editions and firmly established his reputation in the field. In later editions the title was changed to *Applied Economics,* with the South-Western Publishing Company continuing as publisher. The seventh edition was published in 1967. Mrs. Dodd collaborated in preparing the workbooks and tests that accompanied the various editions.

In 1945 the Marine Corps Institute published Dr. Dodd's third edition of *Applied Economics* in paperback form for use in the course in economics offered members of the corps through the instructional program of the institute. The 567-page edition carries the Marine Corps seal on its cover. In 1944 Dr. Dodd collaborated with Louis A. Rice and Augustin Cosgrove in writing *First Principles of Business,* which was published by D. C. Heath and Company.

In 1948 the first edition of *Economics—Principles and Applications,* by J. H. Dodd and Carl Hasek appeared. Published by the South-Western Publishing Company, this well-known college text was used by over three hundred colleges and universities. In 1965 the fifth edition appeared, this time with Thomas J. Hailstones as coauthor. Each edition of both the high school and the college texts involved extensive revision by Dr. Dodd, not to mention the proofreading necessary. In the fifth edition the title was changed to *Economics: An Analysis of Principles and Policies*, the title under which the text is currently published.

In 1953–54 Dr. Dodd served as Fulbright lecturer at the University of the Philippines. Mrs. Dodd accompanied her husband during his stay there. He also served as visiting professor of economics at the summer sessions of the University of Tennessee, the University of Virginia, and Peabody College. He was the author of many articles in professional journals and collaborated in the preparation of Coronet Instructional Films in his field. One year he gave a series of lectures in economics for the American Telephone and Telegraph Company in Washington.

Dr. Dodd retired from his teaching duties at Mary Washington at the end of the 1962 session, at which time he was elected professor emeritus. The following year he served as visiting professor of economics at the United College of the University of Hong Kong. His lectures at New Asia College were translated into Chinese, and a handsomely bound copy was presented to him as a farewell gift.

Dr. Dodd took an active part in the life of the college and the community. He organized Sigma Tau Chi, an honorary fraternity for majors in commercial education, chapters of which were subsequently established in a number of other colleges. He served as consultant for the business education course of study produced by the Virginia State Board of Education during 1936–39. In 1935–37 Dr. Dodd was president of the Southern Business Education Association. He was also a president of the Fredericksburg Rotary Club.

Dr. Dodd died on June 10, 1969, after a fairly long illness. He was buried in Oak Hill Cemetery, with long-time associates serving as pallbearers. He was survived by his wife, Eileen Kramer Dodd.

MILDRED McMURTRY BOLLING

Mildred McMurtry—or Mrs. J. Brawner Bolling as she was known after her marriage in 1937—also came to the college in the fall of 1928. She was born in Indiana where her father had just completed his Ph.D. degree at Wabash College. Mrs. Bolling grew up in the Middle West. At the age of twenty she received the A.B. degree from Colorado College, specializing in classical and modern languages. Her father was dean of the college at the time.

The College in 1928

From Colorado she went to the University of Missouri, receiving the M.A. degree at the end of the 1921–22 session, again with intensive study in languages. For two years she taught at Lamar (Colorado) Union High School before going to the College of Emporia, where for four years (1924–28) she taught Latin, Greek, and French. In 1928 she came to Fredericksburg as professor of foreign languages at the State Teachers College.

She taught all of the foreign languages offered at that time: three classes in French and three in Latin. The college offered at that time no beginning classes in either of these languages. Students were expected to have completed at least two units of high school work to enroll for the intermediate or advanced classes in the language then being offered.

In addition to the six college courses mentioned, each with an enrollment of ten or twelve students, she also supervised student teachers in French and Latin in the Campus Training School. There was no foreign language requirement for any degree at the time. Students who took these languages were usually preparing to teach them, and motivation was high.

Library facilities in foreign languages were decidedly limited. Mrs. Bolling recalls that when she came to the college there were only seven books in French in the library. Three of these textbooks, and one was a translation into English of two French plays.

Mrs. Bolling recalls vividly her first impressions of the college. President Chandler met her at Virginia Hall and walked with her to the Faculty Annex to show her to the room she would occupy. In a gracious and courtly way, he toured the whole house with her and sought to make her feel at home. Only female faculty members resided at the Faculty Annex. It had been the main building of the City Poor Farm before this facility was relocated. The rambling structure was later divided into two parts and moved a short distance to new locations on College Avenue and an adjoining street. Both buildings have since been thoroughly modernized and are occupied as residences by private individuals.

Mrs. Bolling remembers well the two years she resided in the Faculty Annex. The building stood on raised supports without foundation walls or basement. There was nothing to impede the passage of air under the boards of the first floor where her room was located. When the wind blew hard, a small rug on the floor would rise perceptibly as each gust of air came up through the thin flooring.

In those days faculty members were required to receive room and board as part of their compensation. The charge of twenty-five dollars a month was technically added to their salaries, but the college required that it be paid back for maintenance. Under the terms of the teaching contract—and there were actually contracts in those days—the allowance for room and board was to be deducted from the salary check.

Faculty members were expected to take all of their meals in the college dining hall, then located at the rear of the first floor of Willard Hall. The faculty ate in the cross hall in Willard between the student dining hall and the kitchen. Mrs. Bushnell ate with the students. Even married faculty members who lived off campus, such as the Darters and the Cooks, came to the dining hall for their meals.

The post office was located then in the basement of Willard. There was also a college shop called The Little Red Lane, operated by the Alumnae Association.

Mrs. Bolling served as chairman of the department of modern foreign languages until 1967. There was a brief separation into departments of French and Spanish in the 1950s, and she headed the French department, but the two were soon reunited, again under her direction.

In the early 1950s the language houses were started, with special residences assigned for occupancy by juniors or seniors majoring in French or in Spanish. Students agreed to speak only the language of that house during their residence there. Weekly programs, often with visiting speakers, were held under the leadership of the language instructor in charge of the house.

For many years Mrs. Bolling sponsored the French Club. She also served as faculty representative of the local chapter of the Phi Sigma Iota national honorary romance language fraternity. She succeeded Mrs. Bushnell as sponsor of the German Club and remained in this role until the formal dance organizations were discontinued.

During her chairmanship the modern foreign language department became the largest on the campus from the standpoint of the number of faculty employed. Majors in French, Spanish, and German were offered. Course sequences in Italian, Russian, and Portuguese were also available. Two—and later three—years of foreign language credit at the college level or its equivalent were made a requirement for graduation. The department developed a reputation for high standards of accomplishment. Junior year abroad programs for French, Spanish, and German majors became popular.

Mrs. Bolling received a number of academic honors. She was a

The College in 1928

member of Phi Beta Kappa, of Alpha Zeta Pi national honorary fraternity in Romance languages, and of the Order of Academic Palms (Ordre des Palmes Académiques), an honor society of educators in France and the United States. She traveled and studied abroad on several occasions. From 1967 to 1971 she continued to serve as professor of French. During this time she served on the future of the college committee. She retired in 1971.

DEATH OF PRESIDENT CHANDLER

The week preceding the opening of college had been a busy one for President Chandler. On Monday, September 10, he had welcomed the annual teachers meeting of the King George-Stafford school division at the college and congratulated them upon the establishment of accredited high schools in those counties.

On Tuesday, September 11, the teachers of Spotsylvania County held their opening meeting at the college. Again President Chandler spoke, inviting the teachers to use the facilities at the college whenever possible and announcing a new extension course for teachers to be initiated through the cooperation of the University of Virginia Extension Division, the first project of its kind for the local college.

On Saturday afternoon, September 14, the supervising teachers of the training school held their opening meeting and made plans for the use of the new building. The opening faculty meeting of the college staff was held on Sunday evening, September 16.

Shortly thereafter, the college and community were plunged into gloom when President Chandler unexpectedly died. He was stricken with a fatal attack of apoplexy about four o'clock on the afternoon of Thursday, September 20, just as he was returning to his home on College Avenue after a busy day at the office. He was fifty-eight years old.

President Chandler had not been in good health for several months. He had had a severe spell in June and had spent some time in a hospital in Richmond. However, he had shown steady improvement upon his return and showed his old energy in plunging into his numerous responsibilities in connection with the opening of college and the reception of new students.

President Chandler had served the college long and faithfully —as well as brilliantly—from its founding. A professor from 1911 to 1915, dean from 1915 to 1919, and president from 1919 to 1928, he worked indefatigably for the progress and welfare of the institution. Much of its progress was due to his resourcefulness and energy.

During the nine years of his administration, all high school courses were eliminated; a four-year degree program was initiated; a new commercial teacher-training course was added, the only one in Virginia; the summer school was extended to twelve weeks, or a full quarter; additional dormitory space was provided; new facilities for practice teaching were established; new positions were authorized and many outstanding appointments to the faculty and staff were made; the enrollment was more than doubled; and, as a tribute to the late president put it, "a distinctive school spirit was built up." It was an impressive record of accomplishments.

President Chandler's death was a shock to his many friends throughout the state. The Richmond *Times-Dispatch* announced the news with first-page headlines, along with a picture of the popular educator. All activities at the college were suspended until the funeral Saturday. Meanwhile, messages of condolence poured in for Mrs. Chandler and the college authorities.

The body of President Chandler was returned to Bowling Green for interment in the family burying ground there. Pallbearers, active and honorary, the college faculty and administrative staff, and students of the college accompanied the body from the residence on College Avenue to the church in Bowling Green. Funeral services were held at three o'clock Saturday afternoon, September 22, 1928, in the Antioch Christian Church there. Active pallbearers were his associates on the faculty: B. Y. Tyner, W. N. Hamlet, Dr. Roy S. Cook, O. H. Darter, Harry K. Dorset, Dr. J. H. Dodd, Charles A. Edwards, and Dr. C. Mason Smith. The numerous honorary pallbearers included representatives of the Board of Virginia Teachers Colleges, the Rotary Club of Fredericksburg, prominent educators from various parts of Virginia, and local civic leaders. Members of the faculty and student body attended the services.

The death of President Chandler cast a pall over the entire community. Faculty and students were stunned as the news of his passing spread rapidly. Immensely popular among the citizens of Fredericksburg, he had served as president of the Rotary Club and of the Chamber of Commerce and was closely identified with cultural and civic activities of the city. His death was regarded as a distinct loss to the community as well as to the college.

On September 22 the *Free Lance-Star* said editorially: "He was a man whose personality was pleasant and who found life filled with things to smile at, and his was a friendly smile. He had

The College in 1928

friends everywhere and few enemies. In his position as head of the State Teachers College he experienced the friction that always accompanies executive work, but he still kept himself from acrimony and did his work efficiently and without offending others."

The editorial concluded: "He led a useful life and one which will be of value to this and future generations. . . . The community . . . will remember Mr. Chandler as a man who led a blameless life and whose work was a valuable contribution to the advancement and promotion of better citizenship."

President Chandler had received many honors. Just the year before his death he was elected to membership in Phi Beta Kappa at the University of Virginia, a signal recognition of his scholarly leadership at the college. He was one of the two persons in Fredericksburg listed in *Who's Who In America.*

President Chandler was survived by his wife, the former Blanche Montgomery of Warsaw, who had ably assisted and encouraged him in his many duties and responsibilities. The Chandler residence on College Avenue was sold to the college and, for a time, served as the college infirmary. Later, as Anne Fairfax Hall, it was a residence for students. Currently it serves the office of the dean of students.

Mrs. Chandler built a new residence across from the dining hall on College Avenue, where she lived for many years. She continued alert and active, and drove a car when she was well into her seventies. Her declining health prompted her to move to Kenmore Lodge. She died on March 16, 1971, at the age of 91.

RESOLUTIONS OF THE STATE BOARD

At a meeting of the Board of Virginia Teachers Colleges held in Richmond on October 4, 1928, resolutions on the death of President Chandler were adopted. The board also appointed a nominating committee to recommend a successor to Chandler, with the following membership: W. C. Locker, chairman, Robert A. McIntire, Norman Hamilton, Belle Webb, Senator George W. Layman, and Dr. H. M. DeJarnette. The board appointed Dean B. Y. Tyner to perform the duties of the president's office until the election of a successor.

On Sunday afternoon, October 14, 1928, an impressive memorial service in honor of the former president was held in the auditorium of the college in the presence of friends and relatives, as well as the faculty and student body. The *Free Lance-Star* (October 15) described the whole program as "one of simplicity and dignity with a trend throughout that brought near the spirit of President Chandler to those assembled in honor of him."

Under the supervision of Mrs. Bushnell, the stage had been converted into a little chapel with its vested choir on each side of an improvised altar "where soft candlelight played over a huge spray of roses, whose fragrance was the altar's incense." Tributes to Chandler as a citizen of the community were paid by W. J. Ford and, as the leader of the college, by W. N. Hamlet. Their complete addresses appeared in the *Free Lance-Star* on October 15. They are also published in a memorial edition of the *Bullet*, dated November 23, 1928, which contained tributes to him from members of the student body and others.

An editorial in that issue paid an affectionate tribute to President Chandler, saying in part, "without hesitation and with a great amount of pride, all can say that the world is much better for this man having lived in it."

Meanwhile, life went on at the college on the Hill. The first convocation of the year was in the charge of the senior class. Its officers were Peggy Branch, president; Betty Billingsley, vice-president; Grace Pendleton, secretary; and Julia Troland, treasurer. Grace Pendleton gave a short résumé of notable accomplishments of the class in the past, and Peggy Branch discussed plans and resolutions the class had made for the future. The latter included resolves "to 'back' the Student Government Association to the best of its ability" and to take an active interest in all class undertakings.

At the second convocation of the year, the faculty appeared as a group before the student body. Tyner, as acting president, introduced each new member of the faculty, who was asked to respond "in one and only one sentence." Then Mrs. Bushnell spoke on the theme, "What came ye here for to seek?" The *Bullet* reports that her message "left every girl with a new conception of what there is really to be found in college. Her thoughts were inspirational and helpful to all." Mayor W. Marshall King then extended to the new students an earnest and hearty welcome to the city. He urged them to feel at home in Fredericksburg, "even walking up the street with an ice cream cone."

On November 6 the convocation speaker was Acting President Tyner, whose topic was "Some Educational Considerations and Outlooks." After outlining some of the educational theories of the day, he counseled students regarding their own opportunities at the college. He concluded with a challenge to make the most of the privilege offered them.

The Choral Club, under the direction of Eva Taylor Eppes,

made plans to entertain the University of Richmond Glee Club in February. It was also reported as "looking forward to the coming of John Powell, the noted pianist, on April 10." The Scene Shifters, the dramatic organization on the campus, announced that its first play under the supervision of the new director, Roberta Barnett, would be *The Beau of Bath,* to be presented at convocation on November 27. The *Bullet* reported a hard-fought hockey game on October 18 between "the Devil, upheld by the Seniors, and the Billy Goat, championed by the Juniors," which resulted in a victory for the juniors.

With the presidential election imminent, a straw vote among the students emphasized the closeness of the contest between Herbert Hoover and Alfred E. Smith. Hoover won the student vote by a majority of only 20. In these days before television revolutionized the dissemination of news, the *Bullet* reported that "during the course of the evening [when election returns were coming in] and until the 10:30 bell rang, groups of students could be seen standing about in the dormitories, and in the vicinity of a telephone to hear the returns as they came in." It was not until the next morning that they learned of the sweeping victory of Herbert Hoover.

Eva Eppes gave a program of Stephen Foster songs and Negro spirituals, accompanied by Nora Willis at the piano. Both were dressed in "old-fashioned costumes." Mary Phoebe Enders was again chosen as adviser for the class of 1929, having started out with them as sophomores when she came to the college in 1926. In the fall of 1928 the college received a gift of 420 volumes from Frances Thompson, librarian from 1925 to 1928. The collection included complete sets of Dickens, of Macaulay's *History of England,* and "a number of books printed as early as 1800."

In 1928–29 Mollie Vaughan was president of the Student Government Association. Later, as Molly Vaughan Parrish (Mrs. Edward Alton Parrish) she was president of the Alumnae Association (1949–50) and, in 1965, was appointed a member of the Board of Visitors of the University of Virginia. She served later as chairman of the Mary Washington College committee of the board.

DR. COMBS ELECTED PRESIDENT

On November 19, 1928, the nominating committee of the Board of the State Teachers Colleges of Virginia met in Richmond and announced that "after the most careful consideration of a number of leaders in educational work in Virginia," it had decided to present the name of Dr. Morgan Lafayette Combs as its nominee for the president of the Fredericksburg State Teachers College.

Since the committee stated that Dr. Combs's name would be the only one presented to the board at its next meeting, it was assumed that the nomination was equivalent to election. The board took this action as anticipated, and on December 7, 1928, Dr. Combs was officially elected to the presidency of the college to take office forthwith.

THE NEW PRESIDENT

Dr. Combs was born in Honaker, Russell County, on June 11, 1892. He was brought up on a farm in southwest Virginia and received his preparatory education in local schools there. At the age of seventeen, he began teaching in a one-room school, and for the next four years he taught in public elementary and high schools in the southwestern part of the state, serving also as principal of one of the schools.

He then entered the University of Richmond where he received the A.B. degree in 1917. While in college, he served as president of the student government and also headed the Literary Society. Upon his graduation he was appointed superintendent of schools of Buchanan County, a position he held from 1917 to 1922. During his tenure many of the crude one-room schools of the mountain section were consolidated into five- and six-room elementary schools and staffed by well-trained teachers. It was also during this period that he attended the University of Chicago, receiving the A.M. degree there in 1922.

In 1922 Dr. Combs was appointed assistant supervisor of secondary education in the State Department of Education. In less than a year he was promoted to the position of state supervisor, in which he served from 1923 to 1926. In the meantime, he was continuing his graduate study in education. He received the Ed.M degree from Harvard in 1926 and the Ed.D degree in 1927. He also served as professor of secondary education at Boston University during the session of 1926–27.

Upon his return to Virginia in 1927, Dr. Combs was appointed director of research and surveys in the State Department of Education, the position he held at the time of his appointment to the presidency at Fredericksburg. Before coming to Fredericksburg he had taught courses in education during the summer sessions at the College of William and Mary in 1927 and at George Washington University in 1928. He had also served as chairman of the Virginia Committee on Secondary Schools, Southern Association of Colleges and Secondary Schools, from 1923 to 1926.

THE NEW PRESIDENT IS WELCOMED

On the evening of December 19, 1928, the faculty and administration held a formal reception in honor of the new president, Dr. Combs, and his wife. The members of the student body met the new president for the first time as they passed down the receiving line. Wooding's Orchestra furnished background music for the occasion. The college closed for the holidays on Friday, December 21, 1928.

Dr. Combs used to remark that he had never been officially inaugurated. On January 3, 1929, he took over the duties of the president. His picture appeared on the first page of the *Free Lance-Star* of the following day with the caption, "Dr. M. L. Combs, new president of Fredericksburg State Teachers College, who took charge of the institution on Thursday."

Dr. Combs arrived in the midst of a statewide influenza epidemic. Many schools and colleges had closed early for the holidays, and their resumption of classes was only with permission of the State Health Department. The college was permitted to reopen after the Christmas holidays when the assistant state health commissioner, Dr. Roy K. Flanagan, who had "been detailed by the Commissioner of Health to prevent an outbreak of influenza at the college," said that he believed the precautions being taken would prevent the spread of the disease.

When the college reopened on January 3, Dr. Flanagan himself "carefully inspected all students upon arrival, segregating those who were suffering in any degree from respiratory troubles. He also examined all the teachers." The precautions taken were stringent. No visitors were allowed over the weekend, and none of the students or the faculty were permitted to visit Fredericksburg except in extraordinary circumstances and then only when special permission had been given. The high rate of absenteeism at the College Heights Training School and the Falmouth school also under supervision of the college was expected to drop upon the announcement that they were from the health standpoint "the safest places for children at this time."

Since Dr. Combs had been unsuccessful in finding proper quarters in town for himself and his family, a three-room suite on the first floor of Frances Willard Dormitory was made available as a temporary apartment. The family took their meals in the college dining hall.

An account of Dr. Combs's arrival appears in an issue of The *Bullet* (January 31, 1929) devoted largely to events of his first days at the college. "On the morning of January 7th," said the lead story, "when Dr. Combs with his attractive wife and two handsome little boys, Bobbie and Morgan, Jr., entered the dining hall for the first time, they were greeted with a roar of applause."

On Tuesday, January 22, Dr. Combs addressed the entire faculty and student body at the first convocation of the new year. He was introduced by Dr. Elizabeth W. Baker, chairman of the convocation committee. Dr. Combs began his address with a tribute to the late President Chandler. He then spoke of service as the "great commission of life," characterizing it as "the purpose of a school and the chief end of men." He emphasized particularly the nobility and importance of the teaching profession. Dr. Combs stressed unity and cooperation, describing educational work as a "cooperative profession." In a sort of dedication, he said, "if we really want to do it, we can make this college second to none of its kind in the State."

DR. COMBS'S FIRST COMMENCEMENT

The 1928–29 session closed with the commencement exercises on Monday morning, June 2, 1929, in the open-air theatre. Following the processional and several selections by the Glee Club, President Combs introduced the speaker, the Honorable Thomas W. Ozlin, Speaker of the House of Delegates, who spoke with pride of the rich heritage of Virginians.

Dean Tyner then presented thirty-five candidates for the B.S. degree and sixty-five for the two-year diploma. After conferring the degrees and diplomas, President Combs spoke to the graduates, reminding them of the responsibilities that rested upon them and the challenge that the present and future held for them.

It was a pleasant June morning as the sunlight played upon the gathering in the sylvan setting of the open-air theatre. Few persons would have believed that a stock-market crash later in the year would plunge the nation into the Great Depression.

CHAPTER IX

A Period of Change, 1929–1934

STRENGTHENING OF FACULTY

ONE of the first concerns of the new president was strengthening the faculty both in numbers and in academic preparation. When Dr. Combs took office in January 1929, only three members of the faculty held the Ph.D. degree. Several had only the bachelor's degree, and a few had no degree at all. Three years later President Combs was able to report to the board that eleven members of the faculty held Ph.D. degrees. All but two of the others held master's degrees, and those two had done considerable work beyond the bachelor's level and were regarded as having the equivalent of the master's degree.

This upgrading was accomplished in two ways: by insisting that inadequately prepared members of the faculty take leaves of absence for further study and by appointing as replacements or additions to the teaching staff only persons with high academic qualifications. The upgrading of the resident faculty presented some problems. In 1933 two of the training school supervisors were dropped when they had not made any effort to work toward the requisite master's degree. However, other faculty members did enroll for advanced study, either with leaves of absence or as commuting graduate students to institutions in Washington. At one time as many as eight faculty members were going once or twice weekly to George Washington University for graduate courses leading to the master's or doctor's degree.

Much of the upgrading of the academic level of the faculty was accomplished through new appointments, wherever possible, at the doctor's degree level. An improved salary scale made it possibe to attract staff members with strong preparation. Between 1929 and 1932 eight holders of the doctorate were appointed. In 1929 Dr. M. L. Alstetter, Dr. Burt W. Loomis, Dr. George E. Shankle, and Dr. Olive G. Stull joined the faculty. Dr. W. J. Young returned to teach at the college in 1930. Dr. Louise Boillin also joined the faculty that year. In 1932 Dr. Amalia Lautz and Dr. C. G. G. Moss were appointed. Since several of these new appointees were destined to play an important role in the life of the college, a few pen profiles seem appropriate here.

A NEW DEAN

In September 1929 Dr. Michael Louis Alstetter came to the college as acting dean of instruction, registrar, and head of the department of education, in place of Dean B. Y. Tyner, who had been granted a leave of absence. When Dean Tyner resigned during the session, Dr. Alstetter continued as a regular appointee to this administrative and teaching post.

Dr. Alstetter was born in Ohio. He held the B.S. degree from Lima College, the A.B. and M.A. degrees from Ohio State University, and the Ph.D. degree from Peabody College. He had served as high school principal and superintendent of schools in Ohio and in Florida. Before coming to the college in September 1929 as dean of instruction and registrar, he had taught at the University of Florida.

Mrs. Alstetter had also taught at the University of Florida and had been director of the demonstration school there. She became instructor in education on the college staff and also served as elementary supervisor in the Stafford–King George County schools.

GEORGE EARLIE SHANKLE

Among the new appointments President Combs made to the faculty in spring 1929 was that of Dr. George Earlie Shankle as professor of English and head of the English department. For the next twenty-eight years, until his death in 1957, Dr. Shankle occupied this important post.

Dr. Shankle was born in Paris, Tennessee. Records indicate that he entered college at a fairly mature age. He did work at Dickson College in Dickson, Tennessee, and the Hall-Moody Institute at Martin, Tennessee, before beginning a degree program that led eventually to three degrees at the bachelor's level, two at the master's level, and finally the doctorate.

Before coming to the college at Fredericksburg, he had served as head of the English department at Union University, at Mississippi College, and at Oklahoma Baptist University. It was from the last institution that he resigned to accept the new appointment offered him by President Combs.

As his students will testify, Dr. Shankle was a colorful individual. A large, rather portly man until he dieted rigorously in

A Period of Change 161

his last years, he circulated about the campus, greeting students with "Hi, sister" or "Hi, sisters" in a hearty manner. He was not unaware of his role as a campus character, and he encouraged comments on his idiosyncracies. A bachelor throughout his life, Dr. Shankle lived at first in a rented room on Cornell Street and later on College Avenue. Subsequently he purchased a small house on Rowe Street where he lived alone after 1945.

Dr. Shankle had many interests. He liked to paint in a very traditional style. He would buy framed oleos at a Woolworth store and paint over the original picture some scene that he fancied, such as a landscape, still life, or even a copy of a well-known painting. These Shankle pictures, as they came to be known, were given as presents to his friends.

Dr. Shankle was also an accomplished musician. For several years, resplendent in full dress for the occasion, he gave piano or organ recitals at the college. At the student benefits he liked to give female impersonations, one of his favorites being "Pistol-packin' Mama." At his home he was fond of "putting up" fruits and vegetables, and he always had a large supply of food he had processed himself.

Dr. Shankle taught such courses as a survey of English literature and one on Shakespeare. In the latter course he required that every student memorize at least five hundred lines from the plays, a facet of the course that for many students overshadowed their appreciation of Shakespeare as a dramatist.

During his years at the college Dr. Shankle wrote several books. The first was entitled *State Names, Flags, Seals, Songs, Birds, Flowers, and Other Symbols: A Study Based on Historical Documents Giving the Origin and Significance of the State Names, Nicknames, Mottoes, Seals, Flags, Flowers, Birds, Songs, and Descriptive Comments on the Capitol Buildings and on Some of the Leading State Histories, with Facsimiles of the State Flags and Seals.* This reference book of 512 pages was published by the H. W. Wilson Company in 1934. Separate bulletins giving the material by individual states were published for Massachusetts, Minnesota, Virginia, and Washington.

In 1937 the first edition of *American Nicknames, Their Origin and Significance* appeared, a 599-page book of reference published, again, by H. W. Wilson. In his preface Dr. Shankle acknowledged the aid of a former student, Margaret Rose Kalnen, of Castle Hayne, North Carolina (B.S., 1933). In 1941 Wilson published Dr. Shankle's *American Mottoes and Slogans.* In 1945 *Current Abbreviations* appeared under the same imprint.

Dr. Shankle organized and sponsored a club for students majoring in English called the Modern Portias. He was especially proud of the group, and each year he gave a formal dinner for them in the private dining room of a local restaurant. He always said he was writing a novel about life at the college, and to close friends he occasionally read an episode that he planned to include. However, "Little Sisters" was never published, and the manuscript seems to have vanished.

Students and faculty made fun of Dr. Shankle. He was certainly not the stereotyped image of a college professor of that day. However, he dared, as one faculty member put it, to be himself. If he preferred to eat in the kitchen instead of the dining hall of the college, he did so. He never told his age and ignored the state retirement system. He was supposedly "about seventy" when his terminal illness forced him to give up active teaching during the session of 1956–57. He was probably closer to eighty at the time of his death on May 30, 1957. He was buried in Ebenezer Cemetery, four miles northwest of Troy, Tennessee.

CHARLES GEORGE GORDON MOSS

Dr. Moss, one of the most popular professors to teach at Mary Washington, joined the faculty in September 1932 as associate professor of social science. A native of Lynchburg, Dr. Moss received the B.A. degree from Washington and Lee University and the M.A. and Ph.D. degrees from Yale University. Before coming to Mary Washington he had taught history at the Episcopal High School, Wake Forest College, and Farmville State Teachers College.

A handsome, affable, and relaxed person, Dr. Moss was, to use a hackneyed phrase—but most apt in this case—"both a scholar and a gentleman." His classes in American history and English history were sought eagerly. His keen and sincere interest in students, his delightful, slow drawl, his sense of humor, and his high standards of integrity were facets of his personality that endeared him to many.

The *Battlefield* was dedicated to him in 1935, in appreciation of "his spirit of good fellowship, his enduring friendliness, his sportmanship, and his genial humor." The annual was dedicated to him again in 1940, with special mention of "his genial-

A Period of Change

ity . . . , his friendly dignity in the classroom and his cooperative spirit in all campus activities."

Dr. Moss taught at the college for twelve years. He spent one summer in Williamsburg, editing his Yale doctoral dissertation on the plantation system in colonial Virginia for publication as a monograph by Colonial Williamsburg, Inc. When asked what his editorial work involved, he replied, in his customary deep-pitched drawl, "Just removing the trappin's of scholarship."

When World War II came, Dr. Moss was a little too old for active duty. However, he was eager to serve his country. He joined the local company of the Virginia Protective Force and rarely missed a weekly drill. When the Japanese struck at Pearl Harbor, and the fear of invasion or sabotage reached even the East Coast, Dr. Moss helped to guard the bridges into Fredericksburg during the bitter cold weather of December, January, and February 1941–42.

In 1944, the year of Mary Washington's affiliation with the University of Virginia as its liberal arts college for women, Dr. Moss decided to resign and go back to the Farmville State Teachers College, which had been renamed Longwood College, where he became head of the history department.

He was as popular a professor as ever. However, his later years at Farmville had their unpleasant aspects when Dr. Moss became deeply involved in opposing the closure of the Prince Edward County schools in 1959 to avoid the integration ordered by the United States Supreme Court. Dr. Moss did not feel that it was right to shut down the public schools, and he said so with conviction. At the time, this was an unpopular position to take, and some of his friends in the community turned against him. With no thought of personal sacrifice, he continued to speak out for public education.

Time magazine on September 27, 1963, paid tribute to Dr. Moss in a news story entitled "Dickie's Decision," which appeared under the heading of "Integration." The fairly long article contained this interesting paragraph:

Dickie's inspiration comes from his father, Dean Gordon Moss of Longwood College in Farmville, the county seat. For four lonely years, in letters, speeches and interviews, Dean Moss has urged his fellow citizens to reopen public schools. He has been snubbed, ostracized, threatened—all to his son's increasing admiration. Sent earlier to school outside the county, Dickie is putting in his senior year at the free high school for a simple reason: "This was something I could do for my father. He has fought this battle for a long time."

When, finally, the public schools reopened in 1963, Dr. Moss's son was one of 4 white students among the 1,500 blacks at Moton High School. Dr. Moss was accused of forcing him to go there, but soon it became clear that his son enrolled of his own volition because of his admiration for his father and the stand he had taken.

Dr. Moss continued to return to Mary Washington for alumnae homecomings. He had sponsored the class of 1936, and he returned for their reunions in 1956, 1961, and 1971. He also returned for the twenty-fifth reunion of the class of 1940, which he had also sponsored. From 1959 to 1964 Dr. Moss was associate dean and then dean of the college at Longwood. He returned to full-time teaching in 1964, and retired completely in June 1968. He taught history until the very last of his service.

SOUTHERN ASSOCIATION ACCREDITATION

In December 1927 the Association of Colleges and Secondary Schools of the Southern States had rejected the application of the college for recognition on the grounds that the faculty training and salaries were below standard.[1] It was a blow to the college, especially since sister institutions at both Harrisonburg and Farmville were admitted to membership at that time.

President Chandler immediately set about to obtain a new salary schedule and redoubled his efforts to recruit training school and college instructors whose academic credentials included the requisite advanced degrees. In fall 1928 the seven appointments to the faculty included five persons with master's degrees and two with the doctorate (Dr. Elizabeth W. Baker and Dr. J. H. Dodd). Although the academic preparation of the faculty was thereby improved, the salaries still had far to go.

Upon assuming the presidency of the college in January 1929, Dr. Combs set as one of his first objectives the winning of accreditation by the Southern Association. The stamp of approval by this regional accrediting agency was most important in establishing the academic standing of the institution and facilitating the acceptance of its credits by other colleges.

Dr. Combs's appointments for fall 1929 included three more faculty members with doctorates. He was also successful in ob-

[1] Report to Board, Dec. 16, 1927.

taining raises of $360.00 each for seventeen faculty members, but even this increase was not enough to bring all of the full professors to the $3,000 minimum. The college failed to win membership at the December 1929 meeting for this reason.[2]

The obstacle was overcome by a further increase in all salaries for 1930–31 that brought the full professors up to the $3,000 minimum. There was general rejoicing when, at its meeting in Atlanta early in December 1930, the Southern Association admitted the college to full membership, which meant unconditional accreditation. This appears even more significant when it is noted that of the eighteen or twenty colleges applying for admission at that time, only three were approved.[3]

The college had been a class A member of the American Association of Teachers Colleges for some years and, more recently (1930), a member of the National Association of Commercial Teacher-Training Institutions. Accreditation by the Southern Association now placed the college in a more favorable position to attract students, since there was no question about its academic standing.

GOVERNOR BYRD VISITS COLLEGE

On November 13, 1929, the college enjoyed the unique distinction of having a visit from the governor and the governor-elect of Virginia at the same time. Governor Harry F. Byrd and Dr. John Garland Pollard, accompanied by the director of the budget, Colonel J. H. Bradford, were the guests of Dr. Combs.

After a tour of the college buildings, the group had dinner with President Combs in the college dining hall. To the delight of the four hundred students who packed the dining hall, each of the distinguished guests was presented by Dr. Combs and spoke informally, with complimentary and humorous references to each other.

Governor Byrd referred to himself as the setting sun and introduced Dr. Pollard as the rising sun. When Colonel Bradford was introduced, he expressed his feeling of insignificance in the presence of two such luminaries. All expressed their pleasure with the progress the college was making. They left for Richmond that evening.

[2] *Ibid.*, April 15, 1930.　　[3] *Free Lance-Star*, Dec. 6, 1930.

A NEW BOARD

Changes in the Constitution of the Commonwealth of Virginia, effective January 1, 1930, transferred management of the four state teachers colleges from the Board of Virgina Teachers Colleges to the State Board of Education. The teachers colleges board, which had succeeded the old Normal School board when the institutions were changed from normal schools to teachers colleges in 1924, was discontinued as of December 31, 1929.

The last meeting of the Board of Virginia Teachers Colleges was held in Richmond on December 10, 1929, with W. C. Locker, president of the board, presiding. Each of the college presidents spoke briefly at this meeting. Dr. Combs expressed "high appreciation for the sympathy, patience, and cooperation of the Board in dealing with his institution." [4]

Control of the institution passed to the State Board of Education on January 1, 1930. Former Governor E. Lee Trinkle was president of the board. Other members were Rose MacDonald of Berryville, Robert M. Hughes of Norfolk, Herbert H. Harris of Lynchburg, Joseph H. Saunders of Newport News, Thomas G. Burch of Martinsville, and Harris Hart, state superintendent of public instruction, Richmond. Thomas D. Eason, director of teacher education in the State Department of Education, was secretary of the board at the time.

ENROLLMENT INCREASES

A steady increase in enrollment in the college began with the appointment of President Combs. The enrollment in the fall 1928 had been 404. Subsequent fall enrollments, according to the quarterly reports of the president to the State Board of Education show a consistent growth in the number of college students.

In 1929 the fall enrollment was 432; in 1930, 448; in 1931, 511; and in 1932, 620. In May 1933 President Combs reported a total enrollment of 665 for the session. This represented an increase of 50 percent in the number of students in the past three years, despite seriously disturbed economic conditions. Applications for the 1933-34 session were approximately 100 in excess of the dormitory space available. The summer quarter also showed a slight

---

[4] Minutes of the Board, Dec. 10, 1929.

A Period of Change

but consistent increase in number of students. In 1929 the enrollment was 294; in 1930, 329; in 1931, 376; and in 1932, 379. The training school enrollment during this period averaged about 325, which included pupils from the first through the eleventh grades. In addition, the college served a few mature students in evening and extension classes.

The academic qualifications of students also improved. One out of every eight freshman who entered in the fall of 1932 had ranked first or second in her high school graduating class. The student body in 1932–33, the largest up to that time in the history of the college, came from twenty-one states and the Canal Zone. The enrollment increased 15 percent over the previous year. There were 270 freshmen out of a fall enrollment of 620.

Courses in the department of commerce were attracting large numbers of students. An intensive mail campaign addressed to high school seniors in Virginia and other states stressed the need for teachers of commercial subjects and for trained secretaries. One-third of the students in 1932–33 were enrolled in the commerce department for courses in shorthand, typing, bookkeeping, business English, and business arithmetic.

The reputation of the commerce department continued to attract increasing numbers of students. Eventually the enrollment in that department reached seven hundred, or approximately half of the entire student body. With fourteen faculty members it was the largest department in the college. It continued to play a major role in the institution until 1948 when the major in commerce and credit for courses in shorthand and typewriting were discontinued.

ACADEMIC DEVELOPMENTS

Between 1929 and 1934 the chief emphasis academically was upon strengthening the program leading to the two-year-diploma and the normal professional certificate. Graduates of this curriculum were licensed by the state of Virginia to teach in the elementary grades.

In 1929 the normal professional course stressed methodology. There were separate courses on teaching history and geography in the primary grades and in the grammar grades; on teaching reading, language, spelling, and penmanship in the primary grades and in the grammar grades; on teaching arithmetic, again one for the primary grades and one for the upper grades; and even the course in teaching citizenship was divided into primary grades and grammar grades.

All of these courses were offered in the first year. In the sophomore year there were courses in educational sociology, educational psychology, tests and measurements, and principles of teaching elementary grades.

This heavy concentration on professional subject matter left little time for solid academic subjects. Even the courses in English reflected this concern with methodology. English 201–2–3 was Literature for Primary and Grammar Grades; English 211–2–3 was Oral Reading; strangely enough, English 221–2, Contemporary Literature, a course designed to "give a knowledge and appreciation of the best literature of the late nineteenth and twentieth centuries" was an elective.

A vigorous effort to replace the methods courses with content or subject matter courses resulted in a complete revision of the two-year diploma course for elementary teachers. All of the first-year courses in methodology for various subjects and levels were consolidated into a single course in teaching in the elementary school, offered five times a week in the spring quarter.

Courses in English fundamentals, the typical first-year college composition course, replaced the courses in primary literature and oral reading. Arithmetic for elementary grades, actually a review of arithmetic, replaced courses in teaching arithmetic in the primary grades or in the upper grades.

By 1934 the normal professional course had become academically oriented. There were still some professional subject courses, but even these now demanded a high standard of performance. The way was paved for graduates of the two-year program to return to work toward a degree, usually in the summer sessions, without having to make up credit deficiencies in academic subjects required for the B.S. degree.

VIRGINIA ACADEMY OF SCIENCE MEETING

The Virginia Academy of Science held its annual meeting at the college on May 5 and 6, 1933. Over four hundred delegates from colleges and scientific agencies throughout Virginia attended the many sectional and general meetings. Dr. Roy S. Cook was chairman of the general committee in charge of arrangements. The presidential address was given by Dr. T. McN. Simpson of Randolph-Macon College. (The complete text of his address was published in the *Free Lance-Star* for May 6.) Dr. W. A. Kepner of the University of Virginia was elected president for the coming year.

INTERNATIONAL AFFAIRS INSTITUTE

On January 19 and 20, 1934, the International Relations Club sponsored the two-day International Institute, which attracted representatives from every college and university in Virginia. Professor Oscar H. Darter served as general chairman of the institute. Visiting speakers discussed various aspects of the current international scene. The rise of Hitlerism in Germany and fascism in Italy were viewed as producing significant changes in Western civilization by Alden C. Alley, a representative of the National Council for the Prevention of War. Other speakers discussed aspects of the growing crisis in Europe.

SEACOBECK HALL

The need for more adequate and modern dining and kitchen facilities was urgent. At first President Combs considered erecting a dining hall and kitchen on top of the laundry and heating plant structure, which stood immediately behind Willard Hall. However, plans for a more permanent building that would be an impressive and attractive addition to the campus began to take shape. A building on the College Avenue side of the campus, where once the school garden was tended by agriculture students, seemed a commanding and convenient site. Although a small ravine lay in the path to the site, Dr. Combs proposed to erect a bridge that would enhance the natural beauty of the ravine and also provide ready access to the new building.

How to finance the structure was the problem. The country was in the midst of the Depression, and a moratorium on state outlay for nonessentials had been declared. Dr. Combs was not to be deterred, however, and he sought the assistance of his friends in the state government in Richmond.

On June 12, 1930, Governor Pollard authorized the State Teachers College at Fredericksburg to proceed with the construction of the dining halls and kitchen at a cost not to exceed $112,500. Of this amount $41,000 was to be paid out of an anticipated conditional appropriation for this purpose for the year beginning July 1, 1930. Unfortunately, this failed to materialize, so the college found it necessary to pay the $41,000 out of economies in operation. It is interesting to note here that $20,000 was paid on this debt the very first year. It was charged to the maintenance fund of the college. The remainder was taken care of the following year. Meanwhile, construction on the new building had begun. By spring 1931 the first of many buildings to be erected by the new president was ready for occupancy.

When students returned from the Easter holidays they found the new dining hall ready to receive them. It was an exciting change from the dining rooms on the first floor of Willard Hall, which had been in use since the opening of the college.

The new building was named Seacobeck Hall, after an Indian village that had once occupied the spot. The name is an Algonquin word signifying "at the foot of the rock."[5] Undoubtedly this refers to the rock formation marking the fall line in the Rappahannock River below. It was this natural barrier that prevented Captain John Smith from proceeding farther when he journeyed up the river by boat in 1608.

The building stood across a narrow ravine from Willard and Virginia halls, connected with the rest of the campus by an arched viaduct of red brick with stone facing. The main entrance was reached by a series of terraced steps. Two arcs of brick walls led to the north and south entrances.

The facade of the building presented an arc of pillars supporting the roof of the portico. The dining halls on either side also produced an arc effect in their arrangement at angles to the central part of the building.

The center door led into the dome room, or lobby, where an Italian marble fireplace was the first thing to meet the eye. The room was furnished with Chippendale mirrors and tables. Furniture and draperies carried out a scheme of green and yellow coloring. Thick Persian rugs gave a final touch of elegance. Overhead was a brilliantly lighted oval dome, harmonizing with the contours of the room. To the left and to the right a series of double-hinged doorways led into the dining halls, each seating about 250 students. Large windows with rounded arches reached almost to the ceiling.

The spacious kitchen lay behind the Dome Room and between the two dining halls, connected with them by swinging doors. The most modern equipment was installed. There were huge

---

[5] *Free Lance-Star,* April 10, 1931.

A Period of Change

caldrons, a bake oven, gas ranges, and a refrigeration plant. Behind the kitchen were an apartment for the dietitian and offices for the dining hall supervisory staff. A loading platform extended across the back. On the ground floor were classrooms and laboratories for the home economics department. The tea room adjoined, where it could be operated conveniently by the students in that department. Extensive storage space occupied the remainder of the lower floor.

The building was opened formally for inspection on May 19, 1931, when several hundred invited guests attended a reception given by college officials. Dr. and Mrs. Combs headed a receiving line that included Judge Rose MacDonald of the State Board of Education; Dr. Sidney B. Hall, state superintendent of public instruction; and the members of the faculty and staff with their husbands and wives.

ANNUAL RECEPTIONS

With the opening of Seacobeck Hall the practice began of having a reception each spring for friends and patrons of the school. These were occasions on which the president and members of the faculty entertained several hundred guests from Fredericksburg and its environs, with a scattering of visitors from more distant places.

The receiving line of what came to be known as the annual spring reception was headed by Dr. and Mrs. Combs, followed by members of the State Board of Education, the presidents of the other three state teachers colleges, and members of the faculty of the local institution.

One unit of the dining hall was decorated with potted evergreens, which formed a backdrop for the long receiving line. Refreshments of ice cream, cake, and punch were served, with Mrs. Buhsnell presiding at the punch bowl. Afterwards the floor was cleared for dancing, which lasted usually until nearly midnight.[6]

These receptions usually preceded the quarterly meeting of the State Board of Education, held at the college the following day. Former Governor Trinkle was president of the board. He and Mrs. Trinkle were invariably the house guests of Dr. and Mrs. Combs on these occasions. The spring receptions were discontinued when the State Board of Education ceased to be the governing body of the college in 1944.

[6] *Ibid.*, April 27 and 28, 1933.

ANNE FAIRFAX HALL

The residence now known as Anne Fairfax, located on College Avenue just behind the Tri-Unit, was purchased from the widow of President A. B. Chandler, Jr., in 1930 for fifteen thousand dollars. The Chandlers lived there at the time of his death in September 1928, and they owned both the land and the building.

Anne Fairfax has served a variety of purposes. When first purchased, it was used as the college infirmary, with space for about fifteen students. The rooms in Willard used previously for this purpose were converted into housing for students. In 1956 it became the official residence of the new dean of students, Margaret Hargrove. Dean Hargrove lived there until her retirement in 1970 when it was remodeled to serve as offices for the dean of students and her staff.

When the residence of J. H. Chiles, superintendent of Spotsylvania County public schools, was acquired by the college, it was used first as a home economics practice house. Then it was moved from its central location facing the driveway through the college to a location just back of Anne Fairfax and connected with it by a harmonizing covered passageway. The annex, Fairfax Annex as it was called, became the residence of the college physician.

When the new infirmary was completed in 1952, both Anne Fairfax and the annex were converted into small dormitories for students. The annex has continued to serve as a dormitory. In 1970 it was designated as a residence facility for the Student Government Association president and the Honor Council president and their roommates, and it also provides office space for the two presidents.

NEW RECREATIONAL FACILITIES

The Great Depression did not halt expansion and development activities. In fact, full advantage was taken of federal funds appropriated to relieve unemployment to construct both buildings and campus facilities. In 1933 the college was awarded twenty-one thousand dollars under the Civil Works Administration, which was used to employ up to 115 men at times in making improvements on the grounds. It was the first CWA project in this section of Virginia.

When the CWA was converted into the Works Progress Administration (WPA), the college continued to employ a large number of workers. Although the WPA "leaf-rakers" were often the butt of jokes at the time, they accomplished a great deal at Mary Washington College. They were used to build walkways on campus, plant trees and shrubbery, landscape the grounds, and make other improvements. Together with the college maintenance staff the WPA workers constructed new tennis courts, an open-air swimming pool, a field house, and two hockey fields—all located below and west of the old central campus where Willard and Monroe halls stood.

OTHER IMPROVEMENTS

The reports of the president to the State Board of Education constitute an impressive record of improvements to the physical facilities of the college.

When Seacobeck was completed, the space in Willard formerly used for the dining rooms and kitchen was converted into rooms, providing space for fifty-four additional residential students. These alterations, costing $30,175, were financed out of the maintenance fund through economies achieved in operating expenses. The post office was removed from Virginia Hall to the basement of Willard, and the parlors in Virginia were renovated and new furniture purchased. Overhead power lines and poles were removed from the campus, and all wiring placed underground. The college ended the fiscal year June 30, 1931, with a surplus of $44,646. The governor authorized the expenditure of $10,000 of this surplus on roads, walkways, and general improvements.[7]

During the session of 1931-32, the open-air theatre was reconstructed and the stage enlarged. The old faculty annex was sold and moved from the campus to College Avenue. The dean's house, located just a few yards from that of the president, was renovated. It, too, was sold later and moved across campus to a new site on College Avenue.

Four new tennis courts were constructed. Additional kitchen equipment was purchased. Comfortable new seats were installed in the auditorium of Monroe Hall to replace its benches. Betty Lewis Hall and the indoor swimming pool were renovated.

In his quarterly report President Combs stated that the General Assembly had appropriated funds for the new boiler, stoker,

---

[7] Minutes of the Board, Oct. 12, 1931, p. 193.

ice machine, and the improvement of the swimming pool.[8] "All other items were made possible through economy and increased enrollment and paid for out of a surplus in the operating fund of the College."[9]

ROOF GARDEN COMPLETED

During the summer of 1932 a spacious roof garden, with terrazzo floor, was constructed to replace the temporary roof of the swimming pool, which had been designed originally to be the first unit in the projected Student Activities–Alumnae Building.

Winding steps were built on either side of the entrance to the pool, making an attractive access to the roof garden itself. A background of trees in the grove behind it produced a natural setting of beauty by day and especially by night, when the green foliage reflected the glow of lanterns on the parapet surrounding the roof. The structure was made possible by private gifts donated for that purpose.

THE CABIN

A log cabin, a gift of the Athletic Association, was built during the spring of 1932 on a hill in the wooded area some distance behind Willard Hall. It became a popular rendezvous for overnight occupancy on weekends by Athletic Association members or any other group of up to fifteen who made reservations for its use. An open fireplace provided an opportunity for roasting wieners or toasting marshmallows, or simply for conversation around an open fire.

NEW ENTRANCE GATES

In 1936 contracts were let for the construction of ornamental gates marking the entrance to the college at the foot of the hill. Erected at a cost of over three thousand dollars, the construction was financed by donations from graduating classes and from

---

[8] President's Report, Oct. 18, 1932.
[9] Minutes of State Board of Education, Oct. 18, 1932, pp. 204–6.

private individuals. The largest single gift was five hundred dollars donated by Mrs. A. B. Chandler, wife of the former president of the college.

The brick columns and massive iron gates were completed during the Christmas holidays in 1936. Returning students found the new gateway in operation as a beautiful addition to the campus and as a protection against intruders during the hours in the night when the campus driveway was closed to outside traffic.

PROPOSED CONVERSION INTO A LIBERAL ARTS COLLEGE FOR WOMEN

The establishment of a liberal arts college for the women of Virginia, with educational facilities equaling those offered men by the state at the University of Virginia, had long been advocated, especially by women leaders. The matter came up again for discussion during the 1928 session of the General Assembly in connection with a state educational survey and the recommendation that the State Teachers College at Harrisonburg be converted into a liberal arts college for women to be operated under the direction of the University of Virginia.

The General Assembly took no action on this proposal but instead established a commission to study and report to its next session on "the advisability of establishing a liberal arts college for undergraduate women at one of the state teachers colleges, or elsewhere." [10] The commission consisted of nine members, two appointed from members of the Senate by the president of the Senate, three from members of the House of Delegates appointed by the Speaker of the House, and four residents of Virginia, not connected with the state educational system, appointed by the governor. Judge Don P. Halsey of Lynchburg was selected as chairman.

The commission began open sessions in the hall of the House of Delegates in Richmond on November 26, 1929. Delegations from Fredericksburg, Harrisonburg, and Lynchburg, together with many individuals from the state at large and a group representing the alumni of the University of Virginia, met with the commission.

[10] *Acts of Assembly*, 1928, p. 329.

The women speakers, led by Mrs. Beverly B. Munford, a member of the board of visitors of the university, declared that only a liberal arts college for women located at the university itself could ensure equal educational opportunity.

The University of Virginia Alumni Association presented C. Harding Walker of Heathsville, rector of the board of visitors, who read a resolution adopted by the board, setting forth its unqualified opposition to coeducation at the university or the establishment of a coordinate college for women at Charlottesville. It recommended the conversion of one of the present women's colleges in Virginia into a liberal arts college for women to be under the control of the university and to be equal to it in its requirements and standards.

Dr. Edwin A. Alderman, president of the university, endorsed the idea of a liberal arts college for women but earnestly advised against its location in Charlottesville or its immediate vicinity. He expressed his opposition to coeducation at the university, and he specifically mentioned the State Teachers College at Fredericksburg, the one at Harrisonburg, and also Hollins and Sweet Briar as possibilities for conversion into a liberal arts college under the direction of the university.

After several alumni of the university had supported the rector and the president in their opposition to coeducation or a coordinate college at Charlottesville, delegations from Lynchburg and Harrisonburg presented their claims for the location of the women's college there.

Fredericksburg sent a large delegation to the hearing. With Mayor Jere M. H. Willis acting as master of ceremonies, the natural and cultural advantages of the location in Fredericksburg were presented by President M. L. Combs, former Senator C. O'Conor Goolrick, and Judge Alvin T. Embrey. President J. P. McConnell of Radford State Teachers College added his endorsement of the Fredericksburg location.

A full account of the presentations of Mayor Willis, Dr. Combs, Senator Goolrick, and Judge Embrey was published in the *Daily Star* on November 27, 1929. Judge Embrey suggested Mary Washington College as a possible name for the women's university, likening it to the association of Thomas Jefferson with the University of Virginia.

Judge Embrey continued: "The establishment of this University for Women at Fredericksburg under the name of Mary Washington College, in part as a memorial to the noble woman

A Period of Change

who lived and is buried in Fredericksburg would endow the institution with a charm and appeal to all womankind that could be secured in no other way."[11]

The commission proceeded to visit and inspect several of the proposed sites, including Fredericksburg. It reported to the Committee on Schools and Colleges at the 1930 General Assembly. It was against the establishment of a college for women at the university. It did not designate a specific site but recommended that the college be located at Fredericksburg, Harrisonburg, Lynchburg, or Roanoke. No action was taken in the ensuing deadlock.

The General Assembly continued the commission, asking that it report on a site and specifying that the college would be coordinated with the University of Virginia. Each of the four contenders for the college was asked to send in all available data concerning their claims. Mayor Willis submitted many typed pages documenting the request, along with letters from prominent persons endorsing the selection of the college at Fredericksburg.

An attractively illustrated twelve-page brochure was also prepared. Entitled "The Liberal Arts College for Women at Fredericksburg, Virginia," it set forth the many advantages for converting the State Teachers College into the proposed women's college.

FREDERICKSBURG RECOMMENDED

After an extended series of meetings, the Halsey Commission finally recommended that the liberal arts college for women be located at Fredericksburg. The report was hailed with enthusiasm and gratification at the college and in the city. A committee headed by Mayor Willis was appointed to confer with members of the Halsey Commission, officials of the University of Virginia, and members of the General Assembly to determine the best way to obtain approval of the report and the passage of the necessary legislation to put it into effect.[12]

The report recommended an appropriation of $106,000 for the next biennium to make the liberal arts college a reality. A gradual transition was recommended, with additional professors to be employed and more liberal arts courses to be offered. Added im-

[11] *Daily Star,* Nov. 27, 1929.   [12] *Free Lance-Star,* Jan. 5, 1932.

petus to the passage of the legislation was given by a formal resolution of the university board of visitors endorsing the report and the selection of the State Teachers College at Fredericksburg as the coordinate college.[13]

Mrs. B. B. Munford still expressed her opposition to the choice as she believed "it would be impossible for years for the state to bring the proposed women's school there up to a standard comparable with that of the College of Arts and Sciences at the University of Virginia."[14]

Virginia, as well as the rest of the country, was in the very depths of the Great Depression in 1932. All major state appropriations were cut. The governor proposed a 10 percent reduction in all salaries. His earnest plea was to "curtail expenses." He recommended no action on the liberal arts college for women because of the financial situation.

Nevertheless, bills were introduced in both the House and Senate carrying out the recommendations of the Halsey Commission to locate the college at Fredericksburg. Appropriations of $150,000 for the first year and $116,110 for the second year were proposed to facilitate the conversion as opposed to the $106,000 total recommended by the commission.

The University of Virginia Alumni Association strongly supported the bills. Representatives of women's organizations vigorously opposed a location other than at the university. The House of Delegates Committee on Schools and Colleges approved the bill by one vote. The Senate Committee on Institutions and Education approved it by a 9 to 6 vote.

The bill was passed by the House 72 to 21 and by the senate 30 to 9, although Governor John Garland Pollard sent a special message urging that no action be taken until the condition of the state treasury warranted the required appropriation. The measure, as passed, carried no state appropriation.

On March 8, 1932, Governor Pollard vetoed the bill converting the State Teachers College at Fredericksburg into a liberal arts college for women. He cited the condition of the treasury and the uncertainty of a possible appropriation two years later. He also pointed out the need of money for public schools.

Governor Pollard returned the bill with several suggested amendments, which the House refused to accept. His veto followed immediately, and it was sustained by a House vote of 50

---

[13] Jan. 4, 1932.   [14] *Free Lance-Star*, Jan. 8, 1932.

to 36. Thus ended for a time the struggle to convert the institution into a liberal arts college for women.[15]

TWENTIETH ANNIVERSARY OF THE COLLEGE

The celebration of the twentieth anniversary of the opening of the college took place in connection with the commencement exercises on June 5–8, 1931. A souvenir program giving a list of events and the participants was printed for the occasion. A picture of the recently completed Seacobeck Hall appeared on the cover.

Special exercises were held on Saturday, June 6, to commemorate this important event. The day began with the daisy chain processional (class of 1933), followed by Class Day exercises (class of 1931) in the open-air theatre. A luncheon for faculty, alumnae, and visitors was given in Seacobeck Hall.

The anniversary was observed formally in a special program held that afternoon in the open-air theatre. The Honorable E. Lee Trinkle, president of the State Board of Education, presided. President Combs welcomed the three hundred specially invited guests. Dr. Sidney B. Hall, state superintendent of public instruction, then spoke.

The main speaker and guest of honor on that occasion was C. O'Conor Goolrick, who was recognized as being instrumental in bringing the college to Fredericksburg. In his introduction Governor Trinkle referred to Goolrick as "one of Virginia's really prominent men." In a brief and entertaining address, Mr. Goolrick gave an account of the inception of the school. The program concluded with the singing of the alma mater. This program was followed by an elaborate song and dance festival in the central campus at four o'clock. At six-thirty the alumnae dinner was held in the north unit of Seacobeck Hall.

A feature of the banquet was the address given by Professor W. N. Hamlet. The senior professor at the college both in age and in years of service, Hamlet described the opening days of the first session when two still uncompleted buildings constituted the entire physical plant.

Mr. Hamlet was one of the first professors to be selected for the new institution. He had expected to decline the offer, but,

[15] *Ibid.*, March 8, 1932.

in his own words, "When I looked upon this beautiful hill, I saw in perspective what glorious things might be accomplished." He accepted the position. The complete text of his address was printed in the *Free Lance-Star* on July 2, 1931. It is a moving and emotional message of memories of the past and bright hopes for the future. Unforgettable is his tribute to the late President Chandler, "whose heart was so full of love for his college that it forgot to beat."

Next on the program was the presentation of the poetic drama, *Paolo and Francesca,* by students of the college. The four-act play was presented at the west entrance of Monroe Hall. The day concluded with the alumnae dance from 10:30 P.M. to midnight in Frances Willard Hall.

The baccalaureate sermon was delivered by the Reverend Martin Luther Enders, D.D., pastor of the First English Lutheran Church of Baltimore and father of Mary Phoebe Enders, who in a few days was to become Mrs. Jere M. H. Willis, wife of the mayor of Fredericksburg.

Final exercises were held in the open-air theatre at ten o'clock Monday morning, June 8. The commencement speaker was the Honorable George C. Peery, judge on the State Corporation Commission. Judge Peery had served as United States Congressman from 1923 to 1929 and was later to become governor of Virginia. His subject was the Hall of Fame. Dean Alstetter presented forty-one candidates for degrees and fifty-four for the two-year diploma. President Combs awarded the diplomas and delivered a "beautiful and impressive speech" to the graduates. He then declared the twentieth session of the college officially at end.[16]

THE ALSTETTER AFFAIR

During the spring of the 1933–34 session a serious rift developed between the president and the dean of instruction. There were rumors that the dean might be dropped from the staff in a proposed reorganization of responsibilities, but nothing definite came to the notice of the public until the meeting of the State Board of Education at the college on April 26.

At the conclusion of this meeting, it was announced that the governing board of the college had unanimously confirmed the authority of the president to "reorganize the administrative set-up

---

[16] *Ibid.,* June 9, 1931.

A Period of Change

and to make whatever changes and adjustments both in the administrative personnel and teaching staff as he deems desirable and commensurate with the growth and development of the institution." [17]

Three days later, on April 30, 1934, the *Free Lance-Star* carried a front-page story with banner headlines on the nature of the changes to be made and the reasons for them. For some time, according to Dr. Combs, the college had felt the need for a revised system of administration in keeping with the growth and requirements of the institution. Chief among the changes to be put into effect was the elimination of the position of dean of instruction, an office held for the past five years by Dr. Alstetter. Dr. Combs explained that the duties performed by Dr. Alstetter would be transferred to other members of the faculty in a plan to distribute administrative functions more widely. He added that Dr. Alstetter had been given an opportunity to submit his resignation to become effective with the close of the current session.

The news of the elimination of Dr. Alstetter's position was received with surprise and mixed feelings on the Hill and in town. Some faculty members sided with the Alstetters. Others stood loyally backed of the president's action. The Alstetters were popular in Fredericksburg and active in church and community affairs. There was a letter to the editor of the local newspaper calling for an explanation of the whole affair. Resolutions expressing regret at the departure of the Alstetters were passed by both the men's and the women's Bible classes of the Presbyterian Church and published in the *Free Lance-Star*.[18]

The Alstetters left at the end of the session. In July it was announced that both Dr. and Mrs. Alstetter were to teach at George Peabody College for Teachers in the coming year. Their twin daughters, Ruth and Beth, were awarded scholarships at Peabody for 1934–35. Later, Dr. Alstetter went to Washington as educational specialist with the Cooperative Study of Secondary School Standards, a project sponsored by the six regional accrediting agencies. During the next three years he developed the evaluative criteria used throughout the United States by visiting committees of the regional associations to determine the accrediting status of secondary schools that had applied or were already members.

The Alstetter affair was a trying experience for all concerned,

[17] *Ibid.*, April 27, 1934.   [18] May 7 and 9, 1934.

especially for the president of the college. In the absence of any official explanation other than the administrative reorganization, there were various speculations as to the reasons for not retaining Dr. Alstetter on the faculty. Dr. Combs refrained from entering into controversy with Dr. Alstetter's supporters. In time the tensions relaxed and interest subsided. New faculty and staff appointments were made to put the revised administrative organization into effect, and the college continued to grow in numbers, facilities, and prestige under the leadership of President Combs.

THE SESSION CLOSES

May Day in 1934 had an Elizabethan theme. Lula Lee Llewellyn of Newport News was queen of May. All members of the court wore Elizabethan costumes. The entertainment featured Old English folk songs and folk dances, as well as games of chance and feats of skill characteristic of the time.

Finals began with the senior class play on June 1, followed by Class Day exercises and the alumnae dinner and dance on June 2, the baccalaureate sermon on June 3, and commencement exercises on the morning of June 4. There were 145 graduates, the largest class since the founding of the college, 71 with bachelor of science degrees and 74 with two-year diplomas. Dr. S. C. Mitchell, professor of history and political science at the University of Richmond, delivered the graduation address.

College Heights High School, the training school of the college, held its graduating exercises on May 31. The address to the graduates was delivered by Dr. Edward Alvey, Jr., of the University of Virginia. Morgan Combs, Jr., president of the graduating class, presented the gift from the class of 1934.

CHAPTER X

Development Accelerates: New Degrees, Faculty, and Facilities, 1934-1938

A NEW ADMINISTRATIVE ORGANIZATION

THE session of 1934-35 opened with a new administrative setup in operation. With the departure of Dr. M. L. Alstetter at the end of the previous session, President Combs had announced that the position of dean would be discontinued. A new official with the title of director of teacher training was designated as the chief academic officer, serving directly under the president of the college. He would also have the rank of professor of education.

Late in the summer of 1934 Dr. Edward Alvey, Jr., then instructor in education at the University of Virginia and acting chairman of the student teaching program there, was offered the new position. He obtained releases from his commitments to the university and also to the Charlottesville school board, and, late in August, accepted the invitation to come to the State Teachers College at Fredericksburg.

Dr. Alvey was born in Richmond. He received his elementary and secondary education in the schools there, graduating from John Marshall High School in 1920. He entered the University of Virginia that fall, enrolling in the liberal arts program in the College of Arts and Sciences. In June 1923 he was awarded the bachelor of arts degree. His undergraduate majors were economics and philosophy.

After a year's employment in the banking and tobacco marketing businesses, Dr. Alvey decided to "teach for a session." He became principal and teacher of Latin at Warm Springs High School, later consolidated into a new Valley High School at Hot Springs, which he also headed. During the summers he had returned to the University to work on a master's degree program. In 1928 he received the master of arts degree and also joined the faculty of the department of education at the university in a new program of experimental education and teacher training.

In 1931 Dr. Alvey completed his Ph.D. degree, with concentrations in education and in English. He continued to offer courses in the teaching of English, to supervise student teaching in English, and to write and edit professional articles and publications.

He also offered courses each year in the University of Virginia summer quarter. At the time of his appointment in Fredericksburg, he was also serving as representative for the southern states for Phi Delta Kappa, a national honorary educational fraternity. The new position of director of teacher training entailed essentially the same responsibilities that had been exercised previously by the office of the dean. In addition, the new appointee served as head of the department of education and also directed the student teaching program.

STUDENT AGITATION OVER RULES

Early in November 1934, the student body of the college was aroused to a high pitch of excitement by the announcement of new rules governing visits to town. Under the new regulations students were not permitted to ride to and from the college except with their parents, faculty members, or in taxicabs. Previously, students had had the privilege of riding with townspeople. When visiting in town, students were restricted to an area bounded by Lewis, Prince Edward, Charlotte, and Main streets, unless reasonable requirements, spelled out in eight exceptions, necessitated their going beyond this zone. Previously there had been no designation of areas they might visit.

The new rules also allowed night visits to town only on Tuesday, Thursday, and Friday, although there was no change in the number of night visits permitted each month, as set forth in the class privileges. Previously, students had been allowed to visit town any week night except Saturday. While certain new privileges were accorded, including the opening of the library and tea room on Sunday afternoons and permission for freshmen to entertain callers on Sunday nights, the rules governing visits to town overshadowed all else.

There were strong expressions of disapproval as each new provision was read to the student body by Thelma Evans, president of the Student Government Association, at a Monday evening assembly. When pressed for explanations, Miss Evans said the new rules had been given to her by the Joint Council, which consisted of three faculty members (Professor O. H. Darter, Dr. Roy S. Cook, and Frances P. Ramey) and four students (Thelma Evans, Frances Mayes, Ethel Nelson, and Helen Taylor). An effort was made to have Dr. Combs appear before the students;

students who opposed the action were requested to withdraw, and about a quarter of those present left the auditorium. However, further discussion and fear of disciplinary action led the students to conclude that a strike would be unwise. Instead, a committee was named to appeal to the Joint Council for a modification of the restrictions.

After the student body meeting Tuesday night, a session of the Joint Council was called at 10:15 P.M. and lasted until 3:15 A.M. Members of the committee just appointed and other students were called in and questioned at length about their part in the proceedings. As an outgrowth of the midnight session, five students were placed on indefinite probation for "leading the agitation against college authority." (A student on probation was subject to dismissal for infraction of any rule in the handbook of regulations.)

When it become known that Elvira Taylor of Emporia, a senior who was president of the German Club and a leader in student activities, had been expelled for her part in the protest, the campus was thrown into an uproar. As news of her dismissal spread, students assembled in a noisy group outside of Virginia Hall where the president's office was located. After dispersing the throng with threats of severe penalties if they did not return to their rooms, President Combs then went to Betty Lewis Hall where another disturbance was in progress. Again he resolved the situation by sending the girls to their rooms.

In spite of calls for a student strike, no concerted action was taken. Fear of penalties that might be imposed undoubtedly had its influence in quieting overt outbreaks, although a smouldering resentment remained among a considerable number of students. Miss Taylor was escorted from the campus by Mrs. Ramey and left for her home in Emporia. Reporters from Washington and Richmond newspapers interviewed her, and the *Washington Post* carried her picture on the front page.

Meanwhile, there were subsequent interpretations of the new rules by the Joint Council. It was announced that students would be permitted to ride in automobiles with town-girl students and "responsible married men of the city" who were considered as respectable and of mature age. No specific age was mentioned.

The *Free Lance–Star* (November 7, 1934) reported an interview with one student who said that "the girls kind of laughed" when told they could ride with men who qualify as being "mature, married, and respectable." The reporter continued: "She said she did not know just who was considered 'respectable' nor did she know how to identify a married man but she could tell a mature man when she saw him."

"At any rate," the interviewer reported, "she rode back to the college this afternoon with a man who seemed to her to meet all the qualifications, although he did not consider himself mature but in the very bloom of youth and vitality."

The Joint Council met all the next day to consider the proper course of action. That evening the usual Wednesday night convocation was held. At the close of the scheduled program, Dr. Combs rose to address the student body. At first there were some scattered boos and hisses, but he continued to speak and to explain how the new rules had come into being, that 90 percent of the students did not need them, and that he believed strongly in student self-government but that orderly procedure was imperative if it were to succeed.

As Dr. Combs spoke, the students listened attentively. As he continued his explanation their attitude changed. Spontaneous applause followed his one-hour address to the students, and many came forward to tell him of their support in the stand he had taken. With the explanation of the new rules and the reasons for their adoption, the feeling of resentment subsided. Miss Taylor herself, through friends in the student body, urged that nothing further be done in protesting her expulsion. She specifically requested no further demonstrations. Further clarification of the new rules disclosed that they were intended to apply only to "pick-up" rides and not to other forms of riding.

The students met again on Thursday night and, in what the *Free Lance–Star* (November 9, 1934) described as a "sudden and sweeping reversal on the part of many girls," adopted "without objection or dissenting vote resolutions declaring their full support of student government and administrative officers, deploring and condemning certain students for giving erroneous impressions to newspapers, and saying that an apology is due by those individuals to Dr. M. L. Combs, president of the college."

Prior to this special meeting of the student body, the fourth in four nights, student leaders had circulated a request that the resolutions be approved as presented without objections, since such action would be to the best interests of the college and the student body. In reaching this resolution of the week's events, the students, no doubt, had come to realize that they had acted impulsively, that the new regulations were not so unreasonable as they had at first seemed, and that the publicity given the disturbances was unfavorable to the college. Many students had also been advised by parents not to participate in any uprising against those in authority at the college.

By the next day the situation on the Hill was back to normal. There was no outward evidence of the strong feelings that had occasioned such a flare-up earlier in the week. The Joint Council continued its inquiry into the circumstances surrounding the uprising, which had caused the expulsion of one student, the campusing of three others for a considerable period, and the placing of still others on probation. Before the student body meeting Thursday night at which the resolutions were passed, the Joint Council gave audience to the student committee of seven asking for a relaxation of the rules. After a two-hour session with the group, the Joint Council announced that it would consider their requests and make a decision in a short time.

In commenting Friday on the events of the week, President Combs attributed the disorders to "growing pains of student government." He also spoke of outside influences that had swayed students at the college. He said he had received many messages endorsing the stand taken by the school. Dr. Combs pointed out that all decisions reached by the Joint Council had been unanimous, indicating that the four student members supported the views of the three faculty members of the council.

Apparently the whole affair seemed to have been a matter of the methods used. Students said they objected to the way in which the new rules were presented to them. College authorities, in turn, said they objected to the methods employed by the students in seeking to present their reactions to the rules. In any case, the situation soon returned to normal and the student body once more went peacefully about the tasks of the day. Thus ended a week of intense excitement which disrupted work at the college and, for a time at least, threatened to result in open defiance of college regulations.

BACHELOR OF ARTS DEGREE AUTHORIZED

Until 1934 the state teachers colleges in Virginia were essentially institutions for prospective teachers. Four-year graduates were awarded the degree of bachelor of science in education and the collegiate professional certificate. Professional courses, including student teaching, were required of all students, unless, for urgent reasons, the teaching requirement was waived.

In the absence of a state liberal arts college for women, it was argued that the state teachers colleges should not be limited to the professional degree of B.S. in education but should be permitted also to award the bachelor of arts degree to students who desired a liberal arts program.

Pursuant to this request, the State Board of Education late in 1934 invited the state teachers colleges to submit outlines of general requirements, major programs, and course descriptions for a program leading to the degree of bachelor of arts. President Combs appointed a special committee, headed by Dr. Alvey, to draw up general degree requirements for the B.A., and also to outline the specific course requirements in the majors to be offered.

This material was compiled promptly and submitted to a committee of the state board appointed to work with the teachers colleges in making plans for the new degree. At its meeting in March 1935, the State Board of Education officially approved the requirements and programs as set up by the state teachers colleges and authorized their granting of the bachelor of arts degree, but none of the liberal arts requirements were waived for students who added the professional courses.

At that time diplomas carried the words *Bachelor of Arts* or *Bachelor of Science.* In the latter case, if a specialized program were followed, the words *Commerce, Dietetics and Home Economics,* and the like appeared in parentheses under the name of the degree. They were all considered bachelor of science degrees.

Majors for the B.S. degree were offered in English, history, social science, foreign language, mathematics, science, education, commercial education, dietetics and home economics, music, and physical education. Minors were also offered in these same fields, with the addition of philosophy and psychology, then listed as a combination minor in part B of the department of education, psychology, and philosophy.

The major in education was actually in elementary education. Students preparing to teach in high school were required to major and minor in the fields they were preparing to teach. Candidates for the B.A. degree were permitted to add courses in education as electives if they wished to qualify for teaching certificates.

The college continued to offer the bachelor of science degree. It was really a professional degree. The general requirements were eighteen quarter hours in English; eighteen in history and social science; nine in physical and natural science; nine in physical education and hygiene; and thirty in education and supervised teaching. There was a provision that "students specializing in certain fields who do not wish to teach may substitute other courses for Education and supervised teaching."[1] Nearly all of the B.S. graduates took the courses in education and qualified for the collegiate professional certificate. The chief exception was mainly for students majoring in dietetics.

The new program for the bachelor of arts degree emphasized academic courses. Of the 189 quarter hours for the degree, 117 were in required subjects, as follows:

English		18 quarter hours
Foreign Language		27
Latin or Greek	18	
Modern Language	9	
History		18
Social Science		9
Mathematics		9
Science		18
Philosophy or Psychology		9
Physical Education and Hygiene		9

The foreign language requirement was the distinguishing feature of the B.A. degree program. To be admitted to this program, students were required to have completed three high school units in Latin and two in French. Otherwise, they had to complete in college a one-year elementary course in the required languages, which would be credited to the general requirements for a degree but not toward a major.

Candidates for the B.A. degree were required to satisfy the general degree requirements as listed above and also to complete thirty-six quarter hours in a major field and twenty-seven in each of two minor fields. Majors were offered in English, foreign language, history, social science, mathematics, and science. Minors were also available in each of these areas, plus fine arts, music, and philosophy and psychology. The only foreign languages in which majors and minors were available at that time were French and Latin. The college also offered two years of Spanish, beginning and intermediate, and two years of Greek.

Majors and minors were still in large academic areas, such as science or social science. Majors in more specific areas, such as biology, chemistry, and physics, developed later. There was a

[1] *Catalogue*, 1936–37, p. 49n.

major in history alone, but the one in social science included not only history but political science and sociology as basic requirements.

In 1936 the first B.A. degree was conferred. The only one granted that year was awarded to Rebekah Ellis Davidson of Rhoadesville. The following year, 1937, there were 2 B.A. degrees; in 1938, there were 4; and in 1939, 6. Each year the number increased until, by 1944, there were 52 graduates who received the bachelor of arts degree. However, the bachelor of science was still the most popular, with a total of 166 B.S. degrees awarded at the 1944 graduation exercises.

TUITION EXEMPTION FOR VIRGINIA TEACHERS DISCONTINUED

It should be noted here that for many years, the Commonwealth of Virginia exempted from tuition charges at the state teachers colleges all residents of Virginia who promised to teach in the state for at least two years. It also exempted students who had been teachers in Virginia, whose tuition was waived one session for each year they had taught in the public schools of the state.

By 1928 the total charge for Virginia teachers had risen to three hundred dollars for the session, with the increase in fees being used mainly to increase the salaries of the college faculty. Application blanks bound with the catalogues still carried a space for the prospective student from Virginia to obtain a state scholarship exempting her from the tuition charge of thirty dollars a year by agreeing to teach for two years in Virginia. The superintendent of schools in which the applicant lived was required to endorse this application, but approval was invariably given.

Practically all Virginia students agreed to teach and obtained the thirty-dollar waiver of tuition. Each year every city and county superintendent of schools was required to furnish to the State Board of Education a list of newly employed teachers. These lists were checked against the lists of graduates of the state teachers colleges to see if they were "fulfilling their teaching obligation."

This was a tedious and laborious process, and there were many obvious objections to such a procedure. Enforcement of the pledge to teach became more and more lax. Finally, beginning with the session of 1936-37, it was discontinued entirely, and all residents of Virginia were exempted from paying a tuition charge

Development Accelerates

at the state teachers colleges. This step was taken shortly after the State Board of Education authorized the granting of the liberal arts bachelor's degree by the state teachers colleges. The total charge for residents of Virginia in 1936 was $318.00, with an additional charge of $57.00 for out-of-state students. The charges remained at this level for several years.

TRAINING SCHOOL ACTIVITIES

Under the administration of the new director of teacher training, a concerted effort to improve the program for the preparation of teachers was begun. Attention centered on the student teaching experience, then offered in the Campus Training School both in the sophomore year for prospective graduates of the two-year diploma program and in the senior year for degree graduates.

The diploma students taught full time for one quarter (three months) in the elementary grades. Degree graduates preparing to teach in the high school taught at least one hour daily for two quarters, one in their major field, and the other in one of their two minor fields. Degree graduates in elementary education, who had usually taught an entire quarter during their sophomore year, did senior teaching in the elementary grades for two hours daily during one quarter in their senior year.

A staff of fourteen full- and part-time supervisors served as critic-teachers. Seven, including the principal of the Campus Training School, were assigned to full-time supervision of student teachers. The other seven, representing such fields as art, music, physical education, commerce, and home economics, were members of the college faculty who devoted part of the time to the supervision of student teachers in their special field.

Regular conferences of student teachers and their supervisors were held on Wednesday afternoons in the training school. Dr. Alvey arranged the programs for these meetings and introduced the topic for discussion. Both supervisors and student teachers participated actively in these weekly conferences, which were in addition to the frequent, informal discussions that each supervisor had with the students for whom she was responsible.

The state of Virginia had embarked upon an extensive program of curriculum revision for both elementary and secondary schools. The new program placed great emphasis upon the creative planning of teaching units growing out of the interests and needs of pupils. This teacher-pupil planning was expected to replace the usual outline of content to be covered. It demanded both ingenuity and resourcefulness on the part of the teacher.

Since there was demand for teachers qualified to teach the "new curriculum," the instructional program of the Campus Training School was geared to provide the necessary experiences for the student teachers. It became, in truth, a demonstration as well as a training school.

In April 1935 the college published in bound, mimeographed form, the first of a series of bulletins giving a detailed description of the teaching units developed by student teachers and their supervisors in the training school. There were two bulletins of illustrative material published the first year, one for elementary grades and another for secondary. Entitled "Units Illustrating Procedures in Using the Revised Courses of Study in Virginia Elementary [or Secondary] Schools," these bulletins enjoyed wide circulation both among other teacher-training institutions and among public school personnel in Virginia.

These two 1935 bulletins were followed by another set of illustrative units for elementary and secondary schools in 1936, and still a third edition of sample units in 1937. The cooperative effort of many persons, these bulletins were edited and duplicated by the director of teacher training and distributed without charge.

SUMMER PROGRAM FOR TEACHERS

These experiences in using the new Virginia state curriculum were the basis of a summer program for teachers, principals, and supervisors interested in knowing more about the new curriculum and its practical application. Arrangements were made for observation of procedures in using the new materials in the summer school operated by the city of Fredericksburg. This was supplementary to the series of lectures given at the college by Dr. Alvey and by members of the State Department of Education, who were invited as visiting speakers.

A special leaflet describing the program was printed and distributed to schools in the eastern part of the state. An announcement of the program was carried on the first page of the summer school catalogue for 1935. It was expected that the program would attract 25 or 30 teachers. Actually, 125 enrolled, and registration was closed at that figure. The demand for this type of course was such that it was repeated the following summer and again in 1937 and 1938.

It was the beginning of a series of summer workshops for teachers conducted throughout the 1940s that drew to the campus many in-service teachers both for certificate renewal and for professional advancement.

OTHER SUMMER WORKSHOPS

Following the new curriculum summer programs, there were special summer courses in radio broadcasting and in dramatics ("The Little Theatre of the Rappahannock"). The series of summer workshops for teachers included ones in guidance (1948); in elementary education and in art (1949); in mental hygiene and in reading (1950); in physical education, teaching materials, citizenship, and school music (1951).

Special summer courses for teachers interested in certificate renewal replaced the workshops in 1952. The Summer School of Music also began that year. These workshops proved highly popular during the period they were offered. Visiting specialists in various fields were brought in to supplement the regular college teaching staff. The workshop in reading, offered under the direction of a nationally known specialist in this field, drew nearly a hundred participants. One outgrowth of these workshops was the publication of mimeographed handbooks, up to eighty pages in length, of procedures and illustrative materials developed by the group. Each member was given a copy.

NEW DORMITORY FACILITIES

For some time the need for new dormitory facilities had been urgent. Early in 1933 Dr. Combs had sought without success to obtain a Reconstruction Finance Corporation loan of a hundred thousand dollars to construct a dormitory to house a hundred students. A new opportunity to obtain federal funds developed with the creation of the Public Works Administration.

Virginia filed applications for over $3 million for state educational institutions. In November a delegation headed by Governor Pollard and Senator Harry F. Byrd appeared before the PWA board of review in support of the request. Also in the group were the presidents of the six state institutions that would benefit, including Dr. Combs. City Manager L. J. Houston, Jr., and J. M. H. Willis of Fredericksburg also attended the hearing.

There was general rejoicing in the community when it was announced that formal approval had been given to a PWA loan and grant of $360,000 to the Fredericksburg State Teachers College for the construction of dormitories.

Thirty percent of the total, or $108,000, was an outright grant and did not have to be repaid. The balance of $252,000 was a loan at 4 percent interest to be repaid over a period of thirty years out of the income for room rental charges. It was the largest award made to any of the state institutions. It made possible an increase in dormitory accommodations that would almost double the enrollment. President Combs announced that an addition to Virginia Hall would be built and that a group of three new dormitories would be constructed across from Virginia Hall at the south end of what had once been an athletic field.

The architectural firm of J. Binford Walford of Richmond had been commissioned to draw plans for the new buildings. They were most impressive. The main building facing north toward Virginia Hall was distinguished by an imposing portico with massive white columns. On the first floor was a large reception hall, thirty-two by forty-six feet, with a circular stairway leading upwards. A skylight with amber-colored glass extended to the roof. On each side of the reception rooms were large parlors illuminated by crystal chandeliers and wall brackets.

The central building was flanked by two smaller residence halls, connected with it by curved colonnades. The group of buildings provided housing for 208 students, 112 in the central unit and 48 in each of the smaller units. Each bedroom was connected with a bath, and on each floor were kitchenettes and pressing rooms for student use. In the basement were laundry and storage facilities, as well as rooms that for many years were used as voice and piano studios for music students. Construction was begun early in April 1934. The firm of J. F. Barbour and Sons of Roanoke was the successful bidder on the contract. The total cost of the buildings and their equipment was $277,364.

BUILDINGS NAMED FOR DISTINGUISHED WOMEN

The Tri-Unit was completed and ready for occupancy in the fall of 1935. The central portion was named Mary Ball Hall, in commemoration of Mary Ball Washington, George Washington's mother. Authoritative data on the facts of her life are decidedly meager. Even the year of her birth is in dispute, some biographers fixing it as early as 1706, while Douglas S. Freeman, in his monu-

Development Accelerates

mental *George Washington,* reported that it was more likely during the winter of 1708–9.

The daughter of Colonel Joseph Ball of Epping Forest, Lancaster County, and Mary Johnson Ball, she became an orphan at the age of twelve when her mother died. Her father had died when she was three. She was left with enough money to provide for her needs. Until she married at the age of twenty-three, she divided her time between the home of her guardian, George Eskridge, a lawyer and burgess of Westmoreland County, and that of her half-sister Elizabeth, who had married Samuel Bonum.

At the time of his marriage to Mary, Augustine Washington was a widower with three children. He and Mary had six children, of whom George was the eldest. George was only eleven when his father died in 1743, and the rearing of the family fell upon Mary. From 1772 to 1789 Mary lived in the house at the corner of Charles and Lewis streets, which her son had bought for her. She lived only four months after George was inaugurated as President. Her grave on Washington Avenue is marked by an impressive monument, unique in having been erected by women to the memory of a woman.

In the 1940s a group of interested citizens in Fredericksburg and at the college made a strong effort to have a commemorative stamp issued in honor of Mary Ball Washington. The absence of an authentic portrait of her proved to be the greatest obstacle to the realization of this goal. The Post Office Department tended to favor the position that the so-called portraits are later reconstructions of how she might have looked, rather than posed likenesses done during her lifetime.

The smaller dormitories to the right and left of Mary Ball Hall were named in honor of two other famous Virginia women. Mary Custis Hall honors the memory of Mary Anne Randolph Custis Lee, the wife of Robert E. Lee. Her mother was Mary Lee Fitzhugh Custis, daughter of Colonel and Mrs. William Fitzhugh, of Chatham, located just across the Rappahannock almost within sight of the college. Her father, George Washington Parke Custis, was the adopted son of George Washington. He lived at Mount Vernon from 1782 to 1802, when he built and moved to Arlington, named for an old Custis home on the Eastern Shore of Virginia.

Mary Custis married Robert E. Lee in June 1831. She and the young second lieutenant began their married life in modest quarters at Fort Monroe. Mrs. Lee visited Arlington frequently and spent much time there.

By the time she was forty-nine, Mrs. Lee was permanently invalided by arthritis. She had to be pushed in a wheelchair wherever she went. General Lee never ceased to care lovingly for her. She survived him by three years, and in 1873 was buried near him in a crypt in the Lee Chapel on the campus of Washington and Lee University.

Madison Hall was named for Dolly Payne Madison, wife of President James Madison, who, as one biographer remarks, acquired "more fame in her own right than many a President of the United States." [2] Although born in North Carolina, Dolly was descended from prominent Virginia families. When she was only one year of age, her family moved back to Virginia. Until she was fifteen Dolly lived at Scotchtown, Patrick Henry's former home in Hanover County, ten miles west of Ashland.

At the age of twenty-two Dolly married John Todd, Jr., a Quaker lawyer. Upon his death from yellow fever after only three years of married life, the young widow named Aaron Burr as sole guardian of her infant son. It was Burr who introduced Madison to her. The following year the twenty-six-year-old Dolly married James Madison, then forty-three.

Her success as a hostess in the White House is legendary. She had a natural flair for entertaining. In times of crisis Dolly showed courage and presence of mind. She herself saved Gilbert Stuart's full-length portrait of George Washington, delaying her departure from the White House until just before the British troops arrived to sack and burn it.

When Madison retired from the presidency in 1817, he and Dolly lived at Montpelier, in Orange County, until his death in 1836. The following year she returned to Washington where she lived at the northeast corner of Lafayette Square. She was active in the social life of the capital. When she died at the age of eighty-one, "a noted and honored figure," she had that year attended a reception at the White House.

ADDITION TO VIRGINIA HALL

While work on the Tri-Unit was in progress, a third section of Virginia Hall was nearing completion. Also designed by J. Binford Walford, the new addition completed the H-shaped building.

---

[2] Irving Brant, *James Madison* (Indianapolis & New York: Bobbs-Merrill, 1950), 3: 401.

Development Accelerates

A portico with tall white columns faced the new central campus that became known as Ball Circle.

The addition was erected by Doyle and Russell of Richmond at a cost of $72,575. On the ground floor it provided space for student parlors, the college library, and the office and apartment of the dean of women. On the two upper floors were rooms to accommodate fifty-four students. Construction was begun in May 1934 and completed in March 1935.

THE GENERAL ASSEMBLY ENTERTAINED

On February 21, 1936, the college was host to Governor George C. Peery and the members of the General Assembly of Virginia and their wives. The visitors were housed overnight in student rooms in the Tri-Unit, which had just been completed. Student occupants shared the quarters of friends in other dormitories or went home for the weekend.

The General Assembly was in session at the time. The group arrived in a number of chartered buses with police escort in time for a formal dinner in Seacobeck Hall at seven o'clock. Afterwards they were guests at a reception and dance given by the college in their honor.

The next morning, February 22, the visitors were taken on a tour of points of historical interest in the city. After lunch they went to Wakefield for ceremonies commemorating the 204th anniversary of George Washington's birth. On the way they stopped for the planting of the first of two hundred cherry trees to be placed along the highway leading to Ferry Farm, the boyhood home of Washington. Officials of the Japanese embassy were with the party and made the presentation.

The members of the General Assembly and their wives returned to Richmond that evening. All were enthusiastic about the accommodations and entertainment at the college. Before they left, Dr. Combs invited them back when the General Assembly met again in 1938.

The legislators and their wives did return in 1938 for an overnight visit to the college. They arrived on Saturday morning, February 19, in chartered buses, accompanied by Governor James H. Price and other notables. The city of Fredericksburg was host to the group at a luncheon at the Princess Anne Hotel. Afterwards, the party made a tour of historic points in the city. Governor Price laid a wreath at the monument to Mary Washington and also visited Kenmore and the Mary Washington house.

That evening the college was host at a banquet in Seacobeck Hall. A program of music and readings was presented by members of the faculty and student body. Dr. Combs introduced Congressman S. Otis Bland; former Governor E. Lee Trinkle; Delegate Alvin Massenburg, the floor leader of the House; and several other distinguished guests, each of whom spoke briefly. There followed a lively dance in the rotunda of Mary Ball Hall, which lasted until midnight. A buffet supper was served under the direction of the dining hall staff, assisted by students in the home economics department.

Most of the visitors stayed overnight in the Tri-Unit, which had been vacated temporarily for their use. They left Sunday morning to return to Richmond. On Monday the House of Delegates adopted a resolution thanking the college and the city of Fredericksburg for their hospitality.

HOBART C. CARTER

In the fall of 1936 Hobart C. Carter joined the department of mathematics, which then included only one other teacher, W. N. Hamlet. For the next thirty-seven years Dr. Carter offered instruction in mathematics, serving as head of the department for most of this long period. Under his leadership the course offerings were expanded greatly, the number of student majors increased, and the faculty expanded to include eight full-time members.

Dr. Carter held the M.A. and Ph.D. degrees from the University of Missouri. In 1936 his first book, *College Algebra,* was published by Prentice-Hall. This popular text was followed by *Modern Basic Mathematics* (Appleton-Century-Crofts, 1964), a new approach to the study of mathematics at the college level he developed after several years of experimentation with the material in mimeographed form.

Dr. Carter retired from active teaching at the end of the first semester of the 1972–73 session. He died a short time afterwards, on February 24, 1973. Both students and professional colleagues characterized him as a capable and devoted teacher.

TITLE CHANGED

During his first two years at the college, Dr. Alvey held the title of director of teacher training and professor of education. The position of dean of instruction had been discontinued after the administrative reorganization in 1934. However, Dr. Alvey had fallen heir to most of the duties exercised by his predecessor, including the direction of the academic program of the college, preparation of class schedules, planning new courses with department heads, assembling material for the catalogue, and other similar activities associated with the office of the dean.

In 1936, "in accordance with the approval of the State Board of Education and the Governor," Dr. Alvey was designated officially as dean of the college."[3] The new title involved few changes in duties, but merely made clear Dr. Alvey's role at the college. It also involved twelve months' employment, as opposed to the previous nine months plus summer session. Dr. Alvey had taught as a visiting member of the faculty at the University of Virginia during the second term of the 1935 and 1936 summer quarters. Beginning with September 1, 1936, he devoted his full time to the college.

NEW FACULTY MEMBERS

The continued growth in enrollment made increases in faculty and staff essential. Academic offerings were being strengthened and more advanced courses added. A dramatic spurt in enrollment took place in the fall of 1937, when the number of students increased more than two hundred over the previous session.

When applications for admission indicated a record increase, President Combs obtained authorization to add several new staff members. There were nine additions to the faculty in the fall of 1937. Several of them were to play a prominent role in the life of the college in the days ahead. Sketches of three of these men and accounts of their accomplishments follow.

EDGAR E. WOODWARD

In July 1937 Edgar E. Woodward began, as treasurer, a period of service to the college that was to span the next thirty-three years. For this lengthy period of time the financial and fiscal affairs of the institution were entrusted to his capable hands. The business administration of this college became the envy of other state institutions struggling to meet continually increasing costs of operation.

[3] President's Report to Board, Oct. 10, 1936.

Woodward, or "Woody" as he was known to a host of friends and acquaintances, was born in Richmond. He attended John Marshall High School before going to the Virginia Military Institute in the fall of 1923. Subsequently he entered the Ohio State University at Columbus, where he graduated in 1932 with the degree of bachelor of science in business administration. He specialized in accounting.

He joined the state auditor's office in Richmond but spent much of the time in the field auditing the accounts of state institutions. He began to specialize in systems accounting. He drew up the accounting systems for several state institutions, including the Medical College of Virginia and the State Teachers College at Fredericksburg.

He was just completing the installation of the accounting system at this institution when President Combs offered him the position as treasurer of the college. Mrs. John C. Ferneyhough became assistant treasurer and cashier.

From the beginning Woody showed himself to be highly capable and sincerely devoted to his work. More and more responsibilities were entrusted to him. He prepared the biennial budget, in itself a major undertaking. He worked closely with President Combs in obtaining increased appropriations for the college. He always accompanied the president at the budget hearings and appeared with him before legislative committees. He usually went with Dr. Combs to meetings of the governing board of the college and represented the president when he was unable to attend.

During Edgar Woodward's thirty-three years as head of the business office of the college the developments that took place are truly remarkable. The annual budget increased from approximately $500,000 in 1937–38 to $5.5 million in 1970–71. The average salary paid faculty members increased from about $2,000 in 1937–38 to $11,300 in 1970–71.

An extensive building program was in progress during most of his tenure. Conferring with architects, advertising for bids, supervising the progress of construction, and ordering furniture and equipment for the new facilities occupied much of his time.

He served also as director of personnel in charge of staff procurement and supervision for the maintenance of buildings and grounds, and the operation of the dining halls and dormitories, the book store, the college shop, the laundry, and all other noninstructional services. His office handled all personnel records of the college. He worked with the classification and reclassifica-

Development Accelerates

tion of positions, retirement and sick leave affairs, hospital insurance programs, and numerous other details concerned with the operation of a large institution. His office staff grew from two assistants plus student help to eleven titled assistantships dealing with collecting and disbursing all funds, state and private; purchasing; payroll; institutional planning; and the like.

When Woody came to the college, Wallace Alsop was the chief janitorial factotum, Eugene Curtis and a few assistants looked after the maintenance of buildings and grounds, and Clifton H. Reeves and Robert E. Humphries constituted the college police force. Currently, the custodial and maintenance staff totals over a hundred. In addition, there is a security force of nine, headed by Chief Medford Haynes. There are full-time electricians, painters, carpenters, plumbers, and a large grounds staff. The college operates a fleet of sixteen trucks, plus special equipment for grass cutting, snow removal, excavating, and the like.

During his service to the college Edgar Woodward's title changed successively from treasurer to bursar to comptroller. In 1969 he was voted faculty status by action of the board of visitors upon recommendation of Chancellor Simpson.

Woody always had time to talk with anyone who had a problem —a student who needed funds for college fees, a faculty member who desired assistance in filling out hospitalization claims, or an employee on the grounds who was facing difficulties. He was a patient listener and a man of action. Often while the visitor was sitting across from him, Woody would pick up the telephone to call the office or individual who might be able to help him.

Some of the most difficult problems grew out of his responsibility for the actions of the college police force, for decisions relating to unwanted visitors on the campus, petty theft in the dormitories, or, occasionally, charges against students growing out of automobile accidents, checks with insufficient funds, or relations with local merchants.

Woody is extremely reticent in speaking about his own accomplishments. When pressed to answer what he regarded as the most important one, he hesitated and grew more thoughtful. Finally, he said it was the repayment of the temporary loan the governor had authorized the state treasury to make to the college.

In brief, the facts are as follows. From 1948 to 1953 or 1954, the college embarked upon a capital outlay program that involved approximately $4.5 million in new construction. The state appropriation for this work totaled about $2.2 million. The balance was borrowed with special permission of the governor, from the state treasury, to be repaid by economies and savings in operations rather than through the issuance of bonds. If bonds had been issued, the total costs of the capital outlay program would have been increased by at least a million dollars over the life of the bonds.

The governor gave special permission to the college to apply any surplus over operating costs to the reduction of this indebtedness. By 1956, or within eight years, the entire debt of approximately $2 million was paid off. In one year alone (1955) a surplus of $450,000 was achieved through economies in operation and increases in enrollment.

Woody is devoted to his family. In 1936 he married Elizabeth Mitchell, of Fairmont, North Carolina, whom he had met while she was a graduate student at Richmond Professional Institute majoring in social work. At the time RPI's School of Social Service was widely recognized as a pioneer in developing graduate programs in this field.

The Woodwards have three children: Elizabeth Parker (Betty), now Mrs. Donald Holman, who lives in Fayetteville, Tennessee, where her husband practices law; Susan Holly, now Mrs. Peter Kilborn, a resident of Paris for several years, who lives now in New York where her husband is on the staff of *Newsweek;* and Edgar E. Woodward, Jr., now serving a two-year enlistment in the United States Navy, who like his two sisters also attended the University of North Carolina.

Woody is active in the life of the community. He is a past president of the Kiwanis Club, past president of the V.M.I. Club of Fredericksburg, a member of the German Club, and a vestryman and at one time senior warden of St. George's Episcopal Church.

Many former students of the college recall Woody's delightful soft-shoe tap dancing, when, with Dean Alvey at the piano, he executed intricate maneuvers to the tune of "Whispering" and "Twelfth Street Rag." The duo performed many times at class benefits and Christmas parties at the college. Both the soft-shoe tap and the piano accompaniment had an air of uncertainty that produced a kind of suspenseful enjoyment, marked by a thunderous expression of relief at the successful conclusion of the performance.

On one occasion Woody was asked when and where he first acquired his skill. He seemed visibly to turn back the years to his student days at Ohio State. "The University used to put on a rather elaborate annual show in those days. I can't remember just how I got into it. Possibly my fraternity (Tau Kappa Epsilon) was asked to put on a number. Anyway, I had a soft-shoe dance in it, which I practiced and rehearsed so I could do a reasonably good job before we went on the road with the show. I never really had any lessons."

Woody always wears a bow tie. He has hundreds of them. He remarked once that he just liked to buy bow ties. No one can recall ever having seen him wearing a four-in-hand. He also prefers a sport coat for all except especially formal occasions.

Colleagues who have traveled with him can certify to his zest for adventure. On one occasion when he, the chancellor, and the dean were returning by way of Nassau from a meeting in Miami, Woody was entranced with the motor scooters he saw. A short time later he roared up in front of the hotel on what seemed to be his first experiment with this type of locomotion. It took an hour to persuade him of the danger faced by an inexperienced operator in traffic that moved to the left on narrow roads at breakneck speed. He disappeared for a while and returned in a convertible which he had rented for the duration of the visit.

On another occasion Woody and the chancellor boarded a train out of Denver that would take them to the other side of the Continental Divide through the Moffatt Tunnel. They got off at the first stop and awaited a train for the return trip. Since passenger service was infrequent, they decided to accept an invitation to ride in the locomotive cab of a freight train with the crew "in order to see more of the Rockies and the tunnel." Both arrived at their hotel in Denver blackened with soot and smoke but triumphant about their experience.

Since his retirement Woody is indulging in his hobby of woodworking. In a basement workshop in his home on Sunken Road he is turning out footstools and other small articles of furniture. He is happy to have more time with his family. His brave outlook and his joy in living continue undiminished, as does his warmth of feeling for his fellow man.

RONALD W. FAULKNER AND THE BAND

In the fall of 1937 Ronald W. Faulkner came to the college as instructor in music and art, with the specific task of organizing instruction in instrumental music. He succeeded admirably not only in this undertaking but also in developing a concert orchestra, a marching band, and a dance orchestra.

Faulkner was a native of Greeley, Colorado, where his father operated for many years a pharmacy located on the main square. After graduating from high school in Greeley, he attended the Institute of Musical Art in New York City, now the Juilliard School of Music, for the session of 1919–20 where he specialized in instrumental music. For three years he was a flutist in the San Diego Symphony Orchestra and a member of the chamber music society there. He also played in theatre orchestras in that city.

He left California in 1920 to enter the Colorado State College of Education at Greeley where he received the B.A. degree in June 1932 with a major in music. He served as director of instrumental music in the Greeley public schools and also continued his studies at Colorado State College of Education (now Colorado State College), receiving the M.A. degree in August 1937 with a major in art. That fall he came to Mary Washington as instructor in music. He advanced successively to assistant and associate professorships in music. At the time of his death in June 1962, he had just completed his twenty-fifth year at the college.

Mr. Faulkner was a tireless worker. From the very first he taught classes in harmony, composition, and conducting and also spent two to three hours daily with either the orchestra or the band, which were scheduled on alternate afternoons. In his spare time he gave individual lessons in flute, clarinet, and other woodwind instruments, conducted rehearsals for the dance orchestra, and furnished the music for innumerable events at the college or in the city.

In order to provide for instruction in various instruments, Faulkner arranged for leading members of the National Symphony Orchestra in Washington to serve as parttime visiting faculty members, teaching on a fee basis those students who wished to study with them.

In 1939–40 the staff in music was augmented by the appointment of first-desk players in the National Symphony on a parttime basis: Ralph Hersh as instructor in violin and viola, William Brennand as instructor in cello and bass, and Sylvia Meyer as instructor in harp. In the same year Vera Neely Ross, a voice teacher in Washington, was appointed as instructor in voice, and Levin Houston III of Fredericksburg became instructor in piano.

The following year Dr. Charlotte Klein, director of music in St. Margaret's Episcopal Church, Washington, D.C., was appointed instructor in organ, and William D. Troxel of Richmond became instructor in brass instruments.

By 1941-42 the faculty in applied music consisted of Millard Taylor, now concert master of the National Symphony, William Brennand, Sylvia Meyer, Levin Houston, Vera Ross, and Dr. Charlotte Klein, as well as Thomas Cousins of the National Symphony as instructor in brass instruments.

The music faculty at the time consisted of Eva Taylor Eppes, chairman, Marion Chauncey, Dr. Herman L. Reichenbach, and Nora Willis, as well as Ronald Faulkner and the visiting instructors in applied music mentioned above.

Furnishing instruments for the band and orchestra players presented a problem, since the initial expenditure involved promised to be quite large. During Ronald Faulkner's first year the instrumental groups struggled along with what instruments the players themselves owned, plus a small number purchased by the college.

In the fall of 1938 a windfall occurred in the form of a number of instruments of varying quality obtained on loan from the National Youth Administration in Washington, which was then in process of liquidating assets. These instruments were rented on a fee basis for several years until the college was able to purchase instruments of high quality and furnish them free of charge to players in the band and orchestra. In time, as the reputation of the instrumental work at the college grew, more and more students who had been outstanding players in high school enrolled, bringing their own instruments with them and contributing greatly to both solo and ensemble work in the band and orchestral organizations.

Unquestionably the most spectacular of the musical organizations developed by Ronald Faulkner was the Mary Washington Band. In the days before nearly every high school had a band with majorettes, the MWC Marching Band was a decided novelty.

Their first appearance in uniform created a sensation as they marched through the campus. Dressed in short white skirts and blue jackets, with white boots and helmet-type headdress, the Mary Washington all-girl band made a colorful appearance. The drum majorette, selected by student applause in a tryout assembly of candidates, wore a helmet with white plumes as she and her twirlers led the band in the fast march step that Faulkner introduced. Later a color guard was added, completing the ensemble.

When the new band uniforms first made their appearance, one rather prim lady on the faculty complained about the shortness of the skirts. When words of this reached Mr. Faulkner, he said rather drily, "I'm glad she doesn't have to wear one."

The band made its first appearance outside of the city at a parade in Richmond launching a new war loan. On this occasion it led the long parade and marched immediately in front of the governor's car. This was only the first of many appearances in Richmond and in Washington, as well as in Fredericksburg. For many years the band led Thalhimer's Toy Parade, an evening spectacle just after Thanksgiving that marked the beginning of the holiday season.

The band lent its services to many parades and rallies during the years of World War II. For several years it marched in the National Safety Patrol Parade in Washington, the Apple Blossom Festival in Winchester, the Tobacco Festival in Richmond, and similar events, winning numerous awards and prizes.

The Christmas programs given by the combined orchestra and band on the Sunday afternoon just before the holidays became a highlight of the season. The auditorium in George Washington Hall was usually filled a half hour before the program was scheduled to start. When the curtains parted they revealed the members of the orchestra in evening dress before a backdrop that Faulkner had designed for the occasion. A balanced program of popular and classical music appropriate to the season was presented, interspersed with vocal or instrumental solos, and usually a special novelty number.

One of the most popular was a sleigh drawn across the stage by eight prancing reindeer, students dressed in leotards with fluffy cotton tails and wearing antlers fashioned from tree branches, while the band played "Rudolph the Red-Nosed Reindeer."

Every year the program concluded with "I'm Dreaming of a White Christmas." As the lights in the auditorium were dimmed, spotlights played on the stage just above the orchestra as bits of white paper fluttered down from the catwalk above and behind the proscenium arch. The illusion of snow falling was so real that spontaneous applause drowned out the music for a time. Many an eye glistened as the curtain slowly closed to the last notes of a "White Christmas." Hearts were warmed and spirits

Development Accelerates

brightened in an indescribable way. As December rolled around, students would begin to ask, "Will we have snow again this year?" Ronald Faulkner sensed their eagerness, and he never disappointed them.

The snowflakes did prove something of a problem, for some lodged in the banks of lights or the network of ropes just above the stage opening. Occasionally a current of air would dislodge a snowflake or two just when a visiting concert pianist or vocalist was reaching the crescendo. There was never any tittering in the audience, just a smile and a glance exchanged in reminiscence, possibly, of the orchestra's playing "Winter Wonderland" the month before as sleigh bells sounded brightly and snow fell gently on the stage below.

The Christmas concerts were carefully planned and rehearsed. Rarely was there a mishap. However, on one occasion an incident occurred that few will forget. An enthusiastic and capable member of the band was scheduled to play a saxophone solo, "My Regards." She loved the saxophone and was an expert player. The students had nicknamed her "Tootie," and they always enjoyed hearing her play. This time she was obviously nervous as she stepped forward in evening dress in front of the band. Halfway through she stopped, turned to Faulkner who was standing aside and blurted, "I've forgotten it."

Faulkner sensed the tenseness. In his calm and sympathetic way, he said, "Let's start over again." The orchestra once again played its introduction, "Tootie" took over her solo part and played it faultlessly to the end, and in the burst of applause that followed, at least one member of the audience swallowed hard to keep down the lump in his throat.

The marching band was often asked to perform between halves at college football games. It was a featured attraction at games in Richmond, Norfolk, Charlottesville, and Griffith Stadium in Washington.

At one of the Charlottesville appearances, Faulkner had arranged for five students to spell out the word HELLO with large cards as the band marched on the field. He had planned for the girl with the letter o to pretend to be confused and stand to the right of the H, so that the letters spelled out O HELL. Upon discovering her mistake she was to run frantically to the other end, so that the correct word appeared. This was done as planned, the crowd in the stadium laughed heartily at the result, and all applauded as the "unfortunate" girl ran to the other end of the word. Afterwards, some spectators found it hard to believe that it had all been planned. One newspaper account referred to the "amusing error" a member of the band had made in the greeting to the stands.

The dance band was in great demand to play for informal dances, student pep rallies, the annual Christmas dinner, and many other occasions when students gathered and popular music was appropriate. The musicians presented an attractive appearance in their red jackets and blue skirts, playing behind individual music stands which Faulkner had designed and decorated with the MWC emblem.

The band usually featured a vocalist, providing an excellent opportunity for one of the voice majors to develop her singing style and stage presence. Out of these experiences developed professional careers in music and radio for several alumnae of the band. The dance band received many requests to play for dances given by organizations locally and in Richmond and Washington. The pressure of studies at the college permitted the acceptance of only a few of these invitations.

On at least one occasion the group made a tour of high schools in Northern Virginia and in Washington, playing at special assemblies. Such tours did much to stimulate interest among prospective students in the music program and organizations at Mary Washington.

Faulkner's enthusiasm and dedication to his work were unlimited. He was always ready to give of his time and talents to the college. Mrs. Faulkner worked closely with him in his plans and ideas for the band and accompanied them on all of their trips. Each Christmas they gave a party for the band and orchestra members in their home immediately after the concert. The students who played under his direction referred to him as Papa Faulkner, and they regarded him with genuine affection.

In 1947 two of Faulkner's students, Jeanne Crotty and Irene Taylor, wrote "High on Marye's Hilltop," which was subsequently adopted as the official alma mater of Mary Washington College. Faulkner himself composed the music and Ann Mason the words for "The Spirit of M.W.C.," a marching song that was a favorite of the band. Both of these compositions were included in *Mary Washington College Songs,* a songbook published in Boston in 1943 by C. C. Birchard and Company and used for many years in assemblies held in George Washington Hall.

Ronald Faulkner was an accomplished musician as well as a band and orchestra director. He and his daughter, Ronna, often entertained at programs and parties at the college, she seated at the harp and Faulkner standing beside her with his flute. The two together made an unforgettable scene as the clear notes of the flute blended with the caressing accompaniment of the harp strings.

Mr. Faulkner was also a creative artist. His ceramics are still to be seen in offices of the college and in the homes of his friends, gifts of a generous nature. He saved all of his molds and planned upon retirement to open a studio and sell his creations commercially in Florida. However, he died in June 1962, after a brief illness.

E. BOYD GRAVES

Dr. E. Boyd Graves, born in Nebraska, attended Hobart College, in Geneva, New York, for two years, and then transferred to William and Mary where he received his A.B. degree in 1932 with majors in English and French. In 1935 he received his M.A. degree, also from William and Mary. In the meantime he had become an elementary school supervisor as well as a specialist in curriculum. He became a consultant for the Virginia curriculum revision program. For two summers he directed the curriculum laboratory at Delta State College in Mississippi. It was at this time that he came to Mary Washington, in September 1937, as associate professor of education and coordinator of inservice and preservice education of teachers.

Soon after coming to the college, Dr. Graves inaugurated a new program of apprentice teaching in what was at the time a decided innovation in the preparation of teachers. As introduced at the college, the plan provided for students in the normal professional course to spend an entire quarter of their sophomore year as apprentice teachers in one of the cooperating school systems. They were to devote the entire school day to observing and teaching under a participating instructor "selected by the school system because of her outstanding work as a teacher."

Students enrolled in the apprentice teaching program were carefully selected. Not only was a satisfactory academic average required but also favorable reports from faculty members as to personality and probable success as elementary teachers. Students who did not seem to give promise of profiting from the program were advised to transfer to another field of study, or, as some chose to do, to another institution.

Dr. Graves personally visited superintendents and principals to outline the program he had in mind. Conferences with each participating teacher followed. Procedures for providing learning experience for the student teachers and the types of reports to be made on their progress were discussed in detail. Each apprentice teacher met both her supervisor and the school principal before any definite assignment was made. Much depended upon a satisfactory relationship between apprentice teacher and supervisor, for the personal element was an integral part of the program. Students were expected to enter fully into the life of the school, attending assemblies, teachers' meetings, and meetings of school organizations, including the Parent-Teacher Association. In addition to her duties at the school, each apprentice teacher prepared a research paper, usually related to her work in the elementary school classroom.

Students were housed in approved homes in the community, selected by Dr. Graves with the cooperation of local school authorities. The apprentice teachers paid the usual college fees for tuition, room, and board during the quarter they were off campus. The college in turn reimbursed the householder for maintenance at an agreed rate. Each quarter a new group of apprentice teachers went out, often occupying the facilities vacated by the students who had completed their work the previous quarter. At its peak, the apprentice teaching program operated in three cities (Richmond, Alexandria, and Norfolk) and twenty counties, large and small. Schools of all sizes were included.

The new program attracted considerable attention both within the state and elsewhere. Dr. Graves was called upon frequently to lecture or contribute articles describing the operation of the arrangement. Several teacher-training institutions sent observers to Fredericksburg. Most impressive was the enthusiasm of the apprentices themselves. They returned to college classrooms with a new concept of the nature and rewards of teaching. Many of them had left their schools with the definite assurance that regular teaching positions were awaiting them there as soon as their work at the college was completed.

When the normal professional certificate course with the two-year diploma was discontinued in 1942, the apprentice teaching concept was incorporated into the four-year degree program for elementary teachers. It continued in operation until the college was affiliated with the University of Virginia in 1944, at which time a major in elementary education was discontinued. Over the next four years the program was phased out as "technical courses designed for the training of teachers" were eliminated.

Dr. Graves completed his Ed.D. degree at George Washington University in 1947. In February 1948 he began a leave of absence to serve as educational consultant to the Allied Commission for Austria. He was attached to the headquarters staff of the United States forces in Vienna. For the next two and a half years, he directed four programs dealing principally with the indoctrination of Austrian educators in the American brand of democracy.

Upon his return to the college in 1950, Dr. Graves was made chairman of the philosophy department, a position he continued to hold until his retirement in 1969. Under his leadership the department grew to require the services of four full-time staff members. It was the first department in the college to inaugurate an independent study program. It was also the first to use all paperback source readings instead of textbooks in an introductory course.

The philosophy department was the first to supplement the series of visiting lecturers from the University Center in Virginia with its own visiting scholars program and to receive funds from the administration for this purpose. It began the practices of having staff members take turns reading original papers at departmental meetings and of providing for student participation in the selection of new teachers to be recommended for the staff.

In 1957–58 Dr. Graves was elected president of the Virginia Philosophical Association. Later he served as chairman of the Virginia Humanities Association. At the time of his retirement he was head of the Washington Philosophy Club. During his period of service at the college, he was also area director of extension teaching for the School of General Studies at the University of Virginia, serving in this capacity for some ten years.

ALMONT LINDSEY

Almont Lindsey joined the faculty in September 1937. His undergraduate degree was from Knox College, his M.A. and Ph.D. degrees from the University of Illinois. Except for a period of two years when he taught history in England and Germany for the overseas program of the University of Maryland, he has continued to teach at Mary Washington.

Out of Dr. Lindsey's doctoral dissertation on the Pullman strike grew a four-hundred-page book published in 1942 by the University of Chicago Press. It was one of the titles selected for President John F. Kennedy's library of significant publications in the White House. Dr. Lindsey reports that he is still receiving royalties from a paperback edition of *The Pullman Strike,* published later as a Phoenix book by the University of Chicago Press.

Socialized Medicine in England and Wales was published in 1962 by the University of North Carolina Press, and also by the Oxford University Press in England. It received favorable reviews in many publications, both in England and in America, including the *Journal* of the American Medical Association. Although writing, research, and travel engage Dr. Lindsey's spare time, his real love is teaching, as hundreds of his former students remember with gratitude.

CHAPELS AND CONVOCATIONS

During the period from 1930 to 1956 it was customary to have three gatherings of the entire student body each week of the session. On Tuesdays and Fridays there was chapel from 12:30 to approximately 1:00 P.M. and on Wednesday evenings there was a convocation from 7:00 to 8:00 P.M.

Attendance at these meetings was required, although each student was permitted two or three cuts from chapel during the semester and one or two cuts from convocation. Student government representatives stood in the aisles and checked attendance by rows as the programs got under way. Absences were checked against sick lists and against total number of cuts. A student who overcut chapel or convocation was subject to student government penalties. Doors were closed after programs began and late students were turned away.

The chapel programs were by no means entirely religious in nature, although for some time a minister from town conducted a religious service with a brief message at least every fourth meeting, or every two weeks. Other chapel programs were staged by college organizations such as the Y, Alpha Phi Sigma, the Dramatic Club, the Science Club, and the International Relations Club.

At times, members of the faculty would speak on some aspect of their specialty, a trip they had taken, or the significance of some special holiday or event commemorated during the week. Many programs were pure entertainment, such as performances by the college band, the Glee Club, or a modern dance group. Distinguished visitors to the college were often introduced if it happened to be a day for chapel, and they usually responded with a few words to the student body.

Few faculty members, other than the committee in charge, attended these chapel exercises. The scheduling of events was in the hands of a chapel committee, which was also responsible for giving out announcements at the beginning of the period, introducing the speaker or the program, and seeing that the exercises went smoothly.

Convocations were held each Wednesday evening and, as the name implies, were more formal in organization and content. The opening convocation was held the first Wednesday of the session, immediately following two days of registration and preceding the beginning of classes on Thursday. It featured an address to the student body by the president of the college, introduced by the dean of the college, who served as chairman of the convocation committee and presided at all convocations of a formal nature during the session. Members of the faculty sat on the stage at the opening convocation until the group got too large for the space available. It was customary for the president to introduce new members of the faculty on this occasion.

Nearly every convocation was formal in that seniors wore caps and gowns and marched in to occupy seats on the first rows of the auditorium. The program usually opened with the singing of one stanza of "America," followed by a brief Scripture reading and the Lord's Prayer, led by the dean of the college, who then made announcements and introduced the speaker. The program concluded with the singing of the alma mater and the recession of the seniors. In the case of more informal programs, such as concerts by the Glee Club, the college orchestra, the Modern Dance Club, or a dramatic presentation, the religious part of the program and sometimes the formal procession of the seniors were omitted. However, seniors usually preferred the processional, since it afforded them front-row seats for talent performances.

Over the years, many prominent persons were convocation speakers at the college. The list included college presidents; heads of organizations such as women's clubs, historical societies, and civic groups; prominent political leaders in the state, including future or past governors; educational leaders in state and federal service; and, from time to time, visiting lecturers scheduled through the arts program of the Association of American Colleges.

Convocation attendance was required; even the library closed. Usually, attendance was enthusiastic and attention commendable. However, there were times when inconsiderate speakers tried the fortitude of even the most patient. A memorable occasion was the time a certain state senator tediously read an address of over forty pages. Toward the end, one could detect an audible whisper of students counting each page as it was turned.

On another occasion, an eloquent and rhetorical speaker of the old school was reaching the peroration of his address with the words, "From the length and breadth of this gre-at state, from Virginia Beach to ah-ah [marked hesitation while speaker fumbles for the word] Grundy:" When he came out with Grundy after such a critical pause, the entire student body burst into laughter. Students had thought immediately of the senior they called "Grundy" (she hailed from there) who was sitting on the first row.

FORMAL DANCE ORGANIZATIONS

During this period the high point of social activities was reached in the formal dances given by the German Club. The name of the club itself indicates something of the traditional nature of its entertainments, since the organization was modeled after dance organizations, such as the Richmond German, which dominated the social scene in the period preceding World War I.

The German Club was founded by Mrs. Bushnell and President Chandler in 1922. One of its major purposes was to have men at the dances, which its predecessor, the Virginia Reel Club, did not permit. The club consisted of a carefully selected membership of sixty students. A bid to join the German Club was regarded as the highest kind of social recognition at the institution. Election was by secret ballot, and the fortunate recipient of a bid was notified officially by a committee from the club. It was said that the dean of women, as faculty sponsor of the club, made the final decision as to whether or not a girl should be elected to membership.

A distinctive German Club pin, similar to a fraternity or sorority badge, was worn proudly by members of the club. There were no annual dues, but the college made a contribution from the student activities fund toward the cost of the dances, which usually exceeded the fee charged.

German Club dances were strictly formal. Engraved invitations bearing the seal of the organization were sent out well in advance of the fall, midwinter, and spring Germans. The sixty members of the club and their dates formed the nucleus of each dance. Then a specified number of other college students were permitted to sign up for the dance and invite dates to it. When the maximum number had signed up, additional reservations were declined, but their names were placed at the head of the list of guests for the next dance.

The dances were carefully planned for months in advance. A theme for the decorations, the favors to be given, the dinner and supper menus, the orchestra to be booked, and the invitations to be sent—all were discussed in detail. A German Club weekend involved a dinner with one's date in the college dining hall, the dance itself from nine to twelve, and afterwards a supper in Seacobeck for the entire group.

Expensive evening dresses were worn at the German Club formals. Card dances were the rule, and each girl spent days before the event exchanging dances with classmates. Each student wanted her date to have a card well-filled with dances with her friends, reserving always the first and last dances for herself.

A feature of the German was the figure held just before intermission in which only members and their dates participated. These figures were elaborate and were carefully rehearsed beforehand. Each member wore a distinctive corsage or carried an American Beauty rose or was in some other way distinguished from the rest of the group. A red ribbon bearing the words *German Club* in gold letters was worn across the chest of the date of a member.

German Club dances were stately and sedate affairs. The music itself was designed to encourage graceful and dignified dancing, with waltzes and fox trots predominating. There was no jitterbugging or other unseemly demonstrations of wild abandon to music or mood. A floor committee gently warned with a reproving but highly effective look any couple whose dancing was inappropriate.

The dance cards deserve special mention. Each program was distinctive, with a specially designed cover in the color scheme of the dance; an appropriate quotation, such as "Now dance we a measure"; a space for listing the partners for each of the eighteen or twenty dances; and, on the last page, a list of the sponsors of that dance, usually two or three members of the faculty and administration and their wives. A complete collection of these cards from 1934 to the end of the formal dance organizations was kept by the wife of the dean of the college and was placed later in E. Lee Trinkle Library.

Of special interest were the pages in the college annual devoted to the German Club. Frequently printed on paper different from the rest of the yearbook, they often featured such devices as an embossed reproduction of the club emblem, along with a fullpage photograph of the officers, and another page listing the club membership for that year. Needless to say, this section of the *Battlefield* usually attracted attention second only to the dedicatory pages.

As the college grew in numbers, the need for another dance organization became apparent, since only a limited number of students could attend the German Club activities. In 1938, largely through the interest and efforts of Dr. W. J. Young, the Cotillion Club was organized. It was quite similar in its format and operation to the German Club. Membership was limited, selective, and decided by secret ballot. Decorations, invitations, programs, and refreshments were elaborate. Lillie Turman and Ronald Faulkner were among the first sponsors of the club.

One of the earliest and, possibly, the most memorable formal affairs sponsored by the Cotillion Club was a make-believe shipboard dance held in the spring of 1939. Couples entered the dance floor by a gangplank at the foot of the stairs leading down to the Monroe gymnasium. Ships' signal flags were strung across from the balcony rails, and the wire netting below the balcony railing had been decorated with facsimiles of ship life preservers on which the words *S.S. Cotillion* had been painted. The illusion of a dance on shipboard was surprisingly well achieved. The signal flags instead of numbers for the dance cards were an added touch.

On January 20, 1940, the Cotillion Club became the first group to hold a formal dance in the Hall of Mirrors, the new ballroom in the basement of George Washington Hall. The last formal dance in Monroe Gymnasium was the Christmas dance of the German Club on Saturday, December 9, 1939. The spring formal of the German Club was held in the Hall of Mirrors.

The two organizations naturally became rivals, strong rivals. There was often discussion as to whether the Cotillion Club was better than the German Club, and if a girl were so recognized as to receive simultaneous bids from each, which one she should accept. The two clubs continued to dominate the social scene until 1946. In the meantime, it was felt that the college itself should sponsor formal dances that any student could attend. An outgrowth of this attitude was the formation, in 1940–41, of the College Promenade under the sponsorship of a faculty committee.

The new organization sponsored seasonal dances, formal in nature, with dinners and suppers as a part of the weekend. The first promenade was a George Washington's Birthday dance on

February 15, 1941. All of the formal dances were held on Saturday evenings, for it was felt that a Friday night dance might interfere with the preparation for the next day's classes. All dances ended on the stroke of midnight, for there was to be no dancing on Sunday. There was usually an informal tea dance on Saturday afternoon.

Mary Washington College had long been committed to the policy of excluding social sororities. When it became evident that the German and Cotillion clubs had more and more of the aspects of selectivity, such as limited membership, sponsored nomination, election by secret ballot, and a sort of social clique, the student body itself, at the suggestion of the administration, voted to discontinue the formal dance clubs and to substitute a college-sponsored series of dances.

The plan was put into operation in 1948-49 through the appointment by the administration of a formal dance committee, consisting of five students, with three faculty members as advisers. This committee was empowered to select dances, book orchestras, issue invitations, supervise decorations, and in general take care of all duties in connection with these occasions.

The new committee was most successful in its operation. Perhaps one of its most distinctive contributions was the building of each formal dance around a special theme, usually seasonal. College workmen were called in to string lights and hang decorations. First used in the fall of 1952, the new ballroom in Ann Carter Lee, with its enlarged capacity and its many possibilities for ingenious decorative motifs, gave new impetus to the college-sponsored formal dances.

BENEFITS

Weekend absences from the campus were not a problem in the 1920s and 1930s. Everyone was usually present from the beginning of the session to the end, except for the holiday periods.

In the twenties, students were allowed one cut a quarter, known as a dance cut. In order to take advantage of this provision, the fortunate student had to show Mrs. Bushnell the actual invitation to the dance before the cut was permitted.

Since the students were usually on campus every weekend, special efforts were made to provide entertainment for them. Chief among these activities were the various class and club benefits held on Saturday evenings in the auditorium of Monroe.

They were essentially talent shows although original skits were always an important part of the program. Mrs. Bushnell always had to preview and approve all benefits to make sure that they were in good taste.

Students of those days recall vividly the class benefits of their four years. Hours and hours of work went into their production, and the student director was always honored with a special gift presented before the entire audience just after the completion of the last curtain calls. And there were always several curtain calls, for even the less successful efforts were received with enthusiasm by an audience that had come to enjoy and to be amused.

Some of the skits were hilarious. Few students here at the time will forget "The Courtship of Miles Standish," with Dr. C. G. G. Moss in the title role; Mary Frances Rowe, editor of the *Battlefield* and May queen later that year, as Priscilla; and Dr. Alvey, who had just come to the college that fall, as John Alden.

Costumes had been ordered especially for the occasion. Priscilla was demure and charming as a Puritan maiden; John Alden was a scholarly youth in his seventeenth-century knee breeches and silver-buckled shoes; and Miles Standish was forthright and virile in his military outfit with helmet and breastplate. The popular Dr. Moss, with his brawny figure and somewhat gravelly voice, made an impressive figure as Captain Standish. When he rumbled, "Say that a blunt old Captain, a man not of words but of action . . . ," the student body almost wept with laughter.

Later, as Priscilla rose from her spinning wheel and said tremulously, "Why don't you speak for yourself, John?" the auditorium echoed with squeals, for John Alden timidly gathered Priscilla in his arms and pressed her gently to his heart.

One highly imaginative skit involved a group of students who had reached heaven and were looking over the edge of their home in the skies at events taking place below. The stage setting consisted chiefly of white pillows collected from beds throughout the dormitory. Participants lounged among them as if on billows of clouds and pretended to peer over the edge as they floated along.

"We must be over Fredericksburg now: it's raining below" began the opening speech, a reference to the downpour that always seemed to characterize opening days at the college. There followed numerous references to individuals and events below, as seen from the vantage point of the heavenly home. A new arrival brought the latest news of the college to heaven. There was a vivid reminder of regulations when the new arrival was asked if she had signed out. Even in heaven, signing in and out was a part of the daily life.

For several years the junior class sponsored a beauty contest. Proceeds from the sale of tickets were used to finance class activities. The Vogue Varieties presented in December 1944 was typical. There were thirty-seven contestants representing various organizations on the campus, including the Alumnae Daughters Club. Emily Avery represented the Athletic Association. Judges were Miss Bradley, head model, Garfinckel's; the display director of Miller and Rhoads; and the assistant manager of Montaldo's. Skits were presented by the class and piano selections played by Levin Houston between eliminations.

The winner of the contest, June Ellen Minnerly, was designated Miss Mary Washington and received a silver loving cup, engraved later with her name. Scrapbooks of press clippings dating from that time show that her picture appeared in newspapers of Washington, Richmond, and other cities.

PEANUT WEEK

Among the most interesting traditions of the college in its less sophisticated days was Peanut Week. As the time for Christmas holidays approached, excitement mounted, especially among students who had not seen home or family since early September. Room doors were elaborately decorated in each dormitory. Furthermore, scenes of the nativity, of Christmas in other lands, of carol singers serenading, and other imaginative representations were set up in the parlors of each residence hall. Competition was keen. A jury of faculty members evaluated each exhibition and awarded a prize for the best one. There were Christmas carols, programs of Christmas music, and a general breathlessness of excitement and anticipation as the days before the holiday grew fewer. In the midst of it all, Peanut Week came along. It was one way of letting off steam.

The names of all of the students—as well as those of faculty members who wanted to participate—were typed on little slips and put inside peanut shells. Then each student picked a shell and drew the name of her peanut. The secrecy of identity was strictly maintained. Each day for a week the drawer of the name gave her peanut some little present—a candy bar, a box of paper clips, or any little inexpensive gift. Gifts were usually exchanged by means of the college post office which, operated by the institution, involved no payment of fees for mailing. Frequently, a little poem accompanied the gift. A card reading "Your Peanut" was the only clue to the sender.

Finally, at the annual Christmas dinner, more substantial gifts were exchanged, and the name of the peanut was revealed on the card accompanying the present. Until the student body became too large, these gifts were piled beneath the dining hall Christmas tree until distributed or claimed.

THE DOLL SHOW

Another feature of the thirties and forties was the doll show sponsored each year by members of the YWCA just before the beginning of the Christmas holidays. A special committee of upperclassmen organized the freshmen in Willard to produce scenes typical of the Christmas season. These were built in large wooden boxes, with little houses, artificial trees and snow, and dolls dressed in appropriate costumes.

Many hours were spent on their preparation. Themes varied from year to year. Most popular were Christmas in Other Lands, scenes from plays or stories about Christmas, or settings depicting life in various parts of the United States. Prizes were awarded for first, second, and third place. At the conclusion of the event, the dolls were sent to children at the Blue Ridge Sanatorium in Charlottesville and, later, to underprivileged children in Fredericksburg and vicinity.

There were also elaborate Christmas decorations in the parlors and halls of each dormitory. Special themes were carried out in each parlor display. Doorways to each room were decorated, and prizes awarded for the best result. Also awarded was a cup that passed from year to year to the dormitory that produced the best Christmas scene in its parlor.

DAISY CHAIN

Another tradition of days past was the daisy chain, pictured and described in catalogues and viewbooks as "One of the Annual Features of the June Commencement."

The daisy chain was a substantial affair, consisting of thousands of small bunches of eight or ten daisies which were then tied securely around a one-inch manila rope, pressed closely together, to make a solid mass of blooms. It was carried on the shoulders of the two-year diploma graduates—who led the procession at Class Day exercises. Ordinarily the chain was so heavy that a carefully folded towel was placed beneath it on the shoulder of each girl both to protect the white dress of the wearer and to ease the burden of the massed chain of daisies.

During the Class Day program the chain was laid around the sides of the stage in the open-air theatre, forming a backdrop for the participants. At the conclusion of the exercises, the sophomores once more lifted the chain to their shoulders and carried it in procession to the central campus where it was usually hung in loops across the portico of Virginia Hall for the rest of the commencement weekend.

Older faculty members recall the vast fields of daisies that once grew along the roads leading to Fredericksburg. It was the task of the freshmen to gather the daisies, tie them into bunches, and fasten these bunches to the rope to produce the finished chain. For days before the event, a truck from the college shuttled back and forth from the daisy fields carrying large galvanized tubs filled with freshly gathered daisies, which were kept in water until ready for use.

There was always some apprehension as to whether the chain would be finished in time. As the deadline drew near, the area near Willard Hall was filled with students emptying tubs, tying bunches of daisies, and working on the chain. On more than one occasion, the activity continued far into the night, carried on by the light of automobile and truck headlights until the job was finished. The next day, there were the usual exclamations of admiration and approval as the sophomores marched in carrying the lovely burden of flowers. The daisy chain continued to be a feature of Class Day exercises until June 1942, when the awarding of the two-year diplomas was terminated.

HAMLET HOUSE PURCHASED

In 1937 the college purchased from Mr. and Mrs. W. N. Hamlet the frame house on College Avenue they had occupied for many years. The property was acquired for $12,500. The house was remodeled for use as a residence for students. Later, the first floor housed the psychological clinic, where testing and other psychological services were available for public school children of Fredericksburg and the nearby counties, under a contract with the

State Department of Education. This plan afforded practical experience for students majoring in psychology and especially interested in testing and in nonpsychiatric counseling of problem pupils. The program was discontinued when a special clinic was provided at the University of Virginia.

The Hamlet house continued to serve as a training facility for individual psychological testing, such as the administration of the Binet-Simon Test, until in 1965 it became a counseling center.

FACULTY CLUBS

The Faculty Men's Club was organized in 1937, largely through the efforts of Dean Alvey and several other men on the faculty. Professor O. H. Darter was elected as its first president. Monthly luncheon meetings were held throughout the session, at first in the banquet room of a downtown restaurant and, later, in the college tea room. There was usually a guest speaker, often a city or county official or a community leader. Panel discussions of current issues became popular, with such topics as social security or socialized medicine warmly debated by members of the group.

There was an ambitious movement to erect a small building adjacent to the campus, with club rooms on the first floor and an apartment for rental purposes on the second. Plans were actually drawn up for such a building and a site selected. Some members of the group began to lose courage when it was evident that subscriptions to finance the project would be required. The option held on a desirable piece of property was not exercised. Had it been purchased, it would have been worth many times the cost today.

Plans for a faculty house were abandoned entirely when the college made available a basement room where members could meet, relax, read, and smoke. The room was never utilized to any great extent, and finally it was converted to other uses. The club had about a hundred dollars in its treasury. This was turned over to the college to provide financial assistance to any worthy student. It was called the Faculty Men's Club Loan Fund. Interest in the meetings began to wane during the late fifties. When attendance at the luncheons dropped below fifteen, the meetings were discontinued, and the club became inactive.

The Faculty Wives' Club was organized early in 1938. Mrs. Richard M. Kirby was the prime mover in its organization and became its first president. An account in the *Bullet* for March 16,

1938, described a meeting of this "newly-formed group" on Thursday afternoon, March 10, in the Dome Room of Seacobeck Hall. Ronald Faulkner was the speaker. The *Bullet* article listed sixteen members of the new organization.

The Faculty Wives' Club continued to grow in membership and service to the college, particularly in making new faculty wives feel at home. A luncheon welcoming new members is usually held early in October at a local hotel; monthly meetings follow during the session; and the year's activities conclude with a covered-dish luncheon in May. There is a program committee for each meeting. The club publishes an annual directory of its membership. In 1971–72 there were seventy-six active members, five nonresident members, and twenty-four inactive members.

The constitution of the club lists as its objective "to assist the College in friendly relationships; to foster fellowship among club members." Membership is open to the wives of current and retired members of the administrative and teaching staff and to widows of these groups.

STUDENT TEACHING IN CITY SCHOOLS

In the early years of the college, all student teaching was done in the public schools of Fredericksburg and, later, also in the schools of Stafford and Spotsylvania counties. Differences of opinion over policies led to a discontinuance of the program in the city schools, and in 1928 the new campus training school was put into operation.

As the enrollment of the college continued to increase, the facilities of the training school were insufficient to provide the necessary teaching opportunities, with the result that several student teachers were often assigned to the same classroom. From grades one through eleven, every class had student teachers, and each supervisor had five or six students to supervise.

As early as 1935 student teachers in commercial subjects and physical education, and later music and art, were assigned on a trial basis to offer instruction in these fields, under the supervision of the city school teaching staff. Their work proved so satisfactory that early in 1938 negotiations were begun with the city school board for an extension of the program on a broad basis.

President Combs and Dean Alvey met with the school board to outline a plan whereby a limited number of seniors would be assigned to the city schools in the nature of assistants or apprentice teachers to serve with and under the direction of the classroom teacher. In no case would the student teachers actually replace the classroom teacher. The plan had the full endorsement of the city superintendent of schools, Guy H. Brown, who saw many advantages in the arrangement. The school board was also favorably impressed.

As a result of these negotiations a two-year contract was drawn up whereby the college would pay the city five thousand dollars annually, to be used as deemed desirable, for the privilege of having student teachers assigned to elementary and high school classrooms, working under the direction of the regular city schoolteachers. The contract was signed by Paul M. Karsten, chairman of the school board, and President Combs, for the college. Dean Alvey and Superintendent Brown proceeded to work cooperatively in assigning student teachers to staff members in the city schools for the session beginning September 1938. Most of these were placed in high schools, for a new program of off-campus apprentice teaching in cooperating elementary schools had just been put into effect.

President Combs gave notice to the Spotsylvania County school board that the contract for operating the training school as an educational institution for county pupils would be terminated at the end of the 1937–38 session. Plans were made for converting the Campus Training School building into a classroom building to provide sorely needed teaching space, especially for classes in the sciences.

The governing board of the college had approved the use of the training school as a classroom building if and when other arrangements for student teaching were made. As soon as the session ended, workmen began a complete renovation of the building. It was renamed Chandler Hall in honor of the former president of the college, who had worked so hard to obtain funds for its erection.

CHANDLER HALL ADDITION

The training school had been built originally with the idea that a front section facing the college campus would be added, and the building was so designed. This accounted for its uncompleted look on the east side. With the discontinuation of the training school in June 1938, construction on the long-awaited addition was begun immediately. Again, the architectural firm of J. Binford Walford of Richmond was engaged. Four large rooms and a central hallway were added. These new rooms were equipped as modern laboratories—two for biology on the first floor and rooms for chemistry and physics on the second. There were also offices for members of the science department, a balance room for advanced chemistry, and a chemical supply room.

The ground floor of the building was redesigned and equipped for the use of the home economics department. There were two large food laboratories, a small dining room, a clothing and textiles laboratory, and offices for the home economics staff. The post office was assigned to a corner room on the ground floor. Next to it was a new town girls' room. In the rear of the building, porticos were added to replace the stoops. Across the new front of the building was a portico with tall columns matching the architectural style of the other buildings facing Ball Circle.

The total cost of the addition was $54,755. It was ready for use by November 1938. The science laboratories were moved from Monroe Hall, and the vacated space converted into much needed classrooms. The college tea room was moved from Willard to the space on the ground floor of Seacobeck formerly occupied by the home economics department. Another dining hall was also set up in the space formerly occupied by the clothing laboratory.

Later, the tea room was moved to the basement of Chandler Hall. New equipment, including a soda fountain and booths, was installed, and there were showcases and shelves for the display and sale of college souvenirs, stationery, and supplies. The tea room continued to operate in Chandler until the student activities building was constructed. The old tea room in the basement of Seacobeck was redecorated and used for small dinners and parties, with food service from the main kitchen above. It was known as the Tapestry Room.

A NEW NAME

For some time there had been a feeling that a more distinctive name should be given to the State Teachers College at Fredericksburg. In the 1930s there were nearly one hundred state teachers colleges throughout the United States whose specific identity was established only when the location of a given institution was stated. In Pennsylvania, to cite an example, there were ten institutions known as state teachers colleges, with the address an added part of the title.

Another and even more cogent reason for a change in name was that the nature and character of the institution had changed. The preparation of teachers was no longer its sole or even major purpose. As the catalogue for 1938–39 stated:

> The purpose of the college is to provide for the young women of today the opportunity for broad and liberal culture and for training in certain specialized fields of professional, vocational, and technical work, including teaching, business, home economics and dietetics, music, fine and industrial arts, and related fields, thus enabling the student to prepare herself thoroughly and harmoniously for her modern dual capacity of wage earner and home maker. The aim at all times shall be to effect a wise compromise between the demands of a modern, practical, and complex society on the one hand, and the claims of an exclusive and traditional culture on the other.

The program of studies at the college had been broadened, especially since the authorization in 1935 to grant standard degrees in the liberal arts, as well as in professional, vocational, and technical fields. In reality, the institution had become a state college for women, rather than exclusively a teachers college. A change in name seemed not only fitting but actually necessary if the purpose of the institution was to be made clear.

A news story that appeared on the first page of the *Bullet* for February 16, 1938, offered strong arguments for a change in name. Under the heading, "Mary Washington College—Reasons Why We Want Our Name Changed," five reasons were given. In brief, they were:

1. In order to honor Mary Washington, the mother of George, whose life was so closely identified with Fredericksburg where her home and tomb are located.

2. To be more descriptive of the type of service the institution was rendering as a state college for women offering both a liberal education and professional training in certain fields, including teaching.

3. To encourage donations and endowments from private sources.

4. To avoid the confusion that resulted from having four colleges, all named state teachers college, with only the name of the post office address to distinguish them.

5. To enhance the development not only of the college at Fredericksburg but the other state teachers colleges.

Development Accelerates

These arguments carried their weight with members of the General Assembly when action was initiated to change the name of the institutions. Early in the session state Senator S. Bernard Coleman, representing the district in which Fredericksburg is located, introduced in the Senate a bill providing that the State Teachers College at Fredericksburg was to be known thereafter as Mary Washington College (Senate Bill 14).

When committee hearings were held on the proposed legislation, opinion was expressed that the college at Fredericksburg would be given an "unfair advantage" if it were permitted to change to a distinctive name and the other state teachers colleges were not.

At the request of officials at the institution in Harrisonburg, the bill was amended to authorize that college to change its name and proposed that it be known thereafter as Madison College. The bill then passed the Senate without a dissenting vote. A few weeks later it passed the House by a vote of 84 to 3. Both President J. L. Jarman of Farmville and President D. W. Peters of Radford had opposed the bill in the early committee hearings.

In the course of its legislative progress, the bill was further modified to permit the other two state teachers colleges to change their names also if it were considered desirable. As the act was finally passed, the names of the colleges at Fredericksburg and Harrisonburg were both changed, and it was stated further that "the State board of education is hereby authorized and empowered, in its discretion to change the names of the State teachers colleges at Farmville and Radford if, as and when these institutions make application to the State board for such a change." [4]

On March 9, 1938, the bill was signed by Governor James H. Price. Although technically the name legislation would not become effective until ninety days after the adjournment of the General Assembly, the new title was put into effect at once. Catalogues and brochures announcing the college program for the coming session were changed at once to feature the new name. A distinctive blue cover with the words *Mary Washington College* in white Old English lettering replaced the rather drab brown cover that for so many years had carried the name of State Teachers College at Fredericksburg.

The new name met with ready and enthusiastic reception at the college, in the community, and among the alumnae. Plans were made for the diplomas awarded in June to bear the name

---

[4] *Acts of Assembly*, 1938, chap. 73, sec. 942, p. 127.

Mary Washington College. President Combs announced that the commencement would celebrate the thirtieth anniversary of the chartering of the college and also the introduction of the new name.

"THE FOUR WINDS"

A feature of the 1938 commencement exercises was a historical pageant, *The Four Winds,* written and directed by Boyce Loving, head of the department of dramatics at the college. The pageant was an elaborate affair, depicting salient events in the history of Fredericksburg and of the college from the landing of Captain John Smith to the present. A cast of hundreds of students and townspeople were involved in the numerous episodes of the production.

It had been planned to stage the pageant in the open-air theatre of the college. However, rain necessitated its transfer to the auditorium of James Monroe High School, which the city generously made available. Long before the program was to begin, every seat had been reserved. Chairs placed in the aisles filled rapidly. Soon all available standing space was filled, and it became necessary to turn away many would-be spectators. Fortunately, the amplifiers of a public address system recently installed enabled all to hear clearly throughout the packed auditorium.

The pageant opened with a scene reenacting the arrival of Captain John Smith at the falls of the Rappahannock in 1608. There followed a series of episodes depicting milestones in the history of the city, including stirring scenes from Revolutionary, Civil War, and World War I days. Boyce Loving acted as narrator, his resonant voice lending vividness to the action depicted on the stage. Colorful costumes characteristic of the period and effective makeup also contributed to creating a sense of reality.

The *Free Lance-Star* of June 4, 1938, in an enthusiastic account of the pageant, commented:

Dr. Richard Beale Davis was impressive as George Washington, while Miss Esther Barney admirably did the role of Mary Washington, shown in the Mercer Apothecary Shop, in the garden of her home, at the famous Peace Ball, and in the final parting with her distinguished son.

One of the high spots was the episode depicting Mrs. Martha Stevens, played by Mrs. C. D. Binns, ministering to wounded soldiers of both armies during the battle of Fredericksburg. The firing of musketry, the falling of injured soldiers, the calm ministrations of the determined Mrs. Stevens as she moved about the dead and dying gave a realistic idea of the battle which raged here in December 1862.

Mrs. Stevens received tumultuous applause as she ripped strips of cloth from her petticoat to bind up the wounds of the fallen men. Mayor W. Marshall King played the role of Mayor Slaughter, who directed the evacuation of Fredericksburg in 1862, as women, children, and aged men were moved to places of safety.

The first episode that dealt with the college was entitled "March 16, 1908," which was the day on which the General Assembly of Virginia enacted legislation establishing the institution. C. O'Conor Goolrick, in person, reenacted the role he played in the legislature as patron of the bill. He was "warmly applauded."

Life in the early days of the college was depicted by young women wearing dresses of the period, resurrected from attics in Fredericksburg and old trunks at home. The unsophisticated amusements of life in those days delighted the audience as did the costumes of 1911.

As a backdrop for the college scenes, Ronald Faulkner had produced a large sketch of the campus with its various buildings. There was also a thermometer showing the growth of the college from 131 to 1911 to 1,010 in 1938. The "mercury" in the thermometer rose to show the enrollment at the time of the successive episodes. Nora C. Willis and W. N. Hamlet were introduced as having been members of the original faculty of the college.

The entire production was well staged and produced a feeling of accomplishment among all who took part. There were humorous incidents, of course, as when one Indian who participated in one of the early episodes showed up in tennis shoes instead of the moccasin-type footwear that had been requested. His explanation that he could not find the moccasins before leaving for the pageant and that he thought tennis shoes would be "just as good" seemed a little lame. Anyway no one seemed to notice in the general excitement of the encounter with the Seacobeck Indians.

GRADUATION EXERCISES, 1938

Graduation day began with Class Day exercises held in the open-air theatre at 10:30 A.M., Saturday, June 4. As was customary, the academic procession was led by members of the class of 1940 carrying the daisy chain on their shoulders. It was a colorful sight as they moved downhill to the open-air theatre, where the chain itself was laid carefully around the stage to form a background for the events that followed.

The class gift was presented by Elizabeth Trimble to President Combs. It was a substantial check "to be added to the fund to build a fountain in the circle between Mary Ball Hall and Virginia Hall." Miss Trimble was awarded the Kiwanis Cup as the senior who had contributed most to the welfare of the college. The award was presented on behalf of the Kiwanis Club by Guy H. Brown, superintendent of the Fredericksburg schools.

Later in the day the graduation exercises took place, also in the open-air theatre. The address to the graduates was delivered by John Temple Graves II, well-known editor and author, of Birmingham, Alabama. He was introduced by C. O'Conor Goolrick.

Dean Alvey presented the candidates for degrees and diplomas, which were awarded by President Combs. There were ninety-one graduates—fifty-seven B.S. degrees, two B.A. degrees, and thirty-two two-year professional diplomas. The two B.A. degrees went to Anna Mae Harris and Ellen Elizabeth Leonard.

Anna Mae Harris led the class in academic average. A major in mathematics, she had been on the dean's list of honor students every quarter of her four years in college. She received a scholarship awarded by the University of Virginia to enable her to do graduate work there. A few years later, she was to join the faculty of Mary Washington College. When a chapter of Phi Beta Kappa was installed, she was one of three alumnae to be elected to membership.

CHAPTER XI

Progress and Personalities, 1938–1941

A RECORD ENROLLMENT

THE 1938–39 session opened with a record enrollment of 1,160 full-time students, an increase of nearly 200 over the 1937–38 final enrollment of 983. For the first time, a number of the freshmen were housed in approved homes near the college. This, however, did little to relieve crowded conditions in the dormitories, resulting from the markedly increased enrollment. Some complaints were voiced about the lack of space in rooms, poor study conditions, and other difficulties.

A special report on enrollment and housing was made by the president under date of August 16, 1939. Although this report dealt with plans for housing the probable enrollment of 1,300 for 1939–40, it also indicated the conditions that obtained in 1938–39. According to this report, there were 684 rooms in college-owned dormitories, plus 84 in Betty Lewis, making a total of 763 rooms available. There were 1,017 students placed in dormitory rooms, as follows:

Two in a room	318
Three in a room	567
Four in a room	128
One in a room	4
Total	1,017

The difference between the full-time enrollment of approximately 1,300 and the dormitory housing of 1,017 represented day students and the new off-campus housing programs.

OFF-CAMPUS HOUSING

When it was evident that the applications for admission far exceeded dormitory accommodations, the administration decided to waive the requirement that all except local or commuting students be required to live and board at the college. Incoming freshmen were advised by letter that they might obtain living accommodations in approved homes near the college and take their meals in the dining hall. In the beginning, only a few students lived off campus, mainly in homes along College Avenue and the adjacent streets or along Cornell Street just below the college gates, where they would be close enough to Seacobeck for their meals there.

As time passed and the enrollment continued to increase, the number of off-campus students grew. It became necessary to designate a specific staff member to work with these students, and Martha Hardy Anderson was assigned this responsibility. Mrs. Anderson was also an instructor in English and had only limited time to devote to the off-campus students. When she left to join the WAVES in 1944, the supervision of these students was assigned to Margaret Swander (now Mrs. John C. Russell), who had come to the college in 1943 and was attached to the dean of women's office as director of student personnel. Miss Swander was designated director of off-campus students and assigned full responsibility for their placement, adjustment, and general welfare. She proceeded immediately to organize and systematize the entire operation.

Notices in the local paper invited nearby residents to submit proposals for housing students, indicating the type of housing available and the rental charge. After an inspection of the facilities, the location of the house and other pertinent data were listed in mimeographed form and sent to parents of prospective off-campus students. The number of students housed in private homes increased greatly until, during the peak period of this practice, there were between 250 and 300 off-campus students each year.

At first, there was no stipulation that the students remain with their off-campus hostess for the entire session. Householders who had made expensive alterations and purchased room furniture in order to accommodate students were understandably disgruntled when their roomers moved into dormitories as college cancellations or withdrawals made space there available. Consequently, it was agreed that student roomers would be liable for rental charges for the period of the session unless dismissed from the college for some reason.

Considerable difficulty developed over just how much overnight supervision the off-campus hostesses were to exercise over their residents. Enforcement of study hours, weekend permissions, and other pertinent regulations of the student handbook presented a real problem. In some cases, students found themselves crowded into small upstairs rooms with inadequate facilities for study and noise from below. In other instances, students themselves showed a lack of consideration for the family with whom they were living. However, the majority of householders took a genuine interest in the girls living in their homes, and many lasting friendships were formed.

The general picture, however, was far from satisfactory, mainly because off-campus students felt left out of college activities. Class meetings were held in dormitories without any notice to the nonresident students. Often, announcements of events and special opportunities were made only in the college residence halls. Off-campus students felt restricted in making the friendships that their dormitory-housed classmates found such a satisfying aspect of college life.

The University of Virginia board of visitors was unhappy over the arrangement, and some members urged that it be terminated. As additional dormitory facilities became available, the urgency of the situation was relieved. At the end of the 1953–54 session the housing of students in off-campus homes was discontinued.

WESTMORELAND HALL

In October 1938 the contract for another new dormitory was awarded the Goode Construction Company of Charlotte, North Carolina. J. Binford Walford was the architect. Erected at a cost of $147,400 with the aid of a PWA loan and a grant, the new building provided accommodations for 116 students. At the time of its completion it was the most modern of the residence halls. In the basement was space for the storing and construction of stage scenery, as well as costume racks. Many of the sets used on the stage of George Washington Hall were built in the basement of Westmoreland and carried by hand to G.W. to be set up there. No actual construction or painting of scenery was permitted on the stage of the latter.

CORNELL LEASED

Steps were taken to provide other dormitory facilities to relieve overcrowding. In 1940 Cornell Hall, located on the corner of Cornell Street and Kenmore Avenue, about two blocks below the Sunken Road entrance to the college, was leased at an annual rental of $4,850. Originally built as an apartment, Cornell Hall was rearranged in suites for student occupancy. The large basement was converted into a recreation room. It was used to house students until June 1959, when Bushnell Hall was completed. Another apartment house, known as Burke-Hudson after its owners, was leased in 1953-54. Because it was farther from the college, it was used for only a limited time.

GEORGE WASHINGTON HALL

In May 1935 President Combs applied for a PWA loan grant to erect a new administration building, but no action was taken. As the enrollment continued to increase, the need for a larger auditorium became urgent for, in the absence of a larger space, chapels and convocations were held in two sittings, one for freshmen and the other for upper classmen. Classroom space was also in demand, with every available room in use, including basements and other spaces where teaching arrangements could be made.

In the light of these developments, the State Board of Education approved in 1937 a request made to the budget commission for an appropriation of $252,000 for an administration building, auditorium, and classroom building. A conditional appropriation of $150,000 was authorized by the General Assembly in 1938, which was considerably short of the amount needed. Furthermore, there seemed little likelihood that the amount authorized would actually be made available.

Fortunately, a PWA loan and grant of $251,000 became available shortly, along with a loan and grant of $150,000 for a new dormitory. Again, the firm of J. Binford Walford of Richmond was engaged to draw plans for the new buildings. The Southeastern Construction Company of Charlotte, North Carolina, was the successful bidder, and construction began on November 23, 1938. The actual cost of the building was $288,535. When completely equipped, it represented an expenditure of approximately $350,000.

On the first floor were offices for the administrative staff, extending across the front of the building. A foyer just across the hall from the main entrance led into a handsome auditorium seating 1,624 persons. Seats were upholstered in leather. A spacious stage extended across the front of the auditorium, equipped with four movable rows of varicolored border lights, twenty-six backdrops, and an asbestos curtain, embellished with the Washington coat of arms in the center. Above the proscenium arch was the seal of the college in relief. The dominating color of the auditorium was cream rose.

Below the stage were five dressing rooms, each equipped with mirrored dressing tables extending across it. Below the front part of the building was a basement recreation room, with mirrors placed on the four sides of each of the supporting columns. This became the Hall of Mirrors, where, for many years, formal dances and other entertainments were held. The Oak Room for the preparation and serving of refreshments adjoined.

The second floor contained offices of the dean and the registrar, a mimeograph room, a booth for the movie projectors, and storage rooms. The third floor contained five large classrooms, several offices, and a broadcasting studio with control room. The studio was connected with the stage, ballroom, and roof garden, so that broadcasts could be made from any of these points.

Above the third floor the roof garden covered the entire front part of the building. It was the scene of many dances during the spring, summer, and fall. Penthouses for the preparation of refreshments stood on each side.

A handsome portal dominated the front of the building. Each of the massive supporting pillars of Indiana marble weighed 270 tons. A clock adorned the portico and, at fifteen-minute intervals, loud speakers sounded chimes audible throughout the college community.

Construction on the new building continued for most of 1939. Meanwhile, in the fall of 1938, offices of the president, dean, treasurer, and registrar had been moved from Virginia Hall to temporary space in the classrooms of Monroe Hall, pending the completion of the administration building. This move provided space for thirty additional students on the first floor of Virginia Hall.

George Washington Hall was completed in late 1939. It was officially opened on January 11, 1940, with a concert by the National Symphony Orchestra under the direction of Hans Kindler. Just before intermission, Dr. Kindler expressed his pleasure at being able to "christen" the new auditorium. He said he had tested the acoustics with both loud and soft music, and they seemed marvelous. "You have a very fine and wonderful building here," he said.[1] A formal dinner in Seacobeck for the entire student body preceded the program. Members of the State Board

---

[1] *Bullet*, Jan. 12, 1940.

of Education and their wives and other distinguished guests were entertained at dinner in the Dome Room.

In the words of an editorial in the *Bullet* on January 12, it was "a really stupendous happening." The entire audience—1,200 students, the faculty and their wives or husbands, board members, and special guests—were all resplendent in evening dress. A remarkable picture of the audience was taken from the stage and used subsequently in college viewbooks.

In the fall of 1940 Emil Schnellock began work on the murals that were to decorate the front entrance hall of the building. For the next five years, he spent considerable time on this project. A brief description of the murals appears in the section devoted to Schnellock.

Cornerstone-laying ceremonies took place on the afternoon of April 20, 1939, with Governor James H. Price as the principal speaker. He was introduced by C. O'Conor Goolrick. Masonic rites were in charge of Fredericksburg Lodge No. 4, A.F. and A.M., "Washington's Mother Lodge." The Bible used in the ceremony was the one on which Washington took his Masonic oath. Governor Price, former Grand Master of Masons in Virginia, took part in cornerstone ritual before making his address.

Among articles placed in a metal box in the cornerstone were copies of the college catalogue for that session, data on the construction of the building, copies of the *Free Lance-Star*, a copy of the program of the cornerstone laying ceremonies, several current United States coins and stamps, and a copy of the Constitution of the United States.

When Dr. Combs was asked to inspect the cornerstone, he peered all around the sides and edges in a careful examination. Governor Price injected a humorous note when, in the opening remarks of his address that followed, he said he wondered if Dr. Combs was looking for another appropriation.

TENTH ANNIVERSARY CELEBRATION

The tenth anniversary of the appointment of Dr. Combs as president of the college was marked on December 1, 1938, with a banquet given in his honor by members of the faculty and administrative staff and the presentation of a substantial purse in appreciation of his services.

Dean Alvey was in charge of arrangements and presided at the banquet. Appreciation of Dr. Combs's services during such a notable period of development was expressed by Blake T. Newton, a member of the State Board of Education; W. Marshall King, mayor of Fredericksburg; Mrs. Jere M. H. Willis of the Alumnae Association; and Dr. Roy S. Cook and Professor W. N. Hamlet of the faculty.

Dr. Cook outlined the growth of the college and praised Dr. Combs's ability as an educator and executive. Newton characterized the development as remarkable. Mayor King called Dr. Combs "Fredericksburg's best salesman." Mrs. Willis expressed the hope that it would be possible soon to have a member of the college staff in charge of alumnae activities.

Professor Hamlet presented the purse on behalf of the faculty. Visibly affected by the entire unexpected occasion, Dr. Combs modestly attributed much of the advancement of the college to the loyalty and enthusiasm of the faculty and staff, whom he called "the finest group of people I have known." He promised no relaxation in his efforts to serve the college.[2]

A MESSAGE FROM THE DEAN

The *Battlefield* for 1939 carried the following message addressed "To the Seniors of 1939":

It is you who reflect the ideals of your Alma Mater. As you leave Mary Washington College, may you take with you a high resolve to grow intellectually, to serve helpfully and generously, and to seek ever the good life; to think clearly and act constructively; to labor unselfishly for the general welfare. May you have the courage to stand boldly for justice, truth, and freedom—the high loyalties of life. May you have the humility that comes from an ever-broadening conception of the magnitude of human achievement, and the warmth of feeling for one's fellow-man that grows with broadened human understanding and enriched experience. May your life be characterized by sincerity and steadfastness of purpose that countenance no compromise with mediocrity. May your grace of manner enrich and ennoble the daily contacts of life, and may your beauty of spirit gleam like sunlight on water—fresh, bright, wholesome. Finally, may you have an ever-deepening reverence for the eternal verities of life.

EDWARD ALVEY, JR.

EXPANSION CONTINUES

The college continued to grow in student body, facilities, and faculty. The 1939–40 enrollment reached approximately thirteen

---
[2] *Free Lance-Star*, Dec. 2, 1938.

hundred. Sixteen new full-time members were added to the faculty, and two more—Emil Schnellock and Levin Houston III—began teaching that session on what was at first a part-time basis. George Washington and Westmoreland halls were completed and occupied. Also the college continued to prosper financially. The 1939–40 session ended with a surplus of $110,000, accumulated through the excess of collections over expenditures. A surplus of at least $100,000 was anticipated for 1940–41.

A significant factor in the growth of the college was the commerce department which, under the leadership of Dr. Dodd, had become nationally known for the high standard of its instruction and the quality of its equipment. In 1940–41 the department enrolled nearly half of the student body. A faculty of thirteen offered instruction in typewriting, shorthand, bookkeeping, and office practice as a two-year business course for students who wished to combine college education with secretarial training. A four-year course leading to the B.S. degree with a major in commerce was offered both for prospective teachers and for those graduates who wished to qualify for business positions. The dual possibility was most attractive.

The college continued to conduct a statewide contest for high school commercial students, featuring competition in shorthand, typewriting, and other business subjects. These contests brought hundreds of high school students to the college each spring, and many returned as students in the commerce department upon their graduation.

EMIL SCHNELLOCK

Emil Schnellock's connection with Mary Washington College began in 1938–39 when he was invited by President Combs to give a series of lectures on art appreciation. At the time Schnellock was giving lectures on art history at Woodberry Forest School and living at Montebello, the lovely old home of the Leslie Grays, near Orange. He occupied a cottage that had served as the office of the estate in the days when Montebello functioned as a working plantation. He had been invited down from New York to do a series of murals for the historic mansion. His project in the dining room covers all four walls and depicts the homes and figures of a number of residents of the fox-hunting area.

Schnellock was born in Brooklyn, New York, and was of German descent. His acquaintance with the Grays went back to an incident that occurred at Lake George when the Grays were swimming there. Their daughter, Alan, swam out too far and found herself unable to get back. Emil and a friend, who were also swimming, saw her predicament and swam out to rescue her as she was about to drown. The Grays always felt that Emil had saved her life, and he became like one of the family, visiting them at Orange when he had a vacation and even making a trip to Europe with them.

In his early days Schnellock worked as a commercial artist in New York. He did illustrations for the *New York Times* and also designed advertisements and posters. The well-known series of Campbell soup advertisements was one of his creations. He also did cruise and travel posters for steamship lines and similar assignments.

Meanwhile he read both widely and intensively. A close friend has described him as an erudite man. His knowledge of art and literature was prodigious. His formal study did not include college attendance, but he more than made up for this deficiency by his intense zest for knowledge. He was a keen student of history, and he had a rich knowledge of the civilizations of the world at various times. His knowledge of art was absorbed from the books that he read and the circle of friends in which he moved in New York. He had a keen sensitivity for the feelings and personalities of others. When he lectured on art, one felt that he had actually lived and experienced the things he spoke about. For him, art appreciation was a vital, living contact with artists and their works.

Schnellock's first lectures at Mary Washington were offered on an optional attendance basis, without credit, to students who were interested enough to gather in the late afternoon once or twice a week to hear him. The popularity of his lectures, with their rich mixture of art, philosophy, and history, led to the organization of credit courses in art appreciation offered as a regular part of the college curriculum. Schnellock became a member of the faculty first on a part-time basis and later as a full-time instructor. In 1941 he was promoted to an assistant professorship and scheduled to teach art appreciation and mural painting.

Schnellock was not only an instructor in these subjects but was also a sort of painter in residence, although he never spoke of himself in that way. Several of the college buildings reflect his genius and touch even down to the color schemes used for the interiors, which he chose to harmonize with the murals he painted.

Perhaps his most ambitious project was the decoration of the walls of Monroe Hall. On the right wall of the entrance hall from the campus side he painted a map of Virginia in geographical relief colors and beside it the seal of the Commonwealth of Virginia, with its motto "Sic Semper Tyrannis" and its triumphant Virtus standing over the prostrate tyrant. Shortly after this had been completed, Schnellock was asked in a somewhat joking way by a faculty colleague if he had had a model for the semidraped female figure that appears on the seal of Virginia. The two looked together at the mural for a minute. Then Emil turned to his friend and, in his soft, delightful voice, said, "No, I just painted it from memory."

On the other side of the entrance hall he painted a large representation of the colonial seal of England's first colony in America. He used to point out that this had served as the seal of the Old Dominion for over a century and a half, although it is little known today. In fact, many visitors have asked what state it represents.

The remaining walls of Monroe, upstairs and down, were eventually covered with meticulous paintings of the flags and seals of the various states, done against the blue-gray background that Emil loved so well. Students in his mural class did a number of the flags and seals. He encouraged out-of-state students to work on the flag or seal of their own state, and a number of them were so painted. Ronald Faulkner, a member of the music department who was also talented in painting, did the seal of Colorado, his native state.

Emil Schnellock was a deliberate and painstaking artist. He went about his work in a poised but relaxed manner, stopping frequently to stand back and survey his progress. While working on the first floor of Monroe he could often hear the music and rhythmic sound of the physical education classes in dance being conducted in the gymnasium below. One spring when all the windows were open, the sounds came up distinctly from below: "One, two, three, *kick!* One, two, three, *kick!*" Emil paused in his work to listen quietly for a few moments. Then he turned to a friend, and with a wistful smile and a slight shake of the head he said, "My, what vitality!"

His sense of humor was delightful. His observations were accompanied frequently by a sort of gargling chuckle that defies description. On one occasion a small group of faculty members were discussing a play that had been given the night before. Some were concerned that the theme was somewhat unconventional, especially since the heroine refused to marry the man who had seduced her. Another faculty member mentioned the Martha Graham dancers who, at a program given in George Washington Hall a short time before, had acted out what he called a seduction scene right on the stage. "But that was *art,*" another faculty member insisted. Emil, who had sat silently listening to the discussion, said gently and somewhat wistfully, "I'm afraid it's a lost art as far as I'm concerned."

The murals in the main entrance of George Washington Hall are a lasting tribute to Emil Schnellock's genius and his love for the college. He spent many hours in thought and discussion as to how he might best portray the spirit of the institution in graphic form. A cardboard model of the area was constructed. Dozens of preliminary sketches were drawn and discarded before the theme began to emerge. Each figure in the mural became a symbol of life at the college, not only in its academic aspects but in the various activities that made up the life of the institution.

There are orchestra players, dancers, a May queen—each an individual portrait—as well as students poring over books or performing laboratory experiments. The conferring of degrees is depicted with portraitlike figures of the president and dean. An academic procession moves forward above the entrance doors to the foyer. The figure of Wallace Alsop, the custodian of the building, appears in a narrow panel between the information booth and the corridor.

Henry Miller and Emil Schnellock were lifelong friends. They had grown up in Brooklyn together, and they never lost contact with each other throughout the years that Miller lived in Paris and was writing *Tropic of Cancer* and *Tropic of Capricorn.* Miller's letters were carefully preserved by Emil. They fill four large cardboard boxes and are currently in the custody of Schnellock's sister. Most of them have never been published.

Tangible evidence of the close relationship between Miller and Schnellock is the little volume entitled *The Waters Reglitterized* which, written in 1939, was printed in a limited edition by John Kidis in 1950. On the title page appears a sort of dedication, in bold type, reading "From Henry to Emil in moments of inspiration or perplexity, with gratitude for having put me on the right Path." An excellent photographic likeness of Emil appears opposite the title page.

In a preface to the publication Miller wrote: "This little volume, originally written by hand in a printer's dummy, was intended exclusively for my friend Emil Schnellock. It was my pleasure to write several little books in this manner, for my intimate friends, during the last few years of my stay in Paris. . . ."

Miller then expressed his gratification that "after about twenty years of struggle with the medium" he was to be given his first watercolor exhibition in Paris. He likened it to his twenty years of struggle with another medium before he succeeded in getting his first book (*Tropic of Cancer*) published, also in Paris.

Miller continued:

> But to come back to this little document. . . . My primary reason for permitting it to become public now is to pay a debt of gratitude to my old friend and comforter, Emil Schnellock. It was he who inspired me to continue after I had made a start. (I needed plenty of encouragement because in school I had always been given up as hopeless, that is, in the art class.) During my ten years in Paris we maintained a steady and voluminous correspondence. On my return to America, in 1940, I visited my friend Emil in Virginia. One day he brought out a huge trunk crammed with the letters, manuscripts, notes, photos, plans, projects and documents of all sorts which I had sent him over the years. It was a staggering collection and testified more eloquently to our friendship than anything I may say here. Ever since that day I have been trying to find some one in this country with the necessary courage and imagination to publish this material, some one who would do it handsomely, as it deserves to be done.

The above quotations are from a copy of this limited edition that bears the inscription, "To Julien and Elizabeth [Binford] with love and deep gratitude, Emil."

A few of Henry Miller's letters to Emil have been published. Excerpts from a number of letters written from Paris in the 1930s were printed in a limited edition by Bern Porter, of Berkeley, California, with the title *Semblance of a Devoted Past* (copyright by Henry Miller, 1944). The cover is a photographic reproduction of a sketch by Henry Miller, and there are nine illustrations selected from his watercolors. The opening page begins "Dear Emil. . . ."

Emil himself wrote an account of his long and close association with Miller and the adventures they shared. Entitled "Just a Brooklyn Boy," the selection appeared in *The Happy Rock,* a collection of reminiscences of Miller, published by Bern Porter in 1945.

Emil died on November 18, 1958. He seemed to have a premonition of his death. When two of his close friends visited him in the hospital the day before his death, he told them good-bye very gravely. As they closed the door to his room (he hated the noise from the hall), he called them back and waved to them in a final farewell. The next day he was dead.

Emil Schnellock's funeral was held in the residence of the Grays at Montebello. He was buried in the family cemetery there.

LEVIN HOUSTON III

When Levin Houston III joined the faculty in 1939 as instructor in piano, he had already built up a reputation through his classes and recitals in the city of Fredericksburg. Beginning at first on a part-time basis, he soon had his teaching schedule filled from the first morning period until late afternoon. As some students would say, "I couldn't get him this year, but I hope to next session."

He is an extremely versatile and talented person. He is a musician, an artist, a writer, a dancer, and an actor. While a student at Virginia Military Institute, he played the piano in the dance orchestra. Later he organized a dance band that for five or six summers provided entertainment for transatlantic passengers on the *Ile-de-France* of the French Line. Thus began the first of his many trips abroad, especially to France.

The year immediately following his graduation from V.M.I., he taught American history there. Less than twenty-one, he was the youngest instructor in the institute. He also took graduate work in English and drama at Washington and Lee University.

From childhood Levin Houston had been interested in music and in art. He had started studying the violin at the age of five. At V.M.I. he was art editor of the annual, the monthly humorous magazine, and the weekly newspaper. Subsequently he received a scholarship to study painting at the National Academy of Design in New York.

During this period he supported himself through music, earning money as an accompanist for dance classes and concert singers and playing in dance bands. He taught dancing at Arthur Murray's and also acted in four Broadway plays.

At twenty-four he gave up art entirely, deciding that he "could never make a living at it," and became general manager of Oliver Ditson's music publishing house. He retired to Fredericksburg when offered an attractive position at the Sylvania plant had just opened there. At the same time he resumed the study of music, taking piano under Quincy Cole of Richmond. At Cole's suggestion, he began to teach piano.

For the next nine years Houston studied music intensively, either on a part-time or full-time basis. In New York he studied piano under Ray Lev. Later, he studied composition under Roger Sessions and Ernst Kranek.

What had been an avocation now became a vocation. In addition to his piano teaching at Mary Washington, with a series of student recitals each semester, Houston composed extensively, producing in one winter over a thousand pages of music manuscript.

His orchestration of Schumann's "Aufschwung" was played by the Richmond Symphony orchestra. His "Andante" for violin was voted the outstanding composition of the year by the Virginia Federation of Music Clubs. His piano piece, opus 38 no. 1, was played in Carnegie Hall by Ray Lev. Subsequently, he was commissioned to write a clarinet concerto for Artie Shaw.

Levin Houston gave his service generously to the college. He wrote seven ballets for the Mary Washington orchestra, over twenty compositions for the Modern Dance Club, and a number of selections for the Glee Club. As may be gathered, he is a rapid worker. On one occasion he completed a forty-eight-page piano sonata in two and a half weeks, teaching full time all along.

Invited to join the Virginia Music Teachers Association after some of his compositions had been played at a state meeting, Houston soon became president of the organization. He edited and did most of the writing for the bulletin of the association for many years. He also contributed articles on teaching piano for professional journals.

For many years he gave at least one formal piano recital at convocation and entertained many times at assemblies, often on short notice. He took part in many of the benefits of those days.

From his first association with the college, he took an active part in dramatics. For some twenty years he played leading parts in productions of the Mary Washington Players. He was Peter Standish in *Berkeley Square,* the first time a man had played on the stage at Mary Washington. Prior to that time, girls played all the male parts, with hair tucked up under caps or wigs and wearing rather ill-fitting male garments. From *Berkeley Square* on, all male parts were acted by men, usually younger members of the faculty. *Berkeley Square,* incidentally, was the first play presented in the new auditorium of George Washington Hall in 1940.

Levin Houston's other well-remembered roles include Professor Higgins in *Pygmalion,* Death in *Death Takes a Holiday,* the hero-villain in *Kind Lady,* and the lead in *Angel Street.* He also directed several of the plays. During World War II he taught drama classes for a time at Mary Washington.

Local dramatic groups have utilized his talents. During the thirties and again in the sixties he directed plays for Fredericksburg's Drama Club and Little Theatre. For thirteen years he has produced the annual musical show for the Lions Club.

Under the pseudonym of George St. Julian, he has reviewed plays, recitals, concerts, and dance programs for the *Free Lance-Star* for over thirty years. His appraisals of these performances show a rich knowledge of classical and contemporary music, the dance, and the theatre. His reviews of college productions reveal a keen perception of the interplay of setting, dramatic theme, costuming, and action on the stage.

As an outgrowth of a talk before the Rappahannock Valley Garden Club, he began a series of articles for the *Spur,* a small monthly magazine published locally. For over thirteen years he contributed a column entitled "Through the Garden on Hands and Knees." The iris garden at his home on George Street attracts many visitors.

In recent years Houston has resumed his art work. Cards made from his drawings of historic sites in Fredericksburg have been sold by the thousands in the gift shops of shrines in the city. He has also done a number of watercolors and oils of landscapes and still life. Between 1960 and 1965 three one-man shows of his work were held.

Houston continues his keen zest for the fine arts, both as a teacher and as a creative musician, artist, and writer. In 1972 he reviewed 178 books for his weekly book page in the *Free Lance-Star* and also continued the gardening column and reviews of plays and concerts. His tremendous energy and varied talents make each day exciting for him.

MAY DAY PROGRAMS

Until 1968 the celebration of May Day was one of the high points of the session, ranking in importance at this woman's college with the homecoming football game at a male or coeducational institution. The largest crowds of the college year gathered for the occasion, including many parents and alumnae who came from considerable distances. Seats were at a premium, and tickets were carefully allocated, each member of the court being allowed a certain number. Usually a special section was reserved for the faculty.

Preparations were begun far in advance. As early as February tryouts for the May court were initiated. Each of the four classes prepared a list of nominees, conducted promenades, and, as a class, voted for its representatives by secret ballot. The May queen was selected in a special assembly in George Washington Hall. Nominees promenaded in evening dress to appropriate music, while the audience took note of their poise, bearing, beauty, and "queenly presence." After ballots had been checked and collected, they were counted then and there. Student entertainers beguiled the time until the results were announced in an atmosphere of great excitement. The runner-up was designated the maid of honor.

For many years the court consisted of eight representatives from each class, plus the May queen, usually a senior, and the maid of honor. The number was reduced later to four from each class. There was great excitement over the final selections to represent each class. The successful candidates were notified by a special committee who called on them individually and announced the results of the balloting. To be included in the May Court was a highly prized recognition of womanly beauty, charm, and grace.

The dresses for the members of the court were simple in design but carefully tailored. Only fabrics of the best quality were used, and the dresses were expensive. However, few girls failed to obtain the necessary funds from their families, who seemed to share the thrill and excitement of this special day. Colors were carefully chosen to harmonize and to create a pleasing effect when the entire court was assembled on stage. Each participant carried a basket or armload of flowers, also selected with reference to the costume of the bearer. These flowers were expensive, too, but they were provided from student activity funds set aside for the May Day exercises.

The procession always started with heralds, who raised their imitation trumpets as cornets in the orchestra sounded a fanfare. The heralds wore page-boy outfits of silk, with brightly lined scarves. Pages, flower girls, and trainbearers also added glamor to the regal procession. The crownbearer, often the only male in the entire procession, was usually a faculty lad of five or six years who, with outstretched arms, bore the royal diadem on a silk cushion proudly but often uncertainly before him.

The queen's chair was an elaborate rattan affair that for many years served that unique function on the first Saturday in May.

The rest of the year it was stored away ignominiously in a corner of the basement in Monroe Hall. With the passage of time, the queen's chair became rickety. When it finally had to be discarded for a more serviceable but less glamorous draped platform chair the ceremony never seemed quite the same. Somehow, the very fragile nature and the flowing lines of the delicately woven rattan chair seemed to typify the youth and beauty of its occupant on that day in May when her assembled subjects offered their homage.

In 1941 the first of an elaborate series of ballets was presented at May Day. Entitled *Joan of Arc,* the score and libretto were written by Levin Houston, instructor in piano, and the choreography was by Mildred Stewart, head of the physical education department. Featured soloists in the ballet were Myran Russell as Joan, Ann Harris as the dauphin, Lilias Scott as the ballerina, and Edith Donnan as a prankish jester. Ensemble numbers were danced by groups costumed as peasants, ladies and gentlemen of the court, halberdiers, and archers.

Scores of students participated in the production. The colorful costumes were designed by the class in costume design under the direction of William Luther McDermott, of the art department. Emil Schnellock's class in mural painting designed the stage sets and properties, constructed by the class in stage scenery under the direction of Paul Ritter. Makeup was done by the members of Harold Weiss's class in makeup in the drama department. The staging of the entire production—from the heavenly voices heard offstage to the brilliant finale celebrating the coronation of Charles before the cathedral at Rheims—was most effective.

Houston's original music for the entire production set a new standard for May Day performances. As the *Free Lance–Star* observed in a review of the performance on May 5:

Much credit is due Mr. Houston for his varied and brilliant score. Much of the music has an archaic charm, which conveys the period of the ballet. The Peasant Dance, which was used again in the finale, has the authentic sound of an old French folk song, although it is an original composition. Many of the people in the audience went away whistling this tuneful little number. Joan's theme develops from a simple phrase which might have been played on a shepherd's pipe to one of nobility, and dignity. The Pavane and the Archer's Dance were musical highlights.

Rose Ronci, a piano major, served as accompanist throughout the long and difficult score. The printed program listed over fifty dancers taking part in the two-act ballet. In addition, there were members of the Glee Club, the stage crew, the costume and makeup staff, and the May Court, which numbered twenty-four maids plus Jamie Redwood as May queen and Aloise Brill as maid of honor. Dulcy Houston was crownbearer.

The following year, 1942, again marked an elaborate production for May Day, having as its theme Sleeping Beauty. Perhaps some idea of the nature of the production can be gathered from the review appearing in the *Free Lance–Star* on May 4, which read in part:

In traditional story-book manner, the clear notes of the bugle were sounded on the stroke of four o'clock and the May Court processional immediately moved forward through the aisles of the open air theatre. Leading the picturesque procession were the twenty-four maids, wearing gowns of taffeta, fashioned with long buttoned bodices and bouffant skirts trimmed with double rows of cording in varying shades of rose and orchid with which each carried a miniature matching parasol.

The diminutive crown bearer, Richard Nunn Lanier, Jr., clad in a Lord Fauntleroy suit of black velvet with white satin blouse, preceded the maid of honor, Miss Aloise Brill, who wore a frock of green organza and carried an arm bouquet of white iris and mammoth sweet peas. She was followed by two flower girls, whose dresses of pink chiffon organdy with bands of applique were accented with matching bandeaux of fresh flowers worn in their hair.

Enhancing the brunette beauty of the queen, Miss Myran Russell, was her gown of ivory faille taffeta, fashioned on distinctive lines and ending in a long court train. Carrying an ivory wand topped with a single gardenia, she was escorted by her two train bearers, attired in dresses of mauve organza, appliqued with flowers, with which they wore wristlets in varying shades of violet and matching ribbon streamers.

Following the crowning of the queen and before her assembled court, the legend of "The Sleeping Beauty in the Wood" was unfolded as Briar-Rose, the infant princess, was received joyfully by the royal family and presented wondrous gifts by each of her fairy godmothers.

The music for the full-length ballet was composed by Levin Houston. The college orchestra under Ronald Faulkner reached new heights in its interpretation of Houston's brilliant and whimsical score. The dancers were trained and costumed by Mildred Stewart. The Glee Club performed under the direction of Marion Chauncey. As usual, Mrs. Bushnell selected the gowns worn by members of the May Court.

Featured ballerinas were Ann Harris of Fredericksburg as the Sleeping Beauty, Frances Bozelle as Wealth, Margaret Thorp as

Grace, and Frances Wills as Beauty. Later Frances Wills doubled as the prince who awakened Briar-Rose. The ensemble dance numbers were also performed with technical skill and dramatic feeling.

May Day on May 1, 1943, featured another production with original score and libretto by Levin Houston and choreography by Mildred Stewart. *La Zingara* with settings in the Royal Garden of the palace in seventeenth-century Madrid, featured court waltzes and gay gypsy dances. Virginia Morgan was May queen; Dorothy Woodson, maid of honor; and a court of twenty-four maids-in-waiting attended them. The college orchestra under the direction of Ronald Faulkner was now an integral part of the May Day activities. The Glee Club continued to supply choral music and Rose Ronci again served as accompanist. Myran Russell, Ann Harris, and Lilias Scott were featured dancers.

May Day 1944 marked the presentation of *The Thirteenth Egg,* described as a representation of the spirit of revolt against the Victorian idea of a woman's function. Again the music was composed by Levin Houston and choreography by Mary Jane Andrews, a professional dancer as well as physical education specialist who was the new head of the physical education department. Mildred Stewart was overseas as a recreational director with the American Red Cross and was to be among the first to organize activities for the American troops who had landed on the continent in the invasion of Normandy. Leah Rubenette Fleet was May queen that year. The college orchestra now listed its members by instrumental sections, an evidence of the extent to which it had developed.

The Story of Persephone was the title of the 1945 May Day production. Based on the Greek legend, it was an elaborate dance-drama with music by Levin Houston and choreography by Mary Jane Andrews. The first of the nine scenes, "The Land of Pluto," depicted the confinement of Persephone in the Lower World, with various groups of dancers portraying the suffering of the tortured ones. The second described her escape, with Miss Andrews dancing the role of Ceres, goddess of earth. Subsequent scenes involved dances presented by Greek maidens, Egyptian slaves, Apollo and the muses, and finally all the gods and goddesses as they welcomed the spring.

Hundreds of students were involved in the production. The college orchestra was present in full strength, with violins, violas, cellos, contrabasses, flutes, oboe, clarinets, harp, bassoon, horns, trumpets, trombone, and percussion section. As usual, it was under the direction of Ronald Faulkner. The Glee Club, under the direction of Marion Chauncey, consisted of sixty voices. Katherine Griffith headed the corps of ushers. The Maypole dancers were woven into the production and appeared in the fifth scene when summoned by Pan. The May Court itself involved nearly fifty students. There were the queen and her maid-of-honor, thirty-six ladies in waiting (including Ellen Alvey, Sarah Armstrong, Hilda Parks, Dorothy Towles Rowe, and many others), trainbearers, flower girls, and pages.

In 1946 *The Shining Land,* described as a ballet with words and music, was presented on May Day. It involved the cooperation of several departments of the college, with music by Levin Houston, words by Harold Weiss, choreography by Claudia Moore (later Mrs. Charles L. Read), and the college orchestra under the direction of Ronald Faulkner. Both the concert-dance group and the junior dance group participated. A narrator and a speaking chorus provided the accompaniment, which, in the words of the play, celebrated "Peace America . . . and the young giant that is America leads the way to a joy-filled world . . . where nation respects nation."

The Glass Slipper was presented in 1947. Once again Levin Houston wrote the music. Claudia Read, director of the Modern Dance Club and head of the physical education department, did the choreography. Barbara Watson and Mary Sue Dunaway were among the solo dancers. In the customary May Day dance that evening the college orchestra introduced "The Mary Washington Stomp."

Whether on the quadrangle in front of Monroe, the open-air theatre, or the auditorium in George Washington Hall, the procession always moved at a slow, stately pace. The members of the court entered at predetermined intervals, allowing ample time for admiring glances at costumes and grooming and for close-up photographs by family and friends.

Last in line were the maid of honor, walking alone, and the May queen herself, hair carefully coiffed to receive the crown. When all were assembled in a half circle of beauty on the stage, the crownbearer advanced with the royal circle, the maid of honor lifted it carefully and placed it upon the poised head of the queen, proclaiming her the queen of the May. Prolonged applause then broke the spell of the ritual, and the queen lifted her scepter in acknowledgment. Then each member of the court came forward individually to curtsy before the queen and to receive the applause of the audience as she resumed her place in the semicircle. Then the queen said regally, "Let the revels begin," and the entertainment in her honor followed.

During the years preceding and following the ballet performances, a Maypole dance was included, performed usually by members of the classes in folk dancing. The Maypole itself was stored away for use the following year. It is still in the basement of Monroe Hall. Its white paint is a little faded and dusty, but otherwise the May Day symbol seems ready for use if the youthful exuberance of a less sophisticated day again finds expression.

THE MENDEL MUSEUM

In the fall of 1939 there came to Fredericksburg a distinguished citizen and scientist of Czechoslovakia, Dr. Hugo Iltis, founder and for many years (1921–38) head of the People's University in Brno (Brünn), an institution for adult education that was the pride of the new republic. It was there that he had established the world-famous Mendel Museum. An outspoken opponent of Hitler and his racial theories,[3] Dr. Iltis had been forced to flee with his wife and two sons when, at Munich, the fate of his native land was turned over to the Nazis. The Committee for the Relief of European Scientists helped the Iltis family come to America to escape persecution under the Nazi authorities.

Dr. Iltis started his teaching career in the Botanical Institute of the University of Zurich. He received his Ph.D. degree from the University of Prague.

Dr. Iltis became interested in Gregor Johann Mendel while still a student at Brno where Mendel had once taught. He discovered Mendel's original work, including his studies of the inheritance of traits as he worked them out in his garden laboratory with plants and insects. Mendel's own notebooks were an interesting part of the collection. When he left Brno, Dr. Iltis managed to bring with him the most valuable exhibits, including leaves of the pear tree with Mendel's own careful notations on them to record mutations in the fruit.

When he first arrived, Dr. Iltis taught biology at the International School, then located at the Fall Hill estate on the out-

[3] Dr. Iltis's publication of *Der Mythus von Blut und Rasse* (The Myth of Blood and Race) in Prague in 1936, which completely refuted Nazi race theories, made him a marked man for Hitler's revenge. A copy of the publication, inscribed as a presentation in memory of the author, was presented to the E. Lee Trinkle Library by Mrs. Anne Iltis, his wife, in January 1953.

skirts of Fredericksburg. The following fall, in 1940, he joined the faculty of the college as professor of biology and began the establishment of the Mendel Museum on the ground floor of the newly completed E. Lee Trinkle Library.

Dr. Iltis taught two courses in biology and devoted the rest of his time to the museum. He worked tirelessly assembling his material and preparing explanatory posters. Meanwhile, accounts of the Mendel Museum began to appear in local newspapers.[4] Feature stories on the Mendel Museum also appeared in the Richmond *Times-Dispatch* (November 1942), the Washington *Post* (June 16, 1946), and the *Commonwealth* magazine (September 1942), the latter written by Mrs. Dodd.

An excellent oil painting of Mendel was the focal point of the exhibition, surrounded by photographs of the geneticist, the garden of the monastery where his experiments were conducted, and the quarters in which he lived. On exhibit tables were dozens of rare publications relating to Mendel, including a copy of the journal in which he had first published an account of his experiments that eventually resulted in the formulation of the Mendelian laws. A number of Dr. Iltis's own publications were displayed in original or reprint form.

Dr. Iltis took upon himself the task of preparing exhibits that would duplicate all of Mendel's experiments, showing how new types of plants could be developed by selective fertilization. Among the interested visitors to the museum in Fredericksburg was Vice-President Henry A. Wallace, former secretary of agriculture, who had visited the museum in Brno while experimenting with Mendel's theories in developing hybrid corn on a farm in Iowa. Through crossbreeding as described by Mendel, Wallace was able to develop hybrid corn that increased average yields between 50 and 100 percent.

Through his biography of Mendel, later translated into English, and his numerous other writings on the nature and applications of Mendelian laws, Dr. Iltis was largely responsible for the recognition of Mendel as the father of modern genetics.[5] As curator of the museum located at the college, he continued to write and publish articles on Mendel's work and to lecture at

---

[4] See Hugo Iltis, "The Mendel Museum and Its Founder: An Interview with Myself," *Bullet*, Nov. 21, 1942. Also, Rebecca Marston, "Museum at College Memorial to Mendel," *Free Lance–Star*, Sept. 16, 1947.

[5] *Gregor Johann Mendel, Leben, Werk und Wirkung* (Berlin: Julius Springer, 1924); *Life of Mendel,* trans. Eden and Cedar Paul (London: George Allen & Unwin, 1932).

universities. He spoke at the University of Virginia and arranged for students there to visit the museum.

Dr. Iltis was very grateful to this country for having received him as a refugee from his native land and for having provided a place for him to teach and continue to develop his museum. He was a firm believer in the principles of democracy, and he admired the form of democracy that he found here.

Few students will ever forget Dr. Iltis's convocation address on Tomáš Masaryk, the founder of the Republic of Czechoslovakia, which emerged as an independent state following World War I. He and Masaryk had been close personal friends. Dr. Iltis chose the anniversary of the establishment of the republic on October 28, 1918, for a magnificent tribute to the first and longtime president of the republic that he loved, then under the domination of Hitler's Nazis. As Dr. Iltis reached the climax of his address his emotions overcame him. His final words were spoken with difficulty, and he left the platform quickly with tears streaming down his cheeks.

Dr. Iltis was a genial and happy person. He loved people, he loved his family, and he loved his work. Once when asked if he did not regret having to leave his homeland for a different country, he shrugged and smiled replying, "Yes, but then I would not have seen all the interesting flowers and plants and trees that I have found on my walks through the woods of this beautiful countryside."

Dr. Iltis died suddenly of a heart attack on June 22, 1952.[6] He had just retired after a teaching career of forty-six years. He was buried in Oak Hill Cemetery, in Fredericksburg. Without its curator, the Mendel Museum languished. There was no one really to take his place. Subsequently, the entire collection was sold by Mrs. Iltis to the University of Illinois, where it is now housed.

Students at Mary Washington dedicated the 1952 *Battlefield* to Dr. Iltis. The citation read, in part, "because you have shown us the deeper meanings and truer values of learning . . . you have been faced by constant sacrifices and have successfully endured them . . . you have shared with us a brilliance of mind recognized by the world . . . you have found a place and served in this land we inherited . . . you have been a friend and a companion to both students and faculty . . . you have been an inspiration to many as a teacher, philosopher and leader."

[6] *Free Lance-Star*, June 23, 1952.

STUDENT ACTIVITIES, 1940–41

The session of 1940–41 began with the usual orientation program. There was a welcoming party for new students given by the Y. Dr. Combs spoke at the opening convocation, and on Friday evening the traditional Kid Party was held in Monroe Gymnasium. Tryouts were held for the Mary Washington Players. A record number of new members were selected from over two hundred contenders. *Jane Eyre* and *Yellow Jacket* were among the plays scheduled. The Modern Portias began the sponsorship of a literary magazine. The first issue of the *Epaulet* appeared on January 18, 1941.

The annual benefits produced by various classes and organizations were being planned and rehearsed. The music department sponsored a series of concerts and recitals. Among the Lyceum numbers were programs by the Humphrey-Weidman modern dance group, the Littlefield Ballet, and Cornelia Otis Skinner. A marching band was organized by Ronald Faulkner, and tryouts for drum majorettes and baton twirlers were held. The band won its first award in the annual Peanut Festival Parade in Suffolk on January 29.

Dr. Edgar G. Gammon, president of Hampden-Sydney College, opened Religious Emphasis Week. Dr. T. McNider Simpson, dean of Randolph-Macon College, spoke at the Sunday morning service on religion and reality in life.

There were numerous athletic activities. The hockey team participated in the state tournament at Sweet Briar and the national tournament held that year at Williamsburg. The Terrapin Club rehearsed its annual spring pageant. The Modern Dance Club performed for the Society of Virginians in Washington. The Junior Dance Club was organized.

The German and Cotillion clubs had their formal dances in the Hall of Mirrors, newly decorated with masks by Mr. Schnellock and members of his art classes. The recently organized College Promenade held its first formal ball, a George Washington's Birthday dance.

The college sponsored an Easter holiday trip to New York in the new college bus. The total cost, including hotel, transportation, and meals, was twenty-five dollars for each participant. The Glee Club gave its customary spring concert. The theme for May Day centered about Joan of Arc.

The annual was dedicated to Dr. W. J. Young, who had died during the session. There were 194 seniors, including both degree and two-year diploma graduates, the largest class in the history of the college. John Temple Graves II, editor of the Birmingham *Herald-Age,* delivered the address to the graduates.

CHAPTER XII

The War Years, 1941–1945

COLLEGE OPENS

THE college opened in September 1941 with a record enrollment of some 1,700 students and 16 new faculty members. The freshman class, as usual, was the largest, with over 700 members. In a *Bullet* interview (October 3) President Combs reported: "Not only is every available space taken, but there were seven hundred other students who applied and were eligible but could not be admitted because of lack of space." The student body came from thirty-eight states, the District of Columbia, and three United States possessions.

The new faculty members represented twelve replacements and four additions. Dr. Dice R. Anderson joined the faculty as professor of government. He had been president of Randolph-Macon Woman's College from 1920 to 1930 and president of Wesleyan College from 1931 to 1941. Among the other faculty members who came in 1941 were Dr. Raleigh M. Drake, psychology, and Dr. John P. Kirby, English. Dr. Alice L. Edwards, formerly executive secretary of the American Home Economics Association, came to head the home economics department. Dr. Alma C. Kelly, who had written extensively on body movement and posture education, joined the physical education department, then headed by Mildred P. Stewart.

DR. CASTLE AND DR. INSLEY

The faculty of the science department was enlarged by the appointment of William A. Castle and Earl G. Insley, both of whom were to serve as departmental chairmen during a period of unprecedented development in the teaching of the sciences at Mary Washington.

Dr. Castle held a B.S. from Denison University and a Ph.D. from the University of Chicago. Before coming to Mary Washington he had taught biology at Brown University for ten years. He had also been a guest investigator at the University of Chicago.

Dr. Castle's appointment was as professor of biology. When the

The War Years

science department was divided into more specific areas in 1944, he became chairman of the biology department. He headed the department until the year before his retirement in 1969. During this twenty-five-year period the facilities of the department were progressively extended, the course offerings were greatly expanded, and the teaching staff was increased. Cooperative programs in nursing and in medical technology were started, and an interdepartmental major in premedical sciences was established.

During the early 1950s Dr. Castle was secretary of the Ecological Society of America and editor of its bulletin. A member of Gamma Alpha honorary graduate science fraternity, he had served as president of the University of Chicago chapter. He was also a member of Sigma Xi. At Mary Washington he was active in both science and dramatic organizations. He served on many important faculty committees and for several years was a member of the Joint Council.

It is interesting to note that Dr. Castle's three daughters hold a total of eight degrees, including a Ph.D. in molecular physics, a Ph.D. in organic chemistry, and an engineering degree. All have been teachers, mainly at the college level.

Dr. Insley joined the faculty as assistant professor of chemistry. He had received both a B.S. and a Ph.D. from Johns Hopkins, where he also served as an instructor in chemistry and was elected to membership in Sigma Xi national honorary society.

When Dr. Cook died in 1949, Dr. Insley was promoted to a professorship and appointed to head the chemistry department. For the next eighteen years Dr. Insley served in this capacity. During his chairmanship many advanced courses were added, laboratory hours increased, and additional faculty members appointed. Dr. Insley and Dr. Castle, together with their colleagues, designed the chemistry and biology teaching and laboratory facilities in the new science building. For over twenty years Dr. Insley was sponsor of the Mary Washington chapter of Chi Beta Phi.

OPENING ACTIVITIES

The first formal convocation of the 1941–42 session was held in the auditorium of George Washington Hall. After an organ prelude by Edna Reed, Dr. Anderson gave the invocation, and Dr. Alvey, who presided, made a number of announcements. There followed a musical interlude, a selection for flute and harp, by Ronald and Ronna Faulkner.

President Combs delivered a welcoming address to the student body. He wished them happiness and success and urged them to "live a life that is full and abundant, a life that is steeped in the awareness of intrinsic values and in the importance of this present, this day, and this hour."[1] The program concluded with the alma mater, and students filed slowly from the auditorium. Classes began the next day.

On the following Monday evening the Y gave a welcoming party for the freshmen around the outdoor swimming pool at the foot of the hill behind Willard. The path leading downward was illuminated with Japanese lanterns, which gave a soft glow against the fall foliage of the trees. The scene was an entrancing one. The fountain at the center of the large circular pool was illuminated with hidden lights. Lanterns around the edges of the pool furnished illumination and produced picturesque reflections in the water. Soft music was played over amplifiers, as the freshmen were served cider and doughnuts.

There was little time for homesickness. On Friday evening there was the annual Kid Party in Monroe Gymnasium. Big Sisters and their Little Sisters marched hand in hand across campus to Monroe. There the grand march took place, with approximately seven hundred girls dressed in children's clothes, with pigtails and ribbons. Grace Bailey won first prize, and Jane Trevvett and Marjorie Dare were runners-up. The judges were Governor James H. Price, Mrs. Combs, and Colonel Leroy Hodges, executive secretary of the Virginia State Chamber of Commerce.

There were all sorts of activities. Members of the cavalry troop rode in the Dog Mart Parade dressed in formal hunt clothes. There were tryouts for the Mary Washington Players, for drum majorette for the college band. *Mademoiselle* ("The Magazine for Smart Young Women") set up a contest for its College Board on campus.

Evening classes in typewriting, shorthand, accounting, and office practice were begun by the commercial department as a project in adult education for the community. Classes were held on Monday and Thursday evenings from seven to ten. Enrollment was disappointingly small, but it was expected to increase. The new post office station on College Avenue began operation, and E. Lee Trinkle Library was nearing completion.

---

[1] *Bullet,* Oct. 3, 1941.

WAR COMES

The late thirties were a time of increasing uneasiness among both faculty and students as war clouds continued to gather. The storm troopers of Adolph Hitler and the black-shirted Fascists of Benito Mussolini were marching constantly, singing songs of defiance, and saluting with raised arms as they gathered in increasingly large displays of numbers and military strength. In spite of Chamberlain's hopes and assurances, "peace in our time" was not to be our lot. Czechoslovakia was overrun and still the steel-helmeted men rumbled along in their personnel carriers.

The college lost no time in organizing activities to aid the war effort. In January 1942 a program to promote the sale of war savings stamps and bonds among the faculty and student body was begun under the sponsorship of the Student Government Association, with Dr. Alvey acting as adviser.

The campaign was launched at a special convocation held on January 21, at which the Mary Washington College Band played, a trio sang "Any Bonds Today?" and a group from the radio broadcasting class discussed informally the meaning of war savings stamps and bonds. Dr. Alvey outlined plans for the sale of stamps at Mary Washington, which included the erection of a victory booth on the terrace of Ann Carter Lee, where students could purchase stamps at any time during the day. He emphasized the need for organized savings to purchase a regular amount in stamps each week. Virginia Urbin spoke for the Student Government Association, describing ways in which the campaign would be conducted by the students and urging the support and cooperation of all.

The victory booth opened on January 23, with representatives of SGA in attendance in their free periods. The first day's sales amounted to over $60.00. By the end of the first week, a total of $314.00 in stamps had been sold. As one of the first colleges in the country to launch such a program, the activities at Mary Washington received wide publicity. A photograph of the stamp booth, with students eagerly awaiting a chance to purchase, was distributed by the Associated Press and appeared in scores of newspapers. The first issue of the *School Savings News,* published by the United States Treasury Department, featured a picture of the victory booth at Mary Washington and a description of the program. By June 1942, the total sales at MWC had reached

$1,274.45. Meanwhile, similar campaigns for the sale of war savings stamps were begun at several other colleges in Virginia, modeled along the lines of the program here.

The fear of air raids was strong in January 1942. The college took over the twenty-four-hour operation of a plane-spotting station, manned by juniors and seniors. Students worked in pairs for two-hour tours of duty. They were required to report all types of planes seen or heard. They had to learn the types of planes and to be able to describe them.

First-aid organizations were set up in every dormitory in case of an air raid. Monitors and messengers, a transport squad, and emergency first-aid crews were designated. A huge air-raid alarm that could be heard all over the city was installed at the headquarters of the fire department. There were both announced and unannounced practice alerts, when blackout regulations were rigidly enforced. Watchers were stationed on the roof of George Washington Hall to detect violations that allowed even a ray of light from windows or street lamps to penetrate the darkness.

In April 1942 the Mary Washington College Band in blue skirts and white coats led a two-mile-long parade of eight thousand military troops, bands, and civilian organizations, marking the opening of the first big drive for the sale of war stamps and bonds in Richmond. It was a real thrill for every member of the newly organized band, as they marched just behind the police escort between crowds six and eight deep that lined the sidewalks. The governor of Virginia rode in an open car just behind the band.

Registration of students for ration books took place in May 1942 and was conducted as a war service by Sigma Tau Chi commercial fraternity. As the session ended, announcement was made of a "Three-Year Degree Program to Accelerate Training for Urgent Needs of the Nation."[2] In accordance with recommendations adopted by the National Conference of College and University Presidents on Higher Education and the War, arrangements were made for students in any curriculum to complete their degree requirements in three years by attending three general sessions and three summer quarters. Superior students could reduce the time even further by carrying heavier loads.

A special effort was made to encourage high school graduates to enter college in June and thereby complete one-third of a regular session's work before September by summer quarter at-

[2] *Catalogue,* 1942–43, p. 3.

The War Years

tendance. Students who entered in June were assured of preference "in such matters as rooms, accommodations, and financial assistance." A substantial number of high school graduates took advantage of this opportunity.

MILITARY SERVICE

When the nation was plunged into war on December 7, 1941, it was not long before the demands of the armed forces began to draw members from the college faculty. One of the first to leave was Bernard M. Fry, assistant librarian, who was assigned to the Division of Special Information in the Library of Congress. As coordinator of sources of defense information, he rendered valuable service throughout the war years.

By September 1942 seven more faculty members had left for military service. During the next three years, records indicate that, in addition to Fry, the following men on the faculty received leaves of absence for war service: Clifton B. McIntosh, Paul J. Ritter, Charles K. Martin, Lyle S. Hiatt, Stuart Denslow, Arthur L. Vogelback, Donald R. Whitney, Richard M. Kirby, W. L. McDermott, Earl G. Nicks, Charles J. Frick, J. Kenneth Roach, J. Edwin Whitesell, and William Brennand.

This list of fifteen is not a complete roster of faculty men who entered military service in World War II. It includes only those who were recorded as having received leaves of absence for this purpose. Others resigned from the faculty to serve their country without the formality of a leave of absence. The *Battlefield* for 1942 was dedicated to "Members of Our Faculty Who Have Entered the Service of Our Country."

Faculty women also volunteered for military service. Anna Scott Hoye became a commissioned officer in the Air Transport Command, Women's Army Corps, where she was a Link training instructor. She already had a flying license at the time. Dr. Mary Catherine Baker also left the department of physical education at Mary Washington to become an officer in a women's branch of the armed forces. The *Battlefield* for 1944 was dedicated to her.

Martha Hardy Anderson, who had become a member of the college faculty after the death of her husband, Dr. Dice R. Anderson, professor of history at Mary Washington, left to join the WAVES and to be commissioned as an officer. Mildred P.

Stewart left the college on leave to join the overseas staff of the American Red Cross. Her group was among the first to land in Europe shortly after the beginning of the Normandy Invasion.

WAR ACTIVITIES INTENSIFIED

By September 1942 everyone realized the seriousness of the war and the struggle that lay ahead. During the summer Singapore had fallen, the Philippines had been lost after the heroic defense of the Bataan peninsula, Wake Island had surrendered, and even Australia was threatened. Throughout the Pacific the flag of the Rising Sun waved victoriously. When the college began its session that fall there was a marked eagerness to aid the war effort. Brothers, fathers, and sweethearts were already in the service at posts ranging from the frozen tundras of Greenland to the steaming tropics of Tinian and Panama.

The victory booth in front of the College Shoppe was reopened on October 2, 1942, again under the sponsorship of the Student Government Association. The opening was featured with a program of patriotic songs played by the MWC Band, skits by student groups, and singing by a quartet that was later to develop into the Victory Chorus.

The Student Council decided to broaden the base of student participation by dividing activities into six separate committees. The art committee, assisted by the entire Art Club, made posters and placards, and also Christmas cards containing war stamp albums. The organization committee had charge of volunteers for regular duty at the stamp booth, which was open from 8:30 A.M. to 5:00 P.M. each weekday except Saturday, when the hours were 8:30 A.M. to 12:30 P.M. and 7:30 to 10:00 P.M. The publicity committee had as its main duty the constant promotion of the sale of war stamps and bonds on the Hill. The radio committee publicized sales by weekly announcements over the MWC radio program hour. The property committee furnished the necessary materials and supplies for the maintenance of the stamp booth.

The student body continued to raise funds to pay for a mobile kitchen to be sent to England to aid defense units and the victims of air raids. The goal of fifteen hundred dollars was reached by the spring of 1943, and pictures of the unit bearing the name of the college as the donor were posted.

The Victory Chorus was organized in September 1942 under the direction of Jayne Anderson, a junior who was its founder and leader. For the next two years, this carefully drilled chorus of thirty members presented a weekly radio program and sang on numerous occasions for college organizations, civic clubs, and local churches. It aided in many bond rallies and USO programs. The chorus, arranged in the form of a V for victory, became noted for its songs to "uplift the morale" of listeners during this trying period of World War II. The enthusiasm and leadership of Jayne Anderson kept the Victory Chorus at a high level. Its final program, "A Call to Victory and Song," was given in the auditorium of George Washington Hall on May 6, 1944. It was also a farewell for Miss Anderson, who graduated that June. The Victory Chorus disbanded at the end of the session.

THE FLOOD

Three days of rain in Fredericksburg and in the counties north and west of the city had caused the normally quiet Rappahannock River to become a rapidly rising torrent. On Thursday night, October 15, 1942, a cloudburst dropped six inches of rain in two hours. Throughout the next day the river continued to rise. During the early afternoon the force of the water and the debris it was carrying caused two spans of the bridge at Falmouth to drop several inches, completely cutting off U.S. Route 1, the main artery of traffic between Richmond and Washington.

The Free Bridge that furnished chief access from Fredericksburg to the Northern Neck was closed to traffic as huge tree trunks, swept along by the flood, battered its framework. And the river continued to rise. By early afternoon the entire business section of Caroline Street was under water, and boats with outboard motors were rescuing people from apartments above the stores on Fredericksburg's main retail thoroughfare.

The river rose until it reached a maximum of forty-five feet above normal at 5:00 P.M. By this time, water was swirling along Kenmore Avenue where there had once been a canal, and only the tops of cars parked along that street were visible.

Students living in Cornell Hall, a freshman dormitory at the time, showed remarkable calm and poise in the face of the danger. The surging waters rose completely above the basement rooms and lapped at the doors of first-floor rooms. Storage rooms, recreation areas, and the entire basement were under water, with untold damage to furniture and personal belongings stored there.

When it became evident that the dormitory would have to be

evacuated, the Fredericksburg rescue squad removed students in boats to the higher part of Cornell Street where ambulances transported them and their hastily packed suitcases to spaces provided by students living in dormitories on the Hill. There, the refugees were made comfortable with warm blankets and hot tea, while roommates doubled up to provide sleeping space for them.

The power plant supplying the city with electricity was one of the early casualties of the flood, leaving the entire community without current. Only the headlights of automobiles above the flood line and emergency searchlight equipment furnished illumination. All street lights were out, of course, as well as electricity for home lighting, cooking, heating, and the other myriad uses that are so readily taken for granted.

As the waters stopped rising and continued flowing in a forty-five foot crest, an eerie quiet settled over the city. With streets and highways blocked or under water, there was no sound of cars in the flooded areas. Not even the friendly whistle of occasional RF & P trains broke the stillness, for all rail traffic had been stopped. Officials had placed trains of loaded coal cars on the high railroad bridge spanning the Rappahannock to make it more secure against the roaring waters.

Fire broke out in the huge gasoline and fuel oil tanks along the river, ignited by sparks from the grinding metal structures. It was impossible to reach them with fire-fighting equipment or hoses, and the tanks burned brightly during the night, shedding a weird glow over that section of the city.

Fear of looting was another problem, since scores of homes had been left unprotected in evacuated areas. As night fell on the darkened city, an appeal came from Mayor King for the services of the MWC cavalry troop. By midnight Russell Walther had the members of his troop in uniform and on horseback. Serving directly under the command of the Fredericksburg chief of police, the mounted students patrolled the evacuated areas in groups of two throughout the night, watching out for prowlers and directing traffic at the fringes of the disaster area. Their services continued until Sunday night, when state police and soldiers from nearby A. P. Hill Military Reservation arrived in sufficient numbers to aid the local authorities.

Under the leadership of Mrs. Bushnell, some two hundred college students served in the canteens set up in various parts of the city to feed and care for the homeless. The MWC volunteers were stationed in the Presbyterian and Episcopal churches and also aided in giving typhoid shots at the Fredericksburg Court House. The girls worked in shifts of fifteen from 3:30 Friday to 5:30 Sunday, serving food and water to those whose homes were flooded.

Life on the Hill during this period went on under some difficulties. Breakfast was prepared by candlelight Friday morning. There was no electricity or water, but the dining hall staff managed to serve food on paper plates as college students filed in. The absence of running water created a health hazard. With the water supply of the city contaminated, typhoid shots were required as an emergency measure. A team of state health department workers arrived with vaccine and supplies and set up inoculation stations where every student was vaccinated. As soon as power was restored, the dining hall and the College Shoppe arranged to boil water for drinking purposes. Students were warned not to drink tap water and urged to take every precaution against colds and to get enough rest and sleep.

The *Bullet* continued publication throughout the period of the emergency, rendering incalculable service in giving information and publicizing official bulletins. Its editorials counseled the students to be patient and understanding. As the lead editorial on the first page of the October 16 issue pointed out, "We on the hill are most fortunate with just no lights or running water facilities. There are those who have no beds, food, or clothing. There are also many in other parts of the world with even less than that, accompanied by the roar of guns."

Among the casualties of the flood were the presses downtown, on which the *Bullet* was printed. Nevertheless, the staff managed to get out a mimeographed issue on October 16, containing news of the flood and reports of the volunteer work being done by students. The *Bullet* continued publication in mimeographed form at regular weekly intervals until November 16. The *Free Lance–Star* was unable to publish on either October 16 or 17. With electric current restored Saturday night, it produced a special Sunday edition on October 18, carrying accounts and pictures of the flood.

Damage done to homes, industrial plants, and oil tanks constituted the major losses in the flood. Scores of homes were completely wrecked, while many others were severely damaged by mud and water. A total of 750,000 gallons of oil, valued at $275,000, was lost in the burning or washing away of the storage tanks of the Standard Oil Company, the Gulf Refining Company, and the Pure Oil Company, all located on the river front at the lower end of Caroline Street. Heaviest losers among the local industrial plants were the Sylvania Industrial Corporation, the Lafayette Pants Factory, and the Virginia Shoe Company, with damages amounting to hundreds of thousands of dollars.

AID TO THE WAR EFFORT

Transportation offered a real problem with gasoline strictly rationed and trains crowded with troop movements. In accordance with President Roosevelt's request to reduce travel, the college abolished its Thanksgiving and Easter holidays, as did most other institutions. It extended the Christmas holiday from December 15 to January 8. Thanksgiving Day was celebrated on campus with a parade, a variety show, and war bond rally. The presence of the United States Marine Band from Quantico was a feature of the show, part of which was broadcast by the National Broadcasting Company. The war bond rally resulted in approximately $25,000 in sales. This sum was matched by $25,000 in purchases by Benjamin T. Pitts, local owner of a chain of motion picture theaters.

In February 1943 MWC participated in the National Bond Queen Campaign, sponsored locally by the *Bullet* under the general auspices of the Associated Collegiate Press. Each ten-cent stamp entitled the purchaser to cast ten votes for any candidate. Many organizations on the Hill sponsored representatives and conducted vigorous campaigns in support of them. The winner was Catherine Chambliss of Emporia, who had been sponsored by the *Bullet*. She was designated as Campus Bond Queen and her photograph entered in the national contest. Sales of stamps and bonds during the campaign totaled $3,103.50.

Large numbers of students gave blood in a program initiated in February 1943 by the American Red Cross. Throughout the war years, a mobile unit from Washington collected these donations of blood to be converted into plasma for the use of the armed forces. From one hundred to two hundred students participated in each of the periodic blood-donor days.

The faculty as well as the entire staff of the college gave full support to the war effort both by serving and saving. Mary Washington was the first educational institution in Virginia to qualify for the minuteman flag, a blue banner with the white silhouette of a minuteman, which was awarded organizations in which 90 percent of the employees were purchasing bonds systematically

The War Years 267

through the payroll savings plan. Mary Washington had qualified in 1942, but formal ceremonies presenting the flag did not take place until April 28, 1943, when a special celebration was held. At the same time the schools-at-war flag was presented, signifying that 90 percent of the students were purchasing stamps regularly.

Dean Alvey, who presided at the program, reported that 100 percent of the faculty and staff were enrolled in a systematic plan of war bond purchases. Henrietta Hoylman, president of the Student Government Association, gave a report showing that every student living in a college dormitory was participating in the program.

The presentations were made by Governor Colgate W. Darden, Jr., who praised the college for its outstanding record in qualifying for the two flags. The governor said that the achievement at Mary Washington "surpassed that of any establishment or institution in the state," so far as he was aware. President Combs introduced Governor Darden and also accepted the two flags on behalf of the college.

After the ceremony in George Washington Hall, the band led a short parade made up of the college cavalry troop and the cadet corps, to the portico of Monroe Hall, where the blue minuteman flag was raised. Photographs of the presentation and flag raising appeared in both state and national publications and were used in a Treasury Department publication designed to promote the sale of stamps and bonds in schools and colleges. Sales for the session of 1942–43 totaled $7,795.90 exclusive of purchases through the payroll savings plan.

WAR BOND RALLIES

Stamp sales continued through the 1944 summer session. On July 4 the cavalry troop sponsored a war bond auction among the student body, with Russell Walther as auctioneer. Items for sale were donations by faculty members, such as dinners in the homes of professors, movie dates, home-cooked foods and candies, and even serenades by male faculty members. The highest single amount was for a "date with the dean." Isabel LeCompte was the successful bidder, purchasing a $1,000 war bond. She shared with her roommate the dinner engagement at the Alvey home, which she had "purchased." Over $3,500 in sales was realized from the auction.

The fall of 1944 was the occasion of renewed activity in war services at Mary Washington. Under the leadership of the Student Government Association, with the dean of the college as faculty adviser, pledge cards were distributed to the students in all eight dormitories. The weekly distribution of stamps and the collection of money were handled by the house president. Each dormitory took turns in running the stamp booth for a week at the time.

The November 1944 issue of the *Virginia Journal of Education* had as its cover a picture of the stamp booth at Mary Washington. "Colleges at War," a handbook of "suggestions for student and faculty war savings committee" published by the United States Treasury Department, carried the same photograph as its cover design. The handbook featured a description of the stamp savings program at Mary Washington.

The Treasury Department publication reported that "better than 90% of Mary Washington's 1400 students and 100 faculty members buy War Stamps each week . . . 100% of the students in the dorms and 85% of the students who live in town." The article commented, in closing, "the flag [schools-at-war] continues to fly at Mary Washington College because their organization is sound and always on its toes."

On January 17, 1945, the Student Government Association sponsored an elaborate war bond rally for the student body, featuring donations of services and courtesies from members of the faculty and an address by a wounded veteran of World War II. This time some forty-five faculty members donated articles or services to be auctioned off for amounts in war stamps and bonds pledged for purchase at the rally. Emil Schnellock offered to do a sketch of the student; Russell Walther, a free ride on any horse in the stables; Dr. Whidden, to serve dessert to the girl's table in the dining hall; Mrs. Dodd, to clean a girl's room; Mrs. Bolling, to make fudge; Dr. Iltis, a copy of his biography of Mendel personally autographed for the successful bidder; George Elmer Brown, an oil painting to be done by him especially for the occasion. Dr. Kirby offered to carry a girl's books from her dormitory to her first class, while Dr. Cabrera promised a Spanish serenade below a student's dormitory window at night. Once again, Walther and the members of the cavalry troop served as auctioneer and runners. Over $13,600 in war stamps and bonds were sold in the course of the rally.

A high point of the evening was a short address by Lieutenant Robert T. Boody, army air force pilot and veteran of 117 missions in the China-India-Burma theater of the war. Lieutenant Boody, convalescing from injuries that had resulted in the loss of both legs, offered his shoulder bars to be auctioned. The successful bidder insisted on pinning them back on him, as cheers rolled through the auditorium and tears mingled with applause.

Representatives of the Treasury Department in Washington and the Virginia war bond office in Richmond also attended the rally, which was covered by Washington, Richmond, and Fredericksburg newspapers.

REGINALD W. WHIDDEN

Dr. Reginald W. Whidden, professor of English and later dean of the college, joined the faculty in September 1943. He is closely associated with Canada. However, he was born in Dayton, Ohio, where his father, Dr. Howard P. Whidden, was then serving as minister of the First Baptist Church. Shortly thereafter, Dr. Whidden's father returned to his native Canada to accept a college presidency. For twenty-five years the senior Whidden was president of McMaster University at Hamilton, Ontario.

Reg attended elementary and secondary schools in Canada and received his undergraduate degree from McMaster University. He taught in suburban Toronto and also completed his master's degree at McMaster University. Subsequently, he enrolled for further graduate study in English at Yale University where he received the Ph.D. degree in 1937.

During most of this period Dr. Whidden continued to teach English. For eleven years he was a member of the faculty at Denison University at Granville, Ohio. He came from Denison to Mary Washington in the fall of 1943.

Dr. Whidden's interest in Mary Washington College stemmed from the enthusiastic accounts of his good friend, Dr. John P. Kirby, who was teaching here at the time and had also received his doctorate in English at Yale. The two had become acquainted as graduate students. Their wives also became good friends as fellow workers in the Harkness Library while their husbands were in the Yale Graduate School.

When asked what really made him decide to come to Mary Washington, Dr. Whidden pondered his reply. Then, with a smile, he said: "I suppose you might say that the courtesy and good manners of the students here impressed me especially. Then, too, there is something about the cultural atmosphere and traditions of Virginia that appealed to me. And, I might add, the prospect that Mary Washington was to become a part of the University of Virginia was also a factor in my decision to come here."

Dr. Whidden recalls that his salary as full professor was then only $3,000 for the session. He remembers his actual take-home pay his first year as $166.66 a month after various deductions had been made. "It makes my retirement allowance today seem generous, indeed," Dr. Whidden says with a laugh. In those days, department heads received $100 a year extra. Dr. Whidden says he and Dr. Kirby often wondered whether they would ever get to $5,000 a year as professors at Mary Washington.

Dr. Whidden speaks admiringly of the quality of the student body at Mary Washington. Having come from a coeducational university, he noted fewer distractions here to serious study. Students seemed less inclined to complain about serious and demanding work. The academic performance was generally of high quality, because, as Dr. Whidden puts it, "the faculty did not have to adjust to outside demands of athletics and fraternities."

Dr. Whidden began his teaching duties with five classes in English. The following year he began to teach the course in Shakespeare, a favorite both with him and with his students, which he continued to offer even after his administrative duties became increasingly time-consuming. Dr. Whidden's courses were always popular. In fact, it was a problem at times to hold enrollment to a manageable size. He loved to teach. It is what he misses most since his retirement, along with the contacts with individual students and the opportunity to help them with their problems.

In the fall of 1956 Dr. Whidden was appointed assistant dean of the college. He was responsible specifically for the orientation program, for the faculty advisory system, for interviewing students with deficiencies, and, in general, for counseling students at all levels. The following year he was named associate dean.

Dean Whidden and Dean Alvey worked closely together in the academic program of the college. They shared a common reception room on the second floor of George Washington Hall and the same secretarial staff. Mutual confidence and regard characterized the working relationship. The two were warm friends as well as colleagues.

Dr. Whidden's contributions to the academic life of the college were varied and lasting. He was a pioneer in the establishment of the dormitory seminars at Trench Hill and Framar. As early as the fall of 1957 students in Framar began a series of reading,

The War Years

lecture, and discussion sessions, which was followed a year later by the "great books" seminar conducted at Trench Hill.

Although they received no academic credit, all students in these two small dormitories shared in the stimulation created by the programs. Dean Whidden served as coordinator of the residence hall seminars, proposing and requesting faculty members to lead them, obtaining the services of outside lecturers as requested, assisting in preparing and distributing reading lists and topics for discussion, and, in general, sponsoring and encouraging the development of the seminars.

The example set by Framar and Trench Hill was followed in Mary Ball, Bushnell, and Betty Lewis, where groups of students organized their individual reading and discussion projects. All five were under the leadership or direction of a member of the faculty chosen by the group, but they were initiated and carried on by student interest.

Among the faculty members who served as leaders of seminars were Edward D. Lowry, Peter R. Coffin, Myra L. Irby, Daniel H. Woodward, James H. Croushore, Zoe C. Black, Albert R. Klein, James R. Nazzaro, Joseph C. Vance, Samuel H. Phillips, Jr., Miriam Greenberg, Donald E. Glover, Josefa Rivas, George M. Van Sant, Charles A. Sletten, and Thomas Lee Johnson.

The residence hall seminars paved the way for the liberal arts seminars that began to be offered for college credit in 1962–63. Among the early leaders were Sidney H. Mitchell, Van Sant, Mrs. Black, Klein, E. Boyd Graves, Lawrence Wishner, Croushore, Mary Jo Parrish, Elizabeth A. Clark, and Cornelia D. Oliver. In time, the liberal arts seminars were supplanted by independent study programs offered by an increasing number of departments during the 1960s.

Looking back over his years of association with the college, Dr. Whidden expressed his satisfaction at being at MWC when it was developing from a teachers college to a liberal arts institution. Dr. Whidden played a significant role in shaping this transition. To Dean Whidden, the future of the college is, at present, "unclear." He wonders if it can continue to remain small and to emphasize the liberal arts. Possibly, pressures for increasing the enrollment may result in a slightly different type of institution, especially with the advent of coeducation.

Dr. Whidden recalls with amusement his first interview with President Combs. He had spent the previous night with the Kirbys at their home in the country, and he arrived a little late for his appointment. Somewhat flustered at finding the president waiting in his office, Dr. Whidden sought to make apologies for his delay. "And then," Dr. Whidden confesses, "I said, 'I understood you didn't get to the office before ten o'clock anyway.' " Dean Whidden smiles as he continues, "They must have really wanted me here for, even after the remark, I got the job anyway!" It was a happy day for Mary Washington when he did get the job, as numbers of students and colleagues will agree with enthusiasm.

SPANISH FIESTAS

An interesting aspect of life at Mary Washington College in the 1940s and early 1950s was the annual Spanish fiesta held in the spring and occasionally repeated for alumnae homecoming at commencement. The project was initiated by Dr. Louis J. Cabrera, a native of Puerto Rico, who joined the faculty as professor of Spanish in 1943.

At this time students from the Latin American countries began to attend the college in increasing numbers, reaching a high of thirty-five about 1950. Although there had been occasional Puerto Ricans as students whose parents were then residing in metropolitan New York, this new group came directly from their native countries to enroll at Mary Washington.

Dr. Cabrera recalls that two girls from Havana, Maria Raquel Riverý and Ruth Matilde Riverý, were among the first to enroll in 1943. Their father was in the diplomatic service as an attaché to the Cuban embassy in Washington. He had visited the college and was so impressed that he arranged to enroll his daughters. Other Latin Americans stationed in Washington became interested and the word spread, especially among the representatives from Puerto Rico, many of whom Dr. Cabrera knew personally.

As the number of Spanish-speaking students grew, their lack of command of the English language presented a problem. Some were really not prepared for collegiate study in an English-speaking environment. Among the students from Puerto Rico was Providencia (known as "Provi" at MWC) Keelan, who attended Mary Washington from 1941 to 1945 and was awarded the B.S. degree in June 1945. Her father, George W. Keelan, was a professor at the University of Puerto Rico. A native of Massachusetts, Dr. Keelan had spent some time in Puerto Rico, married there, and was then teaching at the University. He agreed to have personal interviews with applicants from the island and report to the admission office on their qualifications, especially their mastery of the English language. For a number of years Dr. Keelan rendered this service for the college and helped to select the students who seemed best qualified for study here.

The vivacious and enthusiastic girls from the Latin American countries tended to gravitate toward each other. The Spanish Club, with Dr. Cabrera as sponsor, was in a real sense a Spanish-speaking club although many other students majoring in Spanish participated. The annual Spanish Night became the major project of the club.

The first Spanish Club operetta was given on January 29, 1944.[3] Dr. Cabrera wrote both the scenario and the script. His guitar playing and singing, in Spanish costume, was a high point of the evening. In fact the costuming was a striking aspect of the Spanish Nights. Girls wrote home for their dresses and shawls, and there was a certain rivalry over the magnificence of the laces and embroidery.

The programs usually featured Spanish songs and dances, dramatizations, and a pseudobullfight, with a snorting bull propelled by two anonymous but energetic students in a highly imaginative replica of *el toro*.

The first Spanish fiestas were held as convocation programs in George Washington Hall with no admission charge. Subsequent productions were staged in Monroe, and the receipts from the modest twenty-five cent admission charged were used to finance activities of the Spanish Club.

The *Battlefield* for 1945 described, in Spanish, the activities of the Spanish Club for that session, which included *una comedia musicale* in which all of the members took part. Officers that year were Nancy Akers, president; Annette Keeler, vice-president; Providencia Keelan, secretary; and Ana Luisa Gonzalez, treasurer.

The fiesta produced as a convocation program on March 5, 1947, was entitled "España Alegre." It included songs and dances from both Spain and Latin American countries. Usually, the setting was an outdoor café in a Latin American country. There were tables and chairs, candles, and wine bottles (empty, of course) and a backdrop representing adobe walls and palm trees. Girls were dressed as boys and served as partners for the tangos. There were also excellent solo numbers performed by members of the Modern Dance Club.

[3] *Bullet*, Jan. 31, 1944.

Strange as it may seem now, there was some criticism of the display of wine bottles on the tables and the eagerness of the students in pretending to pour and drink their alleged contents. However, all was in good fun, and in the spirit of Latin warmth and gaiety. One memorable dance number concluded with each dancer flinging herself into the lap of her "date" as he sat at the table applauding. This aroused some comment afterwards. Dr. Cabrera's reply was classic: "But they were *both girls!*"

In April 1948 the Spanish Club's fiesta took place in the basement gymnasium of Monroe Hall, decorated to represent "Cabrera's Cave." An elaborate program of Spanish songs and dances, a bullfight, and a short play (*Delia and Carlos*) constituted the evening's entertainment. Carmen Zeppenfeldt directed the production, Barbara Watson staged the dances, and Ethel Chrisman was in charge of costumes. In April 1949 the club celebrated the recent anniversary of Cervantes with a pageant depicting scenes from *Don Quixote* and a production of scenes from *The Cave of Salamanca*. Dr. Cabrera directed the pageant, and Ann Osburn directed the play.

In time, more rigid academic selection of students from south of the border and a stricter test of English proficiency led to a gradual reduction in their number. But not before one lovely girl from Puerto Rico, Awilda Rose Valiente, had, as representative of the Spanish Club, been crowned the beauty queen of the college in the annual contest then sponsored as a fund-raising project by the junior class. Señorita Valiente's family gave her a trip to the West Coast as a reward for her achievement.

Dr. Cabrera also taught Portuguese and Italian, when needed, during his years at Mary Washington. However, Spanish-speaking students regarded him as their special confidant, even when the faculty in that language had increased to eight or ten. In 1967 Dr. Cabrera retired with the title of professor emeritus of Spanish. Since then, he has divided his time between a villa near Torremolinas in Spain and his home in Fredericksburg.

ACADEMIC DEVELOPMENTS

In the years following the authorization of the bachelor of arts degree, the academic program was strengthened each year by the addition of new courses in academic subjects and by the development of new departments. Professional courses in education were consolidated or eliminated.

In 1942 the two-year diploma for prospective teachers in the elementary grades was terminated in accordance with a resolution passed earlier by the State Board of Education discontinuing the normal professional certificate. Students in the diploma program were required to complete all requirements by September 1942. After that date, only degree graduates were to be certified as teachers for the public schools in Virginia. Students desiring to teach in the elementary grades would have to earn the bachelor of science degree and the collegiate professional certificate.

The last of the two-year graduates received their diplomas at the graduating exercises in June 1943. There were only nine, all of whom had finished the last requirements in the 1942 summer session. By contrast, there were 196 bachelors of arts and bachelors of science degrees conferred in June 1943.

Until June 1944 students completing the two-year secretarial course received a secretarial diploma. This was discontinued when the college became affiliated with the University of Virginia in 1944. By that year, there were new majors and minors in dramatic arts and speech, in psychology and philosophy, in Spanish, and in applied music.

The course offerings in practically every department had been revised and enlarged. In addition to the majors in French, Spanish, and Latin, the foreign language department began to offer courses in Portuguese, Italian, Russian, German, and Greek. With the hiring of Professor Vladimir V. Brenner in 1945, a former instructor at Harvard, the college became one of the earliest in the country to offer courses in Russian. Dr. Clifton B. McIntosh, a Ph.D. graduate in Spanish and Portuguese from the University of Virginia, returned from two years of duty for the Department of State in Brazil to begin instruction in Portuguese, Dr. Brenner also offered courses in German, and Dr. Louis J. Cabrera offered a course in Italian in addition to his work in Spanish.

Six visiting instructors from Washington, most of whom were members of the National Symphony Orchestra, offered a variety of courses in applied music. Majors in fields such as mathematics, history, and English were strengthened by the addition of many advanced courses. Academic standards in all courses were raised.

Final examinations, once optional, began to be given in almost all courses. In 1946, when the college changed from the quarter to the semester system, a five-day period was set aside for examinations at the end of each semester. At that time, examinations were required to be given in every course. No student exemptions were permitted.

The faculty was also greatly strengthened and enlarged during this period. For example, the English department in 1944 included eight faculty members with the doctorate: two from Yale and two from Peabody, and one each from Harvard, Chicago, Pennsylvania, and New York University.

It was during this period that a group of young Ph.D.s in the English department began the *Explicator,* a monthly publication primarily for college teachers, which featured explanations and criticisms of selected passages in English and American literature. Volume 1, no. 1, of the *Explicator* appeared in 1942 under the editorship of George W. Arms, John P. Kirby, Louis G. Locke, and J. Edwin Whitesell. Its opening sentence declared: *"The Explicator* is for those who like literature. Its province is the literature that everyone knows. Its purpose is to provide a clearinghouse for 'explication de texte.' " The same four men still publish the *Explicator.* Dr. Whitesell is now serving as managing editor. Volume 30, no. 10, appeared in June 1972.

The academic preparation of the faculty in 1944 was a far cry from the early days of the Normal School. Of the twenty-four full professors on the staff, twenty-three held doctorates. The one exception received his doctorate from George Washington University shortly thereafter.

CHAPTER XIII

Coordination with the University of Virginia, 1944-1948

THE GENERAL ASSEMBLY ACTS

FOR many years there had been agitation, especially among women leaders, for the establishment of a state-supported liberal arts college for women. Governor Pollard's veto in 1932 of the bill designating the college at Fredericksburg as the woman's college of the University of Virginia ended the matter temporarily. However, it was revived in 1943 by Governor Colgate W. Darden, Jr.

The governor pointed out the obligation of the Commonwealth of Virginia to provide higher educational facilities for both young men and young women of outstanding ability. He stressed the importance of providing opportunities for women comparable to those for men, especially in the fields of liberal arts and of technical, vocational, and professional education. He suggested that Mary Washington College be consolidated with the University of Virginia as a "college of arts and sciences for women" and that Radford College be consolidated with Virginia Polytechnic Institute.

Interest in the governor's proposals was widespread. During the summer of 1943 he appointed a commission to study these proposals and to make specific plans for their implementation, in order that the plan could be acted upon by the General Assembly of Virginia during the session beginning January 1944. Known as the Commission on the Consolidation of Colleges, the group was headed by J. Sinclair Brown of Salem, former president of the State Board of Education; and David W. Peters, then president of Radford College, was secretary. Other members of the commission were John Lloyd Newcomb, president of the University of Virginia; Julian A. Burruss, president of Virginia Polytechnic Institute; Morgan L. Combs, president of Mary Washington College; Rose M. MacDonald of Berryville, member of the State Board of Education; C. O'Conor Goolrick of Fredericksburg, former state senator and sponsor of the original bill establishing the college at Fredericksburg; and Dabney S. Lancaster, state superintendent of public instruction.

The commission made its report to the governor on December 3, 1943. It recommended that Mary Washington be converted into a college of arts and sciences for women on a par with that for men at the University of Virginia and placed under the direction and control of the university; that the university board of visitors be enlarged to include women members; that the president of the University of Virginia become chancellor of Mary Washington College; and that the title of the chief local administrative officer be that of president. Accompanying this report were drafts of bills designed to enact these recommendations into law. The text of the report was published in the *Bullet* on January 24, 1944.

In his message to the General Assembly on Wednesday, January 12, Governor Darden included in his recommendations the passage of legislation consolidating Mary Washington College with the University of Virginia and enlarging the board of visitors to permit the appointment of four women members.[1] A bill incorporating Governor Darden's recommendations was introduced shortly thereafter in the General Assembly. Known as the McCue-Randolph Bill, after the delegates from Charlottesville who sponsored it, the measure provided:

That the college be known as Mary Washington College of the University of Virginia.

That supervision, management, and control pass from the State Board of Education to the Rector and Visitors of the University of Virginia and that "the college shall hereafter be affiliated with the University of Virginia as an integral part thereof."

That the board of visitors of the university be increased by the addition of four members.

That the president of the University of Virginia be the chancellor of Mary Washington College of the University of Virginia and its chief administrative officer, and that the title of the chief local administrative officer be that of president.

That Mary Washington be converted into a liberal arts college for women, "with the same standards of admission and graduation as obtain for male students in the College of Arts and Sciences . . . located at Charlottesville."

That the conversion be effected during a period not exceeding four years and that students entering the college prior to the effective date of the act be allowed to complete their courses, but that after that date (July 1944) "no student shall be admitted to technical courses designed for the training of teachers except

[1] *Free Lance-Star,* Jan. 12, 1944.

those who can qualify for advance standing, leading to graduation within such period of four years."

That although under the control of the university, appropriations from the state be made specifically to Mary Washington College, to be expended by the board of visitors for its use.[2]

The bill was assigned to the House Committee on Schools and Colleges. After a hearing in which Dr. Combs and others spoke in behalf of the measure, the committee reported favorably to the House of Delegates on February 1.

There was little opposition to the bill on the floor of the House. Only Delegate Russell Weaver of Harrisonburg spoke against it. On February 4, the House passed the McCue-Randolph Bill by an overwhelming vote of 82 to 2. A few days later, on February 12, the Senate approved the bill unanimously. Governor Darden signed it on February 22, 1944. In accordance with the Code of Virginia, the act became effective ninety days after the adjournment of the General Assembly, or about the middle of June.

News of the passage of the bill was greeted with great enthusiasm both at the college and in the city of Fredericksburg generally. A special issue of the *Bullet* appeared on February 28, 1944, with accounts of the growth and development of Mary Washington up to that time, of the history and prestige of the University of Virginia, and of Jefferson as an early patron of liberal education.

The eight-page issue included a full-page advertisement headed "Our Congratulations to the Mary Washington College Faculty and Students on the Merger with the University of Virginia" and signed by sixteen business firms in Fredericksburg. Steps were taken to add "of the University of Virginia" everywhere that the name Mary Washington College appeared. The new catalogue published in April 1944 carried the title *Mary Washington College of the University of Virginia*. A subhead on the titlepage read *The Woman's College of the University of Virginia*.

COMMITTEE ON CONVERSION

Soon after the act became effective, steps were taken to implement its provisions. Both President John L. Newcomb of the University of Virginia, as chancellor of Mary Washington Col-

[2] *Acts of Assembly,* 1944, chap. 54, pp. 55–56.

lege, and President Combs of Mary Washington appointed special committees to study the academic aspects of the merger and make "recommendations concerning changes that . . . should be made to convert the college into a liberal arts college for women of the University of Virginia, under the provisions of the law." [3]

On September 25, 1944, President Newcomb appointed a committee of four, with Dr. George O. Ferguson, dean of the College of Arts and Sciences at the university, as chairman. Other members were Dr. James W. Cole, professor of chemistry; Dr. Roberta Hollingsworth, dean of women and assistant professor of Spanish; and Dr. Karl R. Wallace, professor of speech.

President Combs also appointed a committee of four, headed by Dr. Edward Alvey, Jr., dean of the college. Other members were Dr. Roy S. Cook, professor of chemistry; Dr. John P. Kirby, professor of English; and Dr. Rollin H. Tanner, professor of Latin.

The two committees held a joint meeting in Charlottesville shortly after their appointment. There was considerable discussion as to whether they constituted one committee of eight or two separate committees of four. It was finally agreed that the two committees would work closely together, meet regularly together, and confer constantly with each other, but that the final result was to be a report of the university committee to President Newcomb and the Mary Washington committee to President Combs, to be transmitted by them for final action by the board of visitors on the changes recommended or not recommended.

During the next eight months an intensive study was made of the entire academic program at Mary Washington. Data were assembled as called for, visits to classrooms and inspection of facilities were arranged, and many interviews with departmental chairmen and other instructional staff were scheduled. In the words of the university chairman, Dean Ferguson, in his letter of transmittal, "The authorities at Mary Washington have been wholly cooperative throughout our inquiries, and we hope they know of our lasting appreciation of their never-failing courtesy, patience, and helpfulness." [4]

Members of the university committee enlisted the assistance of a number of their colleagues in Charlottesville in studying various departments of the colleges. Professor Randall Thompson of

[3] Letter of transmittal to President Newcomb, May 28, 1945.
[4] *Ibid.*

the music department and Jack P. Dalton of the Alderman Library were among those who spent quite a bit of time at Mary Washington and assisted in the preparation of the final report.

This final report, a document of sixty-seven pages, was entitled "A Report to the Chancellor of Mary Washington College on Its Conversion into a College of Liberal Arts." It was transmitted to Dr. Newcomb on May 28, 1945, and, for the next three years, it was referred to many times as proposed changes were considered and acted upon, either by the academic officials at Mary Washington or, if board action were necessary, by the board of visitors of the university.

The report made a series of recommendations concerning changes in curricula to carry out the mandates of the law converting Mary Washington into a liberal arts college for women. Because of the importance of these recommendations, they are quoted from the report (pp. 16–17):

Recommendations: Curricula

Chapter 54, *Acts of the General Assembly, 1944*, states in three places, Sections 833-a, 833-d and 833-e, that Mary Washington "shall be converted into a liberal arts college for women." Our recommendations are guided mainly by this provision of the law, and are as follows:

1. That all of the specialized programs or curricula be discontinued, and that the College offer only the degree of Bachelor of Arts.

2. That major programs be offered in Art, Biology, Chemistry, Dramatic Arts and Speech, Economics and Business Administration, English, French, German, History, Latin, Mathematics, Music, Philosophy, Political Science, Psychology, Sociology and Spanish.

That the College should not attempt to offer major programs in Geology, Greek, Italian, Physics, Portuguese or Russian in the next few years.

3. That only nine quarter-hours of work in physical education be counted toward a degree, and, therefore, that a major program in this subject be not offered.

The present degree requirement of nine quarter-hours in physical education should be retained and this work should be taken in the freshman and sophomore years.

4. That credit toward a degree for work in stenography, typewriting and office practice be discontinued.

5. That credit toward a degree for work in home economics be discontinued.

6. That credit toward a degree for work in library science be discontinued.

7. That the Department of Education be discontinued, since the law states that students shall not be admitted to technical courses designed for the training of teachers.

That the course in the History and Philosophy of Education, offered in the Department of Psychology and Philosophy, be retained. This course is broadly cultural rather than a technical course for teachers.

8. That the following changes in departmental organization be made (see detailed departmental recommendations below):
   (1) The Department of Commerce and the Division of Economics of the Department of History and Social Science to be combined into a Department of Economics and Business Administration.
   (2) The Department of Foreign Languages to be divided into a Department of Ancient Languages and a Department of Modern Languages.
   (3) The Department of History and Social Science to be divided into a Department of History, a Department of Economics and Business Administration (see [1] above), a Department of Political Science, and a Department of Sociology. The courses in Geography to be included with Geology in the Department of Physical Sciences (see [4] below).
   (4) The Department of Science to be divided into a Department of Biological Sciences and a Department of Physical Sciences. The Department of Physical Sciences to include Chemistry, Geology (and Geography) and Physics.

Most of these recommendations were adopted by the board of visitors in subsequent meetings in which the Mary Washington conversion was considered. It was agreed that changes would take place over the specified four-year period and that after June 1948 degrees and majors to be discontinued would no longer be offered.

While the committee was studying the academic program, Mary Washington had completed a revision of its degree requirements. The committee endorsed, in general, the new requirements and the provisions for a major program. It recommended greater flexibility in major program requirements and more emphasis upon advanced courses. It also suggested that only the bachelor of arts degree be offered, as noted above in the recommendations.

The elimination of specialized degrees meant that the college would no longer offer a bachelor of arts in education or a bachelor of science in education, a bachelor of music, or any of the specialized degree programs in commerce, home economics, physical education, technical secretarial studies, school music, and applied music.

The report on coordination contained a separate section on each of the departments of the college, with specific recommendations concerning offerings, course sequences, major requirements, and staff. Many of these suggestions were put into effect in the period allocated to the conversion into a liberal arts college.

The committee devoted several pages of its report to the faculty. It recommended nineteen additions to the teaching staff, all in the academic departments of the college. It described faculty salaries as "far too low" and recommended a scale that would provide substantial increases at all levels.

Class size was found to be satisfactory. However, the teaching load of fifteen or sixteen hours a week was felt to be "heavy, particularly in the absence of student assistants." A reduction in teaching schedules was recommended for faculty members with administrative committee work or engaged in research projects. Again, many of these suggestions were followed.

The committee was most emphatic in recommending a larger role for the faculty in conducting the affairs of the college. According to the committee's report (p. 22), "the faculty as a body seems to have practically no functions at all, other than ceremonial."

A quotation from this section of the report (p. 22) indicates how seriously the committee viewed the role of the faculty as a body:

The Faculty should be a legislative body with final authority, under the Rector and Visitors, to pass upon all academic regulations, such as degree requirements, entrance requirements, awards of honors, grading systems, attendance regulations, rules of academic discipline, the courses offered for credit toward degrees, and the granting of degrees. Unless the Faculty has such functions as these, it is hardly a faculty in any democratic sense, but only a group of teachers of classes. It can hardly have any real corporate morale.

There are many faculty committees in the College, appointed to discharge administrative functions such as work with student organizations, the supervision of buildings and grounds, the arrangement of chapel services and of convocation and commencement exercises, the administration of discipline and the furtherance of desirable publicity. But there is no faculty committee on academic legislation, the curriculum, entrance requirements or the administration of scholastic regulations.

We recommend that a fairly large committee on academic legislation be appointed, and that it report to the Faculty on any matters that may properly come before it. We further recommend that all matters of academic legislation be referred to the Faculty for action, and that the Faculty be empowered to act with final authority, subject to the approval of the Rector and Visitors.

A number of important developments resulted from these recommendations. A time for regular monthly meetings of the faculty throughout the year was agreed upon, the dean of the college became the presiding officer at future faculty meetings, and a secretary to keep official minutes during the session was elected at the opening meeting. Later, Chancellor Simpson made the position of secretary of the faculty an appointive office and increased the importance and prestige of the position.

The minutes of each meeting, along with the faculty bulletin, were duplicated and distributed regularly to members of the faculty by the dean of the college. Copies of the minutes were bound and subsequently placed in the archives of the library. Faculty minutes dating from September 17, 1945, are now available in the archives.

A committee on academic standards was appointed to deal on a broad base with academic regulations and affairs. For the next ten years, this committee met at least once a month to consider such matters as grading systems, attendance regulations, rules of academic discipline, new courses and curricula, and degree requirements. Full minutes were kept of each meeting. The committee became the clearinghouse for proposals for strengthening and improving the academic program and standards of the college.

Much of the activity of the monthly faculty meetings grew out of the recommendations made by this committee. At times, its suggestions produced controversy. One restless faculty member who preferred the perfunctory meetings of the old days called it the "committee to prolong faculty meetings."

It was, nevertheless, the beginning of a new era of faculty participation in college affairs. The committee on academic standards rendered valuable service in the academic growth of the institution. The dean of the college worked closely with the committee, both as an active or an ex officio member, in the years that followed its creation.

On June 20, 1945, the Mary Washington College committee, headed by Dean Alvey, made its own report to the president of the University of Virginia. It referred to its role in endeavoring "to assist the committee from the University to the fullest extent in its study of the College."[5] The committee also carried on its

---

[5] Letter of transmittal to President Newcomb, June 20, 1945.

own study of the role of the institution as a liberal arts college for women. The result of its weekly meetings and discussions over a period of several months was a report entitled "A Plan for Mary Washington College as a Liberal Arts College."

In the words of the chairman, "We have studied catalogues of women's colleges of various types, read reports on trends in liberal arts education, and discussed the needs of college women of today as we have observed them. We have proposed a liberal arts college of the comprehensive type as the woman's college of the University of Virginia" (p. 2). Briefly, the report urged a broader conception of a liberal arts education. In the words of the committee, "The difference [between liberal and professional education] lies not so much in the particular subjects taught as in the manner in which they are taught and the goals sought in their teaching" (p. 1).

Perhaps the gist of the committee's argument is found in the following paragraph, quoted from the report (pp. 3-4): "If some of the courses of a liberal arts college also prepare its students for economic competence, the college does not thereby become any less a liberal arts college provided it holds to its true objectives. In fact a person's ability to make a living may be essential to his capacity for leadership in the higher things of life. It may be perfectly in keeping with the aims of a liberal arts college for it to offer courses in Applied Art and Music, in Commerce, in Home Economics, in Theatrical Production, in Education, and in Physical Education."

To support its broader concept of liberal arts, the committee quoted from a symposium on the function of the liberal arts college in a democratic society, published in the *American Scholar* (Autumn, 1944), and from a report of a committee of the American Council of Learned Societies entitled "Liberal Education Re-examined."

The committee gave its support to many of the recommendations of the university committee, including elimination of special degrees in education. It urged the limitation of credit in certain courses (commerce, applied music and art, and physical education except for majors). Its main concern was that the majors in fields such as applied music and art, commerce, home economics, and physical education be continued and a B.S. degree be offered in these fields. However, at least half of the courses taken should be from the regular liberal arts program of the college.

These arguments for a broader conception of liberal arts were placed before the board along with the report of the university committee. The point of view and recommendations of the latter prevailed and were adopted officially by the board. When this action was taken, the academic officials at Mary Washington proceeded immediately to put these changes into effect, with a deadline of June 1948 for ending all course offerings or academic credit specified for discontinuance by the board.

NEW DEGREE REQUIREMENTS

In September 1945 a new program of degree requirements became effective for incoming freshmen. The new requirements permitted greater flexibility in the selection of courses leading to a degree and, at the same time, provided more extensive study in a field of special interest. In lieu of the former requirement of one major and two minor subjects, students were to select a field of concentration or major program to which they were to devote a large part of their time in the junior and senior years.

The new major programs in the various fields required thirty-six semester hours of credit, twenty-four in the subject itself and twelve in specified or approved related fields. Of course, students could, and many did, take more credits in the major subject than the minimum of twenty-four required and usually specified. Requirements for the bachelor of arts degree in semester hours, were now as follows:

English	12
Foreign Language	12
History	6
Natural Science	8
Mathematics or Fine Arts	6
Social Science, Philosophy, or Psychology	6
Health and Physical Education	6
Required courses	56
Major program	36
Electives	34
Total for Degree	126

The bachelor of science degree was available to students completing a major program in biology or chemistry. The requirements were exactly the same as those for the bachelor of arts degree with two execeptions: (1) a modern foreign language (preferably German or French) must be taken to satisfy the language requirement; and (2) instead of having a choice between mathematics or fine arts, the student must complete six semester hours in mathematics.

CURRICULUM CHANGES

As an outgrowth of the studies and report of the committee on coordination, a large number of changes were made in the academic program of the college, many of them effective with the 1945–46 or 1946–47 sessions. Students enrolled in certain programs that would be discontinued after June 1948 were given advance warning of this action. Students were not permitted to enroll for majors in the fields to be discontinued unless they could complete the requirements by June 1948. The college calendar was changed from a quarter basis to a semester basis beginning with the session of 1946–47.

In 1946–47 courses in history and appreciation of art were separated from those in the practice of art. In order to receive credit for the latter students were required to earn an equal number of credits in history and appreciation of art. A major in economics and business administration, consisting largely of courses in the former, replaced the major in commerce. The name of the department itself was changed accordingly. Credit for courses in typewriting, shorthand, and office practice was discontinued entirely. These courses were now listed in the catalogue in a separate section as noncredit secretarial courses.

The 1946–47 catalogue (p. 78) announced that "technical courses designed for the training of teachers will be discontinued after June, 1948." This statement was rescinded later. The department of history and political science was reorganized to provide separate majors in history, political science, and sociology. The 1946–47 bulletin also announced that all courses in library science would be discontinued at the end of the 1947–48 session. This was done.

Credit for courses in applied music was limited to a maximum of twelve semester hours. In order to receive credit for applied music, the student was required to match these credits with an equal number in courses in the theory of music. However, courses in applied music could be taken without credit. No student was permitted to earn more than two credits in Glee Club or choir, or more than four in band and four in orchestra.

The major in physical education was due to be discontinued in June 1948. This decision was later changed and the program continued. Courses in dietetics and home economics were also announced to be discontinued in June 1948. This decision, also, was changed later. Courses in the relatively new department of psychology and philosophy were separated completely, and new majors in philosophy and in psychology were organized.

In 1945 courses in general biology and general chemistry were increased an additional credit each term. In 1946 the old major in science was discontinued, and new majors in biology and in chemistry were announced. Courses in geology and physics continued to be offered and could be taken as related fields in the biology and chemistry majors. The technical secretarial course, a combination of courses in shorthand and typewriting with student clinical practice work in medical offices, was discontinued as of June 1948.

ADMISSION REQUIREMENTS CHANGED

When courses below college level were eliminated from the curriculum in the 1920s, graduation from an accredited high school became the only academic requirement for admission. Later, as applications for admission increased in the early 1940s, preference was given to students ranking in the upper half of their graduating classes. It was not until 1946 that entrance units in specific subjects began to be required.

As an outgrowth of the legislative act affiliating the college with the University of Virginia, which specified the same standards of admission as those for men students at the university, Mary Washington began to require not only high school graduation but credit for at least three units in English and two units in mathematics, not including arithmetic or business mathematics. The remaining units were elective, but credit could not be allowed for more than four units in vocational subjects. A foreign language was not required for admission at that time but, if offered for credit, there had to be at least two units in the same language.[6]

The catalogue stated that preference would be given to students ranking in the upper third of their graduating class. There was a provision for enrolling as special students applicants at

---

[6] *Catalogue*, 1945-46, p. 35.

least twenty-one years of age, who were required to meet all regular admission requirements before they could become candidates for a degree. Only a very few persons were ever admitted as special students under these provisions.

For the next thirteen years, until 1959, these requirements remained in effect. That year the committee on admissions policy added the requirement of two years in a foreign language and reduced the number of credits allowed in vocational subjects to two. In 1960 the committee raised the requirement in English to four units.

TRAINING OF TEACHERS

In accordance with the act of the 1944 General Assembly converting Mary Washington College into a liberal arts college for women, technical courses for the training of teachers were to be eliminated. Accordingly, the college discontinued majors in education and announced that after June 1948, the B.A. in education would no longer be offered.

In interpreting the provisions of the act, the college had also eliminated all courses in education with the result that graduates of the liberal arts program who wished to teach were unable to qualify for other than a temporary teaching certificate, a condition that placed them at a disadvantage as compared with graduates of other liberal arts colleges where such courses were available as electives.

The college made an urgent appeal to the board of visitors to be authorized to offer as electives the courses necessary to qualify for a regular teaching certificate. In support of this request, the Mary Washington committee on coordination, of which Dean Alvey was chairman, prepared a statement for members of the board, part of which read:

As a state institution it would be highly desirable for the graduates of Mary Washington College who may wish to teach to have the opportunity of taking as electives those courses in Education that would enable them to qualify for the Collegiate Professional Certificate. This would in no way change the essential nature of the college as a liberal arts college. All majors would be in academic subjects. It would simply mean that the entry of graduates of this institution into the teaching profession would be encouraged and facilitated.

The outstanding liberal arts colleges for women throughout the United States offer such courses as electives to enable their graduates to teach in the public schools if they wish to do so. In order to meet certificate requirements for high school teachers it would be *necessary* to retain in the program of studies only the courses in Secondary Education and Supervised Teaching, both of which are now scheduled to be discontinued after the session of 1947-48.

The liberal arts colleges of Virginia, public and private, have always prepared a substantial proportion of the public school teachers of this state. In view of the acute shortage of teachers, it seems highly desirable that the state liberal arts college for women make it possible for those of its graduates who wish to teach to take as electives the subjects that will enable them to qualify for a regular, renewable teacher's certificate.[7]

Academic officials of both Mary Washington College and of the University of Virginia were called to appear before the board of visitors to give their views regarding the proposal. It was supported strongly by Dr. Ivey F. Lewis, dean of the University of Virginia, and by Dr. Dabney S. Lancaster, state superintendent of public instruction and an ex officio member of the board. Dr. Lancaster emphasized the shortage of teachers in Virginia and the need to have as teachers the kind of students who would be completing the liberal arts program at Mary Washington.

Members of the board of visitors were impressed and in 1947 authorized the inclusion of the courses necessary to qualify for teaching certificates in the high school academic subjects. When the catalogue announcing courses for the session of 1948-49 appeared, it included two courses in education: Education 311-312 (Secondary Education, six semester hours) and Education 440 (Supervised Teaching, six semester hours). These two courses, together with six semester hours in Philosophy 411-412, History and Philosophy of Education, totaled the necessary eighteen semester hours for certification. According to the catalogue (p. 76), they were "available, as electives, to students majoring in other fields who wished to qualify for the Collegiate Professional Certificate—the highest teaching certificate issued in Virginia."

At its meeting on March 9, 1951, the board of visitors gave authority to reinstate also the course entitled Education 311-312 (Elementary Education, six semester hours), so that graduates of the college could be eligible to teach also in the elementary grades.[8]

The catalogue for 1952-53 (pp. 96-97) outlined a suggested

---

[7] "Statement concerning Qualification of Graduates for Teaching Certificates," pp. 1-2.

[8] Minutes of Board of Visitors, March 9, 1951.

curriculum for students who wish to qualify for teaching in the elementary grades. It showed "how a student majoring in psychology could include in her program the courses that would enable her to qualify for teaching in the elementary grades." This program became quite popular. It soon supplanted the cooperative program in elementary education, for many students did not want to transfer to the University of Virginia at the end of two years in order to be certified for elementary school teaching. It also included many more courses in academic subjects than did the cooperative program leading to the bachelor of science in education at the University of Virginia.

DEGREE IN HOME ECONOMICS REINSTATED

The major program in dietetics and home economics was scheduled to be discontinued after June 1948. However, during the session of 1947-48 the board of visitors reconsidered and authorized the reinstatement of a bachelor of science degree in home economics if it were approved by the faculty.

In a formal vote at its meeting on March 27, 1948, the faculty approved the new major program leading to this degree. It required that all general requirements for the B.S. degree be completed, plus thirty-six semester hours' credit in home economics and related fields, the latter selected from art, biology, chemistry, economics, and psychology. The catalogue with announcements for the session of 1948-49 (pp. 83-84) carried a description of the major program in home economics.

The new program did not qualify the student to teach home economics. After careful study, the Mary Washington College committee of the board of visitors voted unanimously on February 27, 1951, to authorize the college to add the courses necessary for candidates for the degree of bachelor of science in home economics to qualify as teachers in this field. This recommendation was formally approved by the board at its March meeting.[9]

PHYSICAL EDUCATION MAJOR REINSTATED

The major program in physical education was also due to be terminated in June 1948. The major was discontinued for a time

[9] *Ibid.*

and only elective courses offered. However, again the board of visitors yielded to the urging of advocates of a major in this field and, on February 10, 1950, authorized the reinstatement of a major program.[10]

A special announcement of this development was inserted in the catalogue for 1950–51, with a mimeographed outline of course requirements available upon request. A complete description of the major program leading to the degree of bachelor of science in health, physical education, and recreation appeared in the next issue of the catalogue (pp. 95–96).

Students were required to complete all required courses for the bachelor of science degree, plus a thirty-six-semester-hour major program in courses in the department. Students who wished to teach could elect the courses necessary to qualify for the collegiate professional certificate.

[10] *Ibid.*, Feb. 10, 1950.

CHAPTER XIV

Postwar Developments, 1946–1949

EXPANSION CONTINUES

WORLD WAR II halted all construction except that essential for military purposes. However, the college continued to expand its facilities and enlarge its holdings through the acquisition of houses and property immediately adjacent to the campus. Important purchases were made in 1944, 1946, 1947, and 1949.

BRENT HALL

In 1944 the college purchased from Mrs. D. J. Boulware for $50,000 the brick residence she and her husband had erected shortly after World War I. It occupied a commanding site on the central campus diagonally across from George Washington Hall, overlooking a part of the city of Fredericksburg. From the year of its purchase until 1947 it served as the president's home. Subsequently it was converted into a residence hall for students, and since September 1951 it has been the French language house.

The newly acquired residence was given the name of Brent Hall in honor of Margaret Brent, who was born in England in 1601. The family members were prominent Catholics. To escape religious persecution, she and her sister and brothers came to America in 1638, settling at St. Mary's, Maryland. The Brents eventually acquired large landholdings, totaling thousands of acres. The management of these estates fell to Margaret Brent, who proved to be a most capable businesswoman.

In 1650 Margaret moved to Virginia, joining her brother at his home near the mouth of Aquia Creek. By 1655 she owned 2,700 acres, including the site of what is now Fredericksburg. When she died at the age of seventy, her holdings in Virginia totaled 8,764 acres. She is believed to have been buried near her sister in the little cemetery of Aquia, not far from the crucifix on U.S. Route 1 commemorating the pioneer Catholic settlers in Virginia.

FRAMAR PURCHASED

In 1946 the college acquired Framar, the home of Dr. and Mrs. Frank H. Reichel, located on William Street on land adjoining the college. The purchase price of $125,000 included a handsome residence, a five-room guesthouse and garage, a private swimming pool and outdoor picnic area, a rose and boxwood garden, and 7.61 acres of land. The purchase of Framar was particularly desirable in that it made the campus a complete unit extending from William Street to the U.S. Route 1 Bypass in one direction and from College Avenue to Sunken Road in the other.

Framar was built in 1930 and served as the Reichel home until he left for Philadelphia to become president of the American Viscose Corporation, which in 1946 had purchased the Sylvania Corporation in Fredericksburg headed at the time by Dr. Reichel. Framar is a combination of the first names of its builders, Frank and Marion Reichel. It is built of old brick, with handsome solid walnut paneling. The residence served as the president's house from 1946 to 1948, until Brompton was ready for occupancy. It has since been used as a small dormitory for students. During part of this time it served as the Spanish house.

BROMPTON ACQUIRED

In 1946 the college acquired from the heirs of Maurice B. Rowe the handsome brick residence Brompton and 171 acres of adjacent land at a cost of $71,000. The estate also included two small frame houses and a barn, dairy, and garage.

At one time this property belonged to Fielding Lewis, George Washington's brother-in-law. It changed hands several times before it was bought in 1821 by John Lawrence Marye, from whom Marye's Heights got its name.

Brompton is named after a town in England which had offered sanctuary to the Reverend James Marye, grandfather of John Lawrence Marye, who had come from France in the early eighteenth century. The elder Marye came to America shortly thereafter and settled in Fredericksburg, where he taught school (George Washington was one of his pupils) and served as rector of St. George's Episcopal Church.

The exact date of the original building is uncertain. It was built in several stages, with three separate roofs constructed over the central portion as additions were made. Authorities agree that the original structure antedates the American Revolution. The central portion may have been built as early as 1740. In any case, Marye is known to have added extensively to the original four-room two-story central section. The two first-floor rooms to the west and those directly above were added about 1820; the entrance hall with rooms above and the two one-story end wings were added in 1840; and the two-story portico with its flat roof was added shortly thereafter.

Brompton has been described as one of the most historic houses in America. It was the center of the bloody attack on Marye's Heights made by Federal General Burnside in December 1862. Repeated efforts to capture this heavily fortified Confederate position resulted in the loss of 12,653 Federal soldiers, many of whom fell under the withering fire coming from the stone wall along Sunken Road just below the mansion. Confederate losses were 5,309 in an engagement that involved a total of 243,311 men in the two armies. Many of the Northern dead are buried in long rows of graves at the United States Cemetery farther along Marye's Heights toward the east. This is the third largest National Cemetery in the country, exceeded only by the Arlington and Gettysburg national cemeteries in the number of those deceased.

The Federal troops were successful in capturing the heights in the Second Battle of Fredericksburg one year later. The columns, brick walls, and sidings of the building still bear the marks of the bullets and shells fired in the course of the battle. Matthew Brady's wartime photographs show the house used as a Union hospital or dressing station during the battles of the Wilderness and Spotsylvania Court House in 1864. One of the most interesting pictures, now available in postcard form, shows the wounded lying against the house and under the great oak tree nearby, which is still standing today.

After the war, the building was repaired and the surrounding land devoted to farming. Maurice B. Rowe ("Captain Rowe") purchased the property in 1887, and it remained in the hands of the Rowe family until purchased by the state of Virginia in 1946 for the use of Mary Washington College.

For over two years the house underwent extensive restoration. Inside surfaces were removed to the bare brick, and new plaster, lighting fixtures, and heating facilities were installed. Dr. Combs spent many hours planning and supervising the renovation of the house which, upon completion of the work, he was to occupy as the official residence of the head of the college. Expert advice on restoration procedures was given by authorities from Colonial Williamsburg. Nancy McClelland, internationally known interior decorator, gave close supervision to the project. Franco Scalamandre, who wove the draperies for Monticello and other historic buildings, presented Brompton with woven wall coverings of damask and matching draperies.

As the home of the chancellor, Brompton has become the center of many social events for the college, beginning with the receptions for new faculty members and for new students and extending through the year to end with a massive reception and buffet on the grounds for the graduating seniors, their parents and friends, the alumnae, and other guests of the college. Some twenty-five hundred to three thousand persons are ordinarily in attendance.

Dr. and Mrs. Simpson are gracious hosts to numerous college and community receptions and guests throughout the year, and they have made the gardens behind Brompton a delightful place to visit each spring and fall.

The furnishings at Brompton are a harmonious blend of the old and the new. Contemporary paintings help to highlight the beauty of period furniture. In addition to furniture owned by the Simpsons and by the college, there are pieces from Belmont, the Gari Melchers estate now administered by the college. A number of Melchers's paintings are also on display at Brompton.

TRENCH HILL

In 1947 the college purchased from the Jenkins estate for $80,000 the brick residence and seven acres of land just across Hanover Street from the Brompton estate. The residence was situated on an eminence overlooking the city of Fredericksburg. The ground on which it was built had been fought over during the Civil War in the Battle of Fredericksburg in December 1862, and there were still remnants of the trench that had been dug at the time. The new addition to the college facilities was named Trench Hill.

After extensive remodeling, the house became a residence hall for students. At first, the distance from the college dining hall seemed a disadvantage. However, when the dormitory was designated as residence for academically talented students participating in the Trench Hill seminars, it became a mark of distinction to be housed there. Bicycles made the trip to the dining hall less arduous. Furthermore, a feeling of camaraderie developed among the students living there. Their periodic at homes for faculty guests on Sunday afternoons added to the prestige of the group. It has continued to be a desirable residence for students.

SPOTSWOOD PURCHASED

In 1949 the college purchased the residence of Charles F. Beck at the corner of College Avenue and Brent Street, just across from the college gates. The purchase price of $33,000 included three lots and a two-car garage with an apartment above it. The house was named Spotswood in honor of Alexander Spotswood, colonial governor of Virginia. Spotswood has been used for a variety of purposes. At first it was a residence for students. For a time it was used as the Spanish house. Then in 1959 it was designated as the Alumnae House, and it now serves as headquarters of the Alumnae Association.

ADMISSION OF MEN

Until 1929, there is no official record of there having been men enrolled as students in the college; however, envisioning a greater role of service for Mary Washington, President Combs announced that the summer quarter would be open to men and women. In fact, the cover of the bulletin reads, *Summer Quarter, 1929, For Men and Women.*

The catalogue (p. 18) stated that "one of the college dormitories will be reserved for the exclusive use of men students during the summer quarter, provided the enrollment justifies such," and that they would be permitted to take their meals in the college dining hall.

Although only a few men were enrolled that first summer, the number increased slightly the next summer (1930), especially with the understanding that they would be allowed to continue as students in the regular session that followed.

On October 23, 1930, President Combs reported to the State Board of Education that eighteen men, sixteen of whom were boarding students, had been admitted for the session of 1930–31 and had paid their fees.[1] The board refused to sanction this action

[1] Minutes of Board, Oct. 23, 1930.

and ruled that men were not eligible to enroll for the regular session. It agreed to permit these men to finish the current session, but thereafter they would have to "make other arrangements."

On April 11, 1931, President Combs pleaded with the board to extend permission for these men to attend another year (1931–32) in the regular session, with the provision that they were not to be housed on the campus. The board turned down this request.[2]

Men continued to enroll in the summer session. The majority attended during the summers of 1931 through 1938. The number was never large at anytime. The roster for the 1933 summer session lists only twenty-three male students, many of whom were from local or nearby areas.

Resident male students were housed in Betty Lewis Hall, originally constructed as an apartment house but leased by the college to take care of the increasing number of students and also used to provide accommodations for faculty members on a rental basis as the need might warrant.

A number of these men students were able to complete their degree programs through summer school attendance. The Reverend Hunter H. Newman, who already held an A.B. degree from Lynchburg College, received a B.S. degree with a major in social science. He served for many years as pastor of the First Christian Church in Fredericksburg and was proud of saying that both he and his wife had graduated from Mary Washington.

Logan Harding, who had previously attended the College of William and Mary, received a B.S. degree in August 1936, also with a major in social science. He is currently a school principal in Hopewell. Elmer Spence was awarded a B.S. degree in August 1938.

In June 1939 Samuel E. Patton was awarded the B.S. degree, also with a major in elementary education. He had also taken courses at William and Mary and at the University of Maryland.

Probably the record for summer school attendance was held by Emmett Day, who, with the exception of a few courses taken at Radford and through the University of Virginia Extension Division, took all of his work at Mary Washington. He received the B.S. degree in August 1938 after attending eight summer sessions. An enthusiastic and popular member of the student body, he served for many years as an elementary school principal in Fairfax County.

---

[2] *Ibid.*, April 23, 1931.

The number of men attending the summer sessions began to diminish especially after 1938 when, incidentally, the name of the college was changed to Mary Washington. When Mary Washington became the woman's college of the University of Virginia in 1944, the admission of male students was discontinued.

At the end of World War II, the returning veterans taking advantage of the Serviceman's Readjustment Act of 1944, popularly known as the G.I. Bill, began to swamp the facilities for higher education in the United States. Men's colleges and coeducational universities were faced with the problem of enrolling additional hundreds of thousands of students who qualified for various periods of attendance at the expense of the federal government.

To meet the emergency, a number of women's colleges opened their doors to returning veterans. In the spring of 1946, arrangements were made for Mary Washington College to enroll men students who met the admission requirements and were certified officially as eligible for educational assistance under the G.I. Bill.

While a few veterans began their studies in the 1946 summer session, the large majority of them enrolled in the fall. During the first semester, there were a total of twenty-seven male veterans enrolled. Six of them stayed only one semester, while ten continued only for one session. On the other hand, those who remained proved to be serious students, and several graduated from Mary Washington. Among them were Robert H. Combs, the son of the president of the college (B.A., 1948), Robert A. Miller (B.A., 1948), Keith Pitzer, a major in art (B.A., 1950), and Thomas B. Sale, Jr. (B.A., 1950). Combs had previously attended the University of Richmond, and Miller had been a student at the University of Maryland.

The second semester, twenty-one more veterans enrolled, bringing the total number in attendance during the session to forty-eight. A number of the second semester group also graduated from Mary Washington College. James H. Filling and Thomas H. Jenkins, Jr., received bachelor's degrees in 1949, Cleveland K. Rollins in 1950, Marshall W. Pender in 1951, and James M. Randall in 1952.

Only a few veterans began their studies after that first year, the session of 1946–47. The following year, Charles C. Ritter entered the college the second semester, majoring in dramatic arts and speech. He took an active part in stage productions at Mary Washington and in 1951 was graduated with the B.A. degree.

After leaving Mary Washington, Ritter enrolled for graduate

study in dramatic arts and speech, attaining the Ph.D. degree in this field. Currently, he is an associate professor at Ohio State University and, incidentally, serving as faculty adviser to a member of the present faculty at Mary Washington, who is completing his doctoral studies at Ohio State.

The last veteran to enroll was Dennis Chauncey Moriarity, a former marine, originally from Brooklyn, but then living in Quantico. Moriarity enrolled the second semester of the 1953-54 session and attended the college for the next four years, majoring in music and specializing in piano. He was awarded the B.A. degree on June 2, 1958.

During the last two years of his attendance at Mary Washington, Moriarity was the only man attending the college. Newspapers in Washington and Richmond found this of special interest and published illustrated feature stories about "one man among 2,000 girls." Modest and unassuming, Moriarity found these articles a little disconcerting, but he took it all in stride, continuing to devote extra hours of practice to his work in piano and earning extra money for his individual lessons through part-time employment in the dining hall. He never seemed conscious of his role as the last remaining male veteran among the women students of Mary Washington.

The veterans made an excellent adjustment to student life in a predominantly women's college. Although they were not housed on the campus, a number of them participated in college activities, especially plays and benefits.

They were well received by the regular students at Mary Washington. Photographs of the Veterans Club appeared in the *Battlefield* in 1947, 1948, 1949, 1950, and 1951. During these years, there was also a veterans' representative on the Student Council. Among those who served were Sam Pepper (later a member of the Honor Committee at the University of Virginia when he transferred there), Thomas Jenkins, Thomas Vivian, and Charles C. Ritter. A basketball team of veterans played periodically with other teams in the area.

ACADEMIC DEVELOPMENTS

In accordance with its new role as a liberal arts college for women, the college continued to strengthen its majors in academic fields by the addition of new courses on the junior and senior level and the employment of additional faculty members.

Postwar Developments

The history and social science department was further divided into geography, history, political science, and sociology. Similarly, the science department was separated into more specialized subject departments and new majors in biology and chemistry were established.

The foreign language requirements for graduation resulted in great expansion in both the number and variety of courses offered. Perhaps the greatest increase in course enrollment, certainly in terms of percentages, took place in the foreign languages, and many new instructors were added. Both mathematics and fine arts became attractive as majors, especially with the enlargement of course offerings and employment of specialists in certain areas of the fine arts.

As a means of measuring the academic attainment of its students, the college administered the Graduate Record Examination to the entire senior class in March 1948. This is a comprehensive examination requiring three four-hour and one two-hour session. The medians for the college on various parts of the examination closely approximated the national norms for liberal arts colleges for women. They were far above the norms for state teachers colleges for women.

A record of faculty publications was compiled and printed as a bulletin of the college in 1947. Copies of this 68-page bulletin were sent to the libraries of all the better-known colleges and universities in the United States. It also contained a brief record of the training and experience of each member of the 1947–48 faculty.

The committee on academic standards and legislation conducted a number of studies, which were duly reported to the faculty with recommendations for action. One such study dealt with the class attendance of students. During the session of 1947–48 seniors on the dean's list were for the first time given responsibility for their own class attendance and not required to submit excuses for absence. A check of the results of this system disclosed that the average senior on the dean's list missed only three and a third classes the first semester. Under the class cut system she would have been entitled to three cuts anyway, plus absences for illness and other approved causes. In other words, evidence supported the conclusion that these seniors appreciated being given responsibility for their own class attendance and actually missed fewer classes than they had previously.

One of the outstanding academic developments during this period was the inauguration of the honors program.

THE HONORS PROGRAM

The honors program had its beginnings in November 1946 when it was announced that the board of visitors had approved the honors plan adopted by the faculty at its May meeting [3] but recommended it be introduced on a limited scale at first. The faculty thereupon voted to elect a five-man honors committee to initiate the program.[4] Dr. Robert W. Pyle, who had drafted the original plan for honors work and had championed its adoption, was elected chairman. Other members of the first committee on honors were professors Bolling, J. H. Dodd, Kirby, and Reichenbach.

The new committee began immediately to draft a statement of requirements for honors study, to meet with various departments interested in participating in the program, and to prepare student application forms. A fairly elaborate statement of the organization and operation of the program was distributed to faculty members and interested students. An overall average of B and an average of B+ in the major field were minimum academic requirements for eligibility. Each participating department appointed an honors committee to screen applicants, arrange for departmental committees to supervise the work of approved applicants, and to make the final evaluation of the honors project.

Announcements of the new program were made in the spring of 1947. Two applicants were approved for honors work the following session: Betty Bowles in French and Charlotte Dean Smith in history. They were the first two students to graduate with honors, and they were accorded this recognition at the graduation exercises in June 1948. There were eight applicants the following year, of whom only two received the final approval of the faculty committee and their departmental committees on honors work. They were Margaret Hines in biology and Barbara Blackburn in music.

In January 1963, the committee on academic excellence published an attractive brochure giving a description of the honors program and listing the papers and their authors up to that time.[5] A complete list of the authors and titles of honors papers

---

[3] Faculty Minutes, May 20, 1946.   [4] *Ibid.,* Nov. 11, 1946.
[5] "The Honors Program at Mary Washington College of the University of Virginia," published by the college, 1963.

was published in December 1971.[6] Since the inception of the program in 1948 until December 1971, a total of ninety-four students graduated with honors. From 1956 to 1971 seventy students wrote papers in seventeen different fields. There were twelve each in chemistry and English, and six in French; history, Latin and music followed, each with a total of five papers. All of these bound papers have been fully catalogued and deposited in the archives of the library.

JULIEN BINFORD

In the fall of 1946 Julien Binford joined the faculty of the art department as professor of painting. He had taught the previous year at Richmond Professional Institute. A native Virginian, Binford grew up in Georgia and attended school there. In 1928 he gave up his premedical studies at Emory because, as he put it, he did better at anatomical drawing than he did on quizzes. He enrolled for study at the Art Institute of Chicago. His achievements there won for him, upon graduation in 1932, the institute's Edward L. Ryerson Traveling Fellowship.

After some European travel, Binford settled in France where he began to paint the jewellike gouaches that won the admiration and friendship of French writers, poets, and collectors. The famous Parisian art dealer Paul Guillaume wrote of his incontestable talents and arranged exhibitions of his work. Binford's work was widely acclaimed for its imagination, spirit, and originality.

While living in Paris, Binford met and married the former Countess Elizabeth Bollée de Vautibault. Mrs. Binford writes entertainingly, has done research for his mural projects, and posed for several of his best portrait studies. She has been a constant companion and inspiration.

Binford returned to the United States in the mid-1930s and exhibited his work in New York. He and his wife lived for a time in a loft above a factory in the heart of the city, where he continued to work at his easel. His works were handled by the Midtown Galleries, which still represents him and expresses an interest in "all he can let them have."

Meanwhile, Binford purchased an old foundry at Fine Creek

---

[6] "Honors Papers at Mary Washington College of the University of Virginia, 1948–1971," by Barbara Alden, Archivist, E. Lee Trinkle Library, 1971.

Mills, Virginia, which had been begun during the War of 1812 but was abandoned in 1816 when insufficient funds from the War Department prevented its completion. The Old Foundry, as it was known, was overgrown with trees and brush and its walls, three feet thick, were partially crumbled when the Binfords bought it in 1936. At first the couple lived in a shack, which Binford gradually improved by adding rooms, paneling walls, and building a chimney and fireplace. It was six years before the large stone structure was ready to house the couple. Binford quarried the stone to repair the massive walls, added windows, and built a slate roof. Gardens and terraces were added. The development of Fine Creek Mills property continues to be a major interest of the Binfords. His three-story studio is an integral part of the house, and there is a spacious working and storage area.

In his early days at Fine Creek Mills, Binford painted many of his neighbors. Among the best known of these pictures are *The Scythe Sharpener, The Crap Shooter,* and *The Razor Fight.* During World War II Binford was assigned to the navy as artist-correspondent for *Life* magazine. He executed a series of paintings entitled *New York Harbor at War,* which appeared in the November 20, 1944, issue as a six-page section in color and were widely acclaimed.

In Binford's first years at Mary Washington he lived in a cottage at Belmont, the Gari Melchers estate across the river at Falmouth. Mrs. Melchers was very fond of the young couple and made her husband's studio available as a working place for him. Later the Binfords purchased a stone house at the foot of the hill in Falmouth, where they established a large studio. During this period Binford painted seven mural panels for the new building of the Greenwich Savings Bank at Fifty-seventh Street just off Fifth Avenue, in New York. The banking area was designed to display most effectively these murals, which depict colorfully the early history and activities of the city.

Binford has always been an indefatigable worker. His teaching complemented his own productive work as an artist. To students he was a patient, helpful, and encouraging critic, always ready to point out ways of improvement and capable of bringing out the best in each one of them. Scholarships awarded to graduates who have studied under Binford are one evidence of his success as a teacher. From time to time Binford has taken a year's leave of absence just to catch up with his painting, execute commissions that he had agreed to undertake, and work on the house at Fine

Creek Mills. At first his weekends were spent at the Powhatan County house; now he commutes from there for his classes at the college.

Binford is extremely modest. Many persons at the college were unaware of his wide reputation as an artist until a special exhibition of his paintings, drawings, and sculpture was held in the exhibition rooms of duPont Hall from April 7 to May 1, 1971. The project was planned and carried out by students in a new course in the art department, the connoisseurship, research, and gallery course, taught by Mathew Herban III. Students wrote to collectors and galleries for the loan of paintings, collected information, secured photographs, wrote and arranged for the printing of the catalogue, packed and unpacked crates, and arranged the entire exhibition. Some eighty works by Binford were gathered on loan from museums, galleries, and private collections. The exhibition was the occasion of a number of published interviews and feature stories on the artist and his work.[7]

Binford's work is characterized by a sensitivity to light and color, a love of nature, and a feeling of rapport between the artist and the viewer. He is more concerned with relating the basic elements of art—line, color, design, and texture—than in working in a particular style. His work always has a freshness and vitality that well exemplifies Binford's own enjoyment of life and his desire to share its beauty with others.

MATILA GHYKA

A real prince joined the faculty in 1947. Matila Ghyka, K.C.V.O., M.C., was born in Romania, at Jassy, capital of Moldavia, where his family had large estates. He was graduated from the French Naval Academy and served as a midshipman in the French navy, visiting the West Indies, South Sea Islands, and the United States as a youth. Later he entered the diplomatic service of his native country, with assignments that took him to Spain and Persia, and later to Sweden and England.

When World War II changed the status of Romania, Prince Ghyka and his wife, an Englishwoman, began a series of travels to London and many other parts of the world. His writings in

---

[7] See especially, Helaine Patterson, "Art as a Life Style," with photographs by Barry Fitzgerald, *Free Lance-Star,* April 3, 1971, and a review of the exhibition by Levin Houston, *ibid.,* April 8, 1971.

aesthetics led to the awarding of an LL.D. degree by the University of Brussels. He moved to California and became a visiting professor of aesthetics at the University of Southern California in Los Angeles. It was from there that he came to Mary Washington.

In the library at Mary Washington are copies of several of Dr. Ghyka's books, in both French and English. Among them is an English translation of his *Couleur du Monde,* published by William Heineman in London in 1961 as *The World Mine Oyster.* One chapter of this autobiographical work deals with his experiences during the three years (1947–50) he spent as a member of the faculty and a resident of Fredericksburg.

In an amusing way Prince Ghyka recounted his first impressions of the college and its students (p. 313):

Next day brought the ceremony which was my first contact with the *Jeunes Filles en Fleur* of the place, some of whom were going to be my pupils. The Campus, that is, the whole of the domain, park and lawns included, surrounded the pretty Palladian buildings of the College. On a smaller scale, it resembled that of other American Universities I already knew. There were only fifteen hundred students instead of the twelve thousand in my Californian University. My first contact with this virtual gynaeceum of virgins, made me feel rather like a eunuch in a harem—with, of course, an essential difference—but this feeling soon disappeared. Most of the girls were charming and delightfully natural, with all the distinction and manners of Southern young ladies in life as well as in magazine stories. Some were very pretty, often with the dreamy expression and the slim ankles one would attribute to the heroines of Edgar Allan Poe, and the pre-Raphaelite charm of the Ophelias and *Dames sans Merci* of Burne-Jones and Rossetti. Here were not the vitamin-loaded bodies and the concentrated sex appeal of the Californian girls, reminding one of ripening pomegranates or peaches.

The eighteenth-century atmosphere peculiar to Virginia spun a web of elegant courteousness round teachers and students: a chaste, avuncular gallantry on the one side; a trusting coquetry on the other.

Prince Ghyka taught three courses: aesthetics, history of art, and Far Eastern art. In the last-named course he shared with the class the enjoyment of his magnificent collection of jade, which he had brought with him from Europe.

Ghyka found his new students enthusiastic over his theories of art and aesthetics. As he put it in his autobiography (p. 314), "Then I boldly embarked on my own theory of the role of Proportion in Life and Art, its mathematical foundations, including the establishment of the Golden Section and its affinities with the pentagon and the dodecahedron and so on. To my great surprise, the girls in my class, a dozen or so of the most intelligent and most ambitious from the faculty of Philosophy [majors in philosophy] took to my rather abstruse discourses with unexpected gusto and competence." He continued, "It must have been very different from anything they had ever heard before."

PHILIP J. ALLEN

In 1947 Philip J. Allen was appointed professor of sociology. At the time he held an A.B. from Ohio Northern University, an M.A. from Northwestern University, and a B.D. from Garrett Theological Seminary. Later he received the Ph.D. degree from American University.

Dr. Allen's appointment marked the removal of the courses in sociology from the social science department to a new department of sociology that offered a major program. This soon became one of the most popular major fields in the college. The teaching staff was enlarged with the appointment of L. Clyde Carter (Ph.D., Yale) in 1948 and Charles A. Sletten (Ph.D., Harvard) in 1958. Both Dr. Carter and Dr. Sletten, now full professors, have worked with Dr. Allen in building a strong major in sociology. Dr. Carter was made chairman of the department in 1971. The teaching staff now numbers seven and offers twenty-seven courses in sociology. A concentration in social welfare is also available.

In 1963 Dr. Allen edited *Pitirim A. Sorokin in Review*, a five-hundred-page study of the famous sociologist published under the sponsorship of the American Sociological Forum. In 1971 Dr. Allen was appointed to the State Board of Welfare and Institutions. He is also a member of the Advisory Committee on Statistics, United States Bureau of the Census.

PRESIDENT DARDEN INAUGURATED

Upon the retirement of Dr. John Lloyd Newcomb, the second president of the University of Virginia, Colgate W. Darden, Jr., was elected to the presidency. In a formal resolution the faculty of Mary Washington College wrote Mr. Darden on April 15,

1947, expressing their gratification at his acceptance of the position and pledging their "unqualified cooperation."

The new president was inaugurated on October 1, 1947, in the presence of a large audience of distinguished educators and political leaders. The principal address was delivered by Sir Alfred Zimmern, emeritus professor of international relations, University of Oxford. Governor William M. Tuck brought greetings from the Commonwealth of Virginia. A holiday was declared for students and faculty of Mary Washington that they might attend the exercises. The Student Government Association chartered buses for the occasion. A large number of faculty members attended the inauguration. Dr. Combs marched in the academic procession as the official delegate of Mary Washington College.

COLGATE W. DARDEN, JR.

Congressman, governor, United Nations delegate—these were major civic roles of Colgate Darden, the third president of the University of Virginia and also chancellor of Mary Washington College. Mr. Darden, as he preferred to be called, was born in 1897 in Southampton County where he attended secondary schools. His higher education was interrupted by World War I. He entered the French army in 1916 as an American volunteer. When the United States declared war in 1917, he became an officer in the air corps branch of the United States Marines, serving on the western front.

Upon his return to America, Mr. Darden completed his B.A. degree at the University of Virginia and went on to Columbia University where he received both the M.A. and LL.B. degrees. He was awarded a Carnegie Fellowship to Oxford University, where he studied international law during 1923–24. He returned to begin the practice of law in Norfolk. In 1929 he was elected to the General Assembly, where he served two terms. Election to Congress followed, and he was a member of the seventy-third, seventy-fourth, seventy-sixth and seventy-seventh congresses. He resigned to run for governor of Virginia, to which office he was elected in the fall of 1941.

As governor of Virginia during World War II, Darden was active in mobilizing the entire resources of the Commonwealth of Virginia in the struggle against the dictatorships. He personally devoted his time, energies, and talents to projects designed to aid the armed services throughout the struggle. When his term as governor ended in 1946, Darden was elected chancellor of the College of William and Mary. A year later, he was chosen by the board of visitors in April 1947 to head the University of Virginia and also to be chancellor of Mary Washington.

Darden served as president of the university from 1947 to 1959. Upon his retirement, he continued to be active in state and national affairs. His service on the State Board of Education was evidence of his continuing interest in education. He has received a number of honorary degrees.

KURT F. LEIDECKER

In September 1948 Kurt F. Leidecker was appointed to the faculty. He held the B.A. and A.M. degrees from Oberlin College and the Ph.D. from the University of Chicago, where he had specialized in Indian philosophy. Before coming to Mary Washington, Dr. Leidecker had taught at Rensselaer Polytechnic Institute, the Air Forces Academy at Dayton, Ohio, and Lehigh University. His teaching was interrupted by World War II, during which he served in the United States Air Force and Air Technical Intelligence.

From 1948 to 1973 Dr. Leidecker taught philosophy at Mary Washington, sponsored the Oriental Club, and was instrumental in bringing many distinguished visitors to the college. He served as adviser for the pre–foreign service and Asian studies interdepartmental majors. In 1950–51 Dr. Leidecker was a Fulbright Research Scholar in India, and from 1955 to 1957 he was a cultural affairs consultant with the United States Embassy and Information Service in Thailand.

Dr. Leidecker is a member of several international organizations fostering understanding between the Orient and the West, through such institutions as the International School of Vedic and Allied Research, the American Oriental Society, and the Deutsche Morgenländische Gesellschaft. He is known internationally as a Vedantic and Buddhist scholar. His encyclopedic dictionary of Buddhism, now in preparation, represents some fifteen years of research.

COLLEGE BUS

In October 1948, the new luxurious air-conditioned bus was finally delivered. The order had been placed in 1940 but had been canceled because of the outbreak of World War II. Providing accommodations for thirty-seven students, this bus was equipped with reclining seats, wide-view windows, and air-foam upholstery. It was painted in the college colors, blue and white, with the name and seal of the college just below the windows on each side. A committee headed by Margaret Swander was in charge of reservations for the use of the bus and also of a college-sponsored series of trips to historic places.

In the following years the blue and white bus made hundreds of trips to concerts, museums, plays, art galleries, dances at other colleges, athletic events, and a host of other destinations. It transported the college band on scores of its appearances at football games, in parades, and for concerts.

The bus was used regularly for field trips by practically every department, ranging from art to zoology. It made possible a maximum utilization of the rich cultural resources of the nation's capital. There were college-sponsored trips to New York between semesters for many years. Still stalwart and sturdy after hundreds of thousands of miles, it stands parked behind Randolph Hall ready to take students on "officially approved" trips.

COOPERATIVE PROGRAM IN NURSING

The earliest and certainly the most popular cooperative program was the one in nursing, started in September 1949. An intensive curriculum, it required four academic years of work as well as the intervening summer sessions. The first two years were offered at Mary Washington, with six-week summer sessions at the University of Virginia School of Nursing. There followed third and fourth years of work at the university. At the conclusion of the program the student was awarded a degree of bachelor of science in nursing by the University of Virginia.

When the program began in 1952, Helen H. Schultz (later Mrs. Edgar L. Cotting) was the Mary Washington adviser. She was succeeded by Dr. Winifred T. Updike, professor of chemistry, who continued to serve in this capacity until her retirement in 1968. Rebecca T. Woosley, associate professor of health and physical education, then became the adviser.

INTERDEPARTMENTAL MAJORS

During the 1949–50 session the faculty discussed and authorized three interdepartmental majors, the first to be offered at the college. Suggested originally by the dean of the college, the new programs had been considered and recommended by the committee on academic standards. They were officially adopted by the faculty at its meetings on March 30 and May 1, 1949, and put into effect with the opening of the 1949–50 session. They are outlined in detail in the catalogue for 1950–51 (pp. 69–72).

First to be adopted was an interdepartmental major in premedical sciences, designed as an undergraduate program for students planning to enter schools of medicine, dentistry, and medical technology. Leading to the B.A. or B.S. degree, it met the course requirements for admission to practically all medical schools. Dr. William A. Castle was the adviser for the major.

The second interdepartmental major was entitled American Ideals and Institutions. Later, it became known as the American studies major. It emphasized courses in American art, literature, history, government, economics, and sociology. Dr. R. L. Hilldrup was the first adviser for the program.

The third major, entitled Early Humanities, centered about classical civilization and culture. Courses in the art, philosophy, history, and literature of ancient Greece and Rome constituted the basic requirements. Either Latin or Greek was required, and both were recommended. Dr. Laura B. Voelkel (later Mrs. Raiford E. Sumner) was the first adviser, and she has continued to serve in this capacity. The major is now entitled Classical Civilization.

EUGENE C. CURTIS

The entire college community was saddened by the unexpected death on January 13, 1949, of Eugene C. Curtis, superintendent of buildings and grounds. Mr. Curtis, as everyone called him, had joined the college staff in 1915 when he was only twenty-two years old. He spent the rest of his life as an employee of the college. As a youth he had worked for the contractor who erected the first two buildings on the campus.

In Curtis's early years with the institution, he worked under the direction of W. N. Hamlet, then in charge of buildings and grounds in addition to his other duties. As the college grew larger and Hamlet grew older, the major responsibility for the maintenance and operation of the plant fell to Curtis. When Dr. Combs became president he relied heavily upon Curtis. In 1934 he was officially designated superintendent of buildings and grounds, a title he held until his death in 1949.

Eugene Curtis was responsible directly only to Dr. Combs and Edgar Woodward. It was his duty to oversee the maintenance of the entire campus and all of its buildings. He knew the location of every steam line, electric conduit, and water main beneath the grassy surface of the campus. His duties included responsibility for painting, plumbing, carpentry, steam lines, stokers, electrical work, landscaping, masonry, and construction projects.

Woodward once described Curtis as "one of the most versatile and capable men I have ever known." In the early years Curtis did much of the actual work himself. Later, he recruited and supervised mechanics, firemen, truck drivers, and laborers. He worked closely with President Combs in carrying out his plans for landscaping and beautifying the campus.

Curtis was fifty-five when he died. The entire administrative staff and many of the faculty attended his funeral. College officials were honorary pallbearers. Curtis was succeeded by Vincent H. Willetts, who, as superintendent of buildings and grounds, became head of a large staff of carpenters, plumbers, electricians, groundskeepers, and other maintenance personnel employed to provide for the comfort, safety, and well-being of the student body.

MADAME PANDIT SPEAKS

One of the high points of the 1949–50 session was a convocation sponsored by the Philosophy Club on April 26, 1950, at which Her Excellency Madame Vijayalakshmi Pandit addressed a gathering of the entire college. Madame Pandit was introduced by Dr. Leidecker, club sponsor, who spoke to her in Sanskrit before turning to the audience for the formal presentation.

The subject of Madame Pandit's address was "The Place of Women in the Life and Thought of India." She stated her belief in "equality of opportunity for everyone, regardless of race, creed, sex, or religion."[8] She urged the women of the world to point the way to peace. She cited in some detail the progress made by the women of India since, in 1931, the Indian National Congress framed a bill of rights for women guaranteeing complete equality with men. The address was broadcast by Station WRNL, Richmond, and, internationally, by the Voice of America.

[8] *Richmond News-Leader,* April 27, 1950.

At the conclusion of Madame Pandit's address, a group of students placed a garland of flowers on her shoulders. The program concluded with the *Star-Spangled Banner* and the Indian national anthem.

During the ambassador's visit the flag of India flew over the city hall in Fredericksburg. Dr. and Mrs. Leidecker gave receptions for the distinguished visitor at their home and at the Mary Washington House where townspeople were given an opportunity to meet the ambassador.

TWENTIETH ANNIVERSARY CELEBRATION

On January 15, 1949, the twentieth anniversary of the presidency of Dr. Combs was celebrated with a dinner tendered him by the faculty and staff of the college. Greetings to President Combs from the chancellor were brought by the president of the University of Virginia, Colgate W. Darden, Jr., who also served as chancellor of Mary Washington College; from the board of visitors by Mrs. Jere M. H. Willis; from the alumnae by Mrs. Edward A. Parrish, '29; from the students by Barbara Haislip, '49; and from the faculty and staff by Dr. Roy S. Cook. Dean Edward Alvey, Jr., presided.

On behalf of the faculty and staff, Dr. Cook presented Dr. Combs with a silver punch bowl inscribed in appreciation of his outstanding service to the college and his loyalty and devotion to it. Dr. Combs was deeply moved and said the tribute was a full reward for his twenty years of service.

A souvenir program with pictures of Dr. Combs and of Brompton was printed for the occasion. It contained a full-page salute to Dr. Combs as an able administrator, a tireless planner and worker, and as a man of vision who had built up a great institution. Of interest in the souvenir program is a summary, in acrostic form, of the achievements of Dr. Combs. Entitled "Twenty Years of Progress," it listed in compact form the progress made between 1929 and 1949.

Merger with the University of Virginia as liberal arts college for women.
Opportunities for full academic training in a state university system made available to Virginia women.
Residence halls increased from three to fourteen.
Geographical origin of student body expanded beyond Virginia to include thirty-seven states and eight foreign countries.

Academic standards raised in all departments.
Number in graduating class increased from 46 to 240.

Library staff enlarged from one to nine full-time members.
Accessions to library increase size of book collection from 9,900 to 68,000.
Fields or departments of study expanded from ten to thirty.
Admission requirements raised to upper half of high school graduating class.
Yearly expenditures increased from $196,503 to $1,308,892.
Enrollment in regular session increased from 460 to 1,744.
Trinkle Library built to accommodate 150,000 books.
Teaching staff enlarged from 27 to 92.
Earned degrees of faculty members increased from 4 Ph.D's and 11 M.A.'s to 42 Ph.D's and 35 M.A.'s.

Campus extended from 65 to 381 acres.
Offerings in various curricula increased from 87 to 293 courses.
Membership in Association of American Colleges, Southern Association of Colleges and Secondary Schools, and Southern Association of Colleges for Women.
Brompton purchased and restored.
Staff (non-instructional) increased from nine to fifty.

CHAPTER XV

The Early 1950s

NEW RULES IN EFFECT

WHEN the college opened in September 1950, a new dean of students had taken office following the retirement of Mrs. Bushnell. She was Mary Ellen Stephenson, assistant professor of Spanish, who had previously been in charge of the Spanish house. Ruth Seawright Wade moved from her position as reference librarian in E. Lee Trinkle Library to become dean of freshmen. She had also been a hostess in Trench Hill. As the session opened, the two young women announced plans to mingle more closely with students, visiting them in the dormitories and sitting at various tables in the dining hall at meal times. They also announced relaxation of certain college social rules to give more freedom to students.

Beginning with the 1950–51 session, students were permitted to remain on dates until eleven o'clock Saturday night instead of ten-thirty as had been customary. On payment of certain fees, dates were permitted to use tennis, golf, and riding facilities.

Seniors and their dates were permitted to go to the movies together any afternoon and also one evening a week on specified days "in either a public conveyance or by walking." They were required to be back on campus by 10:30 P.M. Students other than seniors could go to the movies on Saturday afternoons with dates provided that two couples went together and they were back on campus by 6:00 P.M. Under certain conditions, two or more upperclassmen and their dates could ride to the movies on Saturday afternoon or go out together for Sunday midday dinner in town. This liberalization of the rules was hailed with great enthusiasm by the student body. It indicates clearly how strictly student conduct was regulated in every detail in the days before "freedom with responsibility" became a slogan.

MORE NEW BUILDINGS

In the early 1950s enrollment continued to increase, the faculty and staff were enlarged, and many new courses and programs were introduced. Most impressive, certainly to outside observers, was the growth in the physical plant of the college. Within the next three years, over $3 million in new construction was completed.

HUGH MERCER INFIRMARY

A new infirmary building had been a goal of the college for some time. When funds for the project became available, the firm of J. Binford Walford and O. Pendleton Wright was engaged to draw plans. Ground was broken on February 7, 1950. After some delays in obtaining material, the new building was finally opened during the session of 1950-51.

The infirmary was named in honor of Hugh Mercer, a native of Aberdeen, Scotland, who practiced medicine in Fredericksburg for some fifteen years. Mary Washington was one of his regular patients, and George Washington is reported to have kept a desk in Mercer's Apothecary Shop as his business headquarters when in Fredericksburg.

Mercer married Isabella Gordon of Fredericksburg, becoming the brother-in-law of George Weedon, proprietor of the Rising Sun Tavern and later a general in the continental army. Mercer himself closed his office and went to war, first as a colonel and later as brigadier general in command of militia from the Middle Atlantic States. He was killed in the Battle of Princeton in January 1777. A monument to General Mercer, erected in 1906, stands on Washington Avenue in Fredericksburg. The original Hugh Mercer Apothecary Shop at 1020 Caroline Street is now maintained as a pharmaceutical museum.

The Hugh Mercer Infirmary was erected immediately behind Willard Hall on a hill overlooking the tennis courts. It represented an expenditure of $250,000 for the building, plus $21,200 for equipment. Some years later (1964) an elevator was added at a cost of $29,000. The new building provided the most modern facilities. Every room was equipped with a private or connecting bath. There were isolation wards, solarium, sun deck, small dining room and kitchen, nurses' quarters, consultation offices, drug room, examining room, and related facilities. There were a nurses' station and kitchenette on every floor.

The Early 1950s

NEW WINGS TO DINING HALL

As the enrollment of the college increased, the need for additional dining facilities became urgent. By the 1949-50 session, when construction on two new units was begun, it had become necessary to serve students in two shifts at both lunch and dinner.

The new wings were completed during the early part of the 1950-51 session. Erected at a cost of $400,000, they provided space for eight hundred additional students. Walford and Wright were the architects. The four wings were named the Blue, Rose, Gold, and Silver rooms. The basement dining room became the Tapestry Room and was the scene of special parties and dinners. Below the new dining units were refrigerators and refrigerating equipment, a completely equipped bakery, and extensive storage rooms.

NEW HEATING PLANT

In 1951 a new heating plant was built on College Avenue just across from the campus proper at Powhatan Street. Designed by Walford and Wright, it was erected at a cost of $220,000. The most conspicuous part of the new plant was an extremely tall brick chimney, visible from miles away, with the letters MWC outlined in white brick near the top.

Unfortunately, even with this high chimney, the coal-burning boilers did not seem to draw well. Neighbors complained about the soot and fly ash that descended upon their homes. Ash-handling equipment and an additional tank were installed later at a total cost of $67,400. In 1969 the entire operation was converted to natural gas, and new boilers were installed at a cost of $242,000. By that time, the central heating plant represented an investment of $649,106. The old heating plant was remodeled to house a central storeroom and shops for the maintenance staff.

ANN CARTER LEE HALL

The student activities building started first with a swimming pool unit, constructed in 1928 with a temporary roof and the expectation that the rest of it would soon be completed. Funds for this purpose were not forthcoming. A more permanent roof was constructed, and in 1946 the structure was completely remodeled at a cost of $47,700. A tiled roof garden, surrounded by a brick and stone parapet wall, was built at this time.

The need for additional physical education and recreational facilities for students led to the construction of a five-story addition behind the swimming pool unit. Bids were let for the new structure on July 11, 1951. Again, Walford and Wright were the architects. The next part of the building represented an expenditure of $700,000, plus $47,482 for equipment. It was completed during the 1952–53 session and occupied that spring.

The new building was a beautiful and impressive structure, especially when illuminated at night. What had been the old roof garden became the outdoor terrace leading to the entrance portico, where tables with large umbrellas were placed during the warmer days of spring and fall, and students could sit out of doors.

Three doorways led into a hall running the length of the building, along which were located offices for the assistant dean of students in charge of social activities, the manager of the College Shoppe, and the Alumnae Association secretary (moved later to Spotswood). At each end of the hall, in an extension overlooking the outdoor terrace, were large lounges for students, containing television sets and magazines.

Just across the hall from the main entrance was the Terrace Room, with soda fountain, food service, and tables and booths seating ninety students or faculty members. This became a popular place for faculty members to have lunch, for a special menu was available at a nominal cost. During evenings and weekends, the Terrace Room was thronged with students and their dates. At formal dances it became the place where refreshments were served during intermission when the weather prevented setting up tables on the outdoor terrace.

At one end of the main floor was the college bookstore. Later it was expanded to include a good selection of trade books offered for sale in what had been Lounge A.

On the floor below were classrooms for physical education, dance studios, offices, and a town girls' lounge. The dressing room space for the swimming pool was also enlarged. On still another level below were bowling alleys and storage rooms. On the floor above the Terrace Room was a large two-story ballroom, which became known as the Gothic Room. It was used for formal dances, recitals, special lectures, teas and bazaars, and faculty meetings. On this floor and the one above were also offices for the Student Government Association, the YWCA, and other college organizations. There was also a faculty lounge. The placement bureau was later moved to this building.

Ann Carter Lee Hall was named in honor of the mother of Robert E. Lee. Her father was Charles Carter of Shirley, then one of the richest men in Virginia. Her great-grandfather was the famous Robert "King" Carter. Her mother was a descendant of Governor Alexander Spotswood. Ann was married in 1793 at the age of twenty to General Henry ("Light-Horse Harry") Lee, hero of the Revolutionary War, governor of Virginia (1791–94), and later a member of Congress. The family lived for eighteen years at Stratford in Westmoreland County, during which time Robert E. Lee was born. Later, the family moved to Alexandria. Mrs. Lee died in 1829 at the age of fifty-six. Her ashes rest in the Lee Chapel in Lexington.

FINE ARTS CENTER

Shortly after the opening of the fortieth session of the college, plans for the laying of the cornerstone of the new fine arts center were completed. Actually, the building had been under construction since January. The exercises were set for Saturday afternoon, September 29, 1951, and were conducted under the auspices of Fredericksburg Lodge No. 4, A.F. and A.M., known historically as George Washington's Mother Lodge.

The program opened with selections by the Mary Washington College Band, which, in full uniform, was arranged in a formation to the right of the speaker's stand. The cornerstone was laid with full Masonic honors and consecrated according to the ritual of that order. Dr. Combs, in ceremonial procedure, requested that the cornerstone be laid in accordance with Masonic rites. After it was cemented and lowered, it was measured with the appropriate tools. It was then consecrated with the corn of nourishment, the wine of refreshment, and the oil of joy and gladness. Dr. Combs then presented a silver-plated and engraved trowel, one of two used in the ceremony, to Mrs. Alfred I. duPont. It was a duplicate of the one that George Washington used to lay the cornerstone of the nation's Capitol.

An address by Colgate W. Darden, Jr., president of the University of Virginia, followed. Introduced by President Combs, the former governor took as his theme the significance of the new structure in enriching the state's facilities for the higher education for women. Citing a long history of neglect in Virginia's provisions for the education of its women, President Darden hailed the new fine arts center as a big step toward the educational equality now being provided by the university's college for women at Fredericksburg. He declared that the new building would be a further means toward producing "infinitely richer and finer women, greater citizens."

After President Darden's brief address, Dr. Combs introduced some of the notables assembled for the occasion. E. H. Russell, former president of the college, paid tribute to C. O'Conor Goolrick and Dr. J. D. Eggleston, former state superintendent of public instruction, for their role in establishing the college at Fredericksburg. "The growth of this institution is beyond any conception I ever had," declared Russell, as he praised Dr. Combs for his part in the development of the college.

Other guests introduced by Dr. Combs were state Senator Robert O. Harris; W. Tayloe Murphy, former state treasurer; State Comptroller Henry G. Gilmer; E. R. Combs, clerk of the state Senate; state Senator Benjamin T. Pitts of Fredericksburg; Francis B. Gouldman, newly elected to represent Fredericksburg and Spotsylvania County in the House of Delegates; Representative Thomas B. Stanley; and Mrs. Alfred I. duPont.

The cornerstone contained issues of the *Bullet,* the *Bayonet,* and the *Epaulet;* a copy of the college catalogue and a schedule of classes; a map of the college; a Masonic pocket piece struck in 1932; and some ten other articles.

Earlier in the afternoon there was a luncheon in the Rose Room in honor of Mrs. duPont, to which some three hundred guests were invited. She was presented with a corsage by the Student Government Association.

The new building was scheduled for completion by June of the following year. The architects were Walford and Wright of Richmond, designers of many other structures on the campus. General contractors were Irons and Reynolds of Washington. The cost of the building was $1,143,556. The new fine arts center consisted of three buildings, connected by colonnaded passageways on either side of the central unit. The middle front unit, with its impressive portico and Greek columns, was named Jessie Ball duPont Hall in honor of Mrs. Alfred I. duPont of Wilmington, Delaware, and Ditchley, Virginia.

A native of the Northern Neck of Virginia, Mrs. duPont was the closest living relative of Mary Ball Washington, mother of the first president, for whom the college was named. Through a generous gift of securities currently valued at over $200,000, Mrs. duPont had established in 1952 the Lalla Gresham Ball Scholarship Fund, in memory of her mother, to provide financial assistance to "worthy and deserving" students from King George, Westmoreland, Northumberland, Richmond, Lancaster, Essex, and King and Queen counties. Mrs. duPont was the third wife of Alfred I. duPont, organizer of E. I. duPont de Nemours and Company and one of the world's wealthiest men. He died in 1935. Her income from his estate in an eleven-year period (1951–62) alone was reported to have totaled $58,800,000.[1] In her later years, Mrs. duPont lived in seclusion at Nemours, the family estate. She died on September 26, 1970.

The new fine arts center is located on the former golf course of the college, facing College Avenue and just north of Seacobeck Hall. The central building, duPont Hall, contains classrooms, offices, four exhibition rooms, and two radio broadcasting studios with control and production rooms. Immediately behind the main building is a two-story auditorium, the Little Theatre, seating 292 persons. Flanking the stage are scenery construction studios, prop storage areas, and scenery lofts. On a lower level are dressing rooms, make-up facilities, and a large costume storage room.

Entrance to duPont Hall is through a large and attractive foyer, the scene of teas and receptions for the opening of art exhibitions, meetings of state and regional scholarly organizations, and other college functions needing a smaller auditorium than the one in George Washington Hall for their general meetings.

The north building, named in honor of the late John Garland Pollard, governor of Virginia, attorney general, college professor, and patron of the arts, is devoted exclusively to music. It contains studios for individual instruction in voice, piano, and string and instrumental music, band practice room, choral practice room, records and listening rooms, offices, and music classrooms, along with storage rooms for instruments and uniforms and other facilities.

The south unit, Gari Melchers Hall, is named in honor of the late Gari Melchers, internationally known artist, whose home, Belmont, is located just across the river from the college at Falmouth. The entire building is devoted to various phases of art,

[1] *Washington Post,* Sept. 28, 1970.

such as painting, sculpture, and ceramics, and to the study of art history. It contains studios on each of its three floors, along with lecture rooms, offices, workrooms, and kilns. It also houses the catalogue and collection of slides, currently totaling more than seven thousand items, which are used in the art history courses.

FINE ARTS FESTIVAL

Both the new fine arts center and the student activities building were dedicated on May 8 and 9, 1953, with an elaborate fine arts festival. On Friday afternoon, May 8, there was an exhibition of the performing arts in the Little Theatre of duPont Hall, consisting of the one-act play *Riders to the Sea,* directed by Albert Klein; a program by the Madrigal Singers, directed by Dr. Stanley F. Bulley; and a series of folk dances by the Concert Dance Club, directed by Mrs. Charles Read. That evening there was a concert in the auditorium of George Washington Hall by the Norfolk Symphony Orchestra, directed by Edgar Schenkman.

The formal dedication exercises took place on Saturday morning. There was an academic procession in which some 120 delegates of universities, colleges, and learned societies participated. The profession formed in the Gothic Room of Ann Carter Lee Hall and proceeded to the south colonnade of the fine arts center, where the exercises were held out of doors.

Dr. Combs presided, President Darden introduced Governor John S. Battle, who presented the new buildings on behalf of the Commonwealth of Virginia. They were accepted by Barron F. Black, rector of the University of Virginia. There were selections by the Glee Club under the direction of Marion Chauncey. Music before and after the ceremony was furnished by the Mary Washington College Band conducted by Ronald W. Faulkner. John Temple Graves II was the special speaker for the occasion.

There followed a luncheon for official delegates and special guests in Seacobeck Hall, an open house at the fine arts center, and a reception at Brompton by President and Mrs. Combs. That evening an alumnae banquet took place in Seacobeck. Then *Pygmalion* was presented in George Washington Hall by the Mary Washington Players directed by Mark Sumner.

It was an impressive dedication of two impressive additions to the college plant, a center for the fine arts and a student activities building, both of them distinguished architecturally and offering excellent facilities.

NEW COOPERATIVE PROGRAMS

The success of the cooperative program in nursing led to the establishment of other similar programs that involved a basic liberal arts program at Mary Washington followed by professional courses at the cooperating institution. In the early 1950s, four additional cooperative programs were established.

Cooperative Program in Elementary Education

This program was inaugurated with the session beginning September 1950. It was designed for students who wished to prepare specifically for teaching in the elementary grades. At the time this program was established, courses in elementary education had been discontinued at Mary Washington. The cooperative program in elementary education provided that the first two years, consisting almost entirely of academic courses, be taken at Mary Washington and that the third and fourth years be taken in the department of education at the University of Virginia.[2] Students completing the program were awarded the degree of bachelor of science in education by the University of Virginia.

The program did not draw a large number of students, especially after Mary Washington reinstated courses in elementary education in 1951 and made it possible for students to qualify for certification at this level. However, the program was continued until 1970–71, with a few students participating each year. Catherine Hook, assistant professor of education at Mary Washington, was the local adviser. When the University of Virginia became coeducational in the undergraduate College of Arts and Sciences in 1971, the need for such a program ceased.

Cooperative arrangements with the University of Virginia School of Education continued, however, with the establishment of an internship program for the preparation of teachers there. Graduates of Mary Washington completed all general and professional requirements for certification except student teaching. They then took an intern year at the university where they were assigned to a cooperating school. With additional course work the requirements of the degree of master of education could be met there.

---

[2] See *Catalogue*, 1950–51, pp. 75–76.

Cooperative Program in Medical Technology

A degree program in medical technology was inaugurated in 1952 in cooperation with the University of Virginia School of Medicine. Dr. William A. Castle was, for many years, the adviser for this program. It provided for three years of study at Mary Washington, followed by a twelve-month period of specialized training in medical technology at the University of Virginia. Upon satisfactory completion of the program, the degree of bachelor of arts in medical technology was awarded by Mary Washington College.

An illustrated brochure was published outlining the program and picturing the facilities at the University of Virginia. The program was quite popular, and it became necessary to limit the number of participants. Later, it was expanded to include training in the Norfolk General Hospital School of Medical Technology.

Degree in Physical Therapy

In 1952 the college inaugurated a program for the preparation of physical therapists in cooperation with the Medical College of Virginia. It provided for three years of liberal arts work at Mary Washington and a fourth year of specialized training at the Baruch Center of Physical Medicine at the Medical College of Virginia. Upon completing the program, the student was awarded the degree of bachelor of science in physical therapy by Mary Washington College.

Dr. Anna Scott Hoye was the first adviser for the program and has continued to serve, but there have been, of course, several changes. The most recent provided for two or three years of liberal arts work at Mary Washington, followed by two years of specialized training in an approved school of physical therapy, at the end of which the degree of bachelor of science in physical therapy was to be awarded by the medical school attended. The other program provided for graduation from Mary Washington with a major in an appropriate field, followed by postgraduate work at an approved school of physical therapy.

Cooperative Program in Speech Correction and Audiology

The demand for teachers and clinical workers with special training in speech correction and audiology led in 1954 to the establishment of the cooperative program in speech and audiology. The program provided that the first three years of work be taken at Mary Washington and the fourth year in residence at the University of Virginia, where the course work consisted mainly in special courses in speech pathology and audiometry, along with clinical methods and practice. Upon completion of the program the student received the bachelor of arts degree from Mary Washington, with a major in speech correction and audiology. An illustrated booklet describing the cooperative program was published by Mary Washington in April 1954.

Albert G. Duke, associate professor of dramatic arts and speech at Mary Washington, has been the adviser of this program since its inception. The title has been changed to cooperative program in speech pathology and audiology.

GRADUATE WORK IN EDUCATION

Beginning with the 1952 summer session, the college offered a few graduate courses that could be applied to the master of education degree offered by the department of education at the University of Virginia. Dual application both to the department of education at the university and to Mary Washington College were required. The student had to be approved for graduate study by the university and also have permission to take the specific courses at Mary Washington. A maximum of two courses (six semester hours) could be taken in any one summer. Not more than twelve credits at Mary Washington could be transferred to the university. The remainder had to be taken in residence there.

During the 1952 summer session two graduate courses in education were offered: Education 114, Mental Hygiene, three semester hours, taught by Mary A. K. Kelly, and Education 116, Theory and Practice of Guidance, three semester hours, taught by Dean Alvey. These courses were also offered in the regular graduate program at the university.

The following summer, two more courses were offered: advanced educational psychology and theory and practice of guidance. In 1954 mental hygiene and school and public relations were offered, again taught by Mrs. Kelly and Dr. Alvey. Two of these courses were again offered in the 1955 summer session. After that year the program was discontinued. Credits earned were recorded both at Mary Washington College and the University of Virginia.

RADHAKRISHNAN SPEAKS

Dr. Sarvepalli Radhakrishnan, then vice-president of the Republic of India (later president), a long-time acquaintance and friend of Dr. Kurt F. Leidecker, was invited by President Morgan L. Combs, at Dr. Leidecker's suggestion, to give the address at the graduation exercises of Mary Washington College on June 1, 1953.

The vice-president came in the company of Bahadur Singh, counselor of the Indian embassy, and Mrs. Singh; Professor M. S. Sundaram, cultural attaché; and others. Brigadier General Bare, USMC, and Mrs. Bare were also present. A luncheon was given in honor of the vice-president in the Dome Room of Seacobeck Hall, and a reception at the Leidecker residence followed later.

The Quantico Marine Band provided music for the academic procession headed by President Combs and Dr. Radhakrishnan, the latter wearing a colorful green and orange academic gown. Members of the vice-president's staff also marched in the procession.

An internationally famous philosopher and scholar, Dr. Radhakrishnan urged the graduates to follow the ideals of Thomas Jefferson—"freedom of politics, freedom of religion, and freedom of thought." Accounts and pictures of the visit appeared in several issues of the *Free Lance-Star*[3] and in metropolitan newspapers. Notices with pictures of the exercises appeared in a number of papers and magazines published in India.

NEW ALMA MATER

Students during the 1930s and 1940s will recall vividly the alma mater with which each weekly convocation closed. The song, beginning "Eager voices singing," was the work of two graduates

---
[3] May 12, 29, and June 1, 1953.

of the class of 1928. Sally B. Walker wrote the words and Mildred P. Stewart, later head of the physical education department at Mary Washington, the music. This alma mater was sung on both formal and informal occasions. Its words were familiar to students and faculty.

A feature of the annual song contest held among the dormitories was the composition of an alma mater, often in the nature of words written to a familiar tune but occasionally with original music as well. Such a song written by two students in the annual song contest became increasingly popular during the latter 1940s. This was "High on Marye's Hilltop," for which Jeanne Crotty and Irene Taylor, both of the class of 1947, wrote the lyrics and composed the music, respectively. Students liked the song and began to sing it on many occasions. Soon there was a movement afoot to make it the official alma mater of the college.

A sheet music copy of the song was drafted by Ronald Faulkner and sent to all of the alumnae chapters for their consideration. The replies indicated a strong sentiment for approving the new song.

The Student Government Association recommended to the Alumnae Association that the new alma mater be made official. When the association held its spring meeting in 1952 at Mary Washington, it adopted "High on Marye's Hilltop" as the alma mater of the college. The song was copyrighted and used to close the commencement exercises in June 1952. "All hail, dear Alma Mater" was now for subsequent student classes the familiar beginning of a tribute in music to the college they loved.

When coeducation came to Mary Washington in 1970, the phrase in the second verse reading "we, your loyal daughters" was, with the permission of the authors and the class of 1947, changed in 1972 to read "we, your sons and daughters."[4]

SUMMER SCHOOL OF MUSIC

In 1952 Mary Washington College launched its Summer School of Music. Its purpose as set forth in the illustrated announcement gives a good idea of the ambitious nature of the project:

With the inauguration of its Summer School of Music, Mary Washington College makes available to both men and women the very finest in music instruction. Combining a distinguished artist faculty with a

[4] *MWC Today*, Aug. 1972, p. 6.

program stressing group activity as well as individual lessons, the highest standards of performance are constantly before the student as model and ultimate goal. Here the professional may receive advanced training, the amateur enhance his musical enjoyment and understanding, the teacher renew his contact with ever changing methods and materials, the high school and college student—and the music student in general—pursue his technical and musical studies on his own particular level but with the constant stimuli of encouraging assistance and inspiring example. . . .

The Summer School of Music offers eight weeks of invigorating music study, music thinking, and music participation. The results of these manifold activities will be demonstrated in a series of public concerts, in which both the students and the faculty will take part. Great music, exciting and challenging, will here set its own standard for realization in performance, and its own incentive for study and practice, through constant exposure and contact.

The college was fortunate in having the services of Edgar Schenkman as director of the music school. For the past three years he had been musical director of the Norfolk Symphony and Choral Association. Schenkman was a highly competent musician. His early training was as a violinist; he had performed extensively both as a soloist and as the leader of his own string quartet, and he was a graduate of the Juilliard School of Music where he had specialized in conducting.

Immediately after his appointment as director, Schenkman began negotiations to assemble an outstanding faculty. His own contacts in the world of music were invaluable. He would report with enthusiasm each new teacher he had "landed." The first session opened on June 16, 1952, with a distinguished faculty of musicians.

Erno Balogh, pianist, was well-known in Europe through extensive concert tours before Fritz Kreisler introduced him to America. His concerts throughout the United States and Canada had been enthusiastically received. He was at the time teaching piano at the Peabody Conservatory of Music in Baltimore.

Marcel Hubert, the cellist, was born in France where, at the age of thirteen, he won first prize at the National Conservatory of Paris. He had appeared in recital or with an orchestra in almost every state in the Union and was currently devoting his time to concert tours.

Irene Kahn, pianist, was a member of the faculty of the Hartt School of Music in Hartford, Connecticut. In addition to her teaching and concert work, she had written several textbooks on musical theory.

Jacob Krachmalnick, violinist, was born in Russia. He had performed extensively as recitalist and as soloist with such orchestras as the Cleveland and the Kansas City. At the time he came to Mary Washington College he was concertmaster of the Philadelphia Orchestra under Eugene Ormandy.

Elemer Nagy was director of the Central City Opera Festival, Colorado, and chairman of the Opera Department of the Julius Hartt Musical Foundation. In the dozen years immediately preceding his summer at Mary Washington he had directed and designed fifty-eight opera productions and served on the faculties of Smith College and Yale University.

Louise Rood, violist and musicologist, was associate professor of music at Smith College. She had given many concerts and written numerous articles on musical subjects.

Hardin Van Deursen, baritone, held degrees in music from Northwestern University and the University of Michigan. He had served as director of voice and chorus at the National Music Camp at Interlochen, Michigan. He was at the time chairman of the music department at the University of Kansas City.

Allen Warner, bassist, held degrees in music from Columbia University. He had appeared in solo recitals, taught at schools of music, and was at the time first bassist with the Norfolk Symphony. The New York Woodwind Quintet had given recitals at Cornell, Princeton, Vassar, the Library of Congress, and in New York concert halls. In the two summers immediately preceding their coming to Mary Washington they had given concerts and conducted woodwind clinics at thirty colleges and universities.

Throughout the eight weeks there was a series of Thursday evening concerts featuring the artist members of the faculty as performers. These programs covered a wide range of vocal and instrumental music, both solo and in chamber ensembles. They were designed to "set a standard of professional music making as an example and an incentive to the students in the School."

An extensive program was offered the very first summer. There were four specialized curricula: for pianists; for violinists, violists, and cellists; for singers; and for conductors who also served as apprentice assistants to the director. A two-week workshop for woodwind and brass players was offered from July 7 to July 18 and a two-week opera workshop from July 28 to August 8.

Individual instruction under such outstanding concert artists was a feature of the program. Leaders in music throughout the state were enthusiastic about the caliber of the faculty that Schenkman had brought to Virginia.

Intensive efforts were made to publicize the program. An illustrated catalogue describing the course offerings and carrying pictures and biographies of the visiting faculties was widely distributed in Virginia and the neighboring states to music clubs, supervisors of school music, and music teachers both public and private. The Music Educators National Conference cooperated in making available its membership lists in order that descriptive folders could be distributed. Although fees were extremely reasonable, funds for scholarships were obtained from interested benefactors. Auditions for these awards were held by Schenkman in Norfolk, Richmond, Lynchburg, Roanoke, and Northern Virginia.

In spite of these efforts, enrollment the first summer was disappointingly small. Perhaps the novelty of the venture was itself an obstacle. Some persons even expressed doubt that artists of this caliber would actually be in Fredericksburg for eight weeks to offer individual instruction in their specialties. A total of fifty-eight persons enrolled for the summer session and the short-term workshops. They ranged in age from junior high school to advanced graduate students. Some were strictly amateur musicians; others were professionals who had come to Fredericksburg for a chance to continue their study for the summer under their regular teachers. The range of ability was great, but practically all enrollees possessed some talent in music, as the public concerts and recitals demonstrated.

There were some problems, as might be expected. The lack of air conditioning during an unusually hot summer made long hours of practice and rehearsal an ordeal at times. Undoubtedly, the public concerts, which were highly praised by musical critics, would have been better attended if the auditorium had been cooler. The project ended its summer with a sizable deficit. However, students were enthusiastic about the opportunities and the instruction they had received, and it was hoped that the following summer would be more successful financially.

In 1953 Schenkman again assembled an outstanding faculty for the Summer School of Music. Josef Gingold, the concertmaster of the Cleveland Symphony who was said to be one of the finest artists performing and teaching in America, taught violin. Joseph Goodman, composer and pianist, had been a graduate student at Harvard and at Yale. He had published numerous works and had appeared as a concert pianist here and abroad.

Norman Lamb, guest instructor of viola, was the principal violist of the National Symphony Orchestra; Hans Neumann, pianist, was on the faculty of the Mannes School of Music in New York; Edith Piper, voice, a former opera singer, was on the faculty of the Juilliard School of Music; the New Art Wind Quintet, which had concertized extensively at institutions such as Princeton, Harvard, Minnesota, the University of Virginia, William and Mary, and the Library of Congress, conducted the workshop for wind players.

The 1953 catalogue for the Summer School of Music carried many pictures of the activities of the previous summer, as well as photographs and biographies of visiting faculty members and course descriptions. In addition, it listed numbers to be performed at each of the Thursday evening public concerts. There was also a two-day festival of music set for August 6 and 7, with both afternoon and evening performances. A season ticket for the Thursday concerts was only five dollars; the entire festival could be heard for only three dollars.

Once again enrollment figures were disappointing. Enthusiasm and morale would have been higher if there had been more students to share experiences, work and play together, and develop an esprit de corps. However, Schenkman's dedication and devotion to the project made a tremendous difference. He was tireless in his expenditure of energy and in the sharing of his talents. From early morning until ten o'clock at night he was busy with individual lessons, class lessons, ensemble and orchestra rehearsals, and the general direction of the school itself.

The Thursday evening concerts, praised highly by music critics, were performed to perfection, thanks to Schenkman's thorough rehearsals, his attention to detail, and his insistence that both technique and interpretation be correct. Mrs. Schenkman, an accomplished violinist, was there to support the ensemble and orchestral programs. The Schenkmans' two children also participated.

Most of the same faculty were back for the 1954 and final session of the Summer School of Music. Charges were still minimal: $107.75 for general instructional fees for the eight weeks, including eight one-hour and sixteen half-hour private lessons plus practice facilities; and $119.25 for room, board, laundry, library, infirmary, and student activity fee for the eight weeks. Nonresidents of Virginia were charged an extra $50.00 tuition. The total charge for the two-week workshop for wind players was only $85.00, which included tuition, room, and board. The charge for the two-week workshop in opera was the same.

Charges were kept as low as possible in order to attract students and to build up a patronage for the school. When the third session showed no appreciable increase in enrollment and produced a substantial operating loss, the project was discontinued. Shortly thereafter Schenkman left Norfolk to become director of the Richmond Symphony Orchestra. He still recalls fondly his three summers of intensive and enthusiastic work at Mary Washington College.

CHAPTER XVI

An Eventful Session, 1953–1954

OPENING ACTIVITIES

The 1953–54 session got under way with the usual orientation activities, opening convocation, and YWCA-sponsored Kid Party. An opening mixer brought students from eight or ten men's colleges, who danced the jitterbug and the bunnyhop to the music of the Southern Collegians from Washington and Lee.

Student leaders were Ann Lewis Payne, SGA president; Betty Baylor, YWCA; and Meechi Yokogawa, Recreation Association. These three organizations played a leading role in acquainting new students with the customs and traditions of the college and helping them become adjusted to a new environment.

ADMINISTRATIVE CHANGES

Several important changes were made in the administrative staff for the dean of women's office. Dr. Mary Ellen Stephenson, who had been serving previously as dean of women, relinquished her administrative duties to become associate professor of Spanish. In her place was appointed Isabelle Lawrence Gonon, who had been counselor of women students at Michigan State University. Mrs. Gonon received her A.B. in languages from Mount Holyoke, and her M.A. in French from Smith College. She had also done graduate work at the Sorbonne in Paris and at Bryn Mawr and Middlebury colleges. She had the academic rank of professor of French at Mary Washington.

Ruth S. Wade, formerly of the library staff, who had served as dean of freshmen since the fall of 1950, was appointed assistant dean of women and her office moved to George Washington Hall.

A newcomer to the college in a newly created position was Virginia Lawrence Payne, with the title of social director. A native of Massachusetts, she had completed the two-year associate in arts degree at National Park Seminary and Junior College and had taken courses in personnel management and merchandising at Columbia University. For the seven years before her arrival at Mary Washington she had been employed by Garfinckel's in

Washington as a buyer and as a fashion coordinator. She began her duties at the college on October 26, 1953.

Five professors were on leaves of absence. Dr. Almont Lindsey, professor of history, was teaching in Europe in the overseas program of the University of Maryland. Dr. James H. Dodd, professor of economics, was lecturing at the University of the Philippines under a Fulbright grant, and Mrs. Dodd accompanied him. Dr. Michael Erdelyi, professor of psychology, also held a Fulbright award and was lecturing at the universities of Vienna and Graz, in Austria. Professor Clyde Carter, of the sociology department, was working on his doctorate at Yale University.

NEW REGULATIONS FOR STUDENTS

Early in the session there was evidence of a growing tension among students, especially over what were regarded as oppressive regulations regarding their dress and conduct. Both were spelled out in detail in the college handbook. For example, the *Bayonet* for 1953–54 (p. 23) stated under the head of "dress": "Jeans and other unconventional apparel are prohibited in the classrooms, studios, laboratories, in setting up scenery for plays, in the dining rooms, and on the campus; are looked upon with disfavor under any conditions; and are not in keeping with the standards and traditions of the college."

Hours for lights out, circumstances under which students might ride in cars, and many other aspects of student life were carefully spelled out in page after page of rules to be enforced by the Student Government Association and the dean of women's staff.

Under the heading, "A Statement of Policy," the first issue of the *Bullet* for 1953–54 carried as an item on the editorial page an interesting discussion of the function of the college newspaper, "drawn up and submitted by the Faculty Committee on the Student Newspaper."[1] After commenting on the importance of reporting campus news accurately, with discretion and good taste, and of maintaining the good name of the college in letters to the editor, the committee gave this advice in the concluding paragraph: "It is a doubtful practice for students to wash their soiled linen in public; to air their grievances in the columns of their college newspaper until every other means of rectifying just complaints, if there be any, have been exhausted." The personnel of the committee is not indicated.

[1] *Bullet*, Oct. 13, 1970.

An Eventful Session

There were a number of minor incidents, petty in themselves but the cumulative effect of which was to increase tension between the students of the college and the officials most directly concerned with the regulation of their life and conduct.

Early in November Mrs. Gonon was called to her home in Maine by the serious illness of her mother. Mrs. Wade, as assistant dean of women, was asked to carry on the work of that office, with the assistance of Mrs. Payne, who also continued as social director.

UNIFORMS FOR STUDENT WAITRESSES

About the middle of November, Mrs. Payne, at the president's request, "investigated the conditions and operation of the Dining Hall" and formulated a plan for improvement that involved the wearing of caps and uniforms by the student waitresses employed there. When this proposal became known, student resentment was immediate and bitter.

Like most colleges, Mary Washington provided part-time employment for a substantial number of students through various services to the institution in the dining hall, library, residence halls, and certain academic departments. Some two hundred student aide positions were awarded annually on the basis of financial need and satisfactory performance. The most numerous and the most remunerative were the positions as waitresses in the dining hall and college tea room. A total of about eighty students were employed in this capacity in the fall of 1953. Hours for waitresses in the dining hall were long, and their duties were demanding. Waitresses ate before or after the rest of the student body. Heavy trays of food and dishes had to be carried for the table service, which was provided before the later change to a cafeteria form of operation. Waitresses worked seven days a week, with one weekend a month free when a substitute took over for them. They earned approximately sixty-five cents an hour.

No stigma was attached to service as a waitress. In fact, some of the most outstanding students in the college earned money for their expenses in this manner. Students did have to hurry from class for their dining hall duties. It was customary for them to don a sort of apron-smock worn over their regular dress. These aprons were kept on racks just inside the closet doors where students could slip them on as they dashed in from class.

Students who had learned of the new uniforms were openly

antagonistic. The most frequently heard complaint was that it demeaned the position of waitress to a servile role. The actual mechanics of donning the regalia three times a day for the dining hall stint was also mentioned. Underlying the whole issue was the developing hostility between students and administration, with increasing resentment at what were regarded as autocratic methods in regulating their life and conduct. The very term "directive" as used in announcing the caps and uniforms proved irritating.

MOUNTING UNREST

The new regulations regarding uniforms were presented to the hostesses at an afternoon session on November 19 by President Combs, who asked their support. Some expressed concern over the difficulty of putting the new directives into effect.

That evening a session with the student waitresses called by the dining hall director proved to be antagonistic and disorderly, especially when the social director attempted to discuss the new regulations. Several students left the meeting, explaining that they had other commitments. Others expressed their opposition to accepting the plan. As an outgrowth of this session, five of the waitresses were notified that their student aide positions had been canceled because of their lack of cooperation.

The president of student government said she had been told by the president that it was her duty to see that the desires and plans of the administration were put into effect. The SGA president disagreed with this point of view, insisting that the role of student government was more than that of an enforcing agency. Turmoil grew as rumors spread and student meetings were held. The breach between administration and student body became steadily wider.

Matters came to a head when Hester Zella Jacobus, one of the hostesses, was called into the president's office and, according to her, accused of "siding with the students." A stormy session followed. Mrs. Jacobus claimed that she was told to "pack her trunk and leave at once" since she was "fired." The president insisted that Mrs. Jacobus had resigned. However that may be, Mrs. Jacobus got in touch with a member of the board of visitors at once and gave her version of what had occurred. She was told to remain in her job until further notice and that an investigation would be made.

THE BOARD OF VISITORS ACTS

Action was begun immediately. During the next three weeks the Mary Washington committee of the board interviewed faculty and staff members and student leaders. Persons interviewed were urged to speak freely in order that causes of the current unrest might be determined. In the meantime word was received from Mrs. Gonon that she was resigning her position as dean of women at the college, and her resignation was accepted.

The situation at the college came to the attention of the general public on December 10, when the Fredericksburg *Free Lance-Star,* in a front-page story headlined "Dining Hall Uniforms, Reported Firing of Housemother Stir MWC," gave a brief account of "rumors and denials" regarding the alleged dismissal of Mrs. Jacobus. The board of visitors met in Charlottesville on December 10 and 11 to hear a report of the Mary Washington committee and to decide what further action should be taken.

A special meeting was called for December 22 to give President Combs an opportunity to be heard. At his request the meeting was transferred to the board room at Mary Washington College. At a session lasting from 10:00 A.M. to 6:00 P.M. the board interviewed various members of the faculty and staff. Dr. Combs presented a written statement to each board member and addressed the board for two hours. At the conclusion of the meeting the board decided that its investigation should be continued.

The board met again on January 8. Meanwhile the Mary Washington College committee continued its investigation, interviewing and writing to former faculty members, alumnae, and former students, as well as conferring with student leaders and staff members currently at the college.

DUTIES OF PRESIDENT REARRANGED

On February 12, 1954, the Mary Washington College committee made its report to the board of visitors at a meeting in Fredericksburg. Jere M. H. Willis and A. W. Garnett, attorneys engaged by Dr. Combs, spent most of the morning with him in his office near the board room where the meeting was being held. Barron F. Black, the rector of the board, conferred privately with Willis several times in the corridor of George Washington Hall. Later, other board members joined in the conferences. Meanwhile, a number of members of the faculty and staff and several student leaders had been asked by the board to be ready to appear.

At the end of a five-hour session, the board released a carefully worded announcement of a unanimously adopted resolution that spelled out a "rearrangement of responsibilities" for Dr. Combs. "Supreme administrative authority" for Mary Washington College was vested in the president of the University of Virginia, Colgate W. Darden, Jr. While retaining the title of president, Dr. Combs was relieved of any authority over "faculty relations, student relations, curriculum, internal budget and control." He was restricted to such duties as "construction and development, solicitation of funds and related matters." President Darden was authorized to delegate and assign other administrative duties to staff members as he saw fit.

President Combs expressed himself as being thoroughly in accord with the reassignment of responsibility made by the board. In a letter signed by him on February 12 he said, in part: "I have read the resolution today adopted by the Board. It has my full approval and the implementation of it will have my full cooperation." [2]

On February 15 President Darden announced that Dean Alvey and Edgar Woodward, the bursar, would divide administrative duties along the lines of functions they had previously handled under Dr. Combs. They were to be directly responsible to President Darden. Dean Alvey was placed in charge of student and faculty relations and curriculum, and Woodward was designated to have direct control over business affairs.

On the evening of February 15 President Darden addressed a meeting of the entire faculty and student body and, with Dr. Combs, Dean Alvey, and Woodward present on the platform, outlined and explained the new allocation of duties. He also announced that Mrs. John P. Harris, Jr., would serve as acting dean of women for the remainder of the session.

THE BOARD'S DECISION IMPLEMENTED

President Darden prepared a memorandum for Dr. Combs outlining the procedures agreed upon by them and suggesting that pertinent parts of the memorandum be sent to members of the

[2] Quoted from the board's résumé of the case, published in the *Free Lance-Star*, April 9, 1955.

C. O'Conor Goolrick, 1876–1960

Edward Hutson Russell, president, 1908–19

Tennis courts, 1912

Glee Club, 1911–12

Russell Literary Society, 1912

Library, 1912

Rifle Club, 1913

The Nightingales, 1914

Midnight Feast Club, 1914

Swimming pool, 1912

Algernon Bertrand Chandler, Jr., president, 1919–28

Mrs. Charles Lake Bushnell, dean of women, 1921–50

Morgan Lafayette Combs, president, 1928–55

The college in 1928

Daisy chain, 1929

College orchestra, 1930

Edward Alvey, Jr., dean of the college, 1934–67; professor and professor emeritus since 1967

The college in 1938

Tenth-anniversary dinner honoring President Combs, December 1, 1938. *Left to right:* Professor W. N. Hamlet, President Combs, Dean Alvey, Mrs. Combs, and Blake T. Newton, president of the State Board of Education

Cornerstone-laying, George Washington Hall, 1940. President Combs escorts Governor James H. Price

Opening convocation, September 1939. *Left to right:* Roy S. Cook, Lillias D. Francis, Eva Taylor Eppes, Walter J. Young, President Combs, Dean Alvey

A scene from *Berkeley Square*, 1940

Mary Washington College Band leading war bond parade, Richmond, 1942

Students serving at Kenmore, Garden Week, 1942

"The Sleeping Beauty," May Day, 1942

E. Lee Trinkle Library

Reference room, E. Lee Trinkle Library, 1955

Part of mural in George Washington Hall painted by Emil Schnellock, 1940

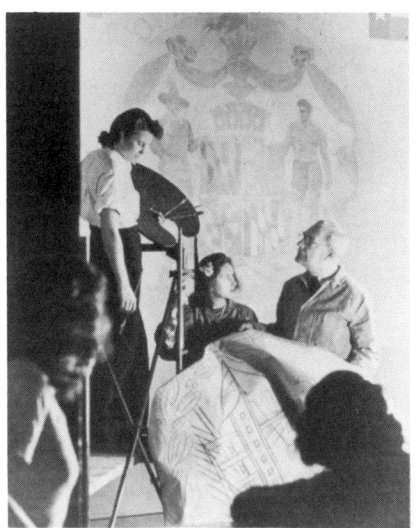

Emil Schnellock and students in mural painting class, 1941

Senior Modern Dance Club group, 1942–43. Anne Harris, Lilias Scott, and Myran Russell

Hoofprints Club, 1947

Brompton

College orchestra, 1947

Cotillion Club figure, Hall of Mirrors, 1946

Jessie Ball duPont Hall, fine arts center

Cornerstone-laying, fine arts center, September 1951. President Combs presents trowel to Jessie Ball duPont.

Dedication of fine arts center, May 1953

Twentieth-anniversary dinner honoring President Combs, January 15, 1949. *Left to right:* Mrs. Alvey, President Combs, Mrs. Combs, Chancellor Colgate W. Darden, Jr., Mrs. Darden, Mrs. Jere M. W. Willis, and Dean Alvey

Class officers, 1948. Presidents: Lois Saunier, senior class; Barbara Haislip, junior class; Carolyn Myers, sophomore class; Sara Katherine Jordan, freshman class

Student waitresses, 1952–53. Nell McCoy, president of Student Government Association, in foreground; Pal Robinson, food service director, serving

Commencement exercises, 1953. Marshals: William A. Castle and Margaret S. Russell

Reginald W. Whidden's class in Shakespeare, 1950

Summer School of Music, 1952. Edgar Schenkman, director, conducts a practice session.

Grellet Collins Simpson, president, 1955—

Belmont

Wallace Alsop retires, July 1956

The Alveys leaving for Europe, February 1957

MWC Marching Band, 1954-55

Reginald W. Whidden, appointed to faculty 1943; associate dean, 1956–67; dean, 1967–71

Margaret Hargrove, dean of students, 1956–69

Mary Ellen Stephenson, appointed to teaching staff 1948; dean of women, 1950–53

Edgar E. Woodward, comptroller, 1937–1970

Chancellor's convocation, September 1960. Dean Alvey presents Alpha Phi Sigma Award to Sandra Kay Gowl.

Sieu Cheng, May queen, 1959

Executive committee, Alumnae Association, 1962. *Front row, left to right:* Irene Lundy Brown, Kathleen Goodloe, Jane Howard Patrick, Mary Annette Klinesmith Kelly; *standing:* Marian Minor, Bettie V. Griffith, Peggy Kelley Reinburg

Liberal arts seminar, 1961–62, George M. Van Sant and Sidney H. Mitchell conducting

Carrol H. Quenzel surveying addition to library, September 1962

After-class discussion with Benjamin W. Early

Julien Binford's painting class

Mildred M. Bolling in language laboratory, 1962

Chancellor and Mrs. Simpson greeting guests at Brompton, 1963

Dr. and Mrs. J. H. Dodd at Christmas dance, 1963

Intermission, Ann Carter Lee Hall, 1964

Seniors serenading the Simpsons

Christmas decorations, December 1963

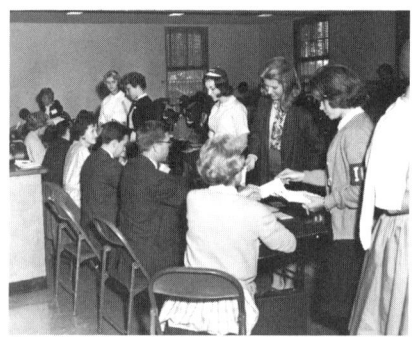
Registration in the sixties

Judicial Council, Student Government Association, 1963-64

Television viewers

Books for sale

A place to study

College life in the middle sixties

Class of 1918, golden anniversary, 1968

Albert R. Klein in Studio 13

Campus scene, 1972

Picnic for new students

Devil-goat rally

Picnic supper

Chancellor Simpson awarding degrees, June 1971

Graduation exercises, 1970

President Simpson at his desk

James H. Croushore, dean of the college

Edward V. Allison, Jr., comptroller

Michael Houston, vice-president

Mildred A. Droste, dean of students

Ruby York Weinbrecht, librarian

A. R. Merchent, director of admissions

Carol Pridgen Gill, president, Alumni Association, 1972–73

The last day

An Eventful Session 339

faculty. On February 22 Dr. Combs distributed a mimeographed statement:

February 22, 1954

TO THE MEMBERS OF THE FACULTY:

Excerpts from letter from Chancellor Darden to President Combs

Mrs. John Harris is to assume the responsibilities of the office of the Dean of Women for the remainder of this session. Mrs. Harris is to be responsible to the Dean of the College, Dr. Alvey, but she is to use as an advisory group the Committee on Student Life and Personnel recently appointed to serve until a Dean of Women can be found. The Committee is as follows: Mrs. Bolling, Chairman, Miss Leonard, Mr. Faulkner, Dr. Hilldrup, Dr. Leidecker and Dr. Parkinson. The function of the Committee is advisory. It is to be called in by Mrs. Harris for advice as to policy and for the settlement of serious student problems as to which she wishes advice.

Care is to be taken to keep and strengthen student government, and nothing contained in the foregoing paragraphs in reference to Mrs. Harris and her advisory committee is to be taken as trespassing on the functioning of this important student activity.

Dean Alvey is to be charged with the direct responsibility of managing the college. In the discharge of his duties, he is to seek the advice and help of the faculty committees now in existence. In all matters having to do with the selection of new faculty members, the promotion of present faculty members and the renewal of present contracts, he is before making a recommendation to the Chancellor for submission to the Board of Visitors, to advise with a special committee which is presently being appointed. This committee, to be known as the Dean's Advisory Council, is to be composed of Dean Alvey, Chairman, Mr. Binford, Dr. Hilldrup, Dr. George Oscar Ferguson, and Dr. Frank Geldard. Dean Alvey's recommendations, upon being sent to the Chancellor for presentation to the Board of Visitors, are to include a statement showing that the recommendations are approved or disapproved by the Committee.

Dr. Ferguson and Dr. Geldard are added to the Committee on Academic Standards. No other changes are made in the college committees.

The placement work heretofore done by the Dean is to be transferred to some person who will be associated with his office.

The Chancellor states that he finds himself in complete accord with the President's suggestion that continued efforts be directed toward lifting academic standards.

Mr. Woodward is to assume responsibility for the business operations. He is to be responsible for the appointment of those students employed in connection with the dining halls and other eating places and is to manage such labor as is required in the operation of the buildings, grounds, power plant, and other activities. In this he shall act through such agents or representatives as he shall select, having due regard for funds available for these purposes. He shall report through the Chancellor to the Board of Visitors.

Newspapers throughout the state headlined the new developments at the college. A news story on the front page of the Fredericksburg *Free Lance-Star* of February 17, 1954, was headed "Long-Time Aides Given Former Duties of Combs." In the same issue an editorial entitled "Brighter Days Ahead," said in part:

Though the final chapter may not yet have been written about the recent startling events at Mary Washington College, our hope is that we can expect a period of relative quiet which will be a welcome respite after the difficult days through which the college has just passed.

In our opinion the Board of Visitors could not have chosen better men than Edward Alvey Jr. and Edgar E. Woodward to take over the chief administrative duties of President Morgan L. Combs. Both have had many years of experience in their respective fields. Both are generally recognized throughout the state as outstanding college administrators. And working together will be nothing new to them, for this is just what they've been doing for many years under Dr. Combs' direction.

With Dean Alvey in charge of student and faculty relations and the college curriculum and Woodward, the college bursar, in control of business affairs, Mary Washington can expect capable and conscientious administration conducive to even greater progress than the school has made in recent years as a liberal arts institution. Initial reaction to Chancellor Colgate Darden's selection of Mrs. J. F. Harris as acting dean of women indicates that this, too, was a wise choice.

THE COLLEGE YEAR CONTINUES

For the remainder of the session, the college operated under the arrangement as outlined. Academic affairs were administered by the dean of the college and financial affairs by the bursar. These two officers worked closely with Chancellor Darden and reported at board meetings on operations at the college.

Recommendations for new appointments to the faculty were made after the credentials of each new appointee had been reviewed by the dean's advisory committee. Dr. Geldard and Dr. Ferguson took a keen interest in their assignment and assisted in the recruitment of well-qualified instructors.

Graduation exercises were held the weekend of May 29–June 1.

An Eventful Session

The Kiwanis Cup was awarded at Class Day exercises on May 29 to Meechi Yokogawa, a native of Tokyo and a dean's list student who had served as president of the Recreation Association.

Mary Ann Dorsey of Charlottesville, president of Alpha Phi Sigma honorary fraternity, won both the Jefferson Cup for her scholarship and service and the Alpha Phi Sigma award for having the highest scholastic average during her four years at the college.

A farewell formal dance was held on the roof garden Saturday night. On Sunday the 178 members of the graduating class heard the Right Reverend A. Hugo Blankenship, Episcopal bishop of Cuba, deliver the baccalaureate sermon at eleven o'clock services at the college. A garden party at Brompton for graduates and their parents and friends followed in the afternoon.

On Monday morning at eleven o'clock the formal graduating exercises were held in the recently redecorated open-air amphitheatre. The main address was delivered by Dr. Charles J. Smith, former president and now provost of Roanoke College. He was introduced by Dr. Combs, who presided at the exercises. Dr. Combs added his own message to the graduates, counseling them to "walk humbly" and not to become embittered. It was the twenty-fifth commencement over which he had presided.

THE SUMMER SESSION

The 1954 summer session got under way on June 14. The cooperative program for graduate study in education leading to the master of education degree at the University of Virginia was again available. The Summer School of Music opened for its second year, again conducted by Edgar Schenkman, with the assistance of a special faculty of outstanding musicians. Other features of the summer session that year included a workshop in ceramics, conducted by Elena Krupenski, and two five-week courses in elementary education designed for teachers interested in certificate renewal. The 1954 summer session showed an increase in enrollment over the previous year. It was concluded on August 6 with two days of final examinations.

CHAPTER XVII

The End of an Era, 1954–1955

OPENING DAYS

THE 1954–55 session opened with the usual orientation activities. Student leaders were Marian Thomas Minor of Richmond, president of the Student Government Association; Dorothy B. Booth of Columbus, Georgia, president of the YWCA; Eileen Marie Cella of Trenton, New Jersey, president of the Recreation Association; Martha Belle Lyle of Goshen, president of the Honor Council; and Carolyn Suzanne Bidwell of Richmond, president of Inter-Club Association.

For the first time, copies of the *Bullet* were printed in advance and sent to all of the incoming students before the opening of college. There were pictures and biographies of the student leaders named above, along with a welcome from each of them and a fairly complete description of the purposes and activities of the organizations they headed. There were messages to the freshman class from both the president and the dean of the college. The president of the freshman class of the previous year gave her advice to the newcomers. There were articles on "How to Make Your Dorm Room Cozy and Attractive," "Clothes Needed," "You May Go to Charlottesville," "MWC Weekends Are Enjoyable," and a "Recipe for MWC Success." The complete orientation program was also included.

As in past years, the orientation program included welcomes by the president and the dean on Monday morning, conferences with faculty advisers in the afternoon, and an evening program presented by the SGA, YWCA, and RA. Freshmen registered Tuesday and that evening heard an address by the dean of women and began freshman training under the Student Government Association.

While upperclassmen registered Wednesday, freshmen heard talks on "Getting Along with Your Roommate(s) and Professors" by Mrs. Dodd, and on "Trinkle Library" by Dr. Quenzel. There were tours of the library and the Mendel Museum. Talks on the honor system, MWC traditions, and a sports program occupied the afternoon. That evening there was the formal opening convocation, and classes began the next day.

RECEPTION FOR NEW STUDENTS

Thursday evening there was a party at the cabin, sponsored by RA. On Friday, the various denominational groups met with ministers at local churches where they were entertained. On Saturday evening, a formal reception for new students was given on the roof garden of George Washington Hall.

An unforgettable experience for new students—and for the faculty, too—in the 1940s and '50s was the annual reception, held on the first Saturday evening of the new session. Promptly at eight, the entire faculty and administrative staff, accompanied by wives or husbands, lined up in a vast arc on the roof garden or, if the weather was inclement, in the Hall of Mirrors. Resplendent in full dress or tuxedo, with formal evening dress for the ladies, the assembled faculty presented a formidable appearance, especially to youthful freshmen as they emerged from the stairs leading to the roof garden.

The line was headed by President and Mrs. Combs, with Dean and Mrs. Alvey next, then department heads, full professors, and so on down the line of academic hierarchy. There was no actual lining up in terms of rank or seniority; it was simply understood that the professors and their wives or husbands would be at the beginning of the line and the newly appointed instructors would stand at the far end.

The president of the student government stood next to Dr. Combs and presented each student by name to the president of the college. Names were passed along in formal introductions as the students progressed slowly down the long line. Every new student—and there were often between six and seven hundred—shook hands with every faculty member until the end of the line was reached. Introductions were usually followed by a polite, "So glad to have you" or "Where are you from?" Any further conversation usually was cut short by the piling up of students waiting to shake hands. Delays in the process were discouraged by faintly audible mutterings of faculty members further down, who were ready to greet the next student. Gaps in the line meant a prolongation of the entire procedure.

A steady flow of students was ensured by setting exact times, such as the second floor of Willard on the stairs at 8:15, the third floor at 8:40, and so forth. The dean of women, in the background, saw that the line progressed evenly and without a break until the entire group of freshmen and transfer students had passed along. Students were told in advance to have an evening dress ready for this formal occasion. For some, it was their first long dress, and their apprehension was often apparent as they faced the prospect before them.

The vista that greeted new arrivals was pleasing and picturesque. Electric lanterns around the parapet gave a mellow illumination to the entire scene. The college orchestra played soft music in the background. Candlelight and silverware gleamed on the white cloths of the buffet tables where bowls of bright red punch and plates of petits fours, ready to be served by students of the home economics department, also in evening dress, awaited the conquerors of the receiving line. Names were curiously garbled as they were passed along in the long series of introductions. Especially difficult were names with unusual pronunciations. Some faculty members simply gave up on passing along the student's name and merely said, "And this is my wife," or "And this is Mrs. Smith." Students related amusing stories of the names by which they were being introduced by the time they reached the last instructor.

Throughout the reception, the orchestra had been playing in the background. There was little dancing of students with each other until the receiving line disbanded and the male faculty members became available. Then wives surrendered their husbands to a waiting group of eager dancers. Young unmarried men of the faculty were particularly in demand as partners, and some could dance only a few steps until the next student cut in. It was a heady experience for both young and old, and their wives graciously stood in little groups on the sidelines to allow husbands to savor the rush to the fullest. Young single instructors, new to an all-girl college, found the entire procedure somewhat disturbing, but in a rather delightful way.

It was pleasant to watch as the sheen of silk evening gowns caught the flashes of reflected light from the lanterns, and white shirt fronts gleamed in sharp contrast to the rich colors of the dresses.

These dances always ended at midnight at the latest. By that time, all but the most ardent dancers had drifted away. It was customary to close with a medley of dreamy selections rather than "Home, Sweet Home," for the latter seemed a little too risky on a freshman's first Saturday night away at college. The usual sequence included "Goodnight, Sweet Heart," "I'll See You in My Dreams," and finally "Aloha-Oe" with its beautiful refrain, "Farewell to thee . . . until we meet again." The notes of the violin

The End of an Era   345

carried the melody in a way that seemed to stimulate soft humming as the dancers concluded their final turns.

Wives then reclaimed their husbands and wraps, and all filed down the flights of stairs to the ground floor of GW where Wallace stood to bid them a final goodnight. "Aloha-Oe" was a pleasant song to hum in a reminiscent way as a sort of extension of the pleasures of an evening under the stars when the trek homeward slowly began.

BIG SISTER–LITTLE SISTER PROGRAM

An important feature of freshmen orientation in those days was the Big Sister–Little Sister program sponsored by the YWCA. In the spring each year students were given an opportunity to sign up for a Little Sister. Then Y workers assigned a new or transfer student to each volunteer unless a special choice was indicated.

During the summer the Big Sister usually corresponded with the new student. Often she met her at the train or bus station upon arrival or, with the trend toward travel to college by automobile, called on her at her dormitory upon arrival.

The Big Sister helped her protégé become acquainted with the facilities and regulations of the college, to make friends among other students, and, at times, to select the courses she wished to take. Later, the assignment of freshmen advisers was taken over by the college, and their training and supervision became a part of the official orientation plan sponsored by the administration.

On the first Sunday after the beginning of classes, the new student and upper-class friend attended church together in what was called Big Sister–Little Sister Church Attendance. The churches of the city were usually jammed as large numbers of students, freshmen and upperclassmen, attended in pairs the church of the new student's choice. More than one minister has been heard to say wistfully, "I wish we could have an attendance like that every Sunday." Nevertheless, many students did go back the next Sunday, and the denominational clubs at the college encouraged their attendance through organized activities and provisions for transportation to and from the college on Sundays and for special occasions.

ADMINISTRATIVE CHANGES

A number of administrative changes were introduced with the fall semester. While Dean Alvey and Edgar Woodward continued to exercise their new responsibilities under Darden, and Dr. Combs remained in charge of development, several new positions were authorized and filled.

Dr. Reginald W. Whidden, professor of English, was appointed assistant dean of the college, to handle freshman academic problems and to run the orientation program. He was assigned an office adjoining that of Dean Alvey in George Washington Hall. Dr. Whidden continued to teach several classes in the English department.

Ruby C. Harris was designated to continue in her role as acting dean of women. Two new assistant deans of women were appointed. Dorothy M. Smith held the A.B. from the University of North Carolina and the M.A. from Syracuse University, with specialization in student personnel work. She was employed in a counseling capacity at Syracuse before coming to Mary Washington as assistant dean in charge of social activities. She was assigned an office in the dean of women's suite in George Washington Hall.

Katherine F. Moran, a native of Georgia, who had recently retired as area recreational director for the Third Army in the European theatre of operations, was appointed assistant dean of women in charge of recreational activities. She was assigned an office and a secretary in the student activities building.

Miss Moran held the bachelor's degree from the College of William and Mary, where she had majored in drama. Her master's degree, also with specialization in drama, was from the University of North Carolina. She had previously taught college courses in dramatics. In the fall of 1958 she began offering the survey of world theatre course, which she continued to teach until her retirement in June 1967.

Miss Moran had charge of recreational activities involving the use of college facilities, such as formal and informal dances, May Days, mixers and special club programs, and the like. She selected and booked the Saturday night movies shown in George Washington Hall. She also scheduled visits to art galleries, plays, music and dance performances, and other trips that involved the use of the college bus. For many years, she arranged and conducted the between-semesters college-sponsored visit to New York.

An innovation in the residence hall setup was the creation of a new position of residence counselor, an idea in which President Darden was keenly interested.

Briefly, the plan was to replace some of the housemothers with women whose academic qualifications would permit their employment on the faculty at the instructor's level and thus provide a more attractive salary. Quarters and board would be provided by the college, and the new appointees would have the responsibility for a certain building. Emphasis was placed upon their interest in and qualifications for counseling students in their residence halls. The counselors were also to teach two college classes in the field of their specialization, as evidenced by at least a master's degree in the discipline.

NEW FACULTY APPOINTMENTS

Fortunately, the college was able to obtain the services of three outstanding young women as residence hall counselors. Cornelia D. Oliver (Mrs. George Brown Oliver) was appointed instructor in art and assigned as counselor to Willard Hall, a freshman dormitory. She held degrees from Smith College and Duke University. She had formerly served as a residence counselor at Holton Arms School in Washington and as registrar at Chandler School for Women in Boston. Before assuming her duties at Mary Washington, she had taught English and Latin at the high school in Ashland, where her husband, then on leave of absence for advanced graduate study in history, was a member of the faculty at Randolph-Macon College.

Although Mrs. Oliver later relinquished her role as residence counselor, much to the regret of the entire campus community, she has continued to serve as a member of the faculty in art history except for a period in which she had a leave of absence for doctoral study. Mrs. Oliver received her Ph.D. degree from the Catholic University of America in May 1972. She is currently associate professor of art. She and her family now reside in Fredericksburg.

Geraldine Ladd, appointed instructor in French and residence counselor in Virginia Hall, had had considerable experience as a teacher of French at both high school and college levels. A native of Kentucky, she had graduated from the University of Iowa and had attended the Alliance Française in Paris, the University of Havana, and the National University of Mexico. For two summers she was in charge of the French houses at Penn State and the University of Wisconsin.

Lucy M. Timmerman, of Athens, West Virginia, was appointed instructor in psychology and residence counselor at the new sophomore dormitory, Ann Mason Hall. A member of the Women's Army Corps in World War II, she had served as residence counselor at Concord College in Athens, West Virginia, and at Winthrop College in Rock Hill, South Carolina. A graduate of Agnes Scott College, she had received her master's degree from Teachers College, Columbia University. She had also attended the New Orleans Baptist Seminary and had been director of religious education in churches in the South.

In addition to these new staff members with administrative or counseling responsibilities, there were several additions to the faculty who have continued their affiliation with Mary Washington.

Mildred Ann Droste later to become dean of students (1969) at Mary Washington, was appointed instructor in health and physical education. Holding degrees from Longwood College and the Woman's College of the University of North Carolina, Miss Droste had taught previously at Virginia Intermont and at Mary Baldwin College.

Mary Jo Parrish, currently associate professor of biology at Mary Washington, was appointed instructor in biology. She had received her B.A. and M.A. from the University of North Carolina and was in the process of completing her studies for the Ph.D. in biology at the University of Virginia.

Sidney H. Mitchell, who held the B.A. degree from Swarthmore College and the M.A. degree from the University of Virginia, joined the faculty in the fall of 1954 as instructor in English. A Phi Beta Kappa graduate, Mitchell continued his studies at the University of Virginia and was awarded the Ph.D. there in 1962. From 1967 to 1970 he served as chairman of the English department. He resigned the chairmanship when his wife, Nancy Heyroth Mitchell, who was then teaching also in the department of English, was appointed assistant dean of the college in charge of academic counseling. At the time of her appointment to this administrative office, Mrs. Mitchell was serving as associate professor of English. She held the B.A. from Swarthmore College, the M.A. from Yale University, and the Ph.D. from Catholic University of America.

On leave of absence for all or part of the 1954–55 session were Dr. Laura Voelkel Sumner, assistant professor of Greek and

Latin, who was a visiting professor at the University of Wisconsin; Dr. Almont Lindsey, professor of history, who was teaching in Germany in the overseas program of the University of Maryland; Dr. Michael Erdelyi, professor of psychology, who held a Fulbright appointment for lecturing in Austria; and Dr. Kurt F. Leidecker, assistant professor of philosophy, who was then in India.

The new plan for residence counselors continued for two or three years. It was abandoned when a new program providing on-the-job training in residence hall managing and counseling for all hostesses was inaugurated in the fall of 1957 by Margaret Hargrove, who became dean of students at that time.

Two of the early residence counselors continued to serve as members of the teaching staff while engaged periodically in further graduate study. Mrs. Oliver has already been mentioned. The other was Myra L. Irby, holder of a B.S. from Alabama State College and an M.A. from Peabody College, who was appointed instructor in history and residence counselor. Mrs. Irby continued her graduate study in history, enrolling for doctorate courses at the University of Virginia. She remained as a full-time teacher in the history department until her death in the spring of 1968. The Myra Irby Memorial Library in history was established in her memory by former students and colleagues in the department.

NEW FEES AND NEW BUILDINGS

Tuition charges were increased with the 1954–55 session for the first time in many years. General college fees for all students were raised from $170 to $270, making the total charges for Virginia students $757 for both semesters, including tuition, room and board, and miscellaneous fees. Out-of-state students now paid a total of $1,097 for the session, with an increase in tuition from $280 to $340.

Interestingly enough, the director of the budget reported that during the previous session the total cost per student at Mary Washington was $1,179, but that income from fees and charges totaled $1,131.[1] In other words, only $48.75 per student came from the state treasury. This compared with state funds of $309, $409, and $535 per student needed to operate the other three state-supported women's colleges.

---

[1] *Free Lance-Star*, Sept. 13, 1954.

For the first time in several years, no students were living off campus in private residences. Newly completed dormitories on the campus had provided space for over four hundred additional students.

Martha Randolph and Ann Mason halls were completed just in time for the opening of college. Erected at a cost of $1,356,000, they provided what the *Free Lance-Star* (September 13, 1954) described as "the newest, costliest and swankiest quarters" on the campus. There were formal lounges, recreation rooms, kitchenettes, laundry and pressing rooms, suites for hostesses, and 178 student rooms. No expense was spared in providing furniture and equipment of the highest quality. These furnishings alone represented an additional outlay of $56,000.

The two main buildings were connected by a circular stone and brick terrace, with additional rooms on the lower floors. An elaborate stone fountain occupied a place midway below the terrace on the side facing the campus. The rooms looking toward the east offered a fine view of the city lying below the College Heights. The group of buildings was christened the Golden Horseshoe.

Mason Hall was named in honor of Ann Thomson Mason, mother of George Mason, well known as the author of the Virginia Bill of Rights. She came from an able and distinguished family. Her paternal grandfather, a lawyer, held the A.B. and A.M. degrees from Cambridge University. Her uncle, a member of Parliament, was recorder of London. Her father, Stevens Thomson, was attorney general of Virginia during Queen Anne's reign and brought his five children to the colony. Ann is described as possessing beauty, intelligence, character, and an amiable disposition. Her husband, George Mason III, was a county lieutenant of Stafford County and had been one of the Knights of the Golden Horseshoe.

Mason was drowned when his sailboat capsized while crossing the Potomac. His young widow never remarried and devoted her energies to rearing her three children. She not only engaged tutors for them but taught them herself the moral precepts of the Bible. Since George Mason III died without leaving a will, the eldest son inherited the whole estate under the laws of primogeniture then in effect. However, the widow's extensive and prudent management and investment of what funds she had proved very profitable, and all the children were well provided for. When Mrs. Mason died in 1762 at the stone mansion on her Chopa-

The End of an Era

wamsic plantation, she was characterized by her rector as "a good woman, a great woman, and a lovely woman."

Randolph Hall was named in honor of Martha Jefferson Randolph, daughter of Thomas Jefferson and his hostess in the governor's mansion from 1819 to 1822. She was born at Monticello, then still under construction. Her mother died when Martha was almost ten, and she became a faithful and devoted companion to her widowed father. She accompanied Jefferson on many of his trips on government business and was with him during his five years of residence in France. When she was just slightly over seventeen, Martha married her 21-year-old third cousin, Thomas Mann Randolph of Tuckahoe, who had been educated at the College of William and Mary and at the University of Edinburgh. They had twelve children. Randolph served in the Virginia House of Delegates and Senate, the United States House of Representatives, and from 1819 to 1822 was governor of Virginia. In her later years Martha lived with her eldest son at Edgehill in Albemarle County. This former hostess at Monticello reported that they all lived comfortably and happily together. She died in 1836.

It was decided to place sophomores in the new halls because so many of them had lived off campus in private houses as freshmen the year before. The 178 rooms were actually designed for 365 students. However, extra beds were installed on a temporary basis, so that a total of 409 students were housed in the Mason-Randolph complex.

LAST OF THE VETERANS ENTER

The new class marked the last entry of veterans before the deadline closing applications from men students as of July 1, 1954. The number of World War II male veterans in attendance had been decreasing steadily, and only five enrolled in the freshman class for the 1954–55 session.

During the previous session the following veterans were attending Mary Washington: Charles Ryland Bowie and Elliott E. Brooks, Jr., of Fredericksburg; Garnet W. Galyen and John H. Prasse of Chancellor; and Thomas I. Dodson and Bernard T. Burchell of Dahlgren. Dr. George E. Shankle was sponsor of the Veterans Club.

A CANDIDATE FOR CONGRESS

As college opened in September, attention throughout the state was centered on Mary Washington with the announcement that Charmenz Lenhart, associate professor of English, would be a candidate for Congress from the Eighth District in opposition to Representative Howard W. Smith. Judge Smith, as he was familiarly called, had a long period of distinguished service in the House of Representatives and was chairman of the powerful Rules Committee.

Reporters from metropolitan newspapers converged on Fredericksburg for pictures and interviews. Since Miss Lenhart had come to Virginia only recently, the question was raised as to her eligibility to seek office as a legal resident of the state. The payment of Virginia poll taxes for the two preceding years was raised as a specific qualification that had not been met.

On September 14, 1954, the *Free Lance-Star* reported that the "blonde, attractive Mary Washington College professor" had been ruled ineligible in an opinion filed by Attorney General J. Lindsay Almond, Jr. However, the state elections board had not acted on the ruling, and the Fredericksburg electoral board sought further advice.

For the next ten days officials in Fredericksburg and at the state capital in Richmond were involved in a series of varying interpretations of Dr. Lenhart's status. There were daily front-page stories in the *Free Lance-Star,* as, in the words of the newspaper, the "hot potato" was passed back and forth. Finally, on September 24, 1954, Circuit Judge Leon M. Bazile ruled that Dr. Lenhart was a qualified voter and candidate and ordered her name printed on the Eighth District ballot for November.

The day of the election Dr. Lenhart released a telegram from President Dwight D. Eisenhower, extending "best wishes for victory" to the Republican-backed independent. However, the Eighth District voters returned Representative Smith to a thirteenth term in Congress by a two-to-one majority. The defeated candidate said she would now work toward "rebuilding the Republican organization" in the Eighth District. Dr. Lenhart continued to teach at Mary Washington until the fall of 1957 when she resigned to accept another position.

ACADEMIC DEVELOPMENTS

During the fall of 1954 the college continued to operate under the "reassignment of duties" ordered by the board of visitors. Dean Alvey handled the academic affairs of the institution, and Edgar Woodward, the financial affairs. Both worked directly under President Colgate W. Darden of the University of Virginia, who was also chancellor of Mary Washington College.

Minutes of faculty meetings during this period indicate that the academic business of the college was proceeding satisfactorily. In October there was a panel discussion on the intellectual stimulation of students. The November meeting was devoted largely to a report of the faculty general cooperative committee on hospitalization plans, given by the secretary of the committee, Fred E. Miller.

The December meeting featured a discussion by Dr. George B. Zehmer, director of the University of Virginia Extension Division, of "The Proposed Development under University Administration of One or More Two-Year Colleges in Outlying Centers," a nine-page report outlining procedures and plans for the development of two-year branches in the Clinch Valley area and in Northern Virginia. Copies of this report had been distributed in advance to department heads at Mary Washington with the request that it be studied and read before Dr. Zehmer's visit on December 1.

As an outgrowth of this discussion, the following resolution was adopted: "Resolved, the faculty of Mary Washington College would look with favor upon receiving transfer students from two-year branch colleges or centers sponsored by the University of Virginia."

At the December meeting the faculty also adopted with two minor changes a report by the committee on academic standards, entitled "Academic Probation and Scholastic Achievement Necessary to Remain in College." It was agreed that these new standards governing academic probation and suspension should be included in the next issue of the catalogue then being readied for the printer.

In February the dean's advisory council launched a study of factors to be considered in making recommendations for faculty promotion for transmission to the president of the university and the board of visitors. Faculty members were requested by questionnaire to evaluate a list of factors as of major, average, or no importance, and to add others, if any, that should be considered. The results of the questionnaire were presented at the February meeting.

When the faculty met on February 14, it heard a comprehensive report on the functions and organization of the faculty general cooperative committee, presented by the chairman, Dr. Oscar H. Darter. The faculty adopted the report after considerable discussion, with two amendments—one proposed by Dr. Whidden, reading "The Committee shall be an agency to represent the Faculty on matters that may arise between meetings of the Faculty," and one by Dr. Bulley providing for staggered terms of one, two, and three years for faculty members elected to this committee. A new faculty salary scale was presented by Dean Alvey, and the faculty formally approved a resolution expressing the "profound satisfaction with the efforts made to improve faculty salaries."

The entire March meeting was devoted to a panel discussion by four selected juniors and seniors on ways of increasing academic and intellectual interests of students at Mary Washington College. The results were summarized later and distributed in mimeographed form to members of the faculty.

At the April meeting the faculty heard reports of the committee on admissions (an increase in number of applications for the next year), the academic standards committee, and the faculty general cooperative committee. These reports, which appeared as appendices to the minutes, incorporated a number of specific suggestions for future action.

AN UNFORTUNATE DOCUMENT

Although the college had continued to function normally under the "reassignment of duties," the man who had headed the institution for twenty-five years became less and less satisfied with the arrangement. Dr. Combs had continued to occupy the president's office at the college but he now spent relatively little time there. While he still enjoyed walking about the campus and buildings, it was evident to close associates that he was not well. The action of the board in relieving the president of most of his duties was not accepted as a lightening of load but rather as a form of punishment or reprimand for what had occurred. "Vindication" was frequently mentioned as the goal to be sought. Unfortunately, this effort took the form of a lengthy mimeographed

The End of an Era 355

document charging certain members of the board, the college administrative staff, and the faculty with having plotted against him to remove him from the presidency.

At the time of the reassignment of Dr. Combs's duties, he had signed a letter to the rector and visitors, under the date of February 12, 1954, which began: "I have read the resolution today adopted by the Board. It has my full approval and the implementation of it will have my full cooperation."

Then on December 9, 1954, Dr. Combs delivered to the Mary Washington College committee at its meeting in Fredericksburg a letter charging a conspiracy against him by five members of the college faculty and staff and the encouragement of this activity by the chairman of the Mary Washington College committee. He asserted that his attorney, Jere M. H. Willis, had acted without his permission in agreeing to the compromise that resulted in the reassignment of his duties on February 12 and that he had signed "under duress" the letter agreeing to cooperate with this arrangement.

About this time there began to be circulated a nine-page mimeographed paper that the board of visitors called a "scurrilous document" entitled "The Whole Story at Mary Washington College." Copies were sent to newspapers, public officials, and influential citizens.

THE BOARD ACTS

Perhaps the effect of this document can be best understood by reference to the text of the board's statement removing Dr. Combs, published in full in the *Free Lance-Star* on April 9, 1955.

This very lengthy report by the board referred to an inquiry made by the *Free Lance-Star* regarding the signatures attached to the document. It was revealed that many of the signers had not understood the type of document they were signing. Although the authorship of the paper was not established, it was brought out that Dr. Combs was aware of its circulation. The board stated that its decision to act was made independently of Dr. Combs's part in this publication, "but it did express its resentment of the completely false charges directed therein."

The board further expressed its grave concern over the repudiation of the agreement by Dr. Combs and his "bitter attack" on members of the college faculty and staff. "It is clear to the Board that continued retention of Dr. Combs in any active capacity at

Mary Washington would be against the best interests of the College. Accordingly, the Board has today [April 9, 1955,] adopted a resolution removing him from office, effective immediately."

The board announced that provision had been made for continued payment of Dr. Combs's salary from private funds of the University until June 11, 1956, at which time he would be eligible for retirement. The board stated further that Chancellor Darden would direct the affairs of the college pending the election of a president in place of Dr. Combs. Meanwhile, Dean Alvey and Treasurer Woodward were directed to exercise the special responsibilities assigned them.

THE END OF A CAREER

Dr. Combs was not well. His condition had by now been diagnosed as leukemia. In July 1955 he entered the hospital of the Medical College of Virginia in Richmond where he died on October 25. He was sixty-four years of age.

The flag at the college was lowered to half mast. Dean Alvey announced that all classes would be suspended the day of the funeral. The body was brought to Brompton to await the funeral service on Friday, October 28. Meanwhile, messages of condolence poured in. In New York, President Darden, then serving as a member of the United States delegation to the United Nations, expressed his deep distress at the news of Dr. Combs's death, adding that he had known for some time that he was gravely ill. "The people of Virginia are in his debt for his services," Darden stated.

The funeral services at Brompton were attended by prominent educators and state government officials. Services were conducted by his longstanding friend, the Reverend Robert F. Caverlee, pastor of the Fredericksburg Baptist Church. Dr. Combs was buried in Oak Hill Cemetery in Fredericksburg.

And so came to an end a career of service to the college that spanned a period of twenty-six years. During this time the institution developed from a small teachers college to an outstanding liberal arts college for women. Its enrollment grew from 460 in 1929 to over 1,500 students, representing thirty-four states and eight foreign countries. The faculty numbered nearly a hundred men and women, 45 percent of whom held the doctorate. There had been only four Ph.D.s on the faculty when Dr. Combs became president. The college had grown from a small group of buildings with modest furnishings to a landscaped campus of 370 acres, with buildings and furnishings that were the admiration of a steady stream of visitors attracted to the college.

During his years at Mary Washington, Dr. Combs was an active participant in educational affairs. In 1933 he was a delegate to the World Federation of Education Associations in Dublin, Ireland. During the summer of 1935 he was one of five American educators appointed to study the educational systems of Germany and Austria, under the auspices of the Carl Schurz Memorial Foundation for the development of cultural relations between the United States and German-speaking countries.

For twenty years Dr. Combs served as a trustee of Bluefield College, a Baptist institution. He was a member of Phi Beta Kappa, Tau Kappa Alpha, Phi Delta Kappa, Alpha Phi Sigma, and the American Legion. In 1952 his achievements were formally recognized by the University of Richmond, which conferred upon him the honorary degree of Doctor of Laws.

As Dr. Quenzel remarked in a sketch of Dr. Combs, published in *Virginia and the Virginia County,* vol. 1, no. 10 (April 1953), Dr. Combs believed that everyone profited when people are exposed to beautiful surroundings, and he sought to implement this conviction in the creation of a college environment of natural and physical beauty. As Dr. Quenzel pointed out, "His widely acknowledged flair for landscaping and the meticulous care he lavished on the minute details of construction deserve part of the credit for the college's unusually beautiful campus."

Dr. Combs's chief interest was the college. It was for him an opportunity to make a lasting contribution to the building of a great institution at Fredericksburg, and he devoted his energies and his talents to this end. His close contacts with political leaders in Virginia and their confidence in him as an educational leader were of great value in his perennial and largely successful appeals for state and federal funds for the buildings and projects he envisioned.

Dr. Combs found his greatest satisfaction in watching things grow, whether they were trees, shrubs, or the buildings of a college campus. The list of buildings and facilities completed during the twenty-six years of his presidency is an impressive one. Equally striking and even more significant was the improvement in the number and academic standing of the faculty.

Dr. Combs's final building project was a science hall, for which he repeatedly sought legislative appropriations. When the building was completed in 1959, it was named in his honor. His portrait, by the Richmond artist David Silvette, is hung in a conspicuous place in the entrance foyer of Morgan Combs Science Hall, facing visitors as they enter. Perhaps it is appropriate here to quote from the tribute, in St. Paul's, London, to Sir Christopher Wren: *si monumentum quaeris, circumspice* (If you seek his monument, look about you).

CHAPTER XVIII

A New Era Begins, 1955–1956

COLLEGE OPENS

THE forty-fourth annual session of the college began in September 1955. The formal opening was preceded by the second annual preschool conference, held on September 16 and 17, with the theme "SGA's Responsibilities in Our College Community." Speakers at the opening session were Dean Alvey and Mrs. John P. Harris, Jr., dean of women. They were followed at later meetings by Marian Minor, the previous year's SGA president, and Dr. Burney Parkinson, chairman of Joint Council.

Panel discussions and group meetings continued the consideration of various aspects of student responsibility and the operation of the Student Government Association. Betty Davies, president of SGA, moderated the panel discussions. Other student officers that year were Elizabeth Poteet, president of the Honor Council; Mabel Virginia Fisher, YWCA president; Hermine Gross, RA president; and Michelle Foley, president of the Inter-Club Association.

The freshmen orientation program began officially with an assembly Monday morning in the auditorium of George Washington Hall, at which new and transfer students were welcomed by Dean Alvey and other members of the administrative staff. Registration followed on Tuesday and Wednesday, and classes for the forty-fourth session began on Thursday, September 22.

On Tuesday evening the Student Government Association, the YWCA, and the Recreation Association gave their annual party for new students in the Monroe Hall gymnasium. While the upper-classmen were registering Wednesday, there were tours of the college's recreational facilities and demonstrations of swimming, tennis, archery, and horsemanship by RA members. On Wednesday evening the first convocation for all students was held. Dean Alvey spoke to the student body and also introduced new members of the faculty and staff.

Friday evening was devoted to a Meet Your Minister program, sponsored by the YWCA. Ministers from the various churches in Fredericksburg met with students of their denomination and welcomed them to their services. In many cases, the entire group was transported by volunteer drivers to the recreational hall of the church where a program and refreshments awaited them.

On Saturday evening the formal reception was given for new and transfer students. It was held outdoors in the Golden Horseshoe between Randolph and Mason dormitories. An innovation that year was a short receiving line consisting of only the administrative officers and their wives or husbands, headed by the dean of the college. The faculty were grouped by departments at various spots on the lawn between Randolph and Mason. Upperclassmen acted as guides and introduced students to faculty members in the academic department in which the freshmen hoped to major. Colored lanterns, orchestra music, and tables of refreshments gave the occasion a somewhat festive air. It was to mark the end of the formal affairs for incoming students, which were discontinued thereafter.

THE ENTERING CLASS

A committee on admissions had reviewed each application carefully. A news story in the college edition of the *Free Lance-Star* (September 19, 1955) reported that the committee turned down 225 applicants for admission to the fall semester for failing to meet the required academic standards. The committee at the time consisted of Edward Alvey, Jr., dean of the college; Reginald W. Whidden, assistant dean; Warren G. Keith, director of admissions; Louis C. Guenther, registrar; Laura V. Sumner, professor of classics; and James H. Croushore, professor of English.

There were some six hundred freshmen and transfer students out of a student body of sixteen hundred. As in the case of many other women's colleges, a falling off in enrollment after the first two years of attendance was evident. Transfer to coeducational universities, enrollment in a cooperative program such as the nursing curriculum, or simply discontinuing higher education after two years were among the most frequently mentioned reasons for not returning.

It is quite possible that the more rigid enforcement of new regulations regarding academic probation and suspension had some effect upon the registration of upperclassmen. Some students withdrew at the end of the previous session when they felt that a declining quality-point average would mean academic probation or suspension in one more semester.

The committee on academic standards was active in proposing

A New Era Begins

and carrying out what the catalogue referred to as "Academic Probation and Scholastic Achievement Necessary to Remain in College."

The schedule of classes that fall discontinued the use of Doctor as a title for faculty members holding the Ph.D. degree. This was pursuant to action by the faculty, passed by a rather small margin, that only Mr., Miss, or Mrs. be used in referring to faculty members in official college publications. Although the new catalogue and subsequent class schedules reflected this decision, most students preferred to call their professors "Doctor" if they held a doctorate, and publications like the *Bullet* and the *Battlefield* continued to use the title.

FIRST ALUMNAE GRANDDAUGHTER

In September 1955 the first granddaughter of a former student enrolled. She was Henryetta DeShields of Richmond, whose grandmother, Virginia Lee Eubank, had attended in the early years of the institution. Miss DeShields graduated in 1958 with a B.A. in art.

There were fifteen daughters of alumnae in the freshman class, making a total of some forty who qualified for the Alumnae Daughters Club.

A lone veteran was in attendance. Dennis C. Moriarity, a former marine, was still continuing his studies with a major in music. Newspapers of the time described him as the "Last of the GI's."

ELECTION OF DR. SIMPSON

In May 1955 the board of visitors appointed a special committee headed by Henry E. McWane of Lynchburg to recommend a new president. Other members were C. O'Conor Goolrick of Fredericksburg; George O. Ferguson, Jr., dean of the College of Arts and Sciences at the university; Benjamin Mears, a Heathsville lawyer; and Dr. John M. Emmett of Clifton Forge, a surgeon.

The committee proceeded to solicit nominations from other members of the board, from the faculty and alumnae of Mary Washington College, and from the faculty of the University of Virginia. Letters requesting nominations were sent to all college presidents in the South and to the heads of outstanding institutions in the nation.

As a result of these efforts, extending over a period of several months, a list of 137 names was compiled for consideration. Further screening resulted in reducing the number of prospects to six, all of whom were interviewed at Charlottesville on September 9 and 10. The committee was unanimous in the choice of its recommendation. It reported to the board at a special session in Charlottesville on September 24. The board of visitors, through its rector, Barron F. Black, announced the election of Dr. Grellet C. Simpson, dean of Randolph-Macon College at Ashland, to be the fourth president of Mary Washington College.

There was no advance hint of whom the committee's choice might be. The *Free Lance-Star* on September 24 cited a "committee source" in reporting that "among the persons nominated for the presidency was the MWC dean, Dr. Edward Alvey, Jr. The source said, however, that Dr. Alvey had written the committee in July, asking that his name be withdrawn from consideration."

In announcing the selection of Dr. Simpson, the committee concluded its report with the words, "It is our firm conviction that Dr. Simpson possesses an abundance of all the qualifications requisite to this position."

THE NEW PRESIDENT

Dr. Simpson was, indeed, well qualified for the position both by training and by experience. A native of Norfolk, he was educated in the public schools there and entered Randolph-Macon College in September 1926.

Upon his graduation with the A.B. in 1930, he served for a year as instructor in English at Randolph-Macon Academy, Bedford. That fall he returned to his alma mater as instructor in English. He was promoted, successively, to assistant professor, associate professor, and professor of English. In the meantime, he had completed his M.A. (1936) and Ph.D. (1949) degrees at the University of Virginia. His teaching at Randolph-Macon College was interrupted for a four-year period during World War II when he served as Field Supervisor, American Red Cross, for Southern Italy, with responsibility for Service to Allied Personnel Families (1944–46).

In February 1946 Dr. Simpson resumed his duties as professor of English at Randolph-Macon College. He also served as director of counseling for the next six years. Actually, he was dean of students, but the title was not used to avoid having two Dean Simpsons, since his cousin, Dr. T. McNider Simpson, was dean of the faculty during this period. In 1952 Dr. Grellet Simpson succeeded his cousin as dean of the faculty, the position he held at the time of his selection to head Mary Washington College.

The new president is, first of all, a scholar with strong academic interests. While pursuing graduate English studies at the University of Virginia, he held duPont and Bradshaw fellowships. His dissertation was written on the manuscript versions of "The Seven Penitential Psalms," ascribed to the early-fifteenth-century poet Thomas Brampton. Dr. Simpson's academic achievements have been recognized by election to Phi Beta Kappa, the Raven Society, and Omicron Delta Kappa. He is a member of the Phi Delta Theta social fraternity.

Throughout his career in various administrative roles at Randolph-Macon he continued to teach. At the time of his appointment to Mary Washington he was teaching a course in drama and one in Chaucer. He announced his intention of continuing to teach in his new role at Mary Washington, and he did offer a course in Chaucer until his administrative duties became too time-consuming.

In 1939 Dr. Simpson married Dorothy Cottrell of Richmond. They have no children. Dr. and Mrs. Simpson are close to each other in many ways. They have worked together to make the home of the chancellor a center of life on the campus for both faculty and students. Associates of Dr. Simpson have heard him say so many times, "Dorothy and I would like . . ." or "Mrs Simpson and I hope that . . . ." It has always seemed a partnership, whether the sphere of activity was social, academic, or recreational.

It was agreed that Dr. Simpson would finish out the semester at Randolph-Macon and assume his new duties at Mary Washington on February 1, 1956. The first appearance of Dr. Simpson locally was at the annual banquet of the Fredericksburg Chamber of Commerce held in Seacobeck Hall on February 18. He declined to be the speaker at an earlier meeting, because he felt that his first address should be to the students of Mary Washington College. Therefore, the annual meeting was postponed until the latter part of February.

Dr. Simpson discussed, in his usual scholarly way, the implications of the sentence, "Our civilization will find its place only in the intellectual and moral solidarity of its inheritors." He emphasized the privilege and responsibility that rest upon us all. A reception for Dr. and Mrs. Simpson preceded the dinner. In an informal receiving line they were introduced to a large number of chamber members and their guests by Dean and Mrs. Alvey.

Meanwhile Dr. Simpson continued to serve as a member of the town council in Ashland and as a steward of Duncan Memorial Methodist Church. In an interview with the press following his election, Dr. Simpson greeted inquiries about his future policies by reasserting his strong belief in the liberal arts tradition as the very foundation of citizenship.[1] The forty-six-year-old president expressed his genuine regret at leaving Randolph-Macon, which had "occupied a commanding spot in my life for the past 29 years." However, the opportunity offered by the appointment at Mary Washington was "too great to be rejected."

President Darden said he considered Dr. Simpson "an excellent choice." President Moreland of Randolph-Macon described his contribution there as of "incalculable value." He continued, "Our regret at losing him is paralleled by our satisfaction in the knowledge that Mary Washington College and higher education in Virginia gain so greatly by his election."[2]

THE FALL SEMESTER

In the fall of 1955 the shrines of Fredericksburg for the first time held open house for students on Saturday and Sunday afternoon, November 5 and 6. In the belief that Mary Washington students should be familiar with the historic place that thousands of persons from many parts of the country visit each year, the governing boards of Kenmore, the Mary Washington House, the James Monroe Law Office, the Hugh Mercer Apothecary Shop, and the Rising Sun Tavern offered free admission upon presentation of a class schedule card for identification. A lecture on historic Fredericksburg at a preceding assembly for new students furnished background information and aroused interest in the opportunity.

The Lyceum series opened with a concert by the National Symphony Orchestra of Washington under the direction of Howard Mitchell. The Mary Washington Players began its 1955–56 season with *A Trip to Bountiful,* followed later in the year by

---

[1] *Free Lance-Star,* Sept. 26, 1955. [2] *Ibid.*

The House of Bernado Alba and *Romeo and Juliet*. The president of the Student Government Association, Elizabeth Louise Davies, more commonly known as Betty, was awarded the Alumnae Daughters Cup at a convocation on October 5.

Early fall activities were many and varied. The Inter-Club Association held an open house at which each organization had a display depicting its activities and a representative to give information to freshman and transfer students. The MWC Band won first place in the 1955 Apple Harvest Festival at Charlottesville. The band held its annual tryouts for drum-major and twirlers.

Clubs were active as usual. The French Club sponsored a speaker from the French embassy. The Spanish Club planned a visit to the Pan-American Union in Washington and sponsored a Spanish movie. The Fencing Club went to Washington to see an exhibition by the Olympic fencing coach. The Art Club sponsored its first exhibition of the session. The Outing Club climbed and hiked on the Skyline Drive with members of the University of Virginia Outing Club.

On October 25, as related earlier, Dr. Combs died in a Richmond hospital after a long illness. His funeral was held at Brompton on October 28.

A New York trip was arranged for the Thanksgiving holiday with Miss Moran in charge. Transportation was provided by the college bus, with overnight accommodations at the Biltmore Hotel. Sightseeing and shopping were crowded into a busy weekend.

CHRISTMAS PROGRAMS

The Christmas concerts of the MWC All-Girl Band were looked forward to from year to year. The 1955 program was typical of the kind of production Director Faulkner staged. The hour's concert included "A Christmas Festival," "The Bells of St. Mary's," "The Christmas Suite," "Dancing Tambourine," and "Teddy Bears' Picnic." Special features were the "Dance of the Reed Flutes," by a trio consisting of Martha Spillman, Sheila Ammerman, and Roberta Holliday; "My Regards," a saxophone solo by Tootie Crandall; and "Winter Wonderland," with Anne Henry and Rudy Bowie as the couple in skating costume. As the "snowflakes" fell softly in the dimmed blue-white lights of the stage, the band concluded its program, as usual, with "White Christmas." The applause was long, thunderous, and appreciative.

The Christmas program of the Glee Club, presented under the direction of Marion Chauncey, was also anticipated eagerly each year. The 1955 concert, held on Sunday afternoon, December 11, was announced as "A Christmas Carol Pageant." The first part featured Christmas carols of many countries—England, Scotland, Spain, Germany, France, Poland—with singers dressed in the costumes of each country coming to the front of the stage as the chorus behind them sang the carol from that country. There were also carols from Appalachia ("Jesus, Jesus, Rest Your Head") and the Huron Indian country (" 'Twas in the Moon of Wintertime"), both plaintive, wistful expressions of religious faith.

The second part of the program was a series of Christmas tableaux, with appropriate carols provided by the Glee Club. The first episode, "The Shepherds," featured Walter Kelly, Carrol Quenzel, and Benjamin Early. The Glee Club sang "The First Noel." The second, "The Wise Men," was presented to precede and accompany the singing of "We Three Kings." The wise men, in period costumes, were Edgar Woodward, Reginald Whidden, and Boyd Graves. Appropriate biblical passages were read by a narrator as each episode unfolded before the audience.

The third episode, "The Manger Scene," preceded the singing of "Away in a Manger." Norma Yarborough played the role of Mary and Albert Duke that of Joseph. The entire cast joined in a grand finale of familiar carols, concluding with "Silent Night" as the stage lights dimmed slowly to a blue glow over the singers.

A reviewer in the *Free Lance–Star* on December 12 described the production in ecstatic terms. He commented especially on the costuming of the girls representing various nations and the costumes of the shepherds and the kings as they "gathered around the manger in awe and adoration of Jesus."

As the audience filed slowly out of George Washington Hall the scene outside was one of beauty and calm. Snow was falling in large flakes, and already the branches of the evergreens were beginning to bend. Lights on the huge Christmas trees near Virginia Hall and across from George Washington gleamed more brightly than ever as the white snow reflected their colors in the winter twilight. "Peace on earth and good will toward men" seemed almost a palpable feeling as guests at the concert walked thoughtfully through the falling snow with the memory of the Christmas carols to brighten their way.

A New Era Begins 367

FACULTY MEETINGS

Faculty meetings were held monthly, usually on the second Monday evening, at seven o'clock in the Little Theatre of duPont Hall, with the dean of the college presiding. A perusal of the faculty minutes for the fall of 1955 indicates a continuing concern with academic practices and procedures. Dr. Whidden reported on the practice of other colleges in accepting D grades for transfer credit. Dr. Castle led a discussion of the basis on which marks should be given. There was difference of opinion on the weight that should be given final examinations. It was agreed finally that no set percentage of the final grade should be expected in all courses.

At other meetings in November and December there were discussions, led by Mrs. Bolling, on the importance of notifying deficient students by giving "deficiencies" at midsemester. Mrs. Dodd led a discussion of the extent to which an instructor's grades should be expected to approximate the normal distribution curve. Miss Hoye discussed the physical therapy curriculum and the cooperative degree programs with other institutions. Mrs. Sumner discussed the honors program.

As the session progressed, there were further studies, reports, and discussions concerning such matters as grading standards, the percentage equivalents of letter grades, programs for gifted students, testing programs, and visiting lecturers.

THE SIMPSONS ARRIVE

Dr. Simpson began his duties at the college on February 1. It is typical of the new head of the institution that one of his first acts was to have removed the rather formidable counter that extended across the length of his outer office in George Washington Hall and in its place to provide comfortable chairs where visitors could wait to see him.

Draperies at the windows, a rearrangement of the furniture, the substitution of bookshelves for locked cabinets—and many other little but deft touches provided a warmth and friendliness that seemed to invite visitors. The door to the inner office usually stood open, and a friendly voice could be heard discussing some problem or project with a student or faculty member. Dr. Simpson was always available, except when important conferences or committee meetings demanded his uninterrupted attention. However busy the day might be, one could always make an appointment for a future visit and be assured of a prompt and cordial reception and an attentive and sympathetic ear at the scheduled time.

Between his election and the assumption of official duties, Dr. Simpson's title had been changed from president to chancellor. The same action of the board of visitors changed the title of Colgate Darden. "Chancellor of Mary Washington College" was dropped as a part of the title of Mr. Darden as president of the University of Virginia. Subsequent publications of the university and of Mary Washington College began to list him as president of the University of Virginia, followed by Grellet C. Simpson, chancellor of Mary Washington College.

Dr. Simpson's first formal meeting with the student body was at a special convocation held on Monday evening, February 6, just after his arrival the latter part of the previous day. The full text of his address, as well as that of all other speeches he has delivered at the college, is preserved in the archives of the library.

Taking the quest for knowledge as the theme of his address, Dr. Simpson stated that education is a personal concern, for it involves the realization of self, the development of the individual, and the exercise of free personality. He characterized education as a matter of the will, for one must have a desire to learn. Knowledge is a means to an end, he emphasized, its final achievement being the good life.

Dr. Simpson expressed his belief in the essential nobility of man. Therefore, a college must support freedom, and students must be given responsible positions. Freedom is the only environment in which knowledge can flourish.

At the end of his address, Chancellor Simpson received a prolonged, standing ovation. Students crowded forward to greet him personally and to express their gratification at his coming to Mary Washington.

The *Bullet* for February 14, 1956, carried a message from the chancellor in the place usually occupied by the editorial. Again, the friendliness and sincere concern of the new appointee were apparent.

After expressing "the joy and the pleasure with which Mrs. Simpson and I have begun our life among you," Dr. Simpson continued:

A New Era Begins

I do hope that you will always feel perfectly free to come to see me both in the office and at home. Mrs. Simpson and I want to know you and want to feel that we are a part of your college life.

Likewise, when you are sincerely disturbed about aspects of college life which are of mutual concern to you and me that you will come and tell me. I will not always be able to do what you suggest. At times, it will be not only possible, but advisable. It is the little things in life that frequently bother us most. Please be frank and straight-forward with me. I will be equally frank with you. We must trust each other. I shall try to play the game fairly, and when I do not obey the rules or the spirit of the rules, I want to know.

In an interview with a *Bullet* reporter, published February 14, Dr. Simpson stated his belief that the purpose of a liberal education is the development of a point of view. Each student should have freedom of thought and action, an understanding of the opinions of others so she can be tolerant, a faith in God, and a broad general knowledge. He spoke of the importance of a liberal education for women, because "they set the cultural pattern of the community." It is the type of education in which a woman learns to use her mind, as well as to acquire facts.

Dr. Simpson said he had no immediate changes of curriculum in mind, but that his goal for the years to come would be the raising of the academic standards of Mary Washington College.

Dr. Simpson attended his first faculty meeting on February 20, 1956. It was his request that it be a regularly scheduled meeting and that he be present largely as an observer.

The official minutes, as recorded by the secretary of the faculty, Dr. Carrol H. Quenzel, are of interest as indicating the tenor of the first remarks of the new chancellor to the assembled body of the faculty: "Dean Alvey introduced Chancellor Grellet C. Simpson, who explained that he regarded faculty meetings as the forum of the Faculty, in which all persons, regardless of rank, seniority or tenure should have an opportunity to be heard. He stated the conviction that his primary task as Chancellor was to increase the effectiveness of the teachers' work. On behalf of Mrs. Simpson and himself he hospitably invited the Faculty to visit them at Brompton. Dean Alvey thanked Chancellor Simpson for his gracious remarks."

A BUSY SPRING

The spring of 1956 was a busy one for Chancellor Simpson. In addition to his many and various activities in a new position at the college, he prepared and delivered a number of addresses. A short time after his Chamber of Commerce address, Dr. Simpson spoke to the Daughters of the American Revolution at their memorial service for George Washington at St. George's Episcopal Church on February 22. He addressed the MWC Alumnae Association at its homecoming on April 7, and the American Association of University Women at its meeting in Richmond on May 3.

A signal honor was paid Chancellor Simpson—and Mary Washington College—when he was invited to deliver the Founder's Day address at the University of Virginia on Jefferson's birthday, April 13, an observance for which all classes at the university are suspended. His subject, "The Liberal Arts 1956: An Essay towards Definition," was a statement of personal philosophy that was to guide the development of Mary Washington College as a center of learning.

Chancellor Simpson emphasized his belief that it is not the subjects studied but the point of view that evolves from such study that determines whether the process has been worth the effort expended. To him, we must think in terms of the liberally educated rather than in terms of liberal education. "The concept of the liberal arts must be dynamic, not static—democratic not aristocratic," he made clear.

Late in April, Chancellor Simpson was asked to judge an open-air art exhibit held in connection with Garden Week. As he descended the worn stone steps leading down to the Market Square in Fredericksburg he lost his footing and fell heavily, breaking his arm.

For the remainder of the session, he went about his manifold duties with the arm in a cast. Just before commencement, he insisted that the cast be removed so that he could preside more readily at graduation.

Commencement exercises began on Friday, June 1, 1956, with the senior picnic at Westmoreland Beach, followed by a "spontaneous" party in Ball parlor that evening. Saturday morning the usual Class Day exercises were held in the open-air theatre. That evening there was a formal dance given by the administration in the Gothic Room, with breakfast served afterwards.

A New Era Begins

Sunday morning the Reverend Harold A. Malmborg delivered the baccalaureate sermon. That afternoon Chancellor and Mrs. Simpson were hosts at a garden party and buffet supper for graduates, their families, and friends. Graduation exercises were held Monday morning at eleven. The commencement speaker was Dr. J. Earl Moreland, president of Randolph-Macon College. Chancellor Simpson presided and conferred 175 degrees, three with honors.

Chancellor Simpson delivered his first message to the graduates, a practice that was to become more and more a high point of the academic ritual. It was a challenge to further growth and development. He closed with the words, "Cultivate your imaginary gardens!" A buffet luncheon at Seacobeck for graduates and their commencement guests concluded the busy weekend.

CHAPTER XIX

The New Chancellor in Action, 1956–1957

THE INAUGURATION

THE inauguration of Dr. Grellet C. Simpson as chancellor of Mary Washington College was the high-point of the 1956–57 academic year; in fact, it was one of the most impressive and colorful ceremonies ever held at the college.

Preparations were begun early in the spring of 1956. An inauguration committee of twenty-one faculty members with Dean Edward Alvey, Jr., as chairman was appointed late in March, and it began work at once.

It was decided that the inauguration was to be a three-day affair, opening with an exhibition of contemporary paintings on Wednesday evening, October 17, and closing with an inaugural ball on Friday evening, October 19. In between were scheduled a symposium, a concert, the inaugural ceremony itself, a luncheon, a fine arts program, and a reception by Chancellor and Mrs. Simpson.

Upon completion of the inaugural plans in broad outline, the members of the general committee then undertook responsibility for various aspects of the celebration, serving as the chairmen of subcommittees to which were added other faculty members and students.

Chairmen and cochairmen of the various committees were: symposium, R. W. Whidden, Mary Ellen Stephenson, Mrs. J. H. Dodd, Carrol Quenzel; inaugural exercises, B. L. Parkinson; concert, Ronald W. Faulkner; invitations, R. E. Sumner; academic procession, James H. Croushore; registration, E. Boyd Graves, Earl G. Insley; hospitality, Mrs. Dodd; inaugural ball, Katherine Moran; arts program, Mark R. Sumner, Benjamin W. Early; exhibits, Julien Binford; printed matter, Miss Stephenson; chancellor's reception, Mrs. J. P. Harris, Mrs. J. Brawner Bolling; luncheon and dinner, Pal Robison; alumnae activities, Mrs. W. H. Lamason; housing, Edgar E. Woodward; publicity, Reynold H. Brooks; and signs, Ronald W. Faulkner.

THE ART EXHIBITION

The art exhibition in duPont Galleries was significant in many ways. It was the first of its kind held at the college, and it also set a precedent for a similar showing of contemporary paintings each fall at Mary Washington.

The frontispiece of the catalogue notes that "this inaugural exhibition is dedicated to Chancellor Grellet C. Simpson, whose imagination made these beginnings possible."

Julien Binford served as chairman of the exhibition committee and jury of awards. He and other members of the committee made several trips to New York to select the fifty paintings representative of the work of distinguished American and European artists. In his foreword to the catalogue, Binford remarked on the appropriateness of such an exhibition to honor the new chancellor, who believed so firmly that "the enjoyment of art in familiar surroundings is the daily need of civilized people." Dr. Simpson himself served as a member of the selection committee.

In view of later developments, a paragraph from the foreword deserves quotation: "From the exhibition, one or more paintings will be bought for the college. It is our hope that throughout the years, as these showings are annually repeated and other purchases are made, a collection of works of art will be formed that will benefit Mary Washington as truly as now does its splendid library."

This fervently expressed hope has been in process of realization. Ever since this first exhibition in 1956 the Mary Washington annuals have become an event looked forward to each year by art circles in Virginia and in Washington. Newspaper reviews have attested to the quality of the painting and the significance of the exhibitions. The annual catalogues are works of art in themselves, and their notes on the character of the collections and on the painters themselves form an interesting commentary on contemporary art.

On Thursday afternoon a symposium on "Woman, Catalyst of Modern Society," was held in the auditorium of George Washington Hall. It was chaired by Dr. Reginald W. Whidden, assistant dean of the college, who had arranged the program and invited the speakers. Dr. Margaret Hargrove, the new dean of students, introduced the individual speakers.

To lead off the discussion Dr. Ashley Montagu, anthropologist and author of *The Natural Superiority of Women,* spoke on

"Woman as Catalyst." He was followed by Marguerite Zapoleon of the Women's Bureau, United States Department of Labor, who discussed "Woman as an Economic Influence." The third and final speaker, Mrs. J. L. Blair Buck, past president, General Federation of Women's Clubs, spoke on "Woman as a Social Influence."

Ashley Montagu's presence on the panel was protested vigorously by, curiously enough, an alumna of the college and her husband. Through letters to college authorities, to the University of Virginia board of visitors, and even to the governor himself, they sought to block his appearance on the program. Dr. Montagu's views on racial integration, including intermarriage, were apparently the grounds on which the protest was based.

When these efforts failed, the protesters announced that they would be present to heckle the speaker. An abortive attempt was made, but the general chagrin of the audience at this interference with the speaker soon silenced the interrupters. Fireworks had been promised during the discussion period that followed, but these fizzled out when Dr. Whidden wisely announced that only questions from undergraduate students at the college would be considered. Students with pads and pencils were in the aisles, and Dr. Montagu was able to select and respond to questions that were germane to the topic of the symposium. In any case, the threat of a demonstration added zest and excitement to a scholarly discussion of the role of women.

That evening Chancellor and Mrs. Simpson entertained the rector and visitors of the university and other distinguished guests at a formal dinner at Brompton. There followed the inaugural concert by Herva Nelli, soprano of the Metropolitan Opera Company. Chancellor Simpson and Dean Alvey had made a trip to New York to engage Miss Nelli's services. She happened to be on concert tour at the time, and they talked and made arrangements with her manager. When Miss Nelli strode forth imperiously onto the stage of George Washington Hall, a stunning blond in a shimmering evening dress with deep décolletage, a surprised gasp escaped the audience. It was difficult to convince some of the inaugural party that she had been selected because of the reviews of the quality of her voice rather than a visual encounter with the prima donna in New York. Miss Nelli opened with "Vaghissima Senebianza" by Donaudy and concluded with "Un Bel Di" from *Madame Butterfly*. This selection from Puccini's opera was a fitting climax to an evening of glorious song.

The next day was the inauguration itself. Delegates from other

The New Chancellor in Action

colleges and universities and representatives from learned societies and educational organizations began to arrive early. Preparations were made to register them at Ann Carter Lee, where facilities for robing were arranged and coffee was served.

In the academic procession were delegates representing 144 colleges and universities, including the presidents of 25 of these institutions. A total of 32 learned societies and educational organizations were represented, 10 of them by their presidents or executive heads. Most of the four-year colleges in Virginia were represented by their presidents.

The processional, Martin Luther's "Ein' Feste Burg," was sung by the combined glee clubs of Randolph-Macon and Mary Washington colleges. Following the national anthem, the invocation was given by Dr. Theodore F. Adams, minister of the First Baptist Church, Richmond. The delegates were then greeted by Frank Talbott, Jr., rector of the University of Virginia, who presided at the inauguration.

Greetings to the chancellor were brought in behalf of the Commonwealth of Virginia by Dr. Dowell J. Howard, state superintendent of public instruction; from the faculties of the University of Virginia by President Colgate W. Darden, Jr.; from the American Council of Learned Societies by Dr. D. H. Daugherty, assistant to the director; from the Association of American Colleges by Dr. William F. Quillian, Jr., president of Randolph-Macon Woman's College; from the Association of Virginia Colleges by Dr. Orville W. Wake, president of Lynchburg College; from the Alumnae Association of Mary Washington College by Margaret L. Reardon, president; and from the student body of Mary Washington College, by Emmaneta Hepford, president of the Student Government Association.

Talbott then presented Dean Edward Alvey, Jr., chairman of the inauguration committee, who introduced the speaker, Dr. Harlan H. Hatcher, president of the University of Michigan.

A former professor of English and later dean of the College of Arts and Sciences at Ohio State University before going to Michigan, Dr. Hatcher chose as his subject, "The Opening of a Door." Most appropriately, he traced the development of education for women, their role in society today, and the implications for higher education as he saw them. Dr. Hatcher mentioned that he came from a campus which had 6,770 women students in residence. For college women, in general, it is "an exciting moment of our history," for so many opportunities await them. As the holder, at the time, of sixteen honorary doctoral degrees,

Dr. Hatcher spoke simply but with authority. Many will remember his characterization of true education as a state of the mind. "We are united and exalted by a common humanity and immortal spirit in a world in which women have a crucial role to play," he said.

Following this address, Colgate W. Darden, Jr., president of the University of Virginia, rose to present Dr. Simpson with these words: "Mr. Chief Justice: I present to you to take the oath of office as Chancellor of Mary Washington College of the University of Virginia, Dr. Grellet Simpson, a young scholar who by character, intellectual attainment and temperament is admirably equipped, in my opinion, to direct the affairs of this center of learning."

The Honorable Edward W. Hudgins, chief justice of the supreme court of appeals of Virginia, then administered the following oath: "I do solemnly swear that I will support the Constitution of the United States, and the Constitution of the State of Virginia, and that I will faithfully and impartially discharge and perform all the duties incumbent on me as Chancellor of Mary Washington College of the University of Virginia, according to the best of my ability; so help me God."

Upon completion of the oath of office, Chancellor Simpson received a standing ovation from the standing-room-only audience in George Washington Hall. He then turned to the lectern to deliver his inaugural address.

Dr. Simpson began with an acknowledgment of the presence of so many delegates from other institutions to honor the college and the university "of which Mary Washington is a very attractive part." Dr. Simpson continued: "In truth, colleges for women are always more attractive than colleges for men—a fact which I fully realized thirty years ago as a student, and which I have rediscovered with happiness after an interval of approximately twenty-five years, during which I had the opportunity to assist in the education of young men."

The new chancellor suggested that his address might be called "Lessons Learned from Literature." Referring to Milton's *Lycidas*, he characterized as the first and most fundamental task of education today the development in students of "the will to think, the will to prepare, the will to serve." Rejecting the notion that one opinion is as good as another, he stressed the importance of the privilege of choice based on intelligent analysis and evaluation. The "informed choice" is an essential characteristic of the educated mind.

The New Chancellor in Action

Dr. Simpson pleaded for a resurgence of what he called the comic spirit in life, so that "we may hear once again the 'tinkling of silver bells' and not merely the blaring of trumpets or the moan of the saxophone." Finally, the chancellor pointed out that the mind of a college is made up of the minds of the faculty as well as those of the students. Teaching becomes an exciting commitment to this development of the minds of youth. As this task engages us, we may "share with the poet Schiller his *Freude, Freude, Freude.*"

Following the singing of the alma mater of the college and a brief benediction by Dr. Adams, the academic procession left the auditorium as the combined glee clubs sang Beethoven's "Hymn to Joy." A luncheon for all of the delegates and guests followed at one o'clock in Seacobeck Hall.

A fine arts program was presented in the Little Theatre of duPont Hall at two o'clock that afternoon. Drama, dance, and choral groups joined in a series of brief presentations to commemorate the inauguration. The Mary Washington Players staged an original one-act play, *More Swift than Larks,* written by Virginia Nettles of the class of 1957 and directed by Mark Sumner, head of the dramatic arts department. It was probably the first student-written play to be staged here. The program continued with "Canterbury Preludes," performed by the Modern Dance Club, under the direction of Mrs. Charles L. Read, to music written by Levin Houston III. It was dedicated to Chancellor Simpson in recognition of his interest in the study and teaching of Chaucer. The arts program concluded with Benjamin Britten's "A Ceremony of Carols," by the Madrigal Singers in costume, directed by Dr. Stanley Bulley. Jeanne Chalifoux was the harpist.

There followed a reception at Brompton at which Dr. and Mrs. Simpson greeted inaugural guests and members of the faculty. Music was furnished by Ronna Faulkner Simpson, harpist, the daughter of Mr. and Mrs. Ronald Faulkner.

The program of events concluded with an inaugural ball held in the Gothic Room of Ann Carter Lee Hall from nine to one o'clock. Students then had an opportunity to greet Dr. and Mrs. Simpson personally, both of them smiling graciously after what must have been an exciting but tiring day. Breakfast was served in Seacobeck Hall immediately following the dance.

The inauguration was not without its lighter moments. Just as the dignitaries to be seated on the stage were robing in the chancellor's office, it was discovered that the mortarboard that had been ordered for one of them was entirely too large. It completely covered the wearer's head and rested rather uncertainly on his eyebrows, where it tilted and shifted as he plaintively asked, "Does it look all right?"

It didn't look all right, and the time was rapidly approaching for the procession to start. The day was saved when the treasurer of the college disappeared across the hall and returned with a handful of tissue paper that was used to stuff the inside of the mortarboard until a reasonably satisfactory fit was obtained. From time to time during the ceremony, the little group on the platform glanced apprehensively at the wearer of the cap, but his headgear survived the entire program although it seemed to teeter precariously with any sudden movement. It took real finesse to remove and replace the cap and its stuffing during the national anthem and the alma mater, but it was done without mishap.

As the participants in the ceremony took their place in the line, the dean noticed that Dr. Simpson's shirt collar was unbuttoned. When his attention was called to this, the chancellor said, "Yes, I know. I unbuttoned it." It was one of the few indications of what must have been considerable tension, quite understandable under the circumstances.

Students were excused from classes on Thursday afternoon and all day Friday. Classes were resumed on Saturday. And so, there ended a beautiful October weekend when, officially, a new era was begun at Mary Washington.

FACULTY COMMITTEE ORGANIZATION

One of Chancellor Simpson's first acts in the fall was to appoint a special study committee, headed by Associate Professor Kenneth Roach, "to investigate and suggest to the faculty a committee set-up through which the faculty would be able to work more efficiently and constructively for the total welfare of the College."[1] This forward step, sometimes referred to in jest as the "committee on committees," resulted in a complete restructuring of this aspect of college life. It provided for genuine participation in college affairs by individual faculty members and also made possible their sharing many responsibilities previously regarded as purely administrative.

[1] Faculty Minutes, Sept. 17, 1956.

In its preliminary report the committee suggested grouping committees into two categories: one concerned with academic problems and procedures and the other concerned primarily with administrative responsibilities for specific aspects of the college program and activities. As the committee continued its deliberations, certain committees were discontinued and others merged. In its final form the report recommended eighteen committees, classified as follows:

I. Area of Academic Policies and Procedures. (These are regular standing committees on matters of joint concern to administration and faculty. They should report to the officially assembled faculty.)
Committee on Academic Counseling and Guidance
Admissions Policy Committee
Curriculum Committee
Faculty General Cooperative Committee
Committee on Faculty Organization and Procedures
Committee on Instruction
Inter-Institutional Committee
Committee on Programs for Superior Students

II. Area of Administrative Responsibility for Specific Aspects of the College Program.
Admissions Committee
Auditing Committee
Catalogue Committee
Commencement Committee
Joint Council
Library Committee
May Day Committee
Orientation Committee
Public Occasions Committee (To be divided into Assembly, Convocation, Lyceum, and Special Events sub-committees)
Student Organizations Committee
Student Publications Committee

The report suggested that every member of the faculty serve on at least one committee, with no one on more than two committees in each grouping. It proposed that each faculty member be given an opportunity to indicate those committees, in order, in which he was most interested—or whether he preferred not to serve on a committee. From these statements data sheets indicating faculty preferences for each committee were to be prepared.

The faculty—and later just the committee on faculty organization and programs—voted to select the personnel of each committee in Group I which it wished to recommend to the chancellor for appointment. Data sheets for faculty preferences for committees in Group II were submitted directly to the administration. Provision was made at the time for student representation on five committees: commencement, publications, May Day, student organizations, and student publications. The faculty general cooperative committee was to continue being elected by the faculty.[2]

The faculty voted to put the proposed plan into operation on February 1, 1957, with the understanding that these committee appointments would carry over through the following academic year (1957–58). Provisions were made subsequently for definite terms of membership, usually three years, with continuity maintained through staggered periods of service. Each committee was empowered to elect its own chairman and secretary. Committees were to complete organization for the following year before the end of each session, so that lists of the committee personnel could be distributed to each faculty member.

This significant report was to pave the way for active participation of the faculty in many aspects of the operation of the college. The duties and responsibilities of each committee were set forth in the original report. Although revisions have subsequently been made as the circumstances warranted, the essential nature of the committee plan of faculty participation in the affairs of the college has remained unchanged.

The adoption of this plan marked the beginning of a new era of faculty responsibility and initiative. Committees met regularly, considered matters referred to or originating with them, kept minutes, and reported to the faculty, often with recommendations for action.

For example, changes in admission requirements, especially in terms of necessary high school units, were studied by the admissions policy committee for their effects on enrollment. As an outgrowth of its investigations, the committee recommended to the faculty certain changes to be discussed fully at one meeting and, if a change in policy were involved, to be voted on officially at the next meeting.

Thus the machinery was set in motion for changes in policy in many areas of college life—academic regulations, student activities, curriculum changes, degree requirements—in a word, the broad spectrum of the operation of the college.

[2] *Ibid.*, Nov. 12, 1956, Appendix E.

The list of committees and their personnel was carried in the catalogue until 1968 when the format of the bulletin was changed.

Reports of committees still provide the major agenda for faculty meetings. Major changes in the college program, such as discontinuance of the majors in home economics and physical education, were discussed long and earnestly at a succession of meetings before a final vote was taken. More recently, such matters as the revision of the college calendar, self-scheduled examinations, and student representation at faculty meetings have been the subjects of committee recommendations and faculty discussion.

A final recommendation of the committee on faculty organization was that the secretary of the faculty be appointed by the chancellor. Upon the adoption of the report, Dr. Carrol H. Quenzel, the incumbent, was officially designated by Dr. Simpson and continued to serve faithfully and efficiently as secretary of the faculty until his death in June 1968.

The report also recommended the appointment of a faculty marshal, who would organize and lead the academic procession at the chancellor's convocation, commencement, and any other such occasions when caps and gowns were worn. The chancellor appointed Dr. James H. Croushore as the first marshal of the faculty. He was succeeded later by Dr. George Van Sant.

In February 1970 Lewis M. Walker, Jr., of Petersburg, a retiring member of the board of visitors of the university, who had been chairman of the Mary Washington College committee of the board, presented a handsome silver mace to the college, to be carried by the marshal in academic processions. It was used first at the graduation exercises in June 1970.

Designed especially for the college by Asprey and Company of London, England, the mace has a slender dark-red leather-covered shaft. The very top of the mace bears the seal of the Commonwealth of Virginia. Immediately below, on top of the enlarged body of the mace, is engraved in circular form: "Presented on Behalf of the Rector and Visitors of the University of Virginia, February 7, 1970."

The four faces of the body have engraved the seal of Mary Washington College on one side, the seal of the University of Virginia on the reverse side, and between on the other two sides, representations of the dogwood bloom, the state flower of Virginia. Immediately above, extending around the four faces of the mace, are the words "Mary Washington College of the University of Virginia."[3] When not in use, the mace is kept in its red, tooled-leather case in the vaults of the college. On important occasions, it is displayed in the rotunda of the library.

ATTENDANCE AT PROFESSIONAL MEETINGS

The adoption of the new plan of faculty committee organization has been treated in some detail because of its significance. However, many other important actions were taken by the faculty during the session of 1956–57.

Representation at professional meetings had long been a matter of concern. In its spring 1956 report, the faculty general cooperative committee noted the lack of a well-defined procedure for granting financial assistance to faculty members attending professional meetings. In the fall of 1956 Chancellor Simpson invited the committee to meet with him and other members of the administration to consider the problem. As a result of these meetings, the chancellor proposed, and the committee endorsed and reported, a plan whereby each department would draw up a list of professional meetings covering the calendar year at which attendance is desired; the faculty members to attend specific meetings would be selected by a vote of the department; and the faculty members selected would submit a request for financial assistance to the chancellor for review.

The report was accepted by the faculty and the plan put into effect immediately. As an outgrowth of this development, Mary Washington College has been represented by one or more faculty members, at college expense, at a wide range of professional meetings. Undoubtedly, this has added to the academic prestige of the institution and to the recognition of the personnel of its various departments.

A recent report reveals faculty membership in approximately 250 professional organizations.[4] During 1970–71, approval was granted to the faculty to attend approximately 140 different professional meetings. From 1968 through 1971 financial assistance for this kind of professional development amounted to $46,336. An impressive list of meetings attended grew out of this substantial aid from institutional funds.

---

[3] In 1972 the following words were engraved on a silver disk just above the stem of the mace: "Mary Washington College became independent of the University of Virginia, 30 June 1972."

[4] Self-Study Report, 1971, pp. 135, 175–82.

Other matters that concerned the faculty during 1956–57 were the improvement of the college bookstore; a further study of the reasons for student withdrawal; the system of class cuts, especially those immediately preceding and following a holiday; and interpretation of what constituted violations of the honor system.

It is interesting to note that at a faculty meeting on January 14, 1957, a discussion of the inadequacy of communication on the campus brought out the need for a telephone switchboard, a campus post office and faculty box delivery, and an information center. All of these proposals were subsequently acted on by the administration. The central telephone switchboard was installed in 1958. The campus mail delivery system and the information center were inaugurated shortly thereafter.

Early in March 1957 Dean and Mrs. Alvey left for a two months' trip to Europe. A going-away party was given them by the faculty, along with a purse to "spend recklessly as they wished." Dr. Whidden, then associate dean of the college, managed academic affairs in Dr. Alvey's absence. The Alveys returned May 5 on the *Independence* after visiting Italy, France, Switzerland, and England "on their own."

A NEW DEAN OF STUDENTS

The 1956–57 session opened with a new dean of students (the title had been changed from dean of women at her request) – Dr. Margaret Hargrove. During the next fourteen years she was to institute important changes in the practices that governed the residential life of students and in the staff that worked with them in the dormitories.

Miss Hargrove was born and reared in Louisville, Kentucky, where she graduated as valedictorian from the Louisville Girls High School in 1921. Four years later she received her A.B. degree from Randolph-Macon Woman's College. She then began a career of high school and college teaching that included E. C. Glass High School in Lynchburg, Ward-Belmont School in Nashville, Tennessee, and Beaver College in Jenkintown, Pennsylvania, where she was also dean of students. Meanwhile, she had earned at Cornell University the A.M. in literary criticism and Renaissance Latin and, in 1937, the Ph.D. in comparative literature and medieval Latin.

In the fall of 1937 she went to Carroll College at Waukesha, Wisconsin, where for the next six years, she was dean of women, professor of classics, and chairman of the department. While there she taught both Dr. Robert Shaw, later professor of mathematics at Mary Washington, and the future Mrs. Shaw. In 1943 Miss Hargrove went with the American Red Cross as director of the area training program, head of the national college division, and official in charge of hiring overseas personnel. She returned to college teaching in 1947 as professor of classics and dean of the college at Lake Erie College. In 1955 Lake Erie conferred upon her the honorary degree of L.H.D. (Doctor of Humane Letters).

A broad opportunity to serve the church came with her appointment as executive secretary of the National Fellowship of Congregational Christian Women (600,000 membership), with headquarters in New York. She left that post to accept the position at Mary Washington as dean of students and professor of classics.

Miss Hargrove had traveled widely, studied in England and Belgium, served as delegate to various international church conferences, and been active in many educational and civic organizations. She was the first woman to be elected an elder in the Fredericksburg Presbyterian Church. She was a member of the Governor's Commission on the Status of Women. She held various offices in the American Association of University Women, the League of Women Voters, the Business and Professional Women's Club, and other organizations. She was a member of Phi Beta Kappa, Mortar Board, Eta Sigma Phi, and Pi Lambda Theta.

Miss Hargrove served as dean of students from July 1, 1956, until her retirement on September 1, 1969. During the first ten years of this period she worked closely with Dr. Mary Ellen Stephenson, a former dean of women at Mary Washington, who now, as assistant dean of students and professor of Spanish, had an office adjoining that of Miss Hargrove on the second floor of George Washington Hall. Miss Stephenson left the office in September 1966 to go to India under the Indian Women's College Exchange Program. Upon her return, she was made chairman of the modern foreign language department.

The new dean of students set as her first goal the strengthening of the Student Government Association. She met at least once a week with the SGA officers and discussed problems and procedures. She championed membership in the National Student Association in order to give the local SGA "a window on the world," as she put it. The dormitories became residence halls and were closely coordinated with SGA leadership.

Miss Hargrove gave particular attention to the upgrading of the residential staff. She worked with deans of women in other state institutions in obtaining better salaries and dignifying these positions. Instead of house mothers, they became head residents, serving in an advisory or counseling capacity rather than as hovering presences over the girls. To achieve these goals Miss Hargrove instituted a program of in-service training, beginning with a preschool conference, first with other staff members and then with student leaders. Semimonthly staff meetings were held throughout the session, at which various members of the faculty and administration, and community leaders as well, spoke and enjoyed a social hour. The group meetings were held in various places in the college and community. Student assistants were provided in the residence halls, offices for head residents were enlarged and, finally, residence complexes were established with a student assistant in charge of one of the buildings.

During Miss Hargrove's tenure Anne Fairfax Hall, then a residence for students, became the official residence of the dean of students. People like Arnold Toynbee, John Gielgud, and Marietta Tree were entertained there. Miss Hargrove continued to teach at least one course in Latin every session. Her favorite was Virgil ("spell it with two i's," she says). She also taught Roman literature in translation.

During Miss Hargrove's years at the college, the first "mixed" dormitories were started, replacing the assignment by class to some residence halls. Bushnell Hall was the first of these "integrated" buildings with a cross section of all four classes represented. Student personnel records were also developed in the dean of students' office, listing activities, offices held, student aide positions, and other information.

These developments took place with the cooperation of many persons, notably the assistant dean of students and the residence hall counselors.

MARY ELLEN STEPHENSON

Mary Ellen Stephenson has made a rich contribution to the life of the college, both as an administrative official and as a professor of foreign languages. A native of Richmond where her mother had been a teacher of Latin, she attended John Marshall High School and Westhampton College of the University of Richmond. Upon receiving her A.B. degree with a major in French she was elected to Phi Beta Kappa and to Mortar Board. She began her teaching career in the Richmond schools. She taught Spanish at Thomas Jefferson High School, and with summer study and leaves of absence, she completed her master's at Middlebury College and the doctor of philosophy at the University of Chicago, specializing in Romance languages.

Miss Stephenson came to Mary Washington in 1948 as a member of the Spanish department. She was instrumental in starting the first language house on the campus, Framar, where, as resident counselor, she organized the new program for Spanish majors who resided there. Upon the retirement of Mrs. Bushnell in 1950, Mary Ellen Stephenson was drafted to become dean of women because of her success in working with students. Although Miss Stephenson was keenly interested in teaching, she left the Spanish house and moved to the dean of women's suite in Virginia Hall. For the next three years, she continued to carry this responsibility while also teaching at least two classes. She relinquished this administrative responsibility in 1953, but, once again, when Miss Hargrove was appointed dean of students, she was asked to come back into student personnel work as assistant to Miss Hargrove. She also continued to teach Spanish.

For the next ten years, as assistant dean of students, Miss Stephenson worked closely with Miss Hargrove. She specialized in counseling students and, in her own words, gave "her full time outside of the classroom to helping them." Her advice and assistance were sought by many students. As an associate remarked, she had an "educated heart." As a Mortar Board member herself, Mary Ellen Stephenson worked actively to bring a chapter to Mary Washington. For many years she sponsored Phi Sigma Iota, the national honorary Romance language fraternity.

In June 1966 she left for a year of teaching French in India at Women's Christian College in Madras. She also helped with their self-study program. Upon her return she asked to go back to full-time teaching. She was appointed chairman of the modern language department, succeeding Mrs. Bolling. The department continued its development, and Japanese was offered as the first Asian language to be taught.

Miss Stephenson has lost none of her interest in students and their problems. As she looks back upon her early days as dean of women, she recalls her practice of sitting with various groups of students at their tables in the dining hall to get to know them better and to share their concerns and problems. Through this and other evidences of genuine interest in students, she was able to bring students and administration into closer relationship.

FIRST CHANGE IN DRESS CODE

In the light of the present permissive atmosphere regarding dress on the campus, it is hard to realize the excitement that greeted the decision that Bermuda shorts, slacks, or pedal pushers could be worn on the campus except: to classes and in George Washington Hall, Seacobeck, Ann Carter Lee, and the library; after 6:00 P.M. Saturday and all day Sunday; on dates after 6:00 P.M. Students were advised not to wear Bermudas while shopping downtown. Residents of Cornell and Trench Hill were asked to cover them with coats when going back and forth to other buildings.

SMOKING RULES RELAXED

Smoking on campus, long limited to the privacy of dormitory rooms and smoking lounges in the basements of academic buildings, came into the open with the provision that students could smoke in the College Shoppe. The permission was greeted with enthusiasm. Students spread the word excitedly, "We Can Smoke in the C. Shoppe!" Although the first days of the new freedom resulted in prolonged sessions over cups of coffee, the smoking privilege soon began to be taken as a matter of course as an accompaniment to a quick snack between classes.

CONVOCATION, ASSEMBLIES, AND VISITING SPEAKERS

The long-time practice of having a Wednesday evening convocation and Tuesday and Friday "chapels" or assemblies each week throughout the session came to an end with the adoption by the faculty of a report providing for four student assemblies and four or five convocations, beginning with the 1957–58 session.[5] The initial proposal included the requirement of student attendance at these meetings. Later this provision was eliminated. The com-

[5] Faculty Minutes, May 13, 1957.

mittee on public occasions also suggested that visiting scholars and artists be invited to appear at places other than George Washington Hall where interested faculty and students could attend their lectures on a voluntary basis. This, too, was adopted and became the basis of the visiting lecturer series.

Through the cooperation of the Richmond Area University Center, later the University Center in Virginia, speakers in many academic fields were brought to the college. Each department was requested to make recommendations for speakers from the published list of available campus visitors. A subcommittee of the public occasions committee, chaired for years by Dr. Benjamin W. Early, the college's representative on the University Center State Committee, made the final selection, arranged the schedule and meeting places for the visitor, and handled details with the cooperation of the academic department that had originally requested the speaker.

Many notable visitors have come to the college over the years through the cooperation of the University Center in Virginia at a cost far less than it would be if they were brought by the institution itself. Dr. Simpson served for a time as chairman of the board of the University Center in Virginia. In the fall of 1971 he was succeeded by President William F. Quillian of Randolph-Macon Woman's College.

In the 1940s and '50s, the college made extensive use of the arts program sponsored by the Association of American Colleges. This subsidized project provided for two-day campus visits by artists and lecturers, who met with classes and informal interest groups and also gave a formal concert or address on the first or second evening of their visit.

The academic disciplines represented ranged from anthropology and archeology to seismology and zoology. One of the first colleges to take advantage of the concert-lecture series, Mary Washington continued to participate for some fifteen years under the general direction of Dean Alvey.

OTHER EVENTS

As the session progressed, various activities enlivened the days. A convocation on October 24 was devoted to the tapping of fifty-four students by eight honor societies in a joint ceremony. The MWC Band again led the annual Thalhimer's Christmas Toy Parade in Richmond on November 15. The annual Christmas concert of the band was given at convocation on Wednesday,

December 12 and was followed by a party for the band members at the home of Mr. and Mrs. Faulkner.

Students took keen interest in the presidential campaign. A mock election at MWC presaged the final result nationally when the Eisenhower-Nixon team won over Adlai Stephenson–Estes Kefauver. Exactly 1,001 students and faculty voted in the successful mock election.

As usual, the National Symphony Orchestra, with Howard Mitchell conducting, opened the 1956–57 Lyceum series. Other attractions presented during the year were the Little Singers of Paris, José Limón and his modern dance group, and the Original Don Cossack Chorus and Dancers. Chancellor Simpson inaugurated the practice of giving free tickets to the concert series to each faculty or staff member and his wife or husband. The complimentary tickets have been continued even after retirement for emeritus members of the faculty.

FAULKNER SPEAKS

William Faulkner, Nobel prize–winning novelist and at the time writer in residence at the University of Virginia, spoke to an interested group of faculty and students in the browsing room of the library on April 25.[6]

A short, grey-haired man dressed in tweeds, he first read a short story, "Shingles for the Lord," and then answered a steady barrage of questions from the audience that overflowed the browsing room.

Faulkner answered questions about the religious symbolism in *The Sound and the Fury,* about the influences of James Joyce and Joseph Conrad, about the situation facing young writers today, and about his own development as a novelist.

A library display on Faulkner's works disclosed the richness of the E. Lee Trinkle collection. An impressive number of his novels and collections of short stories were displayed. The card catalogue of the library lists 118 titles of books by and about William Faulkner.

JUNIOR RING DANCE

The Junior Ring Dance was a high point of the year for members of the class. Planned months in advance, it involved formal in-

---

[6] See article by Judith Townsend, *Bullet,* May 3, 1957.

vitation, dance cards, elaborate decorations, expensive favors, and a well-known orchestra.

Perhaps the best idea of the yearly event can be gathered from an announcement of plans for the 1957 affair that appeared in the *Bullet* on April 5, 1957. It read, in part:

Invitations to the Junior Ring Dance Weekend, to be held April 13, 14 and 15, have been issued by the class. As the social high point of the year for the class of '58, the dance preparations have been planned by Committee Chairmen for many months. As a special feature of the week-end, there will be a class seal designed by Yvonne Lewis, which will be engraved on the top of traveling stud boxes, the Ring Dance favors. Libby Foster, President of the Junior Class, has announced the tentative weekend schedule.

On Friday night, it is hoped that the girls and their dates may get together at one of the clubs in Fredericksburg. From 4:00 to 5:00 on Saturday the 13th, a jazz concert will be given by Tony Pastor and his orchestra on the roof garden of G.W. Following the concert, dinner will be served at 6:30 in Seacobeck. The menu will consist of shrimp cocktail, roast beef, potatoes, broccoli, rolls, coffee, and apple pie.

The formal ring dance will be held from 9:00 to 12:00 in the Gothic Room. Music will be furnished by Tony Pastor and his orchestra, consisting of 13 players and one vocalist. Punch and cookies will be served through the evening by girls from the sophomore and junior classes.

The theme for the ring dance will be "Southern Serenade." This Southern atmosphere will be carried out by a backdrop of a plantation mansion and white trellises and flowers. The mood will be set by soft lights. Tables will be arranged along the sides of the dance floor for the couples. A grand march will lead the couples through the traditional "ring figure," where the girls will receive their MWC rings from their escorts.

Following the dance, breakfast will be served from 12:00 to 2:00 in Seacobeck. Music will be played over the loudspeaker system.

NEW INSTALLATION CEREMONIES

The spring saw the inauguration of a new policy in the installation of members of the Student Council and the Honor Council. Members of Joint Council and representatives of the administration sat on the stage of George Washington Hall along with the retiring officers of the two student organizations. Chancellor Simpson himself presided and presented the SGA President Emmaneta Hepford and Honor Council President Patricia Preston,

The New Chancellor in Action

who administered the oath of office to their successors. As the retiring presidents turned over their responsibilities to the new officers and took their seats again with the seniors, they received a prolonged accolade. It was a fitting recognition of their services to the college, noted by Chancellor Simpson in his introductory remarks.

The processional of the incoming members of the two councils, the active participation of administrative officers—all in cap and gown—the printed programs, and the dignity with which the entire program was conducted made the occasion an impressive one. The retiring SGA president's response and Chancellor Simpson's expression of his faith and confidence in the student leaders added new stature to the role of student government and the Honor Council in the life of the college.

May Day in 1957 included a historical pageant based on actual events that took place in Fredericksburg during the eighteenth century. It was arranged to coincide with the city's week-long celebration of the Jamestown Festival, which marked the 350th anniversary of the first permanent English settlement in America. Through the cooperation of the music, dramatics, and art departments, episodes culminating in the Peace Ball were presented, featuring the Concert Dance Club.

THE SESSION ENDS

Commencement exercises in 1957 marked the separation of Class Day exercises, previously held on Saturday morning of the graduation weekend, from other parts of the program. It was held on Wednesday evening, May 22, at a Class Night observance. Seniors wore caps and gowns. All awards previously made at Class Day were presented at this time, along with the addresses of certain class officers.

Activities of the final weekend began with the Senior Class Night Party in Mary Ball Hall on Thursday evening, May 30, followed, the next day, by the senior picnic at Westmoreland Beach. On Saturday afternoon, June 1, a concert by Buddy Morrow's Orchestra was held on the lawn of Brompton, followed by dinner in Seacobeck and the Senior Farewell Dance in the Gothic Room. The baccalaureate sermon was delivered by the Reverend Frederick W. Olert of Richmond. Chancellor and Mrs. Simpson's garden party and buffet for seniors, their families and guests, and members of the faculty and staff took place Sunday afternoon from five to seven o'clock. Some twelve hundred persons were served.

Dr. Burney L. Parkinson, former president of Mississippi State College for Women, who retired in 1956 after four years as professor of education at Mary Washington, gave the commencement address. His subject was "A Challenge to Active Citizenship and a Continuing Personal Growth." The exercises concluded with Chancellor Simpson's message to the graduates. As in the previous year when the practice was inaugurated, his address was warmly and enthusiastically received.

Hoods were worn for the first time at the 1957 commencement. A faculty committee, headed by Dr. Quenzel, had been appointed to select colors for the hoods and to plan for that part of the graduation ceremony. The aqua-blue and white colors of the college were selected for the lining of the hoods. They provided a pleasing note of color to the black gowns of those receiving bachelor's degrees. The white of the arts degree and the gold of the science degree blended well with the college's colors, and the general result was distinctly pleasing.

There was considerable discussion about how the graduates should receive their hoods. It was finally decided that each row of students would place the hoods on the seniors immediately in front of them, with the marshals hooding the last row. As Chancellor Simpson pronounced the exciting words, "I therefore, declare you bachelors of arts [and, then, of science] of Mary Washington College . . . ," the mass hooding took place. The 244 seniors stood proudly as a wave of applause swept the audience.

In subsequent graduations the practice was changed to have the associate dean of the college and the dean of students hood each student individually just after she had received her diploma and the congratulatory handshake and smile from Chancellor Simpson. This procedure has proved more acceptable and has since been followed.

At the chancellor's convocation each fall, symbolic bachelor's hoods for arts and for sciences are placed in the custody of the president of the senior class and the president of the Student Government Association. The two hoods are then placed on display in the rotunda of the library until the June commencement again involves their use for the entire class.

The class of 1957 requested that its class gift be used to purchase a painting for the college collection. It also suggested that other classes follow this practice.

CHAPTER XX

A Year of Change, 1957–1958

FALL OPENING

Six hundred and twenty-six new students entered the residence halls of Mary Washington College on September 15 to begin their college careers. Of this number, 571 were freshmen and 55 transfers. Later in the week they were joined by 848 returning students. The total enrollment was 1,535, of whom 1,474 were dormitory residents.

Orientation activities began Sunday evening with a welcome from officers of major student organizations. On Monday morning the new students were welcomed by Chancellor Simpson and Dean Alvey. Conferences with faculty advisers followed. That afternoon there were additional sessions with advisers and the administration of placement tests. A party in Monroe gym came after handbook training that evening.

On Saturday afternoon Chancellor and Mrs. Simpson held a reception for freshmen and transfer students at Brompton. This new function took the place of the formal reception that had been held Saturday evening on the roof garden for many years. All members of the faculty and staff, with their wives or husbands, were invited to attend.

NEW PROFESSORS AND NEW COURSES

Returning students in the fall were interested to find fourteen new faculty members, some as replacements for leaves of absences or retirements and others as additions to the teaching staff.

Three new department chairmen were announced by Chancellor Simpson. Dr. Rachel Jane Benton was appointed acting professor and chairman of the physical education department, succeeding Ruth Leonard, who had resigned. Dr. James H. Croushore, a member of the faculty since 1947, was appointed chairman of the English department, succeeding Dr. Shankle, who died after a long illness on May 30, 1957. Dr. Shankle had been head of the English department for twenty-eight years, and he had planned to retire that June. Dr. George E. Luntz was the new chairman of the music department, succeeding Eva Taylor Eppes, who had retired in June.

Dr. Benton came to the faculty from Northwestern University, where she had headed the physical education department for women since 1948. She held the M.A. and Ph.D. from the State University of Iowa.

Dr. Croushore, later to become associate dean (1967) and dean of the college (1971), had come to the faculty in September 1947 from Lehigh University, where he was then teaching. He had previously taught at Mount Union College in Ohio and at Carnegie Institute of Technology. Dr. Croushore had the B.A. and M.A. from Lehigh University and the Ph.D. from Yale University. His specialty was nineteenth-century American fiction.

Under Dr. Croushore's leadership the English department was the first to develop a required reading list for majors in the junior and senior years, the first to require comprehensive examinations, and among the first to make seminar techniques the basis for conducting 400-level courses. Subsequently, the reading lists were abandoned because entering students were more highly selected and had a much richer background of reading.

Other appointments in 1957 included Dr. Daniel H. Woodward as assistant professor of English. He held the B.A. and M.A. degrees from the University of Colorado and soon received the Ph.D. degree from Yale University. He had just returned from England where he had spent the summer completing his dissertation on seventeenth-century English poetry.

Dr. Woodward was to progress rapidly through the academic ranks to a full professorship. In 1964–65 he received a year's leave of absence to go to England for further research on seventeenth-century literature. Upon his return, he continued to teach in the department of English.

After the death of Dr. Quenzel in 1968, Dr. Woodward was named head librarian of the E. Lee Trinkle Library. He assumed the duties in 1969 after a year's leave of absence for graduate study in library administration at The Catholic University of America, where he was awarded an M.S. in library science.

In June 1972 Dr. Woodward left the college to become librarian of the Henry E. Huntington Library and Art Gallery in San Marino, California. His long interest in rare books had greatly enriched the collection of the college. The rare book room was renamed in his honor upon his departure for the **Huntington Library.**

THE NEW CHORUS DIRECTOR

For a time there were both the Glee Club, directed by Marion Chauncey, and an a capella choir, or the Chorus, as it was called later, directed by Eva Taylor Eppes. At the end of the 1955–56 session Miss Chauncey requested to be relieved of the direction of the Glee Club. That fall the Chorus and the Glee Club were merged into a single organization under the direction of Miss Eppes. The name Glee Club was adopted for the combined group. At the end of the session of 1956–57, Miss Eppes retired after thirty-five years on the faculty, having served as head of the music department throughout this period.

A new direction to choral music on the campus was given the following year when Dr. George E. Luntz was appointed acting professor and chairman of the music department.

Dr. Luntz was an accomplished singer and choir director. He had appeared in concert, oratorio, opera, and radio in this country and in concert in Europe. A graduate of the Volkskonservatorium in Vienna, Austria, he held the B.M. and M.M. from the Dana School of Music (now Youngstown University) and a Ph.D. from the State University of Iowa.

The first Christmas concert under Dr. Luntz's direction was presented on Sunday, December 15, at 3:45 P.M. The 90-member chorus performed with members of the Student Organ Guild. The customary candlelight processional and recessional were continued. The selection of songs and the quality of the production were enthusiastically acclaimed.

THE CHORUS

Under Dr. Luntz's capable direction the Chorus became essentially a new organization, known for the excellence of the repertoire, the quality of its rendition, the beauty and faithfulness of tone quality, and the precision of its performance. Many hours of rehearsals went into each performance, but the results justified all efforts that had been expended. Simplicity and unpretentiousness characterized the stage presentations of the new organization. Vestments were abandoned for simple costumes of white shirtwaists and long black skirts. All attention was focused on the effect produced by clear young voices in exquisite harmony.

The Chorus continued the traditional Christmas concert on Sunday afternoon in mid-December and the annual spring concert early in May. Invariably, the musical quality of the selections was high, and their performance technically superb. The reputation of the Chorus spread, and new experiences were in store for the members.

The first of its Christmas concerts, in December 1957, was followed by a trip to Lexington in March, where the Chorus shared a program in the Doremus Gymnasium with the chorus of Washington and Lee University. In April the Chorus joined with the drama and the dance departments in a production of *The Mikado* for the alumnae homecoming. The usual spring concert, this time consisting mainly of sacred music, was presented three weeks later.

The following session the Chorus joined with the University of Virginia Glee Club in the presentation of the seventeenth annual Christmas concert in Cabell Hall on December 16, 1958. The Cathedral Bell Ringers of Virginia presented a prelude of traditional Christmas melodies. Joint concerts with several other universities followed. There were exchange visits with the Georgetown University Glee Club, the University of Richmond Men's Glee Club, and the University of Virginia Glee Club. There were several concerts in the chapels at the Marine Corps base in Quantico and at the Naval Weapons Laboratory in Dahlgren. The chorus was featured in a Lenten service at the Washington Cathedral in March 1961.

A high point of the 1961–62 session was the performance of Berlioz's *Romeo and Juliet* in concert with the Georgetown University Glee Club, under the direction of Paul Hume, and the National Symphony Orchestra, under the direction of Howard Mitchell. Many members of the faculty and students of the college went to Washington on March 13 and 14, 1962. The entire program was recorded and made available to purchasers in a long-playing record album. Reviews were complimentary of the quality of the performance by the sixty-nine-voice group from Mary Washington.

Later that month the first of two concerts was given at the National Gallery of Art in Washington. One of these was a performance of Pergolesi's *Stabat Mater* with the National Gallery Orchestra. The *Stabat Mater* was also presented in George Washington auditorium at Mary Washington.

Three concerts were given at the Pan-American Union in

Washington, two of them in observance of the annual Pan-American Week celebration. The latter were taped and used for subsequent broadcasts from New York.

A review of the 1963 Pan-American Union concert appeared in the Washington *Post* for April 19, 1963, headed "Pan-American Audience Enthusiastic: Mary Washington Chorus Colorful." The review read, in part:

> The Mary Washington Chorus has a full rich sound that is expressive and unusually flexible. Its members can sing moving pianissimos and yet are never timid about projecting solid forte tones.
>
> They have a good sense of pitch and tend to flat only when the tessituras are too high for the sopranos.
>
> It is a credit to their excellent director, George Luntz, that they are well-schooled in the technical aspects of diction, tone production, and phrasing.

In April 1965 the Chorus gave a concert in the auditorium of the Folger Shakespeare Library in Washington. This unique theatre provided an unforgettable setting for the program of largely sacred selections, which concluded with Shakespeare's "Under the Greenwood Tree" and "When Daisies Pied."

One of the away-from-home concerts was presented at Homewood, Baltimore, when the Chorus joined with the orchestra and the glee club of the Johns Hopkins University for a joint program in May 1966. There have been a number of concerts at the Washington Cathedral. During 1970-71 the Chorus also sang at the Pan-American Union in Washington and at the United States Marine Corps Memorial Chapel in Quantico. There were also the usual Christmas and spring concerts at MWC.

In 1960 the music department was accredited by the National Association of Schools of Music. It has maintained a fully accredited curriculum with a variety of courses to meet students' interests and needs. There has been a marked upgrading of standards, including qualifying examinations to take work for credit and jury examinations in applied music each semester. Many graduates of the department of music have successfully pursued graduate study. None has ever been turned down for admission. Alumnae are now engaged in school, college, or private teaching, in church music, or in professional performance.

Dr. Luntz retired in June 1972. Edwin M. Matthias, a new appointee to the music department, took over the direction of the Chorus the following session.

CHANGES IN STUDENT REGULATIONS

The thirty-fourth edition of the handbook appeared with the familiar blue and white cover. However, it was no longer the *Bayonet;* it had been retitled simply *Student Handbook.*

Much more than the title had been changed. There were numerous instances of liberalization or elimination of more restrictive regulations governing student life at the college. For example, lights-out times for sophomores, juniors, and seniors were abolished; freshmen were to have their lights out by midnight except on Saturdays. The specific study-hour quiet period —7:30 P.M. to 10:15 P.M. Monday through Friday, which had been in effect since the early normal school days—was discontinued entirely. Consideration for others was urged as the guiding principle to be observed.

In fact, increased freedom with increased responsibility was characteristic of all of the changes in regulations. Removal of restrictions on trips to town, on drinking at Quantico, on walking with dates on campus, and on other facets of college life had as their basic principle a broader extension of the individual student's responsibilities for her own conduct as well as a recognition of consideration for others as a guide to acceptable standards of dormitory living. This was emphasized in preschool conferences of student leaders and in freshman orientation sessions.

Chancellor Simpson reiterated his belief in obedience to the "unenforceable," an acceptance of the necessity of responsible conduct where regulations give opportunity for free exercise of initiative and self-government.

Equally welcome to both old and new students was a change in regulations that eliminated assigned seats and attendance checking at convocations, assemblies, and student body meetings. Attendance was still "compulsory" for the greatly reduced number of assemblies and convocations. Once again, students were asked to show their willingness to accept responsibility for their own attendance at these gatherings.

Students rejoiced in permission to smoke in Seacobeck after meals. The serving of coffee at dinner added greatly to postprandial conversation and offered an opportunity for welcome relaxation before academic assignments for the following day were undertaken.

NEW CUT SYSTEM

A new cut system was put into effect the second semester. It allowed all students at least as many cuts in a course as there were class meetings a week. For students with a B average (C for seniors) maximum cuts were allowed, which meant that they could miss up to one-fourth of the total class meetings.

In announcing the new cut system, Dean Alvey emphasized that it placed upon the student much greater responsibility for her own class attendance and for keeping up with the work of each course.[1] Absences immediately before or after a holiday would count as two class cuts.

ACADEMIC DEVELOPMENTS

At the October meeting of the faculty Mrs. Bolling, chairman of the admissions policy committee, presented the committee's report revising the regulations governing academic probation and suspension.[2] The chief recommendation was to substitute quality-point deficiency for quality ratio as a means of determining academic standing and to discontinue the practice of deducting quality points for failed courses unless the course was subsequently repeated and passed. The new regulations were adopted by the faculty and incorporated in the next catalogue under the heading "Academic Probation and Scholastic Achievement Necessary to Remain in College."

Of the various committees functioning under the new setup perhaps the most active was the curriculum committee, which usually met as often as twice a month, or, on occasion, weekly, to examine various proposals for new courses and changes in degree requirements. It met with the various departments to hear outlines of content for courses to be incorporated in the revised degree requirements. At various evening sessions the committee met, successively, with the departments of mathematics, philosophy, art, music, and dramatic arts.

In November the faculty heard a report by Dean Alvey, chairman of the curriculum committee, giving the committee's unanimous proposal of a change in degree requirements. Under the new plan students would take six credits in mathematics or

[1] *Bullet,* Oct. 11, 1957. [2] Faculty Minutes, Oct. 14, 1957.

philosophy and six in fine arts (music, art, or dramatic arts).[3] The change separated fine arts from its previous place as a choice with mathematics and added dramatic arts to music and art in the fine arts requirements.

The course in mathematical concepts, ordinarily taken to meet degree requirements, stressed fundamental concepts instead of detailed manipulations. The problems in philosophy course was based on problems in the history of thought.

The new organization of requirements included a breakdown into specific areas of the courses in language and literature, natural science, fine arts, and history and social science. The six credits in health and physical education were shown as additional to the 120 semester hours of academic subjects required for a degree, rather than as an integral part of the total 126. After considerable discussion the new requirements were adopted without a dissenting vote and put into effect for the next entering class in September 1958.

The committee on programs for superior students, with Dr. Quenzel as chairman, prepared a mimeographed statement on requirements for honors programs. It also conducted a series of meetings with various departments concerning their plans for stimulating programs for superior students. As an outgrowth of these meetings, the history department introduced a new reading course. The English department began to require that majors read, by the end of their junior year, ten titles from a carefully selected list and an equal number by the end of the senior year. Students were required to demonstrate by oral examination their familiarity with the books they had read.

At its January meeting the faculty adopted a proposal of the admissions policy committee requiring all applicants for admission for the academic year 1958–59 to take the Scholastic Aptitude Test (morning program) of the College Entrance Examination Board.[4]

INCREASED TUITION FEES

The tuition fees were also increased. The general college fee for all students was raised $25.00, and the out-of-state extra tuition charge was raised from $170.00 to $182.50 per semester. Thus the total charge for a resident of Virginia became $855.00 for the ses-

[3] *Ibid.*, Nov. 11, 1957.   [4] *Ibid.*, Jan. 13, 1958, Appendix H.

sion; for a nonresident of the state, it became $1,220.00. Chancellor Simpson explained that additional funds created by these new charges would be used to increase all teachers' salaries and would enable Mary Washington "to maintain a high standard of academic instruction."

At its final meeting of the year the faculty adopted a recommendation of the committee on programs for superior students and established a new recognition of academic excellence. Students achieving a 2.75 grade-point average in their freshman and sophomore years would be awarded intermediate honors, and students attaining a similar average in their junior and senior years would receive final honors. These programs have proved effective in stimulating high achievement. Certificates of intermediate honors have been awarded to four or five students each fall at the chancellor's convocation, and final honors to a dozen or more graduates at commencement. The names of these students have been starred in the list of graduates.

The committee also recommended that the academic average for the dean's list be raised from a B (2.00) average with no grade below C to a B+ (2.50) average.[5] The proposal was adopted. The number of students usually on this honor roll dropped from 290–300 to 90–100. The dean's list of honor students was first published in 1934–35. Copies were sent to all high schools in Virginia and to every out-of-state high school having graduates attending Mary Washington. In addition, news stories were sent to local papers in the home community of each student honored by inclusion on the dean's list.

At the conclusion of his first full session in office, Chancellor Simpson complimented the faculty on adopting the program for recognizing superior academic achievement. He thanked the committees in general, and the curriculum and the academic counseling and guidance committees in particular, for their constructive work. Chancellor Simpson also called attention to funds available for faculty research and announced that the governor had approved a plan of professional leave for graduate study that provided payment of an amount not exceeding half the salary of each recipient for the period of the leave.[6]

This program has been of great value in upgrading the academic preparation of the faculty. It provided an incentive to young members of the faculty to complete their Ph.D. programs. In the decade 1961–70 thirty instructors participated in this leave

[5] *Ibid.*, May 12, 1958. [6] *Ibid.*

program, with salary expenditures ranging from $6,900 in 1961–62 through a high of $26,750 in 1968–69 to $21,750 in 1970–71. Expenditures for faculty leaves of absences with half pay for advanced study or research totaled $158,665 for the ten-year period ending in 1971. Aids for research other than salary totaled $23,876.[7]

NEW CONSTRUCTION

Bids on a new science hall were opened on September 24, 1957. Chancellor Simpson revealed that they were well within the $725,000 appropriated by the Commonwealth of Virginia for the new structure. It had been decided to defer the construction of observatory and greenhouse features until some later time.

The new building faced toward the city reservoir, which in a short time would be removed to a better location. The area in front of the building would be devoted, in part, to parking space and an extensive lawn. Later, tall poles bearing the flags of Virginia and of the nation were erected in the center of this grassy area, which, with the two new dormitories, created a new quadrangle east of George Washington Hall.

Bids for a new 144-room dormitory, designed to eliminate the use of the rented apartment building known as Cornell Hall, were opened on January 21, 1958. The new building, later named Bushnell Hall, faced the science hall then under construction. Plans for removing the reservoir and clearing and grading the site were being made.

THE SECURITY FORCE

In the early years of the college there was little need for police protection. The school was small and constituted a closely knit community. Men like Eugene Curtis and others on the grounds staff kept their eyes open for suspicious-looking individuals. The dormitories were locked at night. In the early thirties Curtis's son, Jack, was employed for a time as a night watchman. He was not a regular police officer and simply sought the aid of the Fredericksburg police if assistance was needed.

[7] Self-Study Report, 1971, pp. 276–78.

The first regularly commissioned police officer was Clifton H. Reeves, known to every student as Pat, who entered the employment of the college in 1939 and remained as a special police officer until his retirement in September 1964. During his twenty-five years of service, Reeves gave close attention to his duties. He kept an eye on the campus and saw that undesirable visitors were kept out. He was assisted by Robert Humphries, a former employee of the heating plant, who was assigned duty as night watchman and checked certain stations in various buildings. Reeves's picture in full uniform appeared in the *Battlefield* regularly during the 1940s and '50s. He died on May 12, 1967, less than three years after his retirement.

When the extensive building program was begun in 1950-51, it became necessary to increase the security force. William Jordan and William Chewning joined the staff. By 1956 there were four special officers. Of this group, only Chewning was still a member of the staff in 1972, a veteran of over twenty years of service to the college.

Police protection at the college entered a new era in January 1958 with the appointment of Medford D. Haynes to head what became known as the college security force. A former officer of the Fredericksburg police, Chief Haynes proceeded to reorganize and enlarge the force and to extend its sphere of activity to encompass many aspects of service to the college community.

Since 1958 the force of three full-time officers and one part-time has been increased to eight full-time men. There are now two radio-equipped patrol cars tied in with dispatchers both at the headquarters of the city police and at the college security office. Instant radio contact is provided via the college switchboard with the officers on duty. There is close cooperation with city police, as each car can receive the radio telephone messages from another.

The security force provides around-the-clock protection for thirty-six buildings and twenty-two hundred students. From 5:00 P.M. until 2:00 A.M., two patrol cars are in constant operation. Each car averages about a hundred miles a day. Each stays in constant touch by radio telephone with the night-time dispatcher, who is on duty until 7:00 A.M.

Chief Haynes believes that preventive measures are better than punishing wrongdoers. The presence of a constant patrol on the college driveways and immediately adjacent streets does much to discourage prowlers and keep loiterers away. In 1958 there were

104 arrests by college police, primarily involving prowling around dormitories, peeping toms, and indecent exposure. In 1971 there were fewer than twenty arrests, including traffic violations. The program of preventive patrols has paid off in reducing offenses and making the campus safer.

Currently, the security force renders important service in letting students into their dormitories. Doors are locked at midnight on Sundays through Thursdays and at 2:00 A.M. on Fridays and Saturdays. If a student wishes to enter her residence hall after that time, she goes to the security office, signs for a key to her residence hall (the time is carefully noted), and calls back in twenty minutes from her resident hall extension to confirm her arrival. If she does not call within that time, a college police officer is dispatched immediately to that dormitory to see if anything has happened.

Traffic control is a large job, especially when special events are held on campus. In January 1972 there were 684 student cars registered, over half of which had campus parking privileges. There were 530 faculty and staff parking permits, for a total of over 1,200 cars for the 475 spaces available on campus. The security force also operates a motor pool of eleven college cars for official use of faculty and staff, and sees that transportation, with driver, to and from airports is provided if needed.

In 1972 the modern concept of the police as a security and protective force has made the campus a safer place, even with many times the number of students and buildings to be safeguarded. The force is also a public relations agency for the college, as many visitors to the campus on Sundays and holidays will agree.

FALL EVENTS

The second annual contemporary art exhibition opened on November 1, 1957, with a reception for the faculty, administration, and invited guests. Again, art critics from the metropolitan newspapers praised the quality of the exhibition, limited to fifty paintings carefully selected by a college committee headed by Julien Binford.

On October 17 and 18, Mrs. John C. Lang, national treasurer of Mortar Board, visited the college and reviewed with representatives of Cap and Gown and officials of the college the petition for establishing at Mary Washington a chapter of the national senior honorary society.

CHRISTMAS COMES TO THE CAMPUS

Christmas decorations were as elaborate as usual. In Seacobeck stood the traditional huge Christmas tree in the Dome Room, decorated with hundreds of colored balls. Poinsettias on the individual tables and bright red candles surrounded by holly leaves on the serving tables gave a festive look to the entire dining hall.

In Ann Carter Lee there was a silver tree trimmed completely in blue and silver. Dormitory decorations were varied and colorful. First place winner was Randolph Hall, with scenes from China, Holland, Germany, and the United States, thus carrying out the theme of "Christmas around the World." Mason adopted "The Spirit of Giving" as its theme. Underneath a brightly lit tree was a large assortment of gifts and used clothing collected for a needy Fredericksburg family adopted by the dormitory.

Christmas carols echoed over the campus in the late afternoon from the loudspeakers of the public address system atop George Washington Hall. Caroling groups entertained each other with dormitory serenades. The senior class, in caps and gowns, made its usual caroling tour of nearby residences of college administrators, brightening the hearts of deans and chancellor as they stood in doorways to enjoy the soft voices singing in the clear winter air.

FIFTIETH ANNIVERSARY

The fiftieth anniversary of the founding of the college was celebrated with a formal convocation at 11:00 A.M. on March 14, 1958, exactly fifty years to the day after the act establishing the institution was passed by the General Assembly of Virginia. All classes were dismissed for the occasion, and the entire faculty and student body gathered for an impressive program.

The academic procession began with the senior class, led by the president-elect of the Student Government Association and the president of the Honor Council. Members of the faculty, administrative officials, and the official party, each in cap and gown, marched slowly into the auditorium of George Washington Hall. The faculty and staff took their seats among the tiers of chairs that nearly filled the stage, while active participants in the exercises were seated in arm chairs just behind the footlights. Chancellor Simpson presided, flanked by the governor and a former governor of Virginia.

After the invocation by the Reverend Thomas G. Faulkner, Jr., rector of St. George's Episcopal Church, and the singing of the national anthem, greetings to the college on its fiftieth anniversary were conveyed from the Commonwealth of Virginia by the Honorable J. Lindsay Almond, Jr., governor of Virginia; from the Mary Washington College Alumnae Association by Mrs. Peter D. Stokes, president; and from the Student Government Association by Evelyn H. Breeden, president.

The address of the occasion was delivered by Mrs. J. Lindsay Almond, Jr., described in the program as "The First Lady of Virginia." Mrs. Almond entitled her remarks: "Looking at Mary Washington College through Three Doorways—the Doorway of Yesterday or History; the Doorway of Today or Accomplishment; the Doorway of Tomorrow or Hope." The text of her address is preserved in the college archives.

The fiftieth anniversary convocation then proceeded to honor the founder of the college, C. O'Conor Goolrick. In an informal but warm and at times moving manner, Colgate W. Darden, Jr., president of the University of Virginia, delivered "A Tribute to a Founder." He spoke authoritatively of Mr. Goolrick's role in the session of the General Assembly that established the college, and of the successful legislative struggle that he had waged. Darden spoke admiringly of Goolrick's personal qualities. "He has a good mind, unimpeachable character, the courage of his convictions, and the willingness to express them when the situation arises. . . . These endowments . . . insure for him a place in any company of distinguished Virginians." President Darden then presented Goolrick to the assembly. The standing ovation that followed was long and thunderous. Finally, in a voice choked with feeling, Mr. Goolrick acknowledged briefly his appreciation of the tribute that had been paid him.

The program closed with the singing of the alma mater, followed by the recessional, led by Governor Almond and former governor Darden. As other members of the official party, the administrative staff, the faculty, and the senior class, all in academic regalia marched slowly out of the auditorium, there was general agreement that it had been a historic occasion.

A feature of the twelve-page program of the Founder's Day celebration is the complete text of Goolrick's brief history of the college, reprinted from the 1944 *Battlefield*.

The observance of Founder's Day continued with a concert that evening by the Pittsburgh Symphony Orchestra, under the direction of William Steinberg. The *Free Lance–Star* on March 15

A Year of Change

described the interest in the performance by this "wonderful orchestra": "Sensing that this was to be a rare event, an audience filled every seat in the large auditorium five minutes before the scheduled opening of the concert."

On Saturday evening the Emerald Ball, a formal affair, was held in the Gothic Room of Ann Carter Lee Hall, with music by Les Elgart's Orchestra. A duo-piano recital by Ann Farquhar Hamer and Jean Slater Edson, presented Sunday afternoon in the Little Theatre of duPont Hall, concluded the festivities of the weekend.

The Alumnae Association also celebrated the fiftieth anniversary with a Golden Anniversary Banquet, held in the Rose Room of Seacobeck Hall on April 12. Mrs. Peter D. Copes, president of the association, presided and introduced honored guests. The main address was given by President Colgate W. Darden, Jr., who was presented by Chancellor Simpson. A surprise feature of the celebration was a huge birthday cake, which Chancellor Simpson and Mrs. Copes joined in cutting.

VISITING SPEAKERS

Dr. Arnold J. Toynbee spoke at a formal convocation on Tuesday, April 22. His topic was "The Historian: His Inspiration and His Problems." As usual, the library had a display of Dr. Toynbee's publications, including various editions of *A Study of History*.

Among other speakers appearing during the session were Dr. Leonard Carmichael, director of the Smithsonian Institution; John Scott, of *Time* magazine; Ordway Tead, writer on higher education; Vera Brittain, English author; five visiting lecturers from Harvard University; and professors from Princeton, Pennsylvania, Yale, Wisconsin, North Carolina, Pennsylvania State, and other outstanding universities, who spoke to interest groups in the several fields of their specialization.

BERMUDA TRIP

The spring Bermuda trip, sponsored by the junior class to raise money for its Ring Dance, was patronized enthusiastically. Students went by college bus to Washington where they enplaned for the four-hour flight. Accommodations had been arranged at the

Bermudiana Hotel, with three or four girls sharing a room. Planned tours, cruises, water-skiing, and "a tea dance every afternoon" plus shopping and sunning, insured an eventful five-day visit.

MAY DAY—A PAGEANT OF GROWTH

May Day 1958 continued the observance of the fiftieth anniversary of the college, featuring a "Pageant of Growth." The program was a cooperative undertaking of the music and drama departments. The college orchestra, under the direction of Ronald Faulkner, furnished the music; Albert Klein, of the drama department, wrote and staged the program.

A reception by the May Court in the Golden Horseshoe followed. That evening there was a dance in the Gothic Room for all of the visitors. The college dance orchestra furnished the music.

THE MARCHING BAND DISBANDS

On May, 2, 1958, the *Bullet* announced that the Mary Washington College Marching Band was being discontinued and that a concert band would be developed to succeed it. Thus ended the career of the marching group which, since its organization in 1940 under the direction of Ronald W. Faulkner, had won many awards and prizes.

With a tinge of sadness, the *Bullet* reporter remarked that the familiar marching song of the band, "Let's raise a cheer for Mary Washington," would no longer be heard as the uniformed group with its majorettes marched proudly through the campus. However, times had changed, and the colorful procession of musicians all in step had become too commonplace an event by 1958. No longer was a marching band, even an all-girl band, distinctive as when Ron Faulkner started the organization eighteen years before and taught it the intricate maneuvers that so enthralled spectators at football games where the MWC Band was featured between halves. What is now characteristic of practically every football game was a distinct novelty thirty years ago when the carefully rehearsed formations and designs of Faulkner's marching musicians won both admiration and awards.

COMMENCEMENT

Commencement activities for 1958 began with the senior farewell dance on Saturday evening, May 31. On Sunday morning the baccalaureate sermon was delivered by the Reverend Douglas Horton, A.B., B.D., D.D., Litt.D., LL.D., dean of the Harvard Divinity School. Chancellor and Mrs. Simpson held their garden party for graduates and their families and friends that afternoon from five to seven.

The commencement address was given by Mrs. Oswald B. Lord, A.B., LL.D., L.H.D., member of the United States delegation to the United Nations General Assembly. As usual, the speaker was the house guest of the Simpsons at Brompton.

Following the practice begun by the graduating class in 1957, the class of 1958 chose a painting from the MWC contemporary art exhibition for its gift to the college. *North African Village,* a painting by Norman Rubington, was selected by a nine-student committee.

It had been an eventful year for faculty and for students. New academic policies, new student regulations, new faculty appointments, and new construction on the campus made the second full session of the new chancellor a period of development on a wide scale. It was obvious that the college was on its way to a fuller realization of the meaning of a liberal education so earnestly sought by Dr. Simpson. Through his skillful leadership, the progress made was a shared activity in which administrative staff, faculty, and student body all had a part.

Later in June, Chancellor and Mrs. Simpson accepted an invitation to attend the institute for new presidents held at the Harvard Graduate School of Business Administration. Mary Washington College was honored to be represented at this selective eight-day institute.

CHAPTER XXI

Continuing Growth, 1958–1960

A NEW SESSION BEGINS

THE 1958–59 session began with the fifth annual preschool conference held from Thursday through Saturday before the opening of college. Chancellor Simpson and Associate Dean Whidden presented "An Academic Colloquy," Dean Alvey spoke on "The Honor System as an Ideal," and there were numerous panel discussions and conferences. Arranged by Dean Hargrove and SGA representatives, the conference was attended by members of the Student Council, freshmen counselors, presidents of major organizations, class officers, dormitory presidents, and head residents of the various dormitories.

On Sunday, September 14, over six hundred new students arrived. A buffet luncheon in Seacobeck was the first official activity. That evening there was group singing in the outdoor amphitheater. Orientation activities began Monday morning with an assembly in George Washington Hall. Chancellor Simpson greeted the new students. Dean Alvey spoke on the subject, "College Ahead—A Forward Look." Meetings of students with their faculty advisers followed during the morning and afternoon. The first of a series of handbook counseling sessions began at 5:00 P.M.

Returning students were thrilled with a number of changes in handbook regulations. Students were permitted to smoke in Seacobeck at dinner. Bermuda shorts could be worn in Ann Carter Lee between 2:00 and 5:00 P.M. on weekdays. The number of overnights a student could spend away from the campus permitted freshmen during the first semester was increased to nine, with unlimited overnights thereafter if a C average was maintained.

Other orientation activities included an SGA–Honor Council assembly on "Freedom and Responsibility," a college traditions assembly sponsored by Cap and Gown, a student panel program on "Your College Life Is What You Make It," a Big Sister–Little Sister picnic on Saturday afternoon followed by a square dance that evening, and Big–Little Sister Church Day Sunday morning. Sunday afternoon Chancellor and Mrs. Simpson were hosts at a garden party for all new students and faculty at Brompton.

Continuing Growth 411

The second week's activities included the SGA handbook test, the conclusion of honor code training, a Loyalty Night assembly, the Y Penny Carnival, and an informal dance Saturday night in the Gothic Room.

CHANCELLOR'S CONVOCATION

The session of 1958–59 marked the first chancellor's convocation "to establish a tradition of academic excellence at the opening of the college year." On Thursday, September 18, the entire faculty marched in full academic regalia for a formal convocation in George Washington Hall. The subject of the chancellor's address was "The Pursuit of Excellence." Copies were duplicated and given to interested students and faculty members. The text of the address was published later in the bulletin of the Association of American Colleges.[1]

For the first time citations of intermediate honors were presented by Dean Alvey to five students who had maintained a 2.75 grade average for their first two years. The idea of such a convocation originated with the committee on public occasions, which announced at the time that it would be held annually.

CONCERTS, PLAYS, AND A NEW SWITCHBOARD

The concert series for 1958–59 featured the Ballet Russe de Monte Carlo; John Gielgud in a program of excerpts from Shakespearean plays; and the Wagner Opera Company's Production of *La Bohème*.

The 1958–59 season of the Mary Washington Players opened with *Gigi*. Other productions during the year, directed alternately by Mark Sumner and Albert R. Klein, were *The Man Who Came to Dinner, The Tender Trap,* and *Lute Song*.

A new switchboard telephone system was placed in operation on September 1, 1958. Some 135 telephones and 165 extensions now provided telephone coverage for all dormitories and offices, replacing the 45 separate telephones previously used. Six operators worked on shifts to man the new switchboard.

[1] "The Pursuit of Excellence," Association of American Colleges *Bulletin* 44 (1958): 567–70.

DORMITORY DECORATIONS

Dormitory decorations during the Christmas season were an integral part of the preholiday activities. Each year they became more elaborate, and the competition among the residence halls became keener. In 1958 first place was awarded to Cornell Hall by a committee of judges consisting of Dr. James H. Croushore, Pauline King, and Claudia Read. In reporting the results of the competition, the *Bullet* on December 12 characterized the decorations as the most elaborate in years. Hours and hours were devoted to selecting a theme, planning the display, and actually making and arranging the models and materials used.

Perhaps the best idea of these projects can be gained from the *Bullet*'s description of the parlor decorations in the various dormitories:

Cornell's theme is "Christmas Underwater." Grey and white gauze hangs over Neptune's throne in the parlor. Presents are placed in a treasure chest surrounded by cellophane jellyfish, blue lights, shells, and a driftwood branch hung with silver bells, blue balls, and tinsel.

Virginia dorm has chosen the "Golden Glory Christmas" for their theme. Their tree is decorated with gold balls and tinsel. A Nativity scene is placed on the desk, and mistletoe, and holly carry out the theme.

Ball's theme is "Snowbound." Three trees decorate the parlor—one huge tree in the center, and two in front of the windows. Two snowmen guard the center tree and white banks of snow cascade around the railing. Blue lights and snowflakes carry out their theme.

An "Old Fashioned Christmas" is Westmoreland's theme. The tree is decorated with popcorn, cookies, paper chains, and lace doilies, which the girls made themselves. A sleigh sits on the front porch, and a spinning wheel is placed next to a fireplace hung with stockings. Carolers and children complete the picture.

Ann Fairfax Hall is decorated like a home. A red and silver tree, holly on the mantel, and stockings hung from the railing interpret the theme.

Mason's theme of "Gold, Frankincense and Myrrh" is explained with a red tree trimmed in gold. Silhouettes of the three wise men and red and gold crowns are placed in the parlor. A tree with the nativity scene stands in the small parlor.

At the entrance to Randolph stand two pink angels telling their theme of "Hark the Herald Angels Sing." Two trees trimmed in silver and angel hair stand in the parlor. A pink angel watches over the Christ Child, proclaiming "Glory to the Newborn King."

Framar is using the theme of "I'll be Home for Christmas." The

Continuing Growth

dorm is decorated as a home with a tree and packages, stockings, and a basket of greenery on the door.

Trench Hill has used pipe cleaner men playing down the bannister, and a beautifully trimmed tree.

Willard girls have taken "Christmas Carols" for their theme. Their tree has been decorated in blue and silver. A choir of angels stands in front of a stained glass screen, and another angel stands on the porch roof. The girls carried out their theme on their doors, and every third window spells out "Rejoice."

Betty Lewis features gold angels on the door, a tree in the center of the parlor, and mistletoe and holly in the entry.

Marye Hall's theme is the "Nutcracker Suite" and each door is decorated with a part of the story.

In Seacobeck the traditional Christmas tree stands in the Dome Room with other decorations on the tables and chairs. An added bit of interest are the trees and decorations in the east and west entrances.

On campus trees are lighted; at Ann Carter Lee Christmas music is played over a loud speaker in addition to music from George Washington Hall.

ACADEMIC DEVELOPMENTS

The session of 1958–59 was a period of further progress toward the attainment of the goal of becoming a liberal arts college with high academic standards of admission, achievement, and graduation.

At the opening faculty meeting Chancellor Simpson referred to "The Pursuit of Excellence" as the keynote of this academic year. He said that he expected all members of the faculty not only to teach classes for the full period at the scheduled time and to submit grades promptly but also to require a "considerable amount of written work in addition to term papers and, wherever feasible, to require the reading of material beyond that included in textbooks or needed in preparing term papers."[2]

At the October meeting the faculty approved a recommendation of the curriculum committee that a third-year college level foreign language course (a 200-level literature course), or its equivalent in proficiency, be required for either the B.A. or the B.S. degree at Mary Washington, effective with the class entering in the fall of 1959.[3] At the same meeting, the faculty adopted the recommendation of the admissions policy committee that the college require thirteen academic units for admission instead of

[2] Faculty Minutes, Sept. 15, 1958.   [3] *Ibid.*, Oct. 13, 1958.

eleven and that two of the thirteen units be in foreign language.

In the course of the consideration of these new requirements, it was shown that 95.4 percent of the students entering in the fall of 1958 had offered credit for two or more years of foreign language study for admission. Hence, it was felt that "the requirement of an intermediate and an advanced course in foreign language would impose no undue hardship on a great majority of the students and would encourage them to continue the foreign language they had already studied in high school to the extent that some real proficiency is attained." [4]

A major portion of the March meeting of the faculty was devoted to an explanation of the honors program at the University of Virginia. Dr. B. F. D. Runk, dean of the university, and Dean Robert Kent Gooch, chairman of the university committee on honors for twenty-five years, described the program in operation there and answered many questions about the full-time tutorial B.A. in honors and the liberal arts seminars at the university.

The faculty also voted to recommend that the Graduate Record Examination, both area test and advanced test, be given to all nontransfer seniors for a four-year period beginning with the spring of 1960.

An interdepartmental major in Foreign Service had been under consideration for some time. At the April meeting of the faculty the curriculum committee unanimously recommended that it be approved. Considerable discussion followed the distribution by Dr. Kurt F. Leidecker of a ten-page outline of purposes, course requirements, and opportunities for graduates with such a major. By a close margin the faculty adopted the proposal. Before the May faculty meeting the curriculum committee made some changes in the requirements in light of the faculty discussion and changed the title to Pre-Foreign Service interdepartmental major. These changes were approved by the faculty. Subsequently, Dr. Leidecker was designated as the adviser for the new major.

It developed in the next few years that the interest in such a program had not been overestimated. The Pre-Foreign Service major took its place among the popular programs of study in the college. Contacts with the Foreign Service in Washington and with the diplomatic missions of foreign countries provided rich experiences for the majors in this field. Dr. Leidecker continued to serve as program adviser.

As the faculty concluded its last meeting of the year, Dean

---

[4] Letter of Dean to Members of Faculty, Oct. 1, 1958.

Alvey announced that the place of meeting would be transferred in the fall to a large lecture room in the new science building. This ended a series of historic faculty assemblies in the Little Theatre of duPont Hall.

ACADEMIC COUNSELING AND GUIDANCE

As associate dean of the college, Dr. Whidden was in charge of academic counseling. He worked closely with the committee on academic counseling and guidance, the policy-making group of the faculty, in planning orientation programs, advisory services, counseling interviews, and other features of the program that ultimately developed.

Orientation activities became a faculty-administration service early in 1943 when Mrs. John C. Russell, then Margaret Swander, who was director of student personnel, organized the first systematic program. Emphasis was placed upon a two- or three-day orientation session, followed by weekly meetings for freshmen during the fall semester, at which student leaders or faculty members spoke. Juniors and seniors, and later members of the faculty, were used to advise students on their selection of courses prior to registration and to assist in their adjustment to college life.

Building upon this foundation, Dr. Whidden proceeded to expand and develop the advisory services, notably by using members of the faculty more extensively as advisers and by outlining a program of activity for them. The academic counseling program was developed gradually over a period of several years, with the active cooperation of both students and faculty.

FRESHMAN HANDBOOK

One of Dr. Whidden's first projects was a handbook for new students, which supplanted the freshman issue of the *Bullet* previously sent to new students before their arrival.

Among the Columns was the title of the new publication, first mailed to entering students before the beginning of the 1956–57 session. Attractively illustrated with cartoons and drawings, the thirty-page booklet gave practical information on what to bring for one's room and one's college wardrobe, as well as descriptions of the major student organizations and campus traditions. It was published by the Student Government Association.

Frequent revisions kept *Among the Columns* up to date. The last revision was in 1966. The distribution of the freshman guidebook was discontinued when the publication of a much more comprehensive student handbook was begun.

A SURVEY OF PRACTICES

During December and January of the 1958-59 session, Dr. Whidden made a study of academic guidance programs in other institutions similar to Mary Washington. In Virginia he visited Sweet Briar, Randolph-Macon Woman's College, Longwood, Madison, Radford, Westhampton, and William and Mary. A trip to northeastern colleges took him to Hood, Goucher, Vassar, Mount Holyoke, and Connecticut College for Women.

Dr. Whidden made a report on his trip at the January meeting of the faculty. He emphasized that everywhere he found the conviction that the faculty must bear the primary responsibility for academic counseling.[5]

Through a study of methods employed at other institutions the committee on academic counseling and guidance sought to develop a system of academic counseling that would best benefit the individual student. The purpose of the program, according to Dr. Whidden, was to offer sufficient guidance to prevent the student from making mistakes that would result from lack of necessary or needed assistance without making her dependent upon the adviser or failing to take responsibility for planning her own program.

THE NEW ADVISORY PROGRAM

The salient features of the advisory program as it finally developed were: (1) the assignment of a faculty adviser to each new student, preferably one from her proposed major field of study, if indicated on her application; (2) the preparation of a folder of information about each advisee, including high school record, test scores, and other data, and the distribution of these folders to advisers in advance; (3) individual conferences between the adviser and his advisees on the day before registration, so that the adviser could plan the selection of classes and initial the tentative

---

[5] Faculty Minutes, Jan. 12, 1959.

Continuing Growth 417

schedule as having his approval; and (4) a series of meetings of advisers with their advisory groups, usually eight to ten freshmen, at intervals during the session.

The program involved the use of most of the faculty as advisers. It was kept on an optional basis, but there was usually little difficulty in obtaining the seventy-five or eighty persons needed to keep the student-adviser ratio relatively small.

On the day before students arrived, a meeting of faculty advisers was held to distribute folders, make room assignments for conferences with advisees, and give final instructions. Other training sessions were held as needed.

The publication of a faculty advisers' handbook aided materially the development and functioning of the program. First published in 1960, it was revised periodically to provide the latest information on degree requirements, major programs, typical schedules for freshmen, referral services, requirements for teachers' certificates, and other needed data. A most valuable part of the handbook was a detailed outline of "procedures with advisees," listed chronologically as the session progressed with the dates upon which advisers were to make certain reports on their students. Forms were prepared and printed for this purpose.

Any change of classes or schedules had to be approved first by the faculty adviser. He received copies of all student reports, both deficiencies and term grades, and scheduled individual conferences as necessary.

Another innovation was Major Counseling Night, held usually in April. At that time, representatives of each department were available for conferences with students interested in a possible major. Rooms were assigned to each department, and a directory was given freshmen and sophomores. Some departments served refreshments, and on one occasion, the mathematics department was accused of undue proselytizing when a large bowl of punch, surrounded by cookies, met the eager glance of prospective majors.

By the end of the sophomore year, each student was required to declare her major officially and to file and obtain permission to major from the department in which she was interested. From then on, academic counseling became the responsibility of a member of the student's major department. If not the same adviser that the student had had previously, the folder of information, with all accumulated reports, records, and other information, was passed on to the new adviser.

This system continued in operation until the fall of 1971, when assistant deans for counseling and divisional advisers were appointed. At this time the number of faculty advisers was reduced to about thirty.

TRADE BOOK STORE OPENS

Early in 1959 Chancellor Simpson announced that a trade book store would be opened in the alcove next to the College Shoppe. He pointed out that the support of both students and faculty would be necessary to make the project a success. A questionnaire survey made by the committee on programs for superior students indicated that 496 out of the 515 students replying would be willing to support such a store. Beginning modestly in 1959, the bookstore has developed into an integral part of the intellectual life of the campus. A faculty committee has assisted in suggesting worthwhile publications in paperback form that could be purchased inexpensively by students. Prizes have been offered for the best student collection of books on a particular subject or theme, and for the best general collections assembled by a freshman and by a senior.

Currently the college bookstore stocks over three thousand titles, grouped by subject in a spacious room on the ground floor of Ann Carter Lee, formerly occupied by the modern dance studio. Although under the same management as the textbook and college supplies section, it is actually a distinctive part of the operation, with emphasis on building a personal library of readings other than required college textbooks.

Interest in book collecting has continued to grow. During the second semester of the 1971–72 session the library sponsored a book-collecting contest with prizes of thirty, twenty, and ten dollars' worth of books of the students' choice to be obtained from or ordered by the college bookstore. Entries were judged on the quality of the collection, rather than the number or market value of the books. Each student was required to state the theme around which the collection was built, a page or less justifying this choice, and interestingly enough, an annotated bibliography of ten books the student would like to add to the collection. The student's knowledge of the subject selected as demonstrated by an explanatory essay, the selection of books on display, and the choice of books to be added were considered in making the awards. The winning entries were displayed in the rotunda of the library.

NEW ASSEMBLY POLICY

At the April meeting of the faculty the public occasions committee reported that in the future only four formal convocations would be held during the year; namely, the chancellor's convocation in the fall (at which the faculty would wear academic regalia), the Loyalty Night program, the installation of student officers, and the seniors' convocation.

Also, the committee announced that the Class Night exercises were to become the seniors' convocation, held some time before the final graduating exercises, and that awards would be limited to those in which the senior class as a whole is considered in making the award.[6]

It was also agreed that Founder's Day would be observed once each four years rather than annually.

NEW SCIENCE BUILDING

Meanwhile, work on the new science building went forward. Members of the faculty to use the new facilities met, by departments, with the architects to outline the facilities and equipment they would like to have.

The building was readied for occupancy during the summer of 1959. All work in biology, chemistry, physics, geography and geology, astronomy, and mathematics was moved to the new science center.

Space in Chandler previously occupied by these science departments was converted to use by the English department on the top floor and the psychology department on the main floor. New lecture rooms, seminar rooms, and office space became available, and special facilities for laboratory work in psychology were constructed.

FEES CHANGED

A welcome change in college charges was made in 1959 with the elimination of all laboratory and other fees except those for individual instruction in music and horseback riding. Extra charges

---

[6] *Ibid.*, April 13, 1959.

for science, art, physical education, home economics, and typing were discontinued, as was the $12.50 diploma fee.

All differentials in room rent were also eliminated. Beginning with the 1959–60 session, the new fees for all resident students totaled $875.00 for Virginians and $1,240 for out-of-staters.

HALL OF MIRRORS RENOVATION

The first in a series of renovations that was ultimately to eliminate the Hall of Mirrors in the basement of George Washington Hall was begun in January when the area was divided into three basic sections: one to contain the placement bureau, mimeograph room, and mailroom; another to contain the offices of the director of admissions (Michael Houston, at the time), his secretary, and a reception room; and the central portion to continue as a mirrored hall to be used for teas and coffee hours.

When George Washington Hall was being completed in 1939, the basement area occupied by the Hall of Mirrors was first designated as "unexcavated." A change in the architectural plans, made at the request of President Combs, resulted in a new recreational area, used for several years for formal dances and receptions. The supporting columns throughout the area at first appeared to be a problem. However, when each column was encased completely in mirrors, a novel effect of spaciousness and beauty was achieved. The gleaming ceiling with recessed lights and the highly polished hardwood floor added to the sparkle of the new facility, especially when it was filled with dancers in formal dress. In the early years of its existence use of the Hall of Mirrors was limited to formal dances and receptions.

As requirements for additional space became more urgent, the entire area of the Hall of Mirrors was converted into office space. It now houses the data-processing facilities, the central switchboard, the mailing and mimeographing rooms, and various services of the disbursing office. It also houses the offices of the assistant chancellor, Michael Houston, who has continued to utilize part of the reconstructed area which he helped to plan.

COMMENCEMENT

The 1959–60 session ended on June 1, when 230 seniors received diplomas from Chancellor Grellet C. Simpson. The graduation address was given by Colgate W. Darden, Jr., who was retiring as president of the University of Virginia and would be succeeded that summer by Edgar F. Shannon, Jr. The baccalaureate sermon was delivered by Dr. Mary Ely Lyman, former dean of Sweet Briar College.

Chancellor Simpson spoke to the graduates on "The Intimate State of Man." He emphasized that the true test of the worth of an education is "what has merged in the minds and hearts of students and graduates. . . . Education must be dynamic, not static; continuous and expanding; never ending; never tiring; always democratic, not aristocratic. It must somehow add 'new dimensions of enjoyment and grace to life.'"

As the session ended it was announced that bids had been opened for still another new dormitory, a 144-bed facility to be located at the corner of Sunken Road and William Street. This was later named Mary Willis Ambler Marshall Hall, in honor of the wife of Chief Justice John Marshall. It was also announced that the former Spotswood Hall, located on College Avenue just across from the college gates, would be turned over to the Alumnae Association, at a nominal rental, for use as an off-campus Alumnae House, where the offices of the association would be located.

THE ENTERING CLASS

The 1959–60 session opened with the largest enrollment in the history of the college. The 644 freshmen and transfer students had been selected from a total of 1,548 applicants for admission. The freshman class represented what the committee on admissions believed to be the best-qualified applicants out of the 1,395 young women from 377 secondary schools in thirty-six states and nine foreign countries who had sought admission. Over 900 returning students brought the total fall enrollment to 1,607 students, most of whom resided in the college residence halls, when the session got under way on September 13.

NEW BUILDINGS

Returning students found two new buildings awaiting them: the new science hall completed during the summer of 1959 and a new residence hall across from it named in honor of Mrs. C. L. Bushnell, the former dean of women. It was the first time that a dormitory had been named for a living person.

Erected at a cost of $560,000, Bushnell Hall provided accommodations for 160 students. For the first time, as an experiment, students from all four classes were placed in a single dormitory. Later the practice was extended to other buildings. Betty Lewis Hall was completely remodeled during the summer, and many improvements were made.

The new science building, later named the Morgan L. Combs Science Hall by the board of visitors, was erected at a cost of $675,000. With equipment, it represented an investment of about $800,000. Each of the three main floors has a large lecture room with seats arranged in tiers in ampitheatre form, projection equipment, and a large demonstration-lecture table. Each lecture room has an adjacent room where the lecturer can prepare his demonstrations. There are also preparation and storage rooms adjoining each laboratory. An elaborate system of power distribution—the most complete in the state at the time of its construction—makes available to each laboratory a choice of direct or alternating current in voltage ranging from 1.2 to 120. A large control panel in the basement permits routing the desired current to laboratory users just as a telephone switchboard routes calls.

The first floor is devoted largely to biology, with a large lecture hall seating 130, a number of laboratories, and several smaller classrooms. There is also an attractive biology library, as well as adequate office space for the teaching staff.

The second floor is shared by the biology and physics departments. The bacteriology laboratory has an efficient system for handling student experimental materials. Each student has a drawer in an adjoining storeroom. When she reports to class, she simply takes her drawer of material from the storage racks and inserts it in the empty space at her worktable.

The third floor is devoted to chemistry, with, again, a large lecture-demonstration room and a number of laboratories, both for class instruction and individual work by advanced students. There is an elaborate ventilating system to remove fumes. One laboratory designed for special types of work is equipped with a suction hood for each student station. Offices have adjoining workrooms where instructors can prepare demonstrations of experiments or conduct individual research.

The basement houses the mathematics department. It was originally shared with the department of geography and geology until the expansion of the geography offering and the development of

Continuing Growth 423

a major in that field made necessary the removal of this work to the basement of Monroe Hall. There are currently four faculty members in geography and two in geology.

MAJOR IN PHYSICS OFFERED

The completion of the new science building with its facilities and equipment for instruction in physics made a major in this field possible. It was approved by the faculty at its November meeting and announced in the catalogue for the following year. The new major required thirty hours in physics and six in calculus. Other courses had to be chosen in consultation with a representative of the department. A B.S. degree was now available in physics and in mathematics as well as in biology and chemistry.

Materials for individual experimentation facilitated courses on a more advanced level. An electrical control panel at each worktable provided the adjustment of current and voltage so that various experiments could be carried on simultaneously. The new equipment was highly sensitive and made possible extremely accurate and minute measurements. The latest models of such precision instruments as the Kelvin double bridge, the potentiometer, the oscilloscope, and the Van de Graaff machine were now available for student use. Grover P. Burns, head of the physics department since 1948, supervised the ordering and installation of the equipment and planned the major program. Jean A. Edson joined the department in the fall of 1959 on a part-time basis.

The department has continued to develop. In 1971–72 there was a teaching staff of five, with Bulent I. Atalay as chairman. Sixteen courses were offered, including quantum mechanics, solid-state physics, and nuclear physics. The department also offered independent study, seminars, and honors in physics.

INAUGURATION OF PRESIDENT SHANNON

A large delegation of Mary Washington College faculty and staff attended on October 6 the inauguration of Edgar F. Shannon, Jr., as the fourth president of the University of Virginia. At the invitation of Chancellor Simpson, Mary Washington was represented by its administrative officials, at least one representative of each academic department, and all other faculty members who held a degree from either the University of Virginia or Mary

Washington College. All wore academic regalia, marched in the academic procession, and participated in the various activities of the day.

Until just three days before the inauguration was to be held, it was not clear what provisions had been made for the participation of the Mary Washington faculty and staff. When the matter was settled, there was not time to order caps and gowns in the usual manner with the customary two- or three-week notice. Long distance calls to Cotrell and Leonard made clear the desperate nature of the situation. Caps, gowns, and hoods were ordered by telephone, and a college truck was dispatched to Albany, New York, to pick them up. By driving all night, both going and coming, the truck crew got the regalia back just in time for distribution to the MWC representatives before they left by college bus for Charlottesville early in the morning for the ten o'clock ceremony at the University of Virginia.

The inauguration exercises were held on the Lawn at the university. The chief address of the occasion was delivered by Geoffrey Reginald Gilchist Mure, warden of Merton College, Oxford, where the new president had studied. The rector of the university, Frank Talbott, Jr., presided and conducted the installation of Edgar Shannon. Others in the presidential party were Governor J. Lindsay Almond, Jr.; former President Colgate W. Darden, Jr.; and Chancellor Grellet C. Simpson, of Mary Washington College. Delegates from over three hundred colleges, universities, and learned societies marched in the academic procession, and many delivered scrolls of greetings to the university.

In his inaugural address Shannon declared, "I ask for no revolution, but that the faculty and students of the University of Virginia rededicate themselves to greatness and truth." He emphasized that the university should be not only a great state university but a great national one as well.

The inauguration was followed by a luncheon in Newcomb Hall and at 3:30 P.M., a concert by the Philharmonia Hungarica. The Mary Washington College delegation returned to Fredericksburg late that afternoon.

The new president came to the University of Virginia from Harvard in 1956 as associate professor of English. He received his A.B. from Washington and Lee University, where his father was professor of English for many years. President Shannon earned master's degrees at both Duke and Harvard universities. His doctor of philosophy degree was from Oxford where he had been a Rhodes Scholar. Later he was to receive honorary degrees from a number of institutions.

Dr. Shannon had been a navy lieutenant commander in the Pacific in World War II. A short time after his inauguration he was appointed to the board of visitors of the United States Naval Academy. Since that time he has held many offices of national importance. He has been president of the Council of Southern Universities, the State Universities Association, and the National Association of Universities and Land-Grant Colleges. His activities have included membership in the district selection commission for Rhodes Scholars, the board of governors of the National Commission on Accrediting, and the board of directors of the National Council on Education. He is currently a Phi Beta Kappa senator.

A specialist in Victorian poetry, Dr. Shannon announced that he would continue to offer an advanced course in Tennyson and Browning while carrying on the duties of the presidency. Later, he found it necessary to give his full time to administrative work.

HONORARY DEGREE FOR CHANCELLOR SIMPSON

A few days after the inaugural exercises at Charlottesville, Chancellor Simpson went to Ashland to receive the honorary degree of Doctor of Laws from his undergraduate alma mater. In conferring this honor in a convocation on October 9, the president of Randolph-Macon College, Dr. J. Earl Moreland, paid tribute to Dr. Simpson's scholarship, his devotion to liberal studies, and his interest in students over the twenty years that he had served as a faculty member and his four years as dean at Randolph-Macon.

The main address of the occasion was delivered by Colgate W. Darden, Jr., who had recently retired as president of the University of Virginia. Darden referred with pride to the fact that two of the three Randolph-Macon alumni being honored—Chancellor Simpson and Dr. Francis G. Lankford, Jr., president of Longwood College—had been graduate students at the university.

A number of Chancellor Simpson's colleagues at Mary Washington went to Ashland to witness the conferring of the LL.D.

ACADEMIC PROGRESS

In keeping with the theme of the chancellor's convocation—the development of intellectual curiosity—the college continued its quest for an academic environment that would stimulate learning. At the first faculty meeting Chancellor Simpson expressed the hope that the college would continue to stress a "sound, stiff academic program."[7] He introduced seventeen new faculty members, and there were also ten promotions in academic rank.

Tangible evidence of academic progress is the salary scale paid members of the instructional staff. Action taken at the September faculty meeting indicated the extent to which this objective was being attained. By unanimous vote the faculty adopted the following resolution: "That the faculty of Mary Washington College appreciate the continuing improvement in the salary scale, which mirrors the mutual confidence continuing among the faculty, the Chancellor and the other governing authorities."[8]

NEW REGISTRAR

Among the new appointments was that of A. Ray Merchent as registrar and instructor in education, to succeed Louis C. Guenther, who had accepted a position as director of admissions at Wake Forest College. Merchent came to Mary Washington from Longwood College, where he had been director of public relations. A graduate of Emory and Henry, he held the master's degree in education from the University of Virginia.

For the next eight years, Merchent served as registrar and taught courses in education. He advanced in academic rank and in 1967 was made chairman of the education department. Meanwhile he was completing his doctorate in education at the university. In 1968 Associate Professor Merchent was appointed director of admissions, succeeding Michael Houston, who had become assistant to the chancellor. Dr. Merchent continued to teach in the education department.

RESIDENCE HALL SEMINARS

Although the formation of volunteer, noncredit residence hall seminars had been proposed by a small group of students and faculty members and an informal discussion group had met at Framar from time to time during the 1958–59 session, it was Dr. George W. Van Sant of the philosophy department who took the lead in getting the program started in a systematic fashion.

[7] *Ibid.*, Sept. 14, 1959.   [8] *Ibid.*

A graduate of St. John's College where he had been a tutor in the Great Books Program developed there by Scott Buchanan and Stringfellow Barr, Dr. Van Sant envisioned a somewhat similar program for capable and interested students at Mary Washington. He was the organizer and discussion leader of the Trench Hill seminar, which started in the fall of 1959. Dr. Van Sant appeared before the faculty at its opening meeting on September 14 and explained the program. He also expressed the hope that it would someday become an integral part of the curriculum.

The seminar for the first semester was organized around the great works of Western thought. Included for discussion in the weekly seminars were the following publications, all available in paperback editions to be purchased by the students participating: Voltaire's *Candide,* Dostoevski's *Crime and Punishment,* Kierkegaard's *With Fear and Trembling,* Sartre's *Existentialism and Human Emotion,* Freud's *General Introduction to Psychoanalysis,* Conant's *On Understanding Science,* Locke's *Second Treatise of Government, Declaration of Independence* and *Constitution of the United States,* and Calvin's *On God and Political Duty.*

The schedule provided two weeks for the reading and discussion of each great book. On alternate Wednesday evenings, speakers from Mary Washington and elsewhere were invited to visit the seminars and participate in the discussion of the topic under consideration.

Twenty-one students were selected the first year to live in Trench Hill and take part in the program. Fourteen were chosen from more than one hundred applications submitted by students already attending the college. Seven others were picked from incoming freshmen and transfer students on the basis of their records. Thus, all four classes were represented in the group. Dr. Van Sant was assisted by Dr. Zoe W. C. Black, head resident of Trench Hill, who also participated in the project. The success of the Trench Hill program led to its extension to Framar residence hall, where a series of similar seminars was started under the aegis of Dr. Peter Coffin, also of the philosophy department.

The movement continued to grow, especially after the appointment of Associate Dean Reginald W. Whidden as formal coordinator for the seminars. By the 1961–62 session there were five programs in operation. The example set by Framar and Trench Hill was followed in Mary Ball, Bushnell, and Betty Lewis. Later, Marye and Russell were added. The seminars were under the leadership or direction of a member of the faculty chosen by the group, but they were initiated by students and carried on by student interest on a voluntary and noncredit basis. Among the pioneer leaders, in addition to Dr. Van Sant, Dr. Coffin, and Dr. Black, were Dr. Dan Woodward, Dr. Edward Lowry, Myra Irby, Dr. James H. Croushore, Dr. Albert R. Klein, and Dr. Josefa Rivas. Later, Dr. James R. Nazzaro, Dr. Joseph C. Vance, Dr. Samuel H. Phillips, Dr. Lewis P. Fickett, Jr., Dr. Donald E. Glover, Dr. Roger Kenvin, Suzanne Pharr, Dr. Elizabeth A. Clark, and Miriam Greenberg were among those who served as dormitory seminar leaders.

An examination of the lists of books read and discussed indicates the wide range of interests of the students. Modern art, religion, existentialism, communism, modern music, psychoanalysis, current drama, politics, twentieth-century literature – these are representative of the variety of themes about which the readings and discussions of the seminars centered.

As evidence of genuine student interest in intellectual activity, the dormitory seminars occupied a prominent place in the development of a concern for academic excellence. With the advent, in 1961, of the liberal arts seminars for which college credit was available, the dormitory program was phased out gradually. An attractively furnished seminar room was made available in Chandler Hall, replacing the dormitory parlors as the setting for eager and intensive discussion.

BELMONT

In 1960 the General Assembly of Virginia enacted legislation transferring Belmont, the home of the late Gari Melchers at Falmouth, to the custody of Mary Washington College to be maintained as a memorial and art center.

This historic residence is believed to have been built as early as 1761 by the Reverend John Dixon, an Episcopal minister who was for several years professor of divinity at his alma mater, the College of William and Mary. Subsequent owners made sizable additions. The Ficklen family owned the property for ninety-two years, from 1824 until its sale to Gari Melchers in 1916.

Gari Melchers was born in Detroit in 1860. His father, a native of Germany, was a sculptor and decorator who had studied art in Paris before migrating to this country. Gari studied abroad as a youth, spending four years at the Royal Art Academy in Düsseldorf and additional years at the Academy Julian in Paris. In 1886 he received in Paris the first of a long series of awards and decorations for his canvases. He won a grand prize in the Paris International Exhibition of 1889, where he and John Singer Sargent were the only Americans to receive medals for paintings.

Meanwhile, Melchers had settled in a Dutch fishing village on the North Sea where many of his most famous canvases were painted, including *Girl Reading, Mother and Child,* and other interpretations of the life and characteristics of the Dutch people. Many of these canvases were acquired by European museums and collectors.

Melchers lived in Egmond aan Zee for fifteen years, usually spending the winter at a studio in Paris. During this time he made frequent visits to the United States, which he devoted usually to portrait painting. These commissions brought him a lucrative income. In 1895 Melchers was made a chevalier of the Legion of Honor. A long series of titles, decorations, and honors followed in subsequent years. In 1903 Melchers married Corinne Lawton Mackall, a member of a distingiushed Georgia family. Her grandfather had served as minister to Austria, and both her father and uncle had been officers in the Confederate army.

Melchers was professor of painting at the State Academy of Art at Weimar when the outbreak of World War I prompted him to return to his native country. In 1914 he established a studio in New York, which he maintained until his death. The Belmont property was acquired by Melchers in 1916. He built the fieldstone studio, enlarged the mansion, and increased the size of the estate. During his Virginia residence Melchers continued his portraits of prominent citizens. He also painted many studies of local people and scenes of the surrounding countryside.

Melchers died of a heart attack on November 30, 1932. His wife continued to live at Belmont and to take an active interest in the life of the community. In 1942 Mrs. Melchers deeded to the Virginia Museum of Fine Arts as a memorial to her husband the Belmont estate, including the twenty-three-room mansion and its furnishings; an endowment fund of $115,000 for its maintenance; fifty of her husband's paintings, including *The Last Supper,* as a permanent collection; and the power to sell the remainder of his paintings and drawings to add to the endowment of the Gari Melchers Memorial and Art Center at Belmont. The General Assembly of Virginia formally accepted this generous gift and designated the trustees of the Virginia Museum of Fine Arts to administer it.

Mrs. Melchers died on April 7, 1955. Subsequently the trustees of the museum agreed that it was impractical for them to administer the memorial from Richmond. Mary Washington College agreed to operate it on a trial basis from November 1, 1957, to June 30, 1960. Since the arrangement proved satisfactory to all concerned, the 1960 General Assembly enacted legislation, subsequently approved by the courts, transferring the estate and endowment to the Rector and Visitors of the University of Virginia, to be administered by Mary Washington College as a memorial and art center.

Belmont has since been remodeled and has been open during Garden Week and on other occasions when the house and museum attracted interested visitors. The house itself contains a wealth of furniture, paintings, china, and objects of art accumulated by the Melchers. In the fieldstone museum and studio are hundreds of Melchers's paintings and drawings, all catalogued by the college. Included in the collection are such well-known paintings as *The Holland Bride, The Fencer, Girl with Hat, The Lace Cap,* and *The Green Lamp,* all done while the artist was living in Holland. Of particular interest to residents of the Fredericksburg area are his later paintings of his neighbors in Falmouth, such as *The Hunters, In Old Virginia,* and *Nelson Berry's Store.*

The Melchers collection has enriched the foyers, reception halls, and offices of the college. Some seventy of his selected paintings are currently charged out to the library, administration hall, chancellor's residence, and other buildings on the Hill. Other of his paintings are on display currently at the Virginia Museum of Art, the Governor's Mansion, and the University Center in Virginia (Ellen Glasgow House).

FOREIGN LANGUAGE WEEK

In keeping with the emphasis upon the study of foreign languages, both as a major field and as a degree requirement, the college began the observance of Modern Foreign Language Week. Exhibitions and displays of the culture of other countries, lectures by various embassy staff members from Washington, a feature foreign language movie, and the production of plays in other languages characterized the typical program. The February 1960 observance of Foreign Language Week featured a play in Spanish, written by Dr. Josefa Rivas of the MWC faculty, and a play in French, both presented by students majoring in these languages.

Continuing Growth 431

ADDITION TO THE LIBRARY APPROVED

As the book collection increased, the need for additional library space became increasingly urgent. The faculty library committee recommended that the chancellor request a budget appropriation of $430,000 to construct an addition to the present building.

Chancellor Simpson announced to the faculty in September that he had requested such an appropriation in the budget then being prepared by the governor for action by the General Assembly of Virginia. In so doing, Dr. Simpson said that he hoped the faculty would make greater demands on the library, through assignments for individual and independent study, so that the expenditure for additional space, staff, and facilities for books would be justified.

At the March faculty meeting Chancellor Simpson was able to announce that the General Assembly had appropriated $430,000 for the addition to the library, and also $15,000 a year for the purchase of books and periodicals.

THE INTER-CLUB ASSOCIATION

The Inter-Club Association was organized in 1953–54 as the "coordinating unit of club activities and a clearinghouse for the discussion of the problems" of these organizations. "Bootsie" Simpson was the first president, and Dr. Burney L. Parkinson, the first sponsor.

Its first handbook, published in 1958–59, was an eight-page pamphlet giving the officers of the Inter-Club Association, the members of the ICA council, and a brief statement of the purposes of each member organization. The handbook was expanded during the 1960s to include the point system and the requirements for membership and officers of each organization, along with the ICA officers and the members of the council. The ICA publication was discontinued in 1970 when all of this information was incorporated in the revised and enlarged student handbook.

The student organizations committee, headed by Dean Margaret Hargrove, worked actively with the Inter-Club Association to perfect its plan of operation and to increase its responsibility. Currently, the Inter-Club Association is composed of all recognized clubs and honor societies of the college. The presidents of these organizations represent their respective groups at association meetings held three times a year. The ICA council, the governing body, consists of the four executive officers of ICA and elected representatives of the divisions into which clubs are grouped: fine arts, language, science, social science, recreational, religions, and miscellaneous (including Mortar Board and other unclassified organizations). In 1971–72 there were forty-one clubs listed in the student handbook, exclusive of publications and class organizations.

Some of the more recent organizations are the Afro-American Club, the American Civil Liberties Union, the Young Democrats, and the Young Republicans.

The authority of ICA has been extended. Through its council it is responsible for enforcing the point system, arranging the ICA open house for all clubs, scheduling club meetings and activities, presiding over honorary tapping ceremonies, admitting new clubs, and evaluating and coordinating club activities.

A description of the founding and activities of some of the major clubs appears elsewhere.

THE SCHNELLOCK AWARD

The family of Emil Schnellock, for many years associate professor of art at Mary Washington, established a fund to provide a cash sum each year to the outstanding student in painting. Known as the Emil Schnellock Award, it was made for the first time in May 1960 at the annual exhibition of student art.

Joyce Mary Neill and Marjorie Sue Whidden were selected by a special committee to share the award, since their achievements were so nearly comparable. The committee also decided to make the award retroactive and that it be given for the year 1959 to Carolyn Lee Cross. The Schnellock award has been given each year since that time.

THE DARDEN AWARD

The first annual presentation of the Darden Award was made at the graduation exercises on May 29, 1960. The recipient was Maxine C. Foster of Arlington, who earned a four-year average of 2.95 out of a possible 3.00 and had the highest academic average in the graduating class.

The award was established in honor of Colgate W. Darden, Jr., president of the University of Virginia from 1947 to 1959. It consists of a three-inch bronze medal and one hundred dollars in cash. The medal was designed by Gaetano Cecere, the well-known sculptor who was then a member of the art department at Mary Washington. On one side is a profile of Colgate Darden, with the dates of his presidency of the University of Virginia and a small relief of the Rotunda. On the other is a student in cap and gown, a relief of the portico of the library, surrounded by the words "Darden Medal Awarded to [name inserted] for Scholastic Achievement, Mary Washington College of the University of Virginia." The original models of the award are kept in the archives of the college library. One copy of the medal was sent to Mrs. Darden in Norfolk.

With the establishment of the Darden Award, the Alpha Phi Sigma recognition of academic achievement was changed to honor the junior making the highest academic average during her freshman and sophomore years. The presentation is made at the chancellor's convocation at the opening of the session.

THE CHANCELLOR'S MESSAGE TO GRADUATES

Beginning with the graduation exercises in May 1960 the practice of having a visiting speaker for the occasion was discontinued. In its place, the chancellor delivered a message to the graduates. His 1960 address was entitled "The Intimate State of Man."

The texts of these addresses have been preserved in the archives. They constitute a scholarly and thoughtful examination of the goals of education—and of living—and conclude with a warm, personal word to students completing their work at Mary Washington.

CHAPTER XXII

Planning Ahead: The Early 1960s

A NEW DECADE BEGINS

The faculty held its opening meeting of the 1960–61 session in Room 100 of the new science building. In his opening remarks Chancellor Simpson asked the faculty to give attention to the "research climate" of the institution and to the "art of teaching." He introduced some twenty new members of the faculty and staff. Silvia McJilton, president of the Student Government Association, and Vaughan Hargroves, president of the Honor Council, also spoke to the faculty.

The college continued to expand its physical plant. Marshall Hall, a new dormitory at the corner of Sunken Road and William Street, was opened for occupancy. It was named after the wife of Chief Justice John Marshall, Mary Willis Ambler Marshall, whose maternal grandfather had been governor of Virginia and whose father had served as treasurer of the Commonwealth.

It was a time of continuing academic development. Steps were taken to initiate a major in art history. After careful study the curriculum committee approved the rearrangement of courses in the art department to permit either a major in studio art or one in art history.

The admission policy committee recommended that the college require three additional Scholastic Aptitude Tests of all applicants for admission after September 1961. The faculty approved the addition of three area tests from the "afternoon examinations": the English test, a foreign language test, and the writing sample. Thus, both morning and afternoon SAT tests became prerequisite for admission.

An important development was the approval of a twelve-hour teaching load for members of the English department in order that they might have more time to work with students. Chancellor Simpson emphasized that the reduction from a fifteen-hour teaching schedule would be extended to other departments as they demonstrated the need for additional time for student conferences, direction of individual study projects, and other nonlecture types of teaching activity that would justify fewer classroom hours.

LONG-RANGE PLANNING COMMITTEE

At the November 1960 faculty meeting Chancellor Simpson announced the appointment of a long-range planning committee consisting of Dr. Whidden as chairman, Mrs. Bolling, Dr. Insley, Miss Stephenson, Dr. Van Sant, and Mr. Woodward. This was in response to an invitation by President Shannon to appoint a Mary Washington College committee to cooperate with the University's long-range planning committee, headed by Dean Geldard.

Dr. Shannon himself attended the November meeting. He expressed his pleasure at being present at "a faculty meeting of a college that is an integral part of the University." The faculty minutes continue: "He then advocated greater use of the University's facilities by the Mary Washington College faculty and he expressed the hope that able graduates of the College would attend the Graduate and professional schools at Charlottesville. According to President Shannon, retaining a distinguished faculty, encouraging superior teaching and maintaining high academic standards are the central concern of the whole University. He expressed a determination that the University should discharge fully its obligation to the State without sacrificing a national outlook. The faculty was interested to learn that Mary Washington College had a larger number of undergraduate liberal arts students than the University." [1]

The long-range planning committee met regularly and examined many aspects of the college program. It submitted to the chancellor a series of interim reports relating to administrative organization, faculty, educational program, and student life.

The committee did not attempt to involve the college at large in its activities. The chancellor described it as a "free-wheeling group" to think creatively about the future of the college and to submit its recommendations directly to him. The findings in the Self-Study Report of 1962 were considered by the committee in the preparation of its final report. This report was submitted to the chancellor in February 1963. A document of seventy pages, it presented carefully considered recommendations in six areas: instruction, student body, program, administration, financial policy, and plant expansion.

The scores of recommendations are too numerous to summarize here. Under the heading of instruction, the committee

---

[1] Faculty Minutes, Nov. 14, 1960.

recommended additional faculty, increased salaries, more faculty research facilities, sabbatical leave plan, more independent study programs, improvement of the advisory system, establishment of a testing center. Many of these recommendations were made also in the Self-Study Report. Most of them have been put into effect. The committee recommended that the college endeavor to maintain itself at approximately its present size. It also suggested that the college continue to enroll a considerable proportion of out-of-state students. More scholarships, especially as awards for academic excellence, were suggested.

Perhaps the most interesting recommendation, in view of the program of the college, was that the majors in physical education and home economics be eliminated as "inconsistent with the purposes of a liberal arts college." The degrees of bachelor of science in physical education and bachelor of science in home economics should be discontinued. Progress toward these objectives was to occupy the attention of the faculty for a considerable period. Other recommendations included the establishment of majors in religion, anthropology, comparative literature, and geology. The committee urged that grades and academic credit for physical education courses be discontinued.

In the area of administration, the committee recommended that offices of the dean of the college and the bursar be relieved of some of the "inordinate number of responsibilities" the two offices had acquired over the years. Publication of the catalogue, the schedule of classes, the placement bureau, and the awarding of scholarships, which were responsibilities of the dean's office, were specifically mentioned for assignment to other offices or officials. A director of public information, who would also edit college publications, was suggested. The committee also recommended reorganization of the bursar's office and the appointment of a college auditor and a plant engineer. The assistant bursar should serve as director of personnel.

Once again, many of these recommendations were put into effect in the years immediately following. Responsibilities have been reassigned in many cases and new officials appointed. The net result has been a more efficient functioning of the administrative structure of the college.

LIBERAL ARTS SEMINARS ESTABLISHED

The success of the noncredit program of study at Trench Hill dormitory since its inauguration in September 1959 led the committee on programs for superior students to recommend that a liberal arts seminar on a credit basis be established as an integral part of the college program. It was pointed out that the honors program, as successful as it had been, had reached a relatively small number of the able students. Furthermore, it did not become effective early enough in a student's career.

The committee proposed a six-credit Liberal Arts Seminar 1, 2, to be offered selected students in their sophomore year. It would be under the direction of two faculty members, preferably from different disciplines, who would be responsible for planning and conducting the seminars. Requirements for admission would be set up by the committee and application forms drawn up.

The proposal that the six credits, if obtained, could be applied to area requirements provoked long and spirited discussion by the faculty. It was finally agreed that the hours earned could be counted only as elective credits. The program was approved at the April meeting of the faculty to be available in the session of 1961–62.

Dr. Van Sant (philosophy) and Dr. Sidney Mitchell (English) began the seminars that fall. Eighteen students were enrolled the first semester, and sixteen continued with the second semester. Students reported that they found the seminars highly stimulating, but that the amount of reading that they wanted to do in preparation made demands upon study time. In any case, the project had a marked appeal to able students, and also to students who sought a more divergent approach to academic studies.

It was a part of the plan that one new faculty leader would be appointed each year to replace the one finishing a two-year term. It was felt that this would give continuity to the program. The second year (1962–63) Dr. Mitchell and Dr. Black (biology) were the leaders. Dr. Klein (dramatic arts) took Dr. Mitchell's place the following year (1963–64), and Dr. Lawrence Wishner followed Dr. Black in 1964–65. That session a junior year seminar was added, conducted by Dr. Graves.

The liberal arts seminar probably reached its peak development in 1965–66, when sophomore, junior, and senior year seminars were offered by professors L. Wishner and Oliver, Graves and Clark, and Croushore and Parrish. However, enrollments were already beginning to decline, largely because many departments were now beginning to offer independent study programs and senior seminars. The final organization provided for one seminar for freshmen and sophomores and one for juniors and seniors. The seminars were discontinued in 1969–70.

SELF-STUDY INITIATED

For many years, accreditation by the Southern Association of Colleges and Secondary Schools, the regional accrediting agency, was based on meeting a number of quantitative standards set by the association. These standards related to size and preparation of faculty, student-faculty ratio, faculty salaries, expenditures for books, and other data of this kind, which could be supplied in response to an elaborate questionnaire. This periodic report was examined by officials in the main office in Atlanta, and then referred to an accrediting committee of the association for final action. There was a growing feeling that these quantitative standards did not take into account the quality of instruction and that they were somewhat superficial in determining the kind of job that an institution might be doing.

An outgrowth of several years of study was the development of a set of evaluative criteria, by means of which an institution might conduct a self-study of its own program, submit a report to the association, and then have a visiting committee spend several days at the institution discussing the findings of the self-study with faculty, students, and administrative staff. The plan was adopted for the accreditation of secondary schools and, in the 1950s, used at first experimentally and later as a set procedure in the accreditation of colleges and universities. Mary Washington College was among the earlier institutions to cooperate in the new program.

After careful consideration, it was decided in the spring of 1960 to make preliminary organizational plans during the summer and to initiate the study with the opening of the college in the fall. At the October 1960 meeting of the faculty Chancellor Simpson announced the appointment of a steering committee, consisting of three administrative officers and three faculty members. The personnel of the group included:

Dr. Edward Alvey, Jr., dean of the college, chairman
Dr. Margaret Hargrove, dean of students
Edgar E. Woodward, bursar
Dr. James H. Croushore, professor and chairman of the English department
Dr. Laura V. Sumner, associate professor and chairman of the classics department
Dr. Herbert L. Cover, associate professor of chemistry

In announcing the inauguration of the self-study program, Chancellor Simpson stressed the value of the self-examination process and expressed the hope that it "would provide an opportunity to evaluate the innovations made by the college during the past few years." [2]

A manual outlining procedures for the self-study had been prepared by the Southern Association. Over fifty pages of forms had to be filled out, and work on them was begun immediately. In the early stages of the study, each member of the steering committee assumed responsibility for obtaining data on a certain part of the report, utilizing, whenever possible, the services of existing committees of the faculty, and consulting appropriate officials of the college for information and suggestions regarding specific aspects of the self-study. Eight aspects of the institution were studied intensively: purpose, financial resources, organization, educational program, the library, the faculty, student personnel, and physical plant.

For the next fifteen months the college proceeded to examine these eight areas of its operation. Three faculty meetings were devoted in whole or in part to a discussion of proposed statements of purpose of the institution. Finally, on May 8, 1961, the following statement was adopted by the faculty and included in subsequent issues of the college catalogue:

Mary Washington College is a state-supported liberal arts college for women and a part of the University of Virginia. As such, it has an obligation to the people of the Commonwealth of Virginia to provide the best education for those students who give promise of succeeding in College.

As a liberal arts college, Mary Washington stands firmly in the tradition that a broad education in the arts, the sciences, and the humanities, complemented by intensive study in a particular field of interest, is a most appropriate preparation for life and citizenship.

As a college for women, Mary Washington endeavors to provide the best intellectual background possible for the woman of today. It recognizes the importance of the inquiring mind, the significance of aesthetic sensitivity and the necessity of individual and corporate responsibility.

Finally, as a part of the University of Virginia, Mary Washington College has a unique role to fill in Virginia education, and is pledged to the selection of a qualified student body, to the maintenance of a competent faculty and staff, and to the development of the academic and social environment necessary to achieve its goals.

[2] *Ibid.*, Oct. 10, 1960.

As the study progressed, an outline was prepared to guide each department in a thorough study of its purposes, course offerings, teaching procedures, future plans, and staff needs. These departmental reports, totaling some two hundred pages, proved a significant part of the self-study and were used as source material for final recommendations in the section on the educational program.

By the summer of 1961 the self-study had progressed to the point where data were ready for critical examination. Six subcommittees, composed of three faculty members each, were appointed to review each aspect of the report. A series of weekly meetings was set up for the fall. The steering committee reviewed all subcommittee recommendations and finally the entire study was edited, organized, and printed in a 299-page volume, dated March 1962.

Meanwhile, a visiting committee had been appointed, with Dr. Donald C. Agnew, president of Oglethorpe University, as chairman. Dr. Agnew spoke at the March meeting of the MWC faculty, explaining the history and purposes of the self-study program. Copies of the Self-Study Report were distributed to the faculty at its April meeting. The visiting committee arrived on the campus on May 6, 1962, and spent the next four days conferring with administrative officials, faculty, and students; inspecting the library, physical plant, and college facilities; and preparing a report of its findings. In addition to Dr. Agnew, members of the visiting committee were Dean Donald H. MacMahon, Woman's College of Georgia; Dean Ellie Mae Souder, Mississippi State College for Women; Dean Katherine Taylor, Woman's College of the University of North Carolina; and Librarian Charles M. Adams, also of the Woman's College of the University of North Carolina.

It had been explained that the members of the visiting committee, selected from other colleges in the Southern Association, would come "not as critics but as counselors." This point of view was reiterated when the group attended the May meeting of the faculty and were introduced at that time.

The MWC steering committee had prepared a twelve-page summary of "suggestions for study in order that the College may realize its purpose more effectively."[3] Only the most important recommendations can be mentioned here:

[3] See Self-Study Report, March 1962, p. 275.

Appointment of a director of the summer school
Establishment of an office of testing and guidance
Employment of a plant engineer
Use of a computer system
Employment of a scholarship officer
Possible increase in laboratory hours in science courses
The possible elimination of academic credit for courses in Health, Physical Education, and Recreation
A study of the status of a Department of Home Economics in a liberal arts college.
Extension of the 12-hour teaching load to all departments and the employment of additional staff in a number of departments
Additional office space
A program of sabbatical leaves and financial assistance for study beyond the doctorate
More scholarships and additional financial assistance for students
A new dormitory to relieve present overcrowding
A new physical education building to eliminate potentially dangerous conditions and to consolidate all of the work in one building
Conversion to a full cafeteria system in the dining hall

The visiting committee itself, in a twenty-eight-page report on the results of its study and visitation, concurred in nearly all of these suggestions. A large proportion of these recommendations were put into effect subsequently.

In considering the educational program, the committee was agreed that the major programs of the college were consistent with the stated purposes of the institution with two exceptions. It suggested that the following changes be considered: "(a) that the major and the degree program in home economics be eliminated and that courses in home economics be retained as an elective field; (b) that the major program in health, physical education and recreation be eliminated and that the department continue to offer the required courses in the general education program and other suitable elective courses."[4] The two recommendations were to initiate a series of faculty meetings and reports in which the role of these two majors in a liberal arts college would be thoroughly examined.

Many other recommendations of the visiting committee affirmed suggestions that had already developed during the self-study, especially the needs as identified and listed by the study

[4] Report of the Visiting Committee, May 6–9, 1962, pp. 10–11.

groups. In general, the report was highly complimentary. Recurring frequently were such phrases as "there is no apparent problem in . . . ," "sound academic planning," "the College can take pride in . . . ," "the Committee is impressed with the quality of the faculty," "the Committee has favorable impressions of . . . ."

In the annual reports of progress made to the Southern Association after the 1962 visit, it is interesting to note that many proposals and recommendations growing out of the self-study were carried out within the next two or three years.

At the end of the session Chancellor Simpson announced that the Alumnae Association had given the college a check for five thousand dollars for fellowship grants to recent graduates and to faculty members undertaking significant research projects. He characterized this action as a "vote of confidence in the faculty."

The commencement address to the graduates of the class of 1961 was delivered by the Honorable J. Lindsay Almond, Jr., governor of Virginia.

PROGRESS CONTINUES

At the opening faculty meeting in September 1961, Chancellor Simpson introduced twenty-one new faculty members. He announced that Governor Almond had approved a request that the General Assembly appropriate from the general fund an amount sufficient to increase all faculty salaries substantially for the session beginning September 1962. The chancellor urged that all departments move to a twelve-hour teaching load. He insisted that levels of instruction and attainment must be high: no easy freshman courses and no relaxing of standards during the last semester of the senior year.

The admissions policy committee reported that the qualitative requirements for admission were again being raised, effective with the class entering in September 1962. Credit for at least fifteen academic units had to be presented instead of thirteen as formerly, and the mathematics requirement would be three units instead of two, selected from algebra, geometry, and trigonometry.

The long-range planning committee recommended that the curriculum committee undertake a study to "identify courses not in keeping with [the] purposes of the College" and that an effort be made to eliminate unnecessary duplication of courses or course content in the offerings of the college.

A questionnaire evaluation of the effectiveness and impact of Religious Emphasis Week, sponsored for many years by the college Y, was initiated. The results of the inquiry, which disclosed considerable apathy, was one of the factors that led to the discontinuance of this program.

A revision of the faculty handbook, first published in 1949, was underway. The first edition, entitled "Faculty Policy and Procedures," was compiled by a subcommittee of the committee on academic standards, consisting of Dr. Whidden, Dr. Leidecker, and Dr. Castle. Later, the preparation of the handbook was assigned to a special committee, which has sought to keep all material up to date through frequent revisions. It is now published in loose-leaf form.

RETIREMENT PLAN

At the April meeting of the faculty Chancellor Simpson distributed copies of the retirement plan at the University of Virginia adopted by a resolution of the board of visitors on June 19, 1955. He explained that this resolution would be recommended to the board at its meeting on April 14, 1962, as a policy for Mary Washington College. This policy was duly adopted as a plan for all faculty members. Anytime after a faculty member reaches sixty-five, he may be retired on the initiative of either the chancellor or the professor concerned. The retirement age for the chancellor, bursar, and other administrative officers was fixed at sixty-five. Deans and chairmen of departments must be retired at sixty-five also, although they may continue their teaching duties either in whole or in part under the provisions outlined for faculty members. Acceptance of the retirement policy of the college was made a condition of employment for future employees at the time of their election or appointment.

HIGHLIGHTS OF THE 1962–63 SESSION:
NEW FACULTY, COURSES, AND FACILITIES

As the session of 1962–63 opened, there were many new faces on the faculty. Twenty-three newcomers in thirteen departments began their services at the college. Julien Binford was on leave of absence, and Tetsuo Ochikubo was serving as visiting professor of art.

Dr. J. H. Dodd had just retired as professor of economics after thirty-four years of service. He and Mrs. Dodd left for Hong Kong where he was to teach economics for a year at the United College there under a United States State Department grant. Dr. James Russell Nazzaro and Mary Annette Kelly were serving as acting chairmen of the psychology department during Mrs. Dodd's absence.

Twenty-one new courses in ten departments were added, bringing the total number of course offerings in all fields to 265. Among them were the following course titles: Primitive Art, Modern Japan, Readings in Nietzsche, Vertebrate Paleontology, and Atomic Physics.

On September 18 and 19 a total of 1,750 students registered for classes. There were 590 freshmen and transfer students from 220 high schools in twenty-three states and a half dozen foreign countries.

Chancellor Simpson's convocation address was entitled "The Questing and the Questioning." He described Mary Washington as a place "where people learn not so much how to succeed . . . as how to strive. . . . Where the truth is pursued for no other reason than the love of truth and the beauty that emanates from the pursuit."

A week after classes began, Dr. and Mrs. Simpson left for a two-month Mediterranean cruise aboard a Norwegian freighter, his first extended absence from the college since coming to Mary Washington in February 1956. A high point of the trip was a visit to Naples where Dr. Simpson was stationed two years during World War II as head of the Red Cross.

A rash of beanie snatching broke out in the opening days of the session. Medford Haynes, chief of college police, reported that at least thirty-five freshmen lost their beanies the first week. According to Chief Haynes, the cases seemed to be the result of a fad that had developed and grown among some high school boys. In some instances, the boys hid behind walls or bushes, then jumped out and grabbed beanies as the freshmen students walked by. Both local and college police issued warnings that the practice was not a joke but actually theft of personal property. Devotees of beanie-snatching decided that the consequences entailed were too serious for them to continue the practice.

Returning students were delighted to find still new revisions in the handbook regulations. Dormitory closing hours and light privileges were extended. Seniors were allowed to bring cars to the campus, but were required to maintain a C average to keep them the second semester.

There were a number of changes on campus. The addition to the library was still under construction. A new radio-equipped security office had opened in Ann Carter Lee Hall. The college station post office had been enlarged to meet the needs of an increasing student body. An indication of international tensions at the time was the designation of a number of MWC buildings as public fallout shelters.

Experimental work in psychology on a scientific basis became possible in the fall of 1962 when the college opened in Chandler Hall what the acting cochairman of the department, Dr. James Russell Nazzaro, called "the finest laboratory for a school this size on the east coast." Dr. Nazzaro had designed the area and had ordered and installed the equipment. The laboratory consisted of twenty cubicles, with working space for two students in each. They were completely sound- and lightproof, with insulated walls four and a half inches thick. A ventilating system provided fresh air.

The first semester of experimental psychology offered experiments with white rats to study learning processes and behavior. The second semester consisted of experiments involving human beings as subjects. The laboratory contained a variety of electronic equipment, permitting students to work with great accuracy. An open house for interested students and faculty members was held later in the session.

With the October meeting the faculty began the practice of meeting at four-thirty in the afternoon in the ballroom of Ann Carter Lee Hall. Premeeting coffee and refreshments were served at four. This change of time and place was approved enthusiastically by the faculty.

A new policy of term, instead of lifetime, appointments for departmental chairmen was begun with the session of 1962–63. Dr. H. W. Hewetson was named for a three-year term to head the department of economics, replacing Dr. James H. Dodd, who had retired after many years of service. In announcing the new policy, Chancellor Simpson said that all future appointments of department chairmen would be for one, two, or three years. Many of the faculty members heading departments at the time had served for periods ranging from ten to thirty-five years. The term policy would apply only to new appointments.

Interest in independent study programs continued to develop. At the December faculty meeting Dr. John P. Kirby, head of the English department at Randolph-Macon Woman's College and a former member of the Mary Washington faculty, discussed the various programs of independent study available at his institution. He indicated that freshman and sophomore honors programs had been introduced to supplement the senior reading for honors. There are also several other forms of independent study.

Faculty members at Mary Washington were urged by the committee on academic excellence to make greater use of seminars and independent study programs in planning course offerings and major requirements in the various departments. An increasing number of study programs developed in the next two or three years. A handbook on the honors program was prepared for student distribution in January. It listed requirements for the honors programs, as well as the successful honors students and the titles of their papers up to that time.

In December, Chancellor and Mrs. Simpson had their first Christmas party for the faculty at Brompton. The reception rooms of the mansion had been decorated with poinsettias. Silver punchbowls gleamed in the candlelight on tables where plates of Christmas delicacies were constantly replenished. Good fellowship was enjoyed by all. In the years that have followed, the Christmas party at Brompton has become a happy feature of the season for faculty and staff members and their wives and husbands.

In the spring of 1963 the chancellor announced the establishment of a professor emeritus title. To be eligible, a faculty member must have reached retirement age with the title of full professor and must have taught at least fifteen years at the college. The first professors to be elected to emeritus status in the year of their retirement were Oscar H. Darter (1960), Vladimir V. Brenner (1961), James H. Dodd (1962), and Milton H. Stansbury (1963). The college directory for 1971–72 listed fourteen living professors emeriti, all of whom were residing in Fredericksburg.

In March 1963 the Fredericksburg chapter of the American Association of University Women celebrated at Brompton its twenty-fifth anniversary. Four of the members of the original chapter organized in March 1938 were present: Mrs. Brawner Bolling, Mrs. Lawrance Brent, Mrs. Robert H. Tompkins, and Mrs. Edgar T. Van Winckel. Many others of the original group were members of the Mary Washington faculty and have since moved from Fredericksburg. Faculty women at the college have taken an active part in the work of the Fredericksburg chapter. Most of the presidents have come from the teaching staff at Mary Washington.

On October 21, the seventh annual exhibition of contemporary art opened in the duPont Galleries. Reviewers in metropolitan newspapers were enthusiastic about the show, in which abstract paintings predominated.

On November 1 the Inter-Club Association sponsored a tapping ceremony for members of thirteen honorary fraternities and for students to be included in *Who's Who among Students in American Universities and Colleges*. Ethel Armstrong, president of ICA, presided; Dean Edward Alvey extended congratulations from the college.

The concert series for 1962–63 included among its six major attractions a production of *The Book of Job,* by the Everyman Players; *Under Milk Wood;* the National Symphony Orchestra, with Howard Mitchell conducting; and a program by the American Ballet Theater.

Religious Emphasis Week in February featured Dr. D. Elton Trueblood, author of some twenty religious and philosophical books. In April a special exhibition of the works of Gaetano Cecere, distinguished sculptor and member of the art department, was held in the duPont Galleries. Reviewers praised the "quiet strength" of his creations.[5] The Mary Washington Chorus, under the direction of Dr. George Luntz, gave a concert in the Hall of the Americas of the Pan-American Union in Washington in celebration of Pan-American Week.

With the arrival of spring came the awarding of various honors to members of the student body. Linda J. Morrison of Woodbridge, a major in psychology, won a Woodrow Wilson fellowship. Virginia Frances Lucas was selected as the first senior student assistant to work with a head resident, having the specific responsibility of helping new students in Willard Hall to adjust to college life.

Sara Travers (Sally) Tarrant was selected as May queen and presided over the program, which had Camelot as its theme. Kathy Friedman represented Mary Washington as its princess at the Apple Blossom Festival in Winchester. Diane Lovewell of Arlington was Color Girl of the graduating class of midshipmen at Annapolis.

On May 14 Governor Albertis S. Harrison, Jr., and his budget advisers visited the college. Chancellor Simpson explained his goal of providing for the state "a first-rate liberal arts college in the best tradition of colleges for women and for men." Dr. Simp-

---

[5] *Free Lance-Star,* April 3, 1963.

son made it clear that he was seeking quality rather than quantity in student enrollment and that he felt standards of achievement should be high. The governor and his advisers seemed impressed by the chancellor's explanation of his views, especially his concern with quality education.[6]

Alumnae homecoming was held from May 31 to June 2. The Alumnae College, a one-day program of lectures and demonstrations for returning graduates, featured a panel discussion by faculty and administrative personnel, with Chancellor Simpson as moderator, on the subject, "Your Alma Mater in 1963." The first fiftieth reunion of a graduating class brought seven members of the class of 1913 back to the campus.

Degrees were awarded to 288 seniors at the June graduating exercises. Kathleen Joyce Broderick of Alexandria, daughter of a Foreign Service officer, won the Darden Award with an average of 2.99 out of a possible 3.00. The commencement speaker was President Edgar F. Shannon, Jr., of the University of Virginia. The exercises concluded with Chancellor Simpson's message to the graduates. The 1962–63 session was officially at an end.

UNITED STATES–INDIA EXCHANGE PROGRAM

Early in 1963 Mary Washington College was one of a small group of women's colleges, several of which were in Virginia, that sought enriched educational experiences for both their own institutions and for women's colleges in India through the exchange of teachers and administrative staff.

The first meeting of representatives was held in Atlantic City in January 1963. William F. Quillian, Jr., of Randolph-Macon Woman's College, was selected as chairman of the group, with Dr. Elizabeth P. Lam, executive associate of the Committee on International Exchange of Persons, serving as administrator and coordinator of the program.

Plans to initiate the project got under way immediately. After some preliminary work, a team of presidents, consisting of Dr. Quillian, President Anne Pannell of Sweet Briar and Chancellor Simpson of Mary Washington, accompanied by Dr. Lam, administrative officer of the program, went to India in the fall of 1963 for a series of conferences with the heads of women's colleges

---

[6] *Ibid.*, May 15, 1963.

and other officials there. Mrs. Simpson accompanied the group.

The team selected and completed arrangements for exchange programs with six of the women's colleges in India: Indraprastha College and Miranda House, Delhi; Isabella Thoburn College, Lucknow; Women's Christian College, Madras; University Women's College, Hyderabad; and Maharani's College, Bangalore.

The consortium included thirteen women's colleges in the United States: Agnes Scott College, Decatur, Georgia; Barnard College, New York City; Bennett College, Greensboro, North Carolina; Connecticut College, New London, Connecticut; Goucher College, Baltimore, Maryland; Mary Baldwin College, Staunton, Virginia; Mary Washington College, Fredericksburg, Virginia; Mount Holyoke College, South Hadley, Massachusetts; Queens College, Charlotte, North Carolina; Randolph-Macon Woman's College, Lynchburg, Virginia; Sweet Briar College, Sweet Briar, Virginia; Western College for Women, Oxford, Ohio; and Wheaton College, Norton, Massachusetts.

The projected aims of the program were to enrich the curriculum offerings in the colleges of both countries, to identify and cooperate in the study of common educational concerns, and to deepen the understanding and appreciation of faculty and students of another culture.[7]

For the individual faculty member the program offered new professional experiences, travel and residence in a foreign country, and the basis for a feeling of mutuality in relationships of nationals of another culture.

The program provided each year for six Americans to teach in Indian colleges, for six lecturers from there to spend an academic year in residence at an American college (or a semester in each of two institutions), and for intervisitation of three American college presidents and two Indian principals.

The project was financed by grants from the State Department (under Public Law 480) and the Danforth Foundation, along with the stipends paid by the United States colleges to the Indian lecturers and principals. Four of the participating Indian colleges also contributed.

Every effort was made to select carefully the participants in the program. First each cooperating institution was asked to specify fields or services it would like a visitor to fill. This in-

---

[7] See the brochure, "Teaching Opportunities for Faculty of the Cooperating U.S. Colleges in the United States–India Women's College Exchange Program."

formation was compiled and forwarded to the cooperating colleges of the opposite country. Brochures describing the program and detailed application forms were made available to faculty members in each institution who were interested in the openings available and for whom leaves of absence could be arranged.

The selections of the cooperating colleges were then reviewed by the executive committee of that country and, in the case of the Indian applicants, by the United States Educational Foundation in India as well. Then the list and the dossiers of each candidate were circulated among the cooperating colleges, which were asked to indicate, in order, their preferences as to visiting faculty or staff members. The final selection was made by the advisory boards in India, for the American visitors, and the executive committee in America, in the case of the representatives from India.

Early in the program, Mary Washington College took the lead in sponsoring a series of three-day conferences designed to help the American teachers going to India under the program to prepare for their year there; to provide an opportunity for the Indian teachers in this country under the program to comment on their experiences and to make suggestions for the guidance of American colleges having Indian teachers as visiting faculty members the coming year; and to introduce two visiting Indian principals and give them an opportunity to talk with the Americans who would be going to their colleges during the coming year.

Chancellor Simpson and his colleagues organized the conferences and served as chairmen. Meetings were held in 1965, 1966, 1967, and 1968, usually during the spring recess, at Mary Washington College.

Speakers for these conferences included officials of the Bureau of Educational and Cultural Affairs, United States Department of State; of the United States Information Agency; and of the United States Educational Foundation in India. Group conferences provided for close contact between the visiting faculty members, both Indian and American, and the representatives of governmental and educational agencies that could be of greatest assistance. Every effort was made to prepare the visitors for understanding the customs and practices in the new country, as well as its system of higher education. Of special service in the latter respect were the visiting principals from the Indian colleges for women.

Provision was made for the informal association of conference participants at coffee breaks, buffet meals, and, a high point of the social side of the meeting, a dinner at Brompton in honor of the participants.

Among the heads of Indian colleges who participated in these conferences were Principal S. Shridevi, University College for Women at Hyderabad; Principal H. M. Parvathamma, Maharani's College for Women at Bangalore; and Principal Eva Shipstone, Isabella Thoburn College, Lucknow.

There were also conferences in India of a similar nature in which representatives of colleges from both countries took part. In 1966, Chancellor Simpson again went to India to evaluate the accomplishments of the program and also to join in the spring conference of participants in the exchange.

During the years in which the program operated, five professors from Mary Washington participated. The late Dr. Alan S. Pierce, professor of biology, was the first one, conducting seminars in the colleges at Bangalore, Hyderabad, Lucknow, and Madras during the session of 1964-65.

Dr. Pierce was followed the next year by Dr. Roger Lee Kenvin, associate professor of English, who taught at Isabella Thoburn College, Lucknow, in 1965-66. In 1966-67, Dr. Mary Ellen Stephenson, professor of Spanish and then also assistant dean of students, taught at Women's Christian College, Madras.

In 1967-68 Dr. Lewis P. Fickett, Jr., associate professor of political science, was a visiting member of the faculty at Miranda House in Delhi. The following session Dr. Barbara Alden, from the library at Mary Washington, served as librarian at Isabella Thoburn College in Lucknow. Judith Lee Nixon, instructor in health, physical education, and recreation, taught at Indraprastha College, Delhi, for the first semester of the 1968-69 session.

Visiting faculty members from Indian colleges were as follows: Miss R. K. Padmabai, Women's Christian College of Madras, visiting lecturer in English, second semester 1964-65; Dr. Eva Shipstone, Isabella Thoburn College, Lucknow, visiting lecturer in psychology, second semester 1965-66; Joy C. Michael, program officer, United States Educational Foundation in India, visiting lecturer in drama, second semester 1967-68; Mrs. V. Krishna, Miranda House, University of Delhi, visiting lecturer in English literature, second semester 1967-68; Zeba Ansari, University College for Women, Hyderabad, visiting lecturer in literature, art, and philosophy, first semester, 1967-68; Renée V. Singh, Isabella Thoburn College, Lucknow, visiting lecturer in geography, first and second semesters 1968-69.

In response to a request for a reaction to her experiences as a participant in the program, Miss Stephenson wrote:

All of the insights and broadening influences one has from travel were increased many-fold for me by my year as exchange-professor in India. This was because during my time there I belonged to my college community as one of the group. I faced with them their successes and their problems as we face ours in America. It was challenging because Indian educators and students handle their growth and development plans and changes constructively, but in an Eastern, not Western, fashion.

In reply to a similar request, Miss Alden gave this summary of her feelings as a participant:

My experience of India gave me my first intimate knowledge of what it means to belong to a minority group—not only racially (this was of minor importance) but religiously, economically, and linguistically. The last was the most difficult experience, for there was no hope of improving the situation in ten months, nor at my age. Above all in importance, I carried back with me a totally new angle of vision from which to understand my country and my people. This alone made the whole wonderful adventure invaluable to me and convinced me of its importance even more for those younger than I but mature enough to realize the significance of such an opportunity.

Federal funds for the continuation of the project were not available after the session of 1968–69. However, the American Consortium has been continued in the hope that further financing might make possible a renewal of the program. Chancellor Simpson is currently chairman of the American group. The Indian consortium has also continued as an organization. During the summer of 1970 three faculty members from Mary Washington participated in a seminar in India—James H. Croushore, Albert R. Klein, and Samuel T. Emory, Jr.

CHAPTER XXIII

Academic Developments in the Mid-1960s

STUDY OF MAJORS IN HOME ECONOMICS AND PHYSICAL EDUCATION

IN ACCORDANCE with the recommendations of both the visiting committee for the self-study and the long-range planning committee, the college began the study of the relevance of majors in home economics and physical education in a liberal arts college.

The curriculum committee was assigned the task of studying the two programs and making recommendations to the faculty. In a progress report in April 1963, the committee announced that it had divided into two subcommittees to meet with representatives of the two departments. At the May meeting it announced that criteria had been formulated "to which major offerings should conform" and that the two departments had been asked to consider them and prepare written reports. These reports were assembled for the curriculum committee and formed the basis of many of the discussions that followed.

During the session of 1963–64 the curriculum committee held meetings throughout the fall both with the entire home economics faculty in attendance and in executive session. A large body of material assembled by the department in support of its major program was read and discussed by the curriculum committee and later made available in the library to the entire faculty. Finally, by a vote of six to four, the curriculum committee decided on February 4, 1964, to present the following motion to the faculty at its meeting on February 11: "The Curriculum Committee recommends to the faculty that by June, 1968, the major in Home Economics at Mary Washington College be terminated and courses in the Department of Home Economics be offered for elective credit only."[1]

The faculty were requested to weigh the recommendation carefully so that they could vote intelligently at the March meeting. They were urged to examine the two envelopes of pertinent documents on reserve in the library, which might assist them in

[1] Faculty Minutes, Feb. 11, 1964.

making a decision. Chancellor Simpson expressed his confidence in the faculty's ability to decide the question wisely.

At the March meeting a "vigorous and occasionally heated" (faculty minutes) discussion took place. Debate was halted finally when the faculty voted 79 to 46 to continue the consideration of the motion at the next meeting.

Most of the April 14 meeting was devoted to a continuation of the motion to discontinue home economics as a major field. Various faculty members made eloquent appeals for the retention or the elimination of the major. Finally, after calls for the question, the faculty, by secret ballot, voted 77 to 60, with one abstention, to discontinue the major.

On the recommendation of the chancellor, the board of visitors, at its meeting on June 5, 1964, adopted the following resolution:

Resolved by the Board of Visitors of The Rector and Visitors of the University of Virginia that Mary Washington College be and it is hereby authorized to discontinue conferring the degree of Bachelor of Science in Home Economics after June 1968, and that, after September 1964, no student will be permitted to enroll in courses directed towards a degree in Home Economics, except that the degree may be awarded (1) when the requirements have been met after June 1968 on a program begun prior to 30 September 1964, and (2) when in the discretion of the Chancellor an exception should be made.[2]

In the late spring the study of the major program in physical education was begun by the curriculum committee. The department prepared an eighteen-page mimeographed "Reply of the Department of Health, Physical Education, and Recreation to Questions of the Curriculum Committee Concerning the Major Program." A study of this document was on the agenda as the first item of business of the curriculum committee in the fall.

In October 1963 the curriculum committee began its study of the "Reply." The report supported strongly the thesis that a major in physical education and a liberal arts education were not incompatible. In fact, it emphasized that Mary Washington had a unique opportunity in providing such a major within the framework of a good liberal arts program. "We want our students to be both technically skilled *and* culturally competent," continued the statement. It pointed out the staff, courses, and facilities the college had for offering a strong major.

The curriculum committee held a series of long meetings on the elimination of the physical education major. Representatives

[2] Minutes of Board of Visitors, June 5, 1964.

of the department were heard and the data they presented examined. In a progress report presented at the April 1965 faculty meeting the curriculum committee reported that it had "elected, by a vote of 7 to 4, to recommend to the faculty (at the appropriate time) that the existing major program and the degree in Health, Physical Education, and Recreation be discontinued after June, 1969."[3]

This motion was made at the May 19 faculty meeting. A long discussion ensued. The department offered several alternatives, which included the conferring of a regular B.S. for physical education majors rather than the specialized degree. Finally the faculty voted to discontinue both the major and the B.S. in health, physical education, and recreation.

The department had presented two alternative programs for majors in the field, one in dance and the other in the science of movement. A complete outline of major requirements, course content, and supporting evidence for offering a major in dance was presented to the curriculum committee and later distributed to the faculty. At its May meeting the faculty approved the proposed major in dance shortly after it had voted to discontinue the major in health, physical education and recreation.

Action on the proposed major in the art of movement was deferred until fall. Actually, two types of majors had been proposed, one in the art of movement and the other in the science of movement. The former became the basis of the new program in dance, while the latter was retitled as a major in kinesiology.

Discussion of the proposed major extended over a period of several months. Lengthy statements supporting and opposing the major were mimeographed and distributed to the faculty. An extended discussion of the proposal took place at the February 8, 1966, faculty meeting. Finally, at the March 8 meeting, the faculty, voting by secret ballot, passed 91 to 50 a motion to uphold the report of the curriculum committee that a major in kinesiology not be offered by the college.

There were no further attempts to design other types of programs that would, in a sense, replace the discontinued major in health, physical education, and recreation. Dance became the new major program of the department.

The catalogue for 1966–67 (pp. 137–43) carried the announcement that the degree of bachelor of science in health, physical education, and recreation would be discontinued after June

---

[3] Faculty Minutes, April 13, 1965, appendix N.

1969. It also contained a full description of the new major in dance.

Once the new major had been established, steps were taken to develop it into a strong program. An additional instructor in dance was appointed the following session and still another the next year, for a total of four faculty members who had specialized in dance and were giving their full time to instruction in this field.

PROFILES OF ENTERING CLASS

The first general profile of the entering class was published in September 1963. It showed a total of 1,768 students: 527 freshmen, 39 transfers, and 1,202 returning students.

The mean verbal score of the freshmen on the Scholastic Aptitude Test of the College Entrance Examination Board was 549; the mean mathematical score, 532. Both averages were above national norms. Eighty-four percent were in the highest quarter of their graduating class, and 15 percent were in the second quartile, leaving only 1 percent not in the highest half of their class.

By 1964 the mean verbal and mathematic SAT scores had risen to 558 and 547, respectively. By 1965 they were 565 and 555. In 1966 the mean verbal score was 581; the mean mathematical, 575. Ninety-one percent of the 574 entering freshmen were in the highest fourth of their graduating class. In 1967 the mean verbal score was 575; the mean mathematical score, 567; and 97 percent of the freshmen were in the highest two-fifths of their graduating class in high school.

NEW MAJOR IN GEOGRAPHY AND GEOLOGY

Courses in geography and geology had become increasingly popular, and a demand developed for a major in this area. The curriculum committee had deliberated at length before recommending to the faculty, at its meeting in October 1963, that such a major be authorized. There was lively discussion over the desirability of such a combination major, as well as over the size of the teaching staff available, which at the time consisted of two assistant professors—Dr. Samuel T. Emory (geography) and Dr. Samuel O. Bird (geology).

Finally, at its meeting on November 12, 1963, the faculty voted to establish the new major in geography and geology, which required completion of certain courses in both fields.[4] A description of the new major appeared in the catalogue announcements for 1964-65 (pp. 132-34). The interest and enthusiasm of students enrolled in this area of study led to provisions for additional faculty, facilities, and courses.

By 1971-72 there were five full-time faculty members in the department of geography and geology. Twenty-three one-semester courses were available in geography and nine in geology. The need for space to house equipment obtained through the science improvement grant led to a separation of the two areas of study. Geography was moved to rooms 1 and 2 in the basement of Monroe Hall, while geology remained in its basement rooms in Combs Science Building. Increased facilities for laboratory work were provided in each location.

In the spring of 1972 the faculty voted to separate the two areas of study, with a separate major in each field.[5] Professor Samuel T. Emory was appointed chairman of the department of geography, and Professor Samuel O. Bird was appointed to head the department of geology.

KENNEDY MEMORIAL SERVICES

Like the rest of the civilized world, the entire college was shocked by the assassination of President John F. Kennedy on November 22, 1963. A student-sponsored memorial service was held in the auditorium of George Washington Hall on the day of President Kennedy's funeral. Dean Edward Alvey delivered a tribute to the late president, which was published in the *Bullet* on December 14, 1963.

NEW DEPARTMENT OF ECONOMICS AND POLITICAL SCIENCE

On July 8, 1964, Dr. Robert Leroy Hilldrup, professor of history and, for many years, chairman of the department of history and political science, died of a heart attack. The faculty adopted memorial resolutions at its first fall meeting on September 14.

---

[4] *Ibid.,* Oct. 8 and Nov. 12, 1963.   [5] *Ibid.,* April 12, and May 10, 1972.

A reorganization of the offering in social science became effective with the opening of the session of 1964–65. Courses in what had been previously the department of history and political science were regrouped to form a separate department of history, with Dr. Joseph C. Vance as chairman. Courses in political science were transferred to a new department of economics and political science, headed by Dr. Henry W. Hewetson. The new department offered three majors: economics, political science, and political economy. In 1970 Dr. Lewis P. Fickett, Jr., became chairman of the department of economics and political science.

DEPARTMENT OF RELIGION ESTABLISHED

In October 1964 a department of religion was established, with Elizabeth A. Clark (A.B., Vassar; M.A., Ph.D., Columbia University) as chairman. The program provided introductory semester courses in Old and New Testament, followed by a second-year course, The Western Religious Heritage. Four advanced courses of one semester each were devoted to readings in Hellenistic religious literature and that of the Middle Ages and Reformation, the eighteenth and nineteenth centuries, and the twentieth century.

On recommendation of the curriculum committee, the faculty approved a major in religion at its April 1969 meeting.[6] The course offering was expanded considerably and another staff member appointed. Among the courses added were Concepts of God, Studies in Historical Theology, and Theological Ethics. A senior seminar and an independent study program were also established.

CLASS ATTENDANCE

In 1964–65 the faculty adopted on a trial basis a new class attendance system, placing increased responsibility on the student for her own regularity of attendance and eliminating the system of class cuts based on academic average for the previous session. Faculty members were given the authority to excuse absences or to require attendance if a student were doing poorly. They were asked to record absences and report on the final grade sheet the number of absences regarded as excused. Attendance at an-

---

[6] *Ibid.*, March 12, 1969 and April 9, 1969.

nounced tests and final examinations as well as at the last class before and the first class after the college recesses was required, unless specifically excused by the Dean.[7]

After two years of successful trial, the new system was put into effect permanently by the faculty.[8] There was general agreement that elimination of the class-cut system and establishment of a closer relationship between student and instructor regarding absences had improved attendance.

STUDY ABROAD PROGRAMS

During the 1960s junior-year-abroad programs became increasingly popular. In 1964–65 fourteen juniors were studying in France, Spain, Germany, or Austria under the programs sponsored by Sweet Briar College, Hamilton College, New York University, the Institute of European Studies, and the Institute for American Universities. The last-mentioned program, in Aix-en-Provence, France, was particularly popular, and five juniors were there that year. Four were in Spain under the New York University junior-year-abroad program, and two in France under the Sweet Briar program.

IBM REGISTRATION

The use of IBM equipment for registration, preparing class rolls, reporting grades and deficiencies, and recording course information for students' permanent records was introduced in the fall of 1965. The new system was enthusiastically received by both students and faculty.

COMMITTEE ON THE SENIOR YEAR

In 1965 a special committee on the senior year, appointed by the chancellor two years earlier, presented a report to the faculty.[9] The committee, headed by Myra Irby with Nancy Mitchell as secretary, made an exhaustive study of the records of five recent senior classes to chart the number and level of courses taken each year and the credits and quality points earned. It obtained the opinions of seniors regarding major programs, the advisory sys-

[7] *Ibid.,* April 13, 1965.   [8] *Ibid.,* Jan. 10, 1967.   [9] *Ibid.,* Oct. 12, 1965.

tem, and social regulations. Copies of the complete report were distributed to members of the faculty for their information.

COUNSELING CENTER

In 1965, a testing center was established on the first floor of Hamlet House under the direction, on a part-time basis, of Mary Annette Kelly, associate professor of psychology. The demand for services was such that Mrs. Kelly's time at the center was extended more and more each year and her teaching load reduced. Finally, in 1968–69, the operation was made a full-time position and the title changed to counseling center, with Mrs. Kelly as director and Sharon W. Lancaster as assistant to the director. Meanwhile Mrs. Kelly had been officially licensed as a practicing psychologist by the Board of Examiners of the State of Virginia.

The new designation as counseling center is descriptive of its larger role in dealing with the personal and emotional problems of students. Facilities are provided on a free basis, with complete assurance of confidentiality. The majority of students using the counseling service come voluntarily to the center for appointments. Some are referred by members of the college faculty and staff.

The counseling center has rendered rich service to Mary Washington College. Mrs. Kelly has been a sympathetic and capable counselor whose technical knowledge has not overshadowed her genuine interest in the individual as a person and her desire to be of assistance. The demand for her services has resulted in a schedule of appointments filling every hour of the working day. Yet she is always ready to respond to emergencies when they arise.

The center continues to serve as a testing agency for the college, administering both individual and group tests. The center handles the administration of the College Board Examinations, the American College Testing Program, the Graduate Record Examinations, and other national programs as well as batteries of selected tests for individual students.

QUALITY POINT SYSTEM CHANGED

After careful study the faculty voted in October 1965 to accept the recommendations of the committee on academic excellence that the present three-point grading system be changed to a four-point system and that a student's credit ratio be determined on the basis of the number of hours she attempted rather than on the number of hours she passed.[10] The new system went into effect with the opening of the 1966-67 session.

Quality point credit and letter grades for courses in physical education taken to meet degree requirements were eliminated at the request of the department of health, physical education, and recreation, effective June 15, 1967.[11] A system of satisfactory-unsatisfactory would be used to indicate whether course requirements had been met or not. The new plan did not apply to majors in dance.

COURSE IN HEALTH MADE ELECTIVE

At its May 1966 meeting the faculty voted to make elective the course in Health Education 100, Health, which had for so many years been required for a degree. This requirement dated back to the early years of the institution when, as a state teachers college, it was expected to prepare all of its graduates to meet the requirements for a teaching certificate. A course in hygiene, as the health course was then called, was, according to the West Law, required by the Virginia State Department of Education for any type of teaching certificate.

Considerable discussion preceded the elimination of the course in health as a requirement for graduation. The motion was finally carried by a vote of 64 to 36. The credits required for graduation were reduced from 126 to 124. The new ruling became effective with the students beginning their degree programs with the 1966 summer session.[12]

SUMMER SCHOOL IN SPAIN

During the summer of 1966 Mary Washington College conducted its first program of travel and study abroad, primarily in Spain. The theme was "The Living Literature of Spain." The course was conducted by Josefa Rivas (M.A., Rice Institute; Ph.D., University of Valencia), assistant professor of Spanish at Mary

[10] *Ibid.* [11] *Ibid.*, April 11, 1967. [12] *Ibid.*, May 17, 1966.

Washington. It consisted of forty hours of lecture and class discussion, in Spanish, on writers associated with the area being visited by the group.

Dean Alvey organized the trip, handled publicity for the program, registered the students, and accompanied the group as an official representative of the college. During the summer he wrote from Spain a series of articles for the Fredericksburg *Free Lance–Star,* which were collected and reproduced under the title, "Impressions of Spain and Portugal, 1966." A copy of the booklet was sent to each chapter of the Mary Washington College Alumnae Association.

The program sought to offer a new dimension to serious academic study of Spanish literature through the living culture of Spain – its people, places, language, architecture, music, and art. Lectures in the course were carefully planned in relation to the geographic areas visited and their eras of history, art, and literature. In addition to visits to famous museums, monuments, and churches, there were opportunities to mingle with the people and absorb the ideas and customs of another civilization.

Students from other colleges and universities were invited to join the group. The completion of at least one year of college Spanish was required for enrollment. Actually, most of the students were majoring in Spanish. As finally constituted, the group included students from Mary Washington, Meredith College, the University of South Carolina, the University of North Carolina, and the University of Virginia.

The first four days were spent in Lisbon, Portugal, where introductory lectures on the geography and history of Spain were conducted in the evenings. A one-day excursion was made to the Royal Palace at Queluz and the castle at Sintra, called by Byron the most beautiful castle in the world.

A day's journey by train brought the group to Santiago de Compostela, where the next two weeks were spent. During the Middle Ages thousands of pilgrims came there to visit the tomb of St. James, whose body is enshrined in the magnificent Romanesque cathedral begun in the eleventh century. Fonseca University made one of its sixteenth-century lecture halls available for class meetings.

Early in July the group left Santiago for an extended tour of Spain in a chartered bus available at all times for trips to places of literary, historic, or artistic interest. The series of lectures ended when the group left Spain for a final four days in Paris before flying back home. Upon returning to America, each member of the class took a final examination on the lectures and field trips and also submitted a fairly comprehensive essay on some aspect of Spanish culture selected early in the trip so that notes could be taken and material gathered as the program progressed. Three semester hours of college credit were granted upon successful completion of all assignments.[13]

The following year the University of Virginia began a summer program in Spain and invited students from Mary Washington to participate. In view of this development, the idea of repeating the Mary Washington College-sponsored trip was dropped. The University of Virginia project seemed to have its greatest appeal to teachers of Spanish working toward a master's degree. However, one student from Mary Washington participated in the 1967 venture and another when the program was repeated in 1968.

A TENTH ANNIVERSARY

At the faculty meeting on February 8, 1966, recognition was accorded Dr. Simpson upon completion of a decade of service as chancellor of Mary Washington College. In accordance with his wish, there was no special celebration of the tenth anniversary of his coming to the college. However, the occasion provided an opportunity for the faculty to share Dr. Simpson's thinking about days past and days ahead.

Dr. Simpson's remarks on this occasion, as summarized by the secretary of the faculty in the official minutes, are of special interest for the insight they afford into his philosophy of education. The following paragraphs are quoted from the faculty minutes of February 8, 1966:

In recognition of the Chancellor's recent completion of his first ten years as the chief administrative official of the College the Dean mentioned as some of the highlights of the Simpson administration the upgrading of admission standards, the raising of requirements for degrees, the reduction of teaching loads, the improvement of faculty salaries and the creation of a center of hospitality at Brompton. Then Dean Alvey asked Mr. Simpson to discuss the College's progress for the next decade. Mr. Simpson was given a standing ovation by the faculty.

After thanking Mr. Alvey for his gracious remarks, the Chancellor

---
[13] Edward Alvey, Jr., "Our Summer in Spain: A Retrospective Appraisal," *Alumnae News* 19, no. 1 (1967): 3–5.

stated that he was fully aware that what had been achieved had not been accomplished alone. He explained that he had accepted the invitation to come to Mary Washington College because he had been assured that this institution would be permitted to demonstrate something in which he believed strongly, the validity of the undergraduate degree, and because he was to be permitted to provide a liberal arts education for young women comparable to that provided by the Commonwealth of Virginia for its young men.

To Mr. Simpson the greatest achievement was the assembling of a faculty of real scholars and teachers. In looking backward he characterized as the College's most difficult task the clarification of its mission and the implementation of its objectives. He expressed his opinion that the purpose of the College is now more clearly defined and the achieving of its goals much more nearly realized.

The Chancellor predicted that within the next few years colleges must face the necessity of articulating the relevance of a vast amount of knowledge and justifying the uses to which it may be put. He declared that it is our intellectual responsibility to see "that liberal learning will have such relevance to the young in the give and take of their lives that it will open new horizons to them." Mr. Simpson voiced the hope that each faculty member on his own would bring his talents to bear toward the realization of this goal. He warned that this will require dedication, vision, tolerance and sacrifice in a nonfinancial sense. He stressed that we of the Occident desperately needed to develop an understanding of the Asian and African peoples and their rich culture and in furtherance of this end, Chancellor Simpson personally welcomed Miss Shipstone.

He emphasized the need of developing a recognition of the relevance of the creative and performing arts in the liberal arts program. He said that despite the advantages of classifying, categorizing and departmentalizing the frighteningly large body of knowledge, the barriers between disciplines should be broken down. The Chancellor gave this crossfertilization as the explanation of some of the great breakthroughs of knowledge that have been achieved by the natural sciences, and suggested that the social sciences and the humanities might likewise profitably "compete in the best sense of the world."

He characterized the desire of present-day collegians to participate in mapping their education and in self-government as "desirable, commendable and frequently uncomfortable." He declared that "we are here not to work with average people," and that "motivated or unmotivated our students are worth an extra effort on our part." He declared that we were fortunate in having the opportunity to assist in "the awakening of young minds."

The meeting adjourned shortly after Dr. Simpson's remarks. Members of the faculty gathered about him to express appreciation of his decade of such service to the college.

CHAPTER XXIV

New Majors, Degree Requirements, and College Calendar

RECOGNITION OF ACADEMIC ATTAINMENT

IN A FALL 1966 MEETING the committee on academic excellence recommended the recognition of general academic attainment through awards of degrees cum laude, magna cum laude, and summa cum laude, based solely on the student's academic average at Mary Washington. The proposal was debated and discussed at length, and adopted at the January meeting, with academic averages of 3.25, 3.50, and 3.75 specified for the three levels of distinction. It was decided then that the new system would become effective with the graduating class of 1968.

However, when the system was adopted, there was marked dissatisfaction on the part of some faculty members with the use of Latin phrases to describe the level of achievement on a diploma written in English. Before the plan was actually put into effect with the class of 1969, the terminology was changed to With Distinction, High Distinction, and Highest Distinction, based on averages of 3.25, 3.50, and 3.75, respectively.[1]

Students qualifying for these honors have a notation to that effect attached to their diplomas. They are also recognized publicly at graduation exercises when their individual degrees are conferred.

COMPREHENSIVE EXAMINATIONS

For several years the faculty had discussed the pros and cons of comprehensive examinations. Every time the subject had arisen, various questions had been raised about the feasibility or desirability of such a practice. Finally, at a meeting on December 13, 1966, the faculty approved a resolution of the Curriculum Committee authorizing a comprehensive examination in the English department as a degree requirement for majors in that field.

Given four years of experience, the English department discontinued the comprehensive examination requirement after

---

[1] Faculty Minutes, April 9, 1968.

June 1971. The department of religion has continued to require a comprehensive examination for majors at the beginning of the second semester of the senior year, as well as a senior paper.

The psychology department was authorized in April 1969 to require a comprehensive examination for majors. It used for the purpose a test developed by the Educational Testing Service for graduating majors in psychology. The new test was used on a trial basis only. In 1971–72, the department voted to discontinue it.

FIVE-DAY WEEK

At a faculty meeting on March 14, 1967, Dr. Fickett, chairman of the committee on instruction, reported that his committee had been considering the five-day-week proposal for two and a half years and had concluded that it would be a desirable policy. The committee recommended that a special committee be selected to work on the five-day-week proposal.

An ad hoc committee on the five-day-week was appointed by the chancellor. This group, headed by Dr. George Van Sant, made a thorough study of the entire question. Its report considered the incidence of Saturday classes, absences over the weekend, the experiences of other colleges which had adopted a five-day week, and the benefits that would accrue from its adoption at Mary Washington. The committee recommended unanimously that, commencing in the fall of 1968, Mary Washington should schedule classes on a Monday-through-Friday sequence.

Copies of the report were distributed at the January 9, 1968, meeting of the faculty. Dr. Van Sant discussed the report in some detail. He then announced that Chancellor Simpson had approved the committee's recommendation and that beginning in September 1968 Mary Washington College would be on a five-day week. Enthusiastic applause followed this announcement.

Subsequently, the committee presented several plans for a five-day class schedule. Members of the faculty were asked to study the various proposals and indicate their preferences. A track system of fifty-minute class meetings during the morning and seventy-five-minute meetings for afternoon classes, with a fifteen-minute break between periods, was adopted.[2]

Classes were scheduled to begin at 8:00 A.M. and end at 5:30

---

[2] *Ibid.*, March 12, 1968.

P.M. No department was to schedule a second class in the same track until it had filled all other tracks in the weekly schedule. This provision alone did much to eliminate schedule conflicts with other courses in the same department and to insure that hours other than the popular morning ones were being utilized.

GEORGE M. VAN SANT

Dr. George M. Van Sant, chairman of the five-day-week committee and, later, of the committee on degree requirements and the college calendar, received the M.A. and Ph.D. degrees from the University of Virginia where he had been an instructor in philosophy. He joined the faculty at Mary Washington in 1958 as assistant professor of philosophy and progressed steadily through the academic ranks. In 1969 he was made chairman of the philosophy department. His keen interest in academic affairs has resulted in a number of innovations in practices. In 1971–72 he was absent on leave for postdoctoral research with the faculty of philosophy at Cambridge University.

Since 1968 Dr. Van Sant has served as marshal of the faculty. His tall figure stands out in academic processions as he carries the mace with impressive dignity and the military bearing one would expect of a colonel in the Marine Corps Reserve. In faculty meeting his resonant voice has become a familiar sound as he reports for the committees he has headed.

MAJOR IN STUDIO ART

For sometime the college had offered a major in art "with the emphasis on Studio Art" and a major in history of art.[3] In 1967 the board of visitors approved a full-fledged major in studio art, which would consist of twenty-four semester hours of studio art, and twelve semester hours of art history.[4] The history of art major was continued, with a requirement of thirty semester hours' credit in art history courses, including advanced courses in research in the history of art. No studio courses were required for majors in this area.

[3] *Catalogue*, 1965–66, p. 113.   [4] Faculty Minutes, March 14, 1967.

THE GALDÓS SYMPOSIUM

On April 21-22 1967, the department of modern foreign languages sponsored a symposium on Benito Pérez Galdós, the nineteenth-century Spanish author. Arranged by Dr. Carmen L. Rivera, professor of Spanish at the college, the symposium attracted college and university faculty members and students from a wide area. During the two days, eight papers on various aspects of the work of Galdós were presented by university professors from California, Indiana, Florida, Kansas, Minnesota, and other states. The symposium was widely acclaimed for the quality of the papers read and the audience it attracted. Eighteen Virginia and thirty-three out-of-state institutions sent representatives. A collection of the papers read at the symposium was published by the college.

THE PASS-FAIL PLAN

In May 1968, the faculty approved a limited pass-fail plan permitting a student to enroll for one elective course each semester with no grade or quality points recorded.[5] The plan sought to encourage students to experiment with courses outside their major program, without feeling the pressure of earning a certain grade. No student could change to or from a pass-fail status in a course after the initial two-week drop-add period.

COMMITTEE ON THE FUTURE OF THE COLLEGE

A committee on the future of the college was appointed by Chancellor Simpson in September 1967, and its personnel and purpose were announced at the October 10 meeting of the faculty. Selected to serve on the committee were Mildred M. Bolling, Andrew Buni, Mildred A. Droste, George W. Grayson, Jr., Michael Houston, Mary A. K. Kelly, Albert R. Klein, Kurt F. Leidecker, Bernard L. Mahoney, Jr., and Sidney H. Mitchell. Later, Buni and Grayson were replaced by Edward V. Allison, Jr., who succeeded Edgar Woodward as comptroller of the college, and Victor Fingerhut, assistant professor of economics and political science.

---

[5] *Ibid.*, May 14, 1965.

In announcing the committee, Chancellor Simpson explained that "the committee would concern itself with the possibility of co-education here, the impact on the College if the University adopts co-education, whether our College should remain a single-purpose institution, and what should be the administrative relation of the College with the University."[6]

Dr. Simpson disclosed to the faculty that "The Rector and Visitors of the University had established a Committee on the Need or Advisability of Co-education in the College of Arts and Sciences at Charlottesville and that President Shannon on his recommendation had appointed Messrs. Croushore and Klein as our College's representatives on that committee."[7]

In a written memorandum regarding the role of the new committee, the chancellor said, in part:

The work of this committee will not be one such as is usually associated with long-range planning—but rather it will be the work of the committee to recommend to the Chancellor and ultimately to the Board whatever alterations in our present government and program and purpose are needed in order that Mary Washington College will continue to be not only an outstanding institution of higher learning in the last decades of the 20th century but also an academic institution preparing itself to offer to its students the appropriate and necessary intellectual guidance that students in the 21st century will require and find relevant in their era.

The committee will be free—rather encouraged—to discuss appropriate and relevant matters with alumnae, especially the official Board of the Alumnae Association, with members of the Board of Visitors and especially the Mary Washington College Committee of the Board, with members of the faculty and staff, with students and student leaders, with governmental agencies and personnel, especially the State Council of Higher Education, with citizens of the community and Commonwealth, and with other people whose regard and concern for the College are well known.

The committee got to work immediately. During the 1967–68 session alone the committee held twenty-one meetings. It conferred with officers of the MWC Alumnae Association, of the State Council of Higher Education, and of the MWC Student Government Association, as well as with college officials and faculty, active and retired. During the next twenty-four months the committee submitted nine interim reports containing a large number of proposals "intended to initiate actions or studies that

[6] *Ibid.*, Oct. 10, 1967.   [7] *Ibid.*

would keep Mary Washington College attuned to the evolving academic scene." Six of the reports deal with nine specific proposals, none of which involved a radical change from the liberal arts orientation of the college.

Three of the principal topics studied by the committee were the nature of the relationship with the University of Virginia, the role of men students in the future of Mary Washington, and the academic program, including the possible introduction of graduate courses. In both its interim report of June 7 and its final report on the long-range future, the committee proposed that the college continue to work within the university system, in the belief that "not only Mary Washington but the entire university and the State benefit from this present relationship" (p. 12).

After polls of the faculty, students, and alumnae, the committee recommended that men be admitted on a nonresident basis (interim reports of November 14, 1968, and March 21, 1969) to both summer and regular sessions (subsequently approved by the board of visitors) and urged that plans be made to enroll men in "other than a non-residential status" (p. 13). The committee took a stand for offering a limited number of graduate-level courses (interim report of November 14, 1968), not as an "indiscriminate, sprawling extension of the College's current functions," but as individual departments had the "fully qualified faculty and the appropriate facilities and equipment" to provide such instruction (p. 2). The committee cautioned that if graduate courses are made available, the program should not be allowed to jeopardize the principal purpose of the college, the offering of a strong, undergraduate, liberal arts program.

Other recommendations included courses and programs in urban problems and racial relations; automation and computer sciences; and problems of developing nations. The committee suggested that the college utilize its proximity to Washington to create institutes, workshops, or summer intern programs in government, foreign affairs, and area studies. Special summer programs in drama, music, and dance were suggested. Among the proposals for further study were supplemental salary grants from private funds to attract outstanding teachers, more scholarships for out-of-state residents, and the formation of a special standing committee to consider the proper relationship of the college to Fredericksburg and the surrounding area.

The committee transmitted its final report to the chancellor in October 1969. Copies were duplicated and distributed to the board of visitors of the university, the board of directors of the

Alumnae Association, executive officers of the MWC Student Government Association, and the administrative officers and faculty members of the college.

SUPERVISED TEACHING PROGRAM REVISED

Changes in certification requirements for teachers in Virginia, including an increase in the number of contact hours required in student teaching, necessitated a reexamination of the entire plan for the preparation of teachers. The chancellor appointed a committee on supervised teaching, composed of seven members of the faculty and administrative staff, with Dr. B. L. Mahoney of the chemistry department as chairman.

As an outgrowth of the report of this committee, the college adopted an experimental program of off-campus student teaching, beginning with the 1968–69 session. Enrolled students taught full time for one semester in one of several centers located in the Northern Virginia, Richmond, and Fredericksburg areas. College staff members acted as general supervisors, visiting and observing the student teacher in the classroom and conferring with her and with the classroom teacher to whom she had been assigned.

In addition to this supervision, the college staff member also taught a course at the center in foundations of education, for which three semester hours' credit was allowed. Together with the six credits in supervised teaching, the student was able to earn nine semester hours during the semester of her teaching. If she took in addition evening extension work in an approved course offered in that area, twelve credits could be earned.

Obviously, such a program involved schedule conflicts with hyphenated or sequential courses in some departments, which required a full session of study, notably in foreign languages and the sciences. The committee addressed much of its attention to this problem. Through the cooperation of various departments and their chairmen, provision was made for offering such courses on a semester basis or in the summer session, so that the student could spend an entire semester away from the campus without too much hazard to her academic major program.

In cases in which scheduling problems in the major field were apparently insurmountable, provisions were continued for student teaching in residence while other courses were also being taken. Two to three periods for classroom teaching were required of all student teachers in the secondary school; elementary teachers usually taught all day. Students were placed not only in the Fredericksburg schools but also in those of Stafford, Spotsylvania, King George, and even Caroline counties. They furnished their own transportation to and from the schools, returning to the college for meals and room and usually a required course offered for them in the late afternoon. Students doing their student teaching in off-campus centers in the Northern Virginia and Richmond areas made their own living arrangements. Many resided in their own homes if they lived in that area.

Although some problems were encountered, the new program offered so many advantages over the previous provisions for student teaching that it was adopted as a regular policy. The implementation of the new plan, with the employment of the additional faculty necessary to put it into effect, was decidedly a factor in the approval of the teacher-training program of the college by the State Department of Education in every area in which certification had been requested.

In 1970–71, the college program for the preparation of teachers was officially approved by the National Association of State Directors of Teacher Education and Certification. Thus, graduates of Mary Washington who had successfully completed the program of teacher preparation at this institution became eligible for immediate certification in some thirty other states under a reciprocity agreement applicable only to graduates of approved institutional programs.

CREDIT BY EXAMINATION

In May 1969 the faculty approved a plan by which a student could make application to a department chairman for examination in an appropriate course (not an independent study or seminar course), for which she had been neither enrolled nor in attendance.[8] If the examination were passed, the student would receive the credit hours for the course with a grade of P, which would neither raise nor lower the quality-point average. A failure on the examination would result in a grade of incomplete becoming an F unless the student attended and passed the course or an equivalent the next semester.

[8] *Ibid.*, May 14, 1969.

AD HOC COMMITTEE ON DEGREE REQUIREMENTS, COLLEGE CALENDAR

Early in June 1969, the chancellor appointed an ad hoc committee on degree requirements, reform of the college calendar, student loads, and methods of instruction. Dr. George Van Sant was selected as chairman. Although the committee was instructed to report directly to Chancellor Simpson, it began, with his permission, almost immediately to involve both faculty and students as advisers on specific problems to be studied, obtaining their views by questionnaire, general discussions, and evaluations of alternatives.

The committee presented the first part of its report at the March 18, 1970, meeting of the faculty. The 29-page document dealt with the various aspects of the committee's responsibilities. It recommended greater flexibility in major programs and degree requirements, more emphasis upon independent study, an improved advisory service, a simplified grading system, and a revised college calendar.

The report necessitated and received considerable attention. April 29 was designated as a collegewide discussion day. Abstracts of the proposals were prepared and plans made for some forty discussion groups composed of students and faculty members.

The faculty met on two successive days (May 13–14) to consider a number of proposals. Interest centered on changes in the grading system, the degree requirements, and the college calendar. There was also much discussion of self-scheduled examinations. A delegation from the Student Government Association appeared to present their views. Still another faculty meeting was held on May 21 to complete pressing matters of business.

As a result of these discussions and others that followed, the degree requirements were simplified greatly to require two one-semester or one one-year course in each of the following areas: (1) literature (including English and foreign languages); (2) humanities (arts, music, philosophy, and others); (3) social science (economics, history, psychology, and others); and (4) natural science and mathematics.

At least one-third of the courses for graduation were required to be taken in subjects other than the major field for a minimum of forty semester hours. Up to one-third (or a maximum of forty hours) could be required in the major program. Electives made up the remaining credit. The requirement in physical education was reduced to one year. Each student was required to demonstrate competence in English composition. Failure to do so resulted in required attendance in a noncredit writing clinic until released. Each student was also required to demonstrate foreign-language proficiency equivalent to the completion of an intermediate college-level course in the language.

There were also alternate degree programs allowing for greater concentration in the major subject. A special major program allowing flexibility worked out jointly by the student and her adviser could also be followed, if approved by the committee on special degree programs.[9] As a result of these changes, a new advisory system was put into effect, with an increased staff in the office of the dean.

B. S. DEGREE ELIMINATED

On recommendation of the committee on degree requirements, the faculty voted in December 1970 to confer only one degree, the bachelor of arts, effective with the class entering in September 1971.[10] The step was taken because, with the new degree requirements, the distinction between the B.A. and B.S. degree programs no longer existed. The action had no effect upon specific major programs, such as those in the sciences or the various cooperative programs in which professional degrees were offered by other institutions. In the discussion it was brought out that many liberal arts colleges offered only the bachelor of arts degree, and an increasing number of institutions were following the practice.

CALENDAR REVISED

The college calendar was revised to provide two semesters of approximately four months each, with a month's recess between semesters. In 1971–72 classes began September 1, and final examinations for the first semester ended on December 18. The second semester began January 17, and examinations ended May 20.

[9] See *Catalogue*, 1971–72, pp. 73–74.   [10] Faculty Minutes, Dec. 9, 1970.

MAJOR PROGRAMS REVISED

During 1969-70 extensive changes were made in the course offerings in several departments. The entire curriculum of the physics department was restructured, and advanced courses in solid state physics and nuclear physics were offered.[11]

The history curriculum was revised, and many new courses added. For example, there were now separate one-year courses in the history of England, France, Germany, Russia, Spain, modern Japan and China, and modern Southeast Asia. A number of special studies courses in various areas now became available at an advanced level.

MAJOR IN RUSSIAN STUDIES

The Slavic studies committee, appointed by Dean Whidden in the fall of 1968, made its final report at the October 1969 meeting of the faculty. The chairman, Dr. Joseph Bozicevic, recommended that the college offer an interdepartmental major in Russian studies. The new major was adopted at the December faculty meeting and was announced in the catalogue for the following session. A flexible program, it provided for eighteen semester hours' credit in core courses in Russian language and literature and the history of Russia, plus eighteen hours in related courses, including the Russian studies seminar and independent study in Russian (Russian 491). Bozicevic was appointed adviser for the new major.

ASIAN STUDIES MAJOR

At its meeting on March 12, 1969, the faculty approved an Asian studies major as outlined by a committee headed by Dr. Kurt F. Leidecker. The major differed from other interdepartmental majors in that it was built around a core program consisting of four components, all of which were required for the Asian studies major but any of which might be elected by non-majors. Areas covered were South, Southeast, Central, and East Asia.

Required courses for the Asian studies major were: Language

---

[11] *Ibid.*, Dec. 10, 1969.

and Modes of Thought in the Orient, The Religions of the Orient from Animism to Metalogical Systems, The Peoplehood of Orientals, and Values and Ideologies in the Cultures of the Orient.

A wide variety of related courses in art history, political science, history, and philosophy of the Orient were available. An Oriental language had to be taken to meet degree requirements, and two years of Japanese began to be offered. Dr. Kurt F. Leidecker was appointed adviser for the Asian studies major.

RUSSO-ASIAN SYMPOSIUM

Interest in the new majors was heightened by a Russo-Asian Symposium held at Mary Washington on April 21, 1971, and attended by 110 students and professors from fifteen colleges and universities in Virginia and Maryland. Dr. Kurt F. Leidecker, Asian studies adviser, was largely responsible for organizing the symposium. Some twenty-two papers were presented.

MAJOR IN LATIN AMERICAN STUDIES

An interdepartmental major in Latin-American studies was approved by the faculty at its February 1970 meeting. The new program was designed to "give students interested in humanities and/or social sciences an opportunity to concentrate on the Latin American region." [12] An advanced course, Readings and Research on Latin America, and the selection of a Latin American language to meet degree requirements were specified. Also, the student was required to submit an acceptable program of courses. Mary Ellen Stephenson was appointed adviser for the Latin-American studies major.

REVISED STATEMENT OF PURPOSE

In the course of preparing for the visiting committee of the Southern Association of Colleges and Secondary Schools, the committee on the self-study prepared and submitted to the faculty a revision of the statement of purpose carried in official publica-

---

[12] *Ibid.*, Feb. 18, 1970.

tions of the college. At its meeting on March 18, 1970, the faculty adopted the following statement:

Mary Washington College is a state-aided liberal arts college and a part of the University of Virginia. As such, it has an obligation to the people of the Commonwealth of Virginia to provide, without regard to race, creed, or national origin, an educational program of the highest quality.

As a liberal arts institution, Mary Washington College is convinced that a broad education in the arts, the sciences, and the humanities, complemented by intensive study in a particular field of interest, constitutes an excellent preparation for life and citizenship.

The College upholds the values of freedom of inquiry, personal responsibility, and intellectual integrity.

Finally, Mary Washington College is committed to serve with distinction the community, the state, and the nation through the selection of qualified students, the maintenance of a competent faculty and staff, and the development of an appropriate academic, cultural, and physical environment.[13]

COLLEGE SCIENCE IMPROVEMENT PROGRAM

In October 1970 the college was awarded a grant of nearly $250,000 in federal funds by the National Science Foundation for a proposed science improvement program. These funds were matched by some $217,000 from the college to introduce multi-disciplinary and interdisciplinary approaches to the improvement of science education. Dr. Samuel O. Bird, professor of geography and geology at Mary Washington, who was largely responsible for preparing and initiating the proposal, was appointed project director.

Activities proposed included a center for quantitative studies, a Rappahannock River ecology studies program, an advanced linguistics program, a seminar on natural sciences, an X-ray diffraction and fluorescence laboratory, a nuclear laboratory, and various activities involving all of the science departments at the college. The unifying theme for the program was "invigorated, active scholarship for student and faculty, implemented and extended by intensive methods of observation, analysis, and individual interpretation."[14]

Nearly $145,000 of the federal funds for the three-year program were planned to be used for the purchase of scientific equipment,

[13] *Ibid.,* March 18, 1970. [14] *Alumnae News* 2, no. 1 (1970): 1.

$50,000 for faculty research and scholarly activities, and another $45,000 for local course and curriculum studies.[15]

SELF-SCHEDULED EXAMINATIONS

In response to repeated requests from students and after prolonged discussion pro and con at several meetings, the faculty approved a plan allowing students to schedule the examination in a particular course in any of the time periods allotted by the instructor of the course.[16] The students were required to notify the instructor two weeks in advance at what period they wished to take the examination and to sign a pledge to disclose neither the content nor the form of the examination before the end of the examination period.

NEW SUMMER PROGRAMS

A variety of new summer institutes, workshops, and field study programs developed in the early 1970s, largely through the initiative of Dr. Laura V. Sumner, director of summer programs. In 1970 the first statewide arts and humanities institute for rising high school juniors and seniors was held from June 22 until July 12, in cooperation with the Stafford County public schools. Under the direction of Mrs. Sumner, in association with the Virginia Commission of Arts and Humanities, the institute proved highly successful. It was repeated in 1971 and again in 1972, when some one hundred students from across the state were housed at the college and participated in a rich program of activities. Some seventy-five students from Stafford County also participated as a part of a federal program of enrichment for high school juniors and seniors.

A course in marine biology was offered by Dr. William C. Pinschmidt, professor of biology. The six-week, six-credit course was offered in 1969, 1970, 1971, and 1972 at Cross Rip Camp, near Deltaville, Virginia. Dr. Anna Scott Hoye assisted in the program. In 1972 it reached a capacity enrollment of nineteen. The geography department conducted a six-credit field course in the Big Horn Basin, in Wyoming, taught by Dr. Marshall E. Bowen. An

---

[15] *Free Lance–Star*, Oct. 16, 1970.
[16] Faculty Minutes, May 12 and 19, 1971.

Asian studies institute was held during the 1971 summer session, in cooperation with the Virginia Asian Studies Consortium. Dr. Kurt F. Leidecker was the director. The department of education offered an eight-week program in kindergarten education in 1971. The previous summer the department offered a special program for teachers of history and social studies. An institute in history and the social sciences was offered in 1972 in conjunction with the University of Virginia School of General Studies, directed by Dr. Edward F. Shaughnessy of the education department.

Beginning with the 1971 summer session, provisions were made for selected high school students to enroll for college courses. Only outstanding students who had completed their junior year and were recommended by their principal or guidance director were eligible. The arrangements were limited to students within commuting distance in neighboring counties. Full college credit, duly recorded in the registrar's office, was granted for all courses completed successfully. The success of the 1971 project led to its extension to all qualified students residing in Virginia. A special residence hall was provided for them.

THE GRELLET C. SIMPSON AWARD

The Grellet C. Simpson Award for excellence in undergraduate teaching was awarded for the first time at the graduation exercises in May 1972. The recipient was Dr. Carmen L. Rivera, professor of Spanish, who had been a member of the faculty since 1955. Created with a donation by an anonymous friend of the college, the award consisted of a silver rose bowl bearing an engraved likeness of Chancellor Simpson. A cash award also accompanies it. The bowl will be duplicated annually for the winner.[17]

[17] In 1973 Dr. Sidney H. Mitchell, professor of English, received the Simpson Award.

CHAPTER XXV

New Buildings and Art Exhibitions

NEW BUILDINGS

THE 1960s were not only a period of academic development. They marked an equally impressive growth in residential, instructional, and recreational provisions for students and improved teaching and office facilities for the faculty. Actually the building program began to change the campus scene in 1959 when the Morgan L. Combs Science Hall was completed, at a cost of $646,466 for the building and $82,360 for the equipment.

Bushnell Hall was also opened in 1959. Erected at a cost of $445,562 for the building and $58,528 for equipment, the new residence hall provided facilities for 144 students. The year after that, 1960, Marshall Hall was opened, with accommodations for 146 students. Wright, Jones, and Wilkerson of Richmond were the architects. Again, the total cost exceeded $500,000. The building cost $512,461, and equipment totaled $58,528.

These structures were followed later by two more residence halls and a physical education center, the three of which represented an expenditure of nearly $4 million in additional facilities at the college.

RUSSELL HALL

In September 1965 Russell Hall was opened for occupancy. Named in honor of the first president of the college, Edward Hutson Russell, the new dormitory provided space for 179 students. It was designed by Wright, Jones, and Wilkerson and constructed by the Neilsen Company of Harrisonburg at a cost of approximately $800,000, including equipment. The new dormitory was designed in a graceful curve against the hill just below Bushnell and the Golden Horseshoe. It faces the historic Sunken Road.

The interior decorating was done by an alumna, Camilla Moody Payne, '29, who also planned the color schemes and furnishings for Bushnell, Marshall, and Spotswood. Visitors entered an oblong lobby with curving stairways at each end which led to a spacious library above. From there, three sets of double doors led onto a terrace at the rear of the building. An interesting feature was a garden room behind the lobby, on the main floor, with fountain, water lilies, and a willow tree. Lantern-type lighting and patio furniture create the illusion of a garden nook.[1] Provision was made for eight study areas in the new residence hall.

THOMAS JEFFERSON HALL

A landmark passed in 1966 when the city reservoir, long a familiar sight in the eastern part of the campus, was removed and the ground leveled to provide space for a new dormitory. Pneumatic drills dismantled the reservoir, and large chunks of concrete were hauled away for weeks as a new quadrangle began to take shape. Construction on Thomas Jefferson Hall was begun in September 1966. The first dormitory with elevators, it was built by the Thorington Construction Company and furnished by Thalhimer's, both of Richmond. The two contracts totaled $1,201,150. Jefferson Hall was completed in September 1967, just in time for the opening of college. A red brick building with white columns, Jefferson Hall provided accommodations for 195 students. A color scheme of blues and tans was used in decorating and furnishing the lobby, lounges, and small parlors. The thick blue carpeting gave a feeling of elegance as one entered the main reception and entertaining areas.

Rooms were arranged in three sections or clusters on each floor, with study lounge, kitchenette, and bath in each section. Most of the furniture in student rooms was built in. An innovation in the planning of Jefferson Hall was the provision of eleven one-student rooms, in recognition of the fact that some students simply wanted to room alone.

GOOLRICK HALL

In September 1967 construction started on a physical education center to be located off College Avenue between duPont Hall and the U.S. Route 1 Bypass.[2] The new building was named C. O'Conor Goolrick Hall, in honor of the man who was instrumental in having the college established at Fredericksburg. Ac-

---

[1] *Alumnae News* 17, no. 3 (1965): 1.   [2] *Bullet*, Sept. 22, 1967.

tually, the building had been named eight years before ground was broken for its construction. A resolution of the university board of visitors in April 1960 authorized the naming of the proposed building in honor of Goolrick "in partial recognition of the many outstanding services rendered Mary Washington College by this distinguished Virginian."[3] Less than two months later Mr. Goolrick was dead. He died of a heart attack on June 4, 1960, but he had already been told of the honor to be bestowed on him. He was deeply moved and humbly appreciative.

In the years that followed, the new physical education center was passed over three times in the preparation of the state budget. In 1963, when Chancellor Simpson listed the new building as the "number one" need of the college, the estimated cost was between $750,000 and $841,000. By 1966, when the state made $1,252,000 available for this purpose, construction costs had greatly risen. The state later allocated an additional $148,900 for utilities and site improvement. A federal grant of $442,699 was obtained under Title I of the Higher Education Facilities Act. The total cost of the building was $1,755,000, including connections with the heating plant. Equipment cost an additional $53,909. Actual construction was begun during the summer of 1967. The building was designed by Wright, Jones, and Wilkerson and built by Robert M. Dunville and Brothers. It was completed by September 1969.

Goolrick Hall was built on four levels and constructed of red brick with white trim to harmonize with other buildings on the campus. There were a huge gymnasium and an auxiliary gymnasium, a natatorium with a seventy-five-foot swimming pool, several dance studios, a handball court, an exercise room, sun decks, classrooms, offices, and lounges. The new center made possible not only an extensive program of physical education activities and instruction but a recreational program that included both students and men and women members of the faculty.

KIRKLAND MEMORIAL

Largely through the efforts of the late Dr. Richard N. Lanier, a Fredericksburg dentist, a statue commemorating the heroism of Sergeant Richard Kirkland of South Carolina was unveiled on

[3] Minutes of Board of Visitors, April 1960.

September 29, 1965, centered in a small landscaped park on land purchased by the college two years previously. Sergeant Kirkland, called "the Angel of Marye's Heights," risked his life to carry water to dying Northern soldiers lying along Sunken Road during the Battle of Fredericksburg on December 13, 1862. The bronze statue depicts Kirkland bending over and offering water from a Confederate canteen to a wounded Union soldier. The dedicatory ceremony was arranged by the Fredericksburg Civil War Centennial Commission, of which Dr. Raiford E. Sumner of the history department was chairman. Taking part in the dedication was Governor Albertis S. Harrison of Virginia and William P. Fay, Ambassador of Ireland to the United States. A luncheon at Brompton given by Dr. and Mrs. Simpson preceded the ceremony.

HILLDRUP MEMORIAL LIBRARY

As a memorial to Dr. Robert Leroy Hilldrup, long a member of the faculty and chairman of the history department at the time of his death in the summer of 1964, his widow established a library of several hundred books in history for student use. A committee from the history department selected the titles from suggestions submitted by students and other faculty members.[4] The memorial library was placed on special shelves in the student lounge in Monroe Hall, along with sets of the *Dictionary of American Biography* and the *Dictionary of American History,* both given in memory of Dr. Hilldrup by the local chapter of Pi Gamma Mu, with which he had worked for many years.

ANN CARTER LEE

With the removal of the physical education department to Goolrick Hall, major improvements were made in the student activities building. The college bookstore was moved to extensive new quarters on the floor below, in what had been dance studios and offices for the physical education department. Additional space was provided for the trade book section of the bookstore. A day students' lounge was constructed on the floor below the bookstore

[4] *Alumnae News* 18, no. 2 (1966): 2.

in the space formerly devoted to the bowling alley. In anticipation of an increasing number of nonresident students, the new lounge offered much more extensive and attractive facilities for day students. Additional meeting rooms and lounges were provided in other parts of Ann Carter Lee. There were also additional offices for various college staff members, with even a branch of a local bank now located in the building.

With the luxurious new swimming pool in Goolrick Hall now available, the one in Ann Carter Lee was no longer needed. The pool was dismantled, dressing rooms removed, and the entire area completely remodeled. The security office was moved to this new location.

PLACEMENT BUREAU

The renovation of Ann Carter Lee Hall made possible additional space for the college placement bureau. Established originally as an activity of the office of the dean, the demand for the services of the bureau necessitated provisions for special staff and facilities. Isabel Gordon, an alumna of the college, was appointed full-time director in February 1955.

Under Miss Gordon's capable and enthusiastic leadership the bureau has expanded greatly its services to students and alumnae of the college. Credentials are compiled for each senior and copies made available to prospective employers. Visits by representatives of school systems, business and industrial corporations, government agencies, the armed forces, merchandising establishments, and a wide variety of other occupations are scheduled throughout the winter and spring. Students sign up for interviews according to their interests. Many graduates obtain their first positions through the services of the placement bureau.

There is available a large collection of bulletins, folders, and scrapbooks describing careers in fields of interest to women. Each spring a career night has been sponsored with the cooperation of the senior class. Speakers representing various occupations describe employment opportunities and conditions in their respective fields.

The placement bureau staff has grown to three members. Miss Gordon's accomplishments as placement director at Mary Washington have been recognized by her selection as president of the Virginia College Placement Association in 1967 and as president of the Southern College Placement Association in 1972.

SEACOBECK HALL IMPROVEMENTS

Between 1969 and 1972 a series of changes were made in the process of converting to permanent cafeteria operation, which in the fall of 1971 became effective for all food service. What had formerly been the Tapestry Room on the ground floor was converted into another dining unit seating 250 students. Cafeteria installations were completed in all dining units. The kitchen was then completely renovated, with new steam tables and other equipment. The loading area behind the dining hall was concealed by an ornamental brick wall and landscaping. Additional parking space was also provided.

NEW SERVICE BUILDING

Under construction in 1972 was a new service building located on the far side of the golf course near the ravine. The new structure, for which approximately $800,000 in state funds was appropriated, was designed to house all maintenance units of the college, including the laundry, the central supply rooms, the carpentry, plumbing, and painting shops, and all offices for supervisory personnel concerned with plant operation and maintenance.

BETTY LEWIS DISCONTINUED

As of July 1, 1972, the lease of the college on the privately owned Betty Lewis Hall was terminated. Although all dormitory rooms were filled for 1972–73 with a capacity enrollment of twenty-two hundred students, the new residence halls constructed since 1965 made the rental of the building unnecessary. The college has made tentative plans for one more residence hall, but with students of all four classes now permitted to live in town if they wish, construction will not be begun until the residential situation is clarified.

INTERNAL ROADWAYS

Extension of internal roadways on campus was one outgrowth of new construction in the northern part of the campus. A new campus drive, with walkways and lights, was constructed behind duPont Hall, connecting Goolrick and Melchers halls with the central campus. Parking space continued to be a problem, owing to the large increase in both student and faculty cars. New parking areas were built near Monroe Hall, behind duPont Hall, and both in front of and behind Jefferson Hall. Plans are under way for additional campus parking in the area below Willard Hall now occupied by maintenance shops and equipment.

ART EXHIBITIONS

As indicated elsewhere, the first exhibition of contemporary art was held in the duPont Galleries in connection with the inauguration of Dr. Simpson. Dedicated to the new chancellor, "whose imagination made these beginnings possible," the inaugural exhibition in 1956 set a high standard for the many others that were to follow.

The exhibition committee headed by Julien Binford made several trips to New York to select the fifty paintings to be shown. The quality of the works of their choice evoked high praise from metropolitan critics.

Pink Pastures, by Milton Avery, was the first painting to be acquired by the college under the new policy of awarding a purchase prize. The impressionistic nature of the selection caused considerable comment at the time. A watchman employed to guard the collection during exhibition hours confided to several friends his concern over whether the college really "knew what it was doing" when it bought a picture that purported to portray a *pink* pasture. He was also concerned over whether the figure shown was actually supposed to be a cow.

In spite of such misgivings, time has shown that the college purchases were wisely made. *Pink Pastures,* for example, was borrowed later by the Museum of Modern Art for a two-year traveling exhibition. In 1969–70 it was loaned to the Smithsonian Institution for its Milton Avery exhibition and shown in Washington, New York, and Columbus, Ohio. In subsequent exhibitions, other additions were made to the permanent collection, most of which are now worth far more than the prices originally paid.

The catalogues of the exhibitions, beginning with the first one in 1956, are in themselves works of art, with interesting cover designs, photographic reproductions of many of the paintings shown, and carefully prepared notes on the background and works of each artist represented. A complete file of catalogues of the annuals from 1956 through 1965 is in the college archives. Prices of the pictures shown usually ranged from $500 to $4,000 each, with an average of $800 to $1,000. Each year the college awarded two or three purchase prizes, and these paintings became the basis of an impressive collection of modern art. The holdings of the college were further enriched by gifts from senior classes, the alumnae, and interested faculty members. The class of 1959 gave Gustave Foppiani's *Seashore*. The Alumnae Association gave Richard Crist's *View of the Village* in memory of Emil Schnellock.

Julien Binford continued to serve as chairman of the exhibition staff. His wife, Elizabeth, often assisted in the preparation of the catalogues. Members of the art department and other interested faculty members served on the jury of selection and the jury of awards, as well as on the exhibition staff itself. Chancellor Simpson took an active interest and lent a helping hand in each of the exhibitions.

The series of modern art exhibitions ended with the tenth in 1965. Among other paintings acquired by the college during this period, largely through purchase prizes in the annual exhibitions, were: Walter Stuempfig, *Man with Rake* (1956); *Julien Binford, Still Life with Sweet Potato* (1957); Arshile Gorky, *Composition* (1958); Arnold Blanch, *Red and Yellow Landscape* (1959); Emil Schnellock, *Still Life with Red Fez* (gift of artist, 1959); Roger Muhl, *Nature Morte aux Fruits* (1961); Morris Graves, *Bouquet* (1965); Pierre Courtin, *Elements* (1964); Joan Miró, *Nous Avons* (1964); Robert Loftin Newman, *Rest by the Wayside* (1960); James Grant, *Collage in Yellow* (1963); Chi-Kwan-Chen, *Rain* (1962).

The collection now numbers some sixty-two paintings, mainly in contemporary style, which are currently hung in the foyer of George Washington Hall, in several offices in the administration building, and in suitable places in other college buildings.

The duPont Galleries have continued to present outstanding exhibitions. In the fall of 1966 a comprehensive collection of the sculpture of primitive peoples was assembled by Robert D. Kinsman, then assistant professor of art history at Mary Washington. A total of 177 examples of primitive sculpture, mainly of African and South Pacific origin, were loaned by university museums, art collections, and galleries for the exhibition.

The Honorable Hugh Scott, United States Senator from Pennsylvania, who was originally from Fredericksburg, lent his magnificent collection of Chinese art for exhibition in the duPont galleries during March and April 1968. The result of thirty years of enthusiastic collecting, the exhibition presented 138 examples of Chinese art, carefully documented as to dynasty. Metalwork, jade, pottery, and porcelain were displayed. As usual, a reception opened the exhibition, and Senator and Mrs. Scott were on hand for the occasion. Senator Scott's book, *The Golden Age of Chinese Art,* is a definitive catalogue of his collection of T'ang objects.

Other outstanding exhibitions have included "Oriental Art of Fifty Centuries," sponsored by the Oriental Club of Mary Washington College (1958); "An Exhibition of Early Musical Instruments, with Original Prints Showing the Instruments as a Prominent Feature" (1959); "Civil War Centennial" (1961); and "Dada, Surrealism and Today," sponsored by the Museum of Modern Art (1967). There have been special exhibitions of the work of Milton Avery, Julien Binford, Emil Schnellock, Teruo Hara, Dorothy Van Winckel, as well as annual exhibitions of student art.

Two recent exhibitions have attracted wide attention, not only for the works of art themselves but for the descriptive catalogues that accompanied them. Both the catalogues and the exhibitions are the outgrowth of projects undertaken by students in the connoisseurship, research, and gallery course conducted by Mathew Herban III, assistant professor of art.

In March and April 1971 the class organized an exhibition of fifteenth- and sixteenth-century prints from the Rosenwald Collection in the National Gallery of Art, Washington, D.C. The catalogue begins with an essay on techniques used in woodcuts, engravings, and etchings. A picture of each print follows, with detailed information on the artist, subject, technique, collection number, and a bibliography of source material on that item. The catalogue itself is an authoritative reference on prints of that period.

An exhibition entitled "The American Chair" followed early in 1972, again organized and arranged by Mathew Herban and his students. Once more, the catalogue shows intensive research on the development of chair design from 1700 to 1971, the history of each type being traced in this 96-page illustrated publication. The exhibition was an impressive one. The Smithsonian Institution prepared color slides of the entire collection, which were made available for public purchase through its photographic services division.

CHAPTER XXVI

Student Life in the 1960s

STUDENT DEMONSTRATIONS

THE first student demonstration occurred in March 1965 when a number of MWC students, under the leadership of Nan Grogan, who had spent the Christmas holidays in civil rights activity in Mississippi, circled the courthouse for about two hours in an appeal for voter rights.[1] This was the period in which marchers in Mississippi and Alabama were campaigning for integration of facilities in the South and the registration of Negro voters. As they marched in the cold rain, the group sang "We Shall Overcome" and other songs of the civil rights movement. A number of Negro leaders in Fredericksburg joined the marchers.

Later a group of MWC students wrote a letter to the editor of the *Free Lance–Star* (March 17) emphasizing that the demonstrators were not representative of the college at large. The letter ended: "please accept our humble apology for the ridiculous and uncalled for actions of some of our students."

THE MORATORIUM

On October 15, 1969, students throughout the country were urged to participate in a Vietnam Moratorium to demonstrate their desire for an end to the war there. College administrators were requested to suspend classes, but in Virginia, Governor Mills E. Godwin, Jr., made it clear that he did not approve such action in state-supported institutions. Classes were held at Mary Washington, but some professors devoted the period to discussion of topics related to the war. Some twenty-eight faculty members signed a resolution supporting the objective of Moratorium Day.

The focal point of the observance at Mary Washington was a faculty panel discussion in the afternoon, sponsored by the Student Government Association, at which various opinions on the war were expressed and discussed. Throughout the day, arm bands and badges supporting the moratorium were distributed from a booth in Ann Carter Lee Hall. The day ended with a

---

[1] *Free Lance–Star*, March 18, 1965.

candlelight service in Ball Circle at 6:30 P.M., which included discussion, poetry reading, and songs for peace. A faculty resolution commended the Student Government Association on "the manner in which they have chosen to respond to the movement for a student moratorium."[2]

A number of MWC students journeyed by chartered bus to Washington for the huge antiwar demonstration on November 14, 1969. Three juniors walked most of the way via U.S. Route 1 to show their concern for an end to the war.[3] A thirty-six-hour "march against death" from Arlington National Cemetery to the Capitol began on Thursday evening, November 13, in which thousands of college students took part.

ANTIWAR PROTESTS MOUNT

Extension of United States military activity into Cambodia early in May 1970 produced a wave of student protests throughout the country, which culminated in the tragic death of four students at Kent State University, in an encounter with National Guardsmen called out to quell disturbances and halt destruction of property. Some student leaders at Mary Washington called for a boycott of classes and a week-long protest, including rallies to organize antiwar activities and a memorial service for the Kent State students. No strike actually took place, and most professors reported attendance about normal, although study and preparation for classes were seriously interrupted. However, there was none of the violence and destruction that occurred at many other colleges and universities as a result of the extension of the war into Cambodia and the killings at Kent State.

One outgrowth of the tense situation was the canceling of the proposed visit of Mrs. Richard M. Nixon to Kenmore and the James Monroe Law Office on May 6, 1970. A group of students announced that they planned to picket both buildings and to present Mrs. Nixon with a petition protesting the widening of the war into Cambodia.[4] On the evening before Mrs. Nixon's scheduled visit, the White House announced that the President's wife would not make the trip to Fredericksburg. There was general disappointment locally over the cancellation of the visit, and some resentment was expressed by citizens at the action of certain college students that apparently produced this result.

[2] Faculty Minutes, Oct. 8, 1969. [3] *Free Lance–Star*, Nov. 14, 1969.
[4] *Ibid.*, May 5, 1970, p. 1.

About three hundred students signed a letter to Mrs. Nixon apologizing and expressing regret that she had found it necessary to cancel her visit to Fredericksburg.[5] An editorial in the *Free Lance–Star* on June 6 defended the actions of the students. It concluded with these words: "At a time when violence and turmoil has overtaken many of the nation's college campuses, Fredericksburg should be proud of Mary Washington College and its students whose protests have been peaceful."

Although there was no boycott of classes, as at many other institutions, student protests continued throughout the week. A small group staged a march to the main post office where they circled carrying antiwar posters. That weekend more than 140 MWC students journeyed on foot and by car to Washington to join the massive protest being held there. Special editions of the college newspaper were issued daily to keep students up to date on antiwar activities. Debates and panel discussions of United States policy in the Vietnam War were sponsored by campus leaders of the National Student Association and others.

By a narrow margin the faculty rejected a proposal to lift requirements on class attendance and final examinations so that those students who wished could devote more time to activities related to the protests. It was agreed, however, that faculty members could use their judgment in giving grades of "Incomplete" when they felt the circumstances justified them.[6]

STUDENT REPRESENTATION AT FACULTY MEETINGS

In November 1969 the executive cabinet of the Student Government Association addressed a formal request to the faculty that student representatives be permitted to attend its meetings "solely to facilitate communication between students and faculty."[7]

On formal motion the faculty at its December meeting referred the request to the faculty organization and procedures committee. This committee reported back to the faculty at its February and March meetings. The committee did not recommend student representation at faculty meetings "to facilitate communication." It pointed out that there were already many avenues by which students could express their opinions, including the committee on college affairs. The presence of student members on many important faculty committees was mentioned.

[5] *Alumnae News*, June 1970, p. 4. [6] Faculty Minutes, May 13 and 14, 1970.
[7] *Ibid.*, Dec. 10, 1969, Appendix B.

In order that students could be familiar with the proceedings of the faculty, it was agreed that a copy of the minutes of each meeting would be placed in the reserve room of the library by the secretary of the faculty. This practice was followed, and students were able to obtain the minute book simply by asking for it at the desk in the reserve book room.

STUDENT RIGHTS

One outgrowth of the disturbances that racked college campuses throughout the country in the spring of 1970 was an organized effort to obtain more rights for students and to allow them to govern their own conduct. As the *Richmond Times-Dispatch* reported in a Sunday edition, on February 21, 1971, "a sampling of Virginia colleges and universities shows that more codes [governing student conduct] are being reversed right now than in all the decades past. . . . Today, if a student feels his rights have been violated, he's apt to take his college to court."

Like other colleges in the state, Mary Washington students proposed a bill of rights. A long and complicated statement, it included some items that could not be legally authorized by the college. After considerable discussion with student leaders, the chancellor authorized a joint student-faculty committee appointed by himself and by the executive chairman of the Student Association "to study the feasibility of drawing up a Bill of Rights for the entire College community." This ad hoc community bill of rights committee drew up a Statement of Rights and Responsibilities, which was adopted by the student body and the faculty. Chancellor Simpson stated that it would become effective only when passed also by the governing board of the college.

The statement read:

STATEMENT OF RIGHTS AND RESPONSIBILITIES

Members of the College community have responsibilities incumbent upon all citizens, as well as the responsibilities of their particular roles within the academic community.

All members share the obligation to respect the right to freedom of inquiry, of religion, of speech, of press, of peaceful assemblage, of association, and of petition to the institution for a redress of grievances.

The rights of members of the College community shall not be denied or abridged on account of race, color, creed, or sex.

The members of the College community have the right to be secure in their persons, residences, offices, papers and effects, against unreasonable searches and seizures.

All members of the College community have the right to due process in matters concerning discipline or status as members of the College community.

All members of the College community have other responsibilities and rights incident to the educational process and to the requirements of the search for truth and its free presentation.

The enumeration of the rights and responsibilities outlined in this statement shall not be construed to deny or disparage others retained by the members of the College community.

The term "member of the College community" embraces the College as an institution, the faculty as a body, and all members of the administration, faculty, staff, and student body in their official and individual capacities.

STUDENT CHALLENGES

In December 1968 a group of students presented Chancellor Simpson with a list of "challenges," to which he was asked to give a public response. Briefly, the items concerned increasing the number of black students, stimulating the academic caliber of the institution, and improving the judicial system governing the conduct of students. The action of the group was publicized in the *Bullet* and also in the local press on December 13.

In a calm and dignified manner Chancellor Simpson replied to each of the challenges in a statement published in the next issue of the *Bullet,* on January 16, 1969. He answered each challenge specifically, citing evidence to support his statement of the facts in the case. The chancellor showed clearly that there were adequate channels of communication for the expression of varying points of view through the committee on college affairs. However, he expressed his willingness to meet students at any time to discuss the questions they raised. He did protest the "rather unnecessarily self-conscious procedure used to bring these matters to [his] attention."

COMMITTEE ON FACULTY-STUDENT GOVERNANCE

During the summer of 1970 an ad hoc committee on faculty-student governance was appointed by the chancellor to "investigate those areas of responsibility and governance common to both." In a report issued in March 1971, this joint student-faculty committee recommended: (1) student participation in departmental affairs; (2) a college council of eleven members (five faculty and five students, plus the academic dean or his representative) ; (3) a college committee on organization and procedures (five faculty and five students) to be concerned with the selection and appointment of college committees.

The recommendations were discussed at length at faculty meetings following the report, but no definite action was taken. A new faculty-student governance committee with a different personnel dealt with almost the same issues during the latter part of the 1971–72 session.

One outgrowth of their activity was another recommendation that would provide for student participation in departmental affairs. After considerable discussion over the voting provision, the faculty adopted the following motion at its meeting on April 12, 1972: "That all departments develop and implement policies of student participation in departmental affairs, including voting student representation at department meetings. Student representatives are to be elected by their respective departmental majors." [8]

The issue of student representation at faculty meetings remained unresolved, although the committee proposed at the May 1972 meeting of the faculty that the five student members of the committee on faculty-student governance be invited as observers to all faculty meetings during the life of the committee.[9] A vote on the motion was deferred until the fall.

STUDENT PRIVILEGES

As Rose Bennett Gilbert, '60, pointed out in a delightful article in the summer 1970 issue of the *Mary Washington College Quarterly Review* (pp. 3–8) times have indeed changed in the decade since she was a student.

She took note of the interest of students in contemporary affairs, their tendency to question and seek answers, their desire for relevancy in their studies, and, especially, their tendency to ask "why not?" when social regulations were examined. "And if there is no legitimate 'why,' there is no longer a regulation, in most cases," she remarked.

Among the changes she noted were the following:

---

[8] *Ibid.*, April 12, 1972.   [9] *Ibid.*, May 10, 1972.

Students may drink in their rooms. However, there is no "drinking problem."

There are no regulations regarding the dress of students.

Students may entertain men in their dormitory rooms during certain hours.

Students with parental permission may live off-campus in their own apartments.

There are no classes on Saturdays or Wednesday afternoons.

The number of cuts is left to students and their instructors to decide.

When a student goes away overnight, she simply leaves a sealed envelope stating where she can be reached in case of an emergency.

While dormitories are locked at midnight on week-days and 2:00 A.M. on weekends, a student may obtain a key from the Security Office if she wishes to enter the dormitory after closing hours.

Dormitories are now integrated with some black students and with all classes (except freshmen).

Dismissal is no longer automatic for proven violation of the honor system.

The Student Government, now the Student Association, is broadly representative of the entire student body.

Truly, life at Mary Washington changed greatly in the decade of the sixties, especially in terms of the regulation of student conduct from an *in loco parentis* standpoint. The student of today has broad areas of freedom both in her personal life and in her academic program. With this freedom goes a responsibility to be responsive to this opportunity to demonstrate social, intellectual, and ethical maturity.

Mary Washington College continues to offer an opportunity and a challenge. It seeks to develop the incentive and provide the means for the maximum realization of the potentials of its students—academically, culturally, and morally.

LOYALTY NIGHT

Loyalty Night developed as a program designed to acquaint students with the history and traditions of the college. It was characterized by a procession of the seniors in cap and gown, a series of talks or tableaux presented by students, faculty members, or alumnae, and an impressive singing of the alma mater in a darkened auditorium as a spotlight illuminated the college seal at the rear of the stage.

Originally, there was a Loyalty Day during the 1950s which culminated in an evening convocation program sponsored by student leaders. Held early in September, the program was planned with new students specially in mind. For example, the 1957 observance of Loyalty Day ended with a convocation at which presidents of the leading college organizations spoke on loyalty in general and on the significance of *Pro Deo, Pro Domo,* and *Pro Patria* as elements in the seal of the college.[10]

Typical of the later Loyalty Night programs was the one presented on March 11, 1964, when a group of students and alumnae presented "Loyalty through the Decades." Talks and slides described college life in the twenties, thirties, forties, and fifties. According to the *Bullet* on March 14, "The program resulted in a poignant nostalgia which settled over the audience as they reviewed Mary Washington's colorful past." Approximately thirty members of the Alumnae Association representing fourteen chapters were present for the program.

CONCERT SERIES

The concert series continued to schedule outstanding attractions. During 1964–65 the series included a presentation of Shakespeare's *Hamlet* by the Helen Hayes Repertory Company; John Thomas, tenor; the José Limón Dance Company; and the National Symphony Orchestra. The "Little Series" that session included Cilli Wang, comedienne and mime-dancer; Knitzer-Loesser, violin-piano duo; Sahomi Tachibana, Japanese dancer; and the Antiqua Players in a program of early music. There were also twenty visiting lecturers, most of them scheduled through the University Center in Virginia, and five convocations of the student body.

CONFERENCE WITH LEGISLATORS

A five-member delegation from Mary Washington joined some three hundred other Virginia college students in a gathering in Richmond with at least forty members of the Virginia General Assembly for the first Virginia Student-Legislator Forum in April 1971. Governor Linwood Holton and Lieutenant Governor

[10] *Bullet,* Sept. 27, 1957.

J. Sargeant Reynolds were cosponsors of the forum. Such items as social regulations, room visitation privileges, and control of college newspapers were discussed.

Antiwar activities continued on a reduced scale. In April 1971 a rally sponsored by the peace action committee attracted about one hundred students. In April 1972, a small group of students held a silent vigil around a cross and flag-draped box in Ball Circle in memory of those who had died in the Vietnam conflict. Speakers opposed to the war continued to appear on the campus.

READING DAYS

For several years the Student Government Association had been the moving force in the observance of Dead Week. Faculty members were asked not to schedule tests or require term papers in the week immediately preceding final examinations at the end of each semester. Student organizations were not to schedule meetings or other activities during this period. In theory, at least, increased time would be available to prepare for final examinations which usually began after the last day of classes.

In February 1967 the academic affairs committee of the Student Government Association recommended the elimination of Dead Week and the substitution of a two-day reading period without class meetings preceding each examination period. The proposal was accepted enthusiastically by the faculty and went into effect in May 1967.[11] At the April meeting that year the faculty voted to extend the time allowed for final examinations from two to three hours, effective September 1967.[12]

KIWANIS AWARD

In 1923 the newly organized Fredericksburg Kiwanis Club announced that it would award annually a silver loving cup to the senior who, in the judgment of the faculty, had contributed most to the promotion of the interests of the college during her stay at Mary Washington. This annual award soon become the outstanding recognition of service to the college.

In time, a silver bowl suitably inscribed with the name of the winner was substituted for the cup. The recipient was selected by a secret vote of the faculty, the results of which were not an-

[11] Faculty Minutes, Feb. 14, 1967.   [12] *Ibid.*, March 14, 1967.

nounced until the actual presentation was made, usually at the Class Day or Class Night exercises.

Voting for the Kiwanis Award at the faculty meeting on April 14, 1971, resulted in a tie between two graduating seniors. Since there was no provision for a dual award, the first time in many years, no Kiwanis award was made. The two winners were presented checks from the college at the senior convocation.

The Kiwanis Award was discontinued temporarily. In 1972 the senior who was voted to have made the greatest contribution to the interest of the college received a service award in the form of a cash sum presented "on the behalf of the Faculty."

In 1973 the annual Kiwanis Award was resumed. A complete list of the winners follows:

1923 Mrs. George N. Thomas
1924 Maggie Lee Matthews
1925 Charlotte Chappell
1926 Juliet Ritchie Ware
1927 Katherine Micks
1928 Rachel Harriet Wingfield
1929 Grace Taylor
1930 Evelyn Thornton
1931 Aurelia Leigh
1932 Mary Clements
1933 Joan Brickhouse
1934 Nellie Mae Stewart
1935 Polly Eugenia Daniel
1936 Olivia J. Wheeler
1937 Frances Gray Nash
1938 Elizabeth M. Trimble
1939 Mary Alston Burgess
1940 Juanita B. Lassetter
1941 June Stoll
1942 Edna P. Reed
1943 Henrietta Ada Clement
1944 Jayne Anderson
1945 Norma K. Dick
1946 Lelia Jett Marsh
1947 Lillian Irene Taylor

1948 Sarah Margaret Armstrong
1949 Anne White
1950 Sarah Anne Miles
1951 Mary Lee Oliver
1952 Gwendolyn Amory
1953 Constance Mae Bennett
1954 Meechi Yokogawa
1955 Martha Belle Lyle
1956 Elizabeth Louise Davies
1957 Margaret Lee Preston
     Patricia Ann Preston
1958 Ruth McCulloch
1959 Carol Pridgen
1960 Rose Marie Bennett
1961 Sylvia McJilton
1962 Kathleen Sprenkle
1963 Kathy Friedman
1964 Bonnie Grace Ramsey
1965 Mary C. Volk
1966 Grace Marie Bamforth
1967 Patricia Adams Marilla
1968 Amelia Jane Bradley
1969 Patricia Mae Boise
1970 Candace Dawn Whitmer
1973 Martha Ann Welsh

There were no Kiwanis Awards in 1971 and 1972. However, awards based on the same type of voting were made as service awards on behalf of the faculty in these two years: in 1971 to Ann Gamble Jefferis and Marilyn Ann Morgan (dual award because of tie vote) and in 1972 to Mary Elizabeth Saunders.

CHAPTER XXVII

Recent Developments, 1967–1972

ADMINISTRATIVE CHANGES

IN March 1967 Michael Houston, associate professor of history and director of admissions, was appointed assistant to the chancellor. A native of Richmond, he had graduated from Randolph-Macon College a Phi Beta Kappa and had received master's degrees both in history and in communications from American University. Before coming to Mary Washington in 1957 as director of admissions, he had been director of the news bureau and the placement office at Randolph-Macon College. At the March 1967 faculty meeting, Chancellor Simpson announced that Houston would assume his responsibility as assistant to the chancellor immediately and would continue for the present as director of admissions also.[1]

During the summer of 1967, Dr. Alvey retired as dean of the college after thirty-three years in that position. He continued to serve on the faculty as professor of education until 1971, when he retired from active teaching and was elected professor emeritus of education. Dr. Reginald W. Whidden, associate dean of the college for a decade, succeeded Dr. Alvey as dean. Dr. James H. Croushore, professor of English and chairman of the English department, was appointed associate dean of the college.

An extensive reorganization and reassignment of administrative duties was announced by Chancellor Simpson as the 1967–68 session opened. Jane N. Saladin was appointed registrar and director of financial aid. Laura Voelkel Sumner, professor of classics, was appointed director of the summer session. Both offices were placed under the direction of the dean of the college.

Thomas P. Mann was appointed director of information services, a new position under the supervision of the assistant to the chancellor. Houston continued to serve also as director of admissions, with Mann as assistant director, through the 1967–68 session, at which time A. R. Merchent took over as director of admissions. Ann L. Perinchief, a 1967 honor graduate of the college, was appointed administrative assistant to the director of admissions.

[1] Faculty Minutes, March 14, 1967.

The new summer school director had been a member of the faculty since 1948. Dr. Laura V. Sumner received the A.B. degree from Vassar College and the M.A. and Ph.D. degrees from Johns Hopkins University. Before coming to Mary Washington she had taught classics at Wesleyan College in Macon, Georgia.

Mrs. Sumner has served as professor and chairman of the classics department and also as adviser to the interdepartmental major in classical civilization. She has made several trips to Greece for archaeological studies and investigations. She introduced courses in Greek and Roman art and archaeology, including a special studies course in classical archaeology. She has served as visiting lecturer or professor at a number of institutions, and during the summer of 1963 she was a staff archaeologist at Kenchreai, Greece. Mrs. Sumner has been active in numerous civic organizations. From 1960 to 1972 she was a member of the Fredericksburg City Council, the second woman in the history of the city to serve in this capacity. Her husband, Dr. Raiford E. Sumner, is professor of political science at Mary Washington.

Emily A. Holloway, assistant bursar since 1958, was appointed director of student affairs. Lefa Faulkner's duties as director of residential facilities were directly related to Mrs. Holloway's office. Edward V. Allison, Jr., a staff accountant with the F. M. C. Corporation, was appointed business manager, taking over some of the duties of the long-time treasurer, then bursar, then comptroller—Edgar Woodward.

There were thirty-three new faculty members as the 1967–68 session opened. Eleven filled newly created positions, seven were temporary appointments to fill vacancies caused by leaves of absence, ten replaced faculty members who had retired or resigned, and five were visiting lecturers. The total teaching faculty of the college now numbered more than 160.

Margaret Hargrove, professor of classics and dean of students, retired in 1968 after thirteen years of service. Mildred A. Droste, an associate professor of health, physical education, and recreation, and assistant dean of students since 1966, was appointed dean of students, effective July 1, 1968.

She had been a member of the faculty for fifteen years. A native of West Virginia, she had graduated from Longwood College and received the M.Ed. degree from the Woman's College of the University of North Carolina. She had been teaching at Mary Baldwin College at the time she accepted a position at Mary Washington.

ADDITIONAL ADMINISTRATIVE CHANGES

The 1968–69 session opened with still other administrative changes in effect. Dr. A. R. Merchent, former registrar and chairman of the education department, was named director of admissions, succeeding Michael Houston, who had held the position since 1957. Houston continued to serve as assistant to the chancellor, and in October 1971 his title was changed to assistant chancellor.[2]

A native of Roanoke, Dr. Merchent graduated from Emory and Henry College and received the M.Ed. and D.Ed. from the University of Virginia. Before coming to Mary Washington in 1959 he had been director of public relations at Longwood College; before that, he had been assistant director of student aid and placement at the University of Virginia.

Helen R. Thomas was named administrative assistant to the director of financial aid and placed in charge of an expanded student employment program. Audrey Hurlock was appointed recorder and given the responsibility for maintaining all student academic records. Gail G. Braxton was named director of personnel. As indicated elsewhere, Dr. Daniel H. Woodward was appointed librarian to succeed Dr. Quenzel and given a year's leave of absence to complete requirements for a master's degree in library science at Catholic University.

The 1968–69 session began with thirty-six new faculty members, bringing the total to a new high of 175. There were nine appointments to fill newly created positions, three to take care of leaves of absence, and twenty-four to replace faculty members who had retired or resigned.[3]

FURTHER ADMINISTRATIVE REORGANIZATION

In 1970 five members of the college staff, with a total of 145 years of service, retired from their duties. Dr. Reginald W. Whidden, dean of the college and professor of English, retired after a total of twenty-seven years of service. He was succeeded by Dr. James H. Croushore, who had been associate dean. Dr. Nancy H. Mitchell, associate professor of English, was named assistant dean,

---

[2] Mr. Houston died of a heat stroke on Sept. 2, 1973.
[3] *Alumnae News* 20, no. 3 (1968): 15.

with special responsibility for academic counseling. A member of the faculty since 1960, Mrs. Mitchell held a B.A. degree in English from Swarthmore College, an M.A. from Yale University, and a Ph.D. degree from Catholic University.

Edgar E. Woodward, comptroller, retired in 1970 after thirty-three years of service. Edward V. Allison, Jr., business manager since 1967, succeeded him and became comptroller. Claude T. Parcell, Jr., was appointed administrative assistant for fiscal planning and, in 1971, became business manager for auxiliary enterprises. Mervin A. Frantz, formerly personnel officer for the F. M. C. Corporation, was appointed director of personnel early in 1970.

Emily A. Holloway, director of student affairs, retired in 1970 after twenty-two years with the college. Thereupon a number of her duties were transferred to the office of the dean of students, Mildred Droste. The office of the Dean of Students was moved from George Washington Hall to Anne Fairfax Hall, and two new administrative assistants were appointed to aid in the operation of the reorganized office. Claire Talley Booker was assigned to work with student housing. Ruth Willetts, in Anne Carter Lee Hall, was given responsibility for scheduling and implementing student-related activities, along with other duties. Selma Shelton, formerly manager of the college tearoom, became housekeeping supervisor for residence halls. Lefa Faulkner, director of residence halls for many years, had retired at the end of the 1969 summer session.

The admission staff was enlarged in 1970 to include two admission counselors, George F. Dickinson, Jr., and Diane-Louise L. Kenney, who assisted Dr. Merchent in school visitation and processing admission applications.

Guenndolyn A. Beeler, professor and chairman of the department of home economics, retired in 1970 after nineteen years of service. Dr. Eileen K. Dodd, professor of psychology, retired also in 1970 after forty-four years at Mary Washington.

NEW ACADEMIC COUNSELORS

In a major reorganization of the academic advisory system, four new counselors were appointed in 1971: Michael Bass, instructor in biology since 1968; Cornelia D. Oliver, associate professor of art, a faculty member since 1954; Susan J. Hanna, assistant professor of English since 1968; and Rebecca T. Woosley, associate professor of health, physical education, and recreation, a faculty member since 1950.

The greater flexibility and freedom of the new degree program required a more intensive and individualized type of guidance than the one possible under the faculty advisory system previously in effect, when the advisers were also full-time teachers. The advisory staff worked especially with freshmen and sophomores in the planning of their programs. At the end of the second year, students were then referred to the chairman of the department in which they had decided to major. Either he or an assigned member of his department then took over academic counseling. The new counselors were assigned offices in George Washington Hall adjacent to that of the assistant dean of the college for academic counseling. They taught on a half-time basis and devoted the remainder of their time to academic counseling.

In June 1972 Nancy H. Mitchell returned to full-time teaching. Susan Hanna was named assistant dean of the college for academic counseling. A native of Ohio, Miss Hanna received her B.A. from Ohio State University and her M.A. and Ph.D. from the University of Michigan. Before coming to Mary Washington she was employed by the American College Public Relations Association. In 1972 Michael Mery, assistant professor of psychology, and Richard E. Hansen, assistant professor of English, were appointed counselors, while Mrs. Oliver and Miss Woosley were renamed for a second session.

In 1971 Dr. Lawrence A. Wishner, professor and chairman of the chemistry department, was appointed assistant dean of the college, in charge of instruction. A member of the faculty since 1961, Dr. Wishner received his B.S., M.S., and Ph.D. from the University of Maryland. Dr. Wishner also took over the job as director of summer programs, succeeding Mrs. Sumner.

NEW LIBRARIAN

Ruby York Weinbrecht, of the class of 1948, was named librarian to succeed Dr. Daniel H. Woodward and took over her duties on July 1, 1972. In addition to her B.A. from Mary Washington, she received an M.A. in library science from George Peabody College and did further postgraduate work toward the Ph.D. in library science at the Graduate Library School of the University of Chicago.

A former acquisitions librarian at Vassar College, Mrs. Weinbrecht came to Mary Washington from the United States Equal Employment Opportunity Commission where she had been chief of the Technical Information Division since 1967. Her library experience also included service in various capacities with the Library of Congress, Ball State University, and Indiana State University. She has contributed to numerous professional journals and served as editor of *D.C. Libraries.* In 1970–71 she was president of the Mary Washington College Alumnae Association.[4]

SALARY INCREASES

Beginning with the 1969–70 session, faculty salaries were increased again, the eleventh increase in the last fourteen years. The new scale provided a range from $6,700 to $15,000. The average instructional salary was approximately $11,000. In 1970–71, salaries were again raised, ranging from $7,100 to $15,500, with an average of $11,900. Student fees were also increased, bringing the total charges for Virginia students to $1,470 for the session and for out-of-state students to $2,225.

VETERAN DEPARTMENT HEADS

Mary Washington College has had an unusual record of tenure for heads of departments. In the early days of the school, when, at times, one professor constituted the entire department, the designation as head of department seemed superfluous. It was not until increased enrollments and augmented teaching staff resulted in two or more instructors in the same field that the faculty listings in the annual catalogue indicated department heads. Since this practice was not followed consistently in later years, it has been difficult to establish an accurate list of persons who have served as departmental chairmen. Nevertheless, an impressive record of service on the part of these leaders is apparent.

At least thirteen faculty members served as heads of departments, or fulfilled the duties of heads of departments, for twenty-five years or more. The following list is as complete as existing records permit, for the designation as department head was not carried on personnel records before the late 1940s. The depart-

---

[4] *Free Lance–Star,* June 2, 1972.

Recent Developments

ment heads with a quarter of a century or more of service each, have been: Dorothy Duggan Van Winckel, art; William A. Castle, biology; James Harvey Dodd, commerce and later economics; Edward Alvey, Jr., education; George E. Shankle, English; Oscar H. Darter, history and social science; William N. Hamlet and Hobart C. Carter, mathematics; Mildred McMurtry Bolling, modern foreign languages; Eva Taylor Eppes, music; Eileen Kramer Dodd, psychology; Roy S. Cook, science; and Philip J. Allen, sociology.

Almost equaling the above list in years of service as departmental chairmen have been Preston Burns, physics; E. Boyd Graves, philosophy; Rachel J. Benton, physical education; George E. Luntz, music; Guenndolyn A. Beeler, home economics; Earl G. Insley, chemistry; Laura V. Sumner, classics; and Samuel T. Emory, geography. Mrs. Sumner and Dr. Emory were still serving as chairmen in 1972.

FACULTY MEMBERS WITH LONG SERVICE

As of July 1, 1972, at least seventeen other faculty members had served the college for twenty-five years or more. This list of devoted and distinguished teachers follows: Marjorie E. Arnold, physical education; Julien Binford, art; Zoe W. Black, biology; Marion K. Chauncey, music; James H. Croushore, English; Jean Slater Edson, music; William Wayne Griffith, English; Anne F. Hamer, music; Levin Houston III, music; Anna Scott Hoye, physical education and, later, biology; Mary A. K. Kelly, psychology; Walter B. Kelly, English; Almont Lindsey, history; Clifton B. McIntosh, foreign languages; Fred E. Miller, economics; Claudia M. Read, physical education; Reginald W. Whidden, English.

An additional eight had been members of the faculty for at least twenty-four years: Stanley F. Bulley, music; L. Clyde Carter, sociology; Benjamin W. Early, English; Henry W. Hewetson, economics; Edwin H. Jones, foreign languages; Kurt F. Leidecker, philosophy; Mary Ellen Stephenson, foreign languages; and Raiford E. Sumner, political science.

Other faculty members of long service to the college include: Herbert L. Cover, chemistry; Albert G. Duke, speech; Marion A. Greene, foreign languages; Anna Mae Harris, mathematics; Ruby C. Harris, home economics; Rosemary H. Herman, foreign languages; Miriam B. Hoge, foreign languages; Catherine H. Hook, education; Pauline G. King, art; William C. Pinschmidt, biology; Carmen L. Rivera, foreign languages; and Rebecca T. Woosley, physical education.

DESEGREGATION COMES TO MWC

In the spring of 1964 the rector and visitors formally approved a policy of desegregation for Mary Washington College. In May it was announced that the first Negro dormitory student had been accepted for the 1964–65 session and was planning to attend.[5] Previously, there had been two Negroes as day students in the summer sessions.[6] In 1962 Jacquelyn A. Pulliam, a teacher in the Culpeper County public schools, had commuted to attend summer classes. A year later, Gaye Todd, daughter of the first Negro to be appointed to the Fredericksburg city school board, enrolled as a day student. A valedictorian of Walker-Grant High School, she was attending Boston University at the time she registered for two courses in French at the 1963 summer session of Mary Washington.

The first Negro residential student was Kaye Estelle Savage of Richmond, who enrolled in September 1964. A graduate of George Wythe High School, she became a member of the entering freshman class at Mary Washington. Both of her parents were college graduates, and her mother was a teacher in the Richmond public schools. She attended the sessions of 1964–65 and 1965–66. She then transferred to Howard University in Washington, where she graduated with the bachelor of arts degree. In 1972 Kaye Savage, now Mrs. W. Page, was in process of completing her thesis for a master's degree at Howard University. There were three black students enrolled in 1965–66, two in 1966–67, and five in 1967–68.[7]

FIRST NEGRO GRADUATE

In June 1968 a landmark was reached with the awarding of the first diploma to a black student, Venus Romance Jones of Petersburg. When she entered in 1965, she roomed with Kaye Savage, who, the year before, had been the first black dormitory student at Mary Washington. However the two decided to go their separate ways in order to meet more of the other students.

---

[5] Faculty Minutes, May 12, 1964.   [6] *Free Lance-Star*, June 18, 1963.
[7] *Ibid.*, Aug. 21, 1967.

Recent Developments 507

To a reporter Venus Jones recalled Senior Day when, traditionally, seniors could command underclassmen to do their bidding. She asked some friends to dress in "crazy clothes" and pinned on their backs a sign reading, "I am the personal slave of Venus R. Jones." "Things certainly have changed in the last hundred years," an observer exclaimed.[8]

Miss Jones finished requirements for a bachelor of science degree in chemistry in three years and entered the University of Virginia Medical School upon graduation from Mary Washington. On June 4, 1972, she was awarded her M.D. there, and she began interning at Maricopa County General Hospital in Phoenix, Arizona.

FIRST NEGRO STUDENT TEACHER

The first black student teacher was Christiana ("Chris") Hall of Hopewell, who taught chemistry at James Monroe High School in the fall of 1968–69. She received her B.S. degree in June 1969 and became a teacher in the Arlington County public schools. In 1972 she was taking graduate work at Ohio State University.

ENROLLMENT TRENDS

The number of black students began to increase slowly, especially with the appointment of a black counselor, Diane-Louise Kenney, to the staff of the admissions office in 1970. In 1970–71 there were twenty-six black students enrolled. In 1971–72 there were twenty-three black students, of whom only three were day students.

COEDUCATION APPROVED

Chancellor Simpson read to the faculty at its meeting on February 18, 1970, the following resolution adopted by the board of visitors on February 7, 1970, relative to the admission of male applicants to Mary Washington College: "Resolved by The Rector and Visitors of the University of Virginia that the restrictions heretofore placed on the admission of men to Mary Washington College for the regular sessions be and they hereby are uncon-

---

[8] *Ibid.*, June 3, 1968.

ditionally removed, so that commencing with the regular academic session 1970–71 there shall be no restrictions on the admission of male applicants to Mary Washington College other than the same restrictions imposed upon female applicants." [9]

In 1970–71 there were twenty-two male students, only one of whom resided in college facilities. He lived in an apartment on the second floor of Hamlet House. By 1971–72 the number had grown to forty-two, of whom four were residential students. Two were housed in Hamlet House and two in the garage apartment adjoining the Alumnae House.

At the commencement exercises on May 20, 1972, the first men students since post–World War II days graduated from Mary Washington. These latter-day pioneers, all transfers from other institutions, were Raymond Clark Cote, John Bernard Sansone, Joseph Richard Grimes, and Lemuel Gunn. All four had begun their studies at the college after it became coeducational in 1970. All were Fredericksburg residents. Each of the four received thunderous applause from the audience, especially the senior class of 367, when he received his diploma. There were many in the audience who had not realized that the college had become coeducational. As one mother of a graduate remarked to her husband, "There really are men here." [10]

Approximately fifty to sixty men were expected to enroll for the 1972–73 session. Plans were made to house the six or eight resident students of the group in Trench Hill.

KAPPA OF VIRGINIA CHAPTER, PHI BETA KAPPA

The first step toward the organization of a chapter of Phi Beta Kappa at Mary Washington College was taken on December 15, 1964, when at the call of Chancellor Simpson, twenty-three members of the fraternity currently on the faculty and staff of the college met in the board room of George Washington Hall. It was agreed that the following committee should make plans for the organization of a chapter among the Phi Beta Kappa members at the college: James H. Croushore, Laura V. Sumner, Margaret Hargrove, Louis P. Fickett, Jr., Nancy H. Mitchell, and Grellet C. Simpson, honorary chairman.

On January 28, 1965, three members of this committee, Chan-

[9] Minutes of Board of Visitors, Feb. 7, 1970.
[10] *Free Lance-Star*, May 22, 1972.

cellor Simpson, James Croushore, and Louis Fickett, had a conference in Washington with Carl Billman, secretary of the united chapters of Phi Beta Kappa, regarding the procedures by which new chapters are established. This information was reported to the full membership at a general meeting held on March 25, at which time Croushore was elected chairman of the group and Laura Sumner was named secretary.

For the next two years the steering committee continued its activities relating to the establishment of a chapter at Mary Washington. Meetings of the whole group were held at intervals during this period. Application forms were completed and submitted on October 15, 1967. On January 5, 1968, Carl Billman wrote James Croushore that the preliminary application had been approved by the committee on qualifications and that Mary Washington had been selected as one of the nineteen institutions for study during the current triennium.

The preparation of the comprehensive general report occupied the spring and summer of 1968. It was submitted on September 30, 1968. Shortly thereafter, Billman announced that the committee on qualifications had designated two of its members to visit the college during the current session and to report back to the committee. Jewell H. Bushey, professor emeritus of mathematics, Hunter College, and Dr. Mary L. Gambrell, professor emeritus of history and former acting president, Hunter College, visited Mary Washington College on March 20–21, 1969, interviewing college officials, departmental chairmen, selected faculty members, and student leaders.

On January 15, 1970, Billman wrote Croushore on behalf of the committee on qualifications and the senate of Phi Beta Kappa that the application of the Phi Beta Kappa members of the faculty at Mary Washington to establish a chapter of the society at the college had been recommended for favorable consideration at the next triennial meeting and that members at Mary Washington were invited to sign and submit a formal petition. The petition was submitted on February 11, 1970, with the following members as signers: Edward Alvey, Jr., Charles D. Balthis, Mildred McMurtry Bolling, James H. Croushore, Benjamin W. Early, Jean Slater Edson, Lewis P. Fickett, Jr., Diane L. Fishman, Donald E. Glover, Susan J. Hanna, Margaret Hargrove, Rosemary Herman, Miriam Bowes Hoge, Michael Houston, Lucile C. Jones, Albert R. Klein, Helen Reese Luntz, Nancy H. Mitchell, Sidney H. Mitchell, Patricia Pierce, Roberta A. Rankin, Edgar F. Shannon,

Jr., Grellet C. Simpson, Charles A. Sletten, Mary Ellen Stephenson, Laura V. Sumner, Thomas S. Turgeon, Janet M. Whisler, Murat W. Williams, and Daniel H. Woodward.

At the triennial meeting of the council at Indiana University on September 9–11, 1970, the committee on qualifications and the senate recommended that the application of Mary Washington College be approved. Their recommendation was accepted. On September 11, 1970, the college was notified by telegram that the council had approved the establishment of a chapter of Phi Beta Kappa at Mary Washington College.

James Croushore, as chairman of the steering committee, called a meeting of the entire membership for November 23 to effect a permanent organization for the chapter at Mary Washington designated as Kappa of Virginia. At this meeting, committees on foundation and charter members, nomination of officers, constitution and by-laws, and installation ceremony were announced. Elected at a later meeting to serve as officers for the remainder of the academic year 1970–71 were Grellet C. Simpson, president; James H. Croushore, vice-president; and Edward Alvey, Jr., secretary-treasurer.

At a meeting in January 1971, the charter members named six persons to membership in the first elections held by the recently approved chapter. Elected to membership were three alumnae currently serving as members of the faculty: Anna Mae Harris, '36, associate professor of mathematics; Mary Annette Klinesmith Kelly, '44, associate professor of psychology; and Pauline Grace King, '37, professor and chairman of the department of art. Elected as the first honorary members were Eileen Kramer Dodd, professor emeritus of psychology; Lewis Meriwether Walker, Jr., former member of the University of Virginia board of visitors and past chairman of the Mary Washington College committee of the board; and Reginald W. Whidden, former dean of the college and professor emeritus of English.

The new chapter was installed on February 22, 1971, by Dr. Rosemary Park, president of the united chapters of Phi Beta Kappa. The meeting was held in the foyer of George Washington Hall. In the presence of the charter members and the initiates, President Park charged the chapter officers to fulfill certain responsibilities. She then placed the charter of Kappa of Virginia in the hands of Chancellor Simpson, the president of the chapter.

Dr. Park then spoke simply but effectively on the role of liberal education in the world today. She took note of the unusual circumstance of having the chapter at Mary Washington College installed on February 22, the birthday of George Washington, in a building bearing his name. Chancellor Simpson and Dean Alvey then proceeded with the initiation of the three alumnae and three honorary members. A reception and dinner for visiting members of Phi Beta Kappa and the local group followed at Brompton.

In May 1971 the Kappa of Virginia chapter elected its first group of students: twenty-two seniors and one junior. They were initiated later in the month in a ceremony followed by a banquet in Seacobeck Hall. Installed as officers for 1971–72 were Sidney H. Mitchell, president; Thomas S. Turgeon, vice-president; and Miriam Bowes Hoge, secretary-treasurer. The charter of the Kappa of Virginia chapter was framed and hung in the rotunda of E. Lee Trinkle Library.

SEPARATION: A NEW MILESTONE

On Monday, April 10, 1972, Governor Linwood Holton signed Senate Bill 433, providing for the separation of Mary Washington College from the University of Virginia and establishing the college as a completely autonomous institution.

The separation movement first received serious consideration in 1965 when the Report of the Higher Education Study Commission (commonly called the Russell Report after its chairman, John Dale Russell) to the governor and the General Assembly of Virginia observed that the operation of Mary Washington as a four-year branch of the university involved "few advantages and some handicaps to Mary Washington." The report recommended that "at some time in the future, it may be advisable to provide a separate Board of Visitors for Mary Washington College, making it an institution independent of the University of Virginia." [11]

Two years later, in 1967, the status study committee of the Alumnae Association concluded that the college should either become a truly coordinate part of the university or should separate. In October 1969 the committee on the future of the college studied the relationship. While its final report recommended no immediate change, an interim report recognized some inadequacies in the relationship and the "possible need for eventual severance of the connection."

The entire relationship was altered when the University of Virginia began in 1970 to admit women to its undergraduate Col-

[11] *MWC Today*, Feb. 1972.

lege of Arts and Science, ending, in effect, the role of Mary Washington as the woman's college of the University of Virginia. Admission of men to Mary Washington was also authorized.

The Self-Study Report of July 1971, prepared for the Southern Association of Colleges and Secondary Schools, took cognizance of these significant developments. It expressed the view that "the College has reached a stage in development in which the advantages of full autonomy outweigh the disadvantages of severing the existing nominal affiliation." [12]

The movement for separation gained momentum. After conferences and discussions with the faculty and staff, Chancellor Simpson requested the board of visitors to discuss separation. The board, in turn, asked the State Council of Higher Education to study the matter and make recommendations. After due consideration, the council on January 6, 1972, endorsed the separation. At its meeting on February 3, 1972, the board of visitors of the University of Virginia adopted a resolution calling for separation and forwarded it to the General Assembly of Virginia, then in session. State Senator Paul W. Manns introduced the bill, which was passed promptly by the state legislature.

The first two paragraphs of the board's resolution indicate the spirit in which this action was taken. They read:

Whereas the Board of Visitors of the University of Virginia is proud of the advancement of Mary Washington College to its present state of excellence as a component part of the University, evidenced by its offering of undergraduate degree programs in thirty-three fields, by its strong faculty, fine library, and handsome physical plant, and by the granting to the College in 1971 of a chapter of Phi Beta Kappa; and

Whereas the Board is willing to continue in this productive relationship with the College, but recognizes that certain advantages may result hereafter from separate status for the College; especially in view of the recent admission of men and the expectancy of service to the urban corridor as envisioned by the College's recent Self-Study; and. . . .[13]

The new legislation established a governing board of twelve members to be known as the Rector and Visitors of Mary Washington College, to be appointed by the governor, subject to confirmation by the General Assembly. Not fewer than six members are to be alumni or alumnae of the college. No more than three may be nonresidents of Virginia. After the initial period of varying terms, board members are to serve four-year periods, with a

[12] *Ibid.* [13] Minutes of Board of Visitors, Feb. 3, 1972.

maximum of two four-year appointments. The board elects its own rector.

Control of the Melchers estate, known as Belmont, and the James Monroe Law Office–Museum and Memorial Library also passed to the new board.

When the new status of the college became effective July 1, 1972, Chancellor Simpson emphasized that the question was not so much one of separation but of the future role of Mary Washington in furthering higher education in Virginia.

The designation of the chief administrative officer at Mary Washington was changed, and Dr. Simpson once again became president of the college, the title he had had when first appointed. The assistant chancellor, Michael Houston, became vice-president of the college.

On July 1, 1972, Governor Linwood Holton announced the personnel of the first board of visitors of Mary Washington. They include seven alumnae and five men.

The male appointees included two former members of the board of visitors of the University of Virginia: Lewis M. Walker, Jr., of Petersburg, president of the Builders Supply Company, who had previously been chairman of the Mary Washington College committee of the board, and Richard S. Cross of Lafayette Hill, Pennsylvania, a retired investment counselor.[14] Also appointed were Dr. Samuel D. Proctor, former president of Virginia Union University, now a professor at Rutgers University, and Joseph E. Blackburn, former chairman of the State Council of Higher Education, general attorney for the Chesapeake and Potomac Telephone Company at Richmond. The fifth male member was Ralph M. Whitticar III of Fredericksburg, lawyer and vice-chairman of the Fredericksburg planning commission.

The alumnae appointments were as follows: Irene Lundy Brown of Newport News, B.S. 1939, vice-president and treasurer, Fort Eustis Bus Terminal, Inc.; Gwendolyn Amory Cumming of Hampton, B.A. 1952, former public school teacher, former Mary Washington student government president; Donna Henninger Henderson of Troutville, B.S. 1961, assistant principal, Northside High School, Roanoke County; Maria Edmondson Hopper of Fairfax, B.S. 1929, county coordinator of pupil services, Fairfax County public schools; Ann Louise Perinchief of Fredericksburg, B.A. 1967, recently director of alumnae affairs at Mary Washing-

---

[14] Mr. Cross died on Aug. 15, 1972. Patricia Head Ferguson, a 1950 graduate of Mary Washington, was appointed to fill the vacancy.

ton; Joan Whittemore South of Hampton, B.A. 1959, high school teacher; Leah Fleet Waller of Richmond, B.S. 1944, former teacher and former president of Richmond Child Care Centers.

The appointments were from one to four years, subject to confirmation by the General Assembly. Lewis Walker was elected rector when the board held its first meeting on July 28, 1972.

Associations and Organizations

CHAPTER XXVIII

The Alumnae Association

EARLY records indicate that the Alumnae Association was organized in Richmond in 1914.[1] The *Battlefield* for 1915 (p. 139) under the heading "Alumnae Echoes" carried the following account:

Richmond, Va. Acting on the suggestion of Miss Gay Wilson, which was approved by President E. H. Russell, the members of the Fredericksburg State Normal Alumnae, who are teaching in Richmond and vicinity, met on December the eighteenth, and organized themselves into an association known as the "Richmond Chapter of the Fredericksburg State Normal Alumnae."

The purpose of the association is to promote social intercourse and to assist in furthering the interests of the school.

The following officers were appointed: Gay Wilson, president; Ethel Nash, vice-president; Pauline Perry, secretary; May Perrin, treasurer.

Other members, as listed in the *Battlefield* for 1915, were: Helen Phillips, Anne Henry, Buford Lyne, Winnie Walker, Nettie Montgomery Deaderich, Beatrice Ashley, Clare von Hofsten, Belle Pearce, and Mary Deierhoi.

All available records indicate that this meeting in Richmond marked the first formal organization of an alumnae group. It is interesting to note that the *Battlefield* for 1914 (pp. 143–45) under the same heading, "Alumnae Echoes" devoted three pages to activities of graduates of the recently established institution, but there was no mention of any organized alumnae activity. The meeting in Richmond on December 18, 1914, apparently marked the beginning of a formal organization of alumnae.

Gay Vaughan Wilson continued as president of the association for 1914–15 and 1915–16. She married Edward S. Currie, and they went as Presbyterian missionaries to mainland China and later to Taiwan (Formosa), where they spent many years.

[1] On Sept. 23, 1972, the board of directors voted to change the name of the organization to Alumni Association in recognition of the coeducational status of the college.

On February 27, 1970, Mrs. Currie wrote an interesting and informative letter from her home Gayward at Montreat, North Carolina, where she and her husband are now living. Referring to an error in listing her as a member of the class of 1915 in an alumnae publication, she wrote: "I had the privilege of seeing the very beginning of Mary Washington, had supper the first night with the faculty, and was there the next morning for the opening exercises. I graduated in 1913 in the first graduating class. I had the privilege of being the first president of our YWCA. In my senior year I suggested the name which was chosen for our Annual, 'The Battlefield,' and became business manager of the first edition."

Mrs. Currie was pleased to receive copies of the *Alumnae News*. Her affection for the institution has remained strong: "The only chance I've had to visit Mary Washington was during a summer and we just drove around the campus. I still love it." Her letter enclosed a gift to the Alumnae Fund. At the latest word, Mrs. Currie and Ed were still living at Gayward in Montreat. She had just returned from Philadelphia where she had gone to visit her eleventh grandchild.

Under Mrs. Currie's capable leadership, the newly organized association began an active program. A luncheon or banquet was given each year for the graduating class, and occasional reunions were held. At the meeting in June 1916, it was decided that a students' loan fund be started, "since, by this means, the greatest amount of good results could be accomplished." The report continued: "The Association voted for the year 1917 the sum of one hundred dollars, to be raised solely by the dues. November 8th was set apart, henceforth, to be known as Alumnae Dues Day, and, within the space of time between that date and November 30, 1917 the hundred dollars was sent in to the treasurer. Of this response we are very proud, and justly so we think, when it is taken into consideration that we have less than two hundred girls eligible to membership in the Association." [2]

The following alumnae, "having paid the required fee," were enrolled as life members: Jeanette Hess, Gay Wilson, Charlotte Rice, Kathryne Rice, May Perrin, Clara von Hofsten, Nancy Parker, Louise Lewis, Ruth Lord, Margaret Sayre, and Lucy Gouldman.

Mrs. Currie was succeeded as president by J. Louise Lewis, who served for 1916–17 and probably for the following year also, al-

---

[2] *Battlefield*, 1917, p. 124.

though there is no record of officers available. Other officers elected to serve with Louise Lewis were: Marjorie T. Riker, first vice-president, Bertha Scott, second vice-president, Frances Harrell, recording secretary, Grace Beazley, corresponding secretary, Janet LaCrosse, treasurer, and Virginia M. Goolrick of the faculty, advisory member.

Records of the association are missing for the next two years. Apparently, during the participation of the United States in World War I the activities of the Alumnae Association were dormant while the serious business of making the world safe for democracy engaged the attention of all.

It was during this early period that the association began having a meeting in connection with the annual convention of the State Teachers' Association (later the Virginia Education Association), held in Richmond each year at Thanksgiving. These meetings were described as of a "social and business character." The practice of having an alumnae get-together during the fall meeting of the teachers of Virginia has continued until the present time. Currently, the meeting is in the form of an alumnae tea held at a Richmond hotel one afternoon during the convention. The Richmond chapter has usually been in charge.

During 1919 and 1920, a period of some difficulties and transition at the college, there is no record of alumnae activities. The next recorded president of the association was the person who shared with Louise Lewis the yearbook dedication in 1920, Grace K. Tanner, who served in 1920–21. Like Louise Lewis, Grace Tanner was also a member of the faculty of her alma mater at the time. Unfortunately, few records are available regarding activities of the Alumnae Association during her presidency. The *Battlefield* for 1921 contained an interesting account of a meeting held in Richmond at Thanksgiving in connection with the annual state teachers' meeting.

Grace Tanner was succeeded as president by Mary Evans Holman, a graduate of the class of 1920. Miss Holman, now Mrs. William Morris Curd, headed the association for the next two years.

In 1922 plans were projected for an alumnae secretary and for a student-alumnae building. The *Battlefield* for 1922 (p. 115) carried this simple but appealing message as the only item under the heading of "Alumnae":

This page is dedicated to the loyal alumnae of the Fredericksburg Normal School, who are serving with unselfish devotion in the field of education in Virginia, and who individually and in organized groups are making a large contribution to their Alma Mater in raising funds for the establishment in 1922-23 of the new chair of alumnae secretary and are already projecting plans for the construction on our beautiful hilltop beside our exquisite grove of the new Student-Alumnae Building. May God always prosper the work of your hands and hearts and heads.

For the next six years, the raising of funds for what was then called the Student-Alumnae Building occupied the thought and energies of the entire association. Actually, the goal was never reached, but the swimming pool, called the "first unit" of the proposed building, was finally constructed mainly through gifts from alumnae, faculty, and residents of the community. The campaign to raise funds for the structure is described elsewhere in this history. It is important to note here that the Alumnae Association, through pledges and money-making projects of various kinds, raised approximately twenty thousand dollars toward this building during six years of devoted and intensive effort.

During this period the Alumnae Association began the operation of a tea room in the basement of Willard Hall, which was called affectionately The Little Red Lane. All proceeds from the running of the tea room went to the building fund. Operated from 8:30 A.M. to 5:00 P.M. and again at recreation hour in the evening, the tea room was staffed by volunteers from the faculty, student body, and members of the Fredericksburg chapter of the Alumnae Association.

The Alumnae Association in 1922-23 was a very active organization. It boasted a membership of eight hundred, with Mary Evans Holman as president. Local chapters were organized that year in Caroline, Westmoreland, Richmond, Northumberland, Lancaster, Spotsylvania, and Arlington counties and the cities of Hampton, Newport News, Norfolk, Portsmouth, Richmond, and Fredericksburg. All were reported "making great headway—especially financially."

Chapters continued to support the drive for funds. The Fredericksburg chapter raised two hundred dollars through various activities. The Newport News chapter realized fifty-seven from a card party and dessert sale. Richmond City chapter sent in twenty-five dollars from a card party. And so it went, as, little by little, funds were raised for the Student-Alumnae Building.

Among items of interest among alumnae was the news that Anne Harris of Richmond, a graduate of the college, had passed the state bar and been admitted to the practice of law in Virginia. One of the few women lawyers in the state, she received her degree that June from the T. C. Williams School of Law, University of Richmond.

In 1925 Beryl Barber Willis (Mrs. Mason H. Willis) was elected president of the Alumnae Association and served for the next four years. At the time of her election, she was supervisor of the third and fourth grades in the Campus Training School, a position she continued to hold until 1933.

Beryl Willis had attended the Richmond Training School for Kindergarteners and, subsequently, completed the diploma course at Fredericksburg Normal School. Before joining the faculty here in 1924, she had taught for seven years in the Fredericksburg public schools. A warm and enthusiastic person, she was popular both as a teacher and as president of the Alumnae Association. A later tribute to her read:

Organization of the Association was rather loose for many years. Homecoming was held at Commencement with the graduating Senior and Sophomore classes in attendance. (The graduating Sophomores were qualified for teaching in the grade schools only.) Mrs. Mason Willis (Beryl Barber), '29, as president during this long period, held the Association together by the force of her personality and the great affection and esteem for herself held by the graduates for whom she had often been the "critic teacher" or supervisor in the Training School. Miss Elinor Hayes (Mrs. John Nichols), as long time secretary, exercised a like influence. At this time there were no dues and consequently no activities except the banquet at Homecoming.[3]

Mrs. Willis died on March 5, 1970.

Until 1926, "Alumnae Notes," or information under some similar heading was a regular feature of the college annual. These pages carried news of alumnae and, frequently, descriptions of activities of the Alumnae Association.

The drive for funds for the proposed building continued in its intensity, but the goal still seemed far off. Finally, a local drive among citizens of Fredericksburg provided the rest of the funds needed to build the swimming pool part of the structure. As recorded elsewhere in this history, the "first unit" of the new building was completed and dedicated on February 18, 1928, in the presence of a large number of alumnae who had returned for the occasion. Later, the pool was roofed over with terrazzo and used for outdoor dances and parties.

President Chandler died as the college opened in the fall of

---

[3] "Some Historical Highlights of the Alumnae Association mimeographed, April 1961.

1928. Many alumnae attended the funeral or sent letters of condolence to his widow. He was succeeded by Dr. Morgan L. Combs, who took office on January 1, 1929.

On June 1, 1929, an alumnae banquet was held in the dining room of Frances Willard Hall. Molly Coates was program chairman. Rachel Wingfield, president of the association, presided. The new college president, Dr. Combs, brought greetings to the group. There were toasts to various groups during the meal. There were "Echoes from the Dark Ages" by "Alumnae from Far and Near." The college orchestra, under the direction of Mildred McMurtry, played several selections.

During the 1930s, the years of the Great Depression, alumnae publications ceased entirely. In fact, activities of the association were limited largely to the annual banquet and dance held during the weekend of graduation exercises at the college and the Thanksgiving luncheon held in Richmond during the annual convention of the Virginia Education Association, which was attended by a large number of graduates of the college.

Beryl Willis was succeeded as president by Betsy Bassett Sacrey (Mrs. Nymat Sacrey), who served in 1929–30 and 1930–31. The devoted service of the Fredericksburg chapter in carrying on the work of the association during the thirties really kept the organization alive. It was the Fredericksburg chapter which arranged the meetings in Richmond at Thanksgiving and the annual homecoming banquet and dance at graduation. During Betsy Sacrey's presidency a monthly newsletter was mimeographed by the Fredericksburg chapter and regular meetings were held, usually at the college. In 1931 a chapter in Hampton was organized, named in honor of the late President Chandler.

During the next few years all of the officers of the association were from Fredericksburg. In 1931 Betsy Sacrey was succeeded as president by Betty Billingsley (Mrs. D. P. Tillar). In 1932 Katherine Nicks Bernard (Mrs. Edgar Bernard) became president, followed in 1933 by Louise Garnett (Mrs. Richard Goodwin); in 1934 by Phoebe Enders Willis (Mrs. Jere M. H. Willis), who served two terms; and in 1936 by Kathryn Jones Cueman (Mrs. C. W. Cueman).

The alumnae banquet for 1931 celebrated the twentieth anniversary of the founding of the college. It was held in Seacobeck Hall, the newly completed dining hall building, the first structure to be built by President Combs. Dr. Combs welcomed the alumnae and guests. The main address was given by C. O'Conor Goolrick, honored as the founder of the college.

Professor W. N. Hamlet was listed as the honor guest on this occasion. Introduced as the oldest professor at the college—in length of service—Mr. Hamlet responded with a delightful account of the opening days of the school. His complete address was published in the *Free Lance–Star* on July 2 along with an account of his career. He recalled vividly the unpaved streets, the lack of sidewalks, and "the perilous journey from Washington Avenue to the hill, when one had to arm oneself with boards to navigate the mud-puddles and mosquito swamp holes of Cornell Street."

From 1931 on, it became customary to hold an alumnae dinner in Seacobeck at 6:30 P.M., followed by a dance on the roof garden of the swimming pool from nine to twelve with music furnished by Roland Leveque's Orchestra of Fredericksburg.

An authoritative record of Alumnae Association activities during the thirties is found in the record book of the secretary-treasurer from June 1931 to April 1940, now in the files of the association. A review of the minutes shows a continuing effort to establish a scholarship fund and to employ an executive secretary. By the end of the period, both objectives had been attained, with modest funds for scholarships established and a part-time secretary employed.

Officers for 1934–35 and 1935–36 were: Mrs. Jere M. H. Willis, president; Mrs. Roy S. Cook, vice-president; and Elinor L. Hayes, secretary-treasurer. It was at this time that a scholarship fund was officially established (minutes for June 1, 1935). The original amount set up was one hundred dollars, "effective for the second quarter of the 1935–36 session" to be awarded as a loan at 4 percent to a "deserving freshman student" selected by the scholarship committee. The minutes of this period also refer to an "assessment of 25¢ per member" to go to the employment of an alumnae secretary.

In 1937 Clara Boyd Wheeler, '31, became president of the association and served for the next four years. A native of Clifton Forge, she had graduated with a major in social studies and physical education. In 1967, she was to receive the Distinguished Alumna Award. At the time of her election as president of the Alumnae Association, she was associate director of health and physical education for the YWCA in Washington, D.C.

Miss Wheeler brought to the work of the association an energetic and devoted leadership that soon began to show results. The usual Thanksgiving luncheon in Richmond that fall (1937), held at Murphy's Hotel, was unusually well attended. Clara Boyd Wheeler presided. The main speaker was Jesse H. Binford, superintendent of the Richmond city schools.

A special May Day–Alumnae issue of the *Bullet* appeared on

May 5, 1939. In addition to a revised list of members by classes, from 1913 to 1939, there were several pages of fascinating illustrations including pictures of May Days and daisy chains in 1915, 1918, 1926, and 1928, snapshots of the basketball team, and the senior class of 1918. The special edition was the work of the association president, Clara Boyd Wheeler; Lillie Turman, dean of freshmen; and Clara Richards, of the class of 1918.

Meanwhile, the efforts to obtain the services of a part-time secretary began to bear fruit, and plans were under way for a college staff member to undertake the job with a modest salary supplement (fifty dollars a month) from the alumnae. The annual meeting in June 1939 approved such a proposal, and Miss Wheeler agreed to see if Lillie Turman, then dean of freshmen and in charge of Frances Willard Hall, would accept the appointment.

In the fall of 1939 the first issue of the *Alumnae News,* as a separate publication, appeared. It bears the designation "Vol. I, No. 1," and was mimeographed by the commercial department of the college, which, according to the opening announcement, had "graciously consented to mimeograph four issues . . . for 1939–40."

In a message to the alumnae, Clara Boyd Wheeler, the president, announced with pride: "1939 is an outstanding year for the Alumnae. This marks the establishment of an Alumnae office under the direction of a very capable part-time secretary, Miss Lillie Turman, '36. . . . The organization of the work has begun with the office housed in Frances Willard Hall. When you visit the college, you must sign the alumnae register and chat with Lillie concerning the work. . . ." Although the editor of this first news bulletin is not indicated, several messages it contains and requests for news items indicate that it was the work of the new part-time alumnae secretary, Lillie Turman.

There is a brief account of the founding of the Alumnae Association, together with the names of officers of this and other college organizations during the early years of the institution. The remainder of the bulletin consists of news of various alumnae.

Volume 1, no. 3, of the *Alumnae News* appeared in May 1940. In addition to news of alumnae, the issue included a proposed constitution and bylaws, which had been prepared by Mildred Stewart, chairman of the constitution committee. This constitution was adopted at a business meeting of the association held on June 8, 1940.

The Fredericksburg chapter presented a portrait of President

The Alumnae Association

A. B. Chandler to be placed in Chandler Hall. Meetings of the chapter were being held in the town girls' room of Chandler Hall. A monthly bulletin of chapter activities was being sent to each member.

A portrait of William N. Hamlet, one of the members of the original faculty of the institution, was also commissioned during Mildred Stewart's presidency and hung in Chandler Hall. It was the work of A. B. Vondra of Gordonsville, whose two daughters subsequently graduated from the college. Vondra also painted the portrait of President Chandler.

At the annual meeting on June 8, 1940, Mildred Stewart, '28, was elected president to succeed Clara Boyd Wheeler, '31, who had served for four years. Lillie Turman, '36, continued to serve as alumnae executive secretary.

The *Alumnae News* began publication in printed form in fall 1940. It included campus news (the newly organized marching band, the new College Shoppe in Chandler Hall, and the Lyceum program); a description and sketch of the new library (E. Lee Trinkle Library) then under construction; news from several chapters (Tidewater, Norfolk-Portsmouth, Fredericksburg, and a proposed Washington chapter); the constitution and bylaws of the Alumnae Association; and minutes of the annual meeting and the treasurer's report. Expenditures for the year totaled $601.10, including the salary of $250.00 paid the executive secretary.

The new alumnae president, Mildred Stewart, graduated from the college in 1928. She was president of the Student Government Association, vice-president of the YWCA, and business manager of the *Bullet*. Her chief interest, however, was athletics, and she participated actively in various sports. She composed the music to the alma mater: "Eager Voices Rising. . . ."

Mildred Stewart did graduate work at Colorado State College and Columbia University, receiving her M.A. from the latter in 1936. She specialized in dance. Before returning to her alma mater as a teacher in 1938, she taught at Florida State College, Carleton College, and Texas State College for Women. In 1940 she was made head of the department of physical education. She organized the dance programs for many May Day celebrations.

In 1942 Miss Stewart was succeeded as president by Belle Oliver Hart, '22, then living in Washington. An ambitious project of the 1942–43 officers was the publication of an alumnae handbook containing the names and addresses of all active members of the association, and reports of officers and activities from nine local chapters. In 1942–43 there were 280 active members, plus 60 life members. Annual dues were a dollar. Life membership cost twenty dollars, payable in four annual installments. In December 1942 Miss Turman requested to be relieved of alumnae work.

A feature of the 1942–43 year's activities was the organization of the Alumnae Daughters' Club. Founded on April 28, 1943, thirty years after the first class had graduated from the college, the group numbered thirty members and, according to available records, represented the largest number of daughters of alumnae that had attended in any one year up to that time.

Charter members of the organization were: Ruth Birchett, Betty Blackwell, Jean Eleanor Boyle, Anne Bolling Clarke, Doris Mae Clements, Louise Parks Cornwell, Nancy Turner Duval, Rebecca Katherine Engleman, Kathleen Hallet Goffigon, Frances Marie Hale, Betsy Gordon Hilldrup, Jeannette Hutchinson, Virginia Hutchinson, Betty Randolph Jones, Gene Randolph Morris, Betty Randolph Odell, Virginia Elizabeth Peed, Constance Maddox Pusey, Sallie Woodson Scott, Martha Segar Scott, Jeanne Bowman Shade, Frances MacMurdo Stebbins, Thelma Sutton, Frances May Stutz, Virginia Elizabeth Sydnor, Margaret Morris Thomas, Mary Gresham Watkins, Bettie P. Woodward, Frances Virginia Woodward, and Roberta Boxley Woodward.

The organization decided to award annually a cup to the daughter of an alumna who had the highest academic average of the group in the college. The recipient was allowed to keep the cup for one year. An alumnae convocation and Alumnae Daughters' Club reception were held in April. In June 1943, the Alumnae Daughters Scholarship Cup was presented to Kathleen Goffigon, '44, daughter of Kathleen Hallett, '16.

In recent years the Alumnae Daughters' Club has been inactive. The cup is now on display at the Alumnae House. The following record of awards, taken from the engraving on the cup itself, gives the year of the award, the name and class of the recipient, and the maiden name and class of her mother:

1943	Kathleen H. Goffigon '44	Kathleen "Bet" Hallet '16
1944	Sallie Woodson Scott '46	Emma Lankford '14
1945	Bettie Pollard Woodward '46	Lucy Boxley '15
1946	Marguerite Irene Marshall '47	Ethel Beazley '13
1947	Carolyn Jean Sprower '50	Katherine Hackney '27
1948	Carolyn Jean Sprower '50	Katherine Hackney '27
1949	Carolyn Jean Sprower '50	Katherine Hackney '27
1950	Carolyn Jean Sprower '50	Katherine Hackney '27
1951	Mary Hill Chilton '54	Virginia Hill '28
1952	Mary Hill Chilton '54	Virginia Hill '28

1953 Mary Hill Chilton '54	Virginia Hill '28
1954 Ann Lee Dunaway '55	Annie Towles '19
1955 Elizabeth Davies '56	Louise Gordon '29
1956 Joyce Lee Bristow '57	Bates Miller '26
1957 Jacquelin Morton Bragg '60	Susan Baker '32
1958 Jacquelin Morton Bragg '60	Susan Baker '32

In 1944 the Thomas Jefferson Cup was established as an award to commemorate the affiliation of Mary Washington College with the University of Virginia. It is presented each year to "that member of the graduating class who, during her years at Mary Washington College, not only has maintained a high scholastic average, signified by listings on the Dean's List, but has performed a most outstanding service for the College."

The first award was made in 1945 to Ellen Trimble of Hot Springs by Camilla Moody Payne, who served as president of the Alumnae Association in 1945 and 1946. The award has continued to be presented by the Alumnae Association president, usually at the Class Night exercises. The original cup and a second one used later are kept on display at the Alumnae House.

A list of the recipients of the Thomas Jefferson Cup, along with the year of the award, is as follows: Ellen Thompson Trimble, 1945; Janice Corinne Worsley, 1946; Sylvia Iris Francis, 1947; Mary Ann Ross, 1948; Judith Wolling Stone, 1949; Mary Watts Cottingham, 1950; Elizabeth Taliaferro Bunnell, 1951; Virginia Elizabeth Orkney, 1952; Betty Anne Raynor, 1953; Mary Ann T. Dorsey, 1954; Frances Earle Brittle, 1955; Margaret S. White, 1956; Joanne Insley, 1957; Peggy Anne Kelley, 1958; Barbara Ann Jabbour, 1959; Nancy Houston Moncure, 1960; Louise Vaughan Hargroves, 1961; Joan Marie Akers, 1962; Randi Coates Haupt, 1963; Carolyn Ann Hawker, 1964; Judith Anne Sutherland, 1965; Judith Margaret Wells, 1966; Ann Louise Perinchief, 1967; Ann Cecilia Scott, 1968; Patricia Mae Boise and Mary Page Williams, 1969; Marilyn Louise Prebble, 1970; Ann Gamble Jefferis, 1971; and Ann Mitchell Bowling, 1972.

The new president, Camilla Moody Payne, '29, was originally from Fredericksburg. After her graduation she entered the interior designing field in Washington. Meanwhile she received her master's degree in this specialty from George Washington University. She designed the decor and furnishing for the Alumnae House and the public rooms and lounges of Bushnell, Russell, and Marshall residence halls at Mary Washington.

During Mrs. Payne's presidency the financial operation of the association was strengthened and its sphere of activities expanded. For a time she carried much of the responsibility for the operation of the organization in the absence of an executive secretary to succeed Lillie Turman.

At its meeting on April 14, 1945, the directors of the Alumnae Association had decided to set up an Alumnae Fund. A goal of five thousand dollars to be raised during the next two years was set. Funds were to be used for the establishment of an executive secretary. By 1947 these two objectives had been attained, and a broader purpose of the Alumnae Fund as "a growing living endowment, with annual contributions . . ." was envisioned.[4]

Camilla Payne was reelected president for 1946-47. Lindlay Goolrick (Mrs. Segar Hinkle), '44, was appointed national executive secretary. Under her editorship the publication of the *Alumnae News* was resumed. Mary Annette Klinesmith, Camilla Moody Payne, and Mildred P. Stewart assisted her as members of the editorial staff. Volume 3, no. 1, appeared as the "Spring Issue, 1948" with news of the various chapters and pictures of their presidents. Martha McKenney Swope, was elected president for 1947-48.

Homecoming on April 10, 1948, featured the presence of Edward R. Stettinius, Jr., rector of the University of Virginia, and President Colgate W. Darden, Jr. That spring marked the completion of the four-year period set in 1944 for the coordination of the college's academic offerings and degree requirements with those of the University of Virginia.

In 1948 the Alumnae Association was formally incorporated and an official seal adopted. The certificate of incorporation, dated May 9, 1956, is now kept in the vault in the comptroller's office. The official seal consists of two concentric circles of type, with just the year 1948 in the center. The outer circle reads "Alumnae Association Mary Washington College of the University of Virginia." The inner circle reads simply "Fredericksburg, Va." In practice, the association has used the more attractive seal of the college as its customary emblem.

The development of alumnae chapters reached a new high during this period. The following chapter presidents and directors are listed in the spring-summer 1949 issue of the *Alumnae News* (vol. 4, no. 1): Culpeper: Esther James Putnam, '41; Fredericksburg: Mrs. Stuart Graves, '38, Mary Annette Klinesmith, '44;

---

[4] See "The Alumnae Fund," by Mary Annette Klinesmith, '44, and Mrs. Charles S. Payne (Camilla Moody, '29), *Alumnae News* 3 no. 1 (1948): 13-14.

Lynchburg: Jean McCausland, '47, Mrs. T. J. Chaffin, Jr., '45; Greater New York: Jayne Anderson, '44, Helen Kikis, '42; Norfolk: Mrs. Eugene E. Echols, '39, Margaret Lambert, ex '34; Peninsula: Mrs. Ralph G. Newsome, '31, Mrs. Van Anderson, ex '43; Philadelphia: Mrs. Myron M. Jessen, '46, Emily Ribet, '47; Portsmouth: Mrs. Richard Cotten, ex '44, Georgiana Woodhouse, '39; Richmond: Mrs. W. D. Brumble, '44, Betsy Rowe, ex '43; Roanoke: Mrs. Floyd B. Thomas, ex '43, Mrs. Horace Hood III, '39; Suffolk: Ravis McBride, '47, Jean Bell, '47; Washington: Mrs. Richard B. Ransom, '44, Joanna Pappandreau, '40.

A major project of the Alumnae Association in 1949–50 was raising funds to contribute toward the furnishing of the semipublic rooms at Brompton, which, in 1947 had been purchased by the college from the Rowe estate and had just been completely restored and redecorated.[5] Chief fund-raising activity was a concert by Martha Graham and her modern dance group on February 10, 1950, sponsored by the Alumnae Association. About eight hundred dollars was raised and contributed toward the purchase of furniture for Brompton. A Paul Revere silver bowl was also presented to Brompton by the association at that time.

Lindlay Goolrick resigned as executive secretary and editor of the *Alumnae News* shortly after publication of the spring-summer 1949 issue. She was succeeded by Diana M. Tansill, '46, of Fredericksburg. During her tenure a colonial issue of the *Alumnae News* was published as the fall-winter 1949–50 issue (vol. 4, no. 2). It was dedicated to Mildred P. Stewart, retiring faculty adviser of the Alumnae Association. Messages from Barron F. Black, rector of the University, and alumnae president Molly Vaughan Parrish headed the opening pages. Mary Annette Klinesmith succeeded Mildred Stewart as faculty adviser of the association.

Homecoming activities in April 1949 included a formal dinner honoring President Morgan L. Combs upon completion of twenty years as president of the college. The spring-summer 1949 issue of the *Alumnae News* featured the election of Mrs. Edward Alton Parrish (Molly Vaughan, '29) as president of the association. For the next two years, Mrs. Parrish directed the affairs of the organization.

In 1950 the homecoming banquet of the Alumnae Association honored Mrs. Bushnell, who was retiring in June after twenty-nine years of service. The *Battlefield* for that year was dedicated to Mrs. Bushnell in a moving tribute. The Alumnae Association

---

[5] See "Brompton" by Phoebe Enders Willis, *ibid.* 4, no. 2 (1949): 12–17.

presented Mrs. Bushnell with a handsome lapel watch and a life membership in the association. Molly Vaughan Parrish was reelected president for 1950–51.

Because of lack of funds, the association was forced to curtail its activities. Only a part-time secretary could be employed. Since Diana Tansill was not interested in part-time work she resigned and was succeeded in January 1951 by Audrey Ferrell (Mrs. James B. Ferrell), also of Fredericksburg, as acting secretary. The *Alumnae News* (vol. 6, no. 1) was published in March 1951 in greatly abbreviated form as a four-page printed newspaper of slightly smaller than tabloid size. For the next several years, until winter 1955, the *News* was published in this form or as a mimeographed bulletin. Penelope Critzos, '43, edited the 1951 issues of the *News,* with the assistance of Audrey Ferrell.

In 1951 Lillie Turman, '36, long active in the affairs of the association and executive secretary on a part-time basis then, became president. She had become headmistress and administrator of Moravian Seminary at Bethlehem, Pennsylvania, after leaving Mary Washington. In 1951–52 the association was still handicapped by lack of funds. In an "Open Letter from Your President," in the February 1952 issue of the *Alumnae News* (vol. 7, no. 3), Lillie Turman wrote at length about alumnae activities and made an eloquent plea for five-dollar membership payments. Inez Matthews, in the treasurer's office, handled arrangements for homecoming.

The spring 1952 newsletter included a printed insert of the words and music to "High on Marye's Hilltop," by Jeanne Crotty, '47, and Irene Taylor, '47, which was adopted as the official alma mater of the college by the Alumnae Association at the 1952 homecoming. In 1952 Lucille Wheeler of Newport News, long active in alumnae affairs, was appointed to the University of Virginia board of visitors. She served for eight years.

Lillie Turman was reelected president in 1952. That fall Pauline Graves Lamason began work as the new executive secretary. In October the *Alumnae News* reappeared in printed form as an eight-page pamphlet, with a cover illustration of the new fine arts center to be dedicated in May 1953. Also announced with great glee was the designation of space for an alumnae office in the new student activities building then under construction. Annual dues were five dollars; life membership, fifty dollars.

Eloise Caverlee Hughes (Mrs. James Hughes), '40, was elected president in 1953. Pauline Graves Lamason continued as executive secretary. The association now had as its official headquarters

Room 204 in Ann Carter Lee Hall, just across from the Terrace Room, as the college tearoom was then called. Mrs. Lamason resigned in October 1956. There were several temporary appointments in the months that followed.

On April 3, 1954, the homecoming banquet was a formal affair in celebration of Dr. Combs's twenty-fifth anniversary as president. The Alumnae Association presented him with a silver tray at that time.

In 1954 Belva Tune Dunn, '44, past treasurer of the Alumnae Association and active in the organization, was appointed by Governor Stanley to the board of visitors of the University of Virginia. Miss Dunn, later Mrs. Tom Jones, served on the board for eight years, until 1962.

With the June 1954 issue (vol. 9, no. 3), the name of the alumnae publication was changed from *Alumnae News* to *Alumnae Bulletin*. Interest in the Alumnae Association continued to increase. President Eloise Caverlee Hughes reported that charters had been granted to form four new chapters: Maryland Suburban, Peninsula, New Jersey, and Eastern Shore. Increases in membership were impressive, as the table below indicates:

	May 1953	April 1954
Life members	332	385
Paying on life	100	123
Annual members	160	280

The association had the honor of an award at the American Alumni Council Convention in Mississippi for "significant achievement in the use of direct mail to promote alumnae questionnaire response." Class agents for each class from 1913 on were appointed. Reports from various chapters indicated a wide variety of projects.

In the spring of 1955 Margaret Lambert, '34, was elected president to succeed Eloise Hughes. The *Alumnae Bulletin* for spring 1955 (vol. 10, no. 2) reports an invitation from Henry McWane to submit nominations for the president of Mary Washington to succeed Dr. Combs. McWane was the chairman of the board of visitors committee to select his successor. Alumnae activities were burgeoning. The budget for 1955–56 was $7,500, including $2,400 for the salary of the executive secretary. It was a far cry from the few hundreds budgeted just a decade before.

A special issue of the *Alumnae News* appeared in February 1955 (vol. 10, no. 2). It was a well-printed publication of forty pages, with many illustrations and much news about alumnae, newly nominated officers, and plans for homecoming. There were messages from Mrs. Bushnell, then dean of women at Moravian College in Bethlehem, Pennsylvania; Chancellor Colgate W. Darden, Jr.; President M. L. Combs; Dean Edward Alvey, Jr.; Bursar Edgar E. Woodward; and Ruby Cook Harris, acting dean of women. There was also a large picture of the University of Virginia board of visitors assembled in meeting in the board room at Charlottesville.

The fall 1955 issue of the *Alumnae News* announced the election of Dr. Grellet Collins Simpson as president of Mary Washington College. When the winter 1956 number of the *Alumnae News* (vol. 12, no. 2) appeared, it carried messages from President Simpson and Dean Alvey regarding the change in administration. Dr. Simpson expressed his belief in the alumnae as "another means for the greater glory and prestige of Mary Washington." Both he and Dean Alvey looked forward to greeting alumnae at homecoming. This annual event was held on the weekend of April 7. Many alumnae had the privilege of meeting Dr. and Mrs. Simpson at a tea they gave at Brompton on Saturday afternoon, the first of many social occasions for former graduates that the Simpsons were to arrange at homecoming, finals, and other occasions on which alumnae gathered in Fredericksburg.

At the spring homecoming in 1956, the class of 1919 presented a portrait of E. H. Russell, first president of the college. Mr. and Mrs. Russell were present for the luncheon at which the presentation was made. The portrait was hung later in Russell Hall. The association marked the passing of President Morgan L. Combs on October 25, 1955, with formal resolutions of gratitude and respect for his achievements and memory.

On September 1, 1956, the association lost the services of "Polly" Lamason, its efficient executive secretary and for several years editor of the *Alumnae News*. Martha Lyle Pittman was appointed acting executive secretary. She proceeded to make plans for the 1957 homecoming. Meanwhile, a new procedure for voting for officers was established after a survey of practices in other associations. Nominations were to be made well in advance, biographical sketches and ballots sent out with the homecoming bulletin, and the results announced at the homecoming luncheon meeting and the installation held at the banquet.

During the summer of 1957, the executive committee decided

The Alumnae Association

to discontinue the publication of a separate bulletin or news magazine in favor of a special alumnae supplement of the *Bullet,* the college student newspaper. This action was taken largely as an economy measure.

The savings were such as to make it possible to send copies to all former graduates of the college. The first issue appeared on September 15, 1957, and, according to an announcement of the new editorial arrangement, went to almost eighty-five hundred readers. It carried biographies of the officers elected for 1957–58 at the April 1957 homecoming. Margaret Lodge Copes, '32, was president; Jane Hatcher Major, '40, vice-president; Doris Virginia Steele, '52, secretary, and Mary Annette Klinesmith Kelly, '44, faculty adviser. Camilla Moody Payne was appointed chairman of the alumnae endowment committee. Plans were made to increase the fund and to expand its role in the life of the college.

The alumnae supplement for November 22, 1957, indicated the intensity with which the drive was launched and supported. Called the Fiftieth Anniversary Fund, the campaign set four objectives: an Alumnae House on campus; an increased endowment fund; establishment of a scholarship fund; and additions to the college permanent art collection.

Dr. Simpson worked closely with the officers in the formulation of objectives and plans for their attainment. He declared, "By contributing to the Alumnae Association's Fund, a graduate is voting in favor of Mary Washington's future." A special interview with the chancellor indicated his enthusiasm for each objective.[6] It was agreed that the first five thousand dollars raised would be set aside for the Alumnae House.

On March 14, 1958, the fiftieth anniversary of the college was celebrated. Special honor was paid to C. O'Conor Goolrick, regarded as the founding father of the institution. An address was given by Mrs. J. Lindsay Almond, Jr., wife of the governor of Virginia.

Homecoming was held on April 11–13, with Colgate W. Darden, Jr., president of the university, as the principal speaker. A report on the progress of the endowment fund indicated a total of over $2,500 pledged as of March 15, 1958. By homecoming the total had risen to $3,372.00. By July 31, 1958, $4,682.00 had been pledged.

In the fall of 1958 Deborah C. Klein was chosen executive secretary of the association, replacing Emma Timken, '57, who

---

[6] Alumnae supplement, *Bullet,* Nov. 22, 1957.

had served as acting secretary during the preceding year. The Fredericksburg chapter sponsored a fashion show at the college, the proceeds of which went to the alumnae fund. The alumnae supplement for December 12, 1958, contained a salute to Mary Annette Kelly, faculty adviser, as "one in whose footsteps we could wish to follow."

Homecoming 1959 saw the election of Kathleen Goodloe, '25, as president. A feature of the homecoming banquet was an address by Karen Olsen de Figueres, a 1951 graduate of the college, whose husband was president of Costa Rica. Mrs. de Figueres also represented her country as delegate to the United Nations. Homecoming chairman was Jane Hatcher Major, vice-president of the association.

Most exciting news at the 1959 homecoming was that the college had offered to turn over Spotswood Hall dormitory to alumnae for an off-campus Alumnae House. Terms of the offer included a nominal rent and the furnishing of the house by the association.

The offer was eagerly accepted by the alumnae in its business session and plans were made to move August 1 from the office in Ann Carter Lee to the new facility. Spotswood was named for Virginia's colonial governor, Alexander Spotswood. It was built originally by Mrs. E. D. Gould, and later purchased by the college from Charles F. Beck. It had been used for a short time as a Spanish house and was later to house about a dozen art majors. Plans provided for the removal of a panel to make a large reception and meeting room on the first floor. Upper floor bedrooms would be available for alumnae overnight visitors.

With arrangements completed for the occupation of Spotswood as the Alumnae House the first objective of the endowment campaign was realized. Plans to furnish the house went forward with enthusiasm. The acquisition of a headquarters of its own seemed to inject even greater spirit into all activities of the association.

Deborah Klein served as executive secretary for one year. She resigned when her husband took a leave of absence to complete his Ph.D. degree at the University of Denver. In 1959 Bettie V. Griffith (Mrs. William Wayne Griffith) took over the duties of executive secretary and editor of the *Alumnae News*. The November 1960 issue (vol. 13, no. 1) marked the discontinuance of the alumnae supplement to the *Bullet* and the resumption of the association's own publication.

The new *Alumnae News,* edited by Mrs. Griffith and printed

The Alumnae Association

by Whittet and Shepperson of Richmond, was a most attractive publication. The use of blue background with white lettering for the title on the first page, with an appropriate half-tone illustration below, made the first page a delightful innovation and an invitation to read further. The first eight-page bulletin was subsequently expanded to sixteen or twenty pages, as the occasion warranted. It was published regularly four times a year, with color supplements announcing each homecoming. These supplements provided also brief biographies of each nominee for officer or director and official ballots on which to vote.

The illustrations and news columns of the *Alumnae News* from 1960 to the present provide a wealth of information on the activities and development of the association. The year 1960 seemed to mark a turning point in the affairs of the organization, which was destined to grow greatly in prestige and influence during the decade of the sixties.

Homecoming itself in 1960 marked a number of firsts.[7] The date was moved from a weekend in the spring, as had been previously the custom, to commencement time, when other activities were also in progress. For the first time the alumnae had their own house—Spotswood. There was no Saturday evening banquet. Chancellor and Mrs. Simpson invited the alumnae to attend the buffet supper and reception at Brompton on Saturday evening for seniors, their parents and friends, and the faculty. Thereafter, the buffet at Brompton, with Dr. and Mrs. Simpson as hosts, became an established feature of the homecoming activities.

Another significant first was the attainment of the goal set for the endowment fund. The slogan, "$10,000 by Homecoming 1960," became a reality when a gift of eighty dollars from the class of 1915 put the drive over the top. Alumnae who were members of the Cap and Gown were initiated in the newly established chapter of Mortar Board during the 1960 homecoming.

Alumnae activities continued to gain momentum during the year. A record number of alumnae returned to the campus in June 1961 to make the homecoming that year the best attended in the history of the association. A feature of the program was the Alumnae College held on Saturday. Speakers were Sidney Mitchell of the English department, and Dr. Eileen K. Dodd, Dr. Joseph Aposhyan, and Dr. John T. Fauls of the psychology department.

[7] See *Alumnae News* 13, no. 1 (1960) : 1.

At the homecoming luncheon Kathleen Goodloe, president, presented Chancellor Simpson with a check for five thousand dollars to be awarded for graduate or special study to a representative of the college. This was the beginning of what became known later as the chancellor's fund, supported by gifts from the Alumnae Association and used at his discretion to assist students and faculty members in their graduate study programs and projects. The practice of having a banquet luncheon at Seacobeck, at which returning class groups were recognized, awards were made, and a special speaker was heard began at that time.

In 1962 the association made significant strides toward expanding its scope, extending its active membership, and reaffirming its close relationship with the college. A thorough revision of the charter, constitution, and bylaws created structural framework within which new purposes and goals might be pursued. All former students who had attended the college for two semesters became eligible for membership in the association, with privileges both to hold office and to receive publications. Of essential importance was the substitution of annual giving for the rather outdated and restrictive assessment of dues.

The new organizational plan provided for a board of directors consisting of fifteen alumnae elected by the membership to represent both classes and geographical zones. The chairman of the board, as well as several vice-chairmen, were selected from within the board to carry out designated roles of responsibility. The executive secretary (later called the director of alumnae affairs) absorbed the functions of secretary and treasurer of the association. Additional positions on the board included the chancellor of the college, the chancellor's appointee, representatives from the faculty and the senior class. An advisory body known as the Alumnae Council (also represented on the board) was intended to serve as a forum for the discussion of policy, to coordinate chapter activity, and to further understanding between alumnae and the college.[8]

At homecoming 1962 the new plan was adopted enthusiastically by the association. Clara Boyd Wheeler, '31, spoke at the homecoming luncheon. It was followed by the Alumnae College, which was organized into two sections, Modern Foreign Languages, conducted by Mrs. Bolling, assisted by other representatives of

---

[8] In 1972 the Alumnae Council was dissolved, and yet another major revision of the bylaws was undertaken.

The Alumnae Association 537

the department, and Education Today, a seminar led by Dr. Edward Alvey, Jr., Mrs. Paul Hook, and A. Ray Merchent.

An interesting feature of the 1962 reunion was an exhibition of publications by alumnae, assembled and arranged by Dr. Carrol Quenzel. Twenty-nine alumnae were represented by copies of their books and articles in what is believed to be the first such exhibition. A complete catalogue of the exhibition, giving the present position of each alumna represented and bibliographical data on all published works, is on file in the archives room of the library. Since this time, the archivist has compiled an extensive bibliography of published books and articles by alumnae. As of December 1971, forty-three alumnae had varying numbers of publications in the file assembled in the archives room.

In July the newly constituted board of directors selected Jane Howard Patrick, '48, as its first chairman. Mary Annette Kelly was succeeded as faculty adviser by Mildred Cates Jamison, assistant professor of home economics. Mrs. Kelly was named the first chancellor's appointee. Dr. Simpson, who had taken a keen interest in relating the work of the association to the life of the college, expressed gratification in joining the board of directors for the pursuit of shared objectives. In 1962 Mrs. Raynell Goodman Lantor, '41, of South Boston was appointed to the board of visitors, at that time the only woman on the governing body of the university.

By the end of June 1963, a total of 1,269 persons had contributed $10,121.80 to the Alumnae Fund. The first year of the program of annual giving was producing excellent results. In 1961–62 only 4.9 percent of those on the mailing list paid annual dues totaling $1,265. In the first year of annual giving 19.1 percent of the list contributed a total of over $10,000.00. The additional funds made possible an increase in the *Alumnae News* to sixteen pages, the replenishment of the $5,000 scholarship fund, and the establishment of a chancellor's unrestricted fund, which was started with an initial gift of $1,600 from alumnae receipts.

The hundredth day before graduation began to be marked as a special occasion for the senior class. Plans were made for one of the alumnae chapters to entertain seniors on that day. The Fredericksburg chapter began the practice at a tea at Spotswood on February 22, 1963.

The 1963 homecoming was the first at which no registration fee was charged. The Alumnae College featured a panel discussion, "Your Alma Mater in 1963," moderated by Chancellor Simpson. This homecoming marked the first fiftieth reunion of a graduating class of Mary Washington. Seven members of the class of 1913 were present at the luncheon in Seacobeck: Belle Pearce Beverly, Isabel Willis Rowe, Mary Chesley Rowe, Anne Ware Bedinger, Ora Green Tiller, Lucy Kennedy Boyle, and Julia Raiford Urquhart.

In February 1964 Governor Harrison appointed Molly Vaughan Parrish (Mrs. E. Alton Parrish), '29, a former president of the Alumnae Association, to the board of visitors of the University of Virginia. She was appointed to a second four-year term in 1968.

The 1964 homecoming continued the Alumnae College plan with a program on "The Creative Arts in a Liberal Education," arranged by Michael Houston, with the assistance of Albert R. Klein, George E. Luntz, Claudia Read, and Dorothy Van Winckel, followed that evening by a scene from *A Midsummer Night's Dream*. The usual open house was held later at Spotswood.

The annual giving program continued to be highly successful. In 1963–64, Chairman Marian Minor reported 1,605 participants, whose gifts totaled $11,629.22. Homecoming in 1965 featured E. Lee Trinkle Library in the Alumnae College. Peggy Kelley Reinburg, '58, was the new chairman of the board.

In September 1965, Mrs. William Wayne Griffith announced her resignation as executive secretary of the association. During her six years of service, Bettie had guided the association through a period of development and expansion and had seen the group become a vital force in the life of the college. Mrs. Glen Eastridge, office secretary, also resigned as she and her family were moving to Fairfax. Mrs. Griffith and Mrs. Eastridge were succeeded by Mrs. Carrol H. Quenzel as acting executive secretary and Mrs. Edwin Harvie Jones as office secretary, both wives of faculty members.

At homecoming 1966 the Alumnae College featured addresses by President Eva Shipstone of Isabella Thoburn College, Lucknow, India, and Dean Edward Alvey, Jr., of MWC. The Alumnae Association presented to the college an original Chagall lithograph, thus honoring Dr. Simpson's tenth year as chancellor. The homecoming alumnae also presented the chancellor with a check of three thousand dollars for alumnae scholarships and another check for various activities.

There were several firsts. Homecoming Chairman Rose Bennett Gilbert had arranged activities for husbands, and many attended. There was also an off-campus party at the Princess Anne Inn on Saturday night, and this was attended by about two hundred persons. It was the only function for which there was a charge. The first distinguished alumna award was made at the 1966 homecoming. The recipient was Aileen Hirschman Belford (Mrs. Lloyd Earl Belford), '53, an assistant attorney general of Massachusetts. A silver tray engraved with her name and the occasion of its presentation was given to Mrs. Belford by the Alumnae Board chairman, Peggy Kelley Reinburg. Adele Crowgey Giles (Mrs. L. J. Giles, Jr.), '37, was chosen president of the association and chairman of its board of directors. Marian K. Croushore was elected acting executive secretary, replacing Lula A. Quenzel, who was named editor of alumnae publications.

Each year at homecoming the association sent a dozen red roses to Mrs. Bushnell. Her note of thanks in 1966 was written from Bradenton Manor, a retirement home, at Bradenton, Florida. She expressed special appreciation for this reminder of other days in the "newness of (her) surroundings. . . ." Mrs. Bushnell added: "Your understanding hearts will analyze that thought."

A report from President Giles, in the winter 1967 *Alumnae News* announced that at least three hundred individuals were now busily engaged in alumnae affairs as members of councils, committees, or officers of chapters. The cover story in this issue was an account of Mary Washington College's first study abroad program.[9] Spain was selected for this initial project. A contribution from the Alumnae Association supplemented the tuition, fees, and expenses collected from the participants.

In 1967 Dr. Edward Alvey, Jr. retired as dean of the college after thirty-three years of service in that office. He was honored at the homecoming luncheon when the Alumnae Association presented to the library in his honor a two-volume first edition of Dr. Samuel Johnson's *Dictionary of the English Language*, published in 1755. This valuable addition to the collection of the library is now in the rare book room. The alumnae also gave Dr. Alvey a silver tray appropriately inscribed and a citation. The latter read:

The Alumnae Association of Mary Washington College of the University of Virginia present this citation to Dean Edward Alvey, Jr.,

---

[9] See Edward Alvey, Jr., "Our Summer in Spain: A Retrospective Appraisal," *Alumnae News* 19, no. 1 (1967): 3–5.

gentleman, scholar, educator, and friend, whose prestige extends far beyond the borders of Virginia; whose integrity, courage, patience, kindliness, strength of character, and geniality are admired by all who know him; whose multiple activities as Dean will live long in the annals of the College; and whose influence will continue to live in the lives of thousands of Mary Washington students wherever they may be.

Members of the Fredericksburg chapter of the Alumnae Association were hostesses at a reception at Spotswood on May 21, at which Dr. and Mrs. Alvey were presented an inscribed silver bowl. Dr. Alvey was succeeded by Reginald W. Whidden, who had been associate dean of the college. Dr. James H. Croushore was appointed in Dr. Whidden's place. Dr. Alvey continued to teach at the college as professor of education.

At the 1967 homecoming Clara Boyd Wheeler, a former president of the Alumnae Association, received the Distinguished Alumna Award, the second to be conferred. During World War II she had directed the U.S.O. programs in Norfolk and in Washington, D.C. From 1948 to 1956 she worked in Greece, helping the women in that war-torn country to rebuild their YWCA organizations and programs. In Ethiopia, where she spent the next three and a half years, she developed an educational center for women at Addis Ababa. After a period of service with the Institute of International Education, she returned to Y work and became executive director of the Brooklyn, New York, YWCA.

In 1967 the class of 1917 held its Golden Reunion. Fifteen members of that graduating class were present at the luncheon. During 1967–68 officers of the Alumnae Association met with the chancellor's committee on the future of the college. Homecoming in 1968 featured a sixtieth birthday celebration. Dr. Eileen K. Dodd spoke on "The View from Here," consisting of a brief history of the college and an outline of the possibilities for future development. Kathy Friedman Levinson, '63, was elected president of the association and chairman of the board of directors. She had served as president of the Student Government Association in her senior year and had received the Kiwanis Cup as the student who, in the opinion of the faculty and staff, had contributed most to the college during her four years.

Ann Louise Perinchief, '67, became the new executive secretary of the Alumnae Association, succeeding Marian Croushore who for some time had been serving on a part-time basis. Ann Perinchief received the Thomas Jefferson Cup when she graduated in 1967. She had been president of Russell Dormitory, a member of Mortar Board, and program chairman of the Leadership Conference. Upon her graduation she became an administrative assistant in the office of admissions, later becoming assistant director of admissions. She went from this position to her new post, taking over the role as executive secretary on February 1, 1969. Michael Houston, assistant to the chancellor, was appointed liaison for alumnae affairs, and Ann Perinchief's title was changed to director of alumnae affairs.

When the degree of bachelor of science in home economics was discontinued in June 1968 the Home Economics Club voted to present to the Alumnae Association the Reed and Barton Silver Collection, which club members had earned from 1960 to 1968 by conducting an opinion poll for the company. The collection included four sandwich trays, candelabra, a punch bowl, a ladle and tray, and a silver service. The presentation was made by the club president Judy Boyce, at the sixtieth anniversary birthday party.

Homecoming for 1969 provided an Arts Weekend with a student art exhibition and a program by dance majors. Catherine Dryden August, '37, then an official with the National Highway Safety Bureau, received the Distinguished Alumna Award for 1969. An outstanding scientist, Mrs. August was listed before her death in *Who's Who of American Women* and *American Men of Science*.

During the 1969–70 school year, the number of publications sent to alumnae was increased. The Mary Washington College *Bulletin, Quarterly Review,* began publication in magazine form; it contained feature or news articles, chapter news, and other things of interest to alumnae, such as births, deaths, and marriages.

Alternating with the magazine was a newspaper, the Mary Washington College *Bulletin, Alumnae News,* also published four times a year. The newspaper contained articles about the college and alumnae activities, as well as class news. The alumnae publications have been financed by the college, and mailed by the Alumnae Association to all former students. Recently, copies have been sent to all present Mary Washington students and to their parents. The director of information services at the college bears direct responsibility for layout, design, and content.[10]

[10] See *Alumnae Handbook,* 1970, pp. 50–51.

The *Quarterly Review* has consisted largely of special articles, attractively illustrated. The first issue (winter 1969–70) was devoted largely to an in-depth examination of several matters related to the future of the college. Subsequent issues have dealt with the changing life at Mary Washington ("MWC Revisited;" "Into the 70's: A Climate for Change"), new programs and projects at the college; the admission of men; the summer humanities institute; and sketches of retiring members of the faculty and administration.

The new format of the *Alumnae News,* published quarterly in tabloid newspaper size, began publication with vol. 1, no. 1 in December 1969. Devoted mainly to reports of alumnae activities and news from various class secretaries concerning former graduates, the *News* also carries feature stories on developments at the college.

Emma Ziegler Brown, '40, of Richmond had been named to the board of visitors of the University of Virginia in 1966. In 1970 she was reappointed for another four-year term. At this time, also, Molly Vaughan Parrish, '27, a member of the board of visitors since 1964, was named chairman of the Mary Washington College committee.

In 1969–70, Kathy Friedman Levinson served a second term as chairman of the alumnae board. Michael Houston, assistant to the chancellor, continued to serve as liaison for alumnae affairs. Ann Perinchief was director of alumnae affairs; Joy Simpson Toombs, general secretary; and Carolyn McWhirt Whitaker, records clerk. Thomas P. Mann was editor of publications.

In September 1970 a fifty-nine-page alumnae handbook was published by the Alumnae Council. It contained a wealth of information on alumnae chapters, officers and their duties, committees and their responsibilities, and the operation and activities of the Alumnae Association. Olivia Wheeler McCallum, '36, was chairman and Mary Hickle, '66, vice-chairman of the Alumnae Council committee that completed the handbook. The combined effort of many people was involved in its preparation.

The Alumnae Fund has continued to be a vital force in the life of the college. In the absence of any dues, the annual giving program provides funds for the operation of the association and for gifts to the college. The nature and amount of the latter are determined by the board of directors in consultation with college officials. Two groups of donors to the alumnae fund are given special recognition each year: the Chancellor's Circle, composed of alumnae who give five hundred dollars or more in one year, and the Century Club, made up of all who give a hundred dollars a year.[11]

Since the initial presentation of the two-volume first edition of Dr. Johnson's *Dictionary of the English Language* to the rare book collection in honor of Dr. Alvey, the Alumnae Association has made the following gifts in honor of retiring members of the administration: James Boswell's *The Life of Samuel Johnson*, in honor of Dr. Reginald W. Whidden, *The American Drawings of John White 1577–1590 with Drawings of European and Oriental Subjects*, edited by Paul Hope Holton and David Beers Quinn, in honor of Edgar E. Woodward; *Designs for the Pavilion at Brighton Humbly Inscribed to His Royal Highness the Prince of Wales* by Humphrey Repton and his sons, J. A. Repton and G. S. Repton, in honor of Emily A. Holloway.

At homecoming in 1970 the Alumnae Association announced the underwriting of a Distinguished Visitor in Residence. For 1970–71, the program was presented in honor of Eileen K. Dodd and her late husband, James Harvey Dodd. The first visitor chosen by a student-faculty-alumnae committee was the anthropologist Margaret Mead, who was the campus visitor in April 1971. Funds for this project are being provided currently from operating expenses of the association. As increased sums become available, it is hoped that an endowed chair can be established. A program to raise funds through the sale of life insurance policies to alumnae called Quest XX Insured Endowment Plan was initiated.[12]

In 1970 Margaret Lodge Copes, '32, of Accomack County was selected to received the Distinguished Alumna Award. Long active in alumnae affairs, Copes became the first woman to be elected chairman of the Virginia State Hospital Board.

In 1970–71 Ruby York Weinbrecht, '48, assumed chairmanship of the alumnae board. At the time, she was chief of the Technical Information Division of the Equal Employment Opportunity Commission in Washington, D.C. In 1972 she was appointed librarian at Mary Washington College.

In the fall of 1970 Mary Washington was granted a chapter of Phi Beta Kappa. A grant of two hundred and fifty dollars from the Alumnae Fund was instrumental in meeting expenses incident to the organization and installation of the chapter. Kappa of Virginia chapter was formally installed on February 22, 1971, with Grellet C. Simpson, president; James H. Croushore, vice-

---

[11] *Ibid.*, pp. 40–41.   [12] *Alumnae News*, March 1971, p. 2.

president, and Edward Alvey, Jr., secretary-treasurer. Three alumnae were elected to membership initiated at the installation meeting of the chapter: Anna Mae Harris, '38; Pauline Grace King, '37; and Mary Annette Klinesmith Kelly, '44. In June 1971 the first members of the graduating class were chosen for membership. Twenty-three were elected and initiated.

A report on the Alumnae Scholarship Fund made in December 1970 shows that since it began in 1962 nearly twenty thousand dollars in stipends has been granted to seventy-three persons for advanced studies, research, or special educational projects.[13] Grants have been about equally divided among alumnae (25), students (24), and faculty members (24). Funds have been used to assist persons in a wide range of fields. Allocations are made by the chancellor on the basis of written requests. Awards are based on merit and need.

At homecoming in April 1971, Willie Lee Nichols Rose, '47, received the Distinguished Alumna Award. She has been the recipient of many honors. Her dissertation for the Ph.D. degree from the Johns Hopkins University in 1962 received the Allan Nevins Prize, presented annually by the Society of American Historians for the best written scholarly dissertation on a topic of American history. Her book, *Rehearsal for Reconstruction,* received the Francis Parkman Prize for its sound scholarship and literary excellence. In 1968 Mrs. Rose was appointed director of graduate studies for the department of history at the University of Virginia. Currently a professor of history there, she was named to the university's prestigious Center for Advanced Studies during the 1970–71 session.[14]

In 1971 Ellen Duschock, '64, was elected to head the association. A native of New Jersey where she is now teaching, she received her master's degree from the University of Virginia. She was first vice-chairman of the association during 1970–71.

In 1972 Diana D. Koski was named director of alumnae affairs, succeeding Miss Perinchief, who resigned to study law at the College of William and Mary. A graduate of Shepherd College in West Virginia, Mrs. Koski came to Mary Washington from Hood College in Frederick, Maryland, where for three years she had served as alumnae director. The youngest and first nonalumna to hold the position at Hood, she developed a highly successful program of alumnae activities there.

During the session of 1972–73 the name of the Mary Washing-

[13] *Ibid.*, Dec. 1970, p. 4.   [14] For further details, see *ibid.*, April 1971, p. 1.

ton College Alumnae Association was changed to Alumni Association in recognition of the coeducational status of the college. Changes in the organizational structure were also in progress. The association has continued to grow in strength and prestige, as well as in richness of service to the college.

CHAPTER XXIX

Student Organizations

YWCA

As INDICATED elsewhere, the YWCA was one of the very first organizations to be established. After a preliminary meeting in October 1911, at which temporary officers were elected, the group met on November 28, 1911, adopted a constitution, and elected permanent officers.[1] Gay Wilson was president; Julia Raiford, vice-president; Marguerite Dowden, secretary; and Annie Nicholas, treasurer. Various committees were set up and their chairmen chosen, and the organization began operation.

For many years the Y was the most influential organization on the campus. It sponsored devotionals, Mission Study, Bible classes, and other religious activities. It sponsored socials and entertainments throughout the year. A YWCA room was set up in Russell Hall where students could drop in during the day and where the Y cabinet held its meetings. Membership was open to all students, and most of them belonged.

YWCA activities began with a reception to faculty and students at the opening of school.[2] Study classes and devotionals continued throughout the year. There was also a social service committee concerned with community and school projects. The organization helped to support a missionary in India.

By 1915–1916 the YWCA membership had grown to 170 students. There were weekly meetings on Sunday nights, often with outside speakers. Morning watch was held fifteen minutes before breakfast every morning in the YWCA room. There were four Bible study classes in the fall and four Mission Study classes in the spring.[3] The organization made a special point of welcoming new students and making them feel at home. During the summer letters were written to all prospective students. Cabinet members and others began the practice of coming to school early to meet the trains and welcome the new girls. There was, for years, a get-acquainted party for new students on the first Friday night of each quarter.

As early as 1923 the YWCA began to issue a student handbook

[1] "Y.W.C.A. History," *Battlefield*, 1913, pp. 53–56. [2] *Ibid.*, 1915, p. 52.
[3] *Ibid.*, 1916, p. 55.

Student Organizations

containing information not only about that organization but also about the Student Government Association and other college organizations. It carried a detailed list of rules, by classes, and a point system for rating officers in each activity. Later the name was changed to the *Bayonet,* and it became a joint publication of the Student Government Association, the YWCA, and the Athletic Association.

During the 1940s and 1950s, the Y was one of the three main organizations on the campus, ranking in importance with the Student Government Association and the Athletic Association. The Y carried on a wide variety of activities. It sponsored a Kid Party for new students at the beginning of the school year; the Meet Your Minister Night; the Big Sister–Little Sister Church Sunday; a doll show during the week before the Christmas holidays; Religious Emphasis Week; the annual Y Benefit variety shows to raise money for the organization; and a vespers service on Sunday evenings.

During the latter part of the 1960s the YWCA became less of an all-campus organization as a number of its activities were discontinued or were taken over by other agencies. The Interfaith Council did much to coordinate the work of various religious groups. Religious Emphasis Week, once a major project of the college Y, was discontinued in 1963, largely because of a decline in interest in the meetings. An experimental Religious Concerns Program was sponsored during 1963–64, but was not adopted as a permanent project.

The handbook for 1967–68 (p. 91) emphasized Y's role as a service organization and stated that it "exists to serve all students, regardless of faith or creed." In addition to executive officers, there were chairmen listed for committees on campus and community social service, communications projects, publicity, race relations, religious coordination, tutorials, and world relatedness. The possibility of realizing such a broad program of activitiy was seriously impaired when the YWCA was denied its annual allotment from the student activities fund. The reason for this denial, as stated in a letter to Chancellor Simpson, was as follows: "The request made by the YWCA was denied on the basis that it is not a campus-wide organization but should operate as one of the clubs governed by the ICA rather than have an allotment from the student activities fund."[4]

The handbook for 1968–69 simply listed the YWCA among

[4] *Bullet,* July 1968.

religious organizations. The service nature of the group was emphasized, and a fund drive for the World University Service was its major project. After 1969–70 the YWCA ceased to function as an active organization at Mary Washington.

ATHLETIC ASSOCIATION

The Athletic Association was also one of the first organizations to be established.[5] Its first officers were Lottie Broaddus, president; Sex Smith, vice-president; Mary Warner John, secretary; and Ruth Carter, treasurer. All students were considered members of the Athletic Association. During the session of 1911–12 it began the annual spring Field Day, with a trophy cup awarded for the greatest numbers of points in basketball, tennis, and Field Day events.

Basketball was the chief sport in those days, with a large proportion of the students participating as regulars, "subs," or members of one of the class teams. There were also tennis, "krokay," and walking clubs sponsored by the Athletic Association. In 1913–14 softball was added, with the Tigers and the Giants as competing teams. There was also the Rifle Club.

Competitive sports began with the "first basketball game played outside our own gymnasium" on January 30, 1915. The school won a victory over the YWCA team in Richmond, described as "one of the best girls' basketball teams in the State."[6] From then on, basketball became the intercollegiate sport that really aroused enthusiasm. Games with teams from Richmond and Washington and from other colleges drew large and enthusiastic crowds of supporters.

The Athletic Association continued to sponsor Field Day, which included May Day activities. In 1915 the culminating event of the year became a two-day affair, with May Day ("Crowning of the May Queen") on May 15 and Field Day ("Victors Crowned by Queen of May") on May 16.[7] By 1922 May Day was being given prominence as an activity quite apart from Field Day, although it was still regarded as a project of the Athletic Association.

A hockey squad found its place in the annual for 1923.[8] That year the Athletic Association also sponsored a circus and an

---

[5] *Battlefield*, 1913, pp. 58–59.   [6] *Ibid.*, 1915, pp. 55.   [7] *Ibid.*, 1915, p. 54.
[8] *Ibid.*, 1923, p. 131.

Indian club drill team. Hockey became increasingly popular, and began to rival basketball as the chief intercollegiate sport. In 1925–26 there were basketball games with William and Mary, Harrisonburg, Farmville, and the Richmond YWCA team.

Throughout the 1930s and '40s, the Athletic Association was the coordinating agency for all activities of this kind: tennis, dance, archery, swimming, softball, basketball, hockey, hiking, horseback riding, and use of the cabin. There was a chairman for each of these activities, as well as a general chairman of sports. These chairmen and the president, vice-president, secretary, and treasurer of the Athletic Association constituted the Athletic Association Council.

In 1939–40 four new clubs became members of the Athletic Association: the Terrapins (swimming), Hoof Prints (riding), Fencing, and Modern Dance. The president of each group was its representative in the A.A. Council.[9] Badminton, bowling, and ping-pong were added to the sports available at the college.

The Athletic Association functioned as an auxiliary to the department of physical education. Staff members worked actively with each of the clubs devoted to various sports. For example, faculty members who taught swimming worked with the aquacades presented by the Terrapin Club; the instructors in hockey coached the hockey team and arranged tournaments and intercollegiate contests; instructors in tennis helped organize the annual tennis tournament; and, of course, instructors in dance sponsored and directed the programs given by the Modern Dance Club.

Each organization had its own membership requirements and its program of activities. The Riding Club and Modern Dance Club are described in more detail elsewhere. Perhaps a special word should be said also about the Swimming Club, later known as the Terrapin Club. The club sponsored each year a water pageant, with impressive formation swimming to music, and a continuity of plot that tied together individual and group performances. One of the notable productions was "Alice in Waterland," in 1947. The club also participated with marked success in telegraphic swimming meets, winning top place in both southern and national competition.

In 1946–47 the name of the athletic association was changed to Athletic Recreation Association, in accordance with a new emphasis upon recreational activities as well as competitive sports.

[9] *Ibid.*, 1940, p. 190.

While intramural activities were being stressed, team sports were not neglected. The Mary Washington hockey team was undefeated that year in the Virginia State Hockey Tournament at Sweet Briar. ARA continued the sponsorship of Devil-Goat Day, Posture Week, and "the colorful pageantry of May Day." [10]

The session of 1950–51 saw still another change in name, this time to Recreation Association. However, physical education activities received new emphasis with the reinstated major in physical education. There was a "big boom in sports"—golf, hockey, tennis, swimming, horseback riding, modern dance, fecing—all seemed to have attracted increased numbers of participants. RA continued to be the central organization for these activities.

The establishment of the Inter-Club Association brought the entire club program under the general direction of ICA. However, the Recreation Association continued to be the organizing agency for a wide variety of intramural activities, including clubs devoted to individual sports. With the help of staff members in the department of physical education, the Recreation Association formed residence hall teams in many sports and conducted round-robin tournaments. A record was kept of student participation by dormitories, and the Recreation Association Silver Bowl was awarded to the hall with the highest percentage.

The purpose of the Recreation Association was stated in the student handbook for 1971–72 (p. 86) as follows: "Every student at Mary Washington College is a member of this Association, whose purpose shall be to promote wholesome and healthful activity, to stimulate an interest in all forms of recreation, to instill a spirit of enjoyment, to create a spirit of good sportsmanship, and to cooperate with other campus organizations in promoting and maintaining the highest standards of College life." The intramural program in 1971–72 included volleyball, basketball, bridge, tennis, ping-pong, archery, badminton, and softball. Ski trips, judo, and tennis clinics, and mixers were also sponsored.

In conjunction with the physical education department, the Recreation Association sponsored honor teams in field hockey, basketball, swimming, fencing, lacrosse, and tennis. Honor team members participated in intercollegiate competition with many colleges in Virginia and Maryland. Tournament play in these sports often followed the season's schedule. The Recreation As-

[10] *Ibid.*, 1947, p. 200.

sociation has continued to sponsor Devil-Goat activities during the year.

STUDENT GOVERNMENT ASSOCIATION

According to the *Battlefield* for 1915 (p. 64), the Student Government Association was organized December 1, 1914. The first officers were Theresa Inez Lynch, president; Elizabeth Cardwell Chenery, first vice-president; Lucy Lipscomb Duval, second vice-president; and Leam Snow Flippin, secretary. The executive committee consisted of representatives of each of the classes, ranging in number from six members of the senior class to one for the "Sub-Preparatory Class." The annual concluded with this modest statement below the list of representatives: 'The organization has merited much praise for its splendid work. Each girl, having the welfare of the school at heart, has contributed to its success, and it promises to become a permanent factor in the school."

Indeed, it did become a permanent factor. From that time on, the Student Government Association played an increasingly important role in the life of the college. The very next year the *Battlefield* (p. 70) reported "wonderful progress." It continued: "Through the cooperation of the girls it has become stronger than ever before, and, as far as can be reckoned, is a permanent institution."

Its chief purpose seems to have been "seeing that the rules are carried out." The *Battlefield* described the meetings on alternate Monday nights in Room Five, Russell Hall, when wrongdoers were called "one by one, into the august presence of the Executive Committee, who pronounce sentence." There was even then an advisory committee, consisting of President Russell and two faculty members. It is not clear whether they attended the meetings of the executive committee.

By 1921 the Student Government Association was firmly established. An entire page in the *Battlefield* (p. 96) for that year was devoted to a statement by President A. B. Chandler, Jr., the first paragraph of which read:

Student government at the Fredericksburg State Normal School has proven a great success. As administered at this institution, the students are given as large control over their own affairs as they are willing to assume and prove themselves capable of handling efficiently. All matters of discipline are disposed of by a joint council of student government officers and faculty, and the details of home management are entrusted to the student government association. The association interprets the viewpoints of the students and secures a consideration of these viewpoints in the council. The association stands for a high sense of honor and does not tolerate cheating on tests or any other acts of impropriety on the part of students.

President Chandler's hearty and sincere endorsement of the Student Government Association included this tribute: "The administration wishes to record publicly its high appreciation of the valuable services of all the officials of the Student Government Association during the seven years of its life at this institution."

The *Battlefield* for 1922 (p. 73) accorded the Student Government Association first place in order among the student organizations, a practice that was followed for many years. The YWCA officers and chairmen of committees were usually listed on the pages immediately following.

By 1934 the Student Council, as representatives of the student body at large, consisted of a president, vice-president, secretary, and treasurer, plus representatives from each class, dormitory, Y, and the town girls. The first four officers named, along with three faculty members appointed by the president of the college, constituted Joint Council, which acted upon more serious violations of college regulations that might involve campusing, suspension, or even expulsion.

Campusing was a serious penalty in those days. The student was allowed to leave the campus only to attend church Sunday mornings, when she was required to register in the office of the dean of women at the time of her departure and her return. She automatically lost any office she held on campus, and all of the class privileges to which she was entitled. She was not permitted to use the telephone or to relay messages by telephone. Only in case of emergency could these restrictions be lifted, and then by action of either Student Council or Joint Council, whichever one had ordered the campusing.[11]

As one reads these rules, it is obvious why campusing, even for a limited time, was a penalty greatly to be feared. But, in those days a student could be campused for the rest of the quarter for "night riding." Actually, no student was permitted to ride in an automobile except with a member of the faculty, or her family, in a public automobile "for business use" (dental care

[11] *Bayonet*, 1935–36, pp. 60–61.

and the like), or to attend a church service, social, or parties given by local organizations for the college students.

The Student Government Association, through the Student Council and the Joint Council, was the disciplinary body of the college. It also sought to interpret college regulations at regular and called meetings of the student body and to afford a forum at which changes in college rules could be proposed for consideration of the administration which, in the final analysis, decided what modifications would be approved. Consequently, each new issue of the *Bayonet* was read eagerly by returning students to see what changes had been made.

When Chancellor Grellet C. Simpson took office in February 1956 and Margaret Hargrove became dean of students that fall, a new era of student responsibility was begun. In his talks at the leadership conference preceding the opening of college and to the student body at large, Chancellor Simpson stressed the principle of "freedom with responsibility."

Regulations governing student privileges became increasingly permissive, with the understanding that college students were mature enough to live as a community of scholars without having minute details of daily living spelled out. Successive revisions of the student handbook show this trend very clearly. Although the Student Council and Joint Council continued to operate as disciplinary bodies, increased authority was given to the Honor Council. SGA itself was organized into legislative, executive, and judicial departments. There was increased participation in the activities of the National Student Association. A new office entitled NSA coordinator was instituted in 1957–58.

The SGA constitution was revised in 1960–61 to define more clearly the duties and responsibilities of these three departments. Another revision in 1961–62 included in its preamble a statement regarding the obligation of SGA to represent student opinion actively and also to develop and strengthen personal responsibility.

Under the sponsorship of SGA, the first Major Evaluation Night was held on January 4, 1962. Juniors and seniors met to discuss and evaluate their departmental majors. Summary reports were made to the chairman of each department.

In 1965–66 the student handbook began to include an Inter-Club Association section listing the officers and purposes of all student organizations. The list of SGA committees indicates a broad range of activity. The committee on academic affairs began to conduct course evaluations. There were committees on cultural affairs, campus evaluation, leadership conference, and other aspects of college life. SGA began in 1966 to publish a newsletter at weekly or biweekly intervals. Some isssues contain replies to *Bullet* editorials about the role of SGA. The association sponsored a book exchange. It brought speakers on controversial subjects to the campus. It became affiliated with the National Student Association, and a new office called NSA coordinator was created.

The SGA constitution was revised in 1966–67 and again in 1967–68. The latter revision, which became effective the session of 1968–69, established a student Senate, in which all legislative powers of the student government were vested. The reasons cited for establishing the Senate were "to encourage more student participation in SGA, to allow a fairer representation of minority opinion, and to provide a structure which would be tight enough for greater efficiency and open enough to promote free thinking and creativity." [12]

The Senate became the legislative branch of the Student Government Association, with the vice-president of SGA as its presiding officer and the president of SGA as an ex officio member. In general, the plan provided for at least one senator from each residence hall, and one for each additional fifty students. Day students were similarly represented.

The following standing committees were set up in the new program: academic affairs, appropriations, campus evaluation, cultural affairs, elections, handbook, leadership conference, national, state and community contact, orientation, and publicity.[13] This list indicate the wide range of SGA activities directed by the Senate.[14]

In 1970–71 the name of the organization, known for so long as the Student Government Association, was changed to Student Association, in order to indicate more clearly the nature and breadth of its activities.

The Student Association has campaigned for student representatives on faculty committees and for its representatives to attend faculty meetings. There are now student members on most faculty committees, including academic counseling and guidance, curriculum, instruction and academic affairs, public occasions, student publications, and college affairs. Students have been represented on a number of ad hoc committees, such as

[12] *Bullet*, Oct. 14, 1968. [13] *Student Handbook*, 1968–69, pp. 28–30.
[14] See also "The Student Voice Is Changing," *Alumnae News* 21, no. 1 (1969): 6–7.

Student Organizations 555

the five-day-week committee and the committee on degree requirements and reform of the college calendar. Four of the nine members of the committee on special degree programs are students.

In 1970 the chancellor appointed a committee on faculty-student governance at the suggestion of students and faculty "to investigate those academic areas of responsibility and governance common to both." The committee's first report recommended a college council of eleven, to consist of five faculty members, five students, and the academic dean or his representative. In 1972 this proposal was still under consideration.

CHAPTER XXX

The Honor System

From the very beginning, students at Mary Washington College were expected to act honorably. The first annual catalogue (1912, pp. 21–22) carried this interesting statement under the general head of "Discipline":

But few set rules for the government of the students are made. The students are in as large a measure as possible thrown upon their own initiative, and are expected to think and act for themselves; and they are allowed as much liberty of life in the school as is consistent with their work and the inherent idea of higher living. They are taught and encouraged to practice the virtue of self-control. Every student is encouraged to create a desire on her part for the cultivation of the best ideals. No system of petty espionage is exercised over the student body. No such system is desirable or necessary. The life of every student in and out of the school is expected to be lived on a plane of the highest moral considerations.

The honor system will be maintained as fully as is practicable. As a supplement to official government and control, the students themselves have organized a Student Government League, which encourages and enforces honorable conduct in all matters pertaining to school life, and acts as a healthy deterrent to any over enthusiastic or thoughtless students who from such considerations might otherwise be guilty of infractions of the rules.

Every student is expected to exhibit the demeanor of a gentlewoman and to show considerate regard for others. Such a disposition should be the desire and life habit of a well-poised and refined woman.

However, the management will not hesitate, in deserved cases, to administer admonition and reproof. Should the conduct of any of the students justify it or the general good of the school require it, the President will confer with parents or guardians with reference thereto; and in proper cases students will be dismissed from the school.[1]

Apparently the "honor system" referred to was not actually a system but rather a concept of relying upon students to live up to what was expected of them. Failure to do so resulted in action by the administration or, later, by the officers of the student government.

The Honor System

Beginning with the 1921–22 session, students were required to subscribe to a pledge. Damage to property of the school seems to have been the chief concern of the pledge's author or authors:

Every student at this Institution is expected at the beginning of the session to subscribe to the following pledge:

"I do hereby agree, while a student in the Fredericksburg State Normal School, to comply cheerfully with all its regulations in all particulars; and I agree not to deface or injure, by writing or otherwise, any of its furniture, books, walls, or other property. If I should accidentally do damage to any property of the School, I agree to report it promptly to the Social Director or the President, and I agree that such damage shall be assessed and that I will pay for same." [1]

For the next several years, this pledge was carried in the annual catalogues, following the paragraph on student dress. It appeared last in the announcements for the session of 1926–27. Subsequent issues of the catalogue discussed such topics as health, dress, and weekend visits without mentioning an honor pledge.

It was during this period that the increasing influence of the Student Government Association led to an extension of authority over student conduct in general. The student handbook for 1932–33, on a page (p. 19) immediately following that listing the officers of the Student Government Association, carried this quaintly worded statement:

In recognition of the fact that student self-government can be a success only through individual responsibility on the part of each student to uphold the highest standards of honor, the students of the State Teachers College at Fredericksburg, Virginia, in 1924 adopted in word and deed the Honor System as the controlling force in all phases of college life.

Every student upon entrance into this College for registration declares by that very act for a recognition of this system; for a consistent support of its fine principles and standards of behavior, and thereby pledges to keep faith with the Honor System whose ideals can be made real only when a student personnel assumes the responsibility of keeping to splendid behavioristic standards believing in this ratio: That as the student is to the student body, so is the student body to THE HONOR SYSTEM.

It will be noted that the system covered "all phases of college life." No special machinery was set up for handling violations other than the Student Council itself. It could hardly be called an honor system.

[1] *Catalogue*, 1920–21, p. 43. The reference to the "Social Director" was changed later to "Dean of Women."

By 1935–36 the beginnings of an honor system were evident in the following quotations from the *Bayonet* for that session (pp. 28–29):

HONOR SYSTEM

Fredericksburg State Teachers College offers to its girls the opportunity for self-reliance and personal responsibility. This is made possible through Student Government, which gives to each girl a share in student conduct, attitude, and loyalty.

No honor system can be a success without the co-operation of everyone in the student body. Each student is on her honor in regard to others as well as herself.

A new experience awaits the girl at F. S. T. C. who has never been on her own before. She does the right thing because she knows it is the thing to do. The Honor System is a challenge to a girl to be a gentlewoman, and in being one she will uphold the Honor System.

HONOR CODE

I, as a student and citizen of the Fredericksburg State Teachers College, do hereby resolve to uphold the honor of this college by refraining from giving or receiving of academic material in a manner not authorized by the instructor, from the illegal appropriation of the property of others, and from the deliberate and unjustified falsification of facts. I shall do all that is in my power at all times to create a spirit of honesty and honor for its own sake.

In 1938 the name of the college was changed to Mary Washington. During the session of 1938–39, a definite effort was made to develop an honor system that would give emphasis to integrity in academic work. While a broad concept of honesty in all aspects of college life and of obedience to all rules and regulations still seemed to prevail, it was agreed by the faculty to require a pledge on tests, examinations, and term papers, and to trust students accordingly. Enforcement was still in the hands of the Student Council of the Student Government Association.

The all-inclusive nature of the honor system was apparent in the handbook for 1939–40 (pp. 8–9), when the statement referred to "unwritten standards" of conduct that the Student Government Association expected each student to uphold. The pledge that followed was identical with that which first appeared in 1935–36, except for the substitution of the words "Mary Washington College" for "State Teachers College."

A description of the new plan appeared in the college catalogue for 1939–40 (p. 51) under the heading, "The Honor System." It read in part as follows:

The honor system implies that a student is trustworthy and will not violate her pledged word or commit a dishonest or dishonorable act in connection with her college life or classroom work. Every student entering the college is expected to conform to the accepted standards of refined womanhood.

Matriculation at Mary Washington College constitutes an implicit promise and a pledge on the part of the student to familiarize herself with the rules and regulations of the college and student government, and to conform to such regulations so long as she remains in the college.

Pledge.—No test, examination, thesis, or report on parallel reading will be accepted by an instructor which does not contain the following pledge written out in full and signed: "I hereby declare upon my word of honor that I have neither given nor received help on this examination (test or assignment)." The honor system applies not only to classroom work, however, but to other phases of college life involving dishonesty.

Prior to this statement, there had been no mention of an honor system in college catalogues. The system just described was in effect through 1944–45 and appeared in successive issues of the college bulletin during this period.

In 1944 Mary Washington College was affiliated with the University of Virginia as its undergraduate liberal arts college for women. One of the prime recommendations of the joint committee on coordination was that the honor system as operative at the University of Virginia be introduced at Mary Washington. A faculty-student committee headed by the dean of the college drew up an honor plan for Mary Washington, which was officially approved by the rector and visitors of the university and adopted by the college.

At the faculty meeting on February 12, 1946, President Combs announced that the board of visitors of the University of Virginia had unanimously approved the proposed honor system for Mary Washington College with the understanding that it be voted on by the faculty. Dean Alvey was asked to read to the faculty the complete explanation of the organization and procedure of the honor system. The president emphasized that its administration was in the hands of the students, and that it was completely separate from other regulations of the college. A lengthy discussion period followed, in which many questions as to the detailed operation of the system were raised. The responsibility of professors in cooperating with the honor committee was brought out. Finally, the faculty voted by a large majority to adopt the honor system for Mary Washington College.[2]

An explanation of the new honor system was made to the faculty at its meeting on October 15, 1945, by Lelia Marsh, president of the Student Government Association. She gave a summary of the provisions of the honor code and stressed that the honor system was now completely separate from the functions of the Student Government Association. The text of Lelia Marsh's address was incorporated into the official minutes of the faculty.

An explanation of the new honor system appeared in the college catalogue for 1945-46 (pp. 59-60) and also in the *Bayonet* for that year (pp. 13-17). It was modeled closely upon the honor code at the University of Virginia, which dated back to 1842. Its chief difference lay in the composition of the honor committee.

At the University of Virginia the honor committee consisted of the presidents of the various schools (law, graduate, and others) and the vice-president of the school in which the accused was enrolled. At Mary Washington the committee consisted of the presidents of the four classes plus the house president of the dormitory in which the accused resided. Provision was made for the vice-president of the senior class to serve until the president of the freshman class had been elected.

Among the essential features of the new honor system were: (1) its limitation to lying, cheating, stealing, or breaking one's word of honor, rather than an agreement to abide by all college rules and regulations; (2) the use of a specific pledge covering both the giving or receiving of aid on quizzes and examinations; (3) the placing of the enforcement in the hands of the students; (4) a definite procedure for reporting and trying cases involving a breach of the honor system; (5) the option of leaving the college or standing trial for violations; (6) the finality of the verdict, with no gradations of punishment; (7) the obligation of the students to maintain the honor system by investigating suspicious cases; (8) the support of the faculty and administration in delegating such responsibilities to the honor committee.

Intensive efforts were made to acquaint the students with the background and traditions of the honor system. An explanation, which had appeared in the *Battlefield* in 1945 (pp. 23-30), was

[2] Faculty Minutes, Feb. 12, 1946.

reprinted as a pamphlet and distributed to each student.[3] The university also reprinted this account and, for several years, distributed it to entering students there.[4]

Descriptions of the procedural features and the provisions for enforcement appeared both in the college catalogue and in the student handbook. An honor pledge card was designed, and students were required to sign it before registration was complete.

An explanation of the honor system became an important part of fall orientation. The honor committee designated a group of upperclassmen to serve as honor counselors. They met at specified times during the first week with freshmen and transfer students, going over in detail the provisions of the plan and answering individual questions about it.

The culmination of this counseling was an impressive assembly with a speaker on the honor system. At the conclusion of the program, cards on which the signer pledged to abide by this code were distributed to be signed and collected. These pledge cards were checked with registration cards for that session to make sure that every student had signed. No grades or credits were issued by the registrar unless a signed pledge card was on file.

Strangely enough, there was, at first, some reluctance on the part of some of the faculty to accept the honor system in its fullest implications. A few hesitated to leave the room while a test in progress, as they felt it placed "too many temptations" in the way of the students. In time, however, it became clear that the students were proud and jealous of the trust placed in them. Enforcement was conscientious and thorough. There were a few cases each year, mainly of plagiarism, when quotations from references were not carefully acknowledged in term papers. The few instances of required withdrawal under the honor system were, in a sense, an indication that enforcement was decisive and sure.

As time went on, it became apparent that the duties of chairman of the honor committee, especially in its educational program for new students, were more than a class president could carry in addition to her studies and other responsibilities. In 1953 the president of the honor committee was made a separate officer of the student body and the committee was enlarged to six members. The presidency of the honor committee was regarded

---

[3] Edward Alvey, Jr., "An Explanation of the Honor System."
[4] Edward Alvey, Jr., "The Honor System at the University of Virginia."

as one of the most important responsibilities in the college, ranking in prestige with the presidency of the Student Government Association.

Subsequent revisions in the honor system have been mainly in the composition of the honor committee. In 1964–65 the practice of having the presidents of the four classes serve as members of the honor committee was discontinued in favor of having an Honor Council representative elected by each class for that specific purpose. The number of members remained at six, which included also the president of the Honor Council and the house president of the dormitory in which the accused resided or, in the case of day students, the day student representative to the Student Government Association.

In 1968–69 a new constitution drafted under the direction of Laura T. Johnson, Honor Council president, became effective. The membership of the Honor Council was expanded from four to eight, with two representatives elected by each class, plus the president as a nonvoting chairman. The practice of having the house president of the accused sit as a member was discontinued. A local lawyer advised the council in the preparation of its new constitution.

Copies of an explanation of the honor system were reprinted and given every student.[5] In addition, a statement expressing the spirit of the honor system was printed, framed, and hung in every dormitory room. Composed by the author of the explanatory bulletin, the statement reads:

The Honor Code—A Way of Life

The Honor System is fundamentally a code of personal integrity. It means that students of Mary Washington College accept the challenge to make their word of honor a pledge of absolute truthfulness in all matters that fall within the Honor Code. It is a commitment to a way of life characterized by loyalty to the highest ideals of individual and collective ethical responsibility.

The Honor System is based on the principle that human beings can be trusted. This trust not only fosters a college environment of the finest quality but also carries with it the obligation to justify such confidence. It is the responsibility of students at Mary Washington College to maintain the standards of personal honor that makes this resulting freedom possible.

The Honor System makes a lasting impression upon all who have the privilege of living under its influence. Its implementation is the

---

[5] See Edward Alvey, Jr., "The Honor System at Mary Washington College," published by the Honor Council, June 1968.

proof that human conduct is responsive to the noblest type of influence: that of faith in our fellow man. As the embodiment of this principle, the Honor System is indeed

A Way of Life.

In 1969–70, a leaflet describing the honor system was prepared by the honor committee for distribution to students, along with a poster-type explanation of its requirements and procedural features.

A 1969 revision of the constitution of the honor system spelled out in detail the organization of the council, the provisions of the honor system, and the procedures governing investigation and trial.[6]

In 1970 a number of changes in the honor system were incorporated in a further revision of the constitution, which became effective in the 1970–71 session. The most important of these was a provision for varying penalties whenever a violation of the honor code is proved.

As explained in a 1971–72 statement of the honor system, the Honor Council considered each case individually. At its discretion, and according to circumstances, the council could take one of three courses when a violation was proved: (1) waive dismissal; (2) dismiss the student for a semester or a definite length of time, after which he must reapply to the college through the admissions office; (3) absolute dismissal.

These changes in the honor system were the outgrowth of strong sentiment in the student body for a more flexible treatment of violations of the honor code and for more consideration of the circumstances surrounding individual cases.

Every effort has been made to acquaint both parents and students with the honor system. For several years a letter to parents from the chancellor has called attention to this aspect of college governance. The application for admission has been revised to include a brief description of the honor system, reading, in part, "Each student must realize that by accepting admission to Mary Washington, he has acknowledged his commitment to the provisions of the honor code." There follows question number nineteen of the admission application, which reads: "Are you willing to accept the obligations imposed by the Honor System? (Yes) (No)."

Honor system counseling for new students has continued to be an important part of orientation. Pledges to abide by the honor

---

[6] Nov. 10, 1969.

code must be signed, including also the statement of realization that a plea of ignorance will not be accepted. The college catalogue has continued to carry a section on the honor system, including a reference to the honor pledge card. It emphasizes that "registration as a student in the College is not considered completed until this card has been signed. No grades or credits will be released unless the signed honor pledge card is on file."[7]

The honor system has indeed become a way of life at Mary Washington. Evidences of its effectiveness are the mutual trust that characterizes relationships between students and faculty, and the spirit of personal honor and integrity that pervades the student body.

[7] *Catalogue,* 1971–72, p. 45.

CHAPTER XXXI

Clubs and Honor Societies

THE LITERARY SOCIETIES

AMONG the first organizations to be established when the college opened were the literary societies. Both the Russell Literary Society, named after the president of the institution, and the Woodrow Wilson Literary Society, named of course after the incumbent President of the United States, were featured in the first issue of the *Battlefield,* published in 1913.

Such organizations fulfilled a unique role in both secondary schools and colleges during that period. They held regular meetings at weekly or semimonthly intervals, which featured debates, talks by members or visiting speakers, recitations and readings, dramatic skits, and occasionally reviews of books, with refreshments served at the conclusion of the program. As the 1924 *Battlefield* (p. 153) recorded candidly in its account of the Washington Literary Society: "Probably the most enjoyable part of the program is the social hour—just a few minutes given to lively conversation and to the consuming of daintily prepared refreshments."

The literary society of that day was broad in purpose. To quote again the author of the Washington Literary Society's page in the *Battlefield:* "The general aims of the society are to develop literary appreciation, to train in the art of public speaking, and to encourage individual resourcefulness and originality." The Russell Literary Society seems to have been the larger and more prestigious, judging by the size of the groups pictured in the *Battlefield* and the college officials listed as honorary members. After the resignation of President Russell in 1919, the name of the organization was changed to Maury Literary Society, apparently during the session of 1919-20.

Regarding these organizations the catalogues of that period stated under the head of "Literary Societies": "The students have two literary societies, which meet weekly. A large per cent of the students are members, and it is the policy of the school to urge every girl to ally herself with this work. A strong effort is made to conduct the work of the societies along other than stereotyped lines, and to give fresh life and interest to the program every week. These societies have proven very helpful during the past session." [1]

The name of the Woodrow Wilson Literary Society was changed in 1920–21, becoming known as the Washington Literary Society, in honor of the "man who stood for the life, liberty and advancement of the country," [2] and was so closely associated with Fredericksburg.

The literary societies seem to have been discontinued during the 1924–25 session. The last mention of them in the college catalogue was in the announcements for the session of 1924–25, where they are described as meeting biweekly. Although the *Battlefield* for 1924 carried elaborate accounts of the Maury and the Washington, neither society is mentioned in subsequent issues of the annual.

MODERN PORTIAS

For a period after literary societies began to decline in popularity there was no active organization of this type. In 1929–30 what the *Battlefield* (p. 161) described as a literary club," known as Les Savantes, was operating under the sponsorship of Mary McKenzie of the English department.

The following session, 1930–31, Dr. George E. Shankle, who had become chairman of the English department the previous session, started and sponsored an organization of juniors and seniors majoring or minoring in English that became one of the leading clubs on the campus. Known first as the English Club, the group made its first appearance in the *Battlefield* of 1931 (p. 162) with individual pictures of its members and its sponsor. Dr. Shankle was dressed in a tuxedo and sported a moustache. The latter disappeared in time, but the tuxedo remained the characteristic dress of the sponsor in subsequent pictures of the organization. In fact, the very next year the entire membership was pictured in evening dress, seated around the sponsor.[3]

In 1932–33 the name of the organization was changed to Modern Portias. It is by this name that it was best known to students of the thirties and forties. Its purposes, according to the college catalogue, were "to foster the study of English classical literature, to develop a keener appreciation for correctness in

[1] *Catalogue*, 1917–18, p. 37; *Catalogue*, 1918–19, p. 39; *Catalogue*, 1919–20, p. 38.
[2] *Battlefield*, 1924, p. 153.   [3] *Ibid.*, 1932, p. 157.

Clubs and Honor Societies

form and for true merit in the content of literature, and to contribute to the general cultural and social aspects of life at college."[4]

The club met twice monthly, and, again to quote the catalogue, "a formal dinner is given by the sponsor once a year." Pictures of these formal dinners appear as a regular feature of the organization's pages in the annual. They continued to be a highlight of the year for members of the Modern Portias.

SIGMA TAU DELTA

In March 1946 the Modern Portias were superseded by Sigma Tau Delta upon the chartering of Alpha Epsilon chapter at Mary Washington.[5] Dr. Shankle was its adviser. The new organization sought to encourage "literary pursuits" and creative writing. It sponsored convocations, brought speakers to the campus, and arranged trips to Washington to attend important plays. Sigma Tau Delta continued under Dr. Shankle's direction for the next decade as an honor society in English. Upon his retirement from active leadership, interest in the organization seems to have faltered for a time, especially with its new emphasis on writing for campus publications. There was some decline in membership.

In 1965 it was decided that the organization might achieve a broader purpose as an honorary fraternity if it withdrew from the national society. Consequently, in 1965–66 what had been a chapter of Sigma Tau Delta became once again a local organization known as the English Scholastic Honorary. Its purpose continues to be to promote interest in literary achievement. Some experience on a college publication, along with a high average, both in general studies and in courses in English, continues to be required for membership. It is limited to majors in English.

COMMERCIAL CLUB

The Kollege Kommercial Klub started in 1925–26. The *Battlefield* for that session (p. 166) showed a rather large group of students standing on the steps of Monroe Hall and forming the letter K. Ellen Fox was the first president. Honorary members

---

[4] *Catalogue*, 1941–42, p. 64.   [5] *Battlefield*, 1949, p. 123.

were instructors in the recently established commercial department, Alice Curry, Mae V. Powell, and Molly Coates.

The Kollege Kommercial Klub continued under that name for the next nine years. In 1929 Dr. J. H. Dodd became the chief sponsor. The organization was most active in promoting interest in careers in business and in the teaching of commercial subjects. It arranged trips to visit business and government offices in Richmond and in Washington, sponsored statewide contests in typewriting, shorthand, and accounting for high school commercial students, and brought speakers to the campus to address the club.

In 1933-34 the name was changed slightly, with the substitution of C's for K's. The publication of "Commercial Echoes," a newsletter of departmental activities, was begun that year. Dr. Dodd continued as sponsor, with Alice Wakefield and Lola Minich assisting him. From time to time other members of the department joined the advisory staff, but Dr. Dodd remained the guiding force of the organization.

The College Commercial Club grew in number and prestige throughout the thirties. It continued to organize trips to businesses in Washington and Richmond, to bring speakers to the campus, and to sponsor social activities, including an annual banquet. "Commercial Echoes" became a quarterly mimeographed booklet, which carried news of alumnae and accounts of local activities of the organization. *Battlefield* pictures during this period show an increasingly large group each year. Finally, only officers could be shown, along with a list of the members. By 1939 the club included nearly half the student body, for there was an enormous enrollment in classes in shorthand, typewriting, and accounting, as well as a large number of majors in commerce.[6]

SIGMA TAU CHI

In the spring of 1940 the Commercial Club was reorganized as the Alpha chapter of Sigma Tau Chi. Membership was limited to majors in commercial education who had made a general average of at least C with three B's on commercial subjects. The first members were pledged during the 1940-41 session.[7] At the time of its organization it was hoped that Sigma Tau Chi would develop into a national organization. Actually, other chapters

[6] *Ibid.*, 1939, pp. 108-9.   [7] *Bullet*, Oct. 11, 1940.

were established in Michigan and North Carolina, but apparently they flourished for only a limited period.

The Alpha chapter of Sigma Tau Chi, with Dr. J. H. Dodd as sponsor, continued to be a very active organization. A newsletter, the "Steno's Memo," published in the spring of 1942, indicated a variety of projects. There was the usual sponsorship of the Virginia State Commercial Contest; the first State Shorthand Clinic, featuring Louis A. Leslie; a fall banquet; a spring picnic at the Dodds'; and a variety of community service activities related to the war effort. In particular, the organization sent out hundreds of packages of material relating to the sale of war savings stamps for Dean Alvey, then state war savings chairman for the schools and colleges of Virginia.

Sigma Tau Chi continued to be active even after the major in commerce was discontinued upon affiliation of Mary Washington with the University of Virginia as its liberal arts college for women. It became an organization for students majoring in economics. With the retirement of Dr. Dodd in 1963 and the subsequent merger of the department of economics and the department of political science, Sigma Tau Chi ceased to function.

OMICRON DELTA EPSILON

The Virginia Beta chapter of Omicron Delta Epsilon was established on May 30, 1963, largely through the efforts of Henry W. Hewetson, professor of economics, who has continued as its sponsor. A national honorary fraternity in the field of economics with high academic requirements, Omicron Delta Epsilon has over a hundred and fifty chapters, mainly in coeducational or men's institutions. Mary Washington was the first woman's college to receive a charter.

LEADERS' CLUB

The Leaders' Club made its appearance in 1929–30, with Grace Taylor, president of student government, as its first president. It included the presidents of all college clubs and organizations, the editors of all publications, and the house presidents of each dormitory.

Established for the purpose of bringing in closer contact all organizations on the Hill, the Leaders' Club met monthly to discuss problems of mutual interest. For the next fifteen years it functioned in this manner. However, it had no real authority over the formation or functioning of student organizations. It became inactive in the middle forties, and later the Inter-Club Association succeeded it.

INTER-CLUB ASSOCIATION

The Inter-Club Association was formed in the spring of 1950, largely through the initiative of Margaret Swander, later Mrs. John Russell, who was director of student personnel and supervisor of off-campus students at the time.[8] The organization began modestly with monthly meetings of the presidents of all organizations on the Hill. Its purpose—like that of the Leaders' Club, which had become inactive some time earlier—was to coordinate all club activities.

One of the early projects of ICA was the compilation and printing of a college calendar for the session, on which dates and times of club meetings, Lyceum numbers, holidays, and other important information were provided. The project aided greatly in coordinating and systematizing the meeting times of college organizations.

The ICA soon became a major organization on the campus. It began in 1957 the publication of a handbook listing purpose, requirements, and officers of each of the more than sixty clubs then operating. It set up standards for new clubs and saw that existing clubs had constitutions, bylaws, and the other necessities for systematic operation. It began the practice of having an ICA open house, at which each organization had displays of its activities and representatives on hand to discuss its purposes and requirements for membership.

The Inter-Club Association continues to play an important role in the life of the college. The ICA council determines and enforces the point system, sets up a schedule for club meetings, presides over honorary tapping ceremonies, and acts upon requests to organize new clubs. All recognized clubs and honor societies are represented by their presidents at the general ICA meetings held three times during the year. Careful minutes are

[8] *Ibid.*, Sept. 26, 1950.

kept of the decisions reached at monthly meetings of the ICA council.

ALPHA PHI SIGMA

Gamma chapter of Alpha Phi Sigma was installed at Mary Washington College on June 6, 1930, through the interest of Dr. Morgan L. Combs. For many years it was the chief academic recognition society at the college. According to the charter, high school valedictorians and salutatorians were automatically members upon entering the college. Other students were elected on the basis of their academic achievement. All could progress through stages of first, second, and third degree, according to grades and credits earned.

For a quarter of a century, Alpha Phi Sigma carried on an extensive program of activities. It sponsored convocations at which third-degree recipients were honored, brought visiting speakers to the campus, sponsored Lyceum programs began Sunday afternoon film entertainment, held faculty recognition days, gave an annual reception for students on the dean's list, and offered various incentives to scholastic attainment.

A feature of the graduation exercises for years was the presentation of the Alpha Phi Sigma Award, a silver cup inscribed with the name of the senior who had made the highest academic average during her four years' attendance. When the Darden Award was established, the Alpha Phi Sigma Award was based upon the grades made during the first two years and awarded to the junior with the highest average at the opening convocation in the fall.

Dr. M. L. Alstetter was sponsor of Alpha Phi Sigma from its installation in 1930 until he left the college four years later. Eileen K. Dodd succeeded him, and, for the next twenty years, was the enthusiastic and imaginative sponsor of the organization.

Alpha Phi Sigma continues to recognize high academic achievement and to require a high average for membership. With the introduction of intermediate and final honors, the installation of many other honorary societies in various fields, and the extensive public occasions program, many of the chapter's pioneering projects are now carried on through other channels. Throughout the thirties, forties, and fifties, Alpha Phi Sigma ranked as the chief organization for academic recognition.

INTERNATIONAL RELATIONS CLUB

In March 1933 the International Relations Club was organized at the college through the "tireless efforts and infinite interest" of Oscar H. Darter.[9] Established under the auspices of the Carnegie Endowment for International Peace, the local group was one of only thirty in the South at the time. Limited to majors and minors in the department of social science, with at least a B average, the club devoted itself to studying problems of an international nature and to sponsoring lectures on and discussions of these problems. Its programs often featured visiting speakers, trips to IRC state and national meetings, and public forums.

Through the generosity of the Carnegie Endowment for International Peace, the local International Relations Club built up a collection of between a hundred and fifty and two hundred books relating to foreign affairs. These were shelved in a special section in the library where the club members and others could readily use them. These books are now a part of the general collection in Trinkle Library.

Dr. Darter remained the sponsor of the organization for twenty-five years. For a short time in the late fifties it was known as the World Affairs Club. It continued to seek to "broaden and strengthen international relations."[10] In 1959 the club became known again as the International Relations Club. Dr. Myrick H. Sublette, Dr. Joseph C. Vance, and Dr. Victor A. Fingerhut were sponsors during the sixties. The club continues to emphasize international understanding.

HOME ECONOMICS CLUB

Another organization with a long history of service at Mary Washington was the Home Economics Club, founded as the Grace K. Tanner Home Economics Club in 1934–35 for students majoring or minoring in that field. The Home Economics Club served as a catering agency for innumerable dances, teas, and receptions given by the college organizations. It sponsored visits to food service organizations in Richmond and Washington, sponsored state conferences at the college, held fashion shows,

---

[9] *Battlefield*, 1933, p. 143.   [10] *Ibid.*, 1958, p. 146.

Clubs and Honor Societies 573

and entertained distinguished guests. Members were also affiliated with state and national home economics organizations. In 1967 the club gave five hundred dollars toward the international scholarship fund of the American Home Economics Association, to be used to assist a foreign student in graduate study in home economics in the United States.[11]

When the degree of bachelor of science in home economics was conferred for the last time in June 1968, the club was disbanded. At that time the members presented to the Alumnae Association its Reed and Barton silver collection earned by the club from conducting an opinion poll for the company between 1960 and 1968. Valued at well over a thousand dollars, the silver collection included sandwich trays; punch bowl, ladle, and tray; coffee and tea service; centerpiece; and candelabra. The club also gave the library a silver Betty lamp, the symbol of learning. Mildred C. Jamison, club adviser for a number of years, was still serving at the time it was disbanded.[12]

KAPPA OMICRON PHI

The Alpha Chi chapter of Kappa Omicron Phi national honorary home economics fraternity was established at Mary Washington in 1962–63. It had been preceded by a local honorary, Phi Delta Gamma, organized during the 1961–62 session. The honor society sought to "stimulate and recognize high standards of scholarship in Home Economics and to encourage others to strive for the same excellence."[13] Kappa Omicron Phi, with Ruby C. Harris as faculty sponsor, continued to be active at the college until June 1968 when the major program in home economics was terminated.

MODERN DANCE ORGANIZATIONS

For many years, dance activities at the college were considered a part of the physical education program. Courses in dance were listed in the department of physical education. In 1932–33, for example, the catalogue listed Folk Dancing; Beginning and

[11] *Alumnae News* 19, no. 3 (1967): 35.   [12] *Ibid.* 20, no. 3 (1968): 17.
[13] *Student Handbook*, 1965–66, p. 64.

Advanced Clogging; Pageantry and Festivals ("This course is designed primarily for dancing on the May Day Program"); and Beginning and Advanced Interpretive [Dance] ("Grace and skill are developed through simple dances and routines"). This is a far cry from the kind and number of courses available in the major program now offered in dance.

Among the early pictures of dance groups as such, other than as a part of May Day exercises, are photographs of "rhythmic" groups posed for the 1933 *Battlefield* (p. 177). The following year (1934) the *Battlefield* (p. 64) carried for the first time a picture of a dance group in the club section. The caption read "The 'Modern' Dance Club." Theodora Weisner, then a member of the physical education staff, organized the club, which gave a modest Christmas program and attended a dance symposium in Washington. This seems to have been the beginning of a dance organization.

Within another year the Modern Dance Club had expanded its membership to forty-six, apparently including all students taking such courses. Perle Young was sponsor and Helen Shurtleff, president, according to the 1935 *Battlefield* (p. 63). Membership dropped to fifteen the next year, and became more selective. The name was changed to Creative Dance Club and was "sponsored by the Athletic Association." [14] The club continued to sponsor a convocation program, participate in a dance symposium, and take a large part in May Day activities. The name, Modern Dance Club, was resumed in 1937–38, when it also presented "a beautiful program in the open-air theater." [15]

The Modern Dance Club continued to grow in prestige and in the quality of its presentations. In 1940–41 Myran Russell was its president. In 1941–42, when Lilias Scott was president, the group was divided into a Senior Modern Dance Club and a Junior Modern Dance Club. In 1942–43 Ann Harris was president.

During this period Mildred Stewart sponsored the dance clubs. She also taught courses in modern dance and directed the recitals and May Day programs given by the dance organizations. When Mildred Stewart left to go overseas during World War II, Mary Jane Andrews sponsored the dance groups for the next two years. Then in 1945–46 Claudia Moore, later Mrs. Charles Read, took over both instruction and sponsorship of modern dance activities. The *Battlefield* for 1946 referred to her "magnificent leader-

[14] *Battlefield*, 1937, p. 135.   [15] *Ibid.*, 1938, p. 152.

ship and guidance" as sponsor of the Concert Dance Club. Brilliant costuming, careful choreography, and excellent interpretation of themes characterized the performances that became such an attractive feature of the college program.

The Junior Dance Group became an apprentice group for the Concert Dance Club. Throughout the fifties Mrs. Read continued to sponsor the dance organizations. By 1965–66, when a major in dance was authorized, two additional staff members were offering courses in that field. That year, a typical one, the club was one of the sponsoring organizations in a fine arts festival, presented its usual spring concert, arranged master lessons by visiting artists, took an active part in the May Day program, and started Thursday matinees devoted to dance demonstrations.

In 1966–67 the dance group separated from the Inter-Club Association to become a performing group known as the Mary Washington College Dance Company. More recently, Martha Darby, followed by Sonja Dragomanovic, have directed the company and both directed and participated in its dance concerts. Original choreography by both students and faculty characterize these productions. There are also frequent dance workshops in which experimental dances are planned and performed by student groups.

HOOF PRINTS CLUB

Earliest indication of an organized riding group is found in the *Battlefield* for 1934 (p. 51). Known as the Riding Club, it sought "to create more interest on the campus in horseback riding." It sponsored a weekly Sunday morning breakfast ride (leaving at 6:00 A.M.!) and Saturday afternoon "riding tests." The sponsor was Katherine G. Watson, then head of the physical education department. Mallory Huftes was president and Polly Daniel secretary. A group of seven riders appears in the *Battlefield* picture.

Interest in riding grew rapidly. By 1936 there were twenty-five girls riding regularly along the bridle paths of the Battlefield Park.[16] By 1937 the club membership had grown to eighty. Instruction in beginning, intermediate, and advanced equitation was being given by Louise Walraven, the first person to have the title of riding instructor.[17] The entire program was extracurricu-

[16] *Ibid.*, 1936, p. 148.   [17] *Catalogue,* 1937–38, p. 13.

lar, and no credit was given. Club officers were Jacquelin Smith, president; Henrietta Pratt, vice-president; and Dorothy Ramey, secretary. The club sponsored an annual horse show and awarded cups to students excelling in special events.[18]

In 1939–40 the Riding Club became known as the Hoof Prints Club. Beverly Roberts was the first president and Constance Moore, then the instructor in riding, was sponsor. In 1940–41 credit for riding was authorized. It was listed as Physical Education 171, 271, and 371, Beginning, Intermediate, and Advanced Equitation, with one credit each quarter.[19] While riding was no longer merely an extracurricular activity, interest in the Hoofprints Club continued to grow. Russell Walther became instructor in riding and director of Oak Hill Stables in 1940, and for the next fifteen years he taught riding and sponsored the Hoof Prints Club.

Under Walther's leadership the riding program at Mary Washington became outstanding among Virginia colleges. There were spring and fall horse shows, with entries from Virginia, Washington, and southern Maryland. A team from Mary Washington participated in other horse shows and won awards for their horsemanship. Oak Hill Stables developed one small and two large riding rings, and a club house was built for use of the riders and the activities of the Hoof Prints Club.

There were many varied activities each year. In 1941–42 the club participated in the annual Dog Mart Parade in downtown Fredericksburg. Six members dressed in formal hunting attire typified a Virginia hunt club. A month later the club was sponsoring its third annual horse show at the Oak Hill Stables.[20] Membership that year was fifty-five, with Susan Wilson, president; Aloise Brill, vice-president; Marjorie Hudson, secretary-treasurer; and Russell Walther, sponsor.

The number of riders grew amazingly. When Walther was interviewed by the college newspaper in 1950, he reported an enrollment of 135 in riding classes the first semester.[21] Riding was so popular that the physical education department limited to two the number of credits that could be earned in this sport.

There were many other activities besides horse shows. The annual fall possum hunt and the fox-hunting meet attracted wide attention. There were long trail rides, breakfast and supper rides,

---

[18] *Battlefield*, 1938, pp. 142–43.   [19] *Catalogue*, 1940–41, pp. 158–60.
[20] *Bullet*, Oct. 31, 1941.
[21] "Walther Finishing Tenth Year at M.W.C.," *ibid.*, May 2, 1950.

Clubs and Honor Societies

and participation in the Virginia School and College Riding Meet. Monica Dahl began in 1942 a regular column of riding club news in the *Bullet* entitled "Saddle Soap," which was continued for years.

Walther left in 1956. He was succeeded by Michael Kirschner, a graduate of the Officers Training School in Copenhagen, Denmark. Kirschner took over the sponsorship of the Hoofprints Club and continued to carry on the high level of competency that had characterized the performance of MWC riders. In so doing he developed a competitive team that became well known in Virginia and Maryland horse shows. A fourth level of riding instruction has been introduced, but the credit that can be counted toward a degree is strictly limited.

CAVALRY TROOP

In the period following the attack on Pearl Harbor on December 7, 1941, President Combs asked each organization on the Hill to indicate to him how it might contribute to national defense. The Hoof Prints Club decided, at the suggestion of its sponsor, Russell Walther, to organize a cavalry troop among equitation students.

The primary purpose of the organization was to aid the college and the City of Fredericksburg in civil defense work. It was believed that a mounted troop could render important service in the event of an air raid or other emergency. Members were trained in first aid work and handling horses among crowds or in noisy and distracting situations. Uniforms consisted of cotton khaki shirt worn with buff breeches or jodphurs, and necktie and overseas cap also of khaki. There were both mounted and marching units, trained by Walther and members of the local Virginia Protective Force.

The first officers were Susan Wilson, captain; First Lieutenant Aloise Brill, head of the mounted squad; and Second Lieutenant Marjorie Hudson, head of the infantry squad. The first exhibition drill was a part of the May Day program in 1942, with both mounted and marching units participating.[22] Marjorie Hudson of Roswell, New Mexico, became captain in September 1942 and developed the troop to a high degree of efficiency. The mounted unit patrolled city streets during the flood the same year.

When peace came the troop continued its activities. Not only

---

[22] "History and Origin of the M.W.C. Cavalry Troop," *ibid.*, Nov. 16, 1942.

did it lead local parades and perform occasional maneuvers, but it learned many phases of general police work, including photography, fingerprinting, radio, teletype, traffic, and pistol operation. Members of the troop were a familiar sight directing traffic on campus when special events were in progress. Each spring the cavalry troop presented its own gymkhana. It also assisted the Hoof Prints Club at the shows that it sponsored.

Membership grew until in 1950–51 there were two companies, each with its own captain and with a major heading the entire group. *Battlefield*s for this period indicate the colorfulness and enthusiasm of this unique organization.[23] The activities of the troop never failed to interest newspaper reporters and photographers. In the back-to-school issue of the *Free Lance–Star* there appeared a picture of a member of the troop aiming a pistol as the superintendent of police in Fredericksburg looks on.[24]

The cavalry troop continued to function for a short time after Walther left in 1956. It held its last gymkhana at Oak Hill Stables on March 2, 1958. A few days later, on March 6, the organization was formally disbanded because of lack of interest; there did not seem to be further need for such a group.[25]

ALPHA PSI OMEGA

Eta Eta chapter of Alpha Psi Omega was organized in the spring of 1938 through the efforts of Harold Weiss, director of dramatics, who had been a member at the Colorado State College of Education. Weiss served as grand director, or sponsor, of the new honorary fraternity in dramatics. The first officers were Miriam Carpenter, grand stage manager, and Lee-Wingate Keith, grand business manager.

The new organization did not replace the Mary Washington Players but offered a means of recognizing excellence of participation in dramatics. Alpha Psi Omega began the practice of an Awards Night for students who had been active in playwriting and production during the year. It sponsored playgoing trips to Washington, D.C., special productions and programs on

---

[23] "Cavalry Troop," *Battlefield*, 1950, pp. 166–67; *ibid.*, 1955, pp. 196–97; *ibid.*, 1956, pp. 160–61; and *ibid.*, 1957, pp. 158–59.

[24] Sept. 19, 1955, part 2, p. 15.

[25] "Lack of Interest since War's Close Ends M.W.C. Cavalry," *Bullet*, Mar. 28, 1958.

campus, including an annual convocation, and other projects related to dramatics. Several male faculty members who have participated in plays at the college have been elected to membership.

ALPHA TAU PI

Alpha Tau Pi was founded at Mary Washington in 1934 as a national professional fraternity for juniors and seniors specializing in elementary education. Dr. Walter J. Young, professor of education and psychology, was the founder of the fraternity, designed its seal, wrote its ritual, and, as sponsor, conducted the affairs of the organization. It was the hope of the founder that Alpha Tau Pi would become a national organization. The chapter at Mary Washington was designated as Alpha chapter, and active efforts were made to establish chapters at other Virginia colleges. Actually, chapters were started at several other colleges through the interest of Dr. Young. However, the organization failed to achieve national status.

Doris Taylor was the first president of Alpha chapter. She received the Alpha Tau Pi award for 1934–35 in recognition of her scholarship and leadership in elementary education. The following year her successor as president, Greta Hisey, received the award. It was discontinued after the 1935–36 session.

Alpha Tau Pi met in its own quarters in the basement of Custis Hall, which the club furnished and decorated. It sponsored both social events and programs of a professional nature.

Dr. Young continued as sponsor until 1938, when he was succeeded by Dr. E. Boyd Graves, who had become associate professor of education in charge of courses and apprentice teaching in elementary education. Under Dr. Graves's sponsorship Alpha Tau Pi continued to unify interest in elementary education on the campus. It brought prominent speakers to the campus, sponsored visits to observe schools, and made studies of problems of teaching in the state.

Alpha Tau Pi ceased to function on the campus after the session of 1947–48 when, according to the provisions of the act designating Mary Washington College as the liberal arts college for women of the University of Virginia, the major in elementary education was discontinued.

PI SIGMA KAPPA

Pi Sigma Kappa was organized early in 1938 "to encourage interest in types of public speaking, such as informal debating, declamations. . . ." [26] Dr. Almont Lindsey was its sponsor, assisted by Dr. Edward Alvey, Jr., Harold Weiss, and Boyce Loving. Elizabeth Trimble was its first president. The club sponsored intramural contests in speech and debating, and held monthly meetings devoted to speech activities. It also participated in debates with teams from other colleges.

On February 10, 1951, the local organization became the Alpha Eta chapter of Zeta Phi Eta national speech arts fraternity. Officers of the National Council were present for the installation. The fraternity stated among its purposes "the banding together . . . of selected college women interested in maintaining high standards of speech." [27] Betty Jean Snidow was the charter president of the new chapter. Other officers were Anne McClerkin, Nora Lea Hulme, Karen Olsen, Julia Starkey, and Ruth Burrows.

Zeta Phi Eta continued to sponsor activities in speech and drama during the fifties and early sixties, with Mrs. Albert Klein as its sponsor for much of this time. Probably the number of other organizations concerned with dramatics, speech, or both were a factor in a gradual decline in interest in Zeta Phi Eta. There is no longer an active chapter on the campus.

STATION WMWC AND THE MIKE CLUB

When George Washington Hall, the new administration building, was ready for occupancy in November 1939, one of its interesting features was the provision made for radio broadcasting. There was a large, soundproofed major studio, with equipment for sound effects, and a control room with monitoring equipment, two turntables, and facilities for recording and transmitting programs. A direct wire connected the college radio studio with Station WFVA in Fredericksburg, whose transmitting towers were used to broadcast the programs emanating from the college.

---

[26] *Battlefield*, 1938, p. 138.   [27] *Bullet*, March 13, 1951.

Radio was at its peak in 1939-40, and there was much interest in the program of courses and activities instituted by Harold H. Weiss, then instructor in dramatic arts and speech. Courses in beginning and advanced radio broadcasting were offered, and the Mike Club was organized to carry on the work of the new station.

The activities of Station WMWC were extended considerably when arrangments were made to broadcast programs directly from the college studio. Mary Washington became one of the first colleges to utilize telephone wires on the campus for transmitting electric impulses that could be picked up by radio receivers on the campus and in nearby homes. The system, developed by students at the Massachusetts Institute of Technology, utilized frequencies that did not interfere with the normal use of telephone lines for conversational purposes. It was merely necessary to tune radios to the frequency of the college station.

The new system gave a great boost to campus broadcasting. In 1945-46, when the college became a member of the Intercollegiate Broadcasting System, the station was on the air three hours a day. There was a morning program called Dawn Patrol from 8:00 to 9:00 A.M. with music and announcements of time. Then, the station operated again from 3:00 to 5:00 P.M., Monday through Friday.

An idea of the variety of activities can be gathered from the list of personnel given in the *Battlefield* for 1946, when Marion Brooks was station manager. There were directors of programming, of religious activities, drama, music, news, announcing, continuity, artists' bureau, special events, and recording. A radio log showing Station WMWC programs by fifteen-minute intervals was published each week in the *Bullet*. There were morning devotions, classical and popular musical programs, "World News Roundup," interviews, dramatizations, "Campus Life," guest speakers and performers, "Great Hits of Broadway," and the like.

Through its microphones on the stage of George Washington Hall, the studio could record speeches, music, and other events for rebroadcast later. The local station continued to carry many of the college programs for broadcasting to its broader audience of listeners. The studios in G. W. also made records for students or faculty members who requested them.[28] Blank records, enclosed in mailing cartons, were on sale at the College Shoppe. For a fee of

---

[28] "Station WMWC Prepared to Record for School," *Bullet*, March 21, 1950.

twenty-five cents, one could record a piano selection, a poem or an address, or simply a message to a loved one. Many messages and vocal selections were recorded to be mailed to members of the armed forces stationed in lonely arctic outposts or on atolls in the South Pacific.

Dr. Weiss left in 1946 to become chairman of the speech department at Southern Methodist University. There were several short-term successors until, in September 1952, Albert G. Duke was appointed instructor in radio and speech. Under his sponsorship, classes in radio broadcasting and programs over Station WMWC continued to attract interested and talented students.

In 1955–56 Station WMWC moved to the "beautiful new studios in duPont." There were two luxurious studios, with a completely equipped control room in between. Soundproof glass windows made it possible for students to monitor one program while another was being set up in the other studio. As the *Battlefield* for 1956 (p. 152) reported, the new facilities were the "pride of every member" of the Mike Club. Station WMWC was staffed completely by students. It provided an outlet for students in speech, drama, music, and script-writing. The daily programs presented news items, inspirational talks, personality interviews, and college talent. The Mike Club also continued to sponsor regular community broadcasts and public service programs over the local station WFVA.

It was not long before the popularity of the new medium, television, began to change the entire picture. Interest in radio broadcasting began to decline. While the Mike Club continued to broadcast on a reduced scale, there were fewer and fewer students interested in instruction in radio. The courses in radio broadcasting were consolidated into a single one-year course, which soon was offered only in alternate years. In 1962–63 only three students were enrolled. The course was dropped after that year.

The studios in duPont continued to be used for broadcasts by the Mike Club, employing the transmission facilities of stations WFVA and WFLS for broadcasts of a community-service nature. In 1965 the Mike Club produced three weekly programs: "Story Time," a children's program; "Assignment Listening," a musical variety program; and a short news program. Albert Duke continued as club adviser. Finally, in 1969, declining interest in radio production resulted in the discontinuance of the Mike Club. The studios were used for special work in speech. Eventually one studio was converted into a foreign language laboratory.

ART CLUB

An organization with a long history of service to the college is the Art Club, founded in 1942 "to promote and maintain student interest in art." [29] Membership requirements included an overall C average and a B average in art courses.

The club sponsored the student art exhibition for many years. It also helped present the contemporary art exhibitions. The club arranged for trips to art exhibitions in Richmond and Washington, conducted sketching trips to nearby places of interest, and held monthly meetings. For many years, Dorothy Duggan Van Winckel was sponsor. More recently, other members of the art department have served as sponsors of the club.

CAP AND GOWN—MORTAR BOARD

In the fall of 1944, a step was taken that led eventually to added prestige for the college. Under the sponsorship of Mrs. John C. Russell, a local senior honorary society, Cap and Gown, was organized for the purpose of recognizing those students who had "exhibited outstanding qualities of leadership, scholarship, and service during their three years of college." [30]

Among the twelve charter members was Mary Annette Klinesmith, a major in psychology, who was chosen as the first president. She graduated with one of the highest scholastic averages ever made in the college. Later, when she returned after graduate study at Ohio State University to teach in the department of psychology, she was one of the nine alumnae who took part in the installation of Mortar Board.

The new group soon demonstrated its worth as a service organization. One of its first projects was the preparation and publication of a student directory, which was sold at cost. The chapter assisted in freshman orientation by checking attendance at meetings and sponsoring an assembly program on the traditions of MWC. It organized and operated a tutoring service for students with academic difficulties, offered free of charge on an individual, voluntary basis.

Academic excellence was encouraged through the compilation

---

[29] *Student Handbook*, 1965–66, p. 57.
[30] Rose Bennett, "Mary Washington College," *Mortar Board Quarterly*, 1959, pp. 12–15.

of an extensive reading list of books recommended by the chairman of each academic department, which might serve as a guide and stimulus to seniors for post-graduation reading. Cap and Gown played an active part in the establishment of a trade book store on the campus and encouraged students to build their own personal libraries by offering awards for the best student collection in a particular subject.

Early in its history the organization began to sponsor monthly teas for faculty and students in the homes of faculty members. Later it began an annual recognition of students on the dean's list, planning an afternoon reception to honor them and arranging for a speaker to discuss some topic of current interest.

In addition to the activities listed, Cap and Gown arranged for its members to serve as hostesses for the college by greeting visitors and taking them on tours of the campus. Members of the organization took turns in staffing the information booth in George Washington Hall. Visitors to the college will recall the little "On Tour" sign which was placed on the information counter while the Cap and Gown member on duty at that time was conducting a group of visitors on a visit to the library, student activities building, and other facilities of the college.

Under the leadership of Mrs. Russell and Mary Ellen Stephenson, Cap and Gown petitioned Mortar Board for the establishment of a chapter at Mary Washington. The necessary documents were assembled and an inspection visit arranged. Finally, on May 24, 1959, the 103rd chapter of National Mortar Board was installed. A national officer, Mrs. John C. Laird, of Chevy Chase, Maryland, acted as installing official, assisted by Mary Ellen Stephenson, then assistant dean of students, who had been a member of Mortar Board in her University of Richmond days. Nine alumnae members of Cap and Gown were initiated, along with seventeen members of the class of 1959 and thirteen of the class of 1960. A buffet supper in Seacobeck Hall followed, with members of the college administration attending. Mrs. Russell was the first honorary member of the new chapter. Carol Faison was its first president.

Mortar Board has continued the sponsorship and encouragement of academic endeavors. The high point of each year's activities is the tapping ceremony in May, when the organization selects from the junior class the students to be initiated into membership. The honor is highly regarded. The tapping is usually followed by a scholarly address prepared for the occasion by a member of the faculty. The organization also recognizes and presents an award at this time to the sophomore who has made the most outstanding academic record in the college. A reception at Brompton in honor of the new members and their families usually follows. The newly tapped members are always surprised to discover that their parents have been notified in advance and had been sitting in the balcony during the tapping ceremonies.

From time to time Mortar Board has tapped members of the faculty for honorary membership. At the first tapping ceremony conducted by the new chapter on May 2, 1960, Mrs. Grellet C. Simpson and Laura V. Sumner were so honored. Other faculty members have been elected subsequently.

STRAWBERRY LEAF SOCIETY

When Dr. Warren G. Keith joined the faculty in 1945, he organized the Forensic Club, which, as the Strawberry Leaf Society, sponsored a nationally known forensic tournament. The first Grand National Forensic Tournament, as the series of contests was called, held at Mary Washington College took place on April 18–20, 1946.[31] There were contests in debate, declamation, dramatic reading, poetry reading, general oration, extempore speaking, and after-dinner speaking.

Twenty-two colleges and universities, among them the United States Military Academy at West Point, took part in the 1946 tournament. Members of the Forensic Club not only participated in the various contests but handled all local arrangements for the tournament. Dr. Keith served as a knowledgeable adviser who helped the club prepare its invitations and programs, arrange for judges and prizes, and carry on the other work necessary in such a large project.

By 1950 the number of higher institutions participating had grown to fifty.[32] They represented many sections of the country, and now included the United States Naval Academy, as well as institutions like Michigan State University, the University of Texas, Princeton University, Northwestern University, the University of Pennsylvania, and even colleges on the West Coast.

The contests were held during the Easter holidays. All meals were taken in the dining hall, since space was available there at that time. Students from the Strawberry Leaf Society handled registration, housing, and the scheduling of all events. Volunteers

---

[31] *Bullet,* March 26, 1946.   [32] *Ibid.,* March 28, 1950.

stayed on the Hill during the Easter vacation and helped with the various events.

Many contests went on simultaneously, and a large number of judges were necessary. Members of the local service clubs, especially Dr. Keith's Rotary Club, were generous in giving their time and energy to judge the large number of debates, speeches, and readings that characterized the tournament. Many faculty members also helped with the judging.

There were social as well as forensic activities. Dances with an out-of-town orchestra were held on Thursday and Friday evenings. Students who stayed over to help with the tournament reported the time well spent. The large number of men students from other colleges and universities gave a new look to the campus while the tournament was in progress. Members of the Forensic Club not only sponsored the national tournament at Mary Washington but also participated with success in debating contests and tournaments at a number of other colleges.

Dr. Keith had planned and organized and carried major responsibility for the grand national tournament. As professor of history and also director of admissions, he carried a heavy schedule of work and spent much time in the field as a recruiter for the college. Declining health prompted him to obtain the aid of the department of dramatic arts and speech in sponsoring the Strawberry Leaf Society and conducting the Grand National Forensic Tournament in 1956 and 1957. Dr. Keith died on January 9, 1958. The Strawberry Leaf Society and the Grand National Forensic Tournament were discontinued.

RECENT DEBATING ACTIVITIES

Debating once again became popular at Mary Washington during the second half of the 1960s. A team of students led by Penny Penella organized a debating club and enlisted the services of Dr. Louis P. Fickett as coach. The team won awards in statewide and regional tournaments in 1965, 1966, and 1967.

Debate activities languished somewhat while Dr. Fickett was in India. In 1969 the College Debate Club was reactivated.[33] It won a major trophy in January 1971, when the Mary Washington team was named "outstanding first year debaters" at the Presidents Debate Tournament held at Washington and Jefferson Col-

---

[33] *Battlefield*, 1967, p. 182.

lege in Pennsylvania.[34] The trophy was won in competition against twenty teams from eleven Middle Atlantic colleges. In the spring of 1971 the team won outstanding speaker awards in a tournament at Washington and Lee University and also placed second in the Virginia State Tournament at Longwood College.

MU PHI EPSILON

Phi Psi chapter of Mu Phi Epsilon, an international honorary music sorority was installed at Mary Washington on March 2, 1946, with a formal concert, initiation, and banquet. It was established largely through the efforts of Dr. Charlotte Klein, of the music department, who was second vice-president of the national organization at the time, and Vera Neely Ross, also a member of the department. Other faculty members were Anne F. Hamer, Marion Chauncey, and Elizabeth Wysor. Eva Taylor Eppes was initiated at the installation ceremony. Edna Harris was the first president.

Mu Phi Epsilon has continued to "promote musicianship and scholarship." It has sponsored many musical programs and concerts by its student and faculty members, and a scholarship program. It has offered for years an annual scholarship to be used for applied music instruction at the college, and also an award to the most outstanding major in music.

ORGAN GUILD

A Guild student group of the American Guild of Organists was established at Mary Washington in October 1951, through the efforts of Jean Slater Edson, then instructor in organ, who held the degrees of choir master and associate of the A.G.O., awarded by the guild. The District of Columbia chapter, A.G.O., sponsored the group at Mary Washington. Margaret Gooch was the first president. Elizabeth Nalls gave the first student organ recital.

Under Jean Edson's direction the organ guild presented literally scores of recitals for some twenty years, featuring individuals or groups of students. It joined with the chorus, the Madrigal

---

[34] *Free Lance–Star,* Jan. 21, 1971.

Singers, and the college orchestra in presenting programs of music at Christmas, Easter, and other occasions.

CHI BETA PHI

Chi Beta Phi is one of the oldest national honoraries on the campus. Its purpose is the promotion of interest in science. Kappa Sigma chapter was installed on May 19, 1945, largely through the efforts of Mary Rita O'Rourke, a senior majoring in chemistry and Herman J. Bryson, then assistant professor of chemistry and geology, who was its first sponsor.

Chi Beta Phi has always been an active organization. During its first year of operation, 1945-46, with Bettie Woodward as president, it was host to the national convention of the fraternity. An impressive roster of Virginia scientists have addressed meetings of the local chapter. Field trips to the Medical College of Virginia, the Smithsonian Institution in Washington, and the Naval Proving Grounds at Dahlgren are typical excursions. Dr. Earl G. Insley succeeded Dr. Bryson as sponsor in September 1946, and for the next twenty years guided the activities of the organization. Members customarily participated in the college student section of the Virginia Academy of Science.

Chi Beta Phi is well known among the entire student body because of its annual auctions of gifts and services in which both faculty and students have participated enthusiastically. The money raised is used to finance the Cook Memorial Scholarship Fund, established in, October 1949, in memory of Dr. Roy S. Cook, who had died during the summer.[35] Proceeds from these auctions have enabled the organization to make outright grants each year, varying from two hundred and fifty to three hundred dollars each, to two or three students needing financial assistance. Juniors and seniors majoring in biology, chemistry, mathematics, and physics are eligible to apply for the Chi Beta Phi scholarships.

PI GAMMA MU

Pi Gamma Mu, national social science honorary society, is open to students of high scholastic average who are actively interested in

[35] The Minutes of Chi Beta Phi for the meeting on October 27, 1949, at which the scholarships were authorized, also indicate that an auction was suggested as a means of raising money for this fund.

Clubs and Honor Societies 589

the social sciences. Virginia Zeta was chartered at Mary Washington on May 4, 1948, with Sara Margaret Mann as its first president. Dr. Oscar H. Darter and Dr. J. H. Dodd were the prime movers in its establishment and continued to direct its affairs for several years. A B average is prerequisite for student membership. A number of faculty members belong and also take an active part in the monthly discussions of current topics.

SIGMA OMEGA CHI

Sigma Omega Chi, a local honor society for students in sociology, was organized in 1951 by Dr. Philip J. Allen, the chairman of that department, to "extend knowledge of sociology and to encourage its practical application toward wholesome personal and social goals." [36] There is also a Sociology Club "to further interest in sociology." Both organizations sponsor speakers, field trips, and forum discussions.

PSI CHI

Through the efforts of Dr. Eileen K. Dodd, for many years chairman of the psychology department, a chapter of Psi Chi national society in psychology was established on May 20, 1954. Since Mrs. Dodd was overseas at the time, the actual installation was conducted by Mary Annette Kelly and Dr. Thomas Stritch.

The high scholastic requirements of Psi Chi have limited membership somewhat and led to an emphasis on the honorary nature of the organization. It has sponsored visiting lecturers on new developments in psychology and sought to encourage scholarly attainment in this field.

LE CERCLE FRANÇAIS

For many years Le Cercle Français was the chief, or rather the only, foreign language club on the campus. At a time when French was the only modern foreign language in which a major or minor was offered, this organization occupied a leading role in the life of the college.

---
[36] *Student Handbook,* 1971–72, p. 80.

Mildred McMurtry Bolling organized the club as an informal group shortly after she came to the college in 1928. All students taking intermediate or advanced courses in French were eligible for membership. The club gave interested students an opportunity to hear French spoken (meetings were conducted entirely in French), and to study the culture and literature of France. Members viewed French films, reported on articles read in French, and heard native speakers from Washington, often representatives of the French embassy there. The club began the sponsorship of a Foreign Language Week, in which other language clubs joined. Mrs. Bolling sponsored Le Cercle Français for over thirty years, until in 1962 other members of the department began to serve as advisers. Meetings continue to be held monthly, usually in the French house.

EL CLUB ESPAÑOL

In 1940–41, with the appointment of Dr. Clifton B. McIntosh as associate professor of Spanish, the college increased its course offerings in Spanish and began a major program in this subject. The following year Dr. Stuart Denslow was added to the faculty, and under his sponsorship the Spanish Club was organized. Rosemary Fairbank, who lived in Santurce, Puerto Rico, was the first president. When Dr. Denslow left at the end of the session, Dr. McIntosh took over the club sponsorship and served until he left for military leave in 1942–43. Dr. Louis Cabrera joined the staff in September 1943 and became sponsor of the organization. Its name was changed to El Club Hispano-Americano.

Under Dr. Cabrera's leadership the club flourished as a medium of expression and a source of companionship for the Spanish-speaking students. During this period, even the organization's page in the *Battlefield* was written in Spanish. The annual Spanish fiesta sponsored by the club was a feature of college life during the 1940s and early '50s. An account of these programs, written and directed by Dr. Cabrera, appears elsewhere in this narrative.

Upon his return from service, Dr. McIntosh served as a cosponsor of the club. Other members of the growing department also participated in its activities. Dr. Cabrera, however, remained its guiding spirit and its enthusiastic adviser. While the annual fiestas during the years they were held attracted most attention, the club carried on a variety of other activities. There were trips to the Pan-American Union, programs featuring speakers and movies on the Spanish-speaking countries, and exhibitions of Spanish dancing on numerous occasions. The monthly meetings of the club, held in the Spanish house, were conducted in Spanish.

In 1960 the name of the organization was changed back to the Spanish Club. In 1964 it became known as El Club Español, its present designation. Various members of the Spanish department have served as sponsors. The group has continued to carry out its stated purpose: to promote interest in the Hispanic culture and peoples and to be of service to the Spanish department.

OTHER LANGUAGE CLUBS

Der Deutsche Verein was organized to promote interest in the language and culture of Germany. Its activity has varied from time to time, as enrollments in the language have fluctuated. From 1947 to 1951, when Dr. Susanne Engelmann, associate professor of German, served as sponsor of the organization, it carried on an extensive program of public performances of German plays and songs, and celebrations of German festivals. Referred to more frequently now as the German Club, since the dance organization of that name has ceased to exist, Der Deutsche Verein continues to carry on activities of special interest to students in courses in German.

A small but interested group of students in the Russian language carry on the activities of the Russian Club. Dr. Joseph Bozicevic, associate professor of foreign languages, has been its sponsor since 1961.

L'Academia Italiana was organized by Dr. James Mormile in the late forties while he was associate professor of Spanish and Italian. His successors continued to sponsor for several years a club for students in Italian. The organization is currently inactive, since honorary Romance language fraternities have tended to take its place.

For a time there was even a club for students of Portuguese. Club Ruy Barbosa, named after the famous Brazilian author, was organized in 1944–45 by Dr. Clifton B. McIntosh, who taught Portuguese at the time.

ATHENAEUM

On November 13, 1939, the Athenaeum was organized to "stimulate interest in classical studies." Catesby Willis, who taught Latin at the time, was its sponsor, and Eve Catafygiotu was its first president. It is interesting to note that the first president, now Mrs. Peter Topping, went on to earn her M.A. from Radcliffe, was a Fulbright scholar to Greece, and taught Latin and Greek at Wheaton College and the University of Cincinnati.

The Athenaeum was for many years a stimulus to scholarship in the classics. Catesby Willis Stewart continued as its sponsor and directed its activities until 1945 when Dr. Rollin H. Tanner succeeded her. The group became inactive after the session of 1956-57. Its place seems to have been taken by the Archaeology Club, which was organized during the second semester of the 1956-57 session, with Dr. Laura Voelkel Sumner as sponsor.

PHI SIGMA IOTA

The Phi Omicron chapter of Phi Sigma Iota national romance language fraternity, was installed by national officers on April 28, 1950. Dr. H. Logan Cobb, then an instructor in Spanish, and Mildred Bolling, both already members of the organization, were responsible for getting a chapter established at Mary Washington. Dr. Cobb became the first president, and Mrs. Bolling was corresponding secretary. Requirements for admission are unusually high. Specialization in Romance language, plus a 3.5 average in such courses and a 3.0 average overall are required. In 1971-72 eight faculty members and twelve students were members.

ETA SIGMA PHI

Beta Nu chapter of Eta Sigma Phi national honorary classics fraternity, was installed April 27, 1950, through the interest of Dr. Laura Voelkel Sumner, a member of the chapter. The national president conducted the installation service. Nancy Stump was the first president of Beta Nu chapter. Mrs. Sumner has continued to serve as sponsor of the honorary society, which seeks to promote interest in the ideals of the classics. A B average in classical studies is required for membership.

THE PHILOSOPHY CLUB

The Philosophy Club at Mary Washington College was a short-lived venture organized under the sponsorship of Dr. Kurt F.

Leidecker, then acting assistant professor of philosophy and only faculty member teaching in the department of philosophy. It was meant to stimulate interest in philosophy.

The club published a modest mimeographed weekly, The "Philosophic Bull," between October 3, 1949, and February 13, 1950, which commemorated mainly certain philosophers and provided short notices of activities of the club. One of the main events sponsored by the club was a convocation at Mary Washington College on April 26, 1950, at which Ambassador Vijayalakshmi Pandit addressed the collegewide gathering. The club was inactivated at the end of the academic year 1949–50.

THE ORIENTAL CLUB

The Oriental Club of Mary Washington College was founded on April 5, 1954, under the sponsorship of Dr. and Mrs. Kurt F. Leidecker. Its purpose is to provide "opportunities for students of Mary Washington College and invited guests to extend their knowledge and stimulate their interest in the Orient and all things, ideas, persons, and events Oriental."

The Oriental Club has brought scores of outstanding visitors to the college. Prominent among them have been Ambassador C. L. Mehta, of India, in 1954; Ambassador Gunewardene of Ceylon in 1956; Ambassador U Win of Burma, in 1958; and numerous other members of the diplomatic staff of the Asian countries. Dr. and Mrs. Leidecker have usually entertained the distinguished visitors in their home.

There have been dozens of exhibitions of Oriental art, jade, paintings, and rugs, as well as Oriental bazaars and dinners for the benefit of Asian causes. Convocation programs sponsored by the club have included performances of Hindu dances and of the Kabuki dancers and musicians. Members of the Thai embassy presented "A Night in Thailand," with music and dances. The Indonesian Embassy presented a similar program on their country, as did the embassy of India.

The club has made an annual trip to Washington since 1954 and been received and entertained at the embassies of the various Asian countries. It has sponsored films on Asian countries and lectures on Oriental subjects, many of them given by Dr. Leidecker himself. In March 1970 the club presented its extensive and valuable collection of Oriental books to the E. Lee Trinkle Library.

Mary Washington has sponsored several meetings of well-known Oriental societies, such as the Association for Asian Studies for its regional meeting and the Virginia Asian Studies Consortium. The number of courses offered at the college has increased, fluctuating from year to year to between twenty and thirty three-credit courses. An Asian Studies Institute consisting of a seminar on Southeast Asia was held at the college June 21 to July 9, 1971. In all of these courses and activities the members of the Oriental Club have taken a deep interest.

With the establishment in 1969 of the Asian studies major at the college and many related activities, especially of the Pre–Foreign Service major with its visiting speakers and fireside chats conducted with ambassadors from Asian countries and other notables, the Oriental Club has continued to look in new directions to increase still further interest in the Orient among the student body of Mary Washington College.

STUDENT EDUCATION ASSOCIATION

The Student Education Association was organized in 1958 through the interest of Dr. Russell Ratcliffe, then instructor in education, who was its first sponsor. A professional association for college students preparing to teach, SEA members are also student members of both the Virginia Education Association and the National Education Association.

Monthly meetings devoted to speakers, films, and panel discussions on educational problems and practices have characterized SEA activities. The group sponsored programs for Future Teachers of America clubs in neighboring high schools, and SEA members have held office frequently in the statewide organization. Catherine Hook, for eight years a member of the State Board of Education as well as an assistant professor at Mary Washington, has sponsored the Student Education Association most recently.

GAMMA THETA UPSILON

Gamma Theta Upsilon became the newest honorary on the campus when Delta Mu chapter was installed on May 18, 1971. This national geography honorary society seeks to further professional interest in geography. Brenda E. Hinson and Susan T. Liebenow were student organizers, with James B. Gouger of the geography department as sponsor.

OTHER CLUBS

Many student organizations other than those described in some detail have enriched the life of students at Mary Washington. Among them have been the Matthew Fontaine Maury Science Club, the Psychology Club, the Sociology Club, the Physical Therapy Club, the Day Students Club, Mu Alpha Chi (medical technology), and Pi Nu Chi (pre-nursing).

Forty-two clubs and honor societies are listed as members of the Inter-Club Association in the student handbook for 1971–72 (pp. 76–84). They carry on an active program of service and stimulate high standards of achievement. Among the more recently established groups are the Afro-American Club, the American Civil Liberties Union, the Young Democrats, and the Young Republicans. Both of the clubs representing major parties have sponsored speakers and panel discussions on political issues, often with the cooperation of their state and national organizations. Interest in political affairs increased greatly when the privilege of voting in national elections was extended to eighteen-year-olds.

RELIGIOUS ORGANIZATIONS

Major religious denominations have for many years supported a campus representative to work with members of that church attending the larger state colleges and universities. These student workers have operated usually under the direction of a campus education committee of the local church, with financial support and policy direction from a governing body of the denomination. Each usually sponsored an organization of college students belonging to or interested in that particular faith.

Among the early groups active at Mary Washington were the Baptist Student Union, the Wesley Foundation (Methodist), the Newman Club (Roman Catholic), the Canterbury Club (Episcopal), and the Westminster Fellowship (Presbyterian). Pictures of the officers of these organizations began to appear in the *Battlefield* in 1945 (pp. 200–201). There were also active at the time the Hillel Club (Jewish), the Christian Science Organization, the Disciples Student Fellowship, the Lutheran Organization, and the Unitarian Fellowship.

Perhaps best known among the campus student workers was Susie Peach Foster, who from 1945 to 1963 directed the Wesley Foundation at Mary Washington. The daughter of a Methodist minister, she had been a missionary in Korea until the State Department in 1941 requested all American missionaries to return home. She held the B.A. and M.A. degrees in sociology and also had learned the Korean language. Miss Foster was the first director of the Wesley Foundation. She was largely responsible for raising funds for the Wesley Student Center on Dandridge Street, which in 1954 became the headquarters of the Methodist activity at the college.

About the same time the Baptist Student Union acquired a stone building on College Avenue just across from the entrance to Chandler Circle. The little stone house across the road became a familiar sight to students, as it carried on its full schedule of activities. Later the Presbyterians obtained a student center for the Westminster Fellowship on Dandridge Street. Provisions for student activities were a feature in planning the buildings for Trinity Episcopal, St. Mary's Catholic, and Christ Lutheran churches when these congregations located in the college community.

Student religious groups have continued to serve the student body, more and more on an ecumenical basis. In 1970–71 the Campus Christian Center was established in what had been the Wesley (Methodist) Foundation house on Dandridge Street. It was sponsored as a joint project of Methodist and Presbyterian student groups. Its purpose, as stated in the student handbook for 1971–72 (p. 83), was "to help students, faculty, and administration of all faiths develop the religious aspect of their lives while living in our academic community."

CHAPTER XXXII

Publications

THE BATTLEFIELD

THE *Battlefield* has been the most consistent student publication of the college. It made its debut as the college yearbook in 1913, and the annual has appeared each spring ever since except in 1918 when World War I was in progress. In 1919 and 1920 it bore the title *Class Book*.

The *Battlefield* was given its name by Gay Vaughan Wilson (Mrs. Edward S. Currie),[1] who was the business manager of the first issue. The editor-in-chief was Martha Belle Pearce (Mrs. Walter F. Beverly), who, like Mrs. Currie, was one of the early leaders in alumnae activities.[2] Assistant editors of the first issue were Buford Kirkley Lyne and Ethel Louise Taylor. It was dedicated to President E. H. Russell.

In 1932, the year of the Washington Bicentennial, the *Battlefield* was dedicated to George Washington. In 1941 and 1956 the dedication was "To Our Parents"; in 1942, "To the Members of Our Faculty who have entered the Service of Our Country"; in 1946, "To the Making of the Peace"; and in 1953, "To the Student Body."

Several members of the faculty have been honored by repeated dedications. It was dedicated to President Morgan L. Combs in 1930, 1945, 1949, and 1954; to Mrs. C. L. Bushnell, dean of women, in 1923, 1939, 1947, and 1950; and to Dean Edward Alvey, Jr., in 1938, 1955, and 1967. In 1928 it was dedicated to Eileen Lois Kramer; in 1937, to Eileen K. Dodd; and in 1962, to Dr. and Mrs. James H. Dodd. For many years the dedication was determined, after nominations, by a popular vote of the student body. More recently, the annual staff has selected the person to be honored.

The style and format of the annual have varied considerably over the years. Most of the time it has been a rather elaborate publication, profusely illustrated. However, in 1919 and 1920, the

---

[1] See letter to author, Dec. 27, 1971.
[2] Mrs. Beverly died Nov. 5, 1967. See *Alumnae News* 20, no. 1 (1968): 8.

two years when it was known simply as *Class Book,* it was a rather slender volume.

Many of the issues have carried special articles, written at the request of the staff and featured, often with drawings, on the opening pages of the book. In 1944 C. O'Conor Goolrick contributed "A History of Mary Washington College of the University of Virginia," a five-page feature later reprinted on the occasion of the fiftieth Anniversary celebration of the college. In 1945 Dean Edward Alvey, Jr., wrote a special article on "The Honor System." In 1946 Judge Alvin T. Embrey contributed an article on "Brompton," illustrated with drawings and an excellent color photograph of the residence.

Art work has been a striking characteristic of the *Battlefield* almost since its first issue. Most noteworthy, perhaps, is a series of four paintings of college scenes by Julien Binford, reproduced in color and tipped into the 1947 issue as a special feature of the opening pages.

For over twenty years, from the early twenties until 1946, Mrs. Bushnell was usually the sponsor of the *Battlefield.* The word *sponsor* is completely inadequate to describe her role in producing this publication. She selected the cover design and format, personally posed all group and club pictures, called the photographer to record scenes of college activities and views of the campus, wrote much of the copy herself, and in general supervised in detail the entire project.

For many years the only *Battlefield* office was a room in Mrs. Bushnell's suite in Virginia Hall. Much of the material and many of the photographs were kept under wraps until the publication actually appeared. Students of these days will recall Mrs. Bushnell and Judson Smith, either on foot or in Smith's car, taking pictures of nearly every phase of college activity "for the *Battlefield.*" Many of the pictures that appeared were used subsequently in the college catalogues and viewbooks.

Mrs. Bushnell left her mark upon the annual, as upon many other phases of life at Mary Washington. Although her last year as a sponsor was 1946, the *Battlefield* continued to maintain the standard of excellence she had set. Student staff members played an increasingly important role in the production of the book. In recent years it has been essentially a student publication, with the advice and assistance of a faculty committee available when needed.

THE TATTLER

Apparently among the first student publication of a periodical nature was the *Tattler,* published by the Woodrow Wilson Literary Society. It is mentioned first in the *Battlefield* of 1916 as a new publication, with Margaret Irving White (Mrs. James Edwin Bear, Jr.), class of 1917, as the founder and first editor or "chief tattler."

According to a poetic announcement in the 1916 yearbook (p. 73),

> Upon our library shelves you'll find
> Much literature to impress your mind.
> For the frivolous ones there is reading light—
> Stories which are "out of sight,"
> Reference books which will make you sigh,
> Magazines and newspapers piled sky high;
> But different from all of these, 'tis true,
> Is the new publication we bring to you.
> "The Tattler" will tell you many tales
> Of your brilliant remarks and your bitter wails,
> Of your humdrum life on the dear old Hill,
> Of the good times, too, which your moments fill.
> So, hear, the telltale Tattler's tale,
> And give your attention without fail,
> While the Tattler tells its telltale tale.

The 1917 *Battlefield* (p. 75) also listed officers of the *Tattler* under the account for the Woodrow Wilson Literary Society. A two-sentence description read: *"The Tattler,* which is the literary mouthpiece of our society, is published monthly. It is a paper of fun and humor of daily events interesting to all." The term "literary" seemed to have been used rather loosely to describe what was essentially a campus news publication. Unfortunately, no copies can be located, so speculation on its nature and content must suffice. There is no further mention of the *Tattler* after 1917 or subsequent reports of the activities of the Woodrow Wilson Literary Society.

THE BULLET

From all available evidence it seems that the *Bullet,* as the newspaper of the college, began publication in 1921-22. The *Battle-

field (p. 88) for that session has a page of five photographs arranged in a circle around the words, "The Bullet Staff." Strangely enough, none of the individuals are identified. A comparison with the pictures of the seniors reveals that one of them was Mary Lee McNair, a transfer student from Blackstone. Her position in the circle indicates that she was possibly the editor.

The next year's *Battlefield* (p. 153) again pictures the *Bullet* staff, identified this time by name and position. Eva Oliver was editor in chief. It is in the *Battlefield* for 1924 (p. 145) that most information about this early *Bullet* is found. Not only was the complete staff listed, with Mary Rector as editor in chief, but their pictures were displayed against a reproduction of the front page of the December 1923 edition of the *Bullet,* which, according to the masthead, was volume 3, no. 23.

Unfortunately none of these early issues of the *Bullet* can be located. Apparently, it ceased publication after that year, for there is no further mention of such a publication in issues of the annual for the years immediately following. In style and content the *Bullet* of 1921–22, 1922–23, and 1923–24 was much like the newspaper of the same name that resumed publication in 1927.

Strangely enough, a literary magazine known as the *Bullet* began publication a short time after the demise of the newspaper of that name. Volume I, no. 1, of the new *Bullet* appeared in June 1925, with Madeline Milbank as editor in chief. A student publication in magazine form, it featured stories, articles and poems by members of the student body. Three issues were published during the session of 1925–26. A final issue appeared in March 1927.

It was during the session of 1927–28 that the *Bullet* as a literary magazine was succeeded by a college newspaper, again using the same title. Unfortunately no copies of volume 1 of the *Bullet* as a newspaper appear to have survived. There are scattered issues in the files for volume 2, 1928–29, and for the early 1930s. With the exception of a few missing issues, complete files of the *Bullet* from September 1937 to the present are available in the archives.

For the next forty years the *Bullet* chronicled faithfully the events on the Hill. There were the usual news stories, special features, letters to the editor, columnists, and other aspects of student publication that mirrored life at the college. About 1968 the *Bullet* ceased to be primarily a news medium and began to emphasize polemics. It became concerned with issues regarding student rights and privileges, college policies, and involvement in the Vietnam War, taking a strong stand editorially and in its news columns on many controversial issues. It may be said to reflect some of the student unrest of this period. As the session of 1972–73 got under way, the *Bullet* began to provide more coverage of college news. It continued to champion various causes.

THE EPAULET

The *Epaulet,* a quarterly literary magazine, began publication in the fall of 1940 under the sponsorship of Dr. George E. Shankle, then head of the English department, who envisioned such a magazine for the college. The first editors were Ruth Scarlett and Katherine Nutt. For the next twenty-five years the *Epaulet* was published three times a year, with an occasional summer issue also. Printed in attractive format, with good paper and type, it featured short stories, poems, plays, and essays. The contributions were generally of high quality, in accordance with the motto of the *Epaulet,* "Not Words, but Thoughts and the Manner of Expressing Them Make Literature."

In 1947 the format was changed to a larger size publication, with departments for book reviews, theater, dance, and even a "Scrapbag" for humor. Drawings and photographs enlivened issues published during the late forties and early fifties. Dr. Shankle continued as sponsor and was the guiding force, the catalytic agent, behind the publication. When he gave up the sponsorship of the magazine in 1955, it ceased to be a regular publication. Only two issues were printed in 1955–56, and none in 1956–57.

Publication on a regular basis was resumed in 1957. Format varied from time to time. It was now largely handled by interested students, with several members of the faculty serving as advisers. Issues appeared usually three times during the academic year. In 1963 only two issues were published. During this period, various faculty members assisted with the publication: Roger L. Kenvin, James H. Croushore, Pauline G. King, Sidney H. Mitchell, Barbara B. Pollard, and Alan S. Pierce.

In 1965 a new editorial policy gave attention to a "wider range of student interests," including articles on contemporary problems, examples of student art work, and other matters deemed of broader appeal. Apparently, the *Epaulet* did not receive the increased student support it hoped to win with the new policy. Only one slender issue was published in 1968–69. The *Epaulet* eventually ceased publication after that year.

NEW STUDENT PUBLICATIONS

Efforts to resume publication of the *Epaulet* in the fall of 1970 proved abortive. A called meeting of interested students failed to produce any results. However, a new publication, *Polemics,* made its appearance in October 1970. Described in a subtitle as "A Current Affairs and Contemporary Issues Quarterly Publication," *Polemics* began publication with three issues during the 1970–71 session. Leslie Susan Kraus was editor, and Victor Fingerhut, faculty adviser. Articles on current problems of our democracy predominated.

YET, "an independently researched, written, and published student evaluation of Academics at Mary Washington College of the University of Virginia," made its appearance in 1968, with Alexandra Tomalonis as the first editor. It provided student evaluations of courses offered–and the instructor in charge–for the session of 1967–68. It was sold by the staff for one dollar.

Two more issues of *YET* were published, dealing with courses offered in the 1968–69 and 1969–70 sessions. The price was raised to $1.50, but was still insufficient to cover costs. Publication ceased after the 1969–70 session. The *Geiger Counter* appeared in November 1970. It was a general summary of student opinion of college policies rather than of courses and professors.

In 1971–72 two issues of a publication entitled *Aubade* appeared, with Kate Fisher as editor and John Lamph as adviser. Described best, perhaps, as a departure from traditional literary magazines, it presented a selection of poems and stories, drawings and photographs, characterized by a realistic treatment of contemporary themes.

OFFICIAL COLLEGE PUBLICATIONS

Publications of the college began with a bulletin announcing the opening of the State Normal and Industrial School on September 26, 1911, and giving a list of the faculty, description of courses to be offered, charges, and other important information. This was volume I, no. 1, of the *Bulletin,* which has been published continually ever since, usually at least twice a year when announcements of the regular session and the summer session appeared.

Until 1938 the catalogue issues were a uniformly brown color, indistinguishable from hundreds of other college catalogues with inconspicuous, somber covers. However, when the name of the institution was changed to Mary Washington, President Combs decided to have a catalogue that would stand out among others on the shelves of a high school guidance director.

A bright blue cover with old English lettering in white was chosen. When it first appeared, it was described occasionally by officials of other colleges as "gaudy." This pioneer effort to produce a colorful publication soon received the most sincere form of flattery—imitation. In a few years, the majority of college catalogues bore covers in colored stock or made use of color in some fashion. The familiar blue catalogue was published in the same form until 1969, when a newly designed type of publication with in-text illustrations and generally more attractive format took its place.

Other official printed publications included faculty and student directories, schedules of classes, catalogues of art exhibitions in the duPont galleries and book exhibitions in E. Lee Trinkle Library, the dean's list of honor students, the *Alumnae News,* and, most familiar to students, the *Bayonet,* or *Student Handbook.*

The earliest issue of a handbook on file in the archives is a brief pamphlet giving the constitution and bylaws of the Student Government Association, "adopted October 25, 1922." The name "Tyner" is written on the cover. The earliest students handbook extant is one for the session of 1928–29, described as "volume V." It was edited by the YWCA and includes a welcoming message from President Chandler. It contains not only the SGA constitution and bylaws but the rules and regulations governing student privileges and conduct that are usually associated with this publication.

The Y continued to publish the *Student Handbook* until 1933, when it became a joint publication of the SGA, the YWCA, and the Athletic Association. In 1935 the title was changed to the *Bayonet,* a name which it carried until 1957, when it became once again the *Student Handbook.* The changes in rules governing student conduct and privileges are astounding when the 1970–71 edition of the *Handbook* is compared with the *Bayonet* of a generation earlier. Some of the more striking changes are mentioned elsewhere in this publication in the descriptions of the period in which they took place.

Special issues of the college *Bulletin* were published from time to time. One of the earliest is a little illustrated leaflet entitled "The Rappahannock River Country," published in October

1915, as volume 1, no. 3, of the *Bulletin,* and written by Dean A. B. Chandler, Jr. The last three pages are devoted to items of information about the new Normal School. Other issues are devoted to courses of study; teaching suggestions; "War Activities" (1919), dedicated to Captain Gunyon S. Harrison and Private Roy S. Cook; and "An Appreciation of Matthew Fontaine Maury," an address given by President Chandler at the laying of the cornerstone of the Maury monument in Richmond on June 22, 1922. The same issue also contains the address entitled "Maury and the Confederate Navy," delivered on the same occasion by Governor E. Lee Trinkle.

Over the years the college has published many attractive viewbooks and folders. One of the earliest, now in the archives, was a quaint little book of views, suitable for insertion in a small envelope, published in October 1925, which pictures the dining room in Willard Hall, the tea room in the basement, the little swimming pool in Monroe basement, and, among other scenes, students engaged in Maypole dances on the lawn in front of Monroe Hall. In 1930 a rotogravure viewbook showed Chandler Hall and the interior of the new swimming hall at the State Teachers College.

In June 1944, the first of a series of handsome viewbooks bearing the name *Mary Washington College of the University of Virginia* made its appearance. A full-color illustration of the portico of E. Lee Trinkle Library was visible through an elaborate cutout of the front cover. There followed forty-eight pages, 10 × 13 inches in size, of views of the interior and exterior of buildings; scenes from plays, dances, and various student activities; classes in art, music, modern dance, and various sports; the May Court; winter scenes; and scores of other photographs depicting life at the college. New editions with more up-to-date photographs were published in 1946, 1948, 1949, 1951, and 1953.

Many special bulletins have been published from time to time. In 1940 when a new program in applied music was in operation, an illustrated brochure with pictures and brief biographies of all members of the music department was issued. In 1954 there was an illustrated booklet describing the new program in speech correction and audiology offered in cooperation with the University of Virginia.

Beginning with the session of 1957–58, the college began to publish annually a handbook compiled by the Inter-Club Association containing a list of clubs, their purposes, and their officers. This publication was discontinued in 1965 when the *Student*

Handbook began to incorporate all of this information. *Among the Columns* was published as a special handbook for incoming students from 1956 to 1966.

In January 1944 a 60–page compilation of "Faculty Publications" appeared as volume 30, no. 1, of the official *Bulletin*. It also carried biographical information concerning each member of the faculty. A second edition of "Faculty Publications" was compiled in October 1947 and published as volume 33, no. 3, of the *Bulletin*. These are the only two publications of this kind.

In February 1972 the college began to publish officially a combination newspaper-newsletter entitled *MWC Today*, for "Alumnae, Students, Faculty, Staff, Parents, and Friends of the College." This 16–28-page publication, printed in tabloid newspaper size, features news about the activities at the college, announcements of new developments in curriculum and program, stories of faculty activity, descriptions of concerts performed and scheduled, and other information of this kind, much of which might ordinarily have been published by the college newspaper, had the *Bullet* provided better coverage of events on campus.

Parts of each issue are devoted to news and announcements of special interest to alumnae. For readers in general, *MWC Today* provides a rather comprehensive coverage of current activities at the college, including both academic and extracurricular affairs. It is edited by the director of information services.

Any list of official college publications would be incomplete without mention of the weekly "Faculty Bulletin," distributed to all members of the faculty and staff. It was started by the dean of the college about 1940 in response to an expressed need for a weekly schedule of events on campus, with date, hour, and place, and for a medium through which announcements of interest to the faculty could be circulated.

For many years the office of the dean of the college assembled information for the "Faculty Bulletin," mimeographed the material, and prepared copies for mailing. Many faculty members started keeping clipboards for the weekly issues. "Put it in the 'Faculty Bulletin' " became a common plea for anyone with an important announcement for the faculty. In 1967 the preparation and circulation of the "Faculty Bulletin" was transferred from the dean's office to the director of information services.

CHAPTER XXXIII

Dramatics

DRAMATICS occupied a prominent place in college activities long before any courses in this field were included in the curriculum. Perhaps the term *dramatics* is a little too pretentious to describe the amateur efforts that characterized the early days of the college.

The *Battlefield* for 1914 (p. 75) mentioned an active dramatic club that sponsored three productions. On November 21, 1913, the group presented what was called the *Suffragette Convention.* One can imagine the exaggerations and burlesque with which this controversial issue of the time was portrayed. On February 14 the Dramatic Club gave a Valentine's Day program, featuring Saint Valentine and his court, who were "entertained by Cupids and maidens of the Queen of Hearts." On May 2, 1914, the club presented *A Midsummer Night's Dream.* Unfortunately, details are lacking as to the nature and success of this first effort to present serious drama. Apparently, the play was given in connection with the observance of May Day that year.

According to the 1915 *Battlefield,* the main activity of the dramatic club that session was a vaudeville show, featuring the Jumping Jacks and the Down in Michigan Chorus. It is interesting to note that one-third of the proceeds was sent to aid the suffering Belgians. In 1916 the club announced a policy of giving two plays a year, with the proceeds being used to "decorate the school." The group joined the Drama League of America.

By 1917 the club had twenty-two members. It gave a Japanese play, *Abbu San of Old Japan,* in February and *The Ladies of Cranford* in March. The proceeds were used to buy a piece of statuary for Monroe Hall "as a present from the Dramatic Club." This was the statue of Hebe which, for so many years, stood on a pedestal at the intersection of the two main hallways on the first floor. Subsequent, less reverent student generations expressed their lack of respect by occasionally draping a coat about her shoulders, putting crumbled candy wrappers in the bowl she held extended, or coloring her pale lips with red lipstick. The statue was placed in storage in 1960.

In the next two years college productions included *Alice in*

Wonderland (1919) and an operetta presented by the Glee Club entitled *Hiawatha's Childhood*. However, interest in dramatics seemed to wane. The *Battlefield* for 1922 (p. 70) reported, "The revival of dramatics under the head of the English Department [Carrie Belle Vaughan] has been one of the outstanding features of the school year." Several one-act plays were produced. The grand finale of the session was, according to the *Battlefield*, "Van Dyke's beautiful pageant-drama, 'The House of Rimmon,' given by the senior class on the inner court of the campus."

Apparently the hailed revival was short-lived, because, for the next three years, there is no mention of dramatic productions in college publications. Between 1922 and 1925 the head of the English department served as chairman of the dramatics committee. Mary Ethel NeSmith, who had a master's degree from Teachers College, Columbia University, held this position in 1922-23 and 1923-24, and she was followed in 1924-25 by Lulu C. Daniel, a master's degree graduate of the University of Chicago.

In the fall of 1925 Jean Rosborough, a Ph.B. graduate of the University of Chicago, came to the college as professor of English and French and "Adviser to Dramatics." She was a graduate of the Chicago School of Expression and Dramatic Art. Under her sponsorship dramatic activities took on new life.

The Scene Shifters made their appearance as the dramatics organization of the campus. During the 1925-26 session they produced a program of three one-act plays, followed later with *Why the Chimes Rang* and concluded with *What Every Woman Knows*. The following session the Scene Shifters presented *The Torch Bearers, Confessional,* and *The Dover Road*. In 1927-28 the group, also referred to now as the Dramatic Club, presented *She Stoops to Conquer, Little Women* (in collaboration with the College YWCA), and several one-act plays.

In 1927-28 Margaret H. Lakeman became assistant professor with English and dramatics as her fields of concentration. She had studied at the Curry School of Expression in Boston and had previously taught both piano and expression. A new course entitled Vocal Expression and Play Production was introduced in the Department of English. There was also a course in oral reading, which was a required course in the curriculum for primary and grammar grade teaching, and a one-quarter course in reading and public speaking, which was offered as an elective for prospective high school teachers. During the session four dramatizations were given.

In 1928 drama at the college took on a new look with the renovation and refurnishing of the auditorium on the second floor of Monroe Hall. The park-bench seats were replaced with rows of auditorium chairs; new lights were installed both in the auditorium and on the stage, with a panel control box just off stage; a draw curtain of velvet was installed and suitable drapes added; and doors were cut into the classrooms on either side so that these areas could be used as dressing rooms and places where off-stage characters could await their cues.

The audience still entered the middle of the seating areas by double doors on either side of the upstairs hallway. Little attention was paid to fire hazards, even when standees were allowed to block the two main exits. Usually one of these was kept closed, for tickets were always sold and collected at the south door. Actually, there was little danger of fire. No one was allowed to smoke, of course, even on the stage, and the use of lighted candles was forbidden. The few lighting effects used put little strain on the antique wiring installed back in 1910.

Seats in front of the transverse entrance aisle were highly prized, for both visibility and audibility were poorer in the back half of the level-floored auditorium. Spectators in the back half did have the opportunity of seeing and greeting friends as they entered by the midway door in front of them. Occasionally, six or eight students and their dates would seek seats in the rear half, surreptitiously and fearfully holding hands in tense moments of the action on the stage. However, there were always one or two faculty members seated in the back, "just to keep an eye on things."

Mrs. Bushnell always passed upon each presentation, going from the dining hall in her customary dinner dress to the final dress rehearsal, which began, hopefully, at seven. Mrs. Bushnell's stamp of approval was a must before any production. At the end of the rehearsal, questionable lines or actions were pointed out, discussed with the director and cast, and always eliminated if there were any doubt about suitability or good taste.

Of course, the entire play had first been read and approved by the dean of women, but sometimes things can be overlooked or they may appear slightly suggestive when acted out on the stage. There was no hesitation about editing out any lines or scenes in a play that could possibly offend any one.

Since only women took part in the plays, efforts were made to select plays having a predominantly female cast. For example, three of the more memorable productions during this period were *Little Women, The Warrior's Husband,* and *The Cradle Song,* all of which featured a number of women players.

Dramatics

In the fall of 1928, Roberta Louise Barnett had joined the faculty as associate professor of dramatics, in charge of public speaking, reading, and dramatics. She held a bachelor's degree from the University of Missouri and a master's degree from Columbia. She had completed special studies in expression, and she had taught English and dramatics in high school before coming to the college.

Miss Barnett was an enthusiastic and energetic director. Her naturally nervous temperament was inclined to mount in intensity as rehearsals progressed, reaching a crescendo on the night of production. It was obvious that she was deeply involved personally, and the audience respected her for it. The customary comment was "Miss Barnett has certainly put on a good play, hasn't she?" It was her production, from start to finish. The calls for her to come on stage, the wait for her to appear from the wings patting her hair, and the presentation of a bouquet of flowers—and frequently a more lasting gift also—by the lead in the cast were all a part of the closing ritual of each production, as expected as were the customary curtain calls for members of the cast.

For the next eight years Miss Barnett taught courses in play production and oral reading and directed two plays each year. She also taught some freshman English classes. When she left in 1936, she was succeeded by Boyce Loving.

Boyce Loving was talented and versatile. A graduate of the University of Richmond, with a master's degree from Columbia University, he had taught English and dramatics and had written a number of plays. He was engaged both in newspaper work and teaching in Richmond at the time of his appointment as associate professor of dramatic art.

Boyce Loving revised the course in play production and introduced a new course in playwriting (English 375). Courses in dramatic arts were still considered a part of the English department. In addition to these two courses, Loving taught a course in speech correction and interpretation (then required for majors in elementary education) and a section of freshman English composition. He also handled publicity releases for the college, and, with the assistance of Harold Weiss, then a supervisor in the Campus Training School, produced the plays.

The first play under Loving's direction was *The Cradle Song*, presented under the sponsorship of the YWCA. A series of shorter productions included *History in Revue*, five skits written by Loving. These were followed by *Alice-Sit-by-the-Fire*. The climax of the season was the production of *Little Geraldine*, a play about college life written by Loving, which had its premiere on the stage in Monroe Hall. It was later published by Samuel French, the dramatics publishing firm that had purchased another of his plays. In the late spring Loving produced *The Four Winds,* a historical pageant celebrating the thirtieth anniversary of the chartering of the college.

In the spring of 1938 plans were completed to remove the courses in dramatic arts from the English department and to offer a minor in dramatic arts. Play production and playwriting were both expanded to one-year courses. Courses in speech and modern drama, still offered in the English department, were listed to complete the twenty-seven quarter-hours then required for a minor. This marked the beginning of a new department in the college, which was to become the department of dramatic arts and speech offering a major program in this area.

A new era in dramatics began in 1938 when Harold H. Weiss took over the play-producing responsibility at the college. He announced a new policy of producing only well-known plays, even though royalties at times might be high. The name of the producing organization was changed from the dramatics club to the Mary Washington Players. A group of students interested in and willing to work on dramatics was organized as the M. W. Players Apprentices. They built and painted scenery, made costumes and sets, helped with rehearsals, lights, and sound, and became familiar with the play production end of the field.

Largely through the efforts of Harold Weiss, the Eta Eta chapter of Alpha Psi Omega, honorary fraternity in dramatics, was chartered and installed in the spring of 1938. The first officers were Harold Weiss, grand director; Miriam Carpenter, grand stage manager; and Lee Wingate Keith, grand business manager. In the years that immediately followed, a number of faculty members active in dramatic productions were elected to membership. They included Levin Houston III, William A. Castle, Arthur L. Vogelback, E. Boyd Graves, Edward Alvey, Russell Walther, Ronald Faulkner, Jack Warfield, and others.

The following year Harold Weiss was given the title director of dramatic arts. He had served as supervisor of English in the college training school while working also with play production. With the discontinuance of the training school, he was retained on the college staff in this new role. Weiss was a talented actor and director. He held the bachelor's and master's degrees from the Colorado State College of Education, where he had studied dramatics, played the lead in many plays, and had also directed productions. During the summers he had acted in the Little Theatre of the Rockies.

Weiss brought to his new job an enthusiasm and a creative imagination that raised the dramatic productions to a new level. During his first year he produced and directed *Berkeley Square,* probably the most elaborately staged and costumed play ever given at the college. The play was presented on January 18, 1940, before a capacity audience dressed in evening clothes for the occasion.

It was the first play in which men's parts were actually played by men. Prior to Berkeley Square, the men's parts were taken by carefully costumed students, whose wigs and vests did little to disguise the sex of the wearer. Only in Shakespearean plays, which so frequently provided opportunities for Violas to disguise as youths, did the characterizations seem credible. However, men on the stage at the college was subject to one restriction: they all had to be members of the faculty.

This provision had its happy aspect, for it brought to the college stage the versatile and talented Levin Houston, an experienced actor and musician, who was destined to play the male lead in productions of the Mary Washington Players for the next fifteen or twenty years. His characterization of Peter Standish was widely and justly acclaimed as reaching a new peak of excellence in dramatic productions at the college.

Other faculty members in the cast were Arthur Vogelback, later a professor of English at Sweet Briar College; Harold Weiss, who also directed the play; Donald Smith, then college librarian; Alan Pierce, professor of biology; Charles K. Martin, professor of education; and Paul J. Ritter, of the dramatics department.

Contemporary pictures of the production indicate the elaborateness and fidelity of the costumes and stage settings. Eighteenth-century costumes were rented from a New York agency as were powdered wigs, shoes, and other accessories. All scenery was painted by students in the college art classes. The furniture was obtained on loan from the residence of Mrs. Kate Boggs, who insisted that the furniture be not only the period of the play but actually the decade of the 1780s. This attention to detail extended even to the book that Peter Standish picks up from the table. It was one actually published in 1783. Furniture for the stage was insured for twenty-five thousand dollars while the play was in progress. *Berkeley Square* was the first play produced in the auditorium in the recently completed George Washington Hall. Full use was made of the new lighting facilities in producing the gathering shadows of a late October afternoon in the Berkeley Square drawing room. It was not only 1784 but five o'clock in the afternoon of October 23, and the audience felt that it was in that particular room at that particular time.

As the *Bullet* reviewer wrote ecstatically, "January 18, 1940 will go down as a memorable date in the history of Mary Washington College. In a capacity-filled auditorium the cast and crew of *Berkeley Square* presented a performance surpassing all expectations and establishing a precedent more than fitting and complimentary to the magnificence of George Washington Hall. . . ."

Four months of thought and preparation lay behind the success of the production. It established the Mary Washington Players as an outstanding dramatic group whose future productions would be eagerly awaited. The college orchestra gave a new look to college productions by providing overture and intermission selections under the direction of Ronald Faulkner.

Berkeley Square was followed by *Sorority House* that spring, also directed by Harold Weiss. During 1940–41 session the Mary Washington Players produced *Royal Family, Jane Eyre,* and *Yellow Jacket,* the last named brilliantly costumed in Chinese dress.

With the opening of the new radio station on the third floor of George Washington Hall, Harold Weiss became increasingly involved with this aspect of the dramatic arts and speech program. However, he continued to direct and produce plays, now with the assistance of Paul J. Ritter, who from 1940 to 1947 served as assistant professor of dramatic arts and speech, except for a three-year period of military service beginning in 1943, when he was stationed in the Pacific area. A native Californian, Dr. Ritter held an A.B. degree from the University of California and the M.A. and Ph.D. degrees from the University of Southern California. An enthusiastic photographer, he produced a 16-mm movie of life at Mary Washington.

Dr. Ritter and Mr. Weiss worked together in 1941–42 in producing *The Shining Hour* and many one-act plays. Dr. Ritter also directed *Hay Fever,* with Levin Houston III; Dr. Charles K. Martin, Jr., later president of Radford College, and William L. McDermott, of the art department playing leading male roles. Actually, Levin Houston played the male lead in most of these productions.

The United States was at war, and young men were being drafted into military service. The early 1940s Dr. Norman Reid and Don Jones, both experienced in theatricals, were for a short time members of the faculty.

In January 1943 *Kind Lady* was given under the direction of Norman Reid. The sets were described by a writer in the *Bullet* (January 22) as "marvelous." Constructed under the supervision of Donald Jones, the eighteen-foot flats featured prop paintings reproducing paintings by Whistler and other famous artists, which composed the art collection called for by the script. Emil Schnellock and William McDermott worked with their art students in producing these paintings. The atmosphere of the play was aided further by the handsome furniture loaned by local merchants.

As usual, Levin Houston had a leading part in the play as the villain. Mary Vaughan Heazel, in the leading female role, gave a sensitive and highly effective performance. Hilda Parks, according to the reviewer, "shows much talent and will certainly be seen again in the near future."

Other talented student performers during this period were Dorothy Harrington, who starred in *The Warrior's Husband, Jane Eyre, The Shining Hour,* and *Berkeley Square;* Nelle Dawes, who gave a memorable performance as Katherine in *The Taming of the Shrew;* and Kathy Rozmarynowska, who starred in *Pygmalion* and *The Glass Menagerie.*

The 1943 summer session was enlivened by the presentation of *You Can't Take It with You,* by a group that called itself the Faculty Drama Club. Insofar as is known, this was the organization's one and only production. Perhaps the standard set was so high as to discourage future efforts. In any case, the play was enthusiastically received by a large audience of summer students and townspeople.

Emil Schnellock played the role of grandfather Vanderhof, the lovable, philosophical central character of the play, who just decided one day not to go back to the office anymore. Schnellock did more than play the part; he seemed to live the role of grandpa. His reflections on the mad scramble of daily living were essentially an expression of his own kindly, relaxed attitude toward life. Few will forget his prayer for God's blessing upon the family.

In the fall of 1943 Dr. Lucile Charles joined the faculty as assistant professor of dramatic arts. With a Ph.B. from the University of Chicago, a M.A. from Columbia University, and a Ph.D. from Yale University, she was highly qualified academically. Furthermore, she had studied at the Theatre Guild for Acting and had taken an active part in the drama workshop at Yale.

On March 3, 1944, *Quality Street* was staged under her direction. As usual, members of the faculty played the male parts. Levin Houston, the veteran of many Mary Washington productions, was delightful as Mr. Valentine Brown, the lead male role. A trio of Napoleonic soldiers—Boyd Graves, Fred Miller and Edward Alvey—were resplendent in their glittering if somewhat tight uniforms. Carrol Quenzel was suitably garbed as "a gallant" of 1815. The college orchestra under the direction of Ronald Faulkner provided the overture and intermission music.

The prologue was read by Hilda Parks, who, as Hildy Parks, was to become well known for her television network programs. For three years she was a leading figure on one of the quiz shows. Since 1967 she has written the entire script for the annual televised Emmy Awards, which have been widely acclaimed for their excellence.

In December 1944 Dr. Charles produced *The Coventry Nativity Play*. The Choral Club, under the direction of Eva Taylor Eppes, furnished the vocal accompaniment. In the spring a United Nations program of one-act plays provided contributions for the United Nations Relief Fund.

On March 9, 1946, *The Taming of the Shrew* was presented under the direction of Dr. Charles. It was an elaborate production, with five acts and the use of inner and outer stage areas to produce changes of scene as was done in Shakespeare's time. It was a carefully rehearsed and directed production. Russell Walther, an instructor in riding, was in his element as Petruchio, the tamer of the shrew.

In December 1946 *Death Takes a Holiday* was produced, with Levin Houston in the leading role. He also had the lead in *Angel Street,* produced under the sponsorship of Alpha Psi Omega honorary dramatics fraternity in May 1947.

From September 1947 to June 1951, Jack Warfield was in charge of the dramatics department. An experienced actor, he held the A.B. degree from the University of Wisconsin, and an M.A. degree from the University of Minnesota. During Warfield's incumbency, he produced a number of well-known plays, many of which were presented also at other colleges. In fact, an exchange program developed that included the University of Virginia, William and Mary, and Richmond Professional Institute.

Foolish Notion was presented in Charlottesville, while the University of Virginia Players brought one of their productions to Mary Washington. *A Midsummer Night's Dream* was presented also by Mary Washington in the exchange program. In 1949–50 *The Women* was given first at Mary Washington on November 18 and 19, then at William and Mary on November 23, and at the University of Virginia on December 2. In the spring *A Doll's*

House was taken to Richmond Professional Institute and then to Dahlgren Naval Proving Grounds. RPI students presented *The Tempest* at Mary Washington.

Other plays directed by Warfield included *The Late Mr. Early, A Murder Has Been Arranged,* and *The Silver Cord.* The exchange program continued during 1950–51. *The Young and Fair* was given also in Charlottesville. In March 1951 *As You Like It* opened for a two-day run. Warfield's last play was *The Heiress,* given in May 1951. At the end of the session he left to become director of the well-known Pasadena Playhouse in California.

In the fall of 1951 Mark Sumner, a native of Asheville, North Carolina, joined the dramatics department, succeeding Jack Warfield. Mark Sumner had the B.A. and M.A. degrees in dramatics from the University of North Carolina. As a student he had been active in the Carolina Playmakers. He had written and published eight one-act plays, some of which had won the highest awards at the Annual State Drama Festival in North Carolina. During the summers Sumner was producer and director of the historical outdoor drama, *The Lost Colony.* For the next twelve years he was engaged in teaching play production and play writing as well as directing plays at Mary Washington.

During his first year Sumner alternated the direction of plays with Martha Newell, who had joined the faculty in September 1950. *Light Up the Sky* was given in November 1951, under the direction of Martha Newell. This play was followed in February by *Ladies in Retirement,* directed by Mark Sumner. In April, *The Importance of Being Earnest* was given under the direction of Martha Newell. Martha Newell left at the end of the 1951–52 session to return to radio work.

In 1952 Albert R. Klein joined the faculty as instructor in dramatic arts. A native of Council Bluffs, Iowa, he had graduated from the University of Iowa. His master's degree was from the University of North Carolina, where he had specialized in drama. Later he was to earn his Ph.D. from the University of Denver.

For the decade from 1952–53 to 1962–63, Mark Sumner and Al Klein brought a high quality of dramatics to the stage of duPont Hall. The 1952–53 season opened with *Blithe Spirit,* directed by Sumner, with settings by Klein. This production marked the opening of the Little Theatre in duPont Hall on November 6, 7, and 8. It was followed in December by *Years Ago,* with Klein and Sumner providing the direction and setting respectively.

In March 1953, an elaborate production of *King Lear* was

staged, with Klein as director and Sumner as technical director. Sumner also gave a memorable performance in the difficult role of King Lear. Costumes were designed by Debby Klein, and special music composed by Levin Houston. Reginald Whidden was literary adviser. More than forty students, faculty members, and townspeople took part in the play.

Pygmalion was presented April 30, May 1, 2, and 9, 1953, in the duPont Little Theatre. The settings by Debby Klein for the five-act play were particularly effective. Mark Sumner and Al Klein directed, and, as usual, Levin Houston had a leading role as Professor Henry Higgins. The part of Eliza Doolittle was played by Kathy Rozmarynowska, who later received a scholarship for advanced study in drama in London. Incidentally, this was the last play in which Levin Houston acted. Among the notable productions other than those mentioned were: *The House of Bernarda Alba* (1955); *Romeo and Juliet* (1956); *The Curious Savage* (1956); *Caesar and Cleopatra* (1957); *A Streetcar Named Desire* (1957); and *The Great God Brown* (1957). In April 1958, *The Mikado* was produced under joint direction of the dance, drama, and music departments. *The Diary of Anne Frank* was also a noteworthy production of that year.

Other plays presented, with Sumner and Klein alternating as directors, were *The Glass Menagerie, Arms and the Man, Gigi, The Man Who Came to Dinner, The Tender Trap,* and *Harvey.* In *Harvey,* directed by Sumner, one could almost see that great white rabbit that Klein, as Elwood P. Dowd, made so believable in his conversations with him and his solicitude for him.

Masquerade for Linda, an original play by Al Klein, had its premiere before an appreciative audience in the Little Theatre in duPont Hall on May 12, 13, and 14, 1955. A *Bullet* reporter on May 17 described the play as "full of warm charm and freshness of a sunny spring day. Mr. Klein skillfully and delicately wove a plot out of the sweetness of love, the strength of a promise, and the brightness of a gay masquerade."

Mark Sumner resigned in 1963 and subsequently became director of the Institute of Outdoor Drama at the University of North Carolina. He was succeeded by Albert Klein as head of the department of dramatic arts.

A new era of development began under leadership of Dr. Klein. The experimental theatre, later known as Studio 13, was introduced that fall to give drama students an opportunity to work with some of the more unconventional forms of the art. Dr. Klein converted a basement room below the stage, formerly used for costume storage, into an area for the presentation of experimental plays before an invited audience of about thirty-five friends and faculty members. Students of acting, playwriting, and directing were given an opportunity to try out their ideas before the invited critics, who were often asked to fill out evaluation sheets at the end of the performance. In a typical year, fifteen to twenty student-directed experimental or contemporary plays were given in Studio 13.

Dr. Klein's opening production for 1963–64 was *The Crucible,* which he directed. It was followed later in the session by *The Children's Hour* in March and *A Midsummer Night's Dream,* on April 30, May 1, and May 2. The Shakespearean production was an elaborate one. Debby Klein, whose sets had become a feature of the Players' presentations, designed scenery that gave credence to the fanciful happenings on stage that characterize the play. Dances were directed by Martha Darby of the physical education department to music by Lloyd Farrar, of the music department. Overall direction was by Dr. Klein.

The Players began a policy of presenting a children's play each year just before the Christmas holidays. This became a feature of the season eagerly anticipated by children—and by the grownups who accompanied them—not only in Fredericksburg but in nearby counties where school buses brought excited children to the performances.

The activities of the Mary Washington Players were not limited to campus. For several years the college participated in the Virginia College Drama Festivals, where the presentations received critical acclaim.

Roger Lee Kenvin joined the English department in September 1959. He had specialized both in English and in dramatics (M.A., Harvard; M.F.A. and D.F.A., Yale) and in 1966 became associate professor of dramatic arts and speech. Dr. Kenvin directed *Alice in Wonderland* (December 1966); *The American Dream* and *The Chairs* (1967); and a highly successful production of *As You Like It* (1967), with sets by Debby Klein, lighting by Albert Klein, and music by Levin Houston. *Blithe Spirit* (1968) and *Major Barbara* (1968) were also directed by Dr. Kenvin.

Dr. Kenvin took part in several plays. He was J.B. in the play of the same name, Zeus in *The Flies* (1967), and Tom Pettigrew in a 1968 production of *Berkeley Square.* His performance as Bottom in *A Midsummer Night's Dream* (1964) is still recalled fondly by theater-goers who witnessed that production. Dr. Kenvin left the college in 1969 for another position but returned in September 1972 as professor and chairman of the department of dramatic arts.

In 1966 two new developments in the drama department involved the use of a thrust stage, which extended the acting area much closer to the audience and the incorporation of a question and answer period for audience and actors at the end of the first-night performance of each production. As Dr. Klein explained in introducing the discussion period, it was not intended for praise or criticism of individual actors, but rather as an opportunity to discuss the ideas presented and the techniques used by the performers.

An Oriental emphasis was given to the department in 1967–68 when Joy Michael of New Delhi, India, a graduate of the London Academy of dramatic Arts, held a visiting professorship. Mrs. Michael taught a course in modern Indian theater and also directed two Indian plays—*One Day in Ashadh* and *The Ungrateful Man*. She also conducted a seminar in Indian theatre.

Still another innovation by the drama department was a chamber theatre series, sponsored in cooperation with the college library, which on Sunday afternoons, presented rather off-beat plays not usually performed in a regular theatre situation.

A few of the plays produced during this period must be mentioned, for they give an idea of the continuing tradition of excellence in dramatics. *Tartuffe,* presented in March 1969, was one of Dr. Klein's outstanding productions. Again, his wife, Debby, designed and helped to build the sets. Thomas Turgeon, assistant professor of dramatic arts and speech, furnished the technical direction and acted in the play. *The Cherry Orchard* (October 29–November 1, 1969) was one of the last plays directed by Dr. Klein. Many of those who saw this excellent production of Chekhov's masterpiece regard it as a high point in theatrical presentations at the college. The theatre was sold out for the length of the run. Susan Fox's acting as the charming Mme. Ranevskaya, Susan Stumpf's "beautifully designed and executed" costumes, and Mary James Wright's "tasteful settings and furnishings" all contributed to a masterful production. And Benjamin W. Early was "great in the role of Firs, the old house servant."[1]

Incidentally, *The Cherry Orchard* marked the thirty-fourth role of Ben Early, a veteran of the MWC stage. Dr. Early's widely diversified roles have included the singer in *Bird in the Gilded*

---

[1] *Free Lance-Star,* Oct. 30, 1969.

Cage; the blind seer in *Oedipus;* the minister in *The Importance of Being Earnest;* and Throttlebottom in *Of Thee I Sing.* As a colleague has noted, in his long career Dr. Early never failed to contribute his intelligence, taste, and vitality to every role, whether a walk-on part or a lead in the play.

On the morning of October 6, 1970, Dr. Klein was stricken with a heart attack and died while driving his children to school. Fortunately no injury resulted as the car crossed the median strip and struck a bank on the opposite side of the highway. His death was a shock to the entire community. A memorial service attended by faculty and students was held in Trinity Episcopal Church. It was conducted by Rabbi Franzblau and Dr. Robert H. Shaw.

Dr. Klein had made a rich contribution to the college. In the field of dramatics, he had set a high standard for courses in stagecraft, dramatic literature, and creative writing. In addition to his activities in his field of specialization, Dr. Klein had served as a member of the future of the college committee and of the faculty steering committee that was instrumental in obtaining a charter of Phi Beta Kappa for Mary Washington. He had spent the preceeding summer in India in a teacher-exchange program.

An Albert Klein Memorial Fund to provide scholarships for drama majors was established shortly after his death. In May 1971, the memorial committee announced that the theatre in duPont Hall would be named in his honor. The dedication of the Albert Roger Klein Memorial Theatre took place on October 22, 1971. The dedicatory address was made by Chancellor Simpson, who referred to Dr. Klein as one of the truly great. The unveiling of the memorial plaque was followed by the performance of *The Three Sisters,* a favorite play of Dr. Klein's. Proceeds from the subscription performance were allocated to the Klein Memorial Scholarship Fund.

And now at the entrance to the theatre which, in Dr. Simpson's words, "He used to such a great advantage," Dr. Klein is memorialized by a bronze plaque that reads simply:

Albert Roger Klein
Memorial Theatre
October 22, 1971

Since Dr. Klein's death the college has continued to maintain its high standard of theatrical productions. The 1970–71 season included *The Lady's Not for Burning; The Christmas Nightingale,* a children's play; *The Country Wife;* and *America Hurrah.*

A Taste of Honey, presented in March 1970 marked an innovation in its use of six film sequences during scene breaks in the drama to create the mood of the geographical location of the action. Another unique feature of the production was the utilization of original music, played by a jazz combo.

The 1970–71 season marked still another innovation in play production at Mary Washington. *The Country Wife* was the first to make use of a revolving stage that would permit rapid scene changes before the eyes of the audience. Designed by drama instructor Charles Howard, the device was constructed on a strip iron foundation by members of the college course in stagecraft. Research on costumes was conducted as an independent study project.

For some time it had been evident that the separation of the speech courses from the dramatic offerings was desirable because of the heavy burden that fell upon the chairman of the department as organized. This was done during the summer of 1971. Albert G. Duke, who had taught the courses in speech for many years, was appointed to head the new department of speech, while Dr. Turgeon became chairman of the department of dramatic arts. A Phi Beta Kappa graduate of Amherst College, with a doctor of fine arts degree from Yale, Dr. Turgeon had already directed and acted in a number of plays since coming to the college in 1968. The 1971–72 season opened with *The Three Sisters,* followed by *Rumpelstilskin,* a children's play, in December; *The Fantasticks,* a musical; and, in the spring, *Don Juan.*

Of interest to visitors to duPont Hall is the collection of pictures lining the corridors leading to the dressing rooms below the stage. There, in chronological order, are photographs of scenes from dozens of dramatic productions over the past twenty years, collected and framed by Dr. Klein.

CHAPTER XXXIV

The Library

THE EARLY DAYS

WHEN the new Normal School opened in September 1911, the space set aside in the administration building, now Monroe Hall, for use as a library was still in process of completion. President Russell was quoted in the *Daily Star* of September 14, 1911, as saying that he and a faculty committee headed by Professor A. B. Chandler, Jr., would prepare a list of books to be purchased for the library.

The first library was a small room on the right-hand side of the Administration Building, now numbered Room 10 and used as a seminar room. A photograph appearing in contemporary catalogues shows two small tables, with a chair on each of the four sides; one longer table with six chairs, and twelve bookcases of five shelves each. There is also a newspaper rack. Four students are seated at two of the tables, giving the small space an appearance of being well occupied. A large dictionary takes up much of the space on one table. The total seating capacity of the library was twenty-four.

The first book to be placed in the new library was a student's Bible, the gift of Colonel E. D. Cole of Fredericksburg. This is item number one in the first accessions record, where the thousands of books acquired and catalogued over the years are listed in order of their acquisition. The date of this gift is recorded as September 26, 1911. The second book listed in the records is also a Bible, purchased for chapel use and recorded as charged out indefinitely to the chapel desk in the auditorium.

During the fall, large orders of books were placed with various publishers and made available to students upon arrival. It was not until February 1912 that a complete list of accessions up to that time was entered officially in the accession book. A total of 910 volumes were listed as on hand by February 1912.

Among the first books to be acquired were complete sets of Charles Dickens (22 vols.) and Walter Scott (28 vols.), obviously inexpensive editions, as the cost is listed as twenty-eight cents per volume. Other complete sets purchased with the first library funds were the works of George Eliot, Edgar Allan Poe, William

M. Thackeray, and Washington Irving. There were also many paperbound classics, such as Scott's *Ivanhoe,* George Eliot's *Silas Marner,* and Shakespeare's *Julius Caesar,* as well as books such as Plutarch's *Lives,* Longfellow's *Poems,* and Tennyson's *Idylls of the King.*

Woodrow Wilson's *A History of the American People* (5 vols., Harpers, 1902) is one of the interesting items in the first collection of books. The entry in the accession book notes that it was "purchased as premium with magazines" at a cost of twelve dollars for the set.

The majority of books purchased were texts or books related to the courses being offered at the new school. In addition to the usual English classics, there were books on household management, household hygiene, home care of the sick, soils, gardening, insect life, farm animals, personal health, and school sanitation, as well as literally scores of titles on various aspects of methodology. There were also large numbers of books for use by pupils in the high school classes then offered.

The current fiction purchased reflected the reading interests of young college women at that time. Among books purchased with the first appropriation were Mary Johnston's *To Have and to Hold* and *The Long Roll,* John Fox, Jr.'s *The Little Shepherd of Kingdom Come,* Ellen Glasgow's *Voice of the People,* Weir Mitchell's *Red City,* Kate Langley Bosher's *Mary Cary,* Norman Duncan's *Dr. Luke of the Labrador,* and other similar works then popular. Later, novels by Harold Bell Wright, Thomas Nelson Page, George Washington Cable, Frances Hopkinson Smith, and Gene Stratton Porter were purchased.

There were relatively few standard books of reference. The library contained several dictionaries and two sets of encyclopedias. Of the approximately 900 books that constituted the library collection by the end of the first session, some 420 were sample copies of elementary and high school texts accumulated by E. H. Russell during the years he had served as high school examiner prior to becoming president of the new Normal School.

The books given by Russell were published between 1895 and 1910. There are many interesting titles among them. Besides books like Longfellow's *Hiawatha,* Franklin's *Autobiography,* and Whittier's *Snowbound,* we find *Soldier Life in the Army of Northern Virginia* by Carlton McCarthy, published in 1899 by the B. F. Johnson Publishing Company of Richmond. The author of this fascinating account of "life in the ranks" is identified on the title page as "private, Second Company, Richmond

Howitzers, Cutshaw's Battalion Artillery, Second Corps, A.N.V. [Army of Northern Virginia]." The pen and ink illustrations were William L. Sheppard's, "Lieutenant, Second Company, Richmond Howitzers, A.N.V." Particularly poignant is the little sketch entitled "C. S. Buttons Off," showing a Union sergeant removing the symbol of a defeated nation from the worn jacket of a Confederate private.

The book collection, limited as it was, covered a range of material. Both classics and current fiction seem to have enjoyed a high rate of circulation. Reading was a pleasant relaxation on the weekends when there was no radio or television and a trip home, even to a neighboring county, was a rare event except during the holidays.

LIBRARY STAFF AND FACILITIES

For the first four years of the institution no regular librarian was employed. The library was administered by a small faculty committee (three members, later enlarged to five), who selected and ordered the books, recorded their receipt and catalogued them, and in general supervised the entire operation.

Four student assistants were employed to operate the library and to assist in the tasks indicated above. They were carefully selected to carry these responsibilities and were paid a hundred dollars per session, the highest-paid type of student aid. Their compensation was listed as a separate item in the college budget.

In the fall of 1915 the library was moved to a large room in the south end in the front part of the newly completed Virginia Hall, in a room that later became one of the parlors. Subsequently, another smaller room also at the south end of the building was utilized for library purposes.

The library had continued to grow. President Russell's annual report dated June 1913 mentioned a total of 1,700 "well-selected volumes." By the time of the removal of the library to Virginia Hall in September 1915, the book collection numbered about 3,000 volumes. According to the catalogue for 1915–16 (p. 26), "on the shelves of the library are found the very best reference books, works of classical literature, present-day fiction, and current literature." Catalogue descriptions of the library also called attention to the Wallace Library, a public library in Fredericksburg, to which the student body "has access."

With the moving of the library to new quarters in Virginia

Hall, the first regular librarian was appointed. She was Mary S. Yates. Her compensation for the session of nine months was approximately $600.00. Miss Yates had graduated from the Southern Presbyterian College at Red Springs, North Carolina, and had received her training at the Library Training School of the Carnegie Library at Atlanta, Georgia. She did not hold a degree. From September 1915 to June 1917, she had charge of the library. There is no indication as to whether she also taught any classes.

Interestingly enough, the next five librarians who followed her were all graduates of the Library Training School of the Carnegie Library at Atlanta, Georgia, Mary Yates's alma mater. Margaret V. Jones served as librarian from 1917 to 1918; Clara W. Crawford from 1918 to 1920; Mary Vick Burney from 1920 to 1921; Nina L. Morgan from 1921 to 1923; and Sue Vernon Williams from 1923 to 1925. Miss Williams was the only one of the group to hold a degree.

When Miss Williams left in 1925, the chain of graduates of the Carnegie Library School at Atlanta was broken with the appointment of Helen R. Rainey, who had received her training in the Carnegie Library at Mount Vernon, Illinois. She remained at the college only a short time when she was succeeded by Frances Thompson, a graduate of Fredericksburg College, who had attended the University of Virginia Summer School and had received her library training in the library of what was now the State Teachers College at Fredericksburg.

The salary paid librarians at that time was unbelievably low.[1] Frances Thompson received a salary of $900 for the session of 1926–27. In 1927–28 it was raised to $1,000. It was the lowest salary of any "educational employee," considerably less than members of the faculty received and even below the average of $1,400 then paid supervisors in the campus training school.

With the growth in student enrollment, repeated efforts had been made to obtain funds for additional dormitory space. In 1926 the governing board obtained approval of a loan under the Noell Act. This legislation authorized loans from state funds for "self-liquidating" dormitory construction projects at state institutions, with the provision that revenues received from the rental of rooms would be used to repay the loans. Thus, the construction of a second unit of Virginia Hall was made possible.

The new unit was completed on December 15, 1926, and put

---

[1] Annual Reports of President for 1926–27 and 1927–28.

into use immediately. The second and third floors were devoted to rooms for students. The first floor of the new addition provided much needed space for the expansion of the library, which was now moved from the front part of the building to larger quarters extending across the rear of the new unit. The space formerly occupied by the library was converted to use as a student parlor.

Frances Thompson served as librarian for three sessions. When she left in 1928, she gave her collection of over four hundred volumes to the college library. She was succeeded by Rachel Wingfield, a degree graduate of the college, who had taken library training as a graduate student at the School of Library Service, Columbia University. It was at this time that courses in library science began to be offered. Rachel Wingfield was the first to hold the title of librarian and instructor in library training. Dr. Combs had become president of the college on January 1, 1929.

INSTRUCTION IN LIBRARY SCIENCE BEGINS

The catalogue announcement for 1929-30 (p. 91) listed library training as a new course in the English department. Actually, this was only a one-quarter course, for three credits, which was scheduled to be repeated each quarter. The following year it was renumbered as English 280, Library Training, with the same description.[2] The new numbering made it clear that only a one-quarter course was being offered. It will be noted that the course provided laboratory work. Students enrolled worked part time as library aides, preparing books for cataloguing, mending worn volumes, and assisting in various routine duties of that nature. Student aides were employed regularly at the circulation desk to charge and receive books and to man the library during the evening hours.

Rachel Wingfield left early in the 1930-31 session, and on January 15, 1931, she was succeeded by Margaret D. Calhoun, who for the next twelve years served as head librarian, continuing in office until September 11, 1943, when Dr. Quenzel came to the college.

Miss Calhoun was a native of South Carolina. She had attended Randolph-Macon Woman's College and had received the A.B. degree from Birmingham Southern College. She held a B.L.S.

---

[2] *Catalogue*, 1929-30, pp. 96-97.

degree from the School of Library Science at Columbia University and an M.A. degree from George Peabody College. Before joining the faculty at Fredericksburg, she had served as an assistant in the reference department of the Birmingham Public Library and as an assistant in the Columbia University Library. Under Margaret Calhoun's administration, the services of the library were extended and the book collection was gradually enlarged. The course offering in library training was increased.

In the fall of 1930 Grace Taylor was employed as assistant librarian. A major in English, she had had no formal training in library science but had worked as a student assistant in the library prior to her graduation with the B.S. degree in June 1930. For the next seven years, Grace Taylor was a full-time assistant to Margaret Calhoun in the operation of the library. With the help of a small group of student aides, they prepared book orders, catalogued books, manned the circulation desk, and on occasion helped students to find material needed for the preparation of term papers.

Need for additional space was urgent. In 1937, when the third and final unit of Virginia Hall was completed, the library was extended into first-floor rooms immediately to the right of the new entrance facing Ball Circle. This area is now the main parlor of Virginia Hall. New shelves were added and additional reading space provided. There was also more working space for the cataloguing and repair of books.

The selection of books for the library was put on a more systematic basis. Heads of departments were asked to make recommendations periodically for the purchase of books in their specialization. In the later 1930s a budget for library accessions was set up by the bursar, and each department was allocated a portion of the funds available according to its stated needs. Toward the end of a fiscal year, when excess collections indicated a surplus of receipts over expenditures for the operation of the college, a lump sum was often allocated to the library in order that additional titles to build up the collection could be ordered.

It was during this period that the YWCA book collection began to play an increasingly important role in the resources of the library. For many years, the Y had made a practice of spending part of its funds to purchase books of fiction, both standard and current, to provide recreational reading for the student body. Lists of new acquisitions, often with brief annotations, appeared frequently in the *Bullet* and were posted on bulletin boards.

With the opening of the E. Lee Trinkle Library, the collection was moved to the browsing room. By that time it numbered hundreds of volumes. When the Y discontinued the project in the 1950s, the books of fiction were absorbed into the general collection of the library.

A bonanza came to the library when the National Youth Administration was created during Franklin D. Roosevelt's first term as President. Designed as a measure to relieve unemployment and also to make it possible for young people to earn part of the money necessary to attend college, the program included student employment for thirteen hours a week at tasks that would not replace regular staff members. At one time, as many as thirty NYA students worked at various tasks in the library, repairing and rebinding books, cataloguing accessions, writing book orders, and performing many other tasks that made possible the improvement of the library holdings and its services.

In 1933 an advanced course had been added, making possible six quarter-hour credits in library training. Finally, in 1937 the library training courses were expanded to provide twelve quarter-hour credits, which, taken with the courses in children's literature (English 110, three credits) and adolescent literature (English 210, three credits) met the Virginia requirements for certification as a teacher-librarian. Thus, by electing these courses, a major in English, for example, could qualify as a part-time librarian in those high schools whose enrollment was small enough not to necessitate the employment of a full-time librarian.

This continued to be the offering in library training for several years. The technical library courses were taught by Margaret Calhoun, listed in the catalogue as librarian and instructor in library science. Courses in children's literature and adolescent literature were taught by members of the English department.

As the library expanded its collection, it was obvious that additional staff was needed. Trinkle Library was under construction in 1940–41 when George Donald Smith became the first addition to the professional staff, which for so many years had consisted of a full-time librarian, plus student assistants, and, more recently, an assistant librarian without special library training.

Smith was appointed as associate professor of library science. He held the A.B. degree from Colby College and an M.S. from Columbia University. He had also taken library training at the University of Chicago. He remained only one year.

Succeeding Smith in the fall of 1940 was Bernard Fry, who held A.B. and A.M. degrees from Indiana University. He was appointed instructor in library science. During 1940–41 the courses in library training were placed in a separate section under the English department and their title was changed from Library Training to Library Science.

E. Lee Trinkle Library was opened in the fall of 1941. With this new facility available, the library staff was enlarged to four and listed under the administrative section of the catalogue. The offering in library science was expanded to include twenty-seven quarter-hours of course work, which met the requirements then in effect for a minor at Mary Washington.[3] The same offering continued without change until 1948, and then, in accordance with provisions for curriculum changes when the college became the liberal arts college for women of the University of Virginia, all courses in library science were discontinued as being of a "vocational nature."

A NEW LIBRARY BUILDING

Even with the additional space in Virginia Hall, the library facilities were far from adequate for a growing institution. President Combs envisioned a new building that would be outstanding in its architecture, facilities, and equipment. He began to make every effort to obtain a state appropriation for this purpose.

In an eloquent plea addressed to Governor James H. Price on August 15, 1938, President Combs reported in detail on the inadequacies of the present library. Describing the library as "the very heart of an institution of learning," he pointed out that Mary Washington was the only state college in Virginia without a library building.

A year later, President Combs again sought funds for the library, this time in an urgent appeal to the State Board of Education to "pass a resolution urging the governor to release this conditional appropriation of $150,000 (originally for a classroom and administration building) to be used for the construction of a library building at this institution."[4]

On Thursday, October 12, 1939, Governor James H. Price and his budget commission visited the campus to see whether a new library building was needed by the college. Students were asked to assemble in the library rooms in Virginia Hall to demonstrate

---
[3] *Catalogue*, 1942–43, pp. 130–32.
[4] MWC Special Report to State Board of Education, Aug. 5, 1939, p. 2.

The Library

the inadequacies of the facilities. When the visitors entered the library, "amazement shown on their faces as they viewed the crowded conditions," the *Bullet* reported on October 13. They saw students sitting on the floor among the rows of shelves, leaning against walls and window sills, and occupying every bit of available space at the tables, all reading intently.

The commission was impressed. Remarks of "I've never seen anything like it" were overheard as the legislators threaded their way among the throng of students. One visitor remarked, with a twinkle in his eye, that he had never seen so many students in a library in his four years of college.

Former Governor Trinkle took a personal interest in seeing that funds for the library building were made available. He talked with Governor Price in Richmond while the budget for the next biennium was being prepared. When the budget was released later, Governor Price had included funds for the library in his recommendations. When the General Assembly met in January 1940, the $150,000 that had been appropriated conditionally for a "classroom and administration building" at Mary Washington College was reappropriated with the provision that it could be used for a library building.[5]

The use of this appropriation was duly authorized for constructing and equipping the library. This amount was supplemented by approximately $75,000 in college funds, from what were known as "excess collections." Through economies and efficiency of operation, the college had managed to collect revenues in excess of expenditures, and authorization was given by the governor to apply these funds to the new library.[6]

Incidentally, the old library space in Virginia Hall was converted into rooms for students at a cost of approximately $25,000, which was also paid for through excess collections.

With funds for the library now in hand, no time was lost in getting the new structure started. J. Binford Walford of Richmond, the architect who designed the other college buildings erected during the 1930s and '40s, had completed his plans for the new building by July 1940, and specifications were ready for bids. The contract was awarded to Doyle and Russell of Roanoke, and by fall construction was under way. The actual cost of the building was $177,000. Additional furnishings and equipment brought the total cost to over $225,000.

[5] *Acts of Assembly*, 1940, pp. 864–65.
[6] Annual Report of President for Fiscal Year Ending June 30, 1942, p. 3.

President Combs obtained the permission of the State Board of Education to name the new library in honor of former Governor E. Lee Trinkle. Trinkle was a graduate of Hampden-Sydney College, where he won medals in debating and public speaking and made the highest academic average in his class. At the University of Virginia he was a member of Phi Delta Phi law fraternity, won the first Moot Court Prize, and was voted the most influential man in the University student body.[7] He was awarded the LL.B. degree in 1898.

Mr. Trinkle was a highly successful lawyer. He also had varied farming, banking, business, and insurance interests. He represented a group of Southwest Virginia counties in the senate of Virginia from 1916 to 1920. The following year he was elected governor of Virginia by a huge majority.

Governor Trinkle, as he was usually called, and President Combs were close personal friends. Trinkle was a frequent visitor to the college both in his official capacity as president of the State Board of Education and as a guest at receptions, entertainments, and important occasions of various kinds. On these visits he and Mrs. Trinkle were house guests of President and Mrs. Combs.

Governor Trinkle's interest in education was genuine and far reaching. He realized the importance of well-prepared teachers, and, both as governor and as president of the State Board of Education (1931–39), lent the force of his influence to improving facilities for their preparation and standards for their certification.

E. Lee Trinkle died on November 25, 1939, two years before the library bearing his name was completed. He would have been proud of this building, the book collection that it houses, and the services that the library is rendering. It exemplifies his concept of the role of the library in an educational institution.

The E. Lee Trinkle Library was an imposing building, with a handsome Grecian portico. On either side of the central portion there extended large reading rooms. The tall, rounded windows on the first floor gave an impression of spaciousness to the entire structure, as well as affording maximum outside light in the reference and reserve reading rooms. The red brick with white trim and the two-story columns of the main entrance

---

[7] *History of Virginia* (Chicago and New York: American Historical Society, 1924), 4: 6.

harmonized with the other buildings along the central campus driveway.

One entered a large circular rotunda, surrounded by a railed balcony supported by fluted columns. Rising above the second-floor level was a domed ceiling with a blue-glass circular window set in the very top. The total effect was one of spaciousness, dignity, and beauty.

Facing the entrance but across the lobby floor was the receiving and charging desk, with five floors of stacks immediately behind. Shelf space for a hundred and fifty thousand volumes was provided. Study carrels on each floor made possible individual work areas for students or faculty members engaged in research projects. The first floor also provided offices for the librarian, a fairly extensive cataloguing department, and other facilities needed for the operation of the library.

A feature of the rotunda was a large bronze replica of the college seal set in the center of the terrazzo floor. A tradition against stepping on the seal was begun at the time and faithfully observed for several years. In the late 1960s the handing down of the tradition seems to have faltered. A new generation of both faculty and students began to step freely upon the seal in seeking the shortest way to cross the lobby.

Considerable thought was given to furnishing the reading rooms for the new library. The solid walnut tables were designed by Binford Walford and made to order by the Virginia Craftsmen of Harrisonburg, who also made the Windsor chairs to match. The Valley of Virginia firm also made the furniture for the browsing room.

There were also two large reading rooms on the second floor. Immediately above the reference room was the periodical room, while the browsing room occupied the space on the other side. The latter was illuminated by soft lights and reading lamps. A fireplace and wood paneling added to the feeling of warmth. The atmosphere was so conducive to relaxation that it was not unusual to discover students blissfully asleep in the comfortable leather armchairs or stretched full length on a sofa. At times, it was referred to as the "drowsing room."

For many years the pleasant facilities of the browsing room were used for conferences and informal lectures. William Faulkner once spoke there to a fascinated audience that filled every bit of floor space and overflowed into the hallway.

A smaller room on the second floor adjoining the browsing

room was set aside to house a collection of books about Virginia or by Virginians. Some 155 books were placed in the Virginiana collection during the first year. Some important manuscripts, including the charters of Fredericksburg and Falmouth, were later added to the collection.

Courses in library science were conducted in the large room at the far end of the ground floor. The smaller room immediately adjoining (now the archives) was used for Latin and Greek. Classes in these subjects were small and usually sat around a large conference table. Murals depicting Greek and Roman scenes gave a classical atmosphere to the room. They were the work of Emil Schnellock and some of his students in the mural painting class.

It had been planned originally to dedicate the new library on October 25, 1941. However, the United States was in the midst of a vast buildup of resources for national defense, and deliveries of needed materials, especially metal shelving for books, were delayed for weeks. It was well into the session before removal of books from Virginia Hall to the new structure could be undertaken. Plans for a formal dedication were abandoned as the nation mobilized for an all-out effort to win the war.

A TRANSITIONAL PERIOD

Until the library moved into its new quarters, annual reports of library activities were quite informal, consisting mainly of information on accessions, size of collection and other statistical items needed by the president for his own report to the governing body of the institution.

However, as the E. Lee Trinkle Library began to function, annual reports of the librarian to the president became an established procedure. The report of Margaret Calhoun for the fiscal year ending June 30, 1942, showed a marked growth in the size of the collection. Some 4,250 books were received, plus 1,710 federal documents, 120 state documents, and 50 miscellaneous items, making a total of 1,880 printed unbound pieces. By June 1942 the total number of books and pamphlets was 40,862.

Lack of staff to handle the increasing collection of books was still a problem. In her annual report dated July 19, 1943, Miss Calhoun made an urgent request for additional staff, stating that the work load was more than three full-time trained staff mem-

The Library

bers could handle. She also made a strong plea for the installation of a telephone in the library, citing the necessity of communicating with other offices on the campus. She also recommended the installation of a service elevator to replace the hand-operated dumbwaiter used to hoist books to the various levels.

During the summer of 1943 Margaret Calhoun resigned because of poor health. She later became librarian of the Graduate School Library of the United States Department of Agriculture, in Washington, D.C. Subsequently, she was appointed coordinator of reference services for the Alexandria Public Library, in which capacity she was serving at the time of her retirement in 1972.

GROWTH OF THE LIBRARY, 1911–1943

In the early days of the library the collection grew slowly but steadily. From 1915 to 1927 growth continued at a decelerated rate. The ten thousandth book was acquired on February 12, 1930, nearly nineteen years after the opening of the college.

During the 1930s growth averaged a thousand items a year. There were extensive purchases in the early 1940s, just prior to and immediately after the opening of E. Lee Trinkle Library. By November 1943 the collection had reached the thirty-thousand figure shortly after Dr. Quenzel had become librarian.

The following tabulation indicates dramatic growth of the collection. It took nine years (1911–20) to reach 5,000; ten more (1920–30) to reach 10,000; six more (1930–36) to reach 15,000; three more years (1936–39) to reach 20,000; two more years (1939–41) to reach 25,000; and one year and two months (1941–43) to reach 30,000. In 1943 the library began to grow at the rate of 5,000 volumes a year.

EXPENDITURES FOR LIBRARY, 1911–1943

Approximately five hundred dollars was spent annually for library books in the early days of the college. There was no separate listing of expenditures for books in President Russell's report for 1911–12 and 1912–13. They were regarded as school supplies and listed in the expenditures for the school supply room. The auditing committee suggested in 1913 that expenditures for library books be shown separately in future reports, a practice that was followed from then on.

Although the president's annual report for 1912–13 did not list just what was spent for books, it did indicate that two horses were purchased for the farm at a cost of $350.00. Not much more was spent for books.

The president's report for the session of 1913–14 showed an expenditure of $484.71 for library books. Under the heading "Library," the report stated: "The Library has been increased by the addition of about $500.00 worth of books during the session. It is the policy of the school to put about that much in the library every year, thus gradually building it up to a high state of efficiency."

This practice seems to have been rather generally followed. In 1918–19 the president's report simply stated that $800.00 was spent for "books and improvement of library." The same report gave the salary of the librarian as $660.00 for the session of nine months. This was considerably below the average of about $1,200.00 then paid to members of the teaching staff. President Chandler recommended that the salary of the librarian be increased to $1,000.

With the availability of additional space in the middle unit of Virginia Hall (1926–27), library expenditures increased. By 1927–28 a total of $3,985.87 was being expended, of which $2,140.55 was for salaries, $38.71 for library supplies and $1,806.61 for books, magazines, and periodicals.[8]

During the depression years, expenditures for the library were necessarily limited. The president's annual report showed $5,386.19 expended in 1932–33; $4,862.65 in 1933–34; and $4,574.26 in 1934–35. Salaries continued at a low level. In 1933–34, for example, the librarian received a salary of $1,770 for the session of nine months; the assistant librarian (then not professionally trained) received $910 for the session. The student aides were paid less than twenty-five cents an hour.

As plans for a new library building began to take form, expenditures for library purposes began to rise. In 1940–41 total expenditures were $9,052.69;[9] in 1941–42 they totaled $27,693.89, a large part of which was for equipment for the new library building;[10] in 1942–43 expenditures totaled $9,858.22.[11] In September 1943 Carrol H. Quenzel became librarian.

[8] Annual Financial Report, Session of 1927–28.
[9] Presidents Annual Report, July 1941. [10] *Ibid.*, July 25, 1942.
[11] *Ibid.*, Aug. 17, 1943.

CARROL H. QUENZEL

Carrol H. Quenzel joined the faculty as assistant professor of library science. A trained librarian, with a B.S. in library science from the University of Illinois, he offered courses at Mary Washington in reference and bibliography, school library administration, and supervised practice in library science. Students who worked with him during this period found his instruction thorough and stimulating, and many of them went to graduate school to become professional librarians.

Dr. Quenzel was head librarian from the time of his appointment to the faculty. He advanced rapidly to a full professorship. In anticipation of the discontinuance of the professional library courses, his title was changed in 1947 to librarian and professor of history. For the next twenty-one years he taught courses in history in addition to his duties as librarian. In 1960 the title secretary of the faculty was added.

A native of West Virginia, Dr. Quenzel received his B.S. and M.A. degrees from West Virginia University and his Ph.D. in history from the University of Wisconsin. Before coming to Mary Washington College, he had taught in the public schools of West Virginia and at Morris Harvey College.

Dr. Quenzel has been described as an "industrious and indefatigable worker."[12] He contributed extensively to historical quarterlies and library journals. Articles by him appeared in the *Virginia Magazine of History and Biography,* the *Tennessee Historical Quarterly,* the *Southeastern Librarian, West Virginia History,* and the *Ohio Historical Quarterly,* to name a few. He also published numerous book reviews.

He was active in both historical and library associations and was a former president of the Virginia Library Association. When the publication of the *Virginia Librarian* was begun in 1943, he edited it for the first three years. He had served as chairman of the Wallace Library board in Fredericksburg, and at the time of his death he was completing a second five-year term on the state board for the certification of librarians.

Dr. Quenzel's acquaintance with the book collection was amazing. It is said that he had seen five out of six books in the library in some fashion. This is believable, for he personally ordered so many of the books in a collection that grew from some 30,000

---

[12] See tributes to Dr. Quenzel in the *Virginia Librarian* 15, no. 3 (1968): 23-25.

bound volumes to nearly 200,000 during the twenty-five years of his tenure.

In October 1953, Dr. Quenzel prepared a bibliography by subject of the books on India in the college library. Nearly three hundred items are listed. Subsequently in December 1966, he published *A Bibliography of Books, Periodicals and Recordings Pertaining to Asia in the Library of Mary Washington College of the University of Virginia*. This bibliography listed approximately forty-two hundred items, arranged by geographical sections with subject subheads under each.

Another major bibliographical publication was a 250-page volume entitled *Principal Holdings in Art and Architecture in the Library of Mary Washington College of the University of Virginia*. Published in 1967, it was compiled jointly by Dr. Quenzel and Marguerite L. Carder, reference librarian, with the cooperation of the art department. Over forty-four hundred items were listed, classified by periods, by country, and by medium or type of expression. Thirty-eight art dictionaries and encyclopedias in half a dozen languages were listed on the first two pages of this comprehensive bibliography of art publications owned by the library.

In 1951 Dr. Quenzel wrote *The History and Background of St. George's Episcopal Church, Fredericksburg, Virginia*. It was published by the vestry of the church and printed by Clyde W. Saunders and Sons in Richmond, Virginia. The volume contained a wealth of information relating to this historic church. The hundreds of footnotes and citations of sources were typical of Dr. Quenzel's careful research and documentation.

Dr. Quenzel, or Doctor Q as he was known affectionately throughout the college community, became something of a campus legend. His memory for names and detail was amazing. He could greet hundreds of students by name, tell where they were from, and usually add some detail about them. He never forgot a student who had been in any of his classes over the years, and he often had large classes in American history.

His early rising was legendary. He was usually in his office at the library before seven, even during vacation periods. His capacity for productive work was enormous, yet he always had time for friendly contacts with visitors to the library. One never seemed to be interrupting his work. Many faculty members will recall his warm greeting on entering the library and the delight he took in showing them some new acquisition in their fields of interest. He made a point of knowing the reading interests of his

The Library

colleagues and took pleasure in bringing out some new book to show them. "I have the card inside, if you'd like to sign for it." Few could resist his gracious interest in their own reading.

Dr. Quenzel was conservative in dress, manner, and habits. He always wore a hat outdoors, grey felt in winter, panama in summer. His only concession to recklessness in dress was setting his hat at a rakish angle at times. Most of the year he wore a gray suit with vest, and his neckties were always inconspicuous hues.

Dr. Quenzel often took part in dramatic productions at the college. In *Caesar and Cleopatra*, the last one in which he appeared, he played the role of the Egyptian librarian. He brought down the house when he rushed on stage, exclaiming, "O, the library is burning."

On one occasion Dr. Quenzel was describing at a faculty meeting the many demands made on his staff for materials on unusual subjects. "Just recently," he reported, "we were asked for reference material on embalming."

"What kind of course could it have been that the professor assigned reading like this?" asked the president, with some interest.

Before the librarian could manage to think of a reply, a voice from the back of the room, unmistakably that of Emil Schnellock, said in low but clearly audible tones, "It must have been a stiff course."

Dr. Quenzel had a certain dignity and courtliness of manner. He was not one to use first names on short acquaintance, except for his fellow members of the Rotary Club. His manner toward students and colleagues was always respectful, never familiar.

Dr. Quenzel considered himself first of all a teacher. Students in his classes in historical research produced term papers worthy of classification as honors projects. Some of these papers are catalogued among the library holdings. Of especial interest is a carefully documented history of the old Fredericksburg College, known first as "The Assembly's Home and School." He spent many hours helping his students in their research. His corrections on these papers show his regard for careful written expression. He always admired good writing.

Dr. Quenzel spent many of his summers teaching at various outstanding library schools, including the universities of Michigan, Minnesota, Wisconsin, and Florida State, as well as Peabody College in Nashville.

For many years Dr. Quenzel was secretary of the faculty. His minutes provided a careful coverage of important actions. He was always precise. When a meeting ended, he would turn to the dean and say, "What time is it by your watch?" He duly recorded the exact minute of adjournment.

Dr. Quenzel died in his sleep in the early morning of June 3, 1968, just the day after he had taken part in the graduation procession at Mary Washington. Funeral services were held at St. George's Episcopal Church, where he had served on the vestry for many years. He was buried in Oak Hill Cemetery.

DR. QUENZEL'S FIRST YEAR

As soon as Dr. Quenzel became librarian, he plunged immediately into the task of building the book collection both quantitatively and qualitatively. In this effort he enlisted the assistance of subject matter specialists on the faculty, both in recommending books for purchase and in the more tedious job of scanning books on the shelves and recommending titles to be discarded as out-of-date and useless for practical purposes. Through his long tenure as librarian, Dr. Quenzel continued to weed out books for discard, constantly improving the quality of the collection.

The first annual report of the new librarian for the fiscal year ending June 30, 1944, is tangible evidence of the remarkable growth of the library during a single twelve-month period. Exactly 10,001 books were accessioned, an increase of 8,426 volumes over the previous year. When the books yet to be catalogued were included, the number of titles added to the library during the year totaled over 12,000, bringing the total number of books and pamphlets in the collection to over 50,000.

Library services were expanded. A list of books catalogued each month was prepared and distributed to each faculty member requesting a copy. Notice slips were sent to department heads as new books requested by the department were available. Exhibitions of latest books received were kept in the reference room. A file of catalogues from other colleges was set up. Conducted tours of the library were made available as first-year English classes learned the use of various reference materials. During Dr. Quenzel's first year he improved greatly the periodical collection, increasing to 318 the number of purchased and gift subscriptions. Bound files of standard journals were also built up.

Dr. Quenzel set as one of his major goals an increase in student use of the library. He reported proudly that 53,423 books were checked out during his first session as librarian, of which 33,901 were from the main desk and 19,522 from the reserve room.[13] Dr. Quenzel expressed regret that there was no count of books used by readers in the reference room, periodical room, or browsing room, as there had been a decided increase in the use of these facilities.

CONTINUED GROWTH, 1943-68

Perhaps the best characterization of the library during the twenty-five years of Dr. Quenzel's administration is that it was a period of growth and development in number and quality of books and periodicals in the collection, of extension of library services and activities, and of increases in professional and clerical staff.

During the period from 1943 to 1968 the number of bound volumes grew from 35,074 to 185,916; periodicals received, from 225 to 846; and annual expenditure for library purposes from $9,858.22 in 1943 to $166,474.70 in 1968.

LIBRARY STAFF

When Dr. Quenzel became librarian in September 1943, Bernard Fry was still on leave of absence. Mary L. Fleet and Sara Lamon were assistant librarians during the session of 1942-43. They were succeeded in 1943 by Margaret D. Dickinson and Julia M. Lutz. Caroline Willis also served as an assistant librarian during this period.

During the 1940s the library staff increased in number as the book collection and library services continued to grow, from three full-time members in 1943 to thirteen in 1968. Frequent changes in personnel during the early part of this period make a listing of staff members impractical. However, a few individuals should be mentioned. John W. Dudley, now an assistant archivist in the Virginia State Library, was head of cataloguing from 1945 to 1947; Ruth Wade was reference librarian from 1947 to 1949 when she resigned to become dean of freshmen, Marguerite L. Carder joined the staff in 1948; and Marian Reed Watts in January 1952.

Marguerite L. Carder, a graduate of the College of William

[13] Annual Report of the Librarian, July 24, 1944, p. 2.

and Mary, with the B.S. in library science from the University of North Carolina, was a member of the library staff for twenty-one years. Before coming to Fredericksburg she had been a teacher and school librarian in the Roanoke public schools and assistant librarian at the James Kilbourne Library in Ohio. She joined the staff as serials and acquisitions librarian. Two years later she became reference librarian, and from 1950 to 1969 she filled this important role.

In 1958 Miss Carder prepared a handbook to "facilitate and make enjoyable" the use of the library. It gave detailed information on the location and arrangement of the various collections and explained how to locate and charge out books, periodicals, and records. The handbook proved so useful that it was revised and reprinted in 1963, 1966, and 1968.

Marguerite Carder was acting librarian for a two-month period during the 1966-67 session when Dr. Quenzel was hospitalized and convalescent after a heart attack. She acted as head librarian during the entire 1968-69 session while Dr. Daniel Woodward was taking courses in library science at Catholic University. During the summer of 1969 she resigned to be with ill members of her family in Roanoke. She has continued to engage in library work on a part-time basis there.

Marian Reed Watts was a member of the library staff from January 1952 to June 1971. A native of Fredericksburg, she had graduated from Goucher College and also received a B.S. in library science from Drexel Institute. She was on the staff of the library at Teachers College, Columbia University, and of the District of Columbia Public Library before becoming an officer in the WAVES during World War II. She stayed on in the Navy Department as librarian for the Bureau of Naval Personnel in Washington until she resigned to return to Fredericksburg and to become head of circulation at the E. Lee Trinkle Library. Eighteen months later, in September 1953, Mrs. Watts became head of cataloguing, a position she held until her retirement eighteen years later.

A staff manual for E. Lee Trinkle was compiled by Mrs. Watts in 1952-53. Intended primarily for the use of student aides in the library, the manual was revised in 1958 by Mrs. Reed K. Simmons and in 1963, 1966, and 1969 by Renna Cosner.

A substantial proportion of the staff has been with the library for several years. Renna Cosner, circulation librarian, joined the staff in 1959. She is a graduate of Randolph-Macon Woman's College and the University of Michigan Library School. Mrs. Reed K. Simmons, a graduate of Mary Washington, has served as a library assistant since 1955. Mildred Brooks Ray, of the cataloguing department, has been with the library since 1950. Marion Holt, secretary to the librarian, joined the staff in September 1951. In February 1960 Janie M. Kash, a graduate of Randolph-Macon Woman's College, joined the staff as serials clerk.

In the fall of 1962, Barbara Alden joined the library staff, first as an assistant in the cataloguing division and later as the official archivist of the college. A native of Newton Center, Massachusetts, she received her B.A. and M.A. from Wellesley and her doctorate in English from the University of Chicago. In addition to serving as archivist, Barbara Alden has assisted with the rare book collection, arranged exhibitions for the library, and edited and contributed to library publications. During 1968–69 she participated in the U.S.–India Faculty Exchange Program, serving as librarian at Isabella Thoburn College, in Lucknow, India.

More recent additions to the staff are Mary J. Porter, reference librarian, and Diane L. Fishman, staff bibliographer. A graduate of Mary Washington, Mary Porter has an M.A. from George Washington University and the M.S. in library science from Catholic University. Diane Fishman received her B.A. degree from Cornell University and her M.S. in library science from the University of Illinois. Upon the resignation of Mrs. Watts in 1971, Charles D. Balthis, assistant cataloguer, was made head cataloguer. He holds a B.A. from Randolph-Macon College and the M.S. in library science from Catholic University.

SALARIES FOR LIBRARY STAFF

Professional and clerical positions in libraries in state institutions were, for many years, included under the State Personnel Act, which severely limited the salaries that could be paid. It became difficult to obtain staff members under these conditions.

In 1956–57 the positions of both circulation librarian and acquisitions librarian in the library were unfilled, for competitive salaries could not be offered. Sharing Dr. Quenzel's concern over the situation, Chancellor Simpson began to wage an all-out effort to raise salaries. In 1957–58 he enlisted the support of other members of the President's Council of State Colleges and Universities. By 1958–59 the scale was raised slightly. The clerical staff of state librarians received substantial increases in 1959–60. However, it was not until 1962–63 that the salary scale for professional librarians was raised to a level commensurate with the training and ability required for this work. It was largely through Chancellor Simpson's efforts over a long period that this was brought about.

A TYPICAL YEAR: 1959–60

By June 1960, the book collection had grown to 141,247 volumes, a net increase, after discarding 231 out-of-date volumes, of a total of 5,828. Total expenditures for the library that year were $83,799.98. Circulation of books and related materials reached 109,371. Dr. Quenzel reported that a "total 4,268 reference questions were answered; 50 books and dissertations were borrowed from other libraries and 75 were loaned to libraries. Seventy exhibits were arranged."[14]

Since a state appropriation of $430,000 had been made for an addition to the library, the staff devoted much thought and discussion to what should be included in the enlargement and renovation of the building.

In December 1960, Dr. Charles A. Sletten published a detailed survey of the library. Concerned chiefly with determining student use of and attitudes toward the library, it was undertaken as a project by two of Dr. Sletten's classes in methods of social research. Dr. Sletten directed the presentation and interpretation of the material. The survey proved helpful when plans were being made for the addition to the library and the renovation of existing facilities.

The Self-Study Report of March 1962, prepared for the use of a visiting committee of the Southern Association of Colleges and Secondary Schools, devoted a whole section to the library. As in the case of other similar surveys, both faculty and students rated the library staff and services highly. Ninety-seven percent of the faculty gave "excellent" or "very good" ratings on the efficiency and effectiveness of the staff. As with the Sletten survey, student evaluation of the helpfulness of the staff was almost unanimously high.

ADDITION TO LIBRARY

In 1960 the General Assembly appropriated $430,000 for an addition to the library. Chancellor Simpson had given top priority

[14] *Ibid.*, Aug. 25, 1960, p. 3.

to this item in his budget requests. The cost of the addition and its equipment and the alterations made to the existing part of the library totaled some $465,000, or more than twice the cost of the original building.

Library services were carried on without interruption throughout the construction period. The entire wall facing the amphitheatre was removed and heavy cellophane used as a makeshift wall to keep out the wintry blasts. In spite of dust, noise, and cold drafts, the library continued to function. Construction continued throughout the first semester of the 1962–63 session. It was not until the beginning of the second semester that the entire job of construction and renovation was completed.

The new addition increased the capacity of the library from 150,000 to 250,000 books. The added space made possible an open-stack system of library usage long sought by Dr. Quenzel. There were two new 100-foot reading rooms across the back of the building overlooking the open-air theater. The one on the first floor became a new reserve book room, while the second floor room provided more extensive space for periodicals. The former reserve book room was converted into a catalogue and bibliographical reference room, and 280 new card trays were provided.

Rare books were moved to the newly air-conditioned Virginia Room. New twin circulation desks in the rotunda expedited the checking out and return of books. In the older section of the building the heating and lighting were vastly improved. Recessed lighting was installed in the ceilings of all reading rooms. The two subbasements provided greatly increased space for the shelving of books. There were many more individual study carrels, including soundproof booths in which typewriters could be used. An elevator for staff use was installed. The entire new addition was air conditioned.

A NEW LIBRARIAN

Daniel H. Woodward took over the duties as head librarian in July 1969. The previous academic year he had attended, on leave of absence, the library school of Catholic University, where he had received his M.S. in library science in June 1969.

Dr. Woodward was born in Texas. He received his B.A. and M.A. at the University of Colorado and the Ph.D. from Yale University, majoring in English. Dr. Woodward joined the faculty in 1957 as assistant professor of English. He became an associate professor in 1961 and professor in 1966. He was appointed librarian and secretary of the faculty to succeed Dr. Quenzel.

Dr. Woodward believed that a library should strive to attract readers rather than wait for them to appear. He envisioned as a major concern the relevancy of the contents of the library to the program of the college. A collector of seventeenth-century English books himself, Dr. Woodward expressed his hope that the collection of rare books could be enlarged. His point of view is well expressed in an article he wrote for the *Alumnae News,* entitled "On the Relevancy of Rare Books." [15]

During the session of 1964–65, Dr. Woodward was on leave of absence for research in England, primarily on the seventeenth-century poet Robert Fletcher. This opportunity was made available through an Alumnae Association grant.[16] In 1970 Dr. Woodward published an edition of Fletcher's poems and translations.

Upon becoming librarian Dr. Woodward began a series of regular staff meetings at which ways of improving the library and its services were discussed. Through the enthusiastic cooperation of his capable and experienced staff, a number of projects were initiated that brought the library to a new level of efficiency.

THE RARE BOOK ROOM

For some time an MWC collection of rare books had been the goal of Dr. Woodward, then an associate professor of English, and a lover of good books.

During the summer of 1963, Chancellor Simpson appointed a rare book committee consisting of Dr. Woodward, Dr. Sidney H. Mitchell, Dr. Pauline G. King, and Dr. Lawrence A. Wishner of the faculty, and Dr. Gordon W. Jones, local physician, to assist Dr. Quenzel in setting up such a collection.

An account of the development of this project appears in the *Alumnae News.* A room located on the second floor, formerly devoted to the collection of Virginiana, was selected to house the rare book collection. From the start, the committee emphasized that the rare book room was not a museum or repository behind glass barriers, but rather, as Dr. Mitchell, the first chairman, put it, "an integral part of the library, and its contents are purchased

---

[15] *Alumnae News* 21, no. 3 (1969): 5–6.   [16] *Ibid.* 16, no. 4 (1964): 1.

The Library

and cared for solely in order that they may be available to students and faculty for examination, study, and research."[17]

Since the rare book room opened in the fall of 1964, purchases and gifts have enriched the collection greatly. The Alumnae Association had made possible the acquisition of a number of rare volumes, presented as memorial gifts in recognition of a series of retiring members of the faculty and administrative staff. Individual faculty members and friends of the college have contributed books from time to time.

The rare book collection owes much of its value and interest to the enthusiasm of Dr. Woodward, librarian of the college from 1968 to 1972. His knowledge of books and his ability to acquire choice items at a reasonable cost have enabled the college to acquire the nucleus of a collection that by 1972 numbered well over a thousand volumes. When Dr. Woodward departed in June 1972 to become librarian of the Huntington Library, the rare book room was renamed in his honor.

SUBJECT-AREA READING ROOMS

During the 1969–70 session the new librarian made a number of changes in the arrangement of the library. Notable among them were the provisions for the collections in certain disciplines to be shelved in special rooms where interested students could find more readily the material available for reading and study in these fields.

First to be established was the philosophy library in what had been the former browsing room. An art library was established in what had once been the Mendel Museum; a psychology library was set up in Room 1; and a geography library was assembled in Room 3 and the adjoining room.

Other improvements during the year included additional space and shelving for the periodical library, rearrangement in a more functional way of the reference and bibliography collections, and new space for microfilm readers, film cabinets, and the Xerox machine. New record players were installed in booths off the reserve room, convenient to the record collection.

---

[17] Joseph Terrell, "Rare Book Room Open for Students," *ibid*. 17, no. 2 (1965): 1–2.

ARCHIVES

Also during the 1969-70 session, the college archives were established. Room 2 was developed for this purpose, and shelves and cabinets installed. All records and materials relating to the history and development of the college were assembled there. Among the notable accomplishments have been assembling extensive files of faculty and alumnae publications; programs of plays, recitals, concerts, and dance performances; folders of clippings on present and past faculty and administrative officers; and a complete file on all the paintings exhibited, with names of artists, purchase awards, and members of committees involved in the series of modern art exhibitions which took place from 1956 to 1965.

Sets of the college catalogues and bulletins as well as other official publications are shelved there. There are files of the *Bullet,* the *Battlefield,* the *Bayonet,* and the *Epaulet,* along with schedules of classes, copies of the *Alumnae News,* faculty directories, hundreds of photographs, and a mass of other useful information relating to the college over the years.

LIBRARY PUBLICATIONS

Under Dr. Woodward's administration the library began a series of publications designed to acquaint students with its resources and services and to increase interest in its activities.

An Introduction to Reading and Research in Trinkle Library, an annotated bibliography of reference works in the library, was first published in the fall of 1969 and a copy given to each entering freshman. It became the basis for a week-long orientation program for freshmen conducted by all members of the library staff. Revised in 1970 and again in 1971, the bibliography has continued to be useful to both students and faculty members.

Two new series of publications were started in 1969-70. *Trinkle Little Star,* a newsletter designed to stimulate interest in the library and limited to circulation on the campus, appeared in January 1970 and again in April. It included articles on archival matters, bibliographies on selected topics, articles by students and faculty members, and notes about library activities. It is published twice a year.[18]

[18] In October 1972 *Trinkle Little Star* was succeeded by *News and Views from Trinkle.* Volume 1, no. 1 appeared as of that date; four issues a year are planned.

The library's *Occasional Papers* began publication in December 1969. The first issue contained addresses by John B. Blake and Edward Alvey, Jr.—"Of Medical Books and Libraries" and "The Assembly Meets at Jamestown," respectively. Subsequent issues have included articles on a few outstanding exhibitions connected with the library.

Other publications of the library include *Book Odds and Ends*, an annotated bibliography of new books of interest, published periodically, and various bulletins for the information of library users, such as "How to Find U.S. Government Documents." "Newspapers Currently Received," "New Subscriptions to Periodicals," and "Notes about Reserve Books."

EXHIBITIONS

One of the most interesting services of the library for many years has been its exhibitions of books or materials related to some current news event, a lecture or play to be given on campus, or simply a collection of articles, prints, or other materials related to some topic or hobby of literary interest.

Visiting lecturers are delighted to find an exhibition of their books and articles on display when they arrive. The library staff has always taken pride in the number and quality of its holdings of the visitor's publications. Mark Van Doren, for example, was particularly impressed by the display of twenty-odd volumes of his published works. In his delightful way, he remarked, "I don't believe that even Columbia University has this many of my publications."

Two exhibitions during 1962 were of special interest. In March a collection of illuminated manuscripts owned by Harry A. Walton, Jr., of Covington was placed on display. The June 1962 alumnae homecoming was the occasion of an exhibition of alumnae publications in the library. Thirty alumnae were represented in the collection of printed publications assembled by Dr. Quenzel and Bettie V. Griffith, then executive secretary of the Alumnae Association. A catalogue of the exhibition is preserved in the archives.

A book exhibit on the fine arts was arranged in the library in connection with the 1964 Alumnae College, which had as its theme, "The Creative Arts in a Liberal Education." The 1965 alumnae homecoming featured the library. The Alumnae College was devoted to lectures on "The Library—Opportunity for

Individual Excellence." Tours of the library and special exhibits of publications were provided.

A list of recent exhibitions indicate the wide range of topics covered. Among the 1969–70 exhibits were "The Worlds of Dr. Q.," in memory of Dr. Quenzel; "Seventeenth-Century English Poetry in Trinkle Library"; "Printing in Six Centuries"; "A Selection of Works by and about American Negro Writers"; "Wordsworth and the Romantics"; and "Collecting for Anybody: The Works of John Updike."

There have been several rather impressive exhibitions for which catalogues were printed and formal openings held. The first of these was "Illustrations of the History of Medicine: An Exhibition of Books from the Private Library of Gordon W Jones, M.D." The exhibition opened on October 22, 1969, and included an address by John B. Blake on medical books, given in the philosophy library as a feature of the formal opening of this room.

Dr. Jones, a Fredericksburg physician, has served as a member of the rare books committee since its organization. An avid and discriminating collector himself, the exhibition of his rare medical books attracted widespread interest. Requests are still being received for the illustrated, descriptive catalogue of the exhibition.

PLAY READINGS

A series of play readings, the Chamber Theater was initiated in the fall of 1969. Performances took place on Sunday afternoon in the art library. Five programs were given in 1969–70: *The Tragedy of Tragedies, or the History of Tom Thumb the Great; Ubu Roi; A Scrap of Paper; Memorandum;* and *Crime on Goat Island*. During 1970–71 the Chamber Theater presented *The World of Carl Sandburg; Endgame;* and *La Première Famille*.

FACULTY LECTURES

In 1970–71 a new series of faculty lectures entitled Trinkle Library seminars was initiated for Tuesday or Thursday afternoons in the philosophy library. Each speaker prepared a summary of his talk, which was duplicated and distributed to the faculty in advance. Both faculty and students attended, and lively discussions sometimes followed the talks.

Some of the lectures in the 1970–71 series were "The Last Great Renaissance" presented by Bulent I. Atalay; "An Assessment of the Chemical Environment in the Rappahannock River" by Bernard Mahoney; and "Belief Statements and Conscientious Objection," by George M. Van Sant. The series was expanded to ten lectures in 1971–72.

CURRENT EXPENDITURES

During the fiscal year ending June 30, 1971, over a quarter of a million dollars was expended for the library, distributed as follows:

Salaries and wages	$131,442.13
Student aide wages	23,600.94
Books (encumbered: $67,078.84)	55,457.23
Rare books (encumbered: $974.90)	1,213.20
Periodicals	21,665.30
Binding (encumbered: $8,895.80)	7,206.85
Equipment and supplies	4,738.81
Miscellaneous	5,313.37
Total	$250,637.83[19]

It is difficult to realize that for many years during the 1920s the total expenditure for library purposes, salaries, and books was about $7,000 or $8,000 annually.

ACQUISITIONS AND RESOURCES

During the 1970–71 session, acquisitions reached an all-time high of 9,772 volumes. At the same time 1,091 obsolete and defective volumes were weeded out, leaving a net gain of 8,681 volumes. As of June 30, 1971, the collection consisted of 211,087 catalogued volumes. It is the third-largest four-year liberal arts college library collection in Virginia.

The number of periodicals received also reached a new high of 1,223 titles, of which 255 were gifts. Holdings of back issues have also been expanded greatly.

Indications are that by 1974 the book collection will exceed the 250,000-volume capacity of the library. The self-study of 1971 recommended that funds for planning an addition be included in the 1972–74 biennial budget.

[19] Annual Report of the Librarian, 1970–71, p. 10.

AN ALUMNA BECOMES LIBRARIAN

Upon Dr. Woodward's departure in June 1972 to become librarian of the Huntington Library in California Ruby York Weinbrecht succeeded him. A native of South Carolina, she received a B.A. degree with a major in history from Mary Washington College in 1948. Subsequently, she earned the M.A. degree in library science from the George Peabody Library School and completed course and residence requirements for the Ph.D. degree at the graduate library school of the University of Chicago.

A past president of the MWC Alumnae Association, Mrs. Weinbrecht's library experience has been extensive. She has held editing and supervisory positions with the U.S. Department of Commerce and the Library of Congress. She has been acquisitions librarian at Vassar College, regional post librarian with the Army Library Services in Japan, and assistant professor of library science at Ball State University and at Indiana State University.

Before coming to Mary Washington, Mrs. Weinbrecht was chief of the Technical Information Division of the United States Equal Employment Opportunity Commission. Her husband, Standau E. Weinbrecht, is an attorney with the federal government.

GIFTS TO LIBRARY

Over the years the library has been the recipient of frequent and generous gifts of books and other publications. Local citizens have taken an active interest in the library, made use of its facilities, and frequently given valuable books to the collection. To list the more significant contributions would be beyond the limits of this publication. Even to select contributors for special mention is difficult and perhaps rash. However, some names certainly deserve mention.

The late Judge Alvin T. Embrey gave to the library, in March 1943, his outstanding collection of Fredericksburg newspaper files dating back to 1865.[20] Included in the gift were bound volumes of the *Virginia Star*, later the *Fredericksburg Star*, extending from 1877 through 1899, and of the *Daily Star*, later the *Free Lance–Star*, from 1911 to 1938. In July 1945 Kate Doggett

---

[20] *Free Lance–Star*, March 12, 1943.

Boggs of Fredericksburg gave a collection of 270 selected books from the library accumulated by herself and her late husband, Dr. Thomas R. Boggs. Extensive gifts to the library collection have come from John Lee Pratt, C. O'Conor Goolrick, and Dr. Gordon W. Jones. Families of deceased faculty members—Dr. Dice R. Anderson, Dr. Rollin H. Tanner, Dr. Warren G. Keith, to name a few—have given many of their books to the library. Current members of the faculty and administrative staff have contributed generously of books in their special fields. Other benefactors of the library include Elsie Genther, Elizabeth Eckenrode, the Honorable R. Smith Simpson, Mrs. M. J. R. Morris, Mrs. James Ashby, Jr., Mrs. H. I. Brock, Norman Wild, Dr. Richard L. B. Morfit, and the Embassy of India.

The Alumnae Association, as noted elsewhere, has made possible the acquisition of valuable first editions and out-of-print books for the rare book room through its policy of making presentations of highly prized items as memorials to retiring members of the faculty and administrative staff.

CHAPTER XXXV

Gifts to the College

OVER THE YEARS there have been many gifts to the college by alumnae, graduating classes, members of the faculty and staff, and friends of the institution. Whether in money or in other gifts of various kinds, these benefactions have been a constant testimonial of faith in the college, as well as an expression of gratitude for personal benefits derived.

There have been relatively few large gifts to the college, mainly perhaps because of its character as a publicly controlled institution. There are several funds, however, that, through the generosity of their donors, have made possible scholarship funds above and beyond those made available through state and federal loans and grants.

LALLA GRESHAM BALL SCHOLARSHIP FUND

In December 1946 Jessie Ball duPont (Mrs. Alfred I. duPont) established a scholarship fund in memory of her mother, Lalla Gresham Ball, who was a native of Virginia. It was stipulated that applicants be residents of certain counties in the Northern Neck of Virginia or bordering on that area, the ancestral home of the Ball family.

Mrs. du Pont's initial gift of stock was supplemented later by other contributions in cash or securities until, at the time of her death in September 1970, the fund amounted to approximately a hundred and sixty thousand dollars. Income from this principal is used to provide the Lalla Gresham Ball Scholarships.

BIOLOGY SCHOLARSHIPS

In October 1960 a generous but anonymous friend of the college gave $36,900 in securities to provide scholarships to outstanding seniors in biology and biochemistry. The fund also made available financial assistance to graduates of the college planning graduate study in these fields.

CHANCELLOR'S ALUMNAE FUND

In 1961 the Mary Washington College Alumnae Association established the Chancellor's Alumnae Fund with an initial gift of five thousand dollars, to which have been added annually various sums as needed.

Awards are made at the discretion of the chancellor to students, alumnae, and faculty of the college for graduate or special study.

GARI MELCHERS ENDOWMENT

According to the will of Mrs. Gari Melchers of Falmouth, the Melchers estate was deeded to the Commonwealth of Virginia, along with a substantial fund provided for its upkeep. Originally the property was to be administered by the Virginia Museum of Fine Arts. However, by court action in 1961, the control of the estate was transferred to Mary Washington College.

The endowment fund totals about a hundred and thirteen thousand dollars, the income from which is used specifically by the college for the upkeep and operation of the Belmont property.

BOWLEY SCHOLARSHIPS

In September 1962 Elsie Ball Bowley (Mrs. Albert J. Bowley), a sister of Mrs. Alfred I. duPont, gave a total of $65,450 in securities to establish a scholarship fund in memory of her husband, Lieutenant General Albert J. Bowley, and another in memory of Annie Fleming Smith, long executive secretary of the Kenmore Association.

Provisions of the Lieutenant General Bowley award stipulate that the recipient devote a certain amount of her time to the James Monroe Memorial Foundation. In like manner, the recipient of the Annie F. Smith Award is to assist with the activities of the Kenmore Association.

A number of other scholarships have been established as memorials or special awards through private or corporate gifts. There are also state and federal programs providing scholarship assistance.

Index

Index

Abbitt, Frances Emily, 123
Academia Italiana, L', 591
Academic counseling and guidance, 415-18
Academic counselors, 502-3
Academic dress, 392
Academic probation and suspension, 399
Academic recognition, 465
Academic standards, 284, 353, 360-61, 379, 413
A capella choir. *See* Chorus
Accreditation, 164-65, 438
Adams, Charles M., 440
Adams, Theodore F., 375, 377
Administration, 11-12, 69, 181, 183-84, 283, 337-40, 379, 380, 512-13. *See also specific offices and officers*
Administration building, 28, 30, 32, 40-41, 55, 92, 234-35
Admission requirements, 41-42, 288-89, 360, 380, 400, 413-14, 434, 442
Admissions counselors, 502
Adult education, 258
Afro-American Club, 432
Agnew, Donald C., 440
Agricultural program, 76-77
Akers, Joan Marie, 527
Akers, Nancy, 273
Albert Klein Memorial Fund, 619
Albert Roger Klein Memorial Theatre, 619
Alden, Barbara, 451, 452, 641
Alderman, Edwin A., 8, 176
Aldridge, Frederick M., 18
Alexander, Fred M., 145
Allen, Philip J., 307, 505, 589
Alley, Alden C., 169
Allison, Edward V., Jr., 468, 500, 502
Alma Mater, 144, 326-27, 530
Almond, J. Lindsay, Jr., 406, 424, 442
Almond, Mrs. J. Lindsay, Jr., 406
Alpha Epsilon, 567

Alpha Phi Sigma, 127, 571; award, 127, 341, 433, 571
Alpha Psi Omega, 578, 610, 614
Alpha Tau Pi, 96, 579; award, 579
Alsop, Wallace, 109-10, 201, 241
Alstetter, Michael Louis, 159, 181, 571; biographical data, 160; Combs and, 180-81
Alstetter, Mrs. Michael Louis, 160
Alstetter affair, 180-82
Alumnae (Alumni) Association, 132, 150, 318, 487, 651; activities, 522; American Alumni Council Convention award, 531; annual giving, 536, 537, 538, 542-43; banquet, 522; Brompton Fund, 529; Chancellor's Fund, 536, 537, 538, 653; chapters, 520, 522, 528-29, 531; class agents, 531; constitution and bylaws, 524, 525, 536; dues, 530, 537; editor, 539; election of officers, 532; executive secretary (director of alumnae affairs), 519, 523-25, 528-34, 536, 538-40, 542, 544; fellowship grants, 442; founding, 517; Golden Anniversary Banquet, 407; handbook, 525, 542; headquarters, 524, 530-31, 534; honoring of Dean Alvey, 539-40; honoring of Emily A. Holloway, 543; honoring of Chancellor Simpson, 538; honoring of Reginald W. Whidden, 543; honoring of Edgar E. Woodward, 543; incorporation, 529; life membership, 518, 525-26, 530, 531; meetings, 519; membership, 520, 525-26, 531, 536; Phi Beta Kappa grant, 543; program, 518; publications, 541, 542; record book, 523; Reed and Barton Silver Collection, 541; scholarship fund, 518, 523, 537; seal, 528; senior class day, 537; student-alumnae building

Alumnae Association (*cont.*)
  plans, 519; study abroad aid, 539.
  See also Homecoming
Alumnae College, 448, 535, 536-38
Alumnae Council, 536, 542
Alumnae Daughters' Club, 361, 526
Alumnae Daughters Cup, 365, 526
Alumnae Fund, 528, 533, 535, 537, 542
Alumnae House, 297, 421, 533, 534
Alumnae News (Bulletin), 524, 525, 528-32, 534-35, 537, 541, 542. See also *Bullet*
"Alumnae Notes," 521
Alvey, Edward, Jr., 182, 188, 191, 192, 280, 313, 325, 326, 457, 505, 537, 538, 544, 580, 597; on admission committee, 360; biographical data, 183-84; in Combs anniversary celebration, 236; concert-lecture series and, 388; on curriculum committee, 399; as dean of the college, 198-99; as director of teacher training, 183; in dramatics program, 610, 614; in entertainments, 202, 218; Faculty Men's Club and, 222; on faculty salaries, 354; message to class of 1939, 237; nomination for president, 362; in Phi Beta Kappa, 509, 510, 511; report on liberal arts program, 284-85; responsibilities, 338-40; retirement, 499, 539-40; in self-study program, 438; on Simpson inauguration committee, 372, 375; on student teaching, 223, 224; summer session in Spain, 462; on teacher training, 289-90; trip abroad, 383; in war bond program, 259, 267; Whidden and, 270
Alvey, Ellen, 250
American Association of Teachers Colleges, 119, 165
American Association of University Women, 446
American Civil Liberties Union, 432
American College Testing Program, 460
American Guild of Organists, 587
American Ideals and Institutions, 311
American studies, 311
Ammerman, Sheila, 365
Among the Columns, 415-16, 605
Amory, Gwendolyn, 498
Anderson, Dice R., 256, 261, 651

Anderson, Mrs. Dice R. (Martha Hardy), 261
Anderson, Henry W., 79-80
Anderson, Jayne, 262-63, 498, 529
Anderson, Martha Hardy, 232
Anderson, Mrs. Van, 529
Andrews, Mary Jane, 249, 574
Annapolis Color Girl, 447
Ann Carter Lee Hall, 217, 317-19, 483-84
Anne Fairfax Hall, 153, 172, 385
Annie F. Smith Award, 653
Ansari, Zeba, 451
Anthony, Annie I., 28, 36
Antioch College, 1
Antiwar demonstrations, 489-91, 497
Aposhyan, Joseph, 535
Apple Blossom Festival princess, 447
Apprentice teaching, 209-10
Archaeological finds, 18
Archaeology Club, 592
Arms, George W., 276
Armstrong, Ethel, 447
Armstrong, Sarah Margaret, 250, 498
Armstrong, S. C., 7
Arnold, Marjorie E., 505
Art and humanities institute, 478
Art Club, 130, 583
Art collection, 392, 409, 430, 486-87
Art exhibitions, 373, 404, 432, 447, 486-88, 541
Art program, 130, 238, 239, 287, 301, 303-7, 321-22, 341, 434, 467. *See also* Fine arts *entries*
Arts-lecture series, 388
Arts Weekend, 541
Ashby, Frances Goolrick, 15-16
Ashby, James, 24, 54
Ashby, Mrs. James, 651
Ashley, Beatrice, 517
Asian studies program, 475-76, 479
Assemblies, 52, 387, 419
Association of Colleges and Secondary Schools of the Southern States, 164-65
Atalay, Bulent I., 423
Athenaeum, 591-92
Athletic Association, 63, 67, 80, 174, 547, 548-51, 603
Athletic Association Council, 549
Athletic Recreation Association, 549

Index

Athletics. *See* Physical education program; *individual sports*
Aubade, 602
Audiometry, 325
Auditorium, 234-35, 608
August, Catherine Dryden, 541
Augusta Female Seminary, 4
Avery, Emily, 219
Avery, Milton, 488
Awards and honors: Alpha Phi Sigma, 127, 341, 433, 571; Alpha Tau Pi, 579; Alumnae Daughters Cup, 365, 526; Darden, 127, 432-33, 448; distinction awards, 465; Distinguished Alumna, 523, 539, 540, 541, 543, 544; Jefferson Cup, 341, 527, 540; Kiwanis Cup, 230, 341, 497-98, 540; Schnellock, 432; Simpson, 479; Woodrow Wilson, 447

B.A. degree program, 121, 187-90, 286-87
Bailey, Grace, 258
Bailey, Rufus W., 4
Baker, Elizabeth W., 158
Baker, Mary Catherine, 261
Baldwin, Mary, 4
Ball, Joseph, 195
Ball, Mrs. Joseph (Mary Johnson), 195
Ball Circle, 197
Ballets, 247-51
Balogh, Erno, 328
Balthis, Charles D., 509, 641
Bamforth, Grace Marie, 498
Band. *See* Dance band; Mary Washington College Band
Baptists, 3, 6, 9, 51, 595, 596
Barbour & Sons, 194
Barnett, Roberta Louise, 155, 609
Barney, Esther, 228
Bartenstein, Katherine, 47
Basketball, 47, 71, 78, 80, 548, 549
Bass, Michael, 502
Battle, John S., 322
Battlefield, 60, 71, 104, 597-98; dedications, 597; verse, 65-66
Bauman, A. R., 59
Baylor, Betty, 333
Bayonet, 83, 398, 547, 603
Beanie snatching, 444
Bear, Mrs. James Edwin, Jr. (Margaret Irving White), 599
Beauty contest, 219, 274

Beazley, Grace, 519
Beck, Charles F., 297, 534
Bedinger, Anne Ware, 538
Beeler, Guenndolyn A., 502, 505
Belford, Mrs. Lloyd Earl (Aileen Hirschman), 539
Bell, Alden, 13, 20, 25, 26
Bell, Jean, 529
Belmont, 428-30
Benedict, Mary K., 5
Benefits, 217-19, 254
Bennett, Constance Mae, 498
Bennett, Rose Marie, 498
Benton, Rachel Jane, 393, 394, 505
Bermuda, 407-8
Bernard, Mrs. Edgar (Katherine Nicks), 522
Betty Lewis Building Corporation, 112
Betty Lewis Hall, 112-13, 173, 298, 422, 485
Beverly, Mrs. Walter F. (Martha Belle Pearce), 60, 64, 517, 538, 597
Bidwell, Carolyn Suzanne, 342
Big Sister–Little Sister program, 345
Billingsley, Betty, 154
Billman, Carl, 509
Bill of rights, 492
Binford, Jesse H., 523
Binford, Julian, 303-5, 339, 372, 373, 404, 443, 486-88, 505; biographical data, 303-4
Binford, Mrs. Julien (Elizabeth Bollée de Vautibault), 303, 487
Binns, Mrs. C. D., 228
Biology program, 257, 288, 301, 478
Biology scholarships, 652-53
Birchett, Ruth, 526
Birckhead, E. F., 75
Bird, Hugh S., 28, 34, 35, 43, 56
Bird, Samuel O., 456, 457, 477
Biscoe, H. Curtis, 51
Bivens, Willie, 123
Black, Barron F., 322, 337, 362
Black, Zoe W. C., 271, 427, 437, 505
Blackburn, Barbara, 302
Blackburn, Joseph E., 513
Blacks, 506-7
Blackstone College for Girls, 9
Blackwell, Betty, 526
Blankenship, A. Hugo, 341
Blood donors, 266

Board of Virginia Teachers Colleges, 115, 118, 153, 166
Board of visitors, 512, 513
Boggs, Kate Doggett, 650-51
Boggs, Thomas R., 651
Boillin, Louise, 159
Boise, Patricia Mae, 498, 527
Bolling, Mrs. J. Brawner (Mildred McMurtry), 146, 268, 302, 339, 367, 372, 399, 435, 446, 468, 505, 509, 536, 590, 592; biographical data, 148-51
Bonum, Mrs. Samuel (Elizabeth Ball), 195
Boody, Robert T., 268-69
Boogher, Dudley, 111
Booker, Claire Talley, 502
Bookstore, 318, 418
Booth, Dorothy B., 342
Bosher, Kate Langley, 80
Botetourt Springs, Female Seminary, 3-4
Boulware, Mrs. D. J., 293
Bowen, Marshall E., 478
Bowering, A. B., 20, 23, 60
Bowie, Charles Ryland, 351
Bowie, Rudy, 365
Bowles, Betty, 302
Bowley, Albert J., 653
Bowley, Mrs. Albert J. (Elsie Ball), 653
Bowley scholarships, 653
Bowling, Ann Mitchell, 527
Boyce, Judy, 541
Boyle, Jean Eleanor, 526
Boyle, Lucy Kennedy, 538
Bozelle, Frances, 248
Bozicevic, Joseph, 475, 591
Bradford, J. H., 165
Bradley, Amelia Jane, 498
Bradley, Joshua, 3
Bragg, Jacquelin Morton, 527
Bragg, Susan Baker, 527
Branch, Peggy, 154
Braxton, Gail G., 501
Breeden, Evelyn H., 406
Brennand, William, 204, 205, 261
Brenner, Vladimir V., 275, 446
Brent, Mrs. Lawrance, 446
Brent, Margaret, 293
Brent Hall, 131, 293
Brickhouse, Joan, 498
Bridgewater College, 9
Brill, Aloise, 248, 576, 577

Bristow, Bates Miller, 527
Bristow, Joyce Lee, 527
Brittain, Vera, 407
Brittle, Frances Earle, 527
Broaddus, Lottie, 548
Brock, Mrs. H. I., 651
Broderick, Kathleen Joyce, 448
Brompton, 131, 294-96, 529
Brooks, Elliott E., Jr., 351
Brooks, Marion, 581
Brooks, Reynold H., 372
Brown, Emma Ziegler, 542
Brown, George Elmer, 268
Brown, Guy H., 224, 230
Brown, Irene Lundy, 513
Brown, J. Sinclair, 277
Brumble, Mrs. W. D., 529
Bryan, John Stuart, 79
Bryson, Herman J., 588
B.S. degree program, 121, 187, 188-89, 286, 474
Buck, Mrs. J. L. Blair, 374
Buckingham Female College, 3
Budget, 200
Building and grounds. See Maintenance
Building program, 24-28, 30, 39-41, 55, 102, 124, 132-36, 138, 169, 172, 193-94, 200, 201, 233, 238, 293, 316, 350, 402, 419, 421-23, 480, 520, 521, 530
Bullet, 265, 334, 342, 523-24, 533, 599-601
Bulletin, 602, 603-4, 605; "Training School Course of Study," 75
Bulley, Stanley F., 322, 354, 377, 505
Buni, Andrew, 468
Bunnell, Elizabeth Taliaferro, 527
Burch, Thomas G., 166
Burchell, Bernard T., 351
Burgess, Mary Alston, 498
Burke-Hudson, 234
Burney, Mary Vick, 624
Burns, Grover P., 423
Burns, Preston, 505
Burr, Aaron, 196
Burrows, Ruth, 580
Burruss, Julian A., 24, 70, 277
Bursar, 201, 436
Bushey, Jewell H., 509
Bushnell, Mrs. Charles Lake (Nina Gookin), 49, 103, 121, 146, 171, 539; *Battlefield* and, 597, 598; biographical data, 103; as dean of women, 103-8; dramatics program and, 608;

Index

Bushnell, Mrs. Charles Lake (*cont.*) flood service, 264; German Club and, 214; May Day and, 248; retirement, 315, 529-30
Bushnell Hall, 402, 421-22, 480
Business administration, 199, 200
Business administration program, 287
Business manager, 500
Byrd, Harry F., 15, 165

Cabrera, Louis J., 268, 272-74, 275, 590
Cafeteria, 485
Calhoun, Margaret D., 625-26, 627, 632-33
Cambodia, 490
Campus police. *See* Security force
Campus roadways, 485-86
Campus Training School, 138, 191-92
Cap and Gown, 404, 535, 583-85
Carder, Marguerite L., 636, 639-40
Carmichael, Helen W., 121
Carmichael, Leonard, 407
Carnegie Endowment for International Peace, 572
Carpenter, Miriam, 578, 610
Carter, Charles, 113, 319
Carter, Mrs. Charles (Betty Lewis), 113
Carter, Hobart C., 198, 505
Carter, L. Clyde, 307, 334, 505
Carter, Robert, 319
Carter, Ruth, 548
Castle, William A., 256-57, 311, 324, 367, 443, 505, 610
Catalogue, 28, 38, 58, 73-74, 86, 602-3
Cavalry troop, 258, 264, 267, 268, 577-78
Caverlee, Robert F., 356
Cecere, Gaetano, 433, 447
Cella, Eileen Marie, 342
Century Club, 543
Cercle Français, Le, 589-90
Chaffin, Mrs. T. J., Jr., 529
Chalifoux, Jeanne, 377
Chamber Theater, 648
Chambliss, Catherine, 266
Chancellor, 368; assistant, 499, 501; office, 367
Chancellor's Circle, 542
Chancellor's convocation, 411
Chancellor's Fund, 536-38, 544
Chandler, Algernon Bertrand, Jr., 31, 34, 75, 81, 88, 111, 121, 122, 145; as acting president, 91; administration

Chandler, Algernon Bertrand, Jr. (*cont.*) goals, 94; biographical data, 34, 93; fund raising, 132-35; German club and, 214; memorial service, 153-54; portrait, 525; as president, 92, 101-3, 151-53; residence, 77; on student government, 551-52; on student teaching, 136; Bunyan Yates Tyner and, 98-99
Chandler, Mrs. Algernon Bertrand, Jr. (Blanche Montgomery), 153, 172, 175
Chandler, J. A. C., 13, 19, 20, 24, 25, 26, 29
Chandler, John W., 93
Chandler Hall, 83, 138, 224-25, 419
Chapels, 212-14
Chappel, Isabel M., 114
Chappell, Charlotte, 498
Charles, Lucile, 613, 614
Chauncey, Marion K., 205, 248, 250, 322, 366, 395, 505, 587
Chemistry program, 257, 288, 301
Chenery, Elizabeth Cardwell, 71, 551
Chesley, W. S., 70
Chewing, Agnes, 127
Chewing, William, 403
Chi Beta Phi, 83, 257, 588
Chichester, R. H. L., 13, 29
Chiles, J. H., 172
Chilton, Alice, 47
Chilton, Mary Hill, 526, 527
Chilton, Virginia Hill, 526, 527
Choral Club, 154-55, 614
Chorus, 395-97, 447
Chrisman, Ethel, 274
Christian Church, 9
Christian Scientists, 596
Christmas programs, 206-7, 219-20, 365-66, 388-89, 395, 396, 405, 412-13, 446
Church of the Brethren, 9
Civil Works Administration, 172
Clark, Elizabeth A., 271, 428, 437, 458
Clarke, Anne Bolling, 526
Class attendance, 301, 399, 458-59
Class Book, 597, 598
Class cuts. *See* Class attendance
Class Day, 67-68, 221, 391
Classical Civilization, 311
Classical studies program, 591-92
Class Night, 391, 419
Class of 1913, 61, 64, 448, 538

Class of 1914, 62, 67-68
Class of 1915, 62, 73, 535
Class of 1916, 62, 81
Class of 1917, 62, 81, 85, 540
Class of 1918, 62, 81, 87
Class of 1919, 81, 94, 532
Class of 1920, 81
Class of 1921, 81
Class of 1928, 144
Class of 1929, 158
Class of 1931, 180
Class of 1934, 182
Class of 1938, 228, 229-30
Class of 1939, 237
Class of 1941, 255
Class of 1943, 275
Class of 1954, 340-41
Class of 1956, 370-71
Class of 1957, 391-92
Class of 1958, 409
Class of 1959, 487
Class of 1960, 420, 433
Class of 1961, 442
Class of 1963, 448
Class schedule, five-day, 466-67
Clement, Henrietta Ada, 498
Clements, Doris Mae, 526
Clements, Mary, 498
Club Español, El, 590-91
Club Hispano-Americano, El, 590
Club Ruy Barbosa, 591
Clubs, 63, 431-32, 565-96
Coates, Molly L., 98, 119-20, 121, 126, 522, 568
Cobb, H. Logan, 592
Cocke, Charles L., 4
Coffin, Peter R., 271, 427
Cole, E. D., 14, 22
Cole, James W., 280
Coleman, S. Bernard, 227
College Board Examination, 456, 460
College calendar, 474
College Commercial Club, 567-68
College Debate Club, 586
College Entrance Examination Board, 400
College Heights, 18
College Heights Elementary School, 137
College Heights High School, 137, 138, 182
College Promenade, 216-17
Colors, 46

Combs, E. R., 320
Combs, Morgan Lafayette, 176, 182, 277, 280, 571, 597; accreditation objective, 164; administrative achievements, 313-14, 356-58; Alstetter and, 180-81; biographical data, 156-57, 357; building program and, 169, 193-94; death, 356, 365, 532; document regarding responsibilities, 354-56; faculty upgrading and, 159; at fine arts center, 319, 320, 322; illness, 354, 356; on library, 628; portrait, 357-58; as president, 155-58; removal from office, 355-56; residence, 77, 295-96; responsibilities, 337-40; student protest and, 336-37; on student rules, 186, 187; on student teaching, 223, 224; tenth anniversary, 236-37; twentieth anniversary, 313-14, 529; twenty-fifth anniversary, 531
Combs, Mrs. Morgan Lafayette, 258
Combs, Robert H., 299
Combs Hall, 357, 422, 480
Commencement. See Class *entries*
Commerce program, 84, 100-102, 120, 147, 167, 238, 258, 287
Commercial Club, 567-68
"Commercial Echoes," 568
Commission on the Consolidation of Colleges, 277-78
Committee on Student Life and Personnel, 339
Committee on the future of the college, 468-71
Comprehensive examinations, 465-66
Comptroller, 201, 502
Concert band, 408
Concert Dance Club, 322, 391, 575
Concerts, 206-7, 235, 254, 322, 329-31, 364, 374, 377, 388, 389, 395, 396, 411, 447, 496. See also *specific participating groups*
Convocations, 212-14, 257-58, 387, 411, 419, 444, 496
Conway, Vivian, 59
Cook, Roy S., 56, 82, 95, 122, 129, 168, 184, 237, 280, 313, 505; biographical data, 82-84
Cook, Mrs. Roy S. (Virgie Via), 82, 84, 523
Cook Memorial Scholarship Fund, 588

Index

Cooke, Merritt T., 70
Cooperative programs, 323-25
Copes, Mrs. Peter D. (Margaret Lodge), 407, 533, 543
Cornell Hall, 233-34, 263-64, 402
Cornwell, Louise Parks, 526
Cosgrove, Augustin, 147
Cosner, Renna, 640
Cote, Raymond Clark, 508
Cotillion Club, 96, 216-17
Cotten, Mrs. Richard, 529
Cotting, Mrs. Edgar L. (Helen H. Schultz), 310
Cottingham, Mary Watts, 527
Counseling and guidance, 57, 415-18
Counseling center, 222, 460
Courtney, Mrs. Elizabeth, 76
Cousins, Thomas, 205
Cover, Herbert L., 438, 505
Crane, Claris, 46
Crawford, Clara W., 624
Creative Dance Club, 574
Cross, Carolyn Lee, 432
Cross, Richard S., 513
Critzos, Penelope, 530
Crotty, Jeanne, 208, 327, 530
Croushore, James H., 271, 360, 372, 381, 393, 394, 412, 428, 437, 438, 452, 469, 499, 501, 505, 508-10, 540, 543, 601
Croushore, Mrs. James H. (Marian K.), 539
Cuban students, 272
Cueman, Mrs. C. W. (Kathryn Jones), 522
Cumming, Gwendolyn Amory, 513
Curd, Mrs. William Morris (Mary Evans Holman), 519
Curriculum, 20, 42-43, 85, 116-19, 167-68, 188-90, 275, 281-82, 287-88, 300-301, 399-400, 414, 436, 442, 444, 470, 475; accelerated, 260-61. *See also specific subjects*
Currie, Mrs. Edward S. (Gay Vaughan Wilson), 46, 517-18, 546, 597
Curry, Alice, 568
Curry, J. L. M., 7
Curtis, Eugene C., 201, 311-12, 402
Curtis, Jack, 402
Curtis, William, 126
Custis, George Washington Parke, 195
Custis, Mrs. George Washington Parke (Mary Lee Fitzhugh), 195

Cuts. *See* Class attendance
Dadmun, Dora J., 36
Dahl, Monica, 577
Daisy chain, 220-21
Dalton, Jack P., 281
Dance cut, 217
Dance band, 209
Dance organizations, 214-17, 254, 573-75
Dance program, 254, 322, 377, 455-56, 541, 549, 573-75. *See also* Ballets
Daniel, Helen Lane, 47
Daniel, John T., 13, 26, 29
Daniel, Lulu C., 607
Daniel, Polly Eugenia, 498, 575
Dannehl, Theresa, 76
Darby, Martha, 575, 617
Darden, Colgate W., Jr., 267, 277, 278, 313, 319-20, 322, 338, 339, 356, 375, 376, 406, 407, 421, 424, 425; biographical data, 308-9; inauguration, 307-8; title, 368
Darden Award, 127, 432-33, 448
Dare, Marjorie, 258
Darter, Oscar H., 124, 169, 184, 222, 354, 446, 505, 572, 589; biographical data, 128-29
Dating, 53, 142, 144, 315, 398
Daugherty, D. H., 375
Davidson, Rebekah Ellis, 190
Davies, Elizabeth Louise, 359, 365, 498, 527
Davies, Louise Gordon, 527
Davis, Richard Beale, 70, 228
Dawes, Nelle, 613
Day, Emmett, 298
Day Students Club, 595
Deaderich, Nettie Montgomery, 517
Dead Week, 497
Dean (of the college), 160, 183, 199, 269, 270, 436, 499, 501; assistant, 346, 501, 503; associate, 499
Dean of freshmen, 315
Dean of students (women), 103, 172, 315, 333, 338, 339, 346, 348, 383, 500, 502; assistants, 346, 384
Dean's Advisory Council, 339
Dean's list, 301, 401
Debate, 585-87
De Figueres, Karen Olsen, 534
Degree program, 116-18, 120-22, 187-90, 323; graduates, 119, 123-24

Degree requirements, 282-83, 286-87, 399-400, 473-74
Deierhoi, Mary, 517
DeJarnette, H. M., 90, 91, 153
Demonstrations, 489-91, 497
Denny, Collins, 68
Denominational schools. See specific denominations
Denslow, Stuart, 261, 590
Desegregation. See Integration
DeShields, Henryetta, 361
Deutsch Verein, Der, 591
Devil-Goat Day, 550, 551
Dick, Norma K., 498
Dickinson, George F., Jr., 502
Dickinson, Margaret D., 639
Dill, C. C., 87
Dining facility, 18, 169-71, 317
Dining hall regulations, 105-6, 143, 150, 335-37
Director of admissions, 426, 499, 501
Director of financial aid, 499
Director of information services, 499
Director of personnel, 501, 502
Director of public information, 436
Director of residential facilities, 500
Director of student affairs, 500, 502
Director of teacher training, 183, 184
Disciples, 596
Distinguished Alumna Award, 523, 539, 540, 541, 543, 544
Distinguished Visitor in Residence, 543
Dixon, John, 428
Dodd, James Harvey, 126, 238, 302, 334, 446, 505, 543, 568, 569, 589, 597; biographical data, 146-48; retirement, 443-44
Dodd, Mrs. James Harvey (Eileen Kramer), 124-28, 268, 367, 372, 444, 505, 510, 535, 540, 543, 571, 589, 597; biographical data, 124-25; retirement, 502
Dodson, Thomas I., 351
Doll show, 220
Donnan, Edith, 247
Dormitories, 24, 26-28, 30, 32, 39-40, 77, 92, 112-13, 124, 172, 173, 193-94, 221, 231, 233-34, 350, 351. See also Resident Halls
Dormitory, The, 30, 32, 39
Dormitory seminars, 270-71
Dorsey, Mary Ann T., 341, 527

Dowden, Marguerite, 546
Downing, Thomas J., 94
Doyle & Russell, 197, 629
Dragomanovic, Sonja, 575
Drake, Raleigh M., 256
Dramatic Club, 606, 607
Dramatics, 60, 73, 79, 111-12, 155, 180, 193, 218, 228-29, 244-45, 254, 273, 274, 321, 322, 364-65, 377, 411, 578, 606-20, 648. See also Ballets
Droste, Mildred Ann, 348, 468, 500, 502
Dudley, John W., 639
Duggan, Dorothy, 126
Duke, Albert G., 325, 366, 505, 582, 620
Dunaway, Annie Towles, 527
Dunaway, Ann Lee, 527
Dunaway, Mary Sue, 250
Dunlora Academy, 6
Dunville & Bros., 482
DuPont, Alfred I., 321
DuPont, Mrs. Alfred I. (Jessie Ball), 319, 320-21, 652; biographical data, 320-21
DuPont Galleries, 486-88
DuPont Hall, 319-22, 619
Duschock, Ellen, 544
Duval, Lucy Lipscomb, 71, 551
Duval, Nancy Turner, 526

"Eager voices singing," 326
Early, Benjamin W., 366, 372, 388, 505, 509, 618-19
Early Humanities, 311
Eason, Thomas D., 166
Eastern Mennonite College, 9
Eastern Shore Club, 63
Eastridge, Mrs. Glen, 538
Echols, Mrs. Eugene E., 529
Eckenrode, Elizabeth, 651
Eckenrode, Frances Cornick, 119
Economics program, 287, 458
Edmonds, J. W., 13
Edson, Jean Slater, 407, 423, 505, 509, 587
Education program, 188, 209, 274-75, 289-91, 341, 479, 594; cooperative, 323; graduate work, 323, 325-26. See also Teacher training
Edwards, Alice L., 256
Edwards, C. Allmand, 139
Eggleston, J. D., Jr., 13, 24, 26, 320
Electives, pass-fail plan, 468

Index

E. Lee Trinkle Library, 258, 394, 538, 628-32, 642-43; archives, 646; exhibitions, 647-48; play reading, 648; rare book room, 644-45; seminars, 648-49; subject-area reading rooms, 645
Elementary education, 323, 579. *See also* Education program; Teacher training
Elementary schools, 64
Elliott, Louise, 126
Embassy of India, 651
Embrey, Alvin T., 176, 650
Embrey, W. S., 51
Emerald Ball, 407
Emmett, John M., 361
Emory, Samuel T., Jr., 452, 456, 457, 505
Enders, Martin Luther, 180
Enders, Mary Phoebe, 126, 155
Engleman, Rebecca Katherine, 526
Englemann, Susanne, 591
English Club, 566
English program, 270, 276, 394, 434
English Scholastic Honorary, 567
Enrollment, 37, 58, 73, 81, 84-85, 87, 122, 145, 166-67, 199, 229, 231, 237-38, 256, 360, 393, 410, 421, 436, 444, 456
Entertainment, 202, 208-9, 217-19. *See also specific events*
Epaulet, 254, 601, 602
Episcopalians, 50, 595, 596
Eppes, Eva Taylor, 111, 121, 154, 155, 205, 394, 395, 505, 587, 614
Erdelyi, Michael, 334, 349
Eskridge, George, 195
Eta Sigma Phi, 592
Etiquette, 106
Eubank, Virginia Lee, 361
Euliss, Mrs. Emma, 76
Evans, Thelma, 184
Evening program, 120, 122, 137, 167, 258
Examination: comprehensive, 465, 466; credit by, 472; final, 275; self-scheduled, 478
Exchange program, 448-52
Excursions, 54, 59, 72, 78-79, 254, 310, 365, 407-8
Executive committee, 12
Exhibitions, 647-48. *See also* Art Exhibitions
Expenses, 44, 55, 85, 349, 400-401, 420, 504

Explicator, 276
Extension program, 127, 151, 167, 353

Faculty, 28-30, 33-37, 95, 102, 121-22, aries, 56, 95, 164-65, 200, 270, 283, 84, 340, 347-48, 393, 426, 434, 442, 443, 500, 501; appointments, 445; attendance at professional meetings, 382; board for, 56, 149-50; housing, 149; leaves, 334, 348-49, 401-2; professional memberships, 382; promotions, 353-54; record of tenure, 504-6; retirement policy, 443; salaries, 56, 95, 164-65, 200, 270, 283, 354, 401, 402, 426, 442, 504; titles, 361; upgrading, 159, 164, 401
Faculty advisers, 416-18; handbook, 417
Faculty Annex, 149
"Faculty Bulletin," 605
Faculty clubs, 222-23
Faculty committees, 378, 382; student representation, 380
Faculty Drama Club, 613
Faculty exchange program, 448-52
Faculty handbook, 443
Faculty lectures, 648-49
Faculty marshall, 381
Faculty meetings, 284, 353-54, 367, 381, 413-15, 434, 435, 445; student representation, 491-92, 494
Faculty Men's Club, 222; loan fund, 222
Faculty publications, 301, 605. *See also individual faculty members*
Faculty research, 401-2
Faculty secretary, 284, 381
Faculty-student governance, 493-94
Faculty Wives' Club, 222-23
Fairfax Annex, 172
Faison, Carol, 584
Fallout shelters, 445
Falmouth Elementary School, 137
Farmville, normal school, 70, 100
Farmville Female College, 7
Farmville State Teachers College, 163, 164, 227. *See also* Longwood College
Farr, R. R., 7
Farrar, Lloyd, 617
Faulkner, Lefa, 500, 502
Faulkner, Ronald W., 203-9, 216, 229, 240, 248-50, 322, 327, 339, 365, 372, 408, 610; biographical data, 204
Faulkner, Ronna, 208-9

Faulkner, Thomas G., Jr., 406
Faulkner, William, 389
Fauls, John T., 535
Fay, William P., 483
Fees, 28, 44, 349, 400, 419-20, 504
Fellowship grants, 442
Female seminary, 2
Fencing, 549
Ferguson, George Oscar, Jr., 280, 339, 340, 361
Ferguson, Patricia Head, 513n
Ferneyhough, Mrs. John C., 121, 200
Ferrell, Mrs. James B. (Audrey), 530
Fickett, Lewis P., Jr., 428, 451, 458, 466, 508, 509, 586
Ficklin family, 428
Field Day, 63, 66-67, 71, 86, 123, 548
Fiftieth Anniversary Fund, 533
Filling, James H., 299
Fine arts center, 131, 319-22
Fine arts festival, 322
Fingerhut, Victor A., 468, 572, 602
First District Teachers Meetings, 86
Fisher, Kate, 602
Fisher, Mabel Virginia, 359
Fishman, Diane L., 509, 641
Fitzhugh, Janetta, 64
Fitzhugh, St. George R., 22
Fitzhugh, William, 195
Flanagan, Roy K., 157
Fleet, Leah Rubenette, 249
Fleet, Mary L., 639
Flippin, Leam Snow, 71, 551
Flood (1942), 263-66
Florida, higher education for women, 3
Foley, Michelle, 359
Food service, 97, 485
Forbes, Marion C., 28, 37, 53, 66
Ford, W. J., 134, 154
Foreign language clubs, 589-92
Foreign language program, 149, 150, 189, 272-74, 275, 301, 386, 430
Foreign service major, 414
Forensic Club, 585-86
Forrest, W. B., 59
Foster, Libby, 390
Foster, Maxine C., 432
Foster, Susie Peach, 596
Founder's Day, 21, 419
Fountain, 230
"Four Winds," 228-29
Fox, Ellen, 567

Fox, Susan, 618
Framar, 77, 294
Francis, Sylvia Iris, 527
Frantz, Mervin A., 502
Fraser, Margaret Elizabeth, 47, 80
Fredericksburg: flood (1942), 263-66; historic sites, 364; normal school, 10-13, 100; sidewalks, 51
Fredericksburg, Battle of, 18-19, 53, 295, 296, 483
Fredericksburg Alumnae Association chapter, 520, 522, 525, 534, 537
Fredericksburg Civil War Centennial Commission, 483
Fredericksburg College: advertisement, 29; football, 50
Fredericksburg Public School, 74
Fredericksburg State Normal and Industrial School for Women, 13. *See also* Mary Washington College
Freeman, Douglas, 87
French Club, 63, 150, 589-90
French house, 293
Frick, Charles J., 261
Friedman, Kathy, 447, 498
Fry, Bernard M., 261, 627-28
Funding, 10, 13, 25-28, 84, 132-35, 169, 178-79, 201-2, 233, 234, 238, 349, 431, 482, 628, 629

Galdós, Benito Pérez, 468
Galyen, Garnet W., 351
Gambrell, Mary L., 509
Gamma Theta Upsilon, 594-95
Gammon, Edgar G., 254
Gari Melchers endowment, 653
Gari Melchers Hall, 321
Gari Melchers Memorial and Art Center, 429-30
Garnett, A. W., 337
Gates, 174-75
Geiger Counter, 602
Geldard, Frank, 339, 340
General Assembly, 197-98. *See also* Legislation
Genther, Elsie, 651
Geography program, 301, 456-57, 478, 594-95
Geology program, 288, 456-57
German Club, 96, 104, 150, 214-17, 591
Ghyka, Matila, 305-7
G.I. Bill, 299

Index 667

Gilbert, Rose Bennett, 494, 538-39
Giles, Mrs. L. J., Jr. (Adele Crowgey), 539
Gilmer, Henry G., 320
Gingold, Josef, 330
Glass, Meta, 5
Glee Club, 47, 58, 80-81, 248, 249, 366, 395, 607. *See also* Choral Club
Glover, Donald E., 271, 428, 509
Goffigon, Kathleen, 526
Goffigon, Mrs. Kathleen Hallet, 526
Golden Horseshoe, 350
Gonon, Isabelle Lawrence, 333, 335, 337
Gonzalez, Ana Luisa, 273
Gooch, Margaret, 587
Gooch, Robert Kent, 414
Goode Construction Co., 233
Goodloe, Kathleen, 534, 536
Goodman, Joseph, 330
Goodwin, Mrs. Richard (Louise Garnett), 522
Goolrick, C. O'Conor, 10, 14, 19, 25, 26, 29, 67, 111, 176, 179, 229, 277, 320, 361, 522, 651; biographical data, 14-16; death, 482; honors, 406, 533; as legislator, 14-15; loving cup for, 20
Goolrick, Mrs. C. O'Conor (Nannie Osborne Ficklin), 15
Goolrick, John T., 14, 87
Goolrick, Mrs. John T. (Frances Bernard), 14
Goolrick, Virginia May, 28, 36, 89, 519
Goolrick Hall, 16, 40, 481-82
Gordon, Isabel, 484
Gothic Room, 318
Gouger, James B., 595
Gould, Mrs. E. D., 534
Gouldman, Francis B., 320
Gouldman, Lucy, 518
Grace K. Tanner Home Economics Club, 572
Grading system, 367, 460-61
Graduate programs, 323, 325-26, 470
Graduate Record Examination, 301, 414, 460
Graduates' occupations, 90
Graduation. *See specific classes*
Graves, Boyd, 209-11, 271, 366, 372, 437, 505, 579, 610, 614
Graves, Cary, 36
Graves, John Temple, II, 230, 255, 322
Graves, Junia, 67

Graves, Mrs. Stuart, 528
Gray, Leslie, 238-39
Grayson, George W., Jr., 468
Great Depression, 169, 172-73, 178, 522
Green, Mrs. Duff, 134
Greenberg, Miriam, 271, 428
Greene, Marion A., 505
Griffith, Katherine, 250
Griffith, William Wayne, 505
Griffith, Mrs. William Wayne (Betty V.), 534, 538
Grimes, Joseph Richard, 508
Grogan, Nan, 489
Gross, Hermine, 359
Group elective system, 102
Guenther, Louis C., 360, 426
Gunn, Lemuel, 508

Hailstones, Thomas J., 147
Haislip, Barbara, 313
Hale, Frances Marie, 526
Hall, Christiana, 507
Hall, Sidney B., 171, 179
Hall of Mirrors, 235, 420
Hall-Quest, Alfred, 73
Halsey, Don P., 175
Halsey Commission, 177
Hamer, Ann Farquhar, 407, 505, 587
Hamilton, Norman, 153
Hamlet, William N., 28, 34, 56-57, 75, 82, 121, 122, 154, 179-80, 229, 237, 311, 505, 522; bequest to Mary Washington College, 57; biographical data, 34-35; portrait, 525
Hamlet House, 57, 221-22
Hampton Alumnae Association chapter, 522
Hampton Institute, 7
Hanna, Susan J., 502, 503, 509
Hansen, Richard E., 503
Hara, Teruo, 488
Harding, Logan, 298
Hargrove, Margaret, 172, 173, 383-85, 431, 438, 508, 509, 553; biographical data, 383-84; retirement, 500
Hargroves, Louise Vaughan, 527, 434
Harrell, Frances, 519
Harrington, Dorothy, 613
Harris, Ann, 247, 248, 249, 574
Harris, Anna Mae, 230, 505, 510, 544
Harris, Anne, 520
Harris, Edna, 587

Harris, Herbert H., 166
Harris, Mrs. John P., Jr. (Ruby C.), 338, 339, 340, 346, 372, 505, 573
Harris, Robert O., 320
Harrison, Albertis S., Jr., 447, 483
Harrison, Fairfax, 79
Harrison, Gunyon M., 26, 34, 48-49, 84; biographical data, 37
Harrison, Mrs. Gunyon M. (Cleora Segar), 49
Harrison, Mary Rebecca, 49
Harrison, Page, 123
Harrisonburg, normal school (teachers college), 10-13, 70, 100, 118, 227
Harrisonburg State Teachers College, 164, 175, 176
Hart, Belle Oliver, 525
Hart, Harris, 91, 111, 166
Hasek, Carl, 147
Hatcher, Harlan H., 375-76
Haupt, Randi Coates, 527
Hawk, J. C., 67
Hawker, Carolyn Ann, 527
Hayes, Elinor L., 121, 126, 139, 523
Haynes, Medford D., 201, 403
Head residents, 385
Health education program, 461
Heating plant, 27, 317
Heazel, Mary Vaughan, 613
Heck, W. H., 60, 73
Heflin, E. G., 28, 138
Henderson, Donna Henninger, 513
Henderson, J. H., 20
Henry, Anne, 365, 517
Hepford, Emmaneta, 375, 390
Herban, Mathew, III, 305, 488
Herman, Rosemary H., 505, 509
Hersh, Ralph, 204
Hess, Jeanette, 64, 518
Hewetson, H. W., 445, 458, 505, 569
Hiatt, Lyle S., 261
Hickle, Mary, 542
Hicks, Pearl M., 111, 114
Higher education: state-supported, 608; for women, 1-9. *See also specific institutions*
Higher Education Facilities Act, 482
Higher Education Study Commission, 511
"High on Marye's Hilltop," 208, 327, 530
High school department. *See* Preparatory department

High schools, 8, 42
Hilldrup, Betsy Gordon, 526
Hilldrup, Robert Leroy, 311, 339, 457, 483
Hilldrup Memorial Library, 483
Hines, Margaret, 302
Hinkle, Mrs. Segar (Lindlay Goolrick), 528, 529
Hinman, Olive M., 35-36, 60, 62
Hinson, Brenda E., 595
Hisey, Greta, 579
History program, 287, 301, 458, 475, 479
Hockey, 254, 548-49
Hodges, Leroy, 258
Hoge, Miriam Bowes, 505, 509, 511
Holliday, Roberta, 365
Hollingsworth, Roberta, 280
Hollins, John, 4
Hollins College, 3-4
Holloway, Emily A., 500, 502, 543
Holman, Mrs. Donald (Elizabeth Parker Woodward), 202
Holman, Mary Evans, 520
Holt, Marion, 641
Holt, Saxon W., 25, 26
Holton, Linwood, 496
Homecoming, 272, 448, 528-38, 540, 541, 543; alumnae publications exhibit, 537; buffet at Brompton, 535; registration fee, 537; Seacobeck banquet luncheon, 536
Home department, 66
Home Economics Club, 541, 572-73
Home economics practice house, 172
Home economics program, 225, 288, 291, 436, 441, 453-54
Honey, Maggie, 76
Honor code, 558
Honor council, 172, 390-91, 553, 562, 563
Honor counselors, 561, 563
Honor societies, 83, 96, 127, 148, 150, 388, 404, 447, 565-96. *See also specific organizations*
Honors program, 302-3, 400, 401, 411, 437, 446
Honor system, 44, 556-64
Hood, Mrs. Horace, III, 529
Hoods, 392
Hoof Prints Club, 549, 575-77
Hook, Catherine H., 323, 505, 594
Hook, Mrs. Paul, 537
Hopper, Maria Edmondson, 513

Index

Horner, Mrs. M. A., 28
Horton, Douglas, 409
Housekeeping, 502
Housing, 39-40, 125-26, 231-33, 350, 351. *See also* Dormitories; Resident halls
Houston, Dulcy, 248
Houston, Levin, III, 204, 205, 238, 243-45, 247-50, 377, 505, 610; biographical data, 243-44; dramatics programs and, 611-14, 616, 617
Houston, L. J., Jr., 193
Houston, Michael, 420, 436, 468, 501, 509, 538, 541, 542; as assistant chancellor, 499, 501; biographical data, 499
Howard, Charles, 620
Howard, Dowell J., 375
Hoye, Anna Scott, 261, 324, 367, 478, 505
Hoylman, Henrietta, 267
Hubert, Marcel, 328
Hudgins, Edward W., 376
Hudson, C. L., 26
Hudson, Marjorie, 576, 577
Huftes, Mallory, 575
Hughes, Mrs. James (Eloise Caverlee), 530
Hughes, Robert M., 166
Hugh Mercer Infirmary, 316
Hull, D. D., Jr., 70
Hulme, Nora Lea, 580
Humphreys, Anne, 34, 36-37, 52
Humphreys, Milton W., 36
Humphries, Robert E., 201, 403
Hurlock, Audrey, 501
Hutchinson, Jeannette, 526
Hutchinson, Virginia, 566

Iltis, Hugo, 251-53, 268
Independent study, 211, 271, 445-46
India exchange program, 448-52
Industrial arts program, 41, 43, 81, 87
Infirmary, 172, 316
Influenza, 88-90, 157
Insley, Earl G., 256, 257, 372, 435, 505, 588
Insley, Joanne, 527
Installation ceremonies, 390-91
Integration, 163-64, 489, 506
Inter-Club Association, 365, 431-32, 447, 553, 570-71; handbook, 604
Interdepartmental majors, 310-11

Interfaith Council, 547
International Relations Club, 129, 572; International Affairs Institute, 169
Irby, Myra L., 271, 349, 428, 459
Irons & Reynolds, 320

Jabbour, Barbara Ann, 527
Jacobus, Hester Zella, 336, 337
James Monroe Memorial Foundation, 653
Jamison, Mildred Cates, 537, 573
Jarman, J. L., 24, 70, 227
Jefferis, Ann Gamble, 498, 527
Jefferson, Thomas, 351
Jefferson Cup, 341, 527, 540
Jefferson Hall, 481
Jenkins, Thomas H., Jr., 299, 300
Jenkins estate, 296
Jewish students, 596
Jerrell, M. Josephine, 121, 140
Jessen, Mrs. Myron M., 529
John, Mary Warner, 548
Johnson, G. L. H., 112
Johnson, Laura T., 562
Johnson, Thomas Lee, 271
Joint Council, 129, 184-87, 552, 553
Jones, Betty Randolph, 526
Jones, Don, 612
Jones, Edwin H., 505
Jones, Mrs. Edwin Harvie, 538-39
Jones, Gordon W., 644, 648, 651
Jones, Lucile C., 509
Jones, Lynn, 51
Jones, Margaret V., 624
Jones, Mrs. Tom (Belva Tune Dunn), 531
Jones, Venus Romance, 506-7
Jordan, William, 403
Junior Modern Dance Club, 574, 575
Junior Ring Dance, 389-90

Kahn, Irene, 328
Kalnen, Margaret Rose, 161
Kappa Omicron Phi, 573
Karsten, Paul M., 224
Kash, Janie M., 641
Keelan, George W., 272-73
Keelan, Providencia, 272, 273
Keeler, Annette, 273
Keezel, G. B., 10
Keim, Anna, 76
Keith, Lee-Wingate, 578, 610

Keith, Warren G., 360, 585, 586, 651
Kelley, Peggy Anne, 527
Kelly, Alma C., 256
Kelly, Mary Annette Klinesmith, 325, 326, 444, 460, 468, 505, 510, 528, 529, 533, 534, 537, 544, 583, 589
Kelly, Walter, 366
Kemper, A. S., 26
Kenmore, 123
Kenmore Association, 653
Kennedy, John F., 457
Kenney, Diane-Louise L., 502, 507
Kent, Charles W., 73
Kent State, 490
Kenvin, Roger Lee, 428, 451, 601, 617-18
Kepner, W. A., 60, 169
Kid Party, 254, 258
Kikis, Helen, 529
Kilborn, Mrs. Peter (Susan Holly Woodward), 202
King, Mrs. A. M., 76
King, Pauline Grace, 412, 505, 510, 544, 601, 644
King, W. Marshall, 154, 229, 237
King, W. W., 70
Kinsman, Robert D., 487
Kirby, John P., 256, 268, 269, 270, 276, 280, 302, 445
Kirby, Richard M., 261
Kirby, Mrs. Richard M., 222
Kirkland, Richard, 482-83
Kirkland Memorial, 482-83
Kirschner, Michael, 577
Kiwanis Cup, 230, 341, 497-98, 540
Klein, Albert R., 271, 322, 408, 411, 428, 437, 452, 468, 469, 509, 538, 615-17, 618; biographical data, 615; death, 619
Klein, Mrs. Albert R. (Deborah C.), 533, 534, 580, 616, 617, 618
Klein, Charlotte, 205, 587
Kollege Kommercial Klub, 567-68
Koski, Diana D., 544
Krachmalnick, Jacob, 329
Kramer, Eileen Lois, 597
Kraus, Leslie Susan, 602
Krishna, Mrs. V., 451
Krokay Klub, 47
Krupenski, Elena, 341

LaCrosse, Janet, 67, 519
Ladd, Geraldine, 347-48

Lafayette Elementary School, 74
Laird, Mrs. John C., 584
Lakeman, Margaret H., 607
Lalla Gresham Ball Scholarship Fund, 321, 652
Lam, Elizabeth P., 448
Lamason, Mrs. W. H. (Pauline Graves), 372, 530, 532
Lamb, Norman, 330
Lambert, Margaret, 529, 531
Lamon, Sara, 639
Lamph, John, 602
Lancaster, Dabney S., 145, 277, 290
Lancaster, Sharon W., 460
Land-grant colleges, 3
Lang, Mrs. John C., 404
Language houses, 150, 386. *See also specific houses*
Lanier, Richard Nunn, Jr., 248, 482
Lankford, Emma, 63
Lankford, Francis G., Jr., 425
Lantor, Mrs. Raynell Goodman, 537
Lassetter, Juanita B., 498
Latin American Studies program, 476
Laundry, 27
Lautz, Amalia, 159
Layman, George W., 153
Leaders' Club, 569-70
LeCompte, Isabel, 267
Lectures, 59
Lee, Mrs. Henry (Ann Carter), 319
Lee, Robert E., 195, 319
Lee, Mrs. Robert E. (Mary Anne Randolph Custis), 195
Lee Hill School, 136, 137
Legislation, 6-8, 10-13, 25, 27, 69-70, 115-16, 138, 166, 178, 227, 277-79, 511, 512
Leidecker, Kurt F., 309, 313, 326, 339, 349, 414, 443, 468, 475, 476, 479, 505, 592-93
Leigh, Aurelia, 498
Lenhart, Charmenz, 352
Leonard, Ellen Elizabeth, 230
Leonard, Ruth, 339, 393
Leslie, Louis A., 569
Lesner, John A., 13, 25
Les Savantes, 566
Levinson, Kathy Friedman, 540, 542
Lewis, Carlotta, 75
Lewis, Fielding, 113, 123, 294

Lewis, Mrs. Fielding (Betty Washington), 113
Lewis, Ivey F., 290
Lewis, J. Louise, 518, 519
Lewis, Leah Arden, 119
Lewis, Yvonne, 390
Liberal arts program, 300-301; conception of, 285
Liberal arts seminars, 271, 436-37
Librarian, 501, 503-4, 624-25, 643, 650; salary, 624
Library, 30-31, 84, 155, 431, 445, 621-51; acquisitions, 621-23, 625, 626, 632, 633, 638, 639, 642, 649; expenditures, 633-34, 649; facilities, 623-25, 628-29; gifts, 650-51; publications, 646-47; salaries, 634, 641-42; staff, 623-25, 626, 627-28, 632-33, 639-41. *See also* E. Lee Trinkle Library
Library handbook, 640
Library science program, 287, 625-28, 632
Library staff manual, 640
Library survey, 642
Liebenow, Susan T., 595
Lightner, Mary, 123
Lindsey, Almont, 211-12, 334, 349, 505, 580
Literary societies, 47, 80, 565-66
Little Red Lane, 150, 520
Little Theatre, 321
"Little Theatre of the Rappahannock," 193
Llewellyn, Lula Lee, 182
Locke, Louis G., 276
Locker, W. C., 70, 153, 166
Longwood College, 8, 163. *See also* Farmville State Teachers College
Loomis, Burt W., 159
Lord, Oswald B., 409
Lord, Ruth, 518
Lovewell, Diane, 447
Loving, Boyce, 228, 580, 609-10
Lowry, Edward D., 271, 428
Loyalty Night, 495-96
Lucas, Virginia Frances, 447
Luntz, George E., 393-94, 395, 397, 447, 505, 538
Luntz, Helen Reese, 509
Lutherans, 596
Lutz, Julia M., 639
Lyceum series, 254, 364, 389

Lyle, Martha Belle, 342, 498
Lyman, Mary Ely, 421
Lynch, Theresa Inez, 71, 551
Lynchburg College, 9
Lynchburg State Teachers College, 176
Lyne, Buford Kirkley, 517, 597
Lyon, Mary, 2

McBride, Ravis, 529
McBryde, R. J., 20
McCallum, Olivia Wheeler, 542
McCausland, Jean, 529
McClelland, Nancy, 296
McClerkin, Anne, 580
McConnell, John Preston, 70, 176
McCue-Randolph Bill, 278, 279
McCulloch, Ruth, 498
McDermott, William Luther, 247, 261, 612, 613
MacDonald, Rose M., 166, 167, 277
McIntire, Robert A., 153
McIntosh, Clifton B., 261, 275, 505, 590, 591
McJilton, Silvia, 434, 498
McKenzie, Mary, 566
MacMahon, Donald H., 440
McMurtry, Mildred, 522
McNair, Mary Lee, 600
McWane, Henry E., 361, 531
Mace, 381-82
Madison, James, 196
Madison, Mrs. James (Dolly Payne), 196
Madison College, 227
Madison Hall, 196
Madrigal Singers, 322, 377
Mahoney, Bernard L., Jr., 468, 471
Mail delivery, 383
Maintenance, 109-11, 200, 201, 311, 317, 485
Major, Jane Hatcher, 533, 534
Major Counseling Night, 417
Major Evaluation Night, 553
Malmborg, Harold A., 371
Mann, Horace, 1
Mann, Sara Margaret, 589
Mann, Thomas P., 499, 542
Mann, William Hodges, 22, 23, 60
Manns, Paul W., 512
Maphis, Charles G., 23, 26, 59
Marchant, Josephine, 63
Marilla, Patricia Adams, 498

Marsh, Lelia Jett, 498, 560
Marshall, Ethel Beazley, 526
Marshall, Mrs. John (Mary Willis Ambler), 421
Marshall, Marguerite Irene, 526
Marshall Hall, 421, 434, 480
Martha Washington College, 9
Martin, Charles K., Jr., 261, 611, 612
Mary Baldwin College, 3-4
Mary Ball Hall, 194
Mary Custis Hall, 195
Marye, James, 294
Marye, John Lawrence, 294
Marye's Heights, 294
Mary Washington College: accessibility, 22, 39, 51-52; advertisement for, 29; as autonomous institution, 511-14; as coeducational institution, 469, 470, 507-8, 512; conversion to liberal arts college, 278-92; cornerstone laying, 21-24; fiftieth anniversary, 405-7, 533; founding, 10-31; gifts, 652-53; ground-breaking ceremonies, 19-21; as historic site, 18-19, 53; as liberal arts college, 175-80, 277, 278; name, 69, 114-16, 176, 225-28; opening, 27-45; purpose, 38, 226, 439, 441, 476-77; real estate, 18; site, 13, 14, 17-19; twentieth anniversary, 179-80; University of Virginia relationship, 131, 277-92, 470, 527
Mary Washington College Band, 204-8, 254, 260, 322, 365-66, 388-89, 408
Mary Washington College Dance Company, 575
Mary Washington College Songs, 208
Mary Washington Players, 244, 254, 322, 364-65, 377, 411, 610, 612; exchange program, 614-15. *See also* Dramatics
Masaryk, Tomáš, 253
Mason, Ann, 208
Mason, George, III, 350
Mason, Mrs. George, III (Ann Thomson), 350-51
Mason Hall, 77, 350
Mathematics program, 56-57, 198, 301
Matila, Ghyka, 305-6
Matthews, Inez, 530
Matthews, Maggie Lee, 498
Matthias, Edwin M., 397
Maury, Matthew Fontaine, 86
Maury Literary Society, 565, 566

Maury Science Club, 595
May Day, 66-67, 71, 104, 112, 123, 182, 245-51, 391, 408, 447, 548, 574, 575
Mayes, Frances, 184
Mead, Margaret, 543
Mears, Benjamin, 361
Mears, Otho F., 70
Medical College of Virginia, 324
Medical technology, 324
Meet Your Minister program, 359
Melchers, Gari, 296, 428-30; biographical data, 428-29
Melchers, Mrs. Gari (Corinne Lawton Mackall), 304, 429, 430, 653
Mendel, Gregor Johann, 251, 252
Mendel Museum, 251-53
Men students, 297-300, 351, 361, 470, 507-8
Mercer, Hugh, 316
Mercer, Mrs. Hugh (Isabella Gordon), 316
Mercer's Apothecary Shop, 316
Merchent, A. Ray, 426, 499, 501, 537
Mery, Michael, 503
Metcalf, John Calvin, 68
Methodists, 3, 6, 9, 50, 595, 596
Meyer, Sylvia, 204, 205
Michael, Mrs. Joy C., 451, 618
Micks, Katherine, 498
Mike Club, 580-82
Milbank, Madeline, 600
Miles, Sarah Anne, 498
Miller, Fred E., 353, 505, 614
Miller, Henry, 241-42
Miller, Robert A., 299
Mills, Helen, 123-24, 139, 141
Minich, Lola, 568
Minnerly, June Ellen, 219
Minor, J. B., 7
Minor, Miriam Thomas, 342, 359, 538
Miss Mary Washington, 219
Mitchell, Mrs. J. B., 137
Mitchell, S. C., 182
Mitchell, Sidney H., 271, 348, 437, 468, 479n, 509, 511, 535, 601, 644
Mitchell, Mrs. Sidney H. (Nancy Heyroth), 348, 459, 501-2, 503, 508, 509
Mock elections, 389
Modern Dance Club, 273, 377, 549, 574
Modern Foreign Language Week, 430
Modern Portias, 162, 254, 566-67
Moncure, Nancy Houston, 527

Index 673

Moncure, R. C. L., 19, 20, 25
Monroe Hall, 83, 92, 101, 173; murals, 240
Montagu, Ashley, 373, 374
Montague, A. J., 59-60
Moore, Constance, 576
Moran, Katherine F., 346, 365, 372
Moratorium Day, 489-90
Moreland, J. Earl, 371, 425
Morfit, Richard L. B., 651
Morgan, Joy Elmer, 144
Morgan, Marilyn Ann, 498
Morgan, Nina L., 624
Morgan, Virginia, 249
Moriarity, Dennis Chauncey, 300, 361
Mormile, James, 591
Morrill Act, 3
Morris, Gene Randolph, 526
Morris, M. J. R., 651
Morrison, Linda J., 447
Mortar Board, 386, 404, 535, 583-85
Moss, Charles George Gordon, 159, 162-64, 218
Mount Holyoke, 2
Mu Alpha Chi, 595
Munford, Mrs. Beverly B., 176, 178
Mu Phi Epsilon, 587
Murals, 236, 240, 241
Mure, Geoffrey Reginald Gilchist, 424
Murphy, W. Tayloe, 320
Murray, Anne, 123
Music program, 47, 63, 80, 203-9, 243, 275, 287, 321, 327-32, 587-88
MWC Today, 605
Myra Irby Memorial Library, 349

Nagy, Elemer, 329
Nalls, Elizabeth, 587
Nash, Ethel Hester, 62, 517
Nash, Frances Gray, 498
National Association of Commercial Teacher-Training Institutions, 165
National Association of Schools of Music, 397
National Association of State Directors of Teacher Education and Certification, 472
National Bond Queen Campaign, 266
National Science Foundation, 477
National Student Association, 384, 491, 553, 554
National Youth Administration, 627

Nazzaro, James Russell, 271, 428, 444, 445
Neill, Joyce Mary, 432
Neilsen Co., 480
Nelli, Herva, 374
Nelson, Ethel, 184
NeSmith, Mary Ethel, 607
Nettles, Virginia, 377
Neumann, Hans, 330
New Art Wind Quintet, 331
Newcomb, John Lloyd, 277, 279, 280
Newell, Martha, 615
Newman, Hunter H., 298
Newport News Alumnae Association chapter, 520
Newsome, Mrs. Ralph G., 529
Newton, Blake T., 236-37
Nicholas, Annie, 546
Nichols, Mrs. John (Elinor Hayes), 521
Nicks, Earl G., 261
Nightingales, 63
Ninde, M. Louise, 95
Nixon, Judith Lee, 451
Nixon, Mrs. Richard M., 490-91
Norfolk General Hospital School of Medical Technology, 324
Normal Hill, 18
Normal schools, 7-8, 10, 42-43, 69, 114-16; differentiation policy, 69, 71, 99-100, 118-19, 147. *See also* Teachers colleges; *specific schools*
Norris, Sally H., 76, 119
Nursing program, 310
Nutt, Katherine, 601

Oak Room, 235
Oberlin College, 1
Ochikubo, Tetsuo, 443
Odell, Betty Randolph, 526
Off-campus housing, 231-33
Old Foundry, 303-4
Olert, Frederick W., 391
Oliver, Eva, 600
Oliver, Mrs. George Brown (Cornelia D.), 271, 347, 437, 502
Oliver, Mary Lee, 498
Olsen, Karen, 580
Omicron Delta Epsilon, 569
Open-air theatre, 111-12, 173
Operating expenses, 25, 27
Orchestras, 204, 205
Organ Guild, 587-88

Organizations, 46-49, 63, 319. *See also specific groups*
Oriental Club, 593-94
Orkney, Virginia Elizabeth, 527
O'Rourke, Mary Rita, 588
Osburn, Ann, 274
Ozlin, Thomas W., 158

Padmabai, R. K., 451
Page, Rosewell, 73
Page, Mrs. W. (Kaye Estelle Savage), 506
Pageants, 228-29, 408. *See also* May Day
Palmer, Ruth, 126
Pandit, Vijayalakshmi, 312-13, 593
Pannell, Anne, 448
Paperback sources, 211
Pappandreau, Joanna, 529
Parcell, Claude T., Jr., 134, 502
Park, Rosemary, 510
Parker, Nancy, 518
Parking, 404, 486
Parkinson, Burney L., 339, 359, 372, 392, 431
Parks, Hilda, 250, 613, 614
Parrish, Mrs. Edward Alton (Molly Vaughan), 155, 313, 437, 529, 530, 538, 542
Parrish, Mary Jo, 271, 348
Parvathamma, H. M., 451
Pass-fail plan, 468
Patrick, Jane Howard, 537
Patton, Samuel E., 298
Payne, Anne Lewis, 333
Payne, Camilla Moody, 53, 480, 527, 528
Payne, Virginia Lawrence, 333-34, 335
Payroll savings plan, 267
Peabody Fund, 7
Peace Ball, 391
Peanut Week, 219-20
Pearce, Rachel, 64
Peck, Rebekah, 75
Peed, Virginia Elizabeth, 526
Peery, George C., 180, 197
Peirce, Eliza, 67
Pender, Marshall W., 299
Pendleton, Grace, 154
Penella, Penny, 586
Peoples, Charlotte L., 75
Pepper, Sam, 300
Perinchief, Ann Louise, 499, 513, 527, 540-41, 542, 544

Perrin, May, 75, 517, 518
Perrin, Miriam H., 95
Perry, Pauline, 517
Personnel administration, 200-201
Peters, David W., 227, 277
Peters, J. Sidney, 13, 22, 26
Pharr, Suzanne, 428
Phi Beta Kappa, 5, 6, 128, 508-11, 543-44
Phi Delta Gamma, 573
Phi Delta Kappa, 184
Phillips, Helen, 48, 517
Phillips, Samuel H., Jr., 271, 428
Phillips, W. J., 23
"Philosophic Bull," 592
Philosophy Club, 312, 592-93
Philosophy program, 211, 288, 592-93
Phi Sigma Iota, 150, 386, 592
Physical education facilities, 16, 40, 480, 481-82. *See also* Swimming facilities
Physical education program, 2, 47, 52, 55, 58, 63, 66-67, 71, 78, 80, 113-14, 123, 132, 288, 291-92, 318, 436, 441, 453, 454-56, 549, 550, 573, 576. *See also* Athletic Association; *individual sports*
Physical examinations, 52
Physical therapy, 324
Physical Therapy Club, 595
Physics program, 288, 423, 475
Pierce, Alan S., 451, 601, 611
Pierce, Patricia, 509
Pi Gamma Mu, 483, 588-89
Pinschmidt, William C., 478, 505
Pi Nu Chi, 595
Piper, Edith, 331
Pi Sigma, 71
Pi Sigma Kappa, 580
Pittman, Martha Lyle, 532
Pitts, Benjamin T., 266, 320
Pitzer, Keith, 299
Placement bureau, 484
"Plan for Mary Washington College as a Liberal Arts College," 285
Planning committee, long-range, 435-36, 442
Polemics, 602
Political clubs, 595
Political life, 352
Political science program, 287, 301, 458
Pollard, Barbara B., 601

Index 675

Pollard, John Garland, 165, 178, 277, 321
Pollard Hall, 321
Porter, Mary J., 641
Post office, 150, 173, 258, 445
Poteet, Elizabeth, 359
Powell, Mae V., 568
Practice teaching. *See* Student teaching
Prasse, John H., 351
Pratt, Henrietta, 576
Pratt, John Lee, 651
Prebble, Marilyn Louise, 527
Pre-foreign service major, 414
Premedical sciences program, 311
Preparatory department, 4, 5, 76, 102
Presbyterians, 4, 50, 51, 595, 596
President, 13-14, 16, 90-93, 153, 361-62, 513, 531; residence, 28, 77, 294, 295-96; responsibilities, 337-40, 354; salary, 56, 70. *See also* Chancellor; *specific officers*
Preston, Alfred G., 70
Preston, Margaret Lee, 498
Preston, Patricia Ann, 390, 498
Price, James H., 197, 236, 258
Price, John W., 70, 91, 92
Pridgen, Carol, 498
Proctor, Samuel D., 513
Professional Course, 42-43
Professor emeritus title, 446
Psi Chi, 589
Psychological clinic, 221-22
Psychology Club, 595
Psychology program, 288, 445
Psychology testing center, 460
Publications, 602-5; by alumnae, 537. *See also* Student publications
Public education, 7-8. *See also specific systems*
Public Works Administration, 193-94, 233, 234
Puerto Rican students, 272
Pulliam, Jacquelyn A., 506
Pusey, Constance Maddox, 526
Putnam, Esther James, 528
Pyle, Robert W., 302

Quantico, 89, 398
Quarterly Review, 541, 542
Quenzel, Carrol H., 357, 366, 372, 381, 392, 400, 537, 614, 625, 634-38; bio-

Quenzel, Carrol H. *(cont.)*
graphical data, 635-38; death, 394, 638
Quenzel, Mrs. Carrol H. (Lula A.), 538, 539
Quest XX Insured Endowment Plan, 543
Quillian, William F., Jr., 375, 388, 448

Radford, normal school (teachers college), 70, 100, 227
Radford College, 277
Radhakrishnan, Sarvepalli, 326
Radio broadcasting, 580-82
Raiford, Julia, 546
Rainey, Helen R., 624
Ramey, Dorothy, 576
Ramey, Frances P., 129, 184
Ramsey, Bonnie Grace, 498
Randall, James M., 299
Randolph, Thomas Mann, 351
Randolph, Mrs. Thomas Mann (Martha Jefferson), 351
Randolph Hall, 77, 350, 351
Randolph-Macon Woman's College, 5-6
Rankin, Roberta A., 509
Ransom, Mrs. Richard B., 529
Ratcliffe, Russell, 594
Ray, Mildred Brooks, 641
Raynor, Betty Anne, 527
Read, Mrs. Charles L. (Claudia Moore), 250, 322, 377, 412, 505, 538, 574-75
Reading days, 497
Reardon, Margaret L., 375
Receptions, 171, 343-45, 360
Recorder, 501
Recreational facilities, 172-73
Recreation Association, 550
Rector, Mary, 600
Rector, 512, 513, 514
Redwood, Jamie, 248
Reed, Edna P., 498
Reeves, Clifton H., 201, 403
Registrar, 426, 499
Registration, 120, 459
Regular Course, 42
Reichel, Frank H., 294
Reichenbach, Herman L., 205, 302
Reid, Norman, 612, 613
Reinburg, Peggy Kelley, 538, 539
Religion program, 458
Religious Concerns Program, 547

Religious Emphasis Week, 254, 443, 447, 547
Religious life, 50, 142, 144, 212, 254, 443, 447, 547, 595-96
Rennolds, W. G., 24
Repair and maintenance shops, 27
"Report to the Chancellor of Mary Washington College on Its Conversion into a College of Liberal Arts," 281-86
Resident counselors, 347, 349
Resident halls, 293, 294, 296, 297, 298, 384-85, 402, 421-22, 434, 480, 481, 485; integration, 385; student assistants, 385, 447. *See also* Dormitories
Resident hall seminars, 426-28
Reynolds, J. Sargeant, 497
Ribet, Emily, 529
Rice, Charlotte, 518
Rice, Elizabeth, 75
Rice, Kathryne, 518
Rice, Louis A., 147
Richards, Clara, 524
Richmond Alumnae Association chapter, 517, 519, 520
Richmond Area University Center, 388
Richmond College, 6
Richmond Female Institute, 6
Ridge Crest, 77
Riding, 549, 575-78
Riding Club, 575
Rifle Club, 48-49, 63, 548
Riker, Marjorie T., 519
Ritter, Charles C., 299-300
Ritter, Paul J., 247, 261, 611, 612
Rivas, Josefa, 271, 428, 430, 461
Rivera, Carmen L., 468, 479, 506
Riverý, Maria Raquel, 272
Riverý, Ruth Matilde, 272
Roach, J. Kenneth, 261, 378
Roads, 54
Roberts, Beverly, 576
Robertson, A. Stuart, 70
Robinson, C. M., 29
Robison, Pal, 372
Rodgers, J. E., 51
Rollins, Cleveland K., 299
Roman Catholics, 595, 596
Ronci, Rose, 247, 249
Rood, Louise, 329
Roof garden, 174, 235, 318
Rosborough, Jean, 607

Rose, Willie Lee Nichols, 544
Rosebro, John R., 19
Ross, Mary Ann, 527
Ross, Vera Neely, 204, 205, 587
Round, George C., 13, 20, 25, 26
Rowe, Betsy, 529
Rowe, Dorothy Towles, 250
Rowe, Isabel Willis, 538
Rowe, Mary Chesley, 538
Rowe, Mary Frances, 218
Rowe, Maurice B., 17, 22, 294, 295
Rowe's Wood, 17
Rozmarynowska, Kathy, 613, 616
Ruff, Dalia Lam, 95, 97, 121
Ruffner, William H., 7
Rules. *See* Student regulations
Runk, B. F. D., 414
Rural arts department, 41, 43
Russell, Edward Hutson, 14, 19-23, 25, 29, 70; *Battlefield* verse on, 65; biographical data, 16, 34; on commerce program, 101; on fine arts center, 320; newspaper picture, 32, 34; portrait, 532; residence, 77; resignation, 90-92
Russell, George B., 70
Russell, Mrs. John C. (Margaret Swander), 232, 310, 415, 570, 583, 584
Russell, John Dale, 511
Russell, Myran, 247, 248, 249, 574
Russell Hall, 32, 40, 77, 92, 480-81
Russell Literary Society, 47, 80, 565
Russell Report, 511
Russian Club, 591
Russian studies program, 475
Russo-Asian symposium, 476
Ryan, William A., 144

Sacrey, Margaret, 76
Sacrey, Mrs. Nymat (Betsy Bassett), 522
St. Julian, George, 245
Saladin, Jane N., 499
Sale, Thomas B., Jr., 299
Sanders, Muriel I., 139, 141
Sansone, John Bernard, 508
Saunders, John R., 23, 135
Saunders, Joseph H., 166
Saunders, Mary Elizabeth, 498
Sayre, Margaret, 518
Scalamandre, Franco, 296
Scarlett, Ruth, 601
Scene Shifters, 154, 607

Index

Schenkman, Edgar, 328, 330, 331, 332, 341
Schenkman, Mrs. Edgar, 331
Schnellock, Emil, 238-43, 247, 268, 487, 488, 613; biographical data, 238-39, 241, 242-43; murals, 236
Schnellock Award, 432
Scholarships, 85-86, 321, 523, 537, 588, 619, 652-53. *See also specific funds*
Scholastic Aptitude Test, 400, 434, 456
School garden, 76-77
School songs, 63-64
Science Club, 83
Science building, 402, 419, 421, 422, 480
Science program, 30, 83, 225, 256-57, 288, 301, 422-23, 456-57, 477-78, 588
Scott, Ann Cecilia, 527
Scott, Bertha, 519
Scott, Emma Langford, 526
Scott, Hugh, 487-88
Scott, John, 407
Scott, Lilias, 247, 249, 574
Scott, Martha Segar, 526
Scott, Sallie Woodson, 526
Seacobeck Hall, 18, 169-71, 179, 485
Secondary education, 4, 9
Secretarial program, 275, 288
Security force, 201, 402-4, 445
Self-study program, 438-42
Self-Study Report (1962), 435, 436, 440, 512
Semester plan, 474
Seminars, 270-71, 426-28, 436-37
Senior Modern Dance Club, 574
Senior year, committee on, 459-60
Service building, 485
Settle, T. S., 60
Shackelford, V. R., 70
Shade, Jeanne Bowman, 526
Shankle, George Earlie, 159, 351, 448, 505, 566, 567, 601; biographical data, 160-62; death, 393
Shannon, Edgar F., Jr., 435, 509; biographical data, 424-25; inauguration, 423-25
Shaughnessy, Edward F., 479
Shelton, Selma, 502
Shenandoah Collegiate Institute, 9
Shewmake, Oscar L., 70
Shipstone, Eva, 451, 538
Shridevi, S., 451
Shurtleff, Helen, 574

Sigma Omega Chi, 589
Sigma Tau Chi, 148, 226, 568-69
Sigma Tau Delta, 567
Silvette, David, 357
Simmons, Mrs. Reed K., 640
Simpson, "Bootsie," 431
Simpson, Grellet C., 120, 367-69, 370, 388, 409, 424, 538, 543; addresses, 411, 421, 433, 444; biographical data, 362-63; on education, 368, 369, 370, 376-77, 447-48; on faculty responsibility, 413, 442; Founder's Day address, 370; on future of the college, 469; inauguration, 372-78; India exchange program and, 448, 450-51, 452; on library salaries, 641-42; L.L.D. degree, 425; as president, 362; in Phi Beta Kappa, 508-9, 510, 511; residence, 296; on self-study program, 438-39; on student challenges, 493; on student government, 391; on student responsibility, 553; on student rights, 492; tenth anniversary, 463-64, 538
Simpson, Mrs. Grellet C. (Dorothy Cottrell), 363, 585
Simpson, Ronna Faulkner, 377
Simpson, R. Smith, 651
Simpson, T. McNider, 168, 254
Simpson Award, 479
Sinclair, Indie Lowry, 123
Singh, Renée V., 451
Sletten, Charles A., 271, 307, 510, 642
Smith, Annie Fleming, 653
Smith, C. Alphonso, 59
Smith, Captain John, 18, 170
Smith, Charles J., 341
Smith, Charlotte Dean, 302
Smith, C. Mason, 34, 37, 72
Smith, Dorothy M., 346
Smith, E. J., 13, 26
Smith, George Donald, 611, 627
Smith, Howard W., 352
Smith, Jacquelin Randolph, 37, 576
Smith, Judson, 598
Smith, Sex, 48, 548
Smith, Taylor, 72
Smith, William Waugh, 6
Smith College, 3
Smoking regulations, 387, 398
Snidow, Betty Jean, 580
Social director, 333

Social life, 49, 52, 58-60, 64-65, 66, 103-4, 135, 214-17, 343-45. *See also specific events*
Social science program, 301, 457-58, 479, 588-89
Sociology Club, 589, 595
Sociology program, 287, 301, 307
Softball, 63, 548
Song contest, 327
Sororities, 71, 217
Souder, Ellie Mae, 440
South, Joan Whittemore, 514
South, higher education for women, 3
Southeastern Construction Co., 234
Southern Association of Colleges and Secondary Schools, 438
Southern College, 9
Southern Education Board, 8
Southern Seminary, 9
Southwick, Henry, 73
Spain, summer school, 461-63
Spanish Club, 273-74, 590-91
Spanish fiestas, 272-74
Spanish house, 77, 294, 297
Spanish Night, 273
Spanish-speaking students, 272
Speech pathology and audiology, 325
Speech program, 580-82, 585-87
Spence, Elmer, 298
Sphinx, 72
Spillman, Martha, 365
"Spirit of M.W.C., The," 208
Sports, 549-50. *See also specific sports*
Spotswood, Alexander, 319
Spotswood Hall, 297, 421, 534
Spotsylvania County, roads, 51-52
Sprenkle, Kathleen, 498
Sprower, Carolyn Jean, 526
Sprower, Katherine Hackney, 526
Stanford University, 3
Stanley, Thomas B., 320
Stansbury, Milton H., 446
Starke, Anna P., 95, 97
Starkey, Julia, 580
State Board of Education, 166, 171, 180
State Council of Higher Education, 512
State Department of Education, curriculum revision, 145
State Female Normal School (Farmville), 7-8
State Loan Fund, 44

Statement of Rights and Responsibilities, 492-93
State Normal and Industrial School for Women, 32. *See also* Mary Washington College
State normal school certificate. *See* Teaching certificate
State Normal School for Women, 69
State Teachers' Association, 519
State Teachers College, Farmville, 8
State Teachers College, Fredericksburg, 115. *See also* Mary Washington College
State teachers colleges: B.A. program, 187-90; teaching pledge, 44, 190; tuition, 190-91
Stearnes, R. C., 70
Stebbins, Frances MacMurdo, 526
Steele, Doris Virginia, 533
"Steno's Memo," 569
Stephenson, Mary Ellen, 315, 333, 372, 384, 385-87, 435, 451-52, 476, 505, 510, 584; biographical data, 385-86
Steward, Catesby Willis, 591, 592
Stewart, Mildred P., 144, 247-49, 256, 261-62, 327, 524, 525, 528, 529, 574
Stewart, Nellie Mae, 498
Stitch Club, 86
Stokes, Mrs. Peter D., 406
Stoll, June, 498
Stone, Judith Wolling, 527
Stone, Virginia E., 28, 35, 75
Straith, M. Catherine, 35
Strawberry Leaf Society, 585-86
Stritch, Thomas, 589
Strohecker, Mrs. D. H. (John Ruff), 97
Stuart, H. C., 70
Student activities building, 317, 322, 483-84
Student-Alumnae Building, 174, 132-36, 519, 521
Student (Government) Association, 71, 172, 334, 336, 384, 390-91, 415, 489, 490, 491, 495, 497, 547, 551-55, 557, 558, 603; name change, 554; war bond program, 259, 262, 268
Student challenges, 493
Student Council, 262, 552, 553
Student dress, 87, 334, 387
Student Education Association, 594
Student employment, 44, 116, 335, 501
Student government, 339

Index 679

Student Government League, 45
Student handbook, 143-44, 334, 398, 410, 415-16, 431, 444, 553, 603, 604-5
Student health, 88
Student loans, 44, 116, 222, 518. *See also* Scholarships
Student Organ Guild, 395
Student organizations, 546-55. *See also specific groups*
Student personnel records, 385
Student pledge, 557, 559, 561
Student protest, 184-87, 334-37
Student publications, 60, 597-602. *See also specific publications*
Student regulations, 44-45, 53-54, 129, 142-44, 184-87, 315, 334-35, 387, 398, 410, 444, 494-95, 552-53. *See also* Honor system
Student rights, 492
Student teaching, 28, 43, 74-76, 102, 117, 118, 136-38, 140-42, 191-92, 223-24; supervised, 471-72. *See also* Apprentice teaching
Study abroad, 150, 459, 461-63; Alumnae Association and, 539
Stull, Olive G., 159
Stump, Nancy, 592
Stumpf, Susan, 618
Stutz, Frances May, 526
Sublette, Myrick H., 572
Sullins College, 9
Summer session, 122, 145, 166-67, 297, 298, 299, 325-26, 327-32, 341, 478-79; director, 499, 503; in Spain, 461-63; for teachers, 192-93; workshops, 193
Summer School of Music, 193, 327-32, 341
Sumner, Mark, 322, 372, 377, 411, 615-16
Sumner, Raiford E., 372, 483, 500, 505
Sumner, Mrs. Raiford E. (Laura B. Voelkel), 311, 348-49, 360, 367, 438, 478, 499, 500, 505, 508, 510, 585, 592
Sutherland, Judith Anne, 527
Sutton, Thelma, 526
Swanson, Claude A., 10
Sweet Briar College, 5
Sweetser, H. K., 23
Swimming, 549
Swimming facilities, 132, 133, 135, 173, **174**, 317, 520, 521

Swope, Martha McKenney, 528
Sydnor, Virginia Elizabeth, 526

Talbott, Frank, Jr., 375, 424
Tanner, Grace K., 48, 519
Tanner, Rollin H., 280, 592, 651
Tansill, Diana M., 529, 530
Tapestry Room, 225, 317
Tarrant, Sara Travers, 447
Tattler, 599
Taylor, Doris, 579
Taylor, Elvira, 185
Taylor, Ethel Louise, 47, 597
Taylor, Grace, 498, 569, 626
Taylor, Helen, 184
Taylor, Irene, 208, 327, 530
Taylor, Katherine, 440
Taylor, Lillian Irene, 498
Taylor, Millard, 205
Teacher certification, 323, 471, 472
Teachers colleges, 114-15, 166, 225-26
Teacher training, 7, 10, 11, 38, 42-43, 136-37, 167-68, 187, 188, 209-10, 287, 289-91; cooperative program in elementary education, 323; summer institutes, 7. *See also* Education program; Normal schools; Student teaching
Teaching certificate, 43, 85, 136, 289, 290; collegiate professional, 117, 275, 290; normal professional, 117, 167, 210; renewal program, 193, 341
Teaching schedules, 283
Tearoom, 132, 225, 520
Telephone switchboard, 383, 411
Tennis, 47, 549
Terrace Room, 318
Terrapin Club, 254, 549
Terrell, A. L., 24
Textbooks, 55
Theater. *See* Auditorium; DuPont Hall
Theatricals. *See* Dramatics
Thomas, Mrs. Floyd B., 529
Thomas, Mrs. George N., 498
Thomas, Helen R., 501
Thomas, Margaret Morris, 526
Thompson, Frances, 155, 624, 625
Thompson, Randall, 280
Thompson, William E., 81
Thomson, Stevens, 350
Thorington Construction Co., 481
Thornton, Ida **Alsop**, 110-11

Thornton, Evelyn, 498
Thorp, Margaret, 248
Tillar, Mrs. D. P. (Betty Billingsley), 522
Tiller, Ora Green, 538
Timken, Emma, 533
Timmerman, Lucy M., 348
Todd, Gaye, 506
Todd, John, Jr., 196
Tomalonis, Alexandra, 602
Tompkins, Mrs. Robert H., 446
Toombs, Joy Simpson, 542
Topping, Mrs. Peter (Eve Catafygiotu), 591-92
Townes, Myrtle, 75
Toynbee, Arnold J., 407
Traffic control, 404
Training School, 136, 138-42, 167, 224
"Training School Course of Study," 75
Transportation, 39, 54, 72, 81 141, 144, 266, 309-10, 404
Tread, Ordway, 407
Treasurer, 199, 200
Trench Hill, 296-97
Trent, Kate G., 126, 140
Trevvett, Jane, 258
Trimble, Elizabeth M., 230, 498, 580
Trimble, Ellen Thompson, 527
Trinkle, E. Lee, 111, 123, 166, 171, 179; library and, 629, 630
Tri-Unit Dormitories, 19, 194
Troland, Julia, 154
Troxel, William D., 205
Troy Female Seminary, 2
Trueblood, D. Elton, 447
Trustees, 13, 24-26, 55, 69
Tuck, William M., 308
Tufts College, 3
Tuition, 12, 29, 44, 85, 190-91, 349, 400
Turgeon, Thomas S., 510, 511, 618, 620
Turman, Lillie, 216, 524, 525, 530
Two-year diploma, 117-18, 167, 168, 191, 210, 221, 274-75
Tyner, Bunyan Yates, 71, 75, 97, 120, 121, 122, 145, 160; as acting president, 99, 153, 154; biographical data, 97-99; A. B. Chandler and, 98-99; as dean, 97-98
Tyner, Mrs. Bunyan Yates, 99

Ulman, Selma, 76
Unitarians, 596
United Brethren, 9
United Daughters of the Confederacy, 85-86
United States–India exchange program, 448-52
"Units Illustrating Procedures in Using the Revised Courses . . . ," 192
University Center in Virginia, 388
University of Chicago, 3
University of Iowa, 1
University of Michigan, 1
University of Richmond, 6
University of Virginia, 3, 175; admission of women, 511-12; board of visitors, 131, 278, 337-38, 530, 531, 537, 538, 542; as coeducational institution, 176; cooperative programs, 323, 324, 325; Founder's Day, 370; graduate work in education, 325; honors program, 414; honor system, 559, 560; Mary Washington College relationship, 131, 277-92, 470, 511-14, 527; two-year branches, 353
University of Virginia Alumni Association, 176, 178
University of Virginia Extension Division, 151
University of Virginia School of Nursing, 310
University of Wisconsin, 1
Updike, Winifred T., 310
Urbin, Virginia, 259
Urquhart, Julia Raiford, 538

Valiente, Awilda Rose, 274
Valley Union Educational Society of Virginia, 3
Valley Union Seminary, 4
Vance, Joseph C., 271, 428, 458, 572
Van Deursen, Hardin, 329
Van Sant, George M., 271, 381, 426-27, 435, 437, 466, 473; biographical data, 467
Van Winckel, Dorothy Duggan (Mrs. Edgar T.), 124, 129-30, 446, 488, 505, 538, 583
Vaughan, Carrie Belle, 95, 607
Vassar, 2, 3
Veterans, 299, 351, 361
Veterans Club, 300, 351
Vice-president, 513
Victory booth, 259, 262

Index

681

Victory Chorus, 262-63
Vietnam Moratorium, 489-90
Viewbooks, 604
Virginia: higher education for women, 3-9; high schools, 8; liberal arts college for women, 175-77, 277; public education, 7-8; school curriculum, 191-92; state support for education, 6-8
Virginia Academy of Science, 168-69
Virginia Asian Studies Consortium, 479
Virginia Baptist Seminary, 6
Virginia Christian College, 9
Virginia Commission of Arts and Humanities, 478
Virginia Hall, 27, 40, 77, 84, 103, 104, 124, 173, 194, 196-97
Virginia Intermont College, 9
Virginia Normal School Board, 69-71, 87-88, 99, 147. *See also* Board of Virginia Teachers Colleges
Virginia Polytechnic Institute, 277
Virginia Reel Club, 214
Virginia Student-Legislator Forum, 496-97
Visiting lecturers, 388, 407
Visiting scholars, 211
Vivian, Thomas, 300
Vogelback, Arthur L., 261, 610, 611
Vogue Varieties, 219
Volk, Mary C., 498
Vondra, A. B., 525
Von Hofsten, Clare, 517, 518

Wade, Ruth Seawright, 315, 333, 335, 639
Waitress uniforms, 335-37
Wake, Orville W., 375
Wakefield, Alice, 568
Walford, J. Binford, 194, 196, 225, 233, 234, 629
Walford & Wright, 316, 317, 318, 320
Walker, C. Harding, 176
Walker, Lewis Meriwether, Jr., 381, 510, 513, 514
Walker, Sally B., 327
Walker, Susan Dabney, 62
Walker, Winnie, 517
Walking clubs, 47, 63
Wallace, Henry A., 252
Wallace, H. Lewis, 19
Wallace, Karl R., 280

Waller, Leah Fleet, 514
Walraven, Louise, 575
Walther, Russell, 264, 267, 268, 576, 610, 614
War bonds and stamps, 259-60, 266-69
Warden, Henry, 14, 51
Ware, Juliet Ritchie, 498
Warfield, Jack, 610, 614, 615
Warner, Allen, 329
Washington, Augustine, 195
Washington, Mrs. Augustine (Mary Ball), 113, 194-95, 316, 320
Washington, George, 194, 195, 197, 236, 316, 319
Washington, John, 24
Washington Literary Society, 565, 566
Water supply, 52
Watkins, Mary Gresham, 526
Watson, Barbara, 250, 274
Watson, Katherine G., 575
Wattleworth, Charles M., 37
Watts, Marian Reed, 639, 640
Weaver, Russell, 279
Webb, Belle, 153
Weedon, George, 316
Weinbrecht, Mrs. Ruby York, 503-4, 543, 605
Weisner, Theodora, 574
Weiss, Harold, 247, 250, 578, 580, 581, 582, 609, 610-11, 612
Wellesley College, 2
Wellford, E. T., 81
Wells, Judith Margaret, 527
Welsh, Martha Ann, 498
Wesleyan Female College, 2
Westhampton College, 6
Westmoreland Hall, 233, 238
Wheeler, Clara Boyd, 523, 524, 525, 536, 540
Wheeler, Lucille, 530
Wheeler, Olivia J., 498
Whidden, Howard P., 269
Whidden, Marjorie Sue, 432
Whidden, Reginald W., 268, 269-72, 346, 354, 360, 366, 367, 372, 373, 415, 416, 427, 435, 443, 475, 505, 510, 540, 543, 616; biographical data, 269; as dean of the college, 269, 270, 499; retirement, 501
Whisler, Janet M., 510
Whitaker, Carolyn McWhirt, 542
White, Anne, 498

White, Bernice M., 36, 80
White, Brock T., 70
White, Margaret S., 527
White, Peter J., 13, 19, 25, 26
Whitesell, J. Edwin, 261, 276
Whitmer, Cancade Dawn, 498
Whitney, Donald R., 261
Whitticar, Ralph M., III, 513
Who's Who among Students . . . , 447
Wickham, Ruth, 63
Wild, Norman, 651
Willard, Emma, 2
Willard Hall, 32, 39, 77, 97, 150, 173
Willetts, Ruth, 502
Willetts, Vincent H., 312
Williams, Elizabeth N., 95
Williams, Indiana Fletcher, 5
Williams, Mary Page, 527
Williams, Murat W., 510
Williams, R. A., 20
Williams, Sue Vernon, 624
Willis, Beryl Barber, 121, 140
Willis, Caroline, 639
Willis, Jere M. H., 176, 177, 193, 337, 355
Willis, Mrs. Jere M. H. (Mary Phoebe Enders), 180, 237, 313, 522, 523; biographical data, 130-31
Willis, Mrs. Mason H. (Beryl Barber), 521
Willis, M. G., 14
Willis, Nora C., 37, 47, 56, 121, 155, 205, 229
Wills, Frances, 249
Wilson, Susan, 576, 577
Wilson, Woodrow, inauguration, 59
Wingfield, Rachel Harriet, 498, 522, 625
Winston, Helen, 75
Wishner, Lawrence A., 271, 437, 503, 644
Withers, Frances L., 34, 35
WMWC, 580-82
Woman's College of Richmond, 6, 9
Woman suffrage, 59
Women: assumed inferiority of, 1-2; higher education for, 1-9
Woodhouse, Georgiana, 529
Woodrow Wilson Award, 447
Woodrow Wilson Literary Society, 47, 80, 565, 566, 599

Woodson, Dorothy, 249
Woodward, Bettie Pollard, 526, 588
Woodward, Daniel H., 271, 394, 428, 501, 510, 643-45; biographical data, 643
Woodward, Edgar E., 199-203, 366, 372, 435, 438, 500, 543; biographical data, 200; at entertainments, 202; responsibilities, 338, 339-40; retirement, 502
Woodward, Mrs. Edgar E. (Elizabeth Mitchell), 202
Woodward, Edgar E., Jr., 202
Woodward, Frances Virginia, 526
Woodward, Lucy Boxley, 526
Woodward, Roberta Boxley, 526
Woosley, Rebecca T., 310, 502, 506
Works Progress Administration, 172-73
World Affairs Club, 572
World War I, 84-85, 87, 88
World War II, 163, 259-63, 266-69
Worsley, Janice Corinne, 527
Wright, Mary James, 618
Wright, Jones, & Wilkerson, 480, 482
Wysor, Elizabeth, 587

Yale, 3
Yarborough, Norma, 366
Yates, Mary S., 84, 624
YET, 602
Yokogawa, Meechi, 333, 341, 498
Young, Perle, 574
Young, Walter J., 95, 121, 137, 159, 216, 254, 579; biographical data, 95-96
Young, Mrs. Walter J., 96-97
Young Democrats, 432
Young Republicans, 432
YWCA, 46-47, 58-59, 62-63, 72, 79, 80, 126, 142, 258, 345, 359, 443, 518, 546-48; book collection, 626-27; doll show, 220; membership, 546; program, 546, 547; student handbook, 546-47

Zapoleon, Marguerite, 374
Zehmer, George B., 353
Zeppenfeldt, Carmen, 274
Zeta Phi Eta, 580
Zimmern, Sir Alfred, 308